ARCHITECTURE and BUILDINGS

A.K. JAIN

Foreword By:
DIVYA KUSH
President
The Indian Institute of Architects

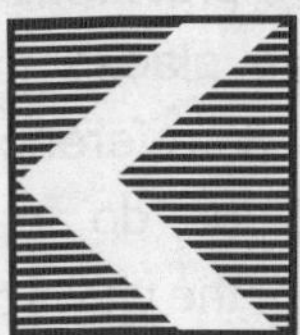

KHANNA BOOK PUBLISHING CO. (P) LTD.
Publisher of Engineering and Computer Books
4C/4344, Ansari Road, Darya Ganj, New Delhi-110002
Phone : 011-23244447-48 **Mobile:** +91-9910909320
E-mail : contact@khannabooks.com
Website : www.khannabooks.com

Dear Readers,

To prevent the piracy, this book is secured with HIGH SECURITY HOLOGRAM on the front title cover. In case you don't find the hologram on the front cover title, please write us to at contact@khannabooks.com or whatsapp us at +91-99109 09320 and avail special gift voucher for yourself.

Specimen of Hologram on front Cover title:

Moreover, there is a SPECIAL DISCOUNT COUPON for you with EVERY HOLOGRAM.

How to avail this SPECIAL DISCOUNT:

Step 1: Scratch the hologram
Step 2: Under the scratch area, your "coupon code" is available
Step 3: Logon to www.khannabooks.com
Step 4: Use your "coupon code" in the shopping cart and get your copy at a special discount
Step 5: Enjoy your reading!

Price: ₹ 450.00

ISBN: 978-93-86173-82-9

Architecture and Building
by A.K. Jain

First Edition: 2021
Reprint: 2023, 2024, **2026**

To view complete list of books, Please scan the QR Code:

Published by:
Khanna Book Publishing Co. (P) Ltd.
CIN: U22110DL1998PTC095547

Visit us at: **www.khannabooks.com**
Write us at: **contact@khannabooks.com**

Printed in India.

PREFACE

An architect is defined as a master builder, one who designs buildings and superintends their erection. Architecture as the art and science of building, design, which the acts as a bridge between the past and future, between technology and humanity, and between ecology and livelihood. Architecture is one of the few professions which strike a balance between technical, artistic, practical, economic and social aspects.

The great master architect Le Corbusier emphasised the 'art' as an integral part of the building design beyond its their practical utility:

"*You employ stone, wood and concrete, and with these materials you build palaces. That is construction. Ingenuity is at work. My house is practical. I thank you, as I might thank railway engineering or the telephone service. You have not touched my heart. But suddenly you touch my heart, you do me good, I am happy and I say: This is beautiful. That is architecture. Art enters in*" Le Corbusier's famous open hand symbolizes and reminds that the architect has to have an open hand, a devata–the compassionate benefactor of all living beings.

Architecture corresponds to the technical achievements, materials and labour available. Egyptian pyramids show the immense strength and scale construction. The Greek construction was entirely 'post and lintel' and maximum spacing of the columns was determined by the amount of labour and largest piece of stone available for roofing. The Romans invented the arch, which allowed large openings to be spanned by smaller elements. It was a milestone in the history of architecture when dome was introduced for roofing. With increasing urbanisation, climate change and depletion of natural resources, the environmental sustainability has emerged a central issue. This needs taking a wide-angle view of the architecture in the context of ecology, environment bio-diversity and natural resources. There is a continual dialect between the habitat and nature, the inside and outside and culture and identity. It is not possible to segregate different constituents of built environment which are all interconnected. The buildings are responsible for consuming about 50% of all resources, 45% of energy, 40% of water and 70% of timber. It is estimated that 60 per cent of buildings which will exist in the year 2030 are yet to be built. This provides a unique opportunity to redefine the architecture for creating a more resources efficient, healthy and sustainable environment.

The book 'Architecture and Building draws a wide-angle perspective on the subject. The purpose is to widen the understanding and horizon of the practitioners and students of architecture.

The time has come to conceive architecture urbanistically and urbanism architecturally. According to Rem Koolhaas, "*Urbanism is something that creates potential and architecture exploits that potential. Urbanism is generous and architecture egotistical.*"

B.V. Doshi believes that "*we cannot look at architecture as merely a product because it is not what one calls a passive space, form or structure. Architecture is an extension of our body. It's not outside of me, it is part of me and we live within it. When you think it is part of yourself then the questions are the food you eat, the life you live, the people you meet and the world in which we live. It is an understanding of culture, aesthetics, climate and space. That's how I understood Corbusier. He would talk about behaviour, attitudes and about climate. He spoke about the relationship between people and the building, about the space, and I think because of that my whole understanding of architecture is different.*"

The architects have been searching for the forms which relate more closely with the context. The architecture needs to infused with the local regional cultural, climatic and artistic characteristics as by Joseph Allen Stein, "*I strongly believe that being modern without being regional is inappropriate and regional without modernism reactionary.*"

It reminds the beautiful words of Osho, 'ego' in the enemy of creativity, twain shall never meet'. An architect has to be humble. He/she is lifelong learner, thinker and performer. By synergy of academics and practice, he/she is able to make a complex problem simple and understand the simple complexities. Above all he/she has a sense of humour that keeps him/her going.

In writing this book, I have benefitted from works and writing's of many organisations and individuals. It may not be possible to acknowledge them individually but all those mentioned in the bibliography given at the end of this book deserve my thanks. I am particularly grateful to who have given me the opportunity to work Ministry of Urban Development, Delhi Development Authority, Delhi-Mumbai Industrial Corridor LTD. Delhi Government, Hyderabad Municipal Corporation, Jaipur Development Authority, and also the UN Habitat, IHS (Rotterdam), JICA, SPA New Delhi, Amity University, TERI, CSE, HSMI, IIPA, INTACH, ITPI and the IIA.

I am grateful to Prof. Divya Kush, President, Indian Institute of Architects for writing a clear and concise Foreword. According to him, this book will provoke the scholars and practitioners to reinvent the subject. The simple language and illustrative nature of the book make it particularly useful for the student. Khanna Books under the leadership of Mukul Seth deserve's a special acknowledgement for transforming an unwieldy manuscript into this beautiful volume.

A.K. Jain

THE INDIAN INSTITUTE OF ARCHITECTS

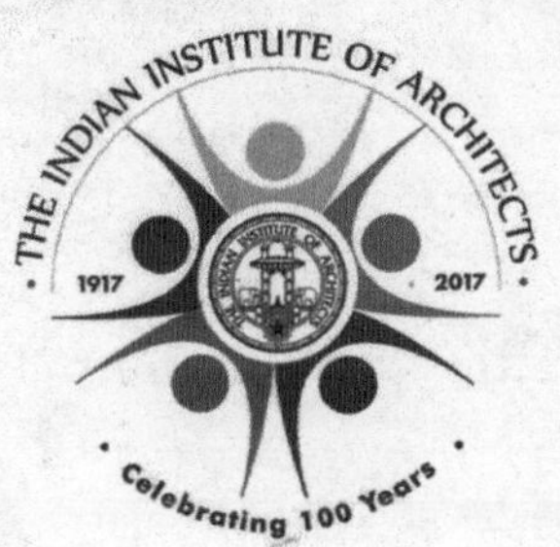

Ar. Divya Kush
President

FOREWORD

Architecture has traditionally been defined as the art and science of building. This to my understanding is a very elementary and inadequate attempt to define the human endeavour which does not limit itself merely to addressing the issue or providing shelter to the mankind, but goes beyond to address the larger concerns of environment, ecology, judicious use of available natural resources and much more in creating a liveable human habitat in complete harmony with the nature.

As a matter of fact, architecture defies any conventional definition as it is continually in the process of assimilating in its domain every field of knowledge and possibility to bring comfort and happiness to the mankinds.

Architect & Planner A.K. Jain with his deep knowledge and over five decades of practical experience is uniquely qualified to discuss and explain in his own original style the lasting influence of architecture and planning in its infinite manifestations, not only in 2D and 3D but as much in its abstract dimensions.

This book is an outcome of his deep personal understanding, knowledge, experience and extensive research of the subject matter and has lot more to offer than its short title "**Architecture and Buildings**" might suggest. I am sure the book will provoke the scholars and practitioners of the noble profession of architecture an opportunity to reinvent the subject. The simple language and illustrative nature of the book make it particularly useful for the students.

Divyakush

President,
The Indian Institute of Architects

CONTENTS

Chapter 1

The Basics of Architectural Design

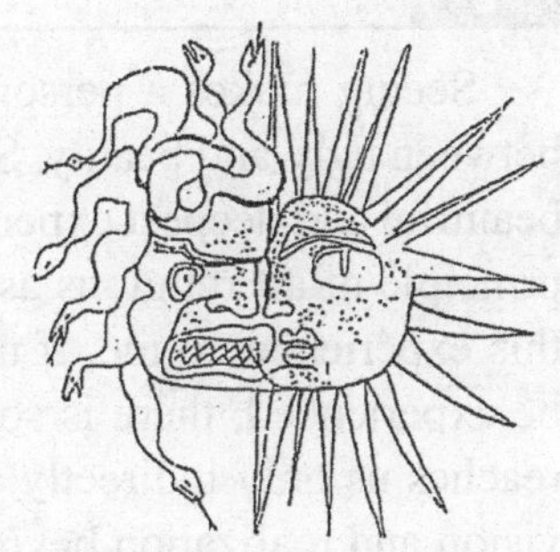

An architect is defined as a master builder one who designs buildings and superintends their erection. Architecture is the art and science of the building structures. Vitruvius gave the classic definition of architecture in pronouncing three conditions of building design, *utilitas*, *firmitas and venustas*, translated as "commodity, firmness and delight." Architecture is one of the few professions which strike a balance between technical, artistic, practical, educational and social considerations. It changes with the socio-economic and cultural development and the technology. Political order, religious beliefs and the level of cultural and educational achievements influence the social structure, hence the architecture.

Architecture is conditioned by the climate. The architect understands the movement of sun, directions of wind, frequency and amount of rain and variations of temperature and humidity for erecting a comfortable building for every season.

Art and science aspects of architecture demand that the architect is both–an artist and a technocrat, which merge seamlessly in the process of design. Technique, derived from the Greek *techne loges,* means knowledge of techniques.

Architectural design is the art of organizing space. It is a visual art that involves seeing the visible and invisible. Seeing and its variations—gazing, viewing, visualizing, looking, absorbing, spectacle, beholding, sighting, perceiving, inspecting and introspecting is the foundation of creation. In our tradition 'Dristhi' means seeing, viewing, beholding, (also with mental eye)...sight, faculty of seeing……the mind's eye wisdom, intelligence….view, theory, doctrine, system…aspects of stars. The right perception (Samyak drishti) means looking at things as they are. The view has to be complete and rounded, which helps in a deeper and integrated understanding.

A group of people decided to go and look at the beauty of the sunset. The scientist saw only the formation of clouds, the astronomer the position of the stars, the environmentalist saw the pollution of the atmosphere and the fashion designer saw the colours of the sky. The child, when asked what he saw, said, "I saw God smile…." The master explained, "The problem was not in the object, the problem was in the seeing. For you can only see what your perception allows you to see."

Seeing leads to perception which removes the darkness and grows into understanding. Understanding triggers the action which gets converted into relationships, peace and happiness. Seeing means awakening, awakening means learning, learning means knowledge, knowledge means understanding, understanding means wisdom, wisdom means awareness, awareness means consciousness of the inside and outside, visible and invisible, real and unreal, and action and inertia. This makes a person a 'seer.' Einstein could see energy in matter and Newton could see gravitational force in a falling apple.

Seeing makes a person to distinguish between false and true, between wrong and right and between ugly and beauty. Seeing and knowledge are manifested in creation and actions."The most beautiful and deepest experience a man can have is the sense of mysteriousness. It is the underlying principle of all religions as well as all serious endeavours in art and science… He who never had this experience, to me, if not dead, then is at least blind. The sense that behind anything that can be experienced, there is something that our mind cannot grasp and whose beauty and sublimity reaches us only indirectly and as feeble reflection, this is religiousness." Seeing is a discovery, a vision and realization beyond what is superficial. In other words an architect is a 'seer', a sadhak, who can see the things as they are and also the invincible. It is this which makes an architect creative.

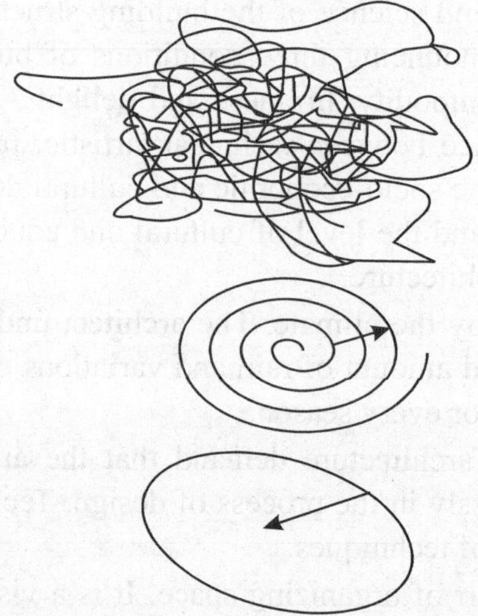

Fig. 1.1. Organisation of thoughts means centring (Paul Klee)

Michelangelo used the perspective approach. If one look the painting of "The Last Supper", one can see that it was done using perspective lines. The painter is using the objective measurement to draw beauty from outside perspective. The impressionist artist Monet oscillated between the nature and the industrial society. He left the studio and went outside into nature. Thus, his paintings show the steam of locomotives in the background of the scene, from fences and bridges, steam and iron, being symbols of modernity in the time of the industrial revolution. The abstractionist like Picasso went further. They swam in nature, jumped out, and painted what they saw. The purpose of the painting was not to copy nature, but rather to show the viewer the sentiment, emotion, the concept the artist saw in nature.

The key point is seeing builds up certain impressions and perspectives, which get translated into understanding and abstractions. These are reflected in one's behaviours, actions and communications. On the other hand, the absence of seeing may results into illusions and hallucinations. These cause the alienation of self from itself, and self from others, producing an irretrievable disaffection where life and death become interchangeable, and where human is reduced to the naked existence deprived of spirited contents. Images of catastrophe are relevant in so far as they act as a disturbing counterpoint to the fake-real of mediated reality, not least because they come across as the substitute for real life.

Visual Perception

There are three kinds of people–visual, auditory and kinaesthetic. The visual people predominantly think and process the experience of life in term of visuals. Architects, painters and photographers are usually visual people. Auditory people process their experiences in term of sounds mostly. Singers and orators are predominantly auditory people. Kinaesthetic people love hands on experience. You can be one, two or all of the three (visual auditory and kinaesthetic) simultaneously depending upon the learning.

The most beautiful experience that we can have is the mysterious. It is a fundamental emotion which stands at a cradle of true art and true science.

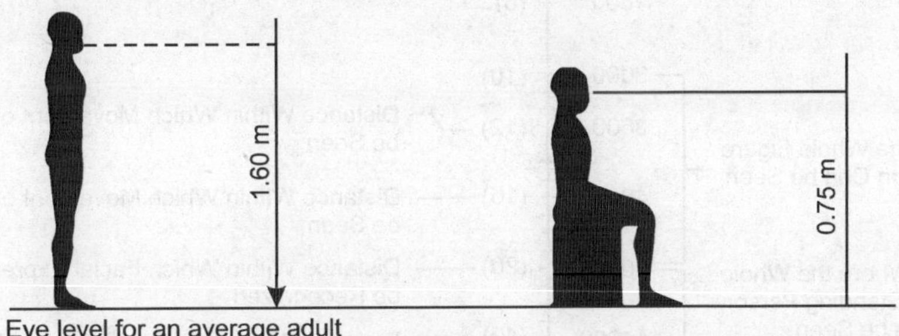

Fig. 1.2. The eye-level of an average adult in a standing position, as well as sitting position, is illustrated on the left. People focus most of their attention at eye level and below during normal perception of their surroundings

Source: *Time Saver Standards for Landscape Architecture*

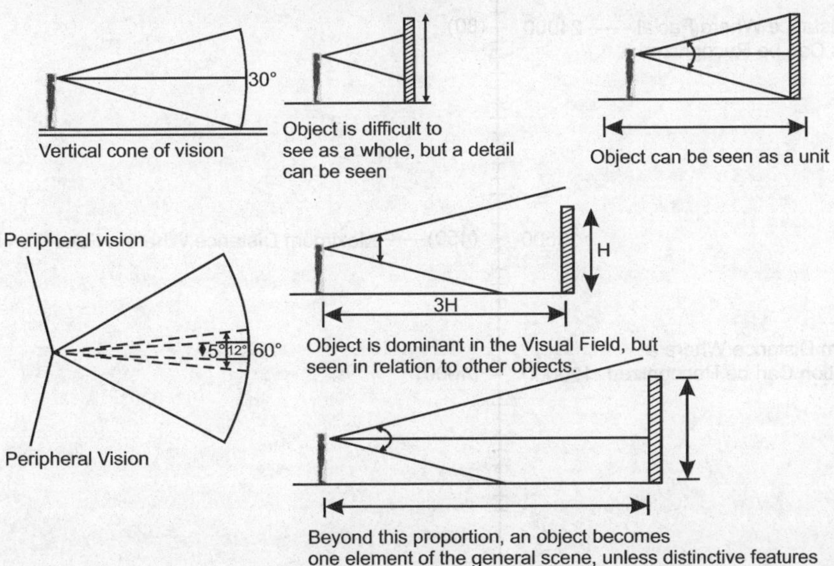

Fig. 1.3. The human cone of vision (*i.e.* the fixed eye) is approximately 30 degrees vertically and 60 degrees horizontally, with angles of acute vision somewhat less than this. Eye levels and cone of vision are especially important in terms of the placement and orientation of signage

Source: *Time-Saver Standards for Landscape Architecture*

People have a strong tendency to use two valued thinking ('it is a hot day' 'the city is polluted'). The two valued scale is very gross, and it is unclear what the boundary between the two value means. Two valued view can be a rhetoric or demagoguery. It simplifies the position to the point of non-reality and leads to illusions. Multi-valued view is to understand real situation with gradation and precision.

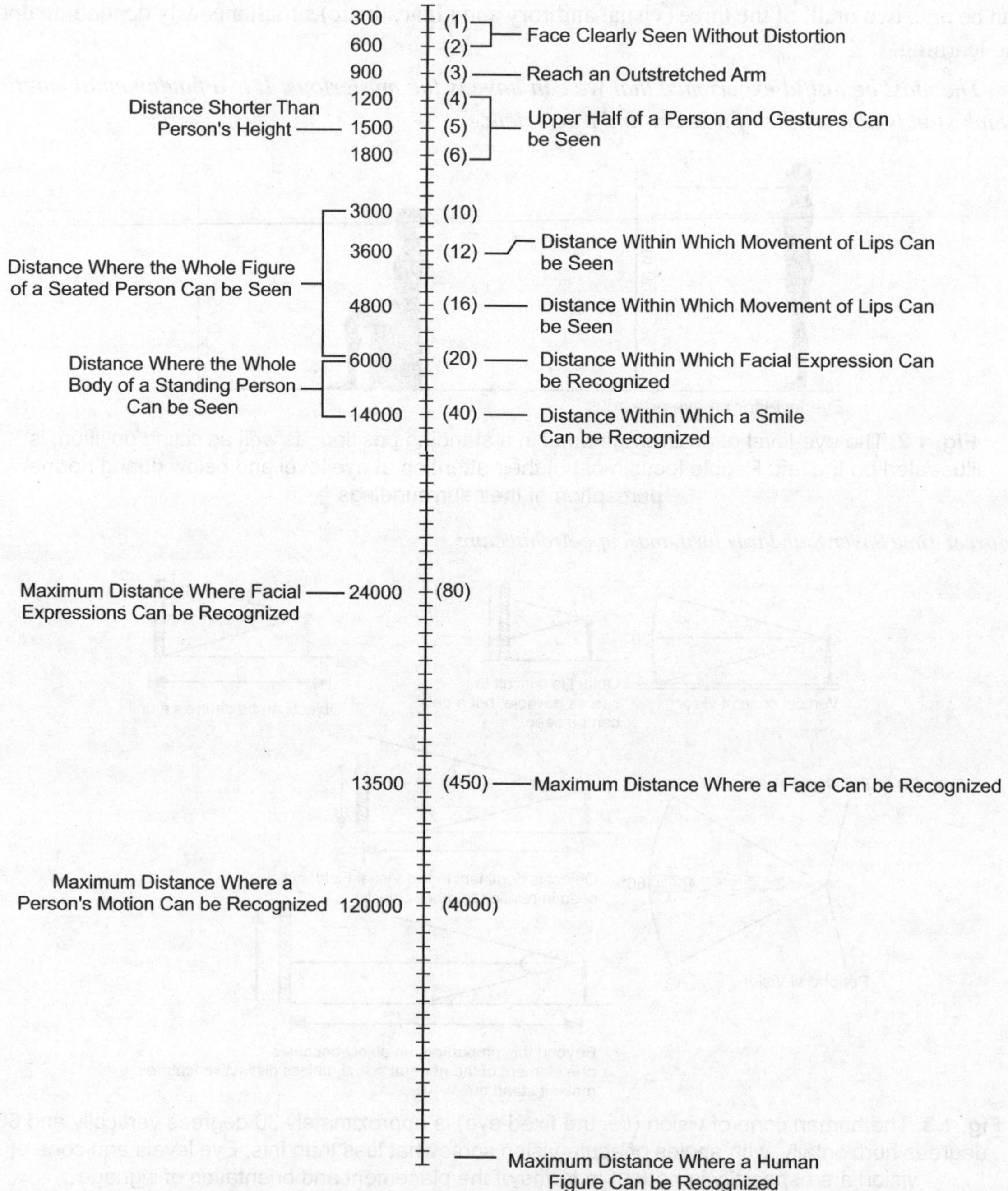

Fig. 1.4. Inherent capabilities of human vision in terms of social communication

Source: *Time Saver Standards for Landscape Architecture*

Visual Perception: An external enclosure is most comfortable when its vertical planes are one-half to one-third as high as the width of the space enclosed. If the ratio falls below one-fourth, the space begins to lack a sense of enclosure.

Social Communication: For a variety of reasons, the scale and form of a space will influence pedestrian behaviour and the type of social communication that may occur within that space. Physical distances that bring people into close proximity, or separate them, are important design considerations.

Settings are meant to be conducive to active social communication, or those meant to allow a certain degree of eye contact possible and probable, within the scale and layout of the setting.

Design Elements

Design elements are the visual units of aesthetics. When it comes to working with elements in a design there are two basic classes to work with, *i.e.* positive forms and negative space. The most basic form is the abstract point or the dot from which build up the lines. The elements of design are:

- Points/Dots
- Lines
- Surfaces/Planes/Shapes
- Form/Volume/Mass
- Pattern/Texture
- Size/Scale
- Space
- Colour/Value

Points or dots and lines have distinct characteristics and functions. In fact most other elements will mimic these fundamental qualities of point, dot, and line in some way so it makes sense for us to understand these two elements before any other. Design elements are the visual units of aesthetic which include point and dots, colour, shape, pattern and texture, volume mass and form.

Points and Dots: A point is a coordinate without any dimensions, without any area. Points are the simplest element of visual design. By definition we can't actually draw a point, since to see one would require it have dimensions. Dots are the building blocks of everything else. Every shape, form, mass, or blob with a recognizable centre is essentially a dot regardless of its size. The defining characteristic of a dot is that it is a point of focused attention. Dots anchor themselves in space and provide a reference point relative to the other forms and space around it. Dots establish a relationship with the space around it. The two most important relationships formed are the proportion of the dot and the space around it and the position of the dot within that space. Dots centrally placed within a composition create symmetry and are neutral and static, through they tend to dominate the space around them. Dots placed off centre create asymmetry. They are dynamic and actively influence the space around them.

As the space between dots decreases the tension between them increases. As that space approaches zero the tiny bit of space itself becomes more important than either dot or any other interval of space on the page. All the tension is held in that tiny bit of space. As dots get closer together they start to be seen as a single object. Their identity moves to that of the single object instead of the multiple identities of distinct objects. One dot overlapping another creates a figure/ground relationship. One dot is now in the foreground and the other is pushed into the background. Overlapping dots form more complex shapes than either of the individual dots. This resulting cluster of dots is in itself a new dot with a different form. Dots together can form an endless variety of arrangement and complexity. The can become lines and curves. They can form complex shapes, patterns, textures, and any other structure imaginable.

Lines: A line can be thought of as points so close together that they lose their individual identity and form a new entity. Since lines can be straight, curved, or irregularly shaped, these depict a track of a point in motion. Vertical lines can stop eye movement. They also equate to power and strength. Horizontal lines symbolize rest and relaxation. Diagonal lines are dynamic and action-oriented. Lines, like points, can direct attention to a specific location in a visual image. Thick lines are more powerful than thin lines. Lines act as borders between ideas, concepts, or steps in a sequence. Lines allow you to quickly visualize an object or idea with a minimum of time and material. By emphasizing basic structure, objects depicted through line drawings are easy to recognize and can be effective for learning. Lines serve a multitude of purposes in visual displays. They also form shapes.

Lines not only connect elements, they can also separate elements. They can connect an element to space or separate it from space. Lines separate and join both spaces and objects. Lines can also cross barriers, protect, and support. A single line travelling in a curve around a fixed, invisible point with an unchanging distance from that point, eventually joins its starting point and becomes circle. A circle is a line until the thickness of the line increases to completely fill the negative space inside the circle. The end points of a line can be seen or appear to move toward infinity. As lines are allowed to enter and leave a format without seeing their endpoints, their sense of movement is reinforced. When one end point is contained within the format, the direction is no longer infinite. It becomes specific to the point and the tension between the end point and the surrounding space is increased.

When two lines join they create an angle between them. This joint or point of connection becomes the starting point to move in 2 different directions along 2 different lines. Multiple joints create a sense of altered direction. Separating lines from each other focuses attention on the individual identity of each line and the interval between them. As the interval between a series of lines and the width of those lines varies, a rhythm is created. Changing the colour or value of the lines can add more complexity to that rhythm. If a line is added to series of lines at an angle and allowed to cross several lines, this sense of depth is increased. It creates perspective. Thick lines placed close together create a thin line in the negative space between them. This negative space line can often become the positive element and the original lines are seen as the new negative space. Lines working together and in rhythm can form patterns and textures.

Colours: Colour is light. Light is electromagnetic radiation over a range of wave-lengths, which makes an impression on the human eye. This range of wave-lengths is the visual spectrum.

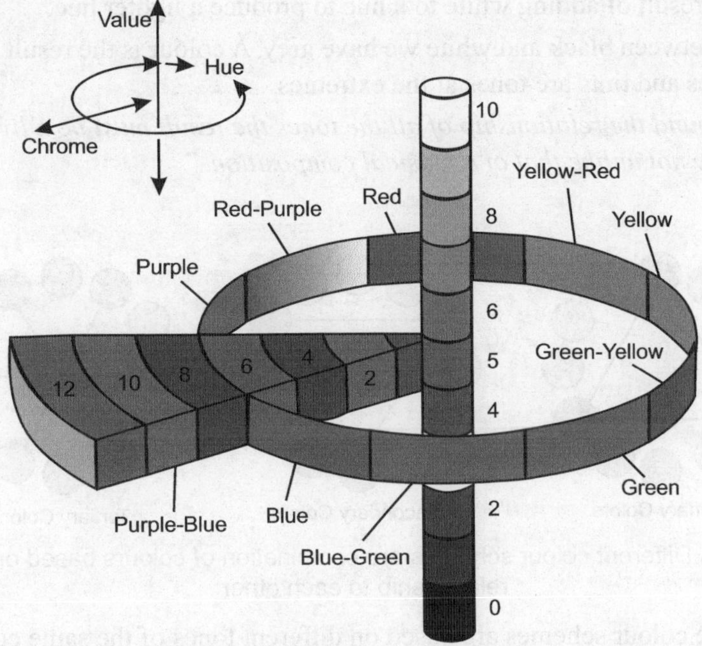

Fig. 1.5. Munsell Colour System

When light hits an object some wavelengths are absorbed and others are reflected. We see the reflected wavelengths of light as colour. When all the wavelengths in the visual spectrum are absorbed we see black and when all are reflected we see white. When some are absorbed and some are reflected we see different colours of the spectrum.

Colour can be described in three ways, by name, by purity, and by value or lightness. We have several terms to help us describe colours in those three ways. The attributes of colour include the following:

- **Hue:** When someone is talking about hue, they are talking about the actual colour of an object. Green is a hue as are red, yellow, blue, purple, etc.
- **Chrome:** Refers to the purity of a hue in relation to grey. When there is no shade of grey in a colour that colour has a high chrome. Adding shades of grey to a hue reduces its chrome.
- **Saturation:** It is the degree of purity of a hue. It is similar to chrome, though not quite the same thing. Pure hues are highly saturated. When grey is added, the colour becomes desaturated.
- **Intensity:** It is the brightness or dullness of a colour. Adding white or black to a colour lowers its intensity. An intense and highly saturated colour has a high chrome.
- **Value/Luminance:** It is a measure of the amount of light reflected from a colour and is basically how light or dark a hue is. Adding white to a hue makes it lighter and increases its value or luminance. Consequently, adding black makes it darker and lowers the value or luminance.
- **Shade:** The result of adding black to a hue to produce a darker hue.

- **Tint:** The result of adding white to a hue to produce a lighter hue.
- **Tone:** In between black and white we have grey. A colour is the result of adding grey to a hue. Shades and tints are tones at the extremes.

"When I have found the relationship of all the tones the result must be a living harmony of all the tones, a harmony not unlike that of a musical composition."

—Henri Matisse

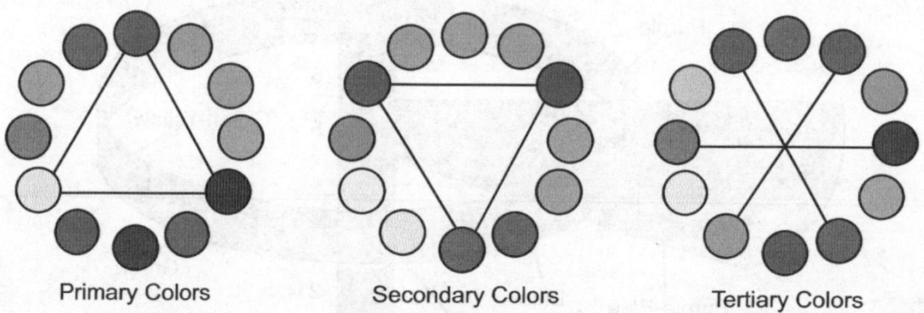

Fig. 1.6. Different colour schemes are combination of colours based on their relationship to each other

Monochromatic colour schemes are based on different tones of the same colour.

Analogous colour schemes are based on colours adjacent to each other on the colour wheel.

Complementary colour schemes are based on colours opposite each other on the colour wheel.

Triadic colour schemes use three colours equally spaced around the colour wheel.

Tetradic/Quadratic colour schemes are created by choosing colours at the corners of a rectangle inscribed on the colour wheel.

Split Complementary colour schemes are created by choosing one colour and then two more colours that are adjacent to the complementary of the initial colour.

Other colour schemes include the following:

Neutral colour schemes include only colours not found on the colour wheel (various tones of brown and grey).

Accented Neutral colour schemes include neutral colours as above and one or more splashes of colours found on the colour wheel.

Natural colour scheme is based on the nature.

Colours are used to attract attention, convey meaning, and generally enhance the aesthetics of design. It can be used to create a visual hierarchy in the design. A small dose of colour that contrasts with main colour will draw attention. It will give emphasis. Warmer colours advance into the foreground while cooler colours recede into the background, which can affect the form and their relationship. Colours play a large role in the design as the colour wheel is a tool for the visual impact.

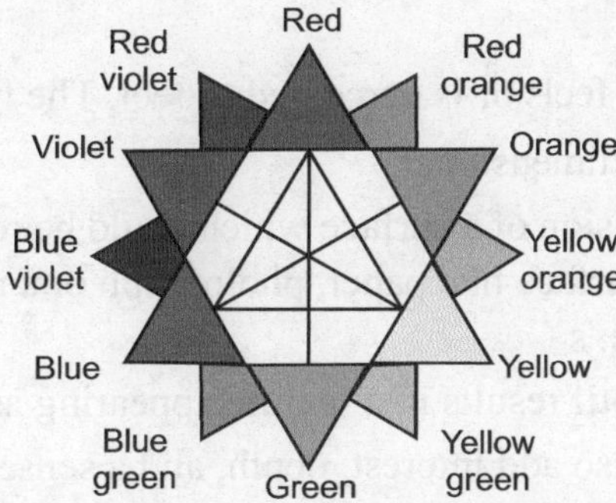

Fig. 1.7. Colour star containing primary, secondary and tertiary colours

Colours can give vibrancy, consistency and interest to a design. It can create a hierarchy of space and buildings and gives a meaning within cultural context.

The attributes of colours comprise:

Shape: A shape is defined as a two or more than two dimensional area that has defined or implied boundary. These are categorised as Geometric Shapes using a compass or ruler, and Organic Shapes that are complex and normally found in nature.

In the two-dimensional world, there are three simple geometric shapes – the square, the triangle and the circle. All other geometric shapes are the combination of these three. There are also more complex organic shapes we see in natural and man-made objects, such as the silhouette of leaves, trees, cars or other everyday objects. Shape is the foundation of form.

The square is the most stable and carries the most visual weight. The triangle is the least stable and displays movement. The circle is nearly as stable as the square and hints at rotational movement.

Circles or dots can be interpreted as either geometric or organic. Shapes or forms that have irregular, complex, and highly differentiated contours are considered organic. Soft, textured forms also appear to be organic shapes as they are seen more like things we see in nature. Variation is an inherent quality of organic forms.

Abstract shapes are simplified or stylized versions of organic shapes. Geometric forms can be arranged organically and organic forms can be arranged geometrically. Either creates tension between the forms and their structure. When we want to convey an organic message, we should emphasize the organic qualities of form and use more irregularity and variety.

Fig. 1.8. Simple geometric shapes

Pattern and Texture

Texture means the way a surface feels or is perceived to feel. The types of texture include:

- Tactile texture is three-dimensional.
- Visual texture is the illusion of a surface which could be rough and three dimensional, but depicted on a smooth surface like paper, photograph or a mirror, no matter how rough the image perceives it to be. s
- Regularly repeating motif results in a texture appearing as a pattern.
- Patterns and surfaces also add interest, depth, and a sense of realism to design.
- Structure or the structural lines can be used to form patterns and textures. The structures we form can be geometric or organic and we can combine geometric forms organically or organic forms geometrically. Each will convey a different message.
- They can call attention to space that takes on a texture or pattern in contrast with the element.

Volume and Mass: For a two-dimensional design, space concerns creating a third-dimension volume and mass. When we make a surface or plane the 3-dimensional we have a volume. Since we live in a 3-dimensional world, volumetric quality to 2-dimensional format gives a sense of realism to a design. Volumes advance when compared to a plane and also carry greater mass and visual weight than planes or surfaces. If we overlap a plane on top of a volume it creates tension between the foreground and background as normal expectations are for the volume to advance and the plane to recede.

The perception of mass is how strongly the element pulls your eye toward it. Through use of mass or weight balance and movement in a design can be controlled. We can add mass to a series of angular planes by rotating them and letting them overlap each other. The overlapped area becomes darker and is seen as containing the mass from multiple planes. The rotation also creates movement.

This change of the pattern or texture emulates the effects of light and shade, in which case the surface or plane becomes a volume with greater mass and weight and naturally appears less flat. Volumes are 3-dimensional and the extra dimension brings with it the perception of mass and weight. A sphere always weighs more than a circle.

In terms of space design, shading can make an object of a two-dimensional surface seem three-dimensional. Highlight, Transitional Light, Core of the Shadow, Reflected Light, and Cast Shadow give an object a three-dimensional look. Linear perspective is the concept relating to how an object seems smaller, the farther away it gets. Atmospheric perspective is based on how air acts as a filter to change the appearance of distant objects.

Form: Form is a three-dimensional object, which has height, width and depth and also has the presence of light and shadows on its surfaces. Broadly, the form can be geometric (man-made) and natural (organic form) or combination of the two.

Principles of Design

The elements of design bring them together into a design for which the following principles are applied:

Unity and Harmony: To achieve visual unity is the main goal of design. When all elements are in agreement, a design is considered unified. No individual part is viewed as more important than the whole design. A good balance between unity and variety must be established to avoid a chaotic or a lifeless design. In architecture unity and harmony can be achieved by:

- **Perspective:** sense of distance between elements.
- **Similarity:** ability to seem repeatable with other elements.
- **Continuation:** the sense of having a line or pattern extend.
- **Repetition:** elements being copied or mimicked numerous times.
- **Rhythm:** is achieved when recurring position, form, size, colour, and use of graphic elements.

Altering the basic theme achieves unity and keeps interest.

"There's got to be enough space in there (between notes) so that the sound will work in an air space. That's what makes the music work."

—Frank Zappa

Without space there is no music. Try to imagine every note playing at the same time or being played so quickly that there is no distinction between one note and the next. You would not have music. You would have a solid wall of noise. As Zappa said, "*You have to leave room for the sounds to be distinguished from each other, to be heard for what they are.*" The same is true about architecture. There has to be enough space.

Space can be used to both separate and connect elements in a design. Wider spaces separate elements from each other and narrower spaces connect elements to reveal relationship between them. Overlapping elements maximize their relationship.

Rhythm, direction, and motion can be created by design flow through space. This involves:

- Creating groupings of elements
- Creating emphasis and hierarchy
- Improving legibility

Space can be used to convey a variety of meanings, some of which include :

- quality – visual, functional, comfort
- solitude – abandonment, loneliness
- cleanliness – simple and neat bleached, washed
- purity – unsullied, unadulterated
- spirituality – sacredness, connection to something greater
- openness – distance, infinity
- calmness – placidity, inaction

Spaces can be active or passive. When the space in a design is symmetrically balanced the space becomes passive, static and formal. When space is asymmetrically balanced, it becomes active, dynamic and interesting.

Fig. 1.9. The Shape of the fish in the water and voids become birds in the sky

Balance: It is a state of tension and equilibrium which may not always be calm. It can be:

- Symmetrical
- Asymmetrical balance produces an informal balance that is attention attracting and dynamic.
- Radial balance is arranged around a central element. The elements placed in a radial balance seem to 'radiate' out from a central point in a circular fashion.
- A mosaic form normally arises from too many elements. Due to the lack of hierarchy and contrast, this can look clumsy.

Day exists in contrast to night. Without cold there is no hot. It is the yin/yang of interconnected opposites. Space is no different. Filled space sits in opposition to negative space, but neither exists without comparison to the other. Both are necessary to create a harmonious balance in a design. When all your design elements crowd each other it is hard to find your way through them. A systematic organization of elements provides visual relief.

Architect Ludwig Mies van der Rohe adopted the motto of "Less is more" to describe his aesthetic tactic of arranging the necessary components of a building to create an impression of simplicity, by enlisting every element and detail to serve visual and functional purposes.

Size, Scale and proportion: Size, scale, and proportion are all related concepts.

- **Size:** the physical dimensions of an object
- **Scale:** the relative size of different objects, or of an object, to a common standard
- **Proportion:** harmony of scale

Scale is about relative measurements. A single object has no scale until it is seen in comparison with something else. Scale can be used to create the illusion of depth as larger elements tend to advance while smaller elements tend to recede into the background. Scale creates perspective in a composition. It can also be an effective way to create icons. A lack of scale leads to a static and boring design. A lack of scale creates competition between elements.

For example, in a small building, the effect of wind may not be a significant problem. As the building grows in size, the wind has a much greater impact. This needs design interventions, structure and building materials that would protect against the horizontal forces of wind add more weight and more vertical force.

Proportion is the relationship between elements with respect to a comparative magnitude. It can create harmony of scale, whether or not the sizes of elements are in agreement of form and balance. Proportion can be used to define symmetry and visual delight, and can create a sense of tension that focuses the eye. Proportion creates rhythm and a sense of harmony or unity in a composition or design. The most universal standard of measurement when it comes to proportion is the human body. People respond emotionally to proportion and if something is out of proportion, it can evoke negative feeling. As such, the design communicates by placing elements in proportion.

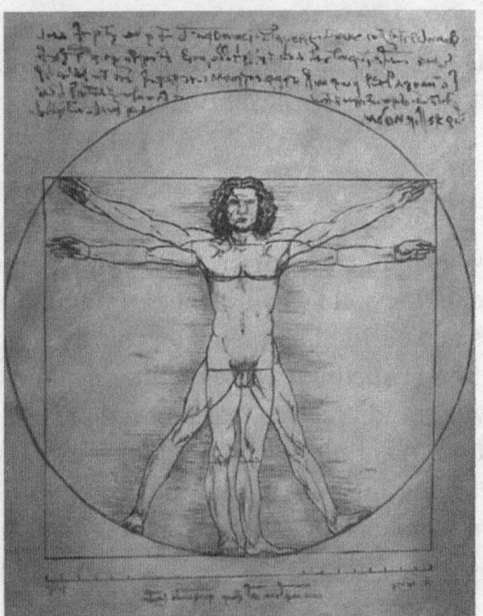

Fig. 1.10. The proportion of human figure by Leonardo-da Vinci

For example, in a house the ceiling door knobs, light switches, etc. are placed at a convenient height as per human proportion. As such, architects use a grid for space design which might be based on the rule of thumb or the golden section. Both are proportional systems for dividing the page as are all grids. The golden section is also called the golden proportion or divine proportion. A design can not be created without thinking about size, scale, and proportion.

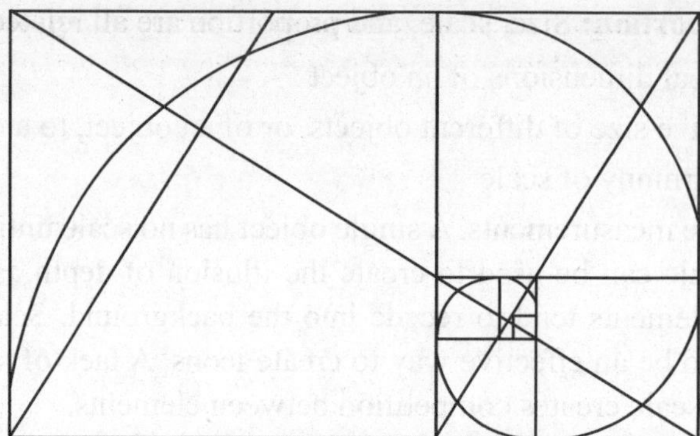

Fig. 1.11. The Golden Section

Similarity and Contrast: A consistent design is an important aspect of an architect's work. Too much similarity is boring, but without similarity important elements will not exist and an image without contrast is uneventful. The key is to find the balance between similarity and contrast. There are several ways to develop a similar environment:

- Structure various components into a composite whole.
- Manipulate forms and shapes to correlate together.
- Express continuity and movement to local areas.
- Develop a style and adhere to it.

Hierarchy: A good design contains elements that lead the eye through each element in order of its significance.

Dominance/Emphasis: Dominance is created by contrasting size, positioning, color, style, or shape. The focal point should dominate the design with scale and contrast without sacrificing the unity of the whole.

Architectural Design Skills

Architects need to have a strong foundation of creative skills, innovation, systems thinking, soft thinking, a blend of theory, technology and performance, communication and managerial skills.Too much focus on formal lectures and curriculum bound teaching marginalizes the creative abilities of the students. The new generation IT mediums, like the internet and CAD, have also contributed in making hand sketching, drawings and creative learning redundant. Many students of architecture are hardly inspired by sculpture, painting, dance, drama, music, poetry, etc. Intellectualism and personal credentials make teaching too overloaded and complex for the tender minds of young students. Gaps exist between academic idealism and pragmatic process. There is a cut-throat competition among the architects and everyone is aspiring to become an island of excellence.

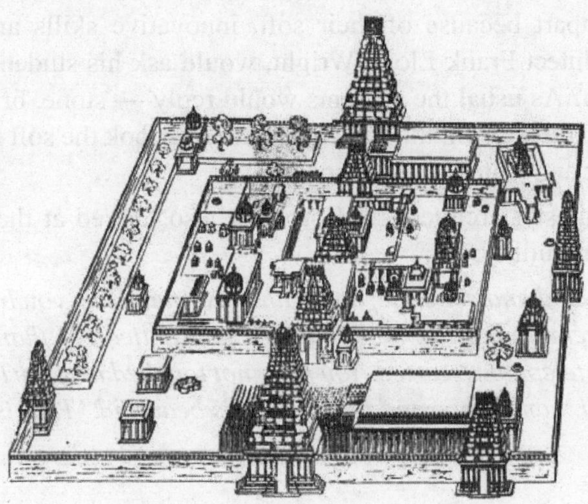

Fig. 1.12. Temple of Thiruvanamalai, Tamil Nadu. Architecture as an element of urbanism and vice-versa. Sketch by Sita Ram (1842)

While education may end after graduation, learning of an architect never stops. Learning is a journey where architect is trained to remain a lifelong student. Learning involves investment of time, energy, finances and other resources. The same student learns many more times by alternative, participatory methods than in a routine classroom/examination style. This implies that the method of learning (and teaching) makes all the difference. This is why some institutes become a brand while many others keep struggling. What needs to be done is to adopt new ways of teaching and learning, where student picks up the most within the available time and understands the process of organisation of space and design.

Soft thinking is like a floodlight. It is more diffuse, not as intense, but covers a wider area. It is easy to pick up solid or something, while the soft things are more difficult to grab-like air and water. Soft skills enable the architect trigger his imagination, fantasy, thinking, innovation and out of box solutions. Soft thinking is metaphorical, mythical, dreaming, approximate, diffuse, humorous, playful and capable of dealing with contradictions. We have heard of Panchatantra fables, which transformed the incorrigible, most unwilling to learn princes into creative and wise young men. This is soft learning.

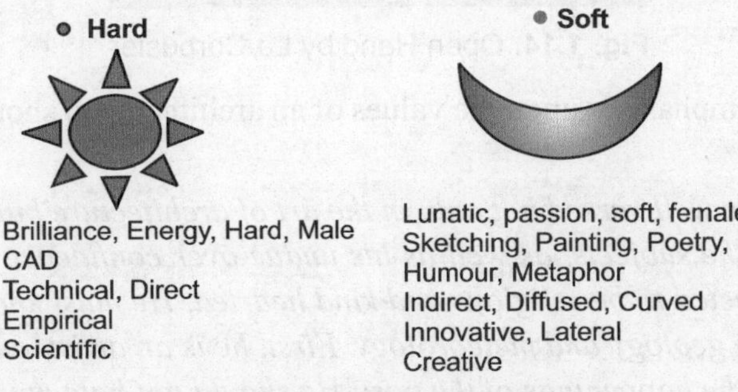

Fig. 1.13. Hard and Soft Skills

The masters stand apart because of their soft, innovative skills and lateral thinking. The celebrated American architect Frank Lloyd Wright, would ask his students — what materials are essential for construction? As usual the students would reply — stone, brick, glass, cement, steel, wood, etc. The master would then tell the students not to overlook the soft materials and ask—what about light and shade, air and water, sun and space?

Likewise, the great master architect Le Corbusier also looked at the buildings beyond their practical physical form and utility:

"You employ stone, wood and concrete, and with these materials you build houses and palaces. That is construction. Ingenuity is at work. My house is practical. I thank you, as I might thank railway engineers, or the telephone service. You have not touched my heart. But suddenly you touch my heart, you do me good, I am happy and I say: 'This is beautiful.' That is architecture. Art enters in."

Values and Ethics

Le Corbusier emphasized on values. His famous open hand symbolizes and reminds the architect that he should be giver with an open hand and heart. This coincides with Indian concept of devata—the compassionate benefactor of all living beings.

Fig. 1.14. Open Hand by Le Corbusier

The Vaastu Shastra emphasises upon the values of an architect who should be an artist and kind hearted:

"An architect must be well versed not only in the art of architecture but also in allied subjects. His weakness in any of the subjects, as well as his undue over confidence in the same manner, is not desirable. He is expected to be religious and kind hearted. He must know the various methods of calculation along with geology and meteorology. First, he is an artist, and then an architect. He should be able to grasp the happenings of the past. He should not hate anybody. He should dislike idleness and discard selfishness. He must have good physique and free from seven types of evil habits, viz. fornication, gambling, violence, harsh speech, swindling, partiality and alcoholism." (Mayamat Ch.5)

The architects are surrounded by visible manifestations but should also be able to see the invisible. The non-manifest lies' embedded in our soul, cultural memory, rituals and history. To draw this infinite source and create a new vision is possible only if an architect can see the invisible by developing soft skills.

Architecture is a performing profession. As such, theory and ideology need to be integrated with the soft skills for creative and lateral thinking. The dreams, fantasy and design innovations relate to time and space in their human, financial, legal, administrative and political context. As such soft thinking is a way to search the context and connections. It would be pertinent to mention that as per UNICEF study 83 per cent learning is by sight and we remember 50 per cent when we see and hear and 90 per cent what we say and do. As such inductive and experimental methods of learning are most valuable for architectural education.

Graphics, visuals, charts, symbols, etc. act as condensed language and the alternative tools of soft skill development. As it is said, each picture is equal to a thousand words, the graphics can express a new way of seeing and putting across the point in a clear, simple way. These are particularly useful for architecture, planning and design professionals.

The architectural education and profession need to closely connect with the realms of ecology, technology, economics, management and humanities. A sense of interdependence can break down the rigid boundaries and make education more human centric, value based and relevant to cultural and environmental context and sustainable development objectives. With a cross-disciplinary education, it is possible to respond to the breadth and depth of the realms of complex interdependence of development. This is necessary for the elimination of redundancy and for the solution of innumerable analytical, conceptual and methodological issues. The layers of development constitute the technology, nature, culture, aesthetic and humanities. The greatest enterprise of the mind has always been the manifestation of the linkages of these constituents. Architects must endeavour developing a creative mindscape which facilitates both, the individual and overall excellence, leading to an attractive and sustainable development.

If you are serious being a good architect, don't be serious. Like a lover, be a bit lunatic and funny. Forget about name and fame, success, intellectualism, career and business. You will discover your originality, dream, song, poetry, symphony and melody. The bedrock of a creative mind is to dream and work with love. To quote Khalil Gibran:

"*And what is it to work with love?*

It is to build a house with affection, as if your beloved were to dwell in that house.

It is to charge all things you fashion with a breath of your own spirit."

Vocabulary, Grammar and Metaphor

According to Adrian Smith, architecture is about relationships. Architecture reflects multifarious and infinite quest to manipulate the built environment. These relationships include the way in which human perceive a need for a building and shelter. They involve understanding of community and how we link community to culture, science and art. Architecture synthesises all these components, along with socio-economic and socio-political forces that shape architecture. Contexualism is integral to the built environment. It reflects and mirrors our interests and preoccupations. The built environment must not just reflect culture, but it must delight those who use it and are affected by it. The built environment is constantly in transition, it is kinetic and it is reminder of the past and predictor of the future. It is an expression of our culture, values and state of our economies and our optimism in the future. The architecture has a vocabulary, grammar and poetics. It has a form, metaphor and space. Grammar is by no means absolute, it is flexible which evolves through time.

In an essay Lewis Mumford wrote *"By his choice of materials and textures and colours, by the contrasting play of light and shade, by the manipulation of planes, by the accentuation, when necessary, of sculpture and ornament, the architect does in fact turn character changes with the hours and seasons, with the functions and actions of spectators and inhabitants. Similarly, he creates in a building a unique work of sculptures, a form one must merely walk around but walk into a form in which the very movement of the spectator through spaces, solids and voids have a powerful aesthetic effect, not known in any other art."*

Cultural and Urban Context

T.S. Eliot in his essay 'Tradition and the Individual Talent' examines how one thinks about context in a culture where there is no longer any assurance on the part of the poet that public has a common cultural heritage, common knowledge of works in the past. A city builds its own body of references, but they are ever changing, continuous, adaptable and in flux. In order to envision, one must first re-vision, re-appropriate and continually update understanding of architectural landscape. The architectural landscape is a kind of tapestry in which many memories forms the character and shape of the buildings and affect the continuity of the form and present. A foreign ideology inserted into an environment can have a cancerous effect on the biology of a city. It can ruin the continuity of a place. The architect approaches the new work with the same respect for the traditional city as a poet has for the tradition in which he works.

An architect's work adds to the continuity of the urban context.

It is worth pointing out that there is always the exception that proves the rule, or as Robert Venturi said "to perceive the deal one must acknowledge the real." Venturi never believed that modern movement was bad thing. Rather, he thought that an international style of making buildings that could be applied in all cases was incorrect.

The Modern movement became a crusade and advances in building technology (e.g. RCC, lifts, steel, cranes, building mechanization, HVAC, etc) were among the major forces behind it. Now the modern movement is part of history. New technology are evolving very rapidly, which are also keeping the traditions alive, making it more efficient and viable and reaffirming a sense of continuity.

Architecture and Culture

The earliest form of architecture existed some 7000 years ago, when man transformed primitive cave shelter into architecture through embellishment by wall paintings, engravings and sculptures, thus establishing architecture. Victor Hugo said, '*During the last several centuries of the World's history 'From the time of pagoda of Hindustan of that Cathedral of Cologne, architecture has recorded the great ideas of human race. Not only religious symbols, but every human thought has its page in that vast book........he who was born a poet became an architect.* 'Hugo's masterpiece, Notre Dame in Paris manifests the idea that architecture was a form of literature that expressed national culture. British writer John Ruskin proclaimed in his celebrated books Seven Lamps of

Architecture that buildings could become '*the embodiment of poetry, life history and religious faith of nations through an architect's hand.*' Like Hugo, Ruskin believed all good architecture is the expression of national life and character.

At the root of their thought was Vitruvian triad of commodity, firmness and delight or utility of structure. It is necessary to connect elements of art (delight) with elements of utility of structure, mechanical and enclosure (commodity and firmness) in order to create architecture, which is connected to a place. Architecture embodied utility as well as poetry. Culture is a complex and contradictory to the modernist urge to reduce complexity to simplicity and universalism. The globalization of architecture resulted in replication of universal design. No longer buildings and cities address the needs of local climate, geography, indigenous materials, culture and environment.

Culture is a way of life, an ancestral history in which religious beliefs, rituals, ceremonies, celebrations, art and crafts, literature, poetry, cuisine, sports, economic status, habitat and memory all play a role, a continuum from one generation to the next, and evolving by technology and invading cultures. Transition occurs as the assimilation of counter cultures take place. When assimilation is resisted, it results in social stagnations and tensions. Conversely, the multi-culturalism allows other cultures their own space and legitimacy.

Architecture has always been a symbol of culture. However, it has become an individual tool of expression and not to build a homogeneous society. Architecture in this era has become an economic tool for investments. Its identity has been largely reduced to the universal buildings of glass and concrete, void of contextual roots. From the expressionless series of misfits, blandness and contrivances, architecture has no roots in the memory of place, no paradigm of design, but a fleeting stylistic fashion. It is void of delight and has become unemotional. It is difficult to find as sense if place.

Only by a search for the meaning of a place through its past, context, climate and culture, we can forge an architecture that provides an environment of richness and collective identity. Cities can achieve a connected indigenous vocabulary enriched by technological innovations and inventiveness.

Contextual architecture represents design in a cultural compatibility, which ranges from the adaptation of architectural styles, elements building facade to design of a building in continuity of the past while responding to the present and future needs, environment, climate, culture, politics and economics.

The Cognitive Perception of Space

The concerns of architects in a wide-angle framework of urban contact and design, ecology and all aspects of function, climate, technology, economy, social, cultural heritage and land. It is necessary to evolve the design which is sustainable and responsive to the land and to the aspirations and culture of the users. The approach to architecture needs to integrate aesthetics, human values and behavior, indigenous knowledge, anthropology and cognitive perceptions of space, environment, ecology, technology, geography, history and social and economic transformation.

According to B.V. Doshi, who started working with Le Corbusier, "*The belief that the psychic experience in architecture is central and that the physical and intellectual experiences are to be developed around them is what fascinates me. My recent work is based on this important realisation.*

Such architecture perhaps, must be specific to a culture and an urge to design a built form rooted in all its aspects to the land where it stands has preoccupied my thinking for several years. This led me to a critical viewing of the traditional architecture of my environment where the holistic experiences were strongly felt."

In his design of the Indian Institute of Management, Bangalore, Sangath at Ahmedabad and Gandhi Labour Institute there is a strong relationship between the earth and the sky. Here the village square form of space gives the place a sense of belonging. Effaced from social disparities, the village complex is an adaptation from the typical village square of India. As Doshi himself remarked, in order to generate a design comprehended at functional, symbolic and notional levels, he adopted the model of a temple of Naudtal, an inner court of a large haveli in Jaisalmer and a typical village square. Likewise in Sangath, the form, light and space are integrated, resulting in a design which is functional, modern and climatic.

Fig. 1.15. CEPT, Ahmedabad, B.V. Doshi

Architecture is not just a building, but the open space around it. Tao Te Ching explains it so eloquently:

> *Though thirty spokes may form the wheel, it is the hole within the hub which gives the wheel utility.*
>
> *It is not the clay the potter throws, which gives the pot its usefulness*
> *but the space within the shape ,from which the pot is made.*
> *Without a door, the room cannot be entered, and without windows it is dark.*
> *Such is the utility of non-existence.*

This means looking beyond functionalism and relate architecture to a larger framework—building, ecology, climate, energy, economy and the culture.

Le Corbusier, the celebrated French-Swiss architect, made one of the most impressive contribution in shaping the Indian architecture. In early fifties he was commissioned to design several buildings and Chandigarh city. His Sarabhai and Shodan Villas and the Mill Owners Building at Ahmedabad and the four majestic buildings of the capital complex in Chandigarh had an incredible impact on Indian architects. It not only helped to regenerate art which was almost lost during the British rule but also provided a stimulus to Indian architects. He threw open the floodgates of revolutionary concepts of form, syntax and aesthetics. Many contemporary Indian architects adopted Le Corbusier's exposed concrete, bold and plastic forms and modular openings and facades.

This started an era of search for the forms which related more closely with the Indian context and regional characteristic. This can be best witnessed in the India International Centre, built in Delhi during early sixties. According to Joseph Allen Stein, the architect, *"I strongly believe that being modern without being regional is inappropriate and regional without modernism reactionary."* Based on human scale, India International Centre (IIC) witnessed integration of both new knowledge, *i.e.* technology with the local culture. The IIC along with the Ford Foundation and the United Nations Children Education Fund building is a beautiful oasis in the sublime setting of historic Lodi Gardens.

Fig. 1.16. India International Centre, New Delhi, Joseph Allen Stein, Architects

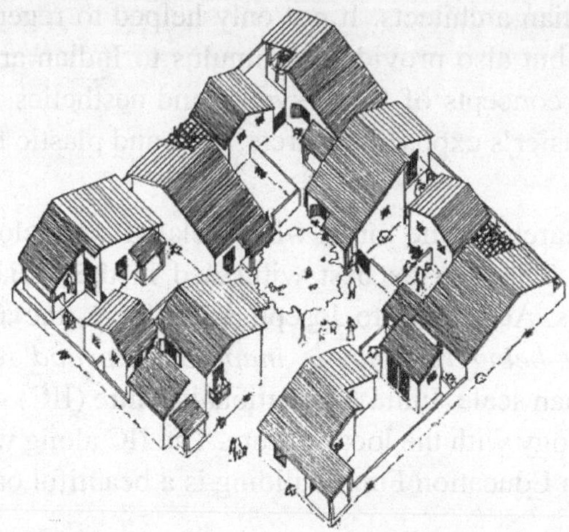

Fig. 1.17. The Artists' Village, Belapur (Architect Charles Correa)

Intrinsic Values in Architecture: We live surrounded by visible manifestations, but it is the invisible that actually adds meaning to our lives. The non-manifest lies embedded in our spirit, cultural memory, rituals and history. To draw this infinite source and create a new vision with the help of today's technology for people and their aspirations is to invent the future. One must look back in order to look ahead. According to Charles Correa, "*we have inherited the cultural accretions of thousands of years. Nothing has been wiped out. New ideas do not replace old ones. They co-exist. Where does Rangoli pattern come from? The Bindi on a Hindu women's fore-head? A woman who wears that mark also wears a nylon sari; the woman who makes mysterious rangoli patterns at her doorstep also watches Hindi films on television. An architect working in such a cultural environment is in a uniquely fortunate position. To carry that tradition forward, all the links with the past, present and alive, in a culture of vast multiplicity, the task of architecture has always been to define the place of the individual in relation to an infinitely cosmos.*"

Fig. 1.18. Kaufman House (Falling Water), Frank Lloyd Wright

Fig. 1.19. Jawahar Kala Kendra, Jaipur (Charles Correa)

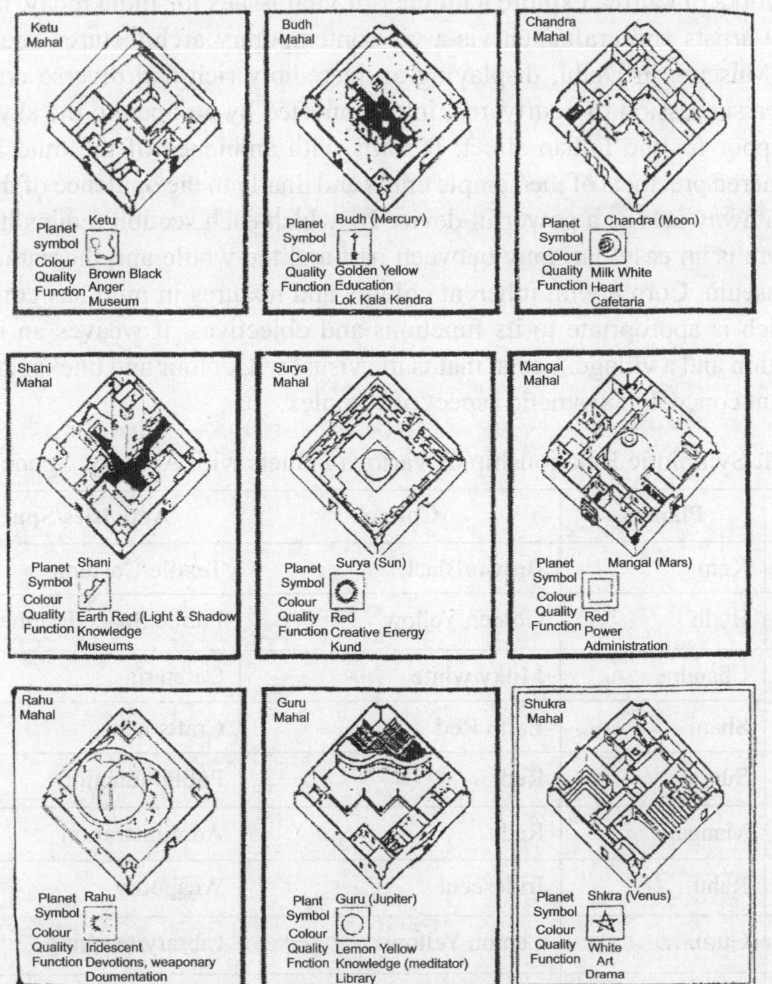

Fig. 1.20. Design process of Jawahar Kala Kendra, Jaipur (Charles Correa)

Fig. 1.21. Bahai Lotus Temple, New Delhi (Fariburz Sahba)

The recent works of Correa explore a number of vital issues for India today, from the position of the traditional artists and craftsmen vis-a-vis contemporary architecture. The galleries of the National Crafts Museum in Delhi, displaying an incredibly rich and diverse crafts of India are arranged around a succession of courtyards, interconnected by an open to the sky pathway which becomes a metaphor for the Indian street. It starts with ambience of the mud houses and then proceeds to the sacred precincts of the Temple crafts and finally to the opulence of the Durbar Crafts. The ritualistic pathway acts as a powerful device by which each section retains its own ambience authenticity. There is an easy harmony between part and the whole and the natural environment. In the Crafts Museum, Correa with inherent colours and textures in mud has conceived a unique atmosphere, which is appropriate to its functions and objectives. It weaves an image of a local vernacular, tradition and a village. Leela, that is the visual wit, colour and unexpected juxtaposition plays an important concept in aesthetic aspect of complex.

Table 1.1. Symbiotic Relationship of Various Planets with Activity, Space and Colours

	Planets	**Colour**	**Activities/Space**
1.	Ketu	Brown/Black	Textile/Costume
2.	Budh	Golden Yellow	Public Space/Exhibition
3.	Chandra	Milky white	Cafeteria
4.	Shani	Earth Red	Craftsmen
5.	Surya	Red	Public function
6.	Mangal	Red	Administration
7.	Rahu	Iridescent	Weaponry
8.	Guru	Lemon Yellow	Library/teaching
9.	Shukra	White	Theatre/Entertainment

Note: This concept has been applied in Jawahar Kala Kendra Jaipur by Architect Charles Correa.

The Library and Headquarters of the British Council in New Delhi is constructed along a pathway, organized along a formal linear axis, a series of layers symbolising the various interfaces, represented by three mythic axes mundi. At the end is the oldest one: the interface with Hinduism, symbolized here by the ancient Vedic Bindu (the source of all energy). In the middle is the interface with the Islam, here represented by the Charbagh (the Koranic Garden of Paradise). The third axis Mundi, brought by the English who arrived with their own mythic beliefs in science and rationality, is a traditional European one.

The Jawahar Kala Kendra, a museum in memory of Nehru, is based on Vastupurush Mandala where architecture has been conceived as a model of the Cosmos. The Mandala invoked here is the Navagraha, which consist of nine squares-each representing a planet (including two imaginary ones, Rahu and Ketu). The city of Jaipur, built by Maharaj Jai Singh was based on this spatial matrix with one of the squares moved because of the presence of a hill. The Jawahar Kala Kendra invokes this original mandala, with one of the squares displaced so as to create a main entrance, recoiling the gesture of the original plan of Jaipur.

In this complex, Correa has conceived architecture from parts to whole and vice-versa. The concept of whole is intrinsic. According to him we can never visualise a building in its entirety. The mental image is synthesised from a sequence of partial views. Jawahar Kala Kendra has been built like a fort in red sandstone with no windows on the facade. This cultural complex is submerged on a local context and environment. The relation of line and shape is simple. The flatness and the horizontal structure of the complex create a spatial envelope. The Vastu Purush Mandal concept gives the whole composition a form of squares and a series of courtyards. The interiors are decorated by Tantra paintings with emphasis on proportions, light and shade effects and architectural balance.

The Inter-University Centre for Astronomy and Astrophysics in Pune has also been conceived by Correa as a model of the cosmos based not on archaic notion, but on the concept of the expanding universe. Thus, one arrives between black (local black basalt), surmounted by even blacker Kuddaph stone, capped by glossy black polished granite, reflecting sky and clouds. Black on black the infinity of outer space. The whole complex is arranged around a central kund symbolizing the ancient archetype for the cosmos which is expanding into peripheral spaces.

In the projects of Charles Correa, colour and animation are combined with building techniques in a unique architectural vision. His projects have a richness that seems undeniably Indian, but there is also a deeper and broader cultural vitality.

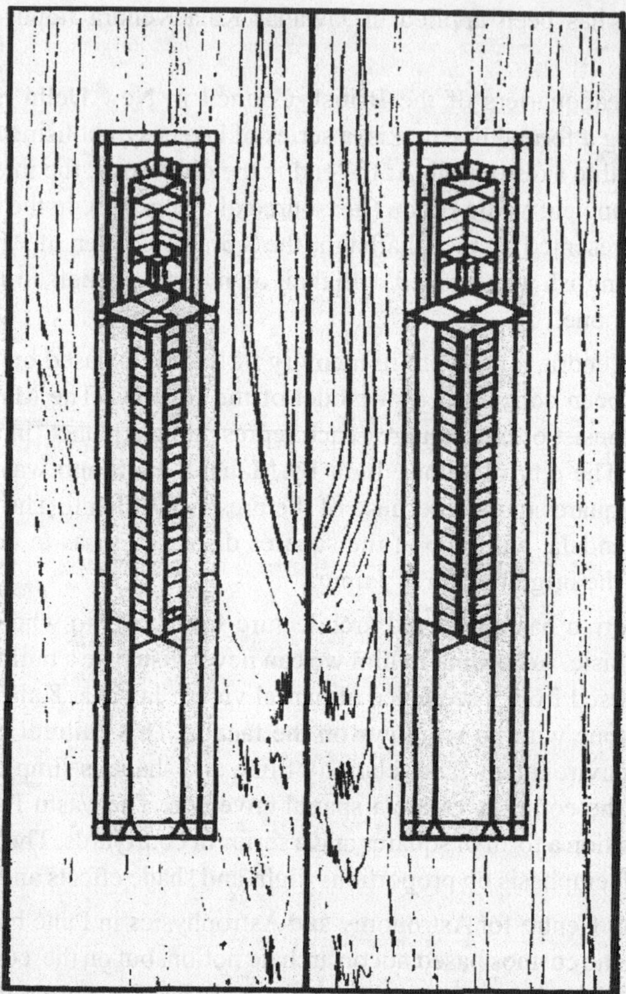

Fig. 1.22. Glazed Door by Frank Lloyd Wright, Robie House, Chicago, 1909

Another striking reinterpretation of spiritual knowledge has been expressed by the Lotus temple, built during the eighties in Delhi. It symbolises the renaissance of intrinsic values of architecture, superseding functionalism. Its architect Fariburz Sahba evolved a unique concept to infuse Bahai ideals into an Indian symbol. The form of the temple represents universal principles and a true symbolism, far from those invented by men but springing from the nature itself. The lotus represents the universe and enshrines the ideas of light and growth. In Indian philosophy, it is associated with the notion of purity and *Sattva*. From *Sattva* springs the *Dharma* and *Gyana*. The tranquil effect created by the Lotus Temple is achieved by arrangement of the petals, geometrical symmetry and the alluring form. The combination of large open spaces all round gives a spacious feeling and lightness to the environment. The nine water pools around the building represent green leaves of the lotus floating on water.

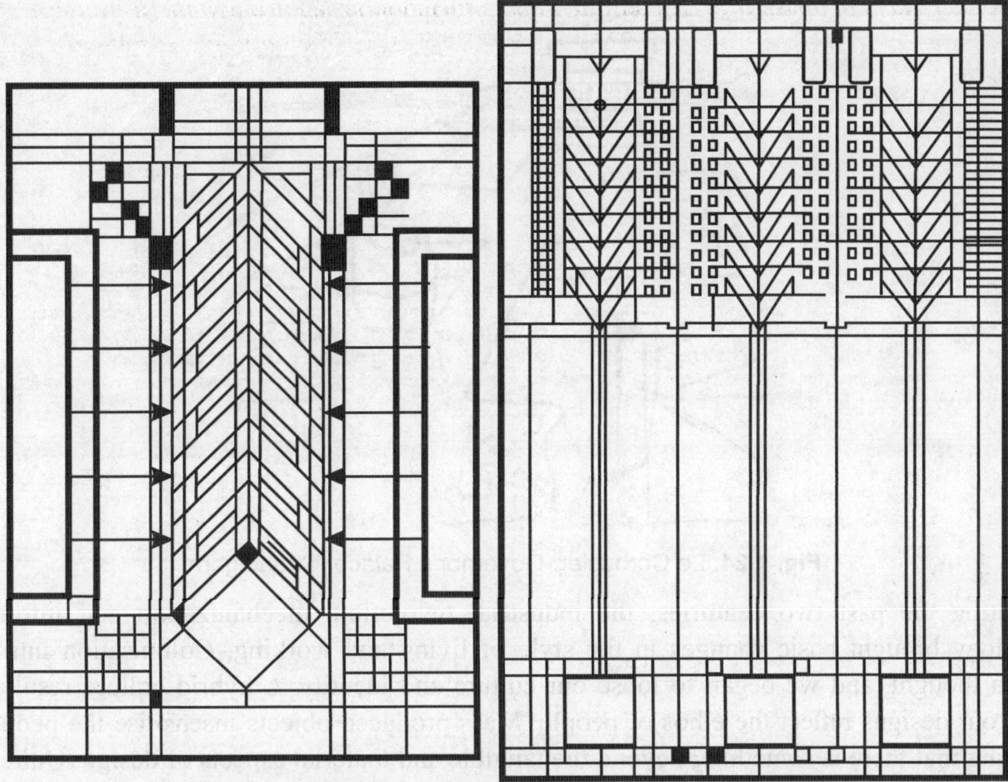

Fig. 1.23. Door and window designs by Frank Lloyd Wright

Changing Concepts of Space

Architecture manifests organization of space and the ability to give shape to an idea. The fascination of design lies in the interplay between the infinite ideas and limited resources which include light, sun, air, rain, building materials, budget and time. Like a musician, the beauty of spatial composition depends upon harmonious orchestration of heterogeneous factors—light and colour, surfaces, comforts, solids and voids, functional and environmental parameters. Designing is like creating a stage set. It should speak and present an individual personality, character and image. Unlike mass produce match box office towers or rubber stamped apartment blocks, the purpose of a design is to give a personal touch and an identity to the faceless space. The recent trends in design indicate a search for emotional and human relationship with the space and the built environment. The human relationship is not just physical, but also in terms of psychological and emotional feelings. In the beginning of the twentieth century, the celebrated architect and progenitor of the modern movement, Le Corbusier employed the human form as a model of harmony and as a module of space. The human relationship with space is much more than mere its physical measurement or scale.

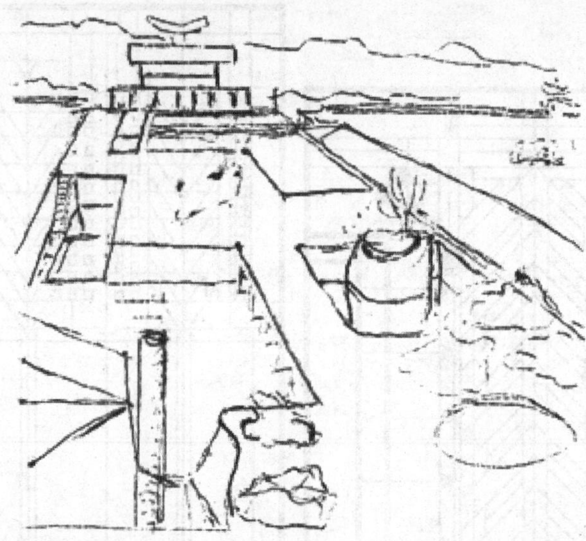

Fig. 1.24. Le Corbusier: Governor's Palace, Chandigarh

During the past two centuries, the industrial revolution, mechanization and information technology brought basic changes in the style of living and working. Colonisation introduced western thought, and we began to loose our culture and identity. A hybrid culture resulted. No longer our designs reflect the ethos of people. Mass produced objects insensitise the people into forgetting that there is something beyond the tangible and material aspects of design. Quite often, in spite of meeting all the functional requirements, using most modern techniques, materials and workmanship standards, the building is uninspiring, lifeless. It is devoid of a feeling of warmth, human consciousness and emotions. Emotions and consciousness are amorphous and ambiguous. A designer has to search for the relationship between consciousness and space. He has to create a living space, a space which is emotionally responsive. This involves a new understanding and expression in terms of design.

The breakthrough in technology has multiplied the space, energy and time. There has been a realisation of "less is more" and the emergence of its practical applications in the form of micro-chips, micro-computers, microwaves, nano-technology, etc. The buildings and services are yet to capture this breakthrough. It is time that new forms of energy, services and construction are evolved. Recharging and recycling must be the key concepts in services and buildings. A new pattern is emerging, shrinking space and time. The network of society, cyber-space, e-topia is changing the familiar borders like inside-outside, private-public, here-there, city-country and yesterday-tomorrow. The built world of space and place is characterized by online exchange of information, interactions, dynamic networks and floating nodes. Recycling of waste water, rain water harvesting, coupled with waterless toilet will save the environment and avoid impending water crisis. Geothermal heating and cooling system by circulating water through a grid of underground wells (100 m deep), where the earth's temperature is constant 15°C, can provide economical and environment friendly solutions to micro-climate and energy needs. The living pattern should manifest a circular metabolism, replacing the existing linear system of input-output.

In his book, "The Road Ahead", Bill Gates says that he is building intelligent systems into his house, located on a hillside overlooking Lake Washington. The spooky house that Bill Gates has been programmed to think. If you were to drive up to the Microsoft billionaire's front door, you'd have an electronic pin clipped to your clothes. It would cause a moving zone of light to accompany you through the house, connecting you to an array of electronic services, so the house can meet and anticipate your every need. As you walk through the corridors, lights in the rooms before you will mysteriously be lit. Your special music will move with you. No one else in the house will hear it. If you get a phone call, only the handset nearest you will ring. Images that you want to summon up will materialise on the walls of rooms just before you walk in and vanish after you ask. The house will memorise all your preferences. If in the past you asked to see paintings by Matisse, you may find these displayed on the walls the next time you enter.

According to Bill Gates, computer-controlled displays of various sizes built into the walls are connected to the information highway, which do away with books, stereo systems, even compact discs and fax machines. Even old photographs will be stored digitally and called up on a screen instead of having to sit in a frame. According to him, new communications will make it easier to stay in touch with people who are geographically distant. The (information) highway will also enable us to find new companions. People once thought of their immediate neighbours as their only community. The telephone allowed us to stretch this and Information Technology is opening up the communications floodgates, where the whole world is becoming a global village.

It is extremely important that the design of space responds to new technologies, communication channels, changing standards of performance and is user friendly. It should be inspiring and reflective. At the same time, a designer has to be conscious of the economic and efficient use of space and materials. The design of space should provide for a built in flexibility for change, growth and variation in functions. With the increasing cost of built-up space, particularly in the metropolitan cities, the need for efficient use of space is becoming more pressing.

Man's experience of space is not only visual but also multisensory. People react to their environment and feel, hear, and smell the space. Today for most people the physical environment, whether at work or home, is frustrating. Quite often, there is unrest in the mind of designers, when they find that in spite of meeting all the functional requirements the house is devoid of a feeling of warmth. This is perhaps the most difficult aspect of design. A designer should be able to visualize the space filled with human form and movements. As such, the study of human form, mind, emotions and spirit becomes critical in place making.

DEBRIEFING QUESTIONS

1. Architecture is the art and science of building. Please explain.

2. Write short notes :

(*i*) Golden Section

(*ii*) Five elements of Prakriti

(*iii*) Visual Perception

(*iv*) Colour system

(*v*) Aesthetics

3. Explain the following design elements:
    - Point, dot, line
    - Surfaces
    - Pattern
    - Texture
    - Form, volume, mass
    - Size, and scale
    - Colours
4. Explain the architectural design principles:
    - Unity, harmony
    - Perspective
    - Continuity
    - Rhythm
    - Composition
    - Proportion
    - Similarity and Contrast
5. Write notes on the following:
    (*i*) Perspective
    (*ii*) Scale and proportion
    (*iii*) Patterns and structure
    (*iv*) Hard and soft skills
6. How architects interprete and understand space and what are its attributes?
7. Explain the role of human dimensions in architectural design.

Chapter 2

Evolution of Architecture in India

The evolution of architecture and human settlements is the manifestation of geographic, economic, political, cultural and social aspirations. These also reflect the level of technology and building resources. The growth of human settlements in the ancient river valley civilizations, such as Indus valley, Mesopotamia and Nile (Egyptian) have triggered the evolution of the architecture and cities. With the colonisation, trade routes, automobiles and industrialisation, a new era of human settlements and architecture was witnessed. A cross-cultural synthesis was seen in Indian cities, with widespread influence of Islamic and colonial morphologies. The colonial imperialism and transition from industrial to post-industrial era, post modern, parametricism and new urbanism concepts have been a turning points in architectural styles. These styles, belonging to different periods of history, bear the stamp of human endeavour and creativity. Indus valley has been a cradle of the Indian architecture. The Great Stupa at Sanchi and the rock-cut caves at Ajanta stand in testimony of the Buddhist architecture. The rock-cut temples of Mahabalipuram, the temples of Kanchipuram, Vijayanagar, Thanjavur, Belur and Halebid mainfest the architectural excellence of the South India.

In north India, a different style of architecture flourished which was called the Nagara style. In central India, the Chandela rulers built a magnificent temple complex at Khajuraho. With the coming of the Muslim rulers, a new architectural style in India—the Indo-Islamic architecture came into existence.

Indus Valley (2300 TO 1600 B.C.)

The earliest human settlements in Indian sub-continent were at Mohenjo-daro, along the Indus River that produced the Harappan culture which persisted from 2300 to 1600 B.C. At its zenith, around 1600 B.C. Mohenjo-daro was a prosperous community of farmers, craftspeople, herders, brick masons, and builders. They cultivated wheat, barley, dates, melons, legumes, and various other crops and husbanded animals, cattle, goats, sheep, pigs, and fowl. To the north of Mohenjo-daro, was situated the town of Harappa in a zone of high agricultural productivity and along the Ravi. The site, with its high ground and alluvium for cultivation, was ideal for the settlement. Due to its location on the Indus river, it was a gateway to the Hindu Kush, Baluchistan and Afghanistan and several trade routes converged on the town. The Indus river afforded boating and communication with the plains. The city was laid with underground drainage and had courtyard houses, public square, markets and granaries.

The mature phase of Indus Valley civilization was the Harappan Civilization. The first of its cities to be unearthed was Harappa, excavated in the 1920s in the Punjab province of British India (now in Pakistan). Excavation of Harappan sites have been ongoing since 1920, with important breakthroughs occurring as recently as 1999. To date, over 1,052 cities and settlements have been found, mainly in the general region of the Ghaggar-Hakra river and its tributaries. Among the settlements, the major urban centre were Harappa, Lothal, Mohenjo-daro (UNESCO World Heritage Site), Dholavira, Kalibanga, and Rakhigarhi.

The inhabitants used gravity flow to convey water from the river via stone channels to open fields below. The Harappan culture of the Indus Valley was a relatively short-lived experience, lasting about 500 years. Theories concerning the cause of the decline range from possibility of a large-scale geological cataclysm and tectonic disturbance, having altered the flow of the lower Indus river.

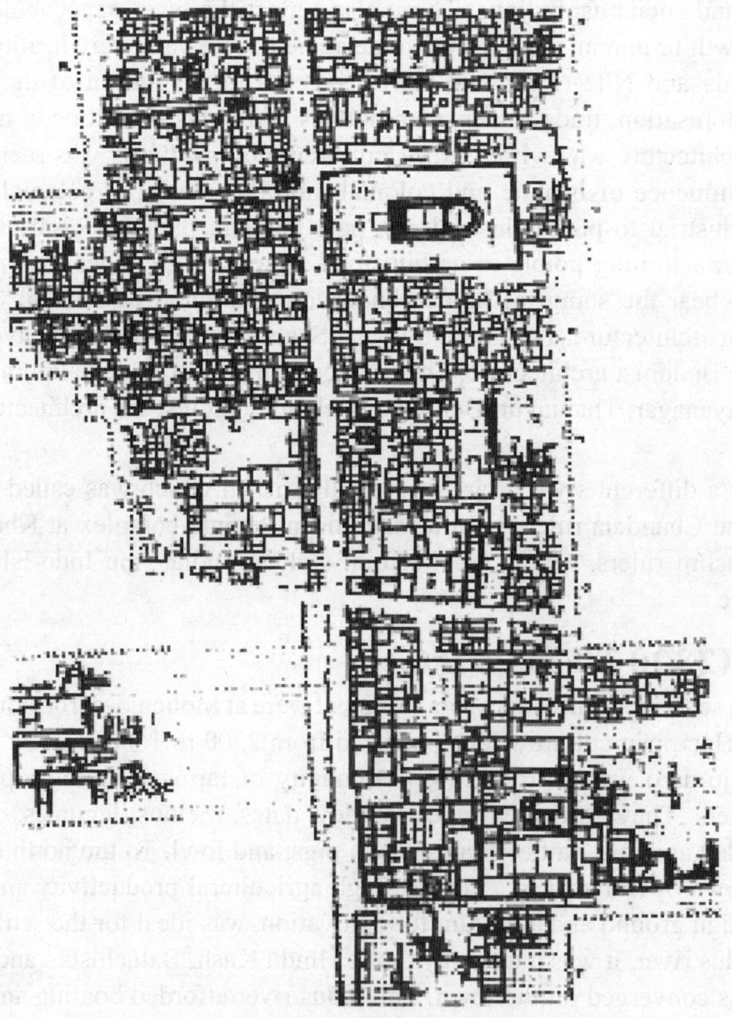

Fig. 2.1. Sirkap Town, Taxila

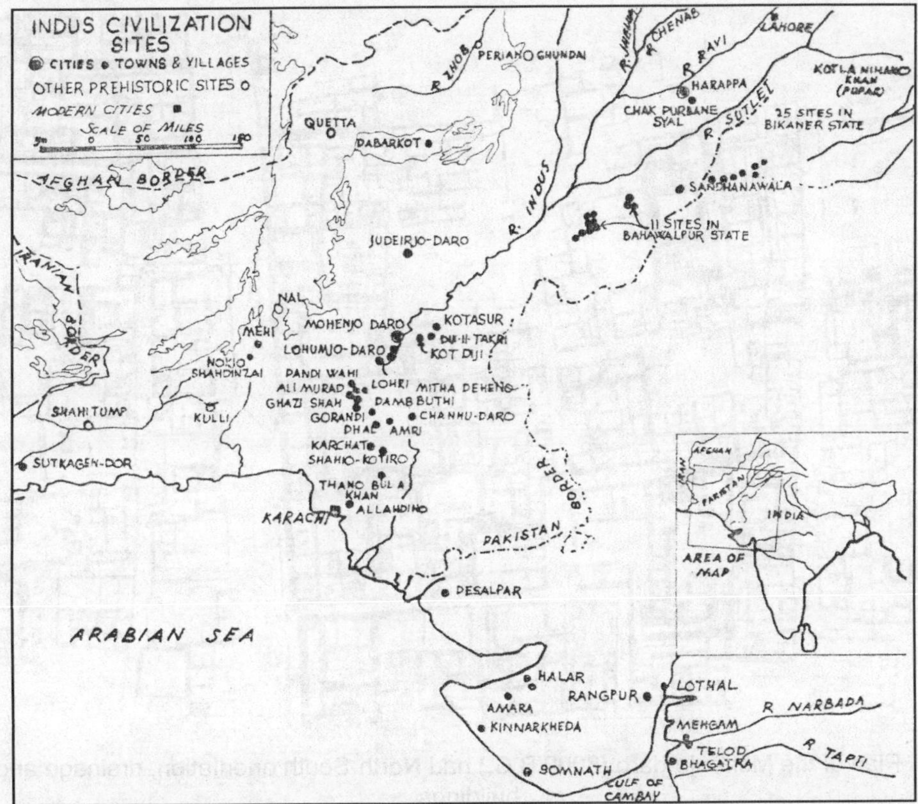

Fig. 2.2. Indus Valley Civilisation Sites

Fig. 2.3. Mohenjo-daro was planned with the world's earliest Sewerage and Drainage System

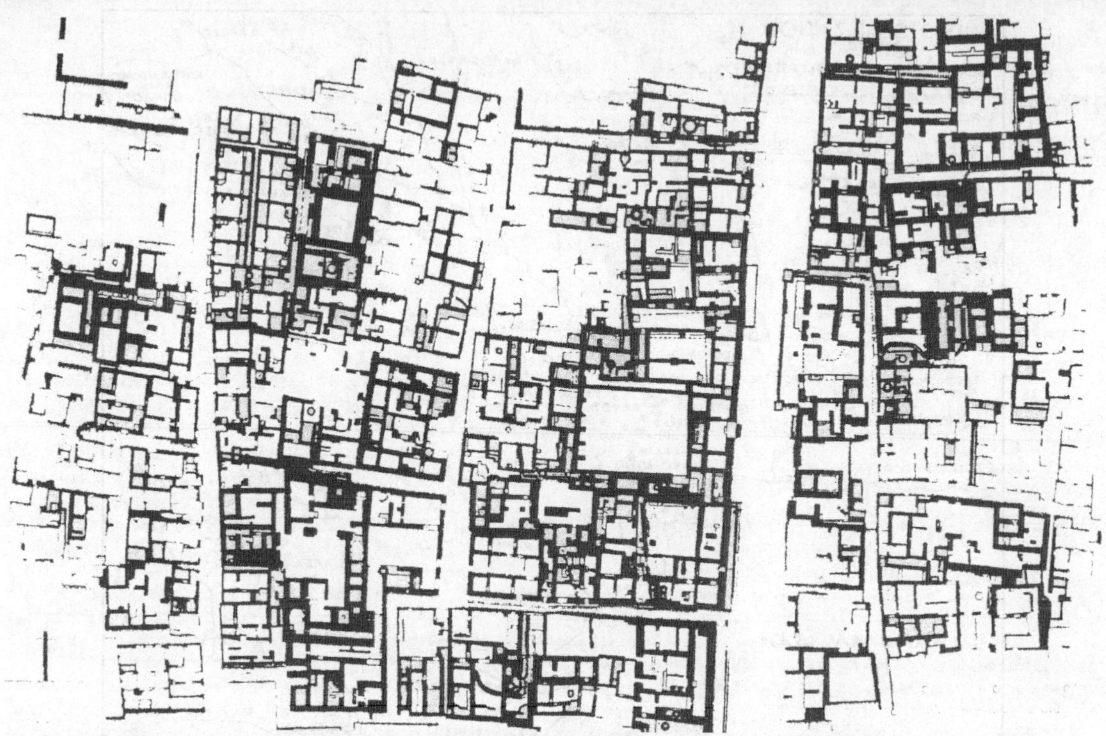

Fig. 2.4. Plan of the Mohenjo-daro (3000 B.C.) had North-South orientation, drainage and brick buildings

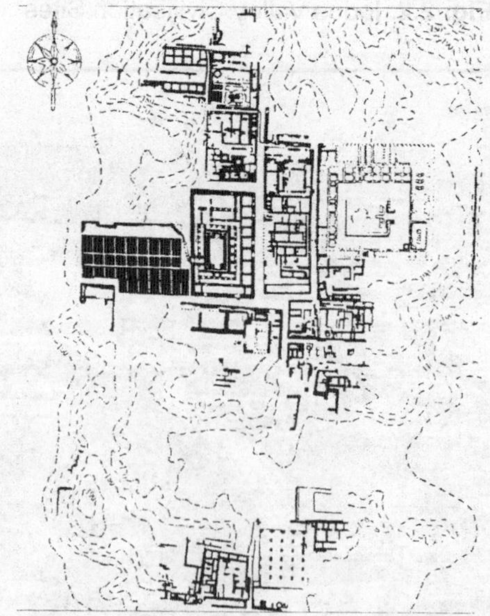

Fig. 2.5. Plan of the Citadel of Mohenjo-daro with Assembly Hall, Stupa and Bath

The decline of the Harrapan culture in the second millennium B.C. shifted the focus to the Ganges River region following the incursions of Aryans from the north between 1500 and 1200 B.C. where large cities developed and metallurgy, agriculture, pottery, jewellery, spices, textiles and other trades propelled the economy. The Vedas chronicled the Aryan way of life. The link between nature and human remains outstanding characteristics of the vedic culture.

Buddhist Period (6th Century B.C.) and Mauryan Empire (324-187 B.C.)

In the 6th Century B.C. Buddhist period began, which corresponds to the period when Persia invaded India and ruled for 200 years over Northern part of India, Alexander, the Great, invaded India in 4th Century B.C. and the contacts between Greece and India were established. Thereafter the Mauryan Empire (324 B.C. to 187 B.C.) was at its glory under Samrat Ashoka and covered almost the whole of India (except Assam and some southern parts), Afghanistan, Baluchistan, Kashmir and Nepal, Buddhism flourished during this period. The Mauryan Empire built magnificent buildings, stupas and temples.

The Buddhist stupa, a dome shaped monument, was used in India as a commemorative monument associated with storing sacred relics. The stupa architecture was adopted in Southeast and East Asia, where it became prominent as a Buddhist monument used for enshrining sacred relics. Fortified cities with stūpas, viharas, and temples were constructed during the Maurya empire (c. 321–185 B.C.). Wooden architecture was popular which is reflected in the rock cut architecture and guard rails *surrounding* a *stupa. Temples*, built on elliptical, circular, quadrilateral, or apsidal plans were constructed using brick and timber. These usually had gateway arches and the *torana*.

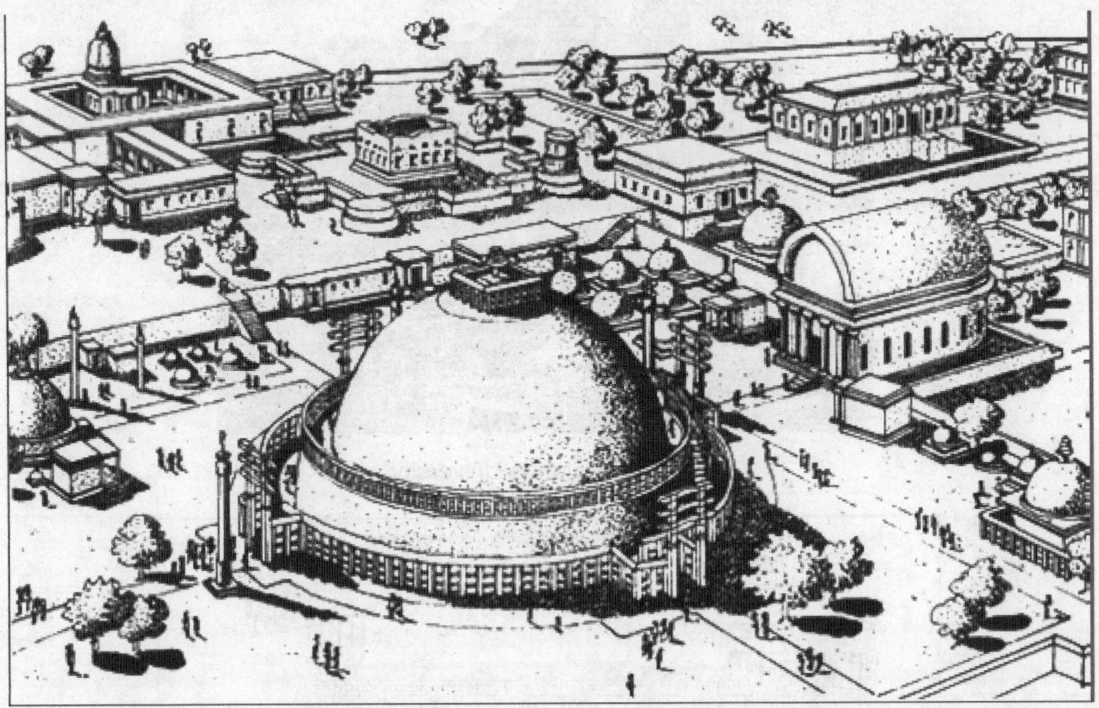

Fig. 2.6. The Budha Stupa, Sanchi, Madhya Pradesh (First Century), the circumambulation determined the form of the stupa

Rock-cut temples and stepwells in India date back to 200–400 A.D. Subsequently, the construction of wells at Dhank (550–625 A.D.) and stepped ponds at Bhinmal (850–950 A.D.) took place. Cave temples became prominent throughout western India, such as Ajanta and Ellora.

The Indian emperor Ashoka (273—232 B.C.) established a chain of hospitals throughout the Mauryan empire. One of the edicts of Ashoka (272—231 B.C.) reads: *"Everywhere King Piyadasi (Ashoka) erected two kinds of hospitals, hospitals for people and hospitals for animals. Where there were no healing herbs for people and animals, he ordered that they be bought and planted."* Indian art and culture has absorbed extraneous impacts by varying degrees and is much richer for this exposure. This cross-fertilization between different art streams converging on the subcontinent produced new forms that while retaining the essence of the past, succeeded in the integrating the old and the new influences.

Cave Architecture

The cave architecture in India is believed to have begun in the third century B.C. These caves were used by Buddhist and Jain monks as places of worship and residence. Initially the caves were excavated in the western India. Some examples of this type of cave structure are Chaityas and Viharas of Buddhists. The great cave at Karle is one such example, where great Chaityas and Viharas were excavated by hewing out rocks. The Karle caves are big in size and the interior is lighted up by great windows.

Fig. 2.7. Nalanda University

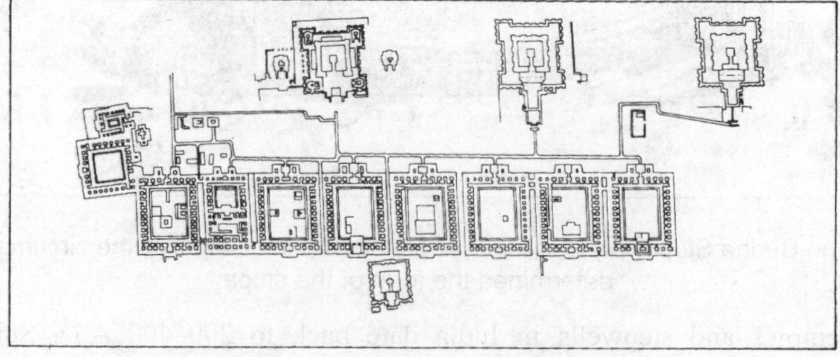

Fig. 2.8. Plan of Nalanda University

Besides the caves at Karle, many caves were excavated at other places. These were excavated not only by Buddhists or Jains but also by Hindus. Some of the famous and prominent caves are at Nashik, Kanheri, Gaya (Barabar Hills), Bhaja, Nagarjunikonda, Badami, Elephanta and Ellora. These caves house some of the amazing murals, sculptures and architectural structures. The Elephanta caves contain Maheshmurti, Shiva in three aspects of Creator, Preserver and Destroyer. This is undoubtedly one of the finest single piece Indian sculptures. There are numerous such great examples of Buddhist, Hindu and Jain rock temples at Ellora but the most spectacular of all is the Kailasha temple. The Kailash temple was hewn out of rocks.

Maharashtra is home to the spectacular and amazing Ajanta and Ellora group of caves. The cave at Ajanta and Ellora were cut out of rock, by hand, and rank amongst some of the most outstanding specimens of ancient Indian architectural heritage. In all there are 34 caves at Ellora and 29 caves at Ajanta.

Ajanta caves were rediscovered in the 19th century by British officers. The Ajanta caves depict the story of Buddhism, spanning the period from 200 B.C. to 650 A.D. The caves at Ajanta served as secluded retreats for the Buddhist monks. Beautiful wall frescos and sculptures speak volumes of the advancement of Indian art in ancient period. Some of the caves at Ajanta house panels depicting stories from the Jatakas, stories about several incarnations of the Buddha. Cave number one contains wall frescos that include two great Bodhisattvas, Padmapani and Avalokiteshvara. Other wonderful paintings in Ajanta are the flying apsara, dying princess and Buddha in preaching mode.

Ellora

At Ellora, 34 caves have been carved into the sides of a basaltic hill. The caves at Ellora contain some of the finest specimens of cave-temple architecture and exquisitely adorned interiors. Structures in the Ellora caves represent the three faiths of Hinduism, Buddhism and Jainism and were carved during 350 A.D. to 700 A.D. The nobility, serenity and grace of Buddha are visible in the Buddhist caves. Ellora caves also contain images of Vishwakarma, the patron saint of Indian craftsmen. The Kailasha temple in Cave 16 is indeed an architectural wonder, the entire structure having been carved out of a monolith.

Rock Cut Architecture

Rock-cut architecture occupies a very important place in the history of Indian architecture. The rock-cut architecture differs from traditional buildings in many ways. The rock-cut art is more similar to sculpture than architecture as structures were produced by cutting out solid rocks. Let's have a look at various specimen of rock-cut architecture in ancient India. Some prominent rock-cut structures of ancient India are Chaityas, Viharas, temples, etc.

Chaityas and Viharas are those rock-cut structures that were hewn out for Buddhist and Jain monks. Chaityas were places of worship whereas Viharas were residence of monks. The Buddhist and Jain monks usually stayed away from the towns therefore they developed Chaityas and Viharas in the hillside. Most of the Chaityas and Viharas were constructed in western India. Some of the prominent places having Chaityas and Viharas are Karle, Nashik, Bhaja and Kanheri. The rugged hills of the Western Ghats were naturally suited to the creation of living space in the hillside. The most remarkable aspect of the rock cut architecture at Karle and other such sites is its close similarity to wood construction. Here, you will find great imitation of every detail of wood in rocks. This throws light on the great skill of Indian craftsmen.

The Rathas at Mahabalipuram are yet another great specimen of rock-cut architecture in ancient India. These Ratha temples at Mahabalipuram were constructed during the reign of Pallava rulers. The Pallavas were founders of the Dravidian style of temple architecture. At Mahabalipuram, scaled-down replicas of actual temples (known as the Rathas of Mahabalipuram or the 'Seven Pagodas') were created. These rathas were sculpted out of monolithic rocks. The Rathas are not very large, the biggest measuring 42 feet by 35 feet, and the tallest is 40 feet high. Most of the Rathas at Mahabalipuram are modeled on the Buddhist Viharas and Chaityas.

Ancient Cities and Villages

Arthashastra written by Chanakya of the Mauryan Empire laid down guidelines in respect of the duties of government, administration and also on town and country planning and housing. The Mansara of the 6th Century A.D. prescribes 8 different types of towns and villages.

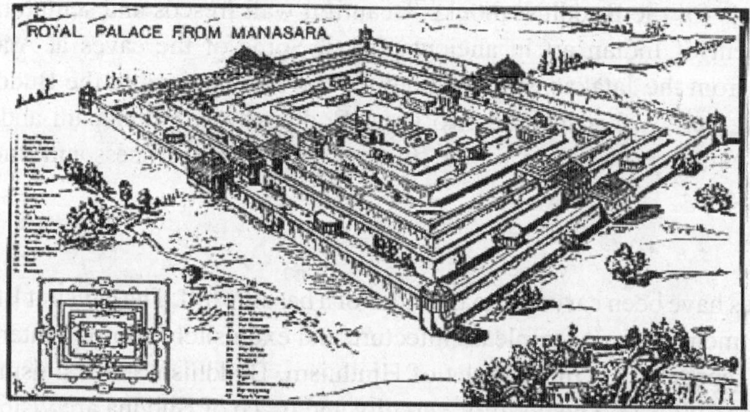

Fig. 2.9. Royal Palace from Mansara

Source: *Prasanna Kumar Acharya, Hindu Architecture in India and Abroad, J K Publishing, Bhopal*

Fig. 2.10. Syncretic Indo-Iranian Art

Fig. 2.11. Ghats of Varanasi along the Ganga, an old Lithograph

The form of a city was derived on the principle of Vãstu shastra. It established an interrelationship of physical form of a settlement with the spiritual, cosmic and behavioural system. It determined the basic form, its location and orientation of various functions in a settlement. It was interrelated with the surroundings, like the planets in the astrological chart. A system of ashtha (8). Navgrah (9 planets), 24 *matrika pithas*, etc. was devised as a numerical symbolism and for orientation and linkages of the settlement system. The Vãstu-Purush-Mandala had been so universal that it could be applied to an altar, a temple, a house, a city or the entire cosmos. The symbol relates physical form with the outer form and the inner vision. The Mandala is not only a spatial axiom but a temporal process as well. It is a module encompassing the principles of organicity: interrelationship of parts, inter-dependence of systems, resonance and synchronicity. Accordingly, the five elements of nature were tied up with the cosmic system.

Fig. 2.12. Bhaktawarpur, Nepal

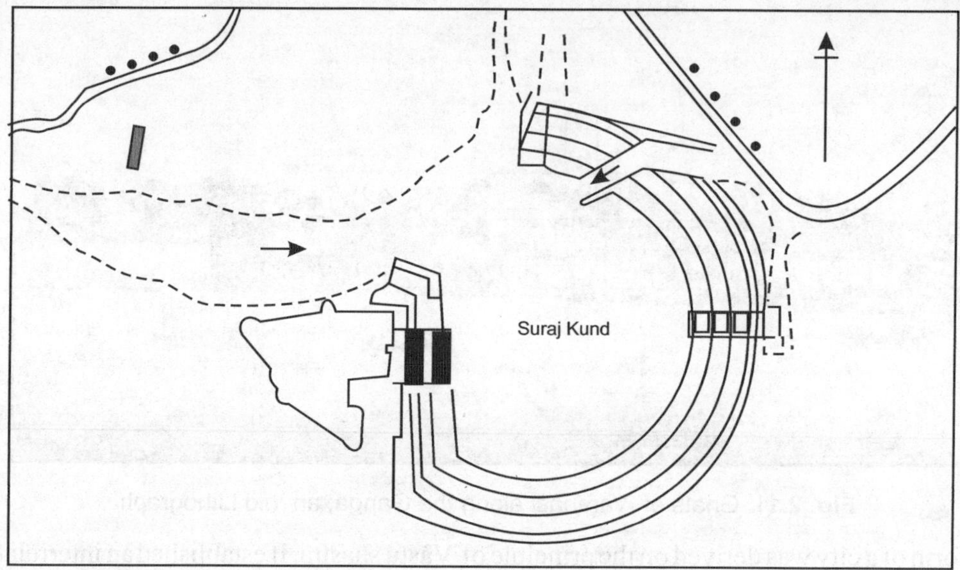

Fig. 2.13. Surajkund (Faridabad) is said to belong to Indraprastha era

In the overall urban fabric, the generic morphology manifests a labyrinthine hierarchy of social organization. It contains an introvert spatial organisation with a system of courtyards and chowks, which enhance frequent contacts and social participation among the residents. These also serve as an efficient means of security, privacy and social control.

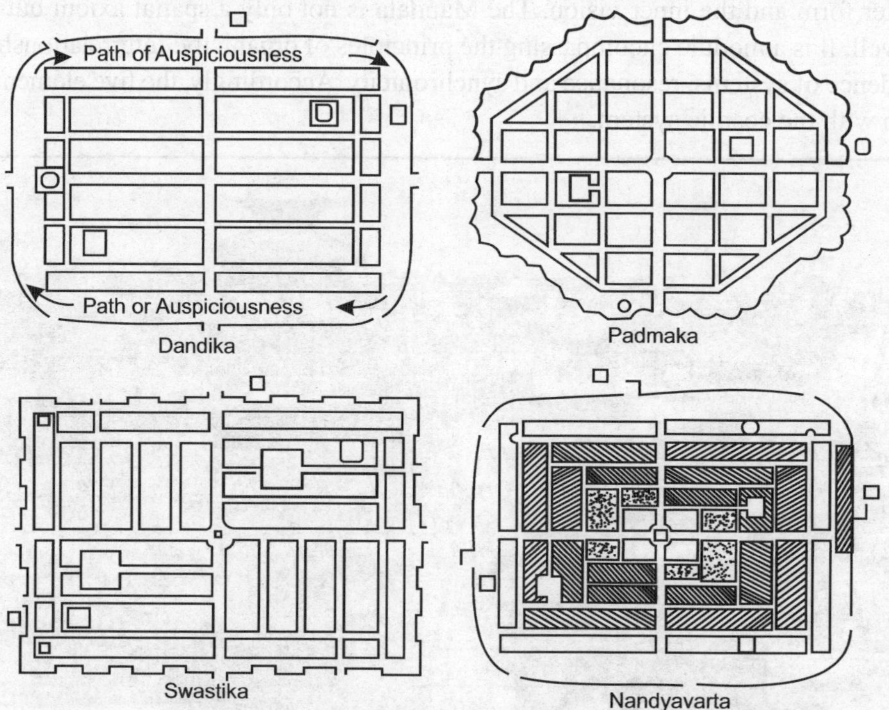

Fig. 2.14. City Patterns According to Mansara. The basic shape of a city was a square with a temple or a palace at the centre and different quarters for people all around it

Fig. 2.15. The Purana Qila excavations in Delhi established the existence of settlement from Late Harappan to Medieval period covering about 2500 years of history

Source: *ASI/INTACH-Delhi a Living Heritage, 2010*

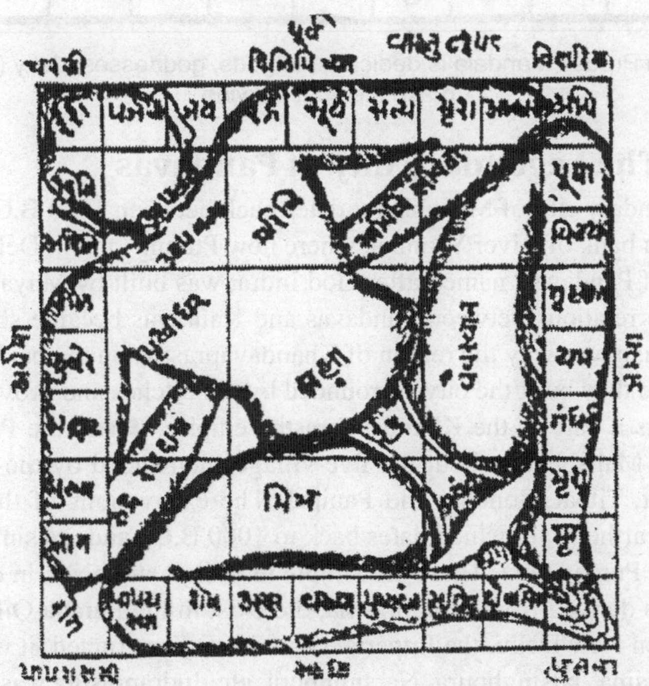

Fig. 2.16. The diagram of Vastu purush mandala is a symbol of the macrocosm. North Kuber-Lord of wealth, South Yama-Lord of death, East Indra-King of Gods, West Varun-Lord of water, North-East Ishana-Incarnation of Lord Shiva, South East Agni-The Fire Deity, North West Vayu-Lord of winds, South-West Pitru-Nairuta or ancestors

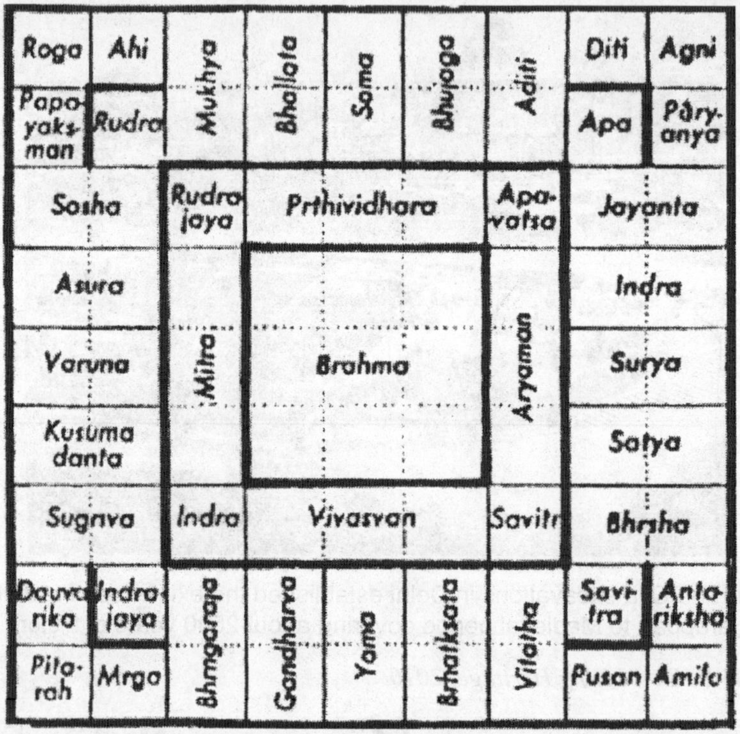

Fig. 2.17. The Vastu Purush Mandala is dedicated to gods, goddesses, deity (even demons), that make the space divine

Indraprastha: The Legendary City of Pandavas

Indraprastha, the legendary city of Mahabharat dates back between 1000 B.C. to 1800 B.C. It was located on the western bank of River Yamuna, where now Purana Qila in Delhi stands. The legend says that the capital of Pandavas, named after God Indra, was built by Maya Danav. According to Mahabharat when the relations between Pandavas and Kauravas became strained, Dhritarashtra, the father of Kauravas, gave away the region of Khandavaprastha on the bank of the river Yamuna to the Pandavas. There they built the city surrounded by the ditches and provided a high defensive wall. Indraprastha was a part of the Khandavaprastha empire, where the Pandavas ruled. There is also a reference in Mahabharat about the five villages demanded by the Pandavas, which are Indraprastha, Baghpat, Tilpat, Sonepat and Panipat. The excavations of these settlements have yielded painted grey earthenware which dates back to 1000 B.C., and are similar to those found in the excavations at the Purana Qila. These are simple in design and black in colour. The village of Indraprastha, which is derived from Indraprastha, did exist in the Purana Qila in the beginning of the 20th century. When New Delhi, the Imperial capital was constructed, it was cleared alongwith other villages like Raisina, Jaisinghpura, Narsimhpura, etc. Indraprastha was stated to be a district Pratiganaas mentioned in a Sanskrit inscription dated 1328 A.D., which is preserved in the Red Fort museum. On the basis of the evidence, it can be said that the society that time was quite advanced and used iron and copper. Tools were made of stone, iron, bones, glass etc. Clay was used to make pots and precious stones were used for the ornaments. The houses were built of mud bricks, wattle and daub.

In the Mahabharat, the description of the Indraprastha is as follows:

"*....The fortress sported massive iron wheel and well laid plan of streets that avoided collision with fate; and it had beautiful buildings of many kind. Thus Indraprastha shone like the image of heaven, like a mass of packed clouds that are encircled by lightning.... Lovely gardens surrounded the city with mango trees, Amratakas, Nipas, Ashoka, Kadambs, Bakulas and Jasmine.... Swarming of the birds of all kinds, always joyous cuckoo. There are houses white like mirrors and all kind of pavilions, lovely painted houses and pleasure hillocks; and many ponds filled with pure water. And most charming lakes redolent with the fragrance of lotuses and water lilies, colourful with wild geese and ducks.... lotus ponds of all shapes and broad and big tanks of great beauty. As they dwelled in their great realm, which was peopled with honest folk, the joy of the Pandavas, great king grew externally, and thus the Pandavas, when Bhishma and the king had displayed the law, became inhabitants of Khandva tract.....*"

In the Mahabharat there is also a reference of the palace built by Pandava which was designed by Maya Danava. It was so beautiful that Duryodhan was envious. Its floor and walls were made of crystal, which gave illusory effect. By this, it was a unique building and looked like a mirror. At the end of Mahabharat war, the Pandavas shifted to Hastinapur and handed over the Indraprastha to the Yadavas. Thereafter the city went into oblivion and became deserted as a mere village. However, the excavations have shown the remains of Maurya, Gupta, Sultanate, Tughlak and Mughal dynasties. The city fort was once again rebuilt by Shershah Suri in the middle of sixteen century and the city was rechristianed as Shershah's City.

The city was planned according to the canons of Mansara, the treatise on town planning and architecture. As a basic principle, a city would be planned within an integral system of broad cosmic cycle. It was inter-related with the surrounding cities, like the planets in the astrological chart. The five elements of nature were also signified by the settlement system. Perhaps the five cities namely, Indraprastha, Bagpat, Panipat, Sonipat and Tilpat signified the 5 elements of nature, namely, air, earth/vegetation, water, fire and space.

Today the lofty remains of Indraprastha are surrounded by the Purana Quila, zoo, Nizamuddin, Humayun Tomb, Exhibition ground, Sunder Nagar and Millennium Park along the river Yamuna and Ring Road. The reign of King Vikrmaditya is identified by the celebrated Kalidas, poet and dramatist. Cities like Ujjain, Patliputra (Patna), Mathura and Shravsti became great centres of learning and culture. Fa Hein, a Chinese traveller who visited India during the 4th Century A.D. wrote that the government was liberal and people had enough food, clothes and housing. Caves at Ajanta and Ellora with unique painting belongs to this period. The famous Iron Pillar at Delhi near Qutab Minar was cast in the 5th Century A.D. King Harshvardhan was the ruler of north India from 606 to 647 A.D. Chinese pilgrim Hiuan Tsang who visited in India during this time recorded that the world renowned university of Nalanda, Bihar, had 8500 students and 1500 teachers.

Temple Architecture of India

Indian temples are classified in three broad types viz. the Nagara or the Northern style, the Dravida or the Southern style and the Vesara or mixed style.

Fig. 2.18. Sun Temple at Konark

The temples of North and South India are distinguished on the basis of some specific features like sikhara and gateways. In the north Indian temples, the sikhara remains the most prominent component while the gateway was generally unassuming. The most prominent features of South Indian temples were enclosures around the temples and the Gopurams (huge gateways). The Gopurams led the devotees into the sacred courtyard. On the other hand, there were many common features in the Northern and the Southern styles. These included the ground plan, positioning of stone-carved deities on the outside walls and the interior, and the range of decorative elements.

The South Indian temple consists essentially of a square-chambered sanctuary topped by a superstructure, tower, or spire and an attached pillared porch or hall (maapa, or maapam), enclosed by a peristyle of cells within a rectangular court. The external walls of the temple are segmented by pilasters and carry niches housing sculpture. The superstructure or tower above the sanctuary is of the kūina type and consists of an arrangement of gradually receding stories in a pyramidal shape. Each story is delineated by a parapet of miniature shrines, square at the corners and rectangular with barrel-vault roofs at the centre. The tower is topped by a dome-shaped cupola and a crowning pot.

Vijayanagara (1336 – 1565 A.D.) was a notable building style evolved by the Vijayanagar empire that ruled most of South India from their capital at Vijayanagara on the banks of the Tungabhadra River. The architecture of the temples built during the reign of the Vijayanagara empire had elements of political authority. This resulted in the creation of a distinctive imperial style of architecture which featured prominently not only in temples but also in administrative structures across the Deccan. The Vijayanagara style is a combination of the Chalukya, Hoysala, Pandya and Chola styles which evolved earlier in the centuries when these empires ruled and is characterised by a return to the simplistic and serene art of the past.

Hoysala architecture has a distinctive building style developed under the rule of the Hoysala Empire in the Karnata (today's Karnataka), between the 11th and the 14th centuries. Large and small temples built during this era remain as examples of the Hoysala architectural style, including the Chennakesava Temple at Belur, the Hoysaleswara Temple at Halebidu, and the Kesava Temple at Somanathapura. Other examples of fine Hoysala craftmanship are the temples at Belavadi, Amrithapura, and Nuggehalli. Study of the Hoysala architectural style has revealed a negligible

Indo-Aryan influence while the impact of Southern Indian style is more distinct. A feature of Hoysala temple architecture is its attention to detail and skilled craftmanship. The temples of Belur and Halebidu are UNESCO world heritage sites. About 100 Hoysala temples survive today.

Some of the best examples of the north Indian style (Nagara style) of temple architecture are the Khajuraho Group of temples, Sun temple, Konark, Sun temple at Modhera, Gujarat and Osian temple, Gujarat. The finest examples of Dravidian style (south Indian style) are temples of Tanjore, Madurai, Mahabalipuram, Badami, Pattadakal, Kanchipuram, Brihadeshwar temple and Thanjavur.

Fig. 2.19. Karle Chaitya Cave (1845 Lithograph)

Fig. 2.20. Kailash Temple, Ellora (8th cent) 1845 Lithograph

Fig. 2.21. Indra Sabha (No.16), Ellora (9th century) 1845 Lithograph

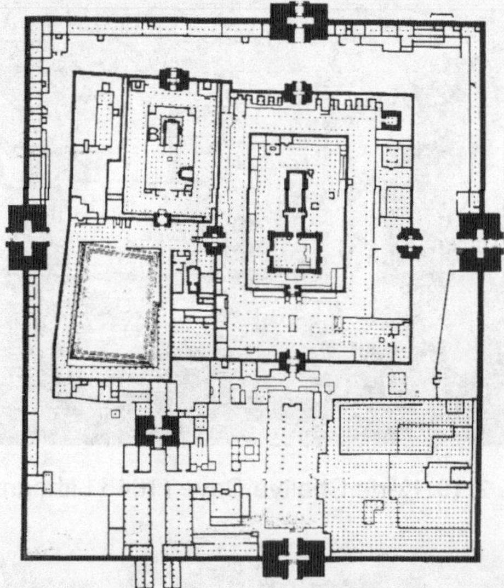

Fig. 2.22. Plan of Madurai Temple

Fig. 2.23. Mahabalipurm from James Ferguson's Illustration of the Rock-cut Temples of India

Fig. 2.24. The Shikara Rath, Mahabalipuram is an example of refined Pallava design, which became a model for temples in the south India

Fig. 2.25. This relief in stone known as 'Arjuna's Penance, at Mahabalipurm represents the austerities Arjuna observed to get the blessings of Shiva, whose image is carved standing next to him. The relief is also known as the Descent of the Ganga

Fig. 2.26. Madurai Temple City

Fig. 2.27. Temple Town of Thiruvannamalai in Tamil Nadu

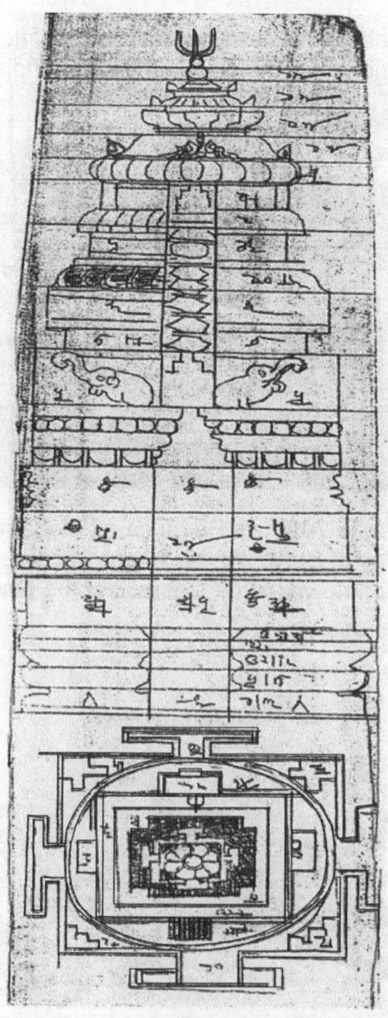

Fig. 2.28. Pillar design (Sri Yantra) from Vastushastra text

Fig. 2.29. Surya Temple, Konark drawing by James Ferguson

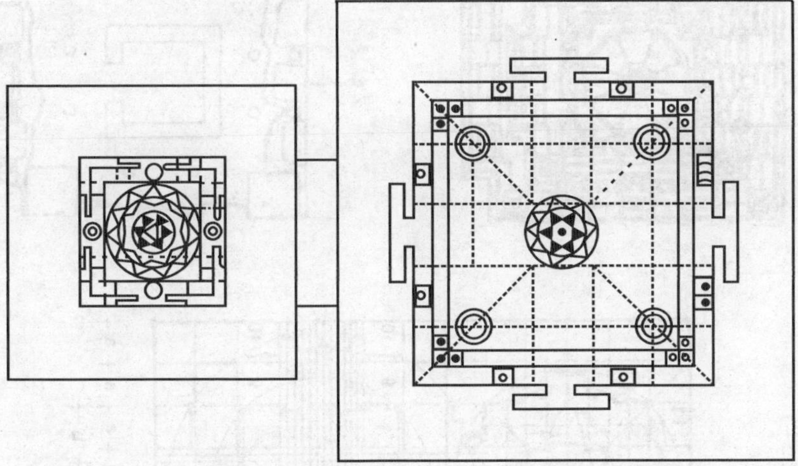

Fig. 2.30. Ground Floor Plan of Sun Temple, Konark showing Yantras

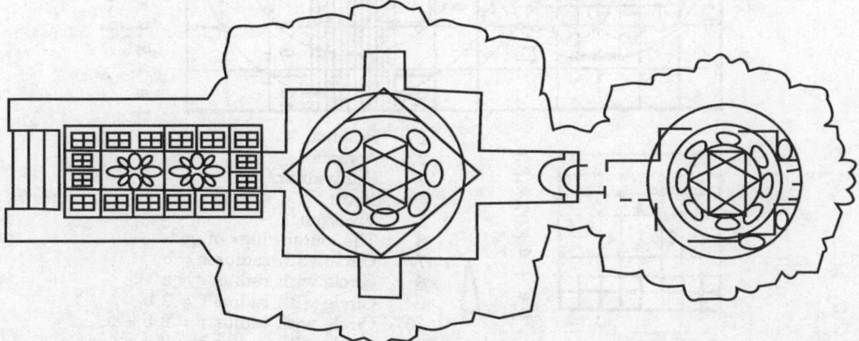

Fig. 2.31. The Sun God, represented by three architectural yantras in Mahagayatri Temple, Odisha

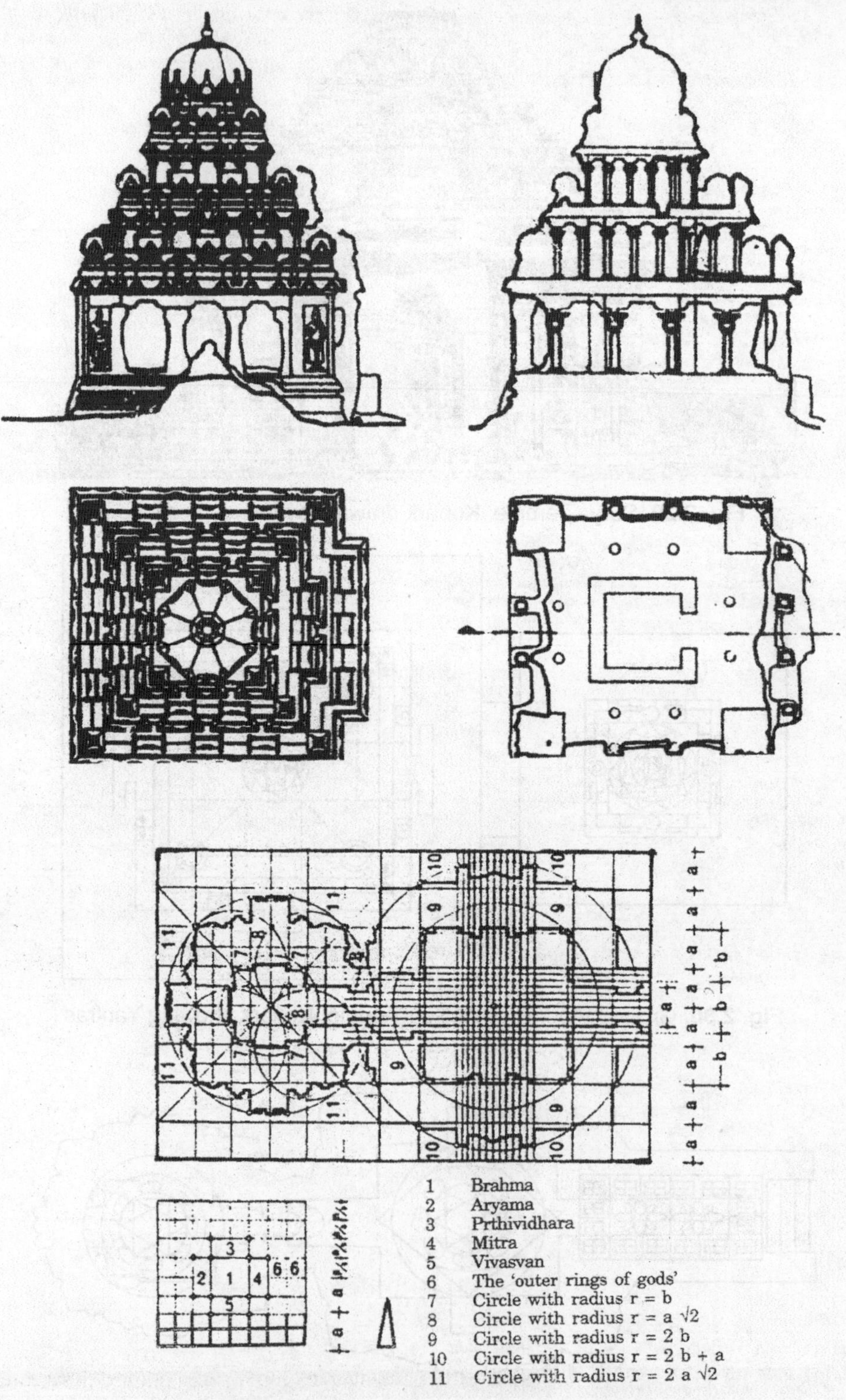

Fig. 2.32. Brahmeshvara temple at Bhubaneshwar

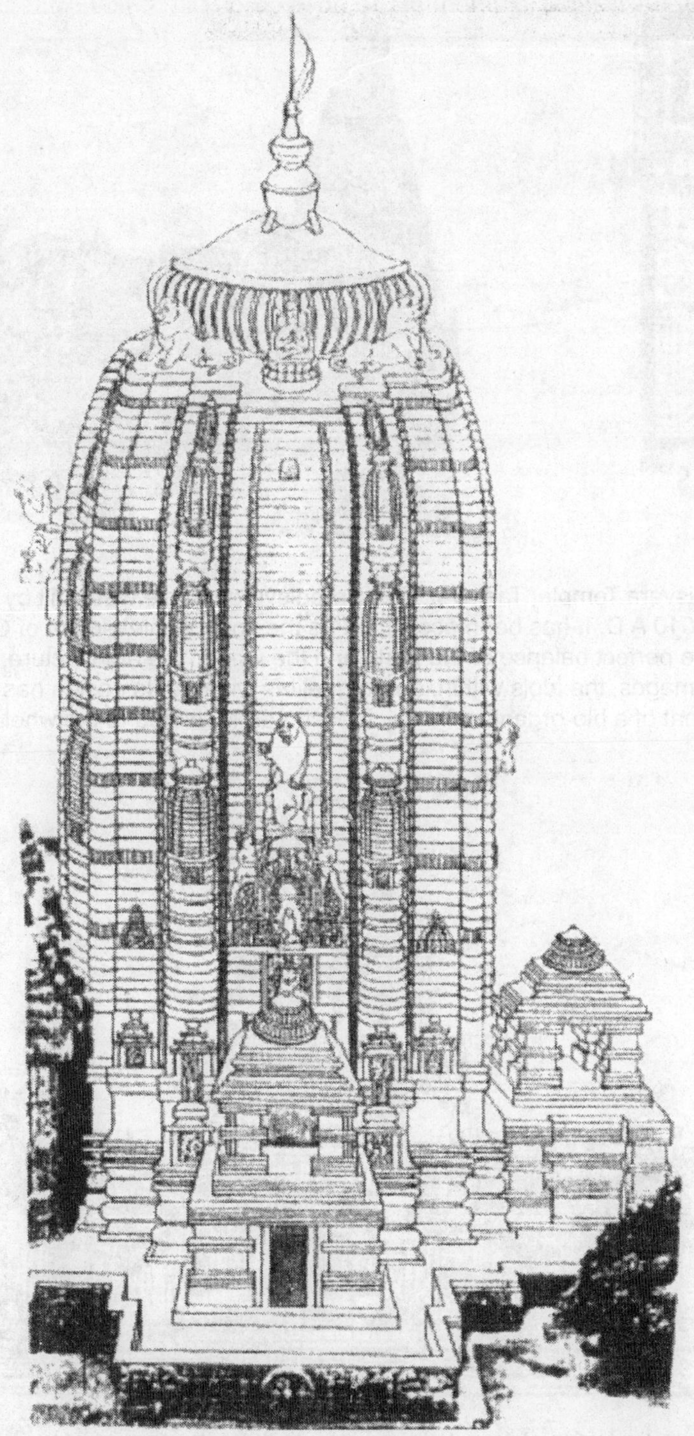

Fig. 2.33. Sun Temple in Konark stands on symbolic solar wheels. It had followed the principles of Ayadi-Shadvarg for proportions and measurement of its six main components - base, columns, entablature, wings, roof and shikhar. The main tower (shikhar) shown in the drawing, collapsed during the last century

Fig. 2.34. Brhadisvara Temple, Tanjavur, The Brhadisvara temple was built by Râjarâja I of the Chola Dynasty in 1010 A.D. It has been acclaimed as the finest achievement of Chola art. Its artistic excellence lies in the perfect balance of the parts and the whole: the architecture, sculpture, painting, stone and bronze images, the idols within, and the reliefs without. Its design has been compared to that of a bio-organism in which each part is related to the whole

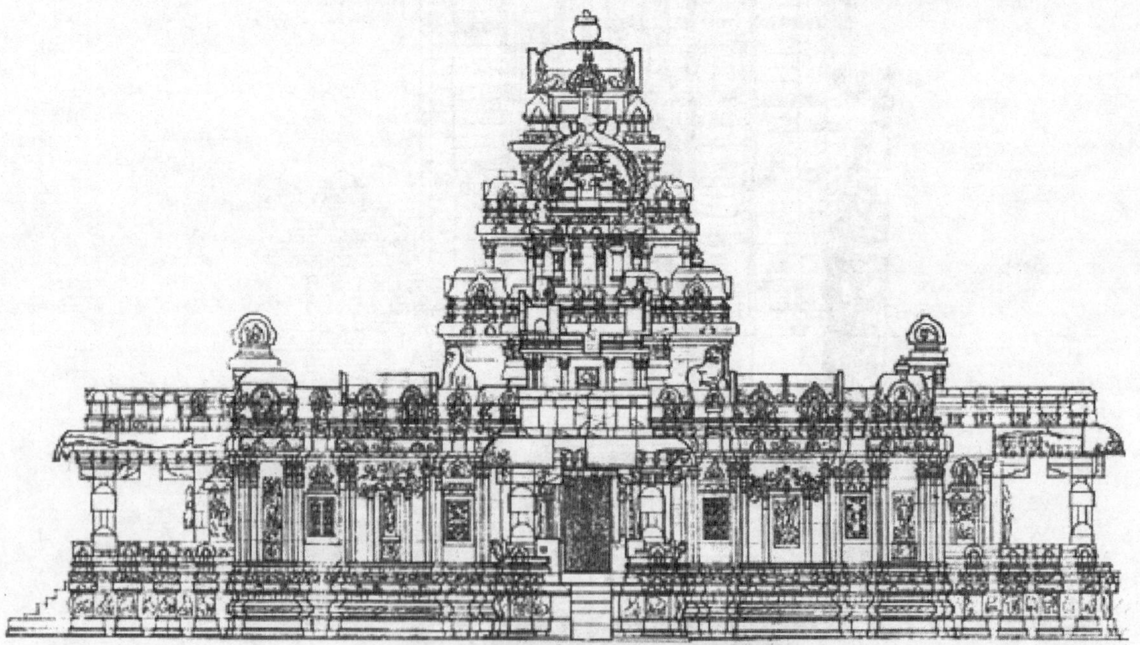

Fig. 2.35. East elevation, of the Virupaksha temple, built by the Queen of King Vikramiditya II to celebrate one of her husband's victories

Source: *Gary Martin, George Michell and Jiri Skopek*

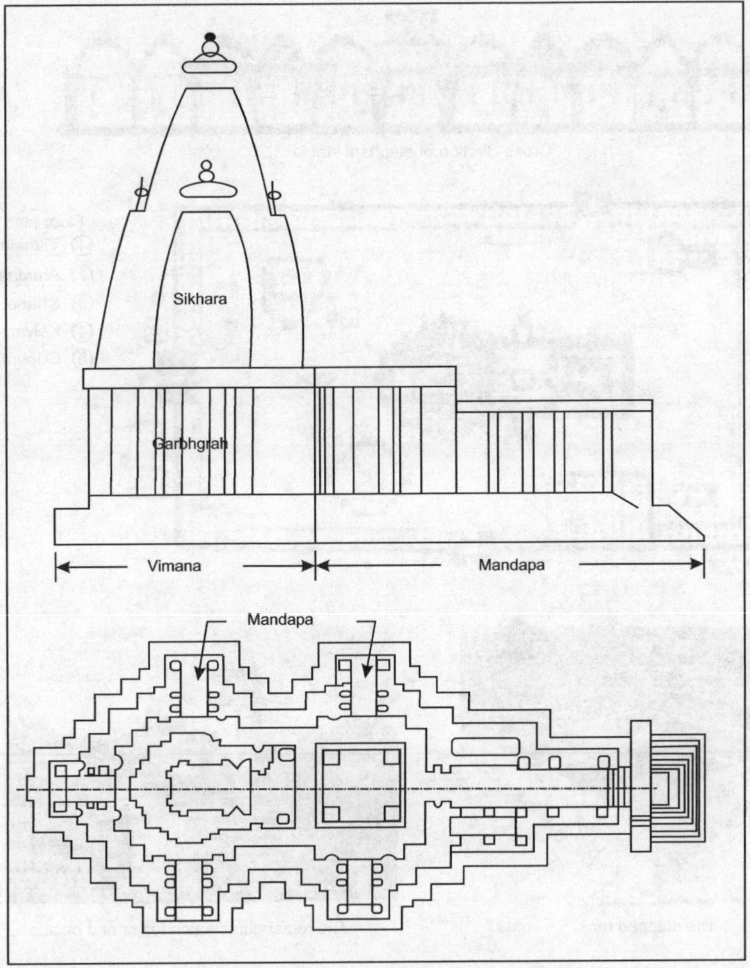

Fig. 2.36. Main components of a north Indian temple (Nagar style)

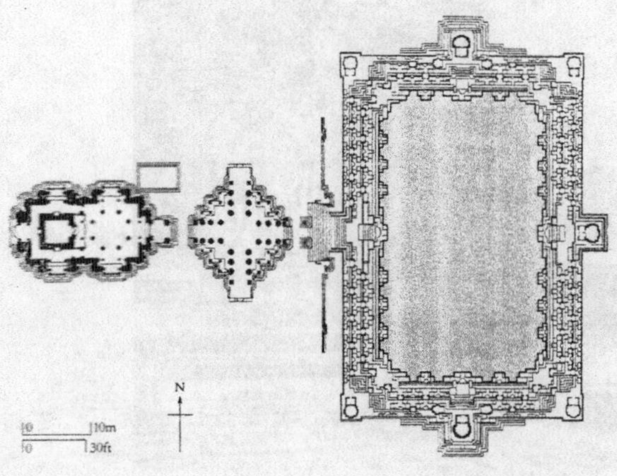

Fig. 2.37. Modhera, Surya temple, Gujarat

Cross-Section of elephant stable

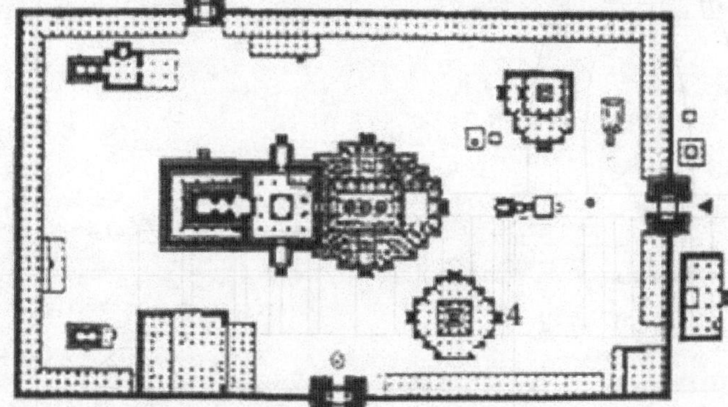

Floor plan
① Vitthala temple
② Amman shrine
③ Chariot
④ Kalyanamandapa
⑤ Gopuram

The stepped tank

The rectangular watch tower and palace

Fig. 2.38. Vitahala temple, Hampi, Vijaynagara

Source: *Kamiya, Takeo (2003), Architecture of the Indian Sub-continent*

Fig. 2.39. Ruda Stepwell, Adalaj (1502)

Source: *Kamiya, Takeo (2003), Architecture of the Indian Sub-continent.*

Vijaynagar (Hampi) echoes the precise measurements which relate to northward Ganga river, Ocean of milk (lake South of Matanga hill), North star, the Celestial pole on the cosmic axis. The north-south line crosses and is tangent to the Tungabhadra river just where it turns north, reminiscent of the northward flow of the Ganga at Kashi. North is the direction of birth and the north-south axis of the city thus acquires a cosmic symbolism, paralleling that of Kashi itself.The axis crosses the remains of an artificial lake that was constructed just south of Matanga hill. This lake, which does not seem to have served any practical needs of the city, may have been a metonym for the Ocean of Milk, one of the great symbols of fertility and cosmogony in Hindu texts. The lake may have been involved in ritual processions between the summit of Matanga hill and the royal centre.

The axis may be symbolic protection of the city by the sage Matanga, which figures prominently in the mythology of the city. The axis establishes a well-defined symmetry by dividing the royal centre into public/private, male/female dualities.

Standing at night in that ceremonial gateway of the royal centre, looking north one sees the North Star, fixed and unmoving, lying directly above the sikhara of the Virabhadra temple on the summit of Matanga hill. As viewed from that spot, the north pole of the celestial sphere is displaced from the sikhara by only 0.8°. The visual symbolism of the night time vista is commanding, and the cosmological symbolism is realised. The north celestial pole lies on the cosmic axis that passes through Matanga hill.

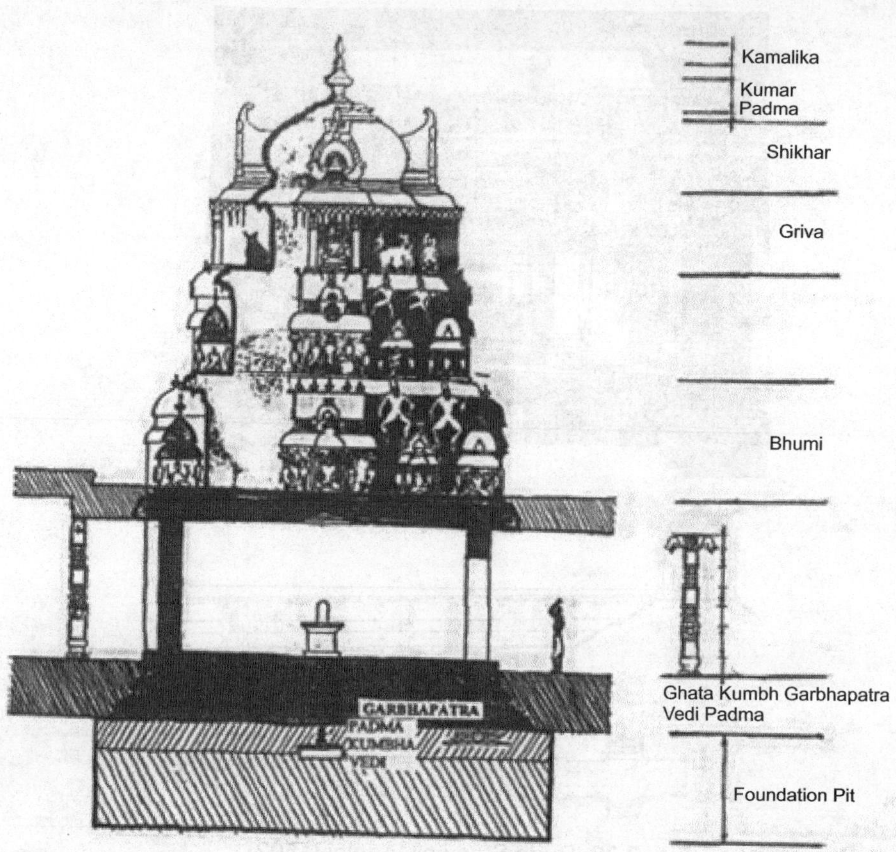

Fig. 2.40. Vimana of Sundareswar

Source: *Kollar L. Peter, Symbolism in Hindu Architecture, Aryan Books, N. Delhi, 2001*

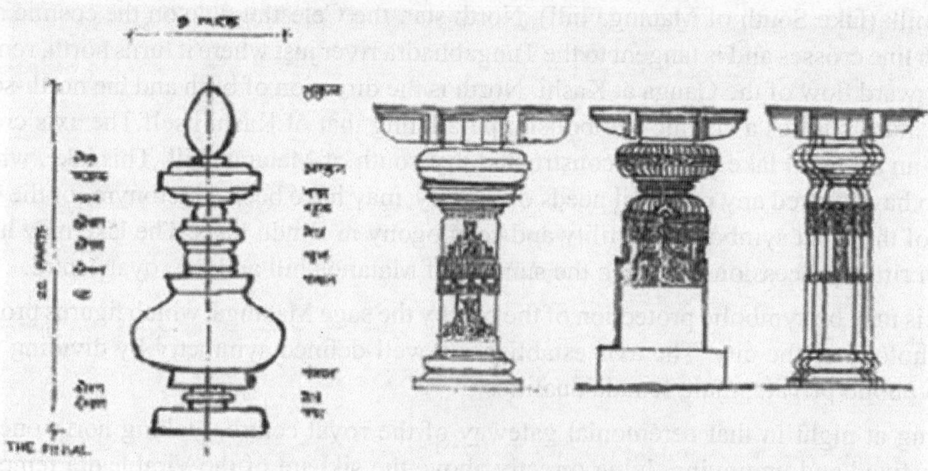

Fig. 2.41. The Finial– Kalasha Column and details from Indian Temple Architecture: From Transformation by Adam Hardy (IGNCA)

Source: *HD Chhaya, Vedic Spirit in Architecture, Architecture+ Design, Sep-Oct., 1988*

Fig. 2.42. Dome (underside), Dilwara Jain Temple, Mt. Abu. Vastu is micro-cosmic representation of macro-cosm, which requires the skills of astronomy, yoga, sculpture, arts, rituals, mathematics and engineering, which all add up in a competent vastu-sutradhar

Fig. 2.43. Sunak Nilakantha Temple, (Tenth century) Elevation (partly reconstructed)

In the overall urban fabric, the generic morphology manifests a labyrinthine hierarchy of social organization. It continues an introvert spatial organisation at the city level, with an extroverted system within the residential cluster. The extrovert spatial character is accentuated by courtyards and chowks, which enhance frequent contacts and social participation among the residents. These also serve as an efficient means of security, privacy and social control.

Fig. 2.44. A wooden door with brass inlay work

Gupta Period (320 A.D. to 570 A.D.)

The fall of Maurya Empire was followed by a period of 500 years of political instability, which was revived during the Gupta Period (320 A.D. to 570 A.D.) under the reign of Samundragupta and his son Vikrmaditya. King Vikramaditya patronized advancement of learning and culture. The period is characterised by growth of trade and industry, which brought in wealth. Caves of Ajanta and Ellora belong to this period and demonstrate the classical Indo-Greek and Gandharva styles of arts and architecture.

The Gupta period is generally regarded as a classic peak of North Indian art for all the major religious groups. Although painting was evidently widespread, the surviving works are mostly the religious sculptures. The period saw the emergence of the iconic carved stone deity in Hindu art, as well as the Buddha and Jain tirthankara figures, often on a very large scale. The two great centres of sculpture were Mathura and Gandhara, the latter the centre of Greco-Buddhist art. Both exported sculpture to other parts of northern India. Unlike the preceding Kushan Empire there was no artistic depiction of the monarchs, even in the very fine Gupta coinages, with the exception of some coins of the Western Satraps, or influenced by them.

The most famous monuments in Gupta style, are the caves at Ajanta, Elephanta, and Ellora, which reflect the monumentality and balance of Gupta style. Ajanta contains by far the most significant survival of paintings from this and the surrounding periods, showing a mature form. The Udayagiri caves record connections with the dynasty and its ministers and the Dashavatara Temple at Deogarh is a major temple, one of the earliest to survive.

Syncretic Architecture

India's connection with Iran goes back to the third century B.C. when the Mauryan Empire modelled itself on Achaemenid Empire of Iran. In Patliputra, the capital of Maurya dynasty, a royal palace was erected on a plan inspired by that of Achaemenid palatial hall at Takht-e-Jamshid (Persepolis). In the wake of Alexander's conquest the Achaemenid and Greek legacy gave rise to the syncretic art and architecture in India. This is reflected by the third century B.C. capital Rampurva in Bihar and Achaemenid capital with sculptures of lions and humped bull. During this time Buddhism extended to East Iranian land under Kushans, besides other countries. Buddhism absorbed Iranian concepts and figural iconography from Hellenistic Iran. This gave birth to a remarkable syncretism in arts, sculpture and architecture.

During the 6th to 8th centuries the traders from Africa and Middle East arrived in Kerala and Gujarat where they established themselves as a part of the fishing and trading community. In the North, the Muslims from Central Asia established themselves by way of conquest that triggered the spread of Islamic culture.

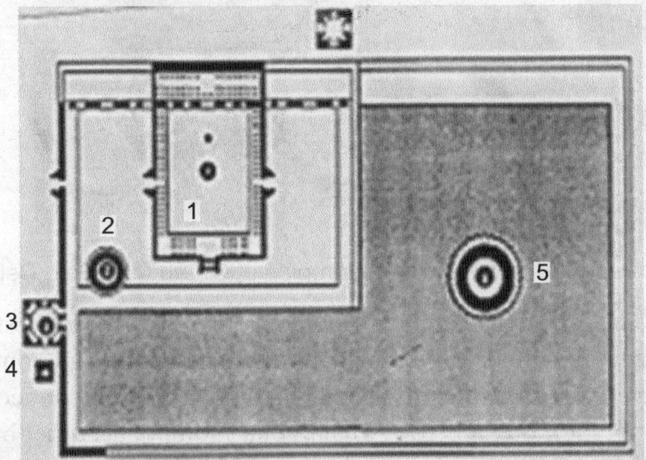

Fig. 2.45. Plan of Qutab Minar Complex Mehrauli, Delhi

Fig. 2.46. Mosque built from recycled pillars of Hindu temples at Qutab Complex, Delhi

In the 11th Century, a ruler of Eastern Iran, Mahmud of Ghazna invaded North-Western India and integrated part of it into Ghaznavid sultanate. Vernacular traditions of the sub-continent are visible in the early mosques, minarets and mausoleums. The Qutb Minar in Delhi, an iconic pillar built in the late 12th century, does not look Iranian. The Arhai din ka Jhompra at Ajmer built in the early 1200s and the tomb of Iltutmish in Delhi which dates back to 1235 A.D. are the torch bearers of syncretic arts and Indo-Iranian aesthetics, where aisles supported by intricately carved pillars adapted or recycled from broken Hindu temples.

Fig. 2.47. Qutab Minar at Mehrauli, Delhi

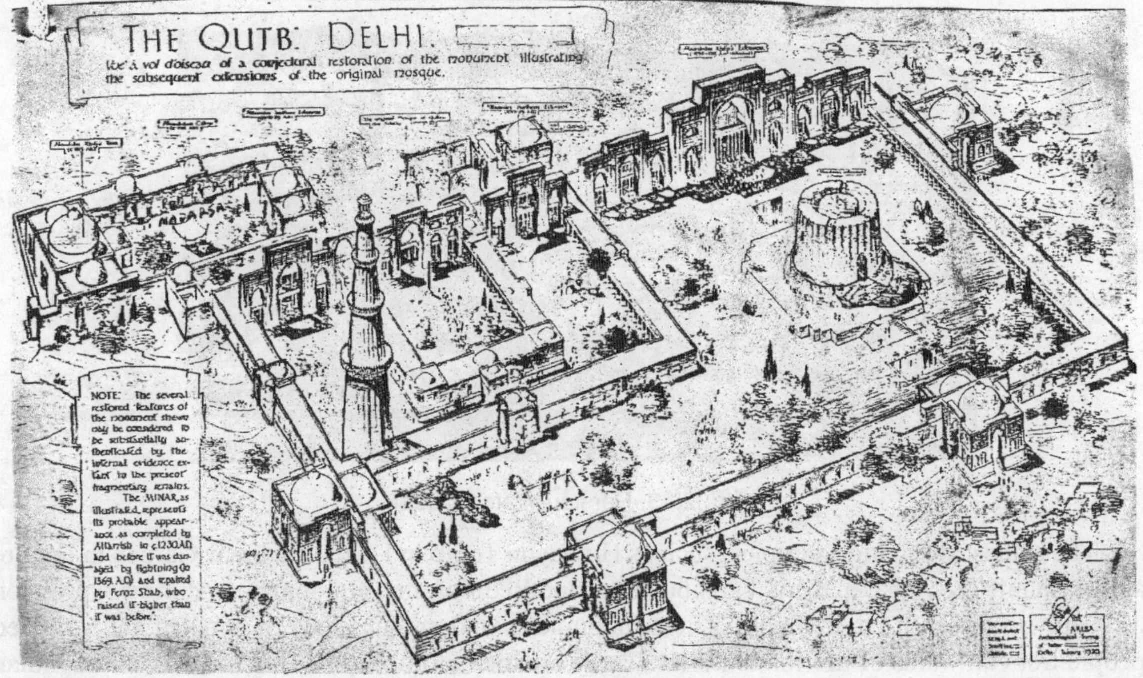

Fig. 2.48. Qutab Minar Complex, Mehrauli, Delhi

Source: *Archaeological Survey of India*

The Mughals

The Mughals, derived from Mongols, traced their ancestry to Chengiz Khan. The Mughal Empire began with Zahir-ud-Din Muhammad Babur (1483-1530) who descended from Taimur. He captured Kabul in 1504 and occupied Delhi and Agra in 1526 after defeating the Lodhis. His father Omar Sheikh Mirza was the ruler of the Fergana Valley, Uzbekistan and brought Timrid heritage as well as the Persian architecture of Samarkand and Herat. Babur's son Humayun (1530-40, 1555-56) and his grandson Akbar (1556-1605) stretched the empire from Kandhar in the north and Bengal in the east. Akbar built the ephemeral capital Fatehpur Sikri (1571-85), besides many other forts, gardens, mosques and tombs. Mughals introduced new ways of city planning, as Emperor Babur upon seizing Delhi declared that "*everywhere that was habitable, should be constructed with waterwheels to create running water and make planned, geometric spaces.*"

The Mughals borrowed frequently from other cultures, adapting elements to their new settings. The resultant Mughal forms of arts and architecture became over time closely interrelated with the wider urban artefacts of its period. Delhi, Lahore and Kabul pre-dated the Mughals, but they were significantly transformed in part during the 16th to early18th centuries. These cities became torch bearer's of a cosmopolitan culture that embraced diverse facets of society, trade and commerce, arts, architecture and culture. The second Mughal emperor Humayun and his successor Akbar were influenced by Nasir-al-Din Tusi's well known treatise Akhlaq-i-Nasiri (1235). It taught respect for diversity and values of justice, tolerance and the pursuit of cultural excellence in the creation of a pluralistic society.

Fig. 2.49. Persian Water Wheel

Their finest surviving examples, such as Humayun Tomb in Delhi, Shalimar Garden in Lahore and Kashmir, Taj Mahal in Agra, Fatehpur Sikri and Red Fort in Agra, remain enduring expression of beauty in the built environment. These monuments and gardens have fascinated and attracted people from all walks of life for centuries. These are the bold juxtapositions of Iranian and Indian designs melting seamlessly. With the accession of Akbar's son Jahangir to power in 1605, these ideals continued to prevail.

The ultimate example of Mughal architecture is the mausoleum, known as Taj Mahal, erected in 1631 over the Shahjahan's Iranian spouse, Mumtaj Mahal. The Taj Mahal garden continued the chahar-bagh model initiated by Humayun's Tomb. Its main garden space has a fourfold plan as does the Taj Ganj village associated with it to the south and the Mahtab Garden to the north. The tomb itself is sited on a high riverfront plinth. The Mahtab Bagh across the river was part of the original composition within a larger landscape.

After the conquest of India by the Muslims, a hybrid urbanscape started. Various cities such as Lahore, Agra, Shahjahanabad, Fatehpur Sikri, Adilabad, Bhopal, Golconda, Hyderabad, Murshidabad and Aurangabad came up. The Taj Mahal (1650) in Agra is a climax of Mughal architecture. Agra on the banks of the Yamuna had as many as 42 river facing gardens. At the Taj Mahal, Shah Jahan's wish to build a lasting memorial to his wife, Mumtaz Jahan, overwhelms the senses in its extravagance. The plan conforms to a char bagh (four square) order, with a main axis connecting a red sandstone entry pavilion. Along both major and cross axes are water channels; the main axis is delineated by rows of cypress tress.

Fig. 2.50. Plan of Char Bagh, Taj Mahal, Agra. Garden is 800 feet wide and 975 feet from the gate to the tomb

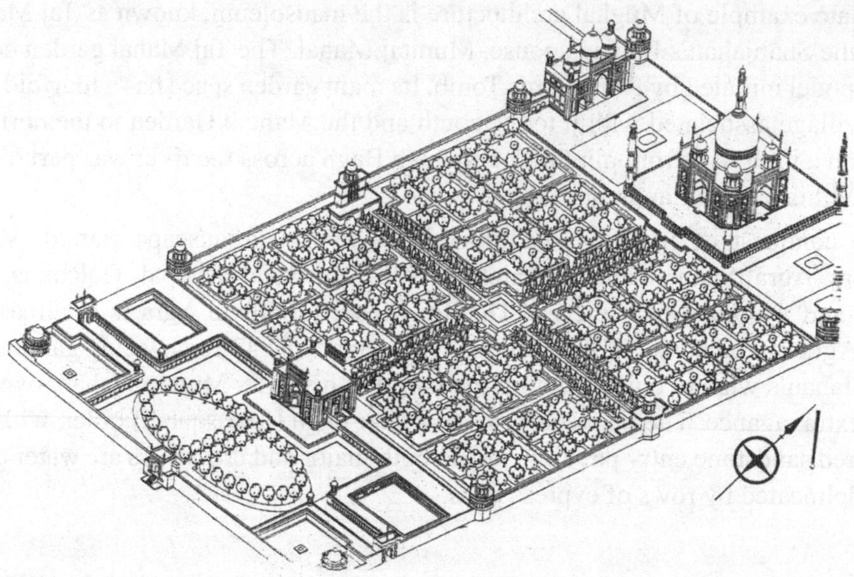

Fig. 2.51. Char Bagh is an integral feature of 17th century Taj Mahal, Agra

Fig. 2.52. Shershah Suri's Tomb, Sasaram

Fig. 2.53. Section and Plan showing placement of domes and chattris at Shershah Suri's Tomb Sasaram

Fig. 2.54. Ghiyas-uddin Tughlaq's Tomb (1325 A.D.) Delhi

Fig. 2.55. Sikander Shah Lodi's Tomb, New Delhi

Fig. 2.56. Pavilion at the Tomb of Safdarjung, Delhi (1841 Lithograph)

Fig. 2.57. A 1841 Lithograph of Safdarjung Tomb, Delhi

Source: *Archaeological Survey of India drawing by J.H Hodgston (1828)*

The Mausoleum of Atgah Khan in Delhi built during Akbar's rule is a fine example of the Hindustani-Iranian style. The stone polychromy, calligraphy and geometric patterns are handled with perfection.

Fatehpur Sikri (the city of victory), where Akbar's son Jahangir was born in 1569, was the capital of Hindustan until 1585, when Akbar moved his seat of empire to Lahore. The Jami Masjid retains elements of Iranian architectural model with rich colours of stone and numerous chattris, which provide an Indian touch. Buland Darwaza, 40 m high gateway has a pink and white palette of tile masonry with the chhatris on its top. The Panch Mahal with its five levels draws on the vernacular heritage of Sind. The colonnaded structure open on all sides acts as a transition building between the semi-public spaces that surround the Daulat Khana courtyard.

Fig. 2.58. Humayun Tomb, New Delhi

Set within the Jami Masjid, the white marble Salim Chishti tomb occupies a prominent position opposite the Buland Darwaza, which was built to honour the Sufi saint, who predicted the birth of Jahangir. The Anup Talao is profusely ornamented chamber, referred to as a pavilion of the Turkish Sultana. Akbar used this structure to receive visitors and honoured guests. The Anup Talao or peerless pool was built on wide platform to the north of the imperial apartments (mahal-i-khas) courtyard. The mini tank and canal cools the air in the vicinity of the royal living quarters. Diwan-i-Khas is a small building with a massive ornamental column at its centre upon which sits a massive capital with four jali lined bridges. It is said that this structure was used for religious and cultural discussions or as a music house. Diwan-i-Aam (public audience hall) was the place where the emperor made his daily public appearance and was also used for court ceremonies and the reception of guests.

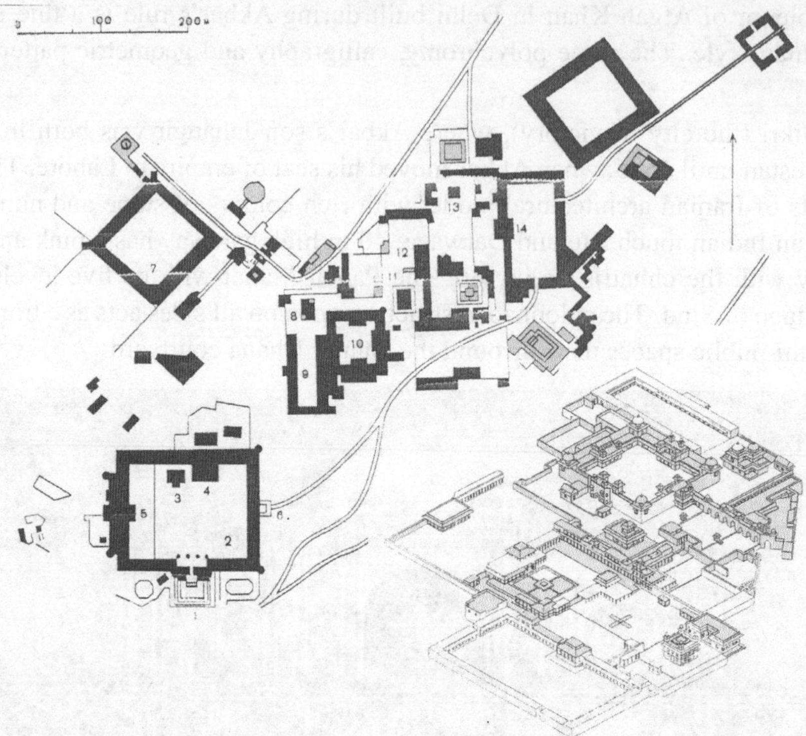

Fig. 2.59. Mugal emperor Akbar built the royal complex of Fatehpur Sikri between 1571 and 1585. It was built upon a hill but the top was flattened out to create a horizontally spread out citadel-spaces demarcated through level differences and plane punctured walls. The labyrinthine structure is woven together through the contiguity of the floors and unity of materials

Fig. 2.60. Panch Mahal, Fatehpur Sikri

Fig. 2.61. Itmad-ud-Daulah's Tomb, Agra

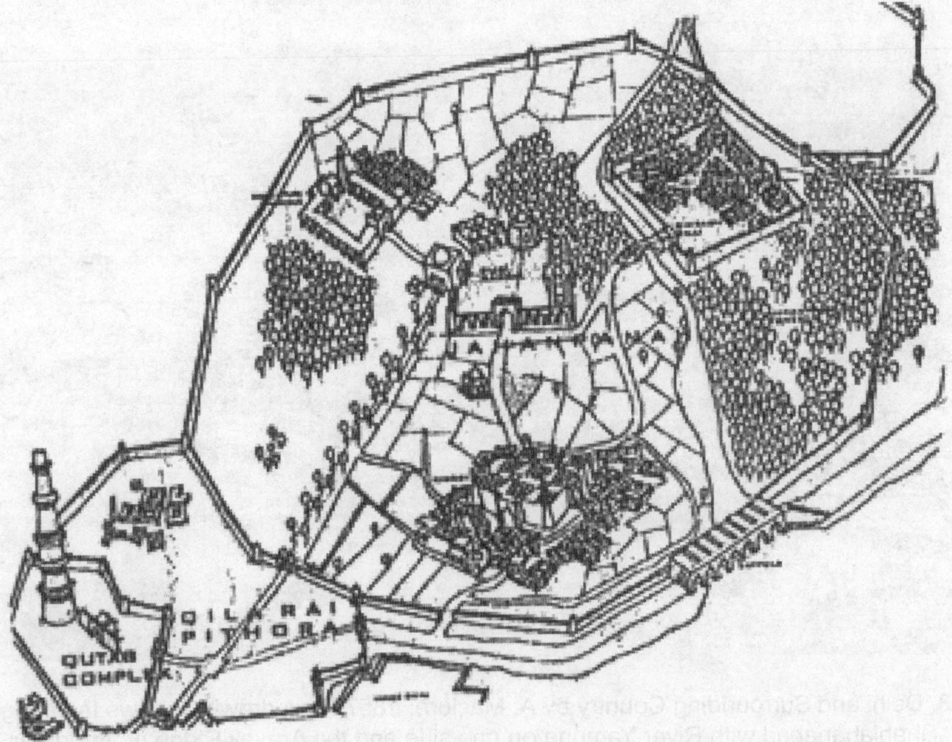

Fig. 2.62. Historic cities of Delhi Mehrauli, Quila Rai Pithora, Jahanpanah and Siri had large parks within and around them

Shahjahanabad

Shahjahanabad built during 1638-1656, immortalises Shahjahan. Its centrepiece was shopping boulevard Chandni Chowk, along with the Red Fort, the royal Fort and the Jama Masjid, the royal mosque. Shahjahan built the magnificent city of Shahjahanabad with wide streets and parks, which were located along the river and to the north of the Indraprastha, said to be the city of the Pandavas, around which Ferozshah Kotla, Humayun Tomb, Nizamuddin, Purana Kila, Tughlakabad and Mehrauli exist. The city wall had 14 gates connecting it to various highways leading to Agra, Kabul, Lahore, Ajmer, Calcutta, Delhi (Mehrauli), Kashmir, etc. and other gates commemorated its great predecessors (Turkman, etc.). Shahjahanabad is still a thriving city, which has embraced various syncretic cultures during last 380 years.

Shahjahanabad was planned along the river Yamuna, which was a major source of water and was used for navigation, connecting Agra, where the earlier Mughal capital existed. Ali Mardan canal supplied water to the city and the river had numerous ghats all along. It also provided a natural defence to the city. The Walled City encloses an area about 1700 acres having Jama Masjid and Red Fort as the nodal points. Three main boulevards radiated from Red Fort. The first was Chandni Chowk with a canal in the middle; the second was the Jama Masjid while the third one led to Delhi Gate. The other three main streets radiated from Jama Masjid towards Chandni Chowk, Ajmeri Gate and Turkman Gate. It was reputed to be one of the most beautiful cities in the orient.

Fig. 2.63. Delhi and Surrounding Country by A. Maclure, 1857. This drawing shows the integration of Shahjahanabad with River Yamuna on one side and the Aravali Ridge on the other

The spatial form of the Shahjahanabad comprises introvert open spaces, narrow lanes, compact and high density. The variety of land uses has richness of activities round the clock. The organic character of the city is striking, strongly reminiscent of pattern of nature. The power of indigenous form of the walled city derives from a spatial context where the intimacy of physical expression results from a close packing of components. Behind blank walls and dark narrow alleys 30 to 40 per cent of the spatial envelope is in the series of internal courtyards, where most of the activities of living take place. The spatial structure of the community corresponds to its occupational division. The unclean occupations cluster on the periphery—low lying areas or in the west. The trade and business of the dominant groups occupy the prime locations, usually high lands, central areas or north side. The patches of occupational clusters are separated by open ground and community facilities, e.g. chowk, chopal, temple and bazaar, allowing all levels to interact. Sometimes the boundaries are simply common walls of houses, courtyards, or streets between groups of houses.

The settlement structure represents a closely knit orthogonal fabric with an introvert character. The clusters are clearly defined in terms of social structure. An inhabitant traditionally relates to his Mohalla, i.e. a geographical area that defines the spatial pattern of the community. Increasing social mobility now makes it difficult to relate the occupation of a man to his Mohalla, but groups related by practice or customs and geographic origin continue to cluster in specific Mohallas.

Fig. 2.64. Jama Masjid (Shahjahanabad), 19th Century Lithograph by John Daniel

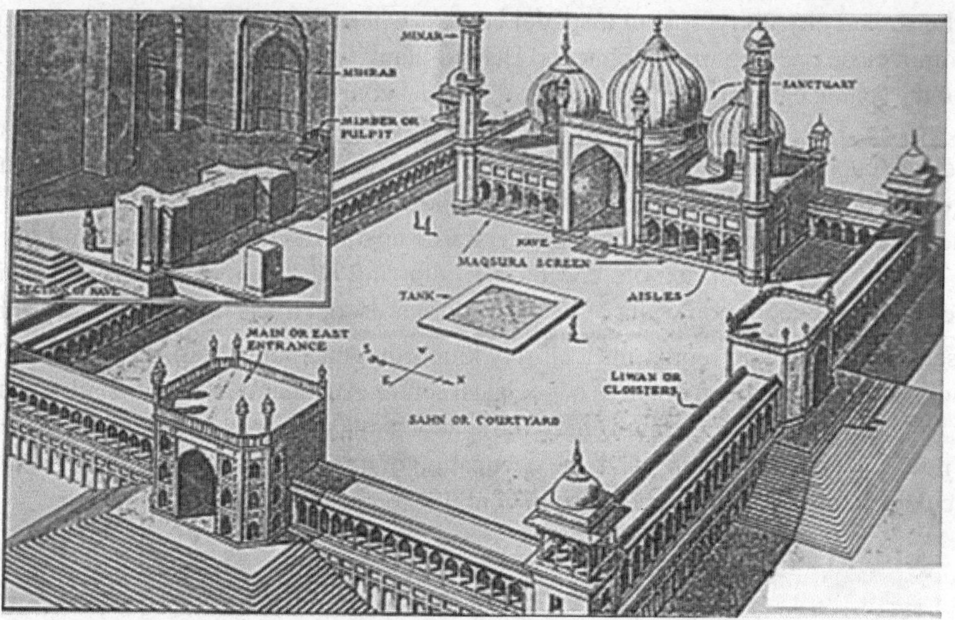

Fig. 2.65. Jama Masjid, Shahjahanabad, Delhi (1650-56), was not only one of the largest mosques in the world, but also a prototype

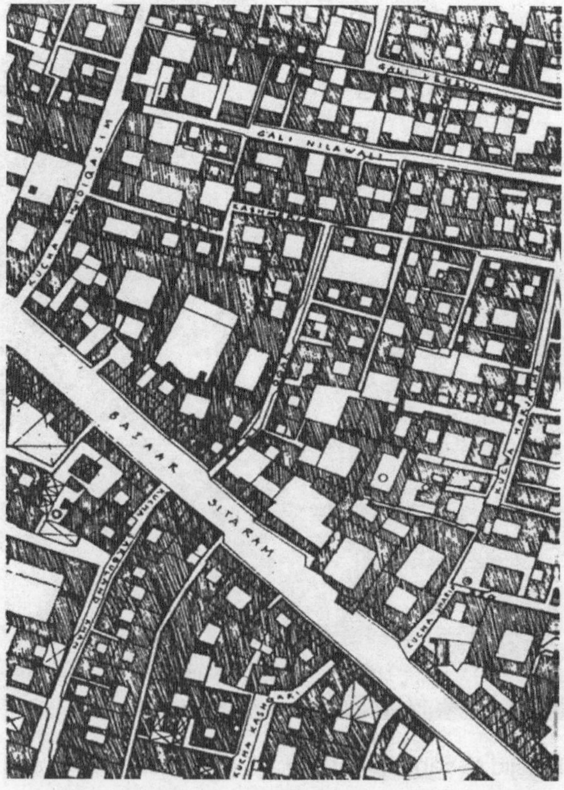

Fig. 2.66. Shahjahanabad: one-third of the area is under courtyards that cool the mohalla and houses

Fig. 2.67. Chandni Chowk, Delhi (1957)

The traditional spatial structure has a sieve like porous form. Closely knit fabric of structures help to keep out the harsh sun and provides shaded courtyards and streets. During the night, the open courtyards radiate out the heat and creating a cooling effect. Thus the form, based upon the principle of thermal comfort through passive means, presents a framework of energy conscious design. The indigenous settlement is a working model of closely knit and self-contained community. Its spatial structure is a logical outgrowth of viable set of social and economic norms governing the community and individual behaviour. The focal point of mohalla in this traditional morphology is the chopal. This is often a semi-public open space at the junction of streets, or at the termination of gali, which acts as a connector between different mohallas and communities. Though chopals apparently appear as left over spaces in a confined environment, the fact that there is no encroachment is an indication of the great value that the community attaches to them. The chopal has a sacrosanct and symbiotic imagery, where the elders and community leaders often meet to take the decisions and to exchange information. Its sanctity is accentuated by a temple or a mosque, invariably located adjacent to the chopal. Around the chopal there is generally a communal or service activity (like a well) serving to daily needs. There is general community agreement and unwritten principle of its use and sequence of events: washing of clothes, playing, smoking hookah, meetings or occasional festival, marriage or other rituals. The temple or a mosque is not only a place of worship but serves as an institution of learning and a centre of community activities.

Fig. 2.68. Facade of Chawri Bazar, Delhi

The custom of purdah required that women be shielded from the gaze of passers-by, as such a street face high blank walls, and women's courtyards are located in the rear. The privacy is protected by a series of spatial envelopes according to the spatial continuum. First degree of privacy is provided by the interior courtyard which is the exclusive domain of women. Second degree of privacy is defined by the land outside the door, which is accessible to the members of family and their relations. Third degree of privacy is the boundary of the Mohalla, which is the domain of the local residents. These zones of privacy are reflected in a sequence of public, semi-public and private domain of spaces, including streets, chowks and the chopal. The degree of privacy increases with the depth. Within a house, the privacy increases on upper floors and intermediate terraces.

An outside observer sees the irregular streets as a pattern of dark voids between buildings and is apt to arrive at an erroneous conclusion. Behind the narrow dark lanes, bounded by blank walls, are sunny courtyards where most of the activities take place. The courts act as the node of horizontal and vertical circulation. The transitional elements, e.g. veranda, entrance and gate are highly pronounced, while the services are located on the periphery of the houses.

After the arrival of East India Company, the Mughal empire started flickering. After the defeat in 1803, the Mughal Emperor Akbar II (1806-37) was a protectorate of East India Company. Shahjahan's jewel Peacock Throne had left India. Bahadurshah II was the last Mughal Emperor enthroned in Red Fort, below the emblematic scale of justice carved into white marble wall. The king of the world was now simply powerless king of Delhi. With the uprising of 1857 his reign and Mughal empire came to an end. The East India Company was replaced by British Crown. As Mughal rule waned and British authority gradually assumed control of India. Besides exploiting the country's resources, they introduced industries anew pattern of irrigation for agricultural, canal systems, communication, railways and other transportation systems.

Other Cities

Besides Mughal cities, many other cities were coming up in various parts of the country, e.g. Rajasthan (Ajmer, Jaipur), Central India (Mandu, Burhanpur, Aurangabad), Gujarat (Ahmedabad, Baroda, Surat), South India (Hyderabad, Golconda, etc.).

Fig. 2.69. Palitana, the holy place of Jains, presents a unique sight with over 800 temples crowned with marble spires dotting the hill slope. Having faced destruction from the invaders, the hill was enclosed with high walls

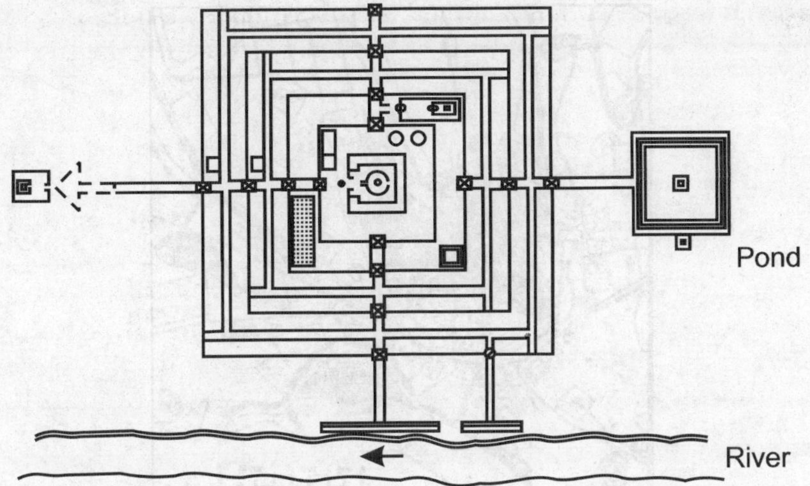

Fig. 2.70. Schematic Plan of a Temple City according to Manasara

The Manasara (Vastu Shashtra) provides the geometric concept of vastu purush mandala, which translates prakriti into physical form. The Vãstu Purusha Mandala depicts the position of various planets on a time-space dimension which provides basic principles of spatial organisation.

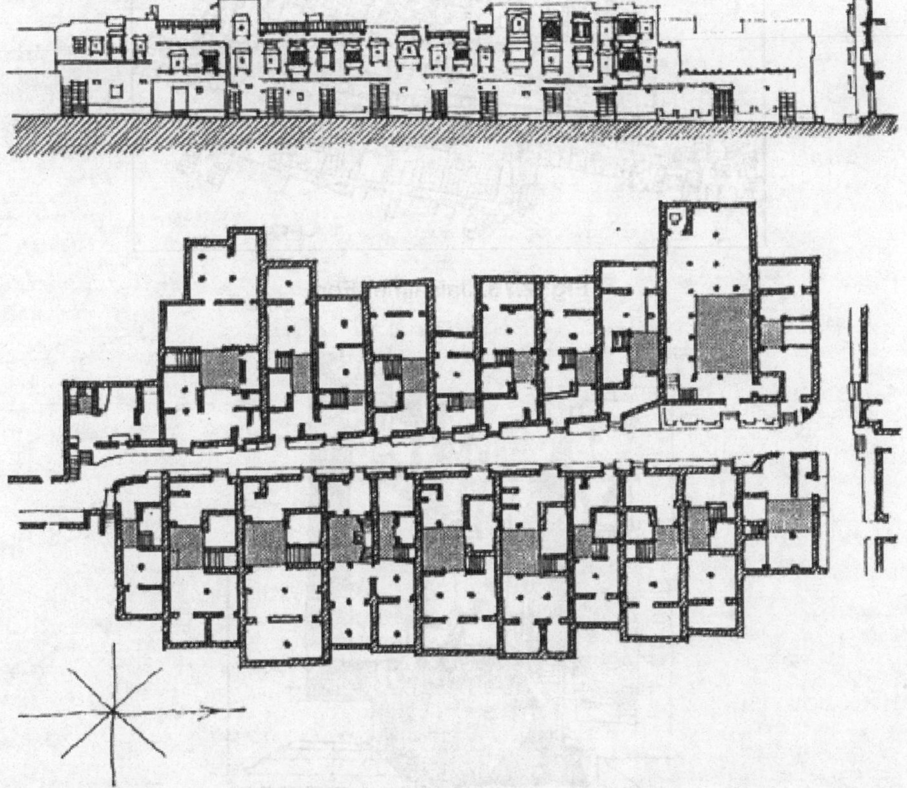

Fig. 2.71. Jaisalmer: Typical residential street (after Kulbhushan Jain)

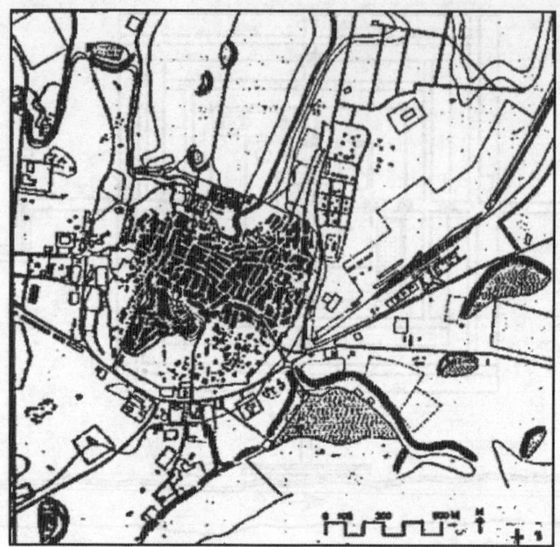

Fig. 2.72. Plan of Jaisalmer

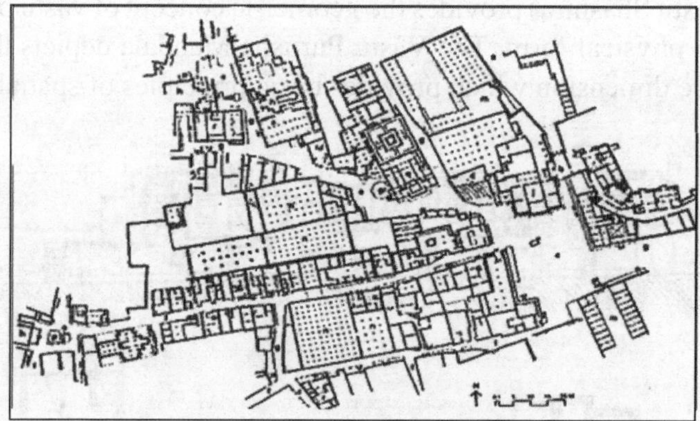

Fig. 2.73. Jaisalmer Fort

Fig. 2.74. Jaisalmer: the urban pattern responds to local culture and micro-climate

Fig. 2.75. The street picture, Jaisalmer

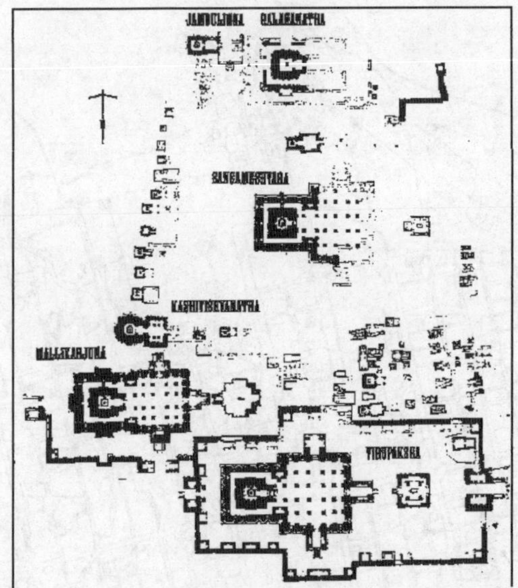

Fig. 2.76. In Pattadakal, all the temples face east. To the east the Malaprabha river flows northwards. The incomplete Sangameshvara temple is probably the earliest building on site dating from the beginning of the eighth century, followed by the Virupaksha and Mallikarjuna temples.

Source: *Pattadakal: City of Temples, Architectural Review*

The form of a city was derived on the principles of Vãstupurush Mandal. It established an interrelationship of physical form of a settlement with the spiritual, cosmic and behavioural system. It determined the basic form, its location and orientation of various functions in a settlement. It was interrelated with the surroundings, like the planets in the astrological chart. A system of ashtha (8), Navgrah (9 planets), 24 matrika pithas, etc. was devised as a numerical symbolism and for orientation and linkages of the settlement system.

In the overall urban fabric, the generic morphology manifests a labyrinthine hierarchy of social organization. It continues an introvert spatial organisation at the city level, with a highly extroverted system within the residential cluster. The extrovert spatial character is accentuated by courtyards and chowks, which enhance frequent contacts and social participation among the residents. These also serve as an efficient means of security, privacy and social control.

In traditional Indian cities courtyards and squares have been important climatic and socio-cultural space. There are city squares, chaurahas, and neighbourhood squares. In Jodhpur, Sardar Market square is the largest square, built by Maharaja Sardar Singh with shops and five-storey clock tower in the centre. Juni Mandi Square is a neighbourhood chowk, which is informal and organic.

The centre of city is Brahmsthan, the divine space according to the concept of Vãstu Purusha Mandala. Surrounding the temple were the residences of Brahmins, the priests the higher castes and went on decreasing towards the boundary. All the roads originated from the temple towards the periphery. The character was maintained as per importance of the street and the inhabitants in it. The individual dwelling units were based on the category and occupations of people.

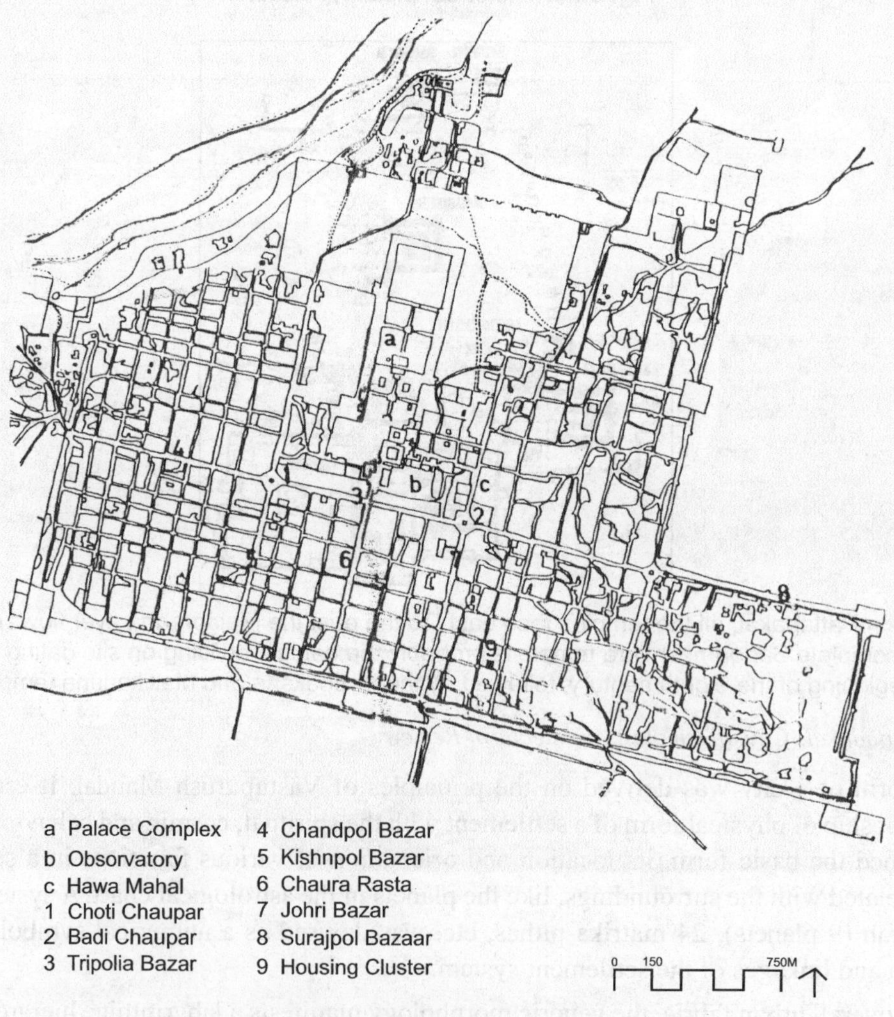

Fig. 2.77. Plan of Jaipur (1725 A.D.)

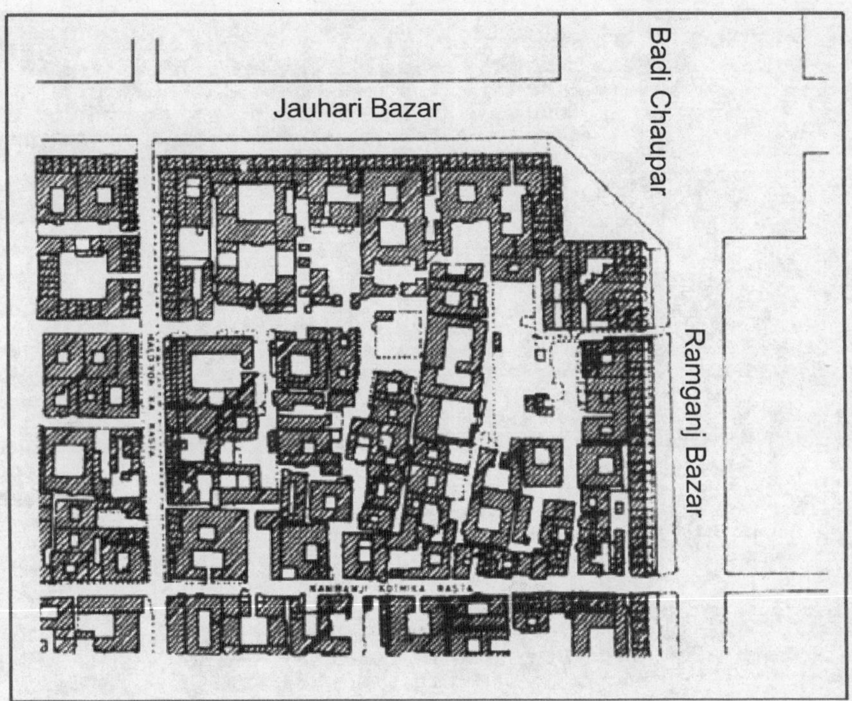

Fig. 2.78. Inner City Plan, Jaipur comprises modules of Mohallas based on occupations with dwellings having courtyards for privacy and shade. At the junction of the roads is the chaupar (public square) with a tree, water point or a well, shops, temple and other facilities (Yatin Pandya)

Fig. 2.79. Jantar Mantar, Jaipur

Source: *Discovering Jaipur, Jaipur Virasat Foundation, 2006*

Fig. 2.80. Hawa Mahal 18th Century, Jaipur

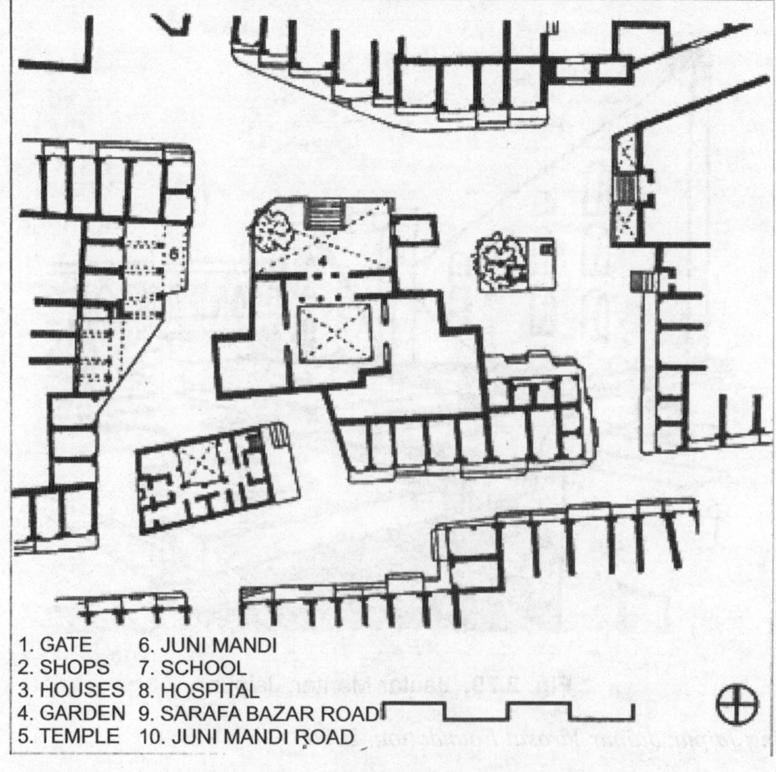

Fig. 2.81. Juni Mandi Square in Jodhpur

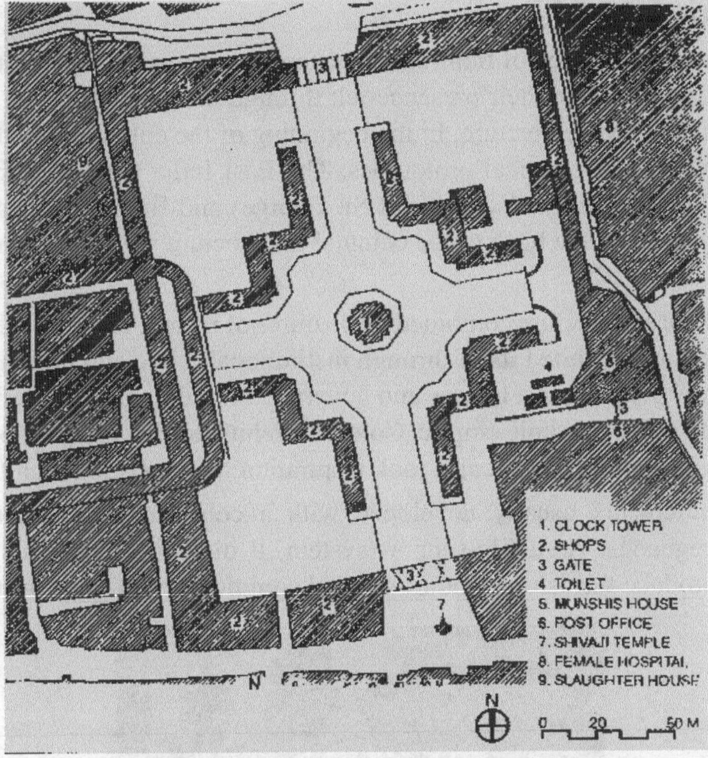

Fig. 2.82. Sardar Market Square in Jodhpur

Source: *Jain, Kulbhushan*

Maratha Architecture (17th to 19th Century)

The Marathas ruled over most of Maharashtra from the mid-17th to the early 19th centuries. Old forms returned with this 'renewal' of Hindu architecture, infused by Sultanate and later the Mughal tradition. The architecture of Maratha period was planned with courtyards suited to tropical climates. The Maratha architecture is known for its simplicity, visible logic and austere aesthetic, made rich by beautiful detailing, rhythm and repetition. The aisles and arcades, punctuated by delicate niches, doors and windows create space in which the articulation of open, semi-open and covered areas is effortless and enchanting.

Sikh Architecture

Sikh architectural style is characterized with values of progressiveness, exquisite intricacy, austere beauty and logical flowing lines. Due to its progressive style, it is constantly evolving into contemporary styles. Although Sikh architecture was initially developed for the gurudwara, its style has been used in many non-religious buildings. Sikh architecture was distinguished for its many curves and straight lines; Shri Keshgarh Sahib and the Sri Harmandir Sahib (Golden Temple at Amritsar) are prime examples.

Colonial Indian Architecture

Like all other aspects, colonization of India started a new chapter in Indian architecture. The Dutch, Portuguese and the French made their presence felt through their buildings but it was the English who had a lasting impact on architecture. In the beginning of the colonial rule there were attempts at creating authority through classical prototypes. The East India Company founded Presidency towns of Calcutta (Fort William) Madras (Fort St. George) and Bombay. These were transplants of classical, ideal cities and gave birth to the colonial architecture which culminated into the Indo-Saracenic architecture.

The Indo-Saracenic architecture combined the features of Hindu, Islamic and Western elements. The colonial architecture exhibited itself through institutional, civic and utilitarian buildings such as post-offices, railway stations, rest houses and government buildings. Such buildings began to be built in large numbers over the whole empire. Colonial architecture in India followed developments not only from English architecture but also took inspiration from existing architecture in India.

Preindustrial settlements usually developed with a coherent and balanced set of forces, endogenous and exogenous. As a life-support system, it did not often reach optimal levels of amenity, but it did produce furnishings, buildings and communities of great aesthetic consistency.

Fig. 2.83. Gothic style was popular in Colonial buildings in Mumbai

From the mid-nineteenth century, it became a norm for the Anglo-Indian church builders to follow the model set by the revivers of the many combinations of Gothic in England. This can be seen in the Mutiny Memorial Church at Kanpur and the last Garrison Church in New Delhi. The East India company also undertook various development projects such as railways, canals, hill stations, cantonments, dak bungalows, mess, clubs, etc.

The Italian Gothic was seen to be well adapted to conditions in India. The architecture style recommended by Sir Gilbert Scott for Bombay University proved crucial in making the colonial architecture look more 'Indian.' Perhaps this was the beginning of an Imperial style that reached its apex at New Delhi. The great public building campaign launched in Bombay in the second half of the nineteenth also resulted into great development of colonial architecture. In this phase Sir Gilbert Scott's buildings were significant products. Other remarkable landmarks built during this phase were William Emerson's Crawford Market, the Bombay High Court and the Victoria Terminus (now Shivaji Terminus).

The Victoria Terminus, once the headquarters of the Great Indian Peninsular Railway, was the culminating masterpiece of the phase. It was increasingly hybrid in style. The Classical and Baroque style furthered the innovation in architecture. Its best exponent was Walter Carnville's Calcutta General Post-office. In Victoria Memorial, William Emerson tried to emulate the Taj Mahal in material if not in form. The Victoria Memorial in Calcutta, is the most effective symbolism of British Empire, built as a monument in tribute to Queen Victoria's reign. The plan of the building consists of one large central part covered with a larger dome. Colonnades separate the two chambers. Each corner holds a smaller dome and is floored with marble plinth. The memorial stands on 26 hectares of garden surrounded by reflective pools.

French (1673 to 1954)

The French colonized Pondicherry in Tamil Nadu and transformed it into a flourishing port-town. The town was built on the French grid pattern and features neat sectors and perpendicular streets and divided into two sectors, French Quarter (Ville Blanche) and the Indian quarter (Ville Noire). French styled villas were styled with long compounds and stately walls, lined houses with verandas, large French doors and grills. Infrastructure such as banks, police station and Pondicherry International Port still hold the French presence.

French expanded their empire by colonizing coastal towns, Yanam in Andhra Pradesh, Karaikal in Tamil Nadu and Mahe in Kerala with a French atmosphere of quiet towns around beaches. French spellings on signage and traffic signs still remains.

Dutch (1605 to 1825)

The Dutch entered India for trade in the early 17th century. During their 200 years in India, they colonized Surat, Bharuch, Venrula, Ahmedabad, Malabar Coast and Kochi. Surat had a Dutch factory in 1630s, Bharuch was a Trading Post of the Dutch East India Company which also had a Dutch cemetery. In Venrula a warehouse was built for 3000 guilders by Leendart Janszoons and a castle for the protection of the Dutch. In Ahmedabad, the Dutch cemetery lies on the bank of Kankaria lake. It holds a mix of Indian and European styled graves, with domed tombs, pyramids, and plain grave stones. In Malabar Coast Kochi; the Dutch Palace (Mattancherry Palace) was originally built by the Portuguese, it fell into the hands of the Dutch when the Portuguese lost control of Kochi. Dutch cemetery-runs parallel to the beach and is the oldest European cemetery in India. It holds 104 tombs that visually narrate the Dutch influence in architecture during the era. The cemetery is guarded by heavy walls and the entrance pillar still carries the original calligraphic inscription "1724" David Hall. – The residence of the famous Dutch Commander and Governor of Kochi, Adriaan van Reed Drakestein was built in 1695. The hall has been restored as a cultural centre and art café for young, visual and performing artists. Bastion bungalow, a Dutch style building near the Fort Kochi beach, was built to protect the harbour. Thakur House was built overlooking the sea as a club. Sadras 17 km from the rock cut temples of Mamallapuram is another Dutch settlement. Pullicat lake 55 km north of Chennai is a million years old and the second largest lagoon in India. It was the most important trading post of the Dutch. They built two cemeteries. One was ruined due to negligence and at the entrance is flanked by stone pillars, having 76 tombs. Images of skeletons are carved onto the gravestones, symbolizing life and death.

Portuguese (1498 to 1961)

The Portuguese arrived as merchants in the 1498 and were driven by a Catholic missionary zeal than gaining power in India. The Portuguese gained a foothold in Goa and ruled for 400 years, before being defeated and evicted by Operation Vijay (1961).

Portuguese presence in Goa still remains evident. Colonizers' missionary spirit built many cathedrals, churches, basilicas and seminaries. The Basilica of Bom Jesus (Good Jesus), Old Goa, former capital during the Portuguese rule, the three storied Renaissance style church, was built of plaster and laterite in 1605. It holds the mortal remains of St. Francis Xavier. The interior is built in a Mosaic-Corinthian style and adorned with wood and gold leaf. The walls embrace old painting of saints and the floor is laid with pure white marble.

The Portuguese Catholic houses faced the street with unique ornamental windows opening onto verandahs. Bold colours were painted on houses constructed with distinct identity, allowing the sailors to recognize their houses from sea. The covered porches and verandas were designed for socializing. Front doors were lined with columns and railings were popular in embellishment.

The interiors of Goan-Portuguese houses consisted of elaborate patterns with tiles imported from Europe and a false ceiling of wood. The walls were painted with bright colours contrasting to the earthy coloured furniture. The walls were made out of mud or laterite stone and coloured with vegetable and natural dyes. Gate posts and compound walls were carved with great detail.

Presidency Cities of India

During 1612–1757, the East India Company set up factories and trading posts in India, mostly in coastal areas. Surat, set up in 1608 was the company's first headquarters. It was followed by Machilipatnam on the Coromandel coast, and other coastal cities. During 1757–1858, the Company gradually acquired sovereignty over large parts of India, and established the Presidencies at Madras, Bombay and Calcutta. North-Western Provinces was added later with its headquarter at Allahabad, then at Agra from 1834 to 1868. Hooghly, Calcutta was founded by Job Charnock in 1686, where the Presidency of Fort Williams was established. Fort St. George was established in 1785 as the headquarter of Madras Presidency. Their provinces increased after the British East India Company defeated local rulers in the wars and annexed their empires.

Fig. 2.84. Madras: Fort St. George (1785 A.D.)

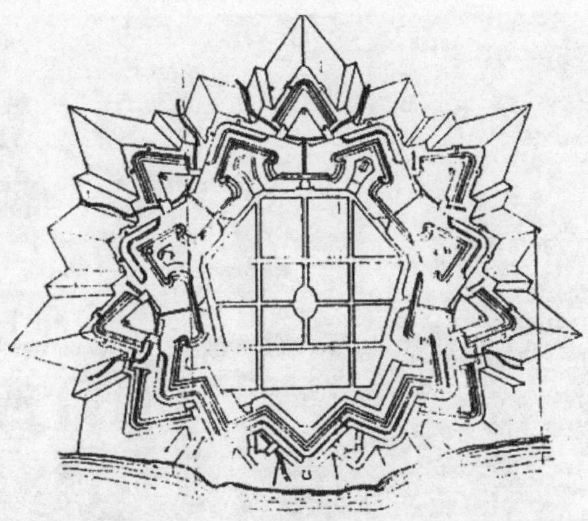

Fig. 2.85. Fort Williams, Calcutta (1686 A.D.)

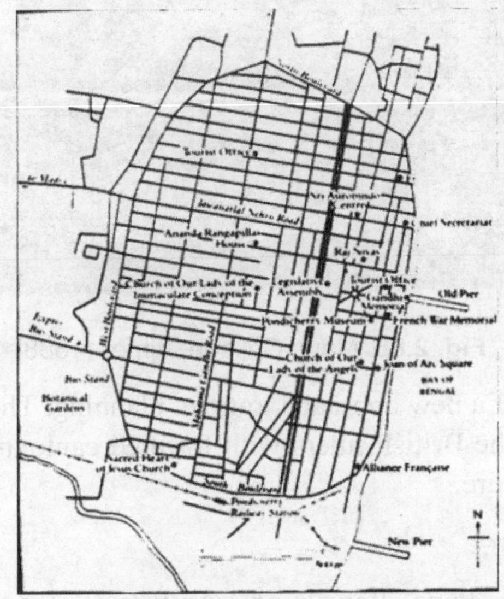

Fig. 2.86. Pondicherry

Fig. 2.87. Pondicherry–A Street in French Quarter

Fig. 2.88. Mayo College, Ajmer (1888)

This was the beginning of a new approach to town planning. The cities and buildings built by the British were mainly for the British rulers with fortified cantonments and had no relationship with the local people and culture.

Cantonments

Many cities such as Meerut, Pune, Rawalpindi, Ambala, Belgaum, Bangalore, Secunderabad Delhi, Kanpur, Bathinda,Peshawar, Ramgarh, Sialkot and Trichy contained large cantonments of the former British Indian Army. Meerut was established in 1803 and was for 150 years the biggest cantonment in the region. Earlier the cantonments in India were viewed as semi-permanent, but by the turn of the 20th century they became permanent garrisons, and were further entrenched via the military reforms of Lord Kitchener in 1903 and the Cantonments Act of 1924. At present 62 notified cantonments and 44 unlisted Garrisons/Cantonments exist in India. These generally have a grid iron pattern, large parade grounds, parks, bungalows and barracks, mess and clubs, boulevards, mall roads, Sadar Bazar with clock tower, schools, hospitals and dispensaries, military training centres, churches, barracks, etc. General pattern is low-rise and low-density development.

Hill Stations

The British rulers also developed several hill stations and cantonments and a new landscape of race courses, cricket clubs, tennis courts and public parks emerged. The pattern of classical, decorative gardens, avenues, mall roads and boulevards was introduced. After the revolt of 1857 the British sought escape from the locals and Indian heat and return to home country without leaving India. The hill stations were developed for the purpose, with the object to reproduce the home country in India. This is illustrated by Lord Lytton's statement about Ootacamund in the 1870s, *such beautiful English rain, such delicious English mud. Shimla was made the summer capital of India in the 1860s and hill stations "served as vital centers of political and military power, besides providing refuge as "places to rest and recuperate from the arduous life on the plains."* The hill stations reached their zenith in the late nineteenth century, which were as many as 40 in numbers.

New Delhi

On December 12,1911 at the historic Delhi Durbar, King George V, Emperor of the British Empire proclaimed that the capital of India would henceforth be Delhi instead of Calcutta. A temporary capital complex was built in the area now known as Delhi University and the Old Secretariat during 1912-15. Delhi Town Planning Commission (DTPC) was constituted to plan the new capital, comprising of G.S.C. Swinton, Edwin Lutyens and J.A. Brodie. There was continued debate regarding whether the city should be located north or south of Old Delhi, and finally it was decided to locate the new city on Raisina Hill, between the Ridge and the River, towards South of Shahjahanabad. The reasons were primarily a healthy and naturally drained site, as compared to low lying northern site at Kingsway Camp and also that the new city at a higher ground will dominate the urban landscape.

Imperial Delhi was laid out by Edwin Lutyens as a garden city covering 8,200 acres to accommodate a population of 65,000. It was accessible from the Walled City only through two underpasses, Minto and Hardinge Bridges. Beyond this, New Delhi was laid in a geometric pattern over a triangular base formed by the Connaught Place, Viceroy House and India Gate. With its wide avenues, double row of trees, the Central Vista called Kingsway (now Rajpath) was the centre-piece of the new city. The residential areas were planned with lower and middle income employees to the north of the vista and senior British officials to the south, in an hierarchical pattern.

The Connaught Place was conceived as the city centre, with its location in the geographical centre of Old and New Delhi. It was to act as a link between two Delhis and a Railway Station was laid adjacent to it in order to link the city to the region. The Viceroy Palace on the Raisina Hill was the focal point for the entire city. To the south of the fashionable shopping centre of Connaught Place and along river Yamuna, the India Gate, National Stadium and recreational activities were planned.

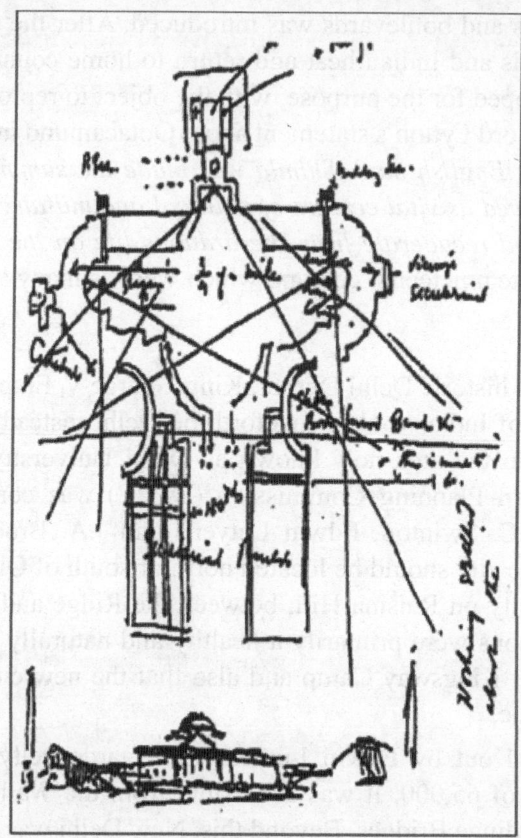

Fig. 2.89. Edwin Lutyens initial sketch of Capital Complex (June 1912)

Source: *Jain A.K. (1994) The Cities of Delhi, Management Publishing Co.*

The plan of New Delhi is geometrical in shape with hexagonal and triangular patterns. The plan can be viewed in 2 parts—a rectangular grid or main central axis that has the monumental government buildings and the hexagonal layout that focuses on the local and residential aspects of the city. The central axis, which was known as Kingsway, now called Rajpath, runs through the layout of the new city with several avenues and streets radiating from it. It was designed by Lutyens as a processional avenue that linked the Viceroy's Palace now the Rashtrapati Bhavan at the west end to the War Memorial Arch or India Gate and the canopy of George the V at the east end of the axis. Rajpath is a picturesque, broad road flanked by large, shady trees and ornamental ponds on either side of it. The central Vista and the vast green avenues accentuated the grandeur and superiority of the new city. The panorama of monumental buildings enveloped within a rich landscape is unique. The Central Vista has become almost symbolic of New Delhi as a stage of the world's largest democracy. The grand vista has remained to function as a ceremonial path during the celebrations of the Republic Day Parade held annually on the 26th of January when the avenue comes alive. The Secretariats were planned flanking the Viceroy House on two sides.

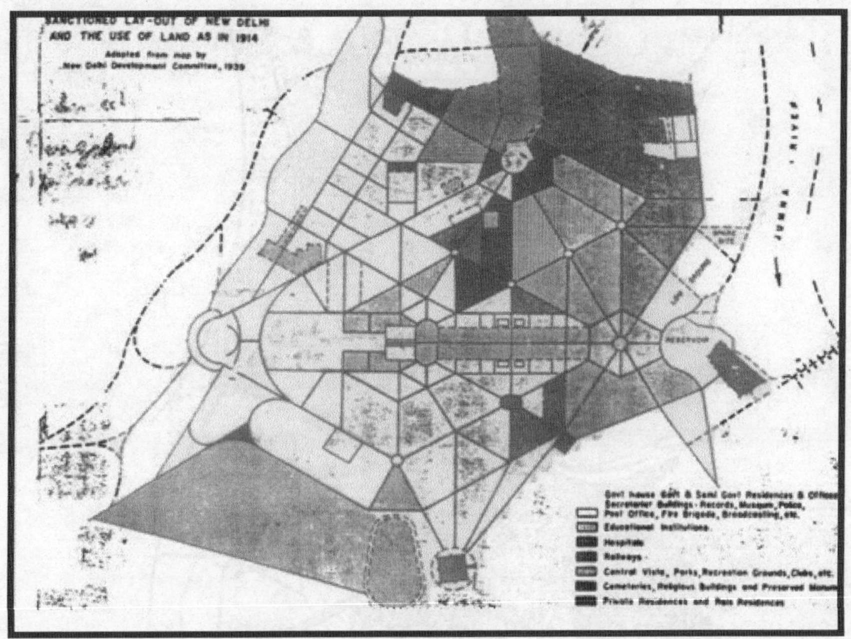

Fig. 2.90. Layout of New Delhi in 1914

Source: *A.K. Jain (2010) Lutyens Delhi, Bookwell Publishing., New Delhi*

Fig. 2.91. Elephantine Security Post, built in red sandstone at Viceroy House, designed by Edwin Lutyens. Photograph by A.K. Jain

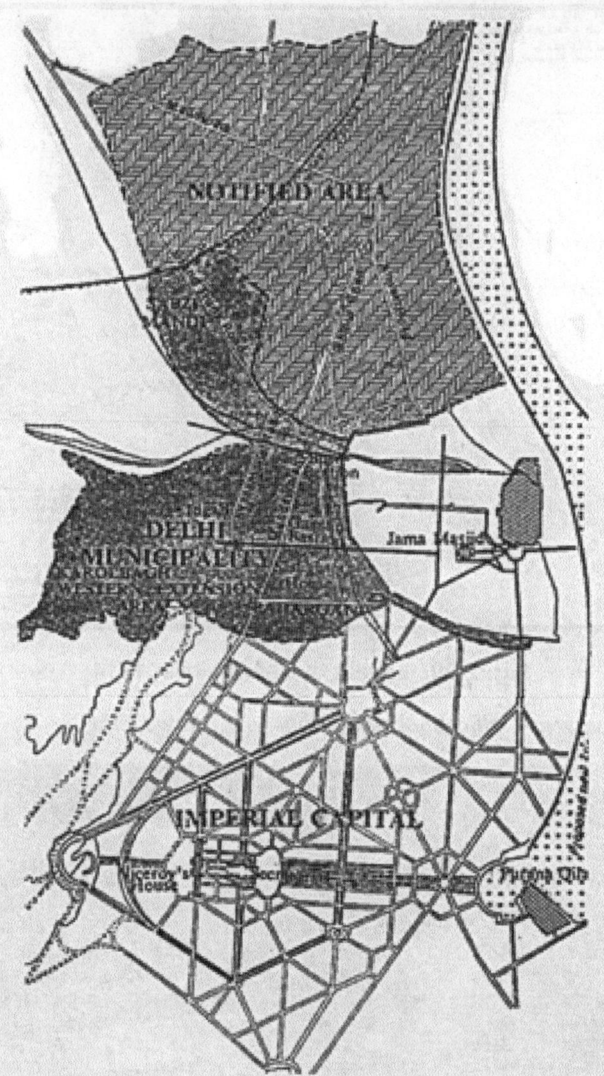

Fig. 2.92. Delhi Municipality Notified Area, Imperial City and Western Extension, 1914

Source: Jain A.K. (2010) Lutyens' Delhi, Bookwell, New Delhi

The capital complex is an architectural ensemble of unique value. Lutyens visualized a grand vision, highlighting the supremacy of the British rule. A hexagonal pattern linked the major activities of the triangular base, viz., governmental, commercial and recreational, at the apex of the triangle and the residential areas in the hexagonal. This provided a visual continuity of the new city with the monuments of ancient capital, like the Purana Quila, Jama Masjid, Safdarjung Tomb, Ferozshah Kotla, Lodhi Tombs, etc. The city was nestled between two ecological features of the site, which were river Yamuna on the East and the Aravali ridge on the West. Lutyens' plan was to landscape a vast expanse joining the river Yamuna and the Ridge. The water pools of the India Gate were surrounded by a number of palaces and a stadium. The city was conceived as a vast park with buildings hidden by trees.

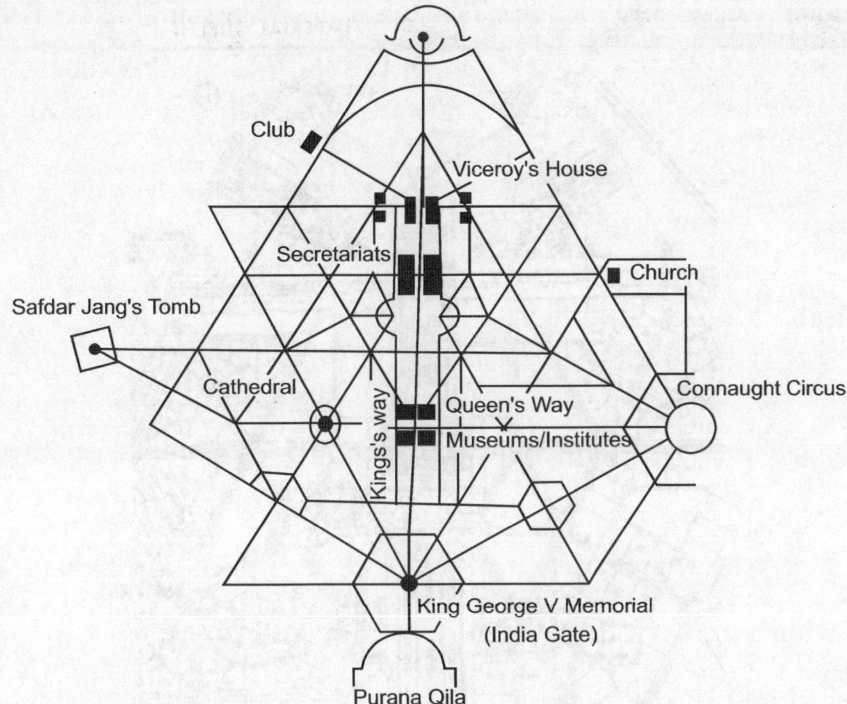

Fig. 2.93. While planning New Delhi, Lutyens conceived a garden city with buildings below tree height except the buildings in the monumental grid i.e. along the Central Vista. India Gate and Government Complex were linked by a monumental grid, known as the Central Vista. The India Gate, symbolic city gate was planned on the river side, while the Capital Complex dominating the skyline was placed at the Raisina Hill. A hexagonal grid provided visual continuity of the city with the ancient monuments, like Purana Qila, Jama Masjid, Safdarjung Tomb, Ferozshah Kotla, Lodhi Garden, Humayun Tomb, etc. The new Capital was carefully placed between two natural feaures of the site, viz. River Yamuna on the East and the Ridge towards the West

Fig. 2.94. Central Vista, the centre-piece of New Delhi

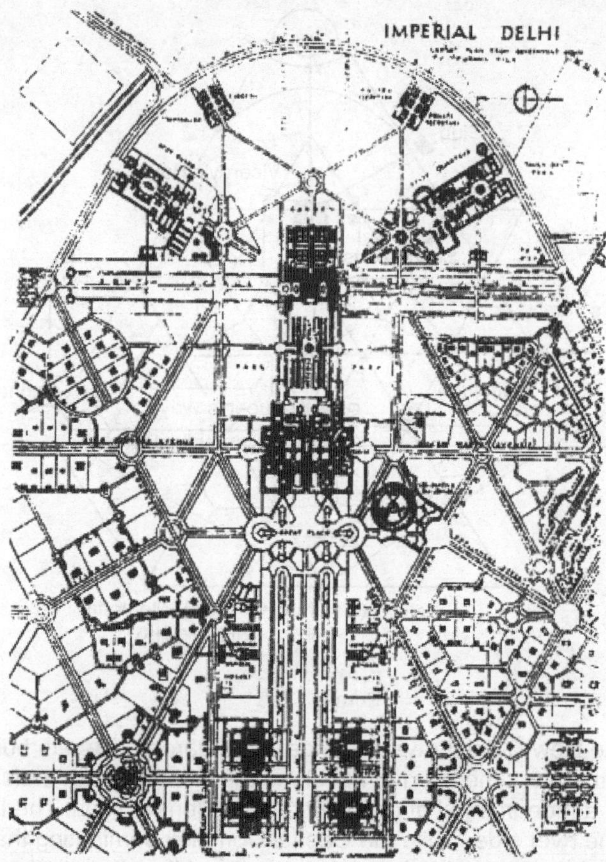

Fig. 2.95. Layout of the Viceregal Estate and Capital Complex at Raisina Hill

Source: *Central PWD, New Delhi*

Fig. 2.96. Landscape had been an integral part of the design of Imperial Capital (New Delhi). The Mughal Garden in Viceroy House was designed by Edwin Lutyens. It combined the concepts of British garden and Mughal Charbagh

Lutyens enjoyed using geometrical shapes in his designs and architectural plans. In his plan for New Delhi the triangle, hexagon and square are used frequently. These geometrical forms were also used by Lutyens' predecessors, the Mughals. The hexagon is commonly used in Mughal architecture, a perfect example of which can be seen in the inlay work in red sandstone and white marble at Humayun's Tomb. Although Lutyens never had much respect for Indian cities and its architecture, it seems that gradually he began to appreciate India's greatness, as reflected by the following lines inscribed on Jaipur Column at the Viceroy Palace:

"Endow your thoughts with Faith

Your deeds with courage

Your life with sacrifice

So all men may know the greatness of India:"

Various roads cross this main avenue at right angles, but the general street pattern is diagonal to the main axis. The system of diagonal avenues in Delhi provides directness of movement for vehicular traffic which has much to commend it.

In contrast to a compact and introverted Walled City, the new city was designed on an extrovert and low density pattern. With a maximum density of 25 persons per acre, no attempt was made to relate the new to the old city. The plan proposed large plots of 1 to 6 acres (with some plots even bigger) for residential development. However, the city remained deserted and looked barren for decades. In attempts to populate the deserted New Delhi, housing allowance given to government employees working in New Delhi was refused to those residing outside it. Businessmen were given incentives to open their shops in the Connaught Place. To service and maintain the new city, the New Delhi Municipal Council was constituted in 1916, but it did not become effective until 1925.

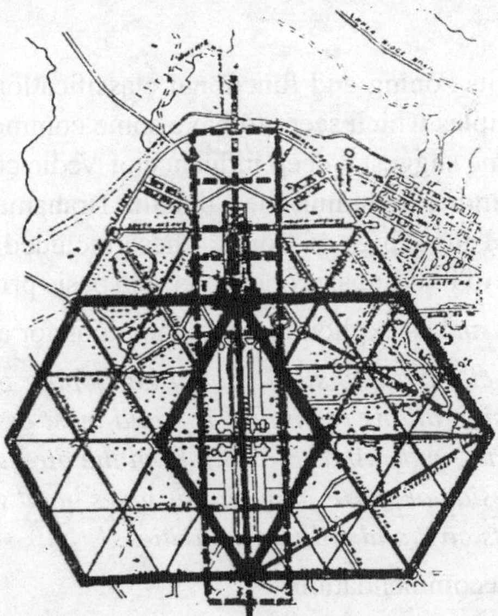

Fig. 2.97. The plan of New Delhi is superimposition of two distinct geometric systems. The rectangular grid is monumental and relates to the major scale of Government buildings. The hexagonal system is local and residential

Source: *A Greenburg, 1969, Lutyens' Architecture Restudied, in Perspecta,12, Connecticut*

When the Imperial Delhi was formally inaugurated in 1931, it indeed was discerned to be an Anglo-Indian Rome. Lutyens, who was deeply influenced by the Greeco-Roman roots of city planning and architecture faithfully followed them in the design of New Delhi. In spite of the fact that in the West "modern architecture", with new materials, functional emphasis and changing concepts of structural engineering, was raising a storm, Lutyens ignored it while planning and building the New Delhi. However, despite Lutyens' own ignorance of Indian architecture, it is intriguing that the plan of New Delhi is not very alien to the principles of Mansara.

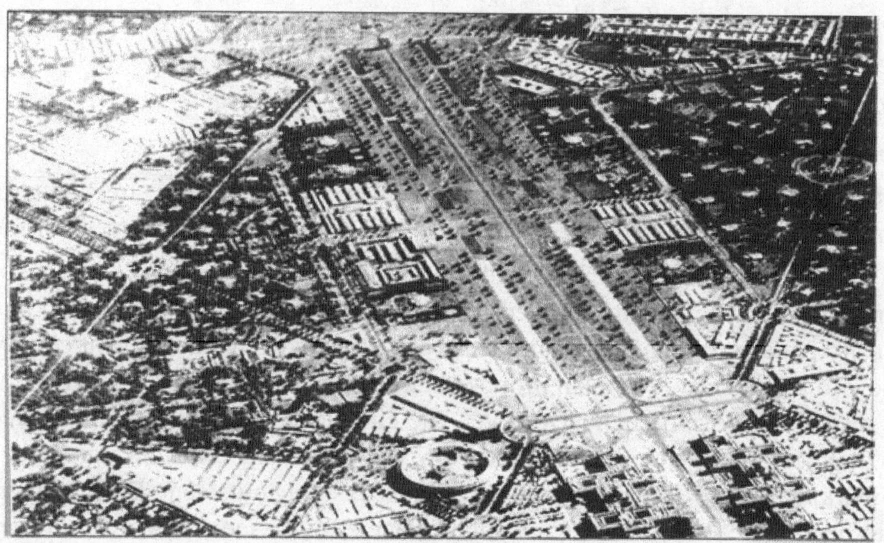

Fig. 2.98. The Central Vista, New Delhi (1931)

Source: *CPWD Archives*

The location of the city, its zoning and functional classification coincide quite well with the traditional Indo-Roman principles which seem to have some common interaction. The mythology and rituals of Greece and Rome suggest a deep influence of Vedic culture. It is believed that many of the epics and Shastras in India, including the Sthpatha Brahaman were composed at a period contemporary with the rule of the Kings of Rome. These included many canonical books which dealt with the rules and rituals of buildings, proportions, and basic principles of settlement planning.

In the 'Politics', Aristotle makes explicit recommendations for a site:

"The land upon which a city is to be sited should be sloping that we must just hope to find, but we should keep four considerations in mind. First and most essential the situation must be a healthy one. A slope facing east, with winds blowing from the direction of sunrise, gives a healthy site, rather better than the leeside or north, though this gives good weather. Next it should be well situated for carrying out all its civil and military activities."

Vitruvius makes similar recommendations:

"The choice of a healthy site must come first. Such a site will be high, neither misty nor frosty, the climate neither too hot nor too cold, but temperate. There should be no marshes in the neighbourhood. If the town is on the coast and exposed either to the south or the west it will not be healthy...In founding towns, in short, beware of districts where hot wind can blow on the inhabitants."

In the fifth century B.C., Hippocrates formulated the basic principles of city planning. This might have been a revolutionary period as earlier cities were more organically developed. It was after Hippocrates that the selection of site of a city, its orientation, topography and health aspects of ground became important considerations, besides its military necessities. Rome was founded on the Palatine hill, overlooking the valley of the forum. Street layout to the direction of the winds emerged an important facts of planning. Vitruvius, following his Greek preceptors, warns that *"if the streets run straight in the direction of the winds then their constant blasts rush in and ...... sweep the streets with great violence. The lines of houses must therefore be directed away from the quarters from which the winds blow, so that they may strike against the angles of the blocks and their force be broken up and dispersed."*

Vitruvius described a sixteen rayed-tablet arrangement for orienting the main streets at an oblique angle in the strongest winds. 300 years after Vitruvius, Oribasius modified the principle of orientation and recommends the following:

"When streets are parallel in a town, some in length and some in breadth, the first running from east to west, the others from south and north, so that they pierce the town through length and breadth without any obstacles, and none of the winds meet any building which might obstruct its course.... (the town will be) well aired and sunlit, healthy and clear. For all the winds, Boreas and Notus, Eurus and Zephyrus, which are the dominant and most regular winds, sweep through the streets without meeting obstacles and pass freely without causing any disturbance... This kind of plan also makes the town a good sun trap because at sunrise and sunset, and sun lights up the streets which run east-west, and at midday those that run north south..."

However, the logic continued to be interspersed with faith, rituals and symbolism Lutyens' geometry conveyed a monumental classical style combined with the concept of Ebenezer Howard's Garden City, which was making waves in England during that time. Several Maharajas also engaged the British architects and engineers for planning their capital cities and palaces such as Mysore, Baroda, Jaipur, Jodhpur, Indore, Hyderbad, etc. These were the show-pieces of splendour and royal affluence with a few lone voices, such as Patrick Geddes, a natural and social scientist, who maintained the indigenous metaphor of city design in his "conservative surgery" approach.

Patrick Geddes in India

Patrick Geddes was in India from 1907 to 1919. Before arriving in India, Patrick Geddes had no specific knowledge of the culture of India. Soon he learnt about it and his work reflects his perceptivity about the Indian city, revealing the deepest insight and the sympathy for the people. Four years before he arrived at Gateway of India, Bombay, the great durbar in Delhi in 1911 marked the apex of Imperial rhetoric, created by plan of Lutyens and architecture of Baker, a city of bungalows, fountains, avenues, palaces and esplanade. The Imperial style got the Colonialist message and it left the borrowed cultural heritage. The old city was seen as a slum fit for clearance.

However, method adopted by Geddes was based on an analytical approach to the issues of urban planning based on social humane concerns. Patrick Geddes, anti, rhetorical approach based on the understanding of the spirit of the place and small adjustments, not magniloquent clearances, on rationalisation of the existing rather than grandiose work of engineering. His plans were moderate in terms of cost and population in planning. He was disturbed by the cities growing without the concern of health, clogging up all their common spaces, overcrowding and segregation of different castes. British planners overcame the problem of congestion by cutting broad boulevards through the crowded districts, while using traditional city gardens for railway stations, industry and power houses. However, Patrick Geddes stated that "Architecture always claimed to be regulator of the arts, and rightly so, town planning in its turn claims to be regulator of architecture. If this is true, then another truth is also inescapable that Civic is the regulator of Town Planning—so to perceive the ideals that create the city and keep it alive is supreme task of a civic awareness matured through historical studies and transformed into a science. "For Geddes, people are the principal term of reference in town planning. If it is to be successful it must be folk planning. This means its task is not to coerce people into new places against their associations, wishes and interests. Instead its task is to find the right places for each sort of people, places where they will really flourish. To give people, in fact, the same care that we give when transplanting flowers, instead of harsh evictions and arbitrary instructions to move on, delivered in manner of officious amateur policeman, Geddes did not favour either the Romantic conservatives linked to Sir Walter Scott of the Oxford Movement, Ruskin Morris, and Sir Gilbert Scott, aggressive architects inspired by Haussmann and led by Stubben. Geddes suggested that city planning must be based on Civic and Diagnostic Surveys. In a brief note on Ahmedabad, where he was asked to give his opinion on circle of city walls, a careful analysis of ring of walls is essential, with precision of a botanist and sensitivity of an architect.

In 1914, Patrick Geddes gave a report on planning of the Walled City of Delhi (Shahjahanabad). He advocated the 'civic survey' as a tool of 'Conservative Surgery' to improve the dilapidated, congested city. Intensive surveying led to working out the minimum number of the most dilapidated houses to be pulled down for creating open spaces within the congested areas and also allowing ventilation for each surrounding house. The few families displaced were to be resettled with a basic standard of housing and environmental hygiene. Thus he advocated slum rehabilitation and improvement in place of clearance, and greenfield development. He strengthened the need for creating Urban Improvement Trusts.

Fig. 2.99. Indore: Expansion of the New Industrial City in the North-East Quadrant under Geddes Plan

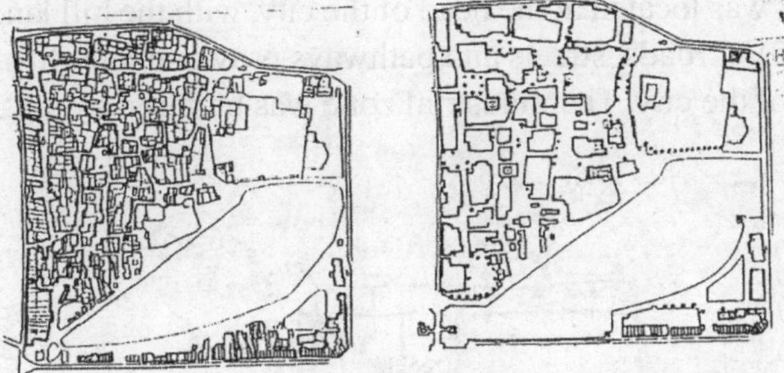

Fig. 2.100. Conservative Surgery applied to Balrampur, 1917

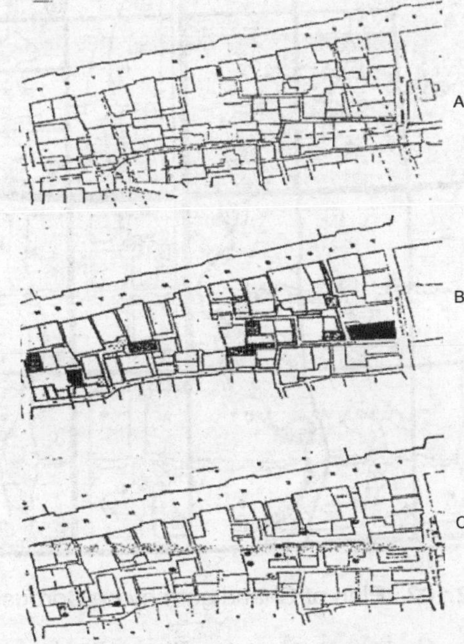

Fig. 2.101. Tanjore: (*a*) Municipal Council Plan, (*b*) and (*c*) Patrick Geddes plan with application of the theory of conservative surgery

Chandigarh

Chandigarh, the capital of Punjab and Haryana was designed by Le Corbusier. It was based on his concept of city as a human system, comprising the head, heart and hands, with roads as the veins. It echoes Corbusier's vision of the city, its human engagement and urban landscape. In the great Indian cities of Mughals, the water flowing from the mountains and rainwater was collected into lakes, reservoirs and channels, where the gardens were located (e.g. Shalimar Bagh in Srinagar). Le Corbusier applied the same principle in Chandigarh Plan. Corbusier's plan for Chandigarh established lake Sukhna that impounds the water flowing from the Shivalik hills and a leisure valley along an existing stream cutting across the city. It cuts through the city, bringing the landscape in the midst of the city. This has become an ecological asset for the city, besides a source of drainage, recreation and protection of bio-diversity.

The capital complex was located at the head of the city, with the hill landscape in the backdrop. A hierarchical system of V-7 roads, streets and pathways provided mobility to its citizens. The City Centre was at the heart of the city. The industrial zone was buffered by an 'invioable' green belt.

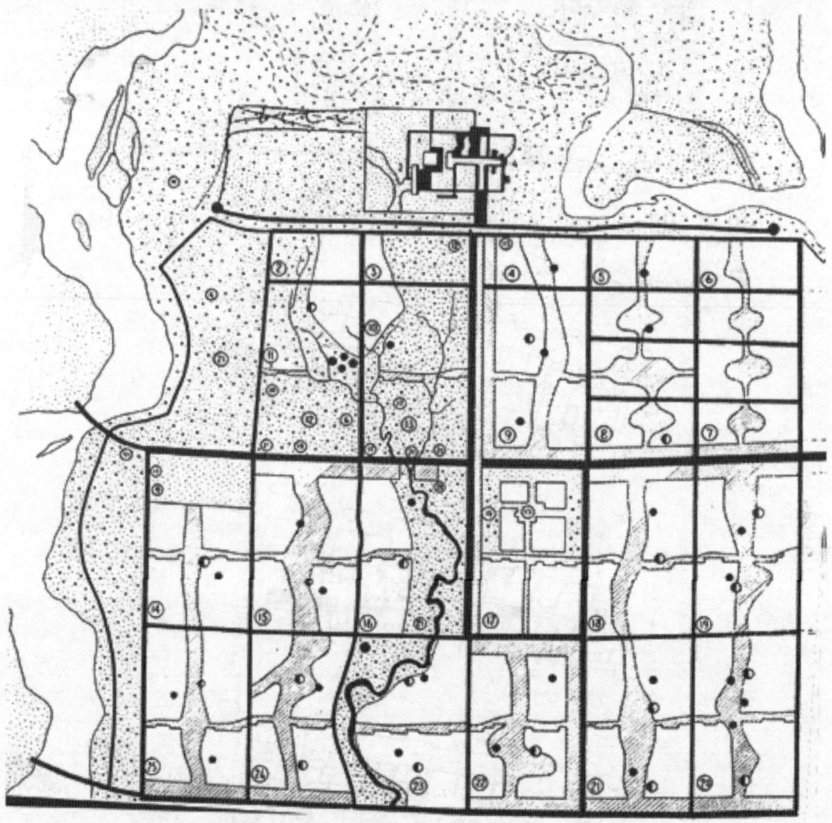

Fig. 2.102. Plan of Chandigarh by Le Corbusier

Source: *Boesiger, W. (Ed.) 1999, Le Corbusier—Complete Works, Birkhauser Publishers, Basel*

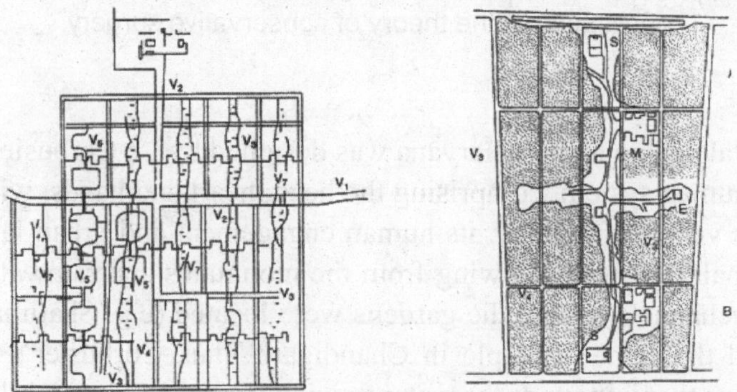

Fig. 2.103. Le Corbusier's road classification, V1 cross country, V2 branch to city, V 3 sector divide, V 4 sector connector, V5 local spine, V6 buildings, V 7 pedestrians through interlinked greens

Source: *Boesiger, W. (Ed.) 1999, Le Corbusier—Complete Works, Birkhauser Publishers, Basel*

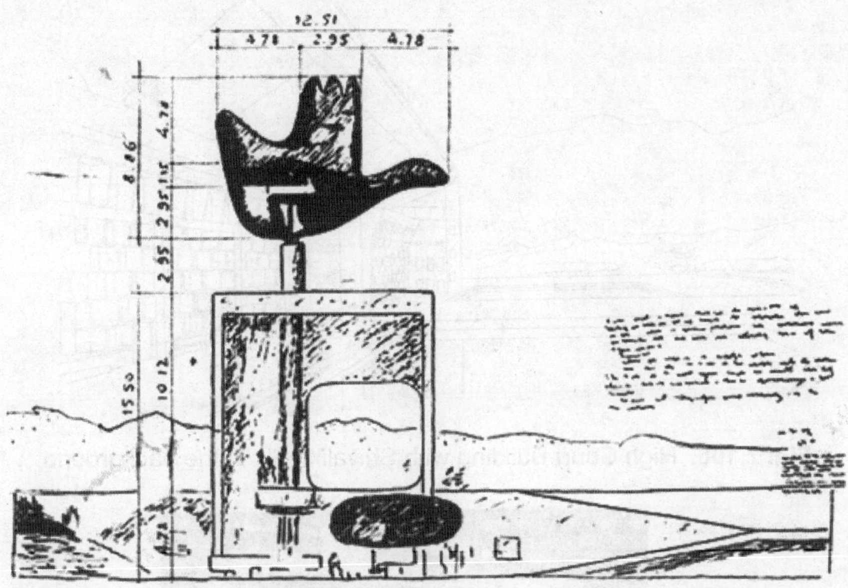

Fig. 2.104. Open Hand Monument in Chandigarh by Le Corbusier is based on philosophy of man as a giver (devta) with an open hand

Fig. 2.105. The Capital Complex (Secretariat Building) by Le Corbusier

Fig. 2.106. High Court Building with Shivalik Hills in the background

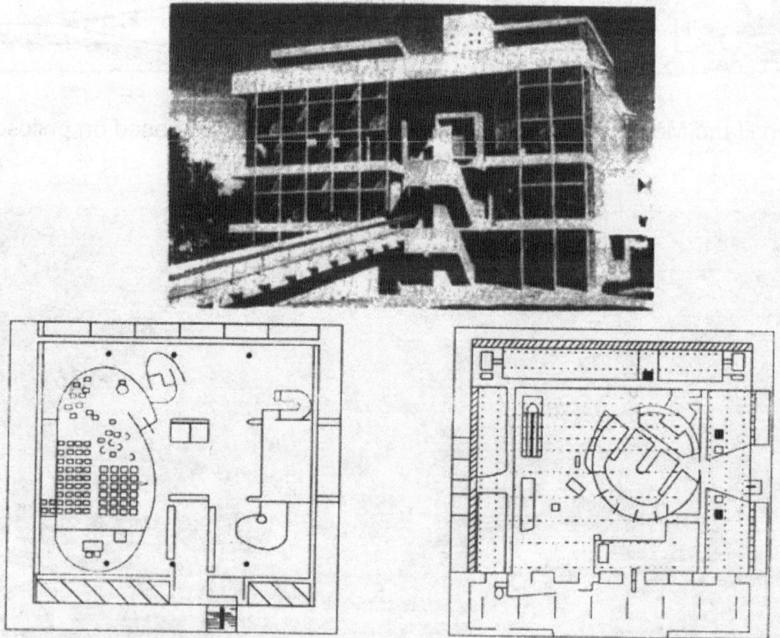

Fig. 2.107. Le Corbusier's building for the Mill Owners' Association in Ahmedabad has walls of brise-soleil on the east and west facades. The hall is indirectly lit by reflections from the ceiling. The building is kept cool by a garden and a water reservoir on the roof

Le Corbusier, the celebrated French-Swiss architect, had his own contribution in shaping the Indian architecture. In early fifties he was commissioned to design several buildings and Chandigarh city. His Sarabhai and Shodan villas and the Millowners Building at Ahmedabad and the four majestic buildings of the capital complex in Chandigarh had an incredible impact on Indian architects. It not only helped to regenerate art which was almost lost during the British rule but also provided a stimulus to Indian architects. He threw open the floodgates of the concepts of form, syntax and aesthetics.

Although now on the wane, many Indian architects adopted Le Corbusier's exposed concrete, bold and plastic forms and modular openings. Even Gandhinagar, the new capital of Gujarat, was adapted from his plan of Chandigarh. On the other hand, there were the architects who were searching for the forms which related more closely with the Indian context. The prevailing trend of traditional modernism with emphasis on regional characteristics can be best witnessed in the India International Centre, built in Delhi during early sixties.

According to Joseph Allen Stein, the architect, "*I strongly believe that being modern without being regional is inappropriate and regional without modernism reactionary*." Based on human scale, India International Centre (IIC) witnessed integration of both new technology with the local culture. The IIC along with the Ford Foundation and the United Nations Children Education Fund building is a beautiful oasis in the sublime setting of historic Lodi Gardens.

Now architecture is at the cross-roads. In this age of specialization, architecture has metamorphosed into several disciplines. This has resulted into a fragmented approach and disruption of age old traditions. There is a paradigm shift in the perceptions and process of design.

DEBRIEFING QUESTIONS

1. What are the predominant styles of historic Indian Architecture?

2. Highlight the salient features of architecture and planning of:
   (*i*) Indus Valley
   (*ii*) Buddhist Culture
   (*iii*) Rock-cut temples

3. Explain the concept of town planning as enunciated by Vastu Shastra/Mansara.

4. What are the salient features of Indo-Islamic architecture?

5. Describe the architecture of the following:
   (*i*) Sanchi Stupta
   (*ii*) Taj Mahal, Agra
   (*iii*) Red Fort, Delhi
   (*iv*) South Indian Temple towns, such as Madurai, Vijay Nagar and Tanjavur
   (*v*) Sun Temple, Konark
   (*vi*) Tomb of Shershah, Sasaram

6. Describe the architectural styles:
   (*i*) Jaisalmer
   (*ii*) Fatehpur Sikri
   (*iii*) Jaipur
   (*iv*) Shahjahanabad

7. What are the distinct features of Colonial Indian Architecture?

8. Explain the architectural styles of:
   (*a*) Edwin Lutyens and Herbert Baker in New Delhi
   (*b*) Le Corbusier in Chandigarh

9. What is the importance of historic architecture while designing modern buildings?

Chapter 3

History of Architecture and Human Settlements

Cities and buildings keep alive culture and the memories. They are not just the material remains of the contemporary society, but are the living things of the people, their economy, knowledge, arts, faith, morals and customs. They also provide lessons how the ruler, architects, builders and society addressed the issues of dichotomy between urban and rural, natural and built form and synergy among community development, climate, security, safety, employment and economy.

The history of architecture can be traced back to river valley civilizations of Egypt, Mesopotamia, India and China which attempted to immortalise dead and also the culture. About 2000 years ago classical style of architecture were developed. These had a global impact on the architecture, settlements, fortifications and religious architecture. Gradually new forms of building developed with the invention of arch, vault and dome together with use of mosaic, murals, cluster columns intersecting vault roof, clear story windows, flying buttress, stone and metal trellis, etc. Subsequently the Renaissance, Baroque, Rococo and Neo-Classic styles appeared with ribbed dome, lantern dome, etc. This was followed by the classical, modern and post-modern architecture and parametric style using fluidity, modulation and closer engagement with the ecology, ergonomics and aesthetics.

Egypt, Nile Valley (3000 B.C. and Later)

Egyptian pyramids, tombs and surrounding settlements are some of the earliest evidences of architecture in the Nile valley. Ramses III, during his reign between 1182 and 1151 B.C., engaged the slaves to build pyramids, cities and gardens. The Egyptian culture revolved around Pharaoh, the lord. The concept of life after death led to the construction of the pyramids. The settlements grew along the Nile river. The pomp and splendour of pharaoh led to development of advanced construction technologies of stone cutting and carving. At El Amarna along the Nile larger private residences had come up as shown by paintings on the walls of tombs near Thebes. A typical mansion at El Amarna and other locations enclosed as large as three-quarters of an acre, their own gardens which also provided food.

With more dependence on urban life, humans were relatively free from immediate dependence on the agriculture and maintained an interplay of social structure and division of labour, which epitomized a new relationship between humans and the urban space.

Fig. 3.1. The Pyramids of Egypt epitomise the human strength and determination

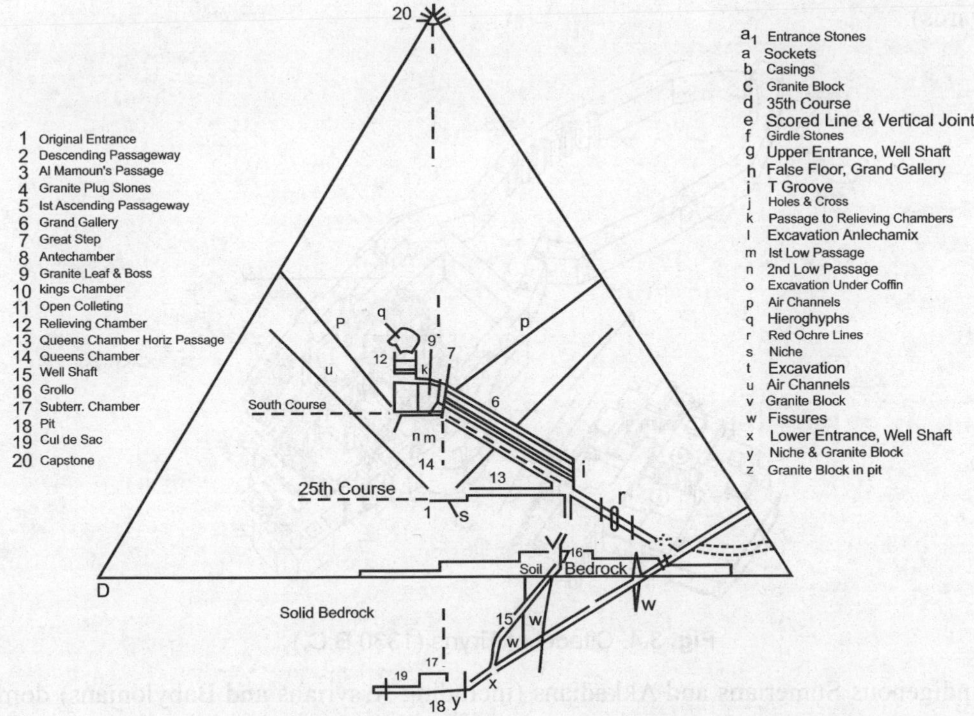

Fig. 3.2. Great Pyramid-Cross Sectional Diagram

Fig. 3.3. Perspective Interpretation of the Mural of an Egyptian Garden

Mesopotamia Civilisation

Mesopotamia civilisation evolved mainly in the land between the river Tigris and Euphrates. The region witnessed the rise of several ancient civilizations like the Sumerian (5000 to 2330 B.C.), the Akkadian, Babylonian (2330 to 525 B.C.), Assyrian empire (1800 to 613 B.C.) and Persian (525 B.C. onwards)

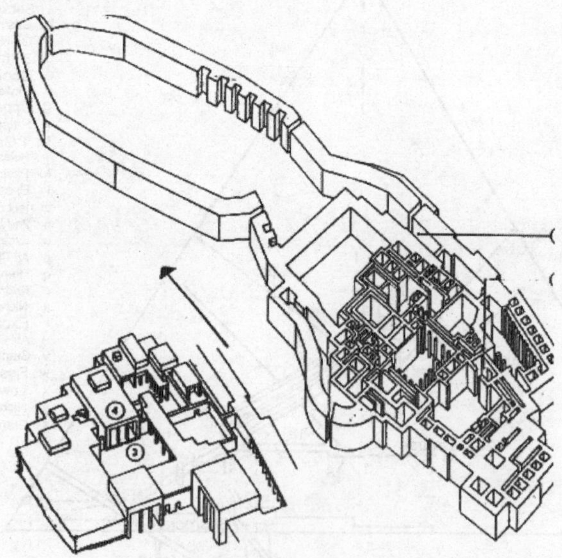

Fig. 3.4. Citadel of Tiryns (1330 B.C.)

The indigenous Sumerians and Akkadians (including Assyrians and Babylonians) dominated Mesopotamia from the beginning of written history (c. 3100 B.C.) to the fall of Babylon in 539 B.C., when it was conquered by the Achaemenid Empire (the first Persian Empire). It fell to Alexander the Great in 332 B.C. and after his death, it became part of the Greek Seleucid Empire. Mesopotamia is the site of the earliest developments of the Neolithic Revolution from around

10,000 B.C.. It has been identified as having inspired some of the most important developments in human history, including the invention of the wheel, the planting of the cereal crops and the development of cursive script, mathematics, astronomy and agriculture.

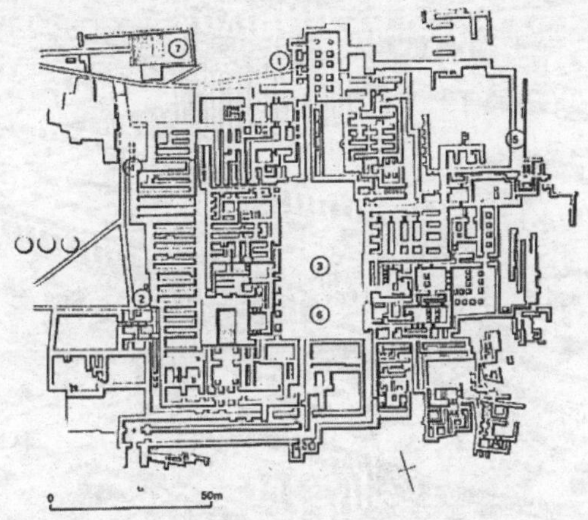

Fig. 3.5. Knosses, Crete (1550 B.C.)

Ancient Mesopotamia

The word Ziggurat is an anglicized form of the Akkadian word ziqqurratum, the name given to the solid stepped towers of mud brick. It derives from the verb zaqaru, 'to be high.' The buildings are described as being like mountains linking Earth and heaven. The ziggurat at Ur, excavated by Leonard Woolley, is 64 by 46 meters at base and originally some 12 meters in height with three stories. It was built under Ur-Nammu (c. 2100 B.C.) and rebuilt under Nabonidus (555-539 B.C.) to eight stories.

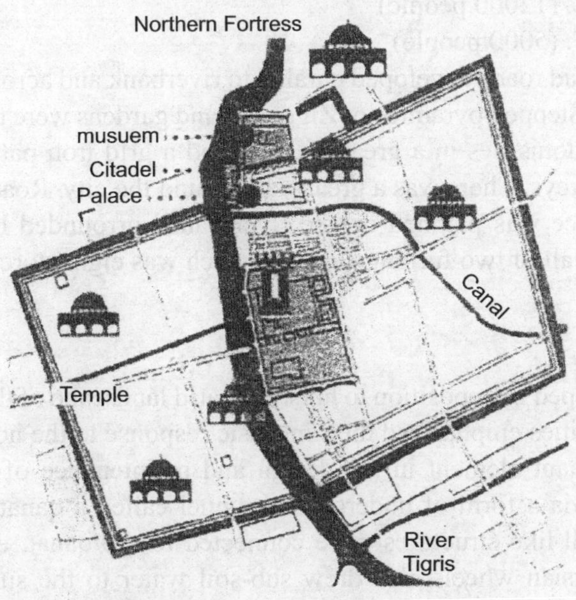

Fig. 3.6. Plan of Babylon Fortified City

Nebuchadnezzar (605-562), who reigned for 43 years, extended political control all over the Mesopotamia. He reconstructed Babylon in elaborate style and restored many temples throughout Babylon.

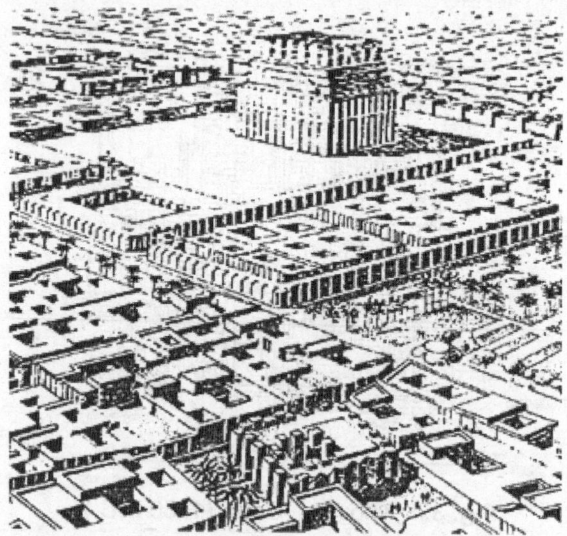

Fig. 3.7. Babylon Ziggurat (200-323 B.C.)

Sumerian and Babylonian Civilization

Sumerian cities were protective and compact and their development was horizontal, adapted well to climate. The market was the centre. River was an important element of the city and served for transportation. Some examples of Sumerian cities are given below:

Ur-Babylon 2000 B.C. (2000 people)
Khafage 2700 B.C. (12000 people)
Eshnunna 2300 B.C. (5000 people)

The Sumerian cities had roads developed parallel to riverbank and across them. The cross roads were frequently stepped. Stepped pyramids or Ziggurats and gardens were the highlights of the city.

Ur-Babylon by Herodotus lies in a great plain. It had a grid iron pattern of 120 feet square. The houses had 3 to 4 storeys. There was a great wall around the city. Roads were all straight with bronze gates. Royal palace was planned on the river bank surrounded by great wall, Ziggurat, (temple) surrounded by wall of two furlongs length, which was eight storey high and was made of bricks.

Persian Culture

Persian cities were developed in opposition to harsh and arid landscape of the Iranian Plateau. Their ethereal and delicate qualities emphasized their intrinsic response to the hot and arid environment. The water was an important element in the design and maintenance of the cities and gardens. Irrigation was provided via a form of underground tunnel called a qanat, that transported water from a local aquifer. Well-like structures were connected to the qanat, enabling the drawing of water. Animal-driven Persian wheels also drew sub-soil water to the surface. In Persia, Darius the Great developed "paradise garden" and the Hanging Gardens of Babylon were renowned as a Wonder of the World.

At the beginning of the ninth century, Baghdad was reputed as one of the wealthiest city in the world, famous for its tiled buildings and houses with gardens and pools. It was the fairy-tale city of Arabian Nights. Tenth-century visitors describe the palace as having two gardens, pools lined with shiny pavilions with lawns with numerous trees. The Arabs had maintained the existing Persian canal systems, so the Euphrates River basin had remained well-populated and prosperous. However, due to the capricious whims of rulers, Baghdad declined when abandoned by the Caliph Mutasim (833-842), who built a new city at Samarra.

Before building his palace at Samarra, Caliph Mutasim constructed a system of waterways and planted groves of date palms with an irrigation network. Spread over four hundred acres, of which 172 acres were gardens, the Jawsaq Palace had vaulted halls, extensive quarters for a large harem and luxurious private quarters for the king. The largest palace ever constructed in the Islamic world and occupied for only a few years, it was built of unbaked brick with a flat mud roof and quickly became a ruin when abandoned. The remains reveal chambers decorated with murals and built around courts with fountains and aromatic plants. Arab historians describe a large garden on the opposite bank of the river linked to the palace by a bridge of boats. For this garden the Caliph imported plants from all corners of the empire.

The early Caliphs enjoyed hunting. In this pursuit, they built hunting lodges and Pairidaeza near royal hunting grounds. The Arab conquerors had succumbed to the charms of the Persian garden and absorbed them into the new Islamic culture. The tradition of the enclosed Persian garden with its crossed water course and symbolic trees spread with Islam throughout Egypt and the Maghrib to India, Sicily and Spain. The Persian garden form intergrates the paradise or hunting park of the Achaemenids with the bagh or smaller decorative garden area, sometimes within the paradise garden and the bagh tradition came about.

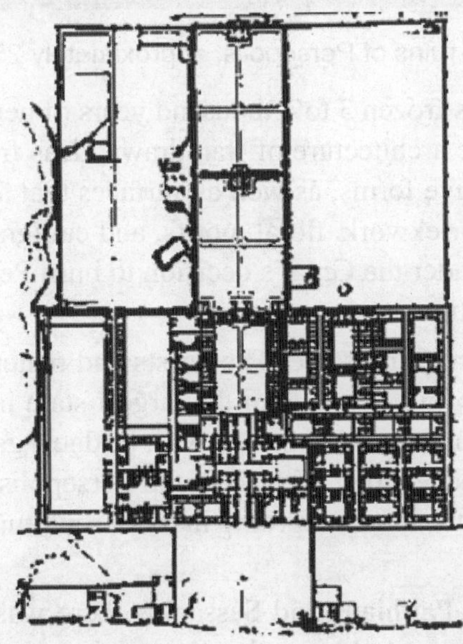

Fig. 3.8. Samarra, Bulkawara Palace (849-859), of which J.D. Hoag has written: "Besides the river a quadripartite garden flanked by pavilions overlooking the water was probably on international evocation of the Koran's paradise suggested also by the mosaic vines of the nearby portal." This is one of the earliest example of Chahar Bagh concept

Persian Architecture

Fig. 3.9. The ruins of Persepolis, approximately 2500 years old

The Persian architecture has frozen 3 to 4 thousand years of heritage of various civilizations of the Iranian plateau. The Islamic architecture of Iran draws ideas from its pre-Islamic predecessor, and has geometrical and repetitive forms, as well as surfaces that are richly decorated with glazed tiles, carved stucco, patterned brickwork, floral motifs, and calligraphy. Iran has suffered its share of destruction, including Alexander the Great's decision to burn Persepolis, yet there are sufficient remains of its classical architecture.

The Achaemenids built on a grand scale. The artists and materials they used were brought in from practically all territories of what was then the largest state in the world. Pasargadae set the standard; its city was laid out in an extensive park with bridges, gardens, colonnaded palaces and open column pavilions. Pasargadae along with Susa and Persepolis expressed the authority of The King of Kings, the staircases of the latter recording in relief sculpture the vast extent of the imperial frontier.

With the emergence of the Parthians and Sassanids there was an appearance of new forms. Parthian innovations fully flowered during the Sassanid period with massive barrel-vaulted chambers, solid masonry domes, and tall columns. This influence was to remain for years to come. The roundness of the city of Baghdad in the Abbasid era, for example, points to its Persian precedents such as Firouzabad. The two designers who were hired by Al-Mansur to plan the city's design were

Naubakht, a former Persian Zoroastrian who also determined that the date of the foundation of the city would be astrologically auspicious, and Mashallah, a former Jew from Khorasan. The ruins of Persepolis, Ctesiphon, Jiroft, Sialk, Pasargadae, Firouzabad, Arg-é Bam, and thousands of other ruins may give us merely a distant glimpse of what contribution Persians made to the art of building.

The fall of the Sassanid Empire to invading Islamic forces ironically led to the creation of remarkable religious buildings in Iran. Arts such as calligraphy, stucco, mirror and mosaic work became closely tied with architecture.

In the old Persian architecture, semi-circular and oval-shaped vaults were used, leading Safavi architects to display their extraordinary skills in making massive domes. Domes can be seen frequently in the structure of bazaars and mosques, particularly during the Safavi period in Isfahan. Iranian domes are distinguished for their height, proportion of elements, beauty of form, and roundness of the dome stem. The outer surfaces of the domes are mostly mosaic faced, and create a magical view. Safavi Isfahan tried to achieve grandeur in scale (Isfahan's Naghsh-i Jahan Square is the 6th largest square worldwide) and built tall buildings with vast inner spaces. However, the quality of ornaments decreased in comparison with those of the 14th and 15th centuries.

The great mosques of Khorasan, Isfahan, and Tabriz used local geometry, local materials, and local building methods to express in their own ways the order, harmony, and unity of Islamic architecture. And thus when the major monuments of Islamic Persian architecture are examined, they reveal complex geometrical relationships, a studied hierarchy of form and ornament, and great depths of symbolic meaning.

Ancient China (2000 B.C.–800 B.C.)

The dawn of civilisation in China is associated with many mythological as well as historical facts. The Xia Dynasty 2000 to 1600 B.C. marked an evolutionary growth between Neolithic culture and the typical Chinese urban civilisation of the Shang dynasty. Shang dynasty 1700-1027 B.C. and the Zhou dynasty (770-221 B.C.) were considered to be the founders of Chinese culture, politics and economic development.

City of Beijing was founded in 800 B.C. in approximately same location. The capital of China was located in the Northern part of north China plain. The city now extends over an area of 10,000 sq. km with a population of over 8 million. The original city had a layout similar to the one in the Ming Dynasty. In the centre lies the group of palaces called the forbidden city, where entry of common people was not allowed. Imperial palaces lie to the south of it. Surrounded the imperial palaces is a square called the inner city, which is criss-crossed by main streets intersected by lanes called hutongs. The north south and east west streets divide town in blocks, performing the function of social control.

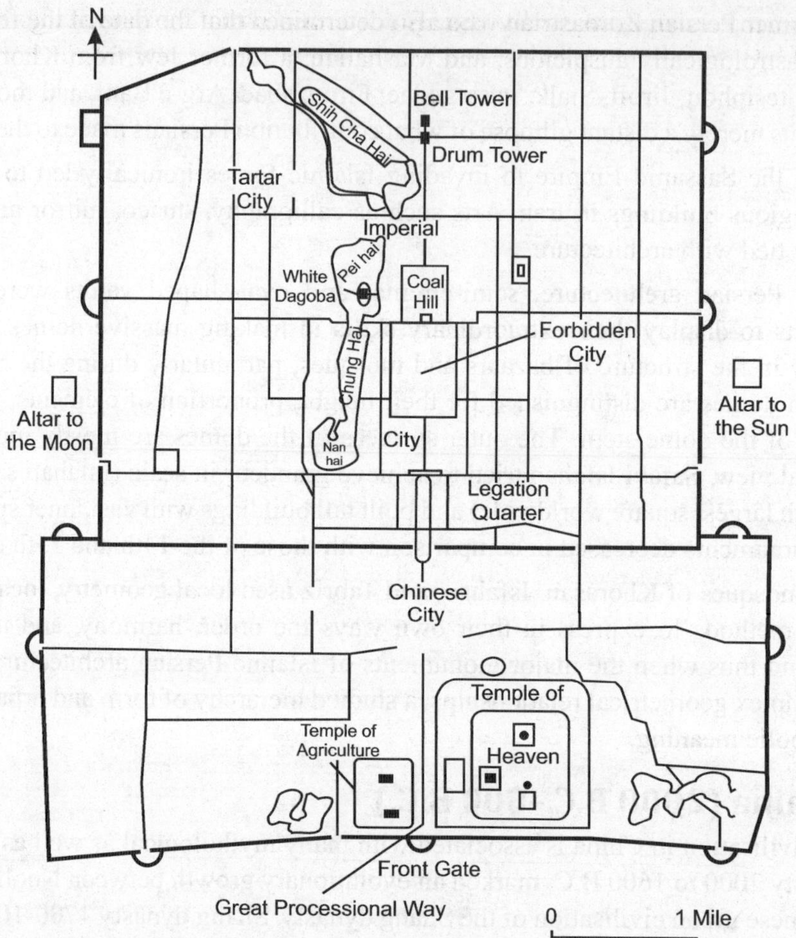

Fig. 3.10. Beijing 1st Century B.C.

From the Neolithic era, Longshan Culture, Bronze Age era and Erlitou culture, the earliest rammed earth fortifications exist, with evidence of timber architecture. The subterranean ruins of the Palace at Yinxu date back to the Shang Dynasty (c. 1600 B.C.–1046 B.C.). In historic China, architectural emphasis was laid upon the horizontal axis. Chinese architecture stresses the visual impact of the width of the buildings. The deviation from this standard is the tower architecture of the Chinese tradition, which began as a native tradition and was eventually influenced by the Buddhist buildings which came from India. Ancient Chinese tomb model representing multiple story residential towers and watch towers date to the Han Dynasty (202 B.C.–220 A.D.). However, the earliest Chinese pagoda is the Songyue Pagoda, a 40 m (131 ft) tall, circular brick tower built in Henan province in the year 523 A.D.. From the 6th century onwards, stone-based structures became more common, while the earliest are from stone and brick arches found in Han Dynasty tombs. The Zhaozhou Bridge built from 595 to 605 A.D. is China's extant stone bridge, as well as the world's oldest stone, open-spandrel, segmental arch bridge.

There were certain architectural features that were reserved solely for buildings built for the Emperor of China. One example is the use of yellow roof tiles; yellow having been the Imperial color. Yellow roof tiles still adorn most of the buildings within the Forbidden City. The Temple of Heaven, however, uses blue roof tiles to symbolize the sky. The roofs are almost invariably supported by brackets, a feature shared only with the largest of religious buildings. The wooden columns of the buildings, as well as the surface of the walls, tend to be red in colour.

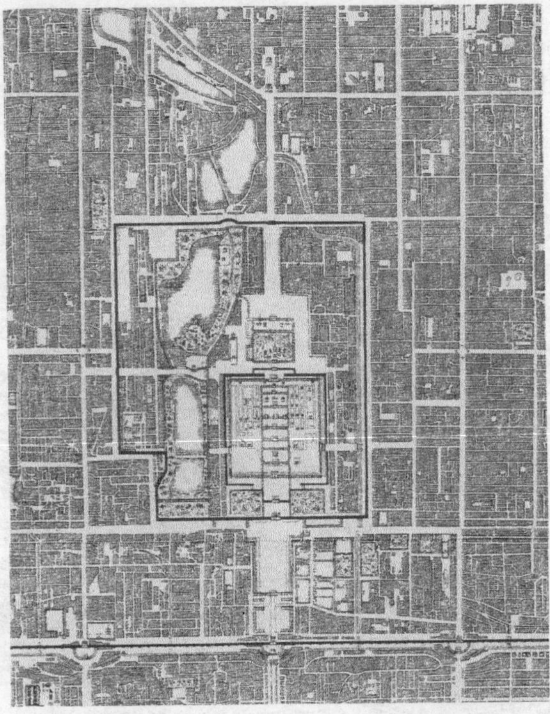

Fig. 3.11. Most ancient Chinese cities were based on an orthogonal grid with a north-south orientation. Beijing and the Forbidden City and Gardens are examples of the traditional Chinese planning

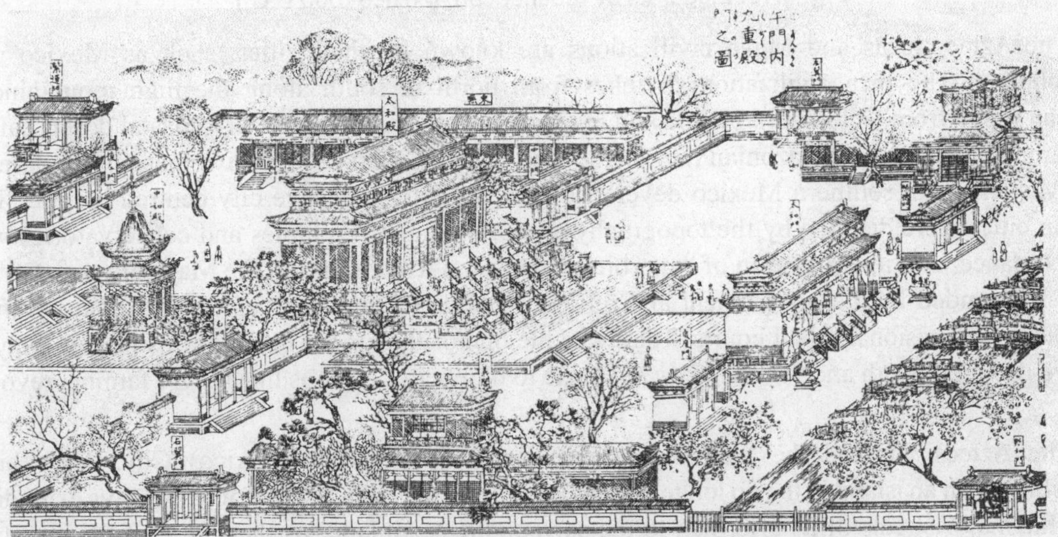

Fig. 3.12. Beijing was planned with gardens and integrated with nature

Source: *Bacon, Edmund N, The Design of cities, Penguin Books*

South American Architecture

The Mississippian culture developed in the central portion of the American continent from 500 to 1400 A.D. where various urban cultures emerged. The most notable among the cities was Teotihuacan, which had at least 125,000 residents in 500 A.D.. This city was organized on a grand plan centred upon a main street which was referred as the Street of the Dead. This 300 feet wide thoroughfare connected ceremonial pyramids and public structures with a market and ruler's residence. To the west and east of the street residential blocks were laid out following a precise, pre-planned grid pattern.

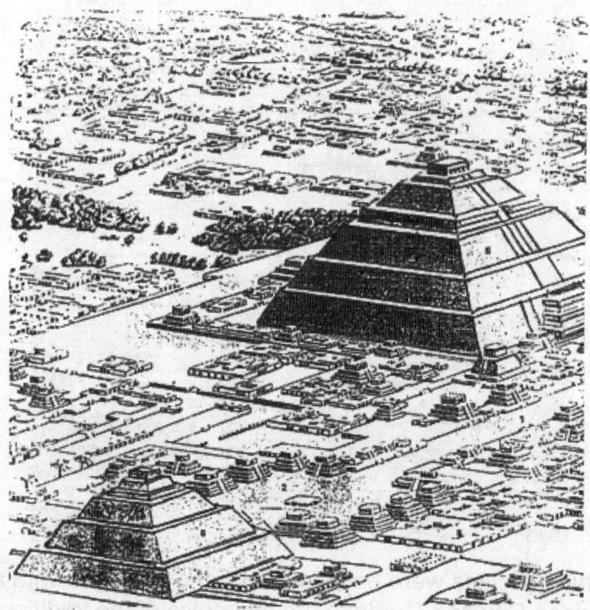

Fig. 3.13. Ziggurats at Teotihuacan, Mexico (500 B.C.)

The Aztac, Incas and Maya civilizations are known by their cities, such as Mexico and Tenochtitlan. The Inca civilization stretches from north to south along the high mountainous Andean range from Colombia to Chile and reached west to east from the dry coastal desert called Atacama to the steamy Amazonian rain forest. The city of Cuzco had massive masonry buildings. The Mayans from southern Mexico developed agriculturally intensive city centred empire. The Mayan cities were dictated by the topography and orientation of temples and conservatories was in accordance with interpretation of the orbits of the stars. At the heart of the Maya city existed the plaza surrounded by the government and religious buildings, the royal acropolis, great pyramid temples and occasionally ball courts. Tikal was the one of the largest cities of this period. Mayan culture declined in 8th and 9th centuries A.D. due to number of reasons like severe famine, revolts, etc.

The Aztecs adopted the planning principles of Teotihuacan (Mexico) City. They built Tenochtitlan on an island in the no longer extant Lake Texcoco, with a series of causeways extending from the major streets of its grid plan to the surrounding mainland. At the centre of the city, two major streets crossed at the location where the temples, plaza of the city, mercantile and ceremonial functions were located. On the perimeter of the island and on adjoining shorelines of the mainland the Aztecs refined the Chinampa field system for agricultural production. The Mississippians developed Cahokia which follows several planning principles found at Teotihuacan. The city was laid out in a grid having modules of 57 meters, as Teotihuacan Cahokia lacked a ceremonial street, but had a Grand Plaza, enclosed by a series of smaller mounds, which was adjacent to Monks Mound. Cahokia's residential areas were clustered into neighbourhoods built around small plazas.

Fig. 3.14. An overview of the central plaza of the Mayan city of Palenque (Chiapas, Mexico)

Fig. 3.15. The Mayan Temple El Castillo

The Incas developed an extensive road system and rope bridges. Much of architecture at the former Inca capital Cuzco shows both Incan and Spanish influences. The famous lost city Machu Picchu is the best surviving example of Incan architecture. Another significant site is Ollantaytambo. The Inca were sophisticated stone cutters whose masonry used no mortar.

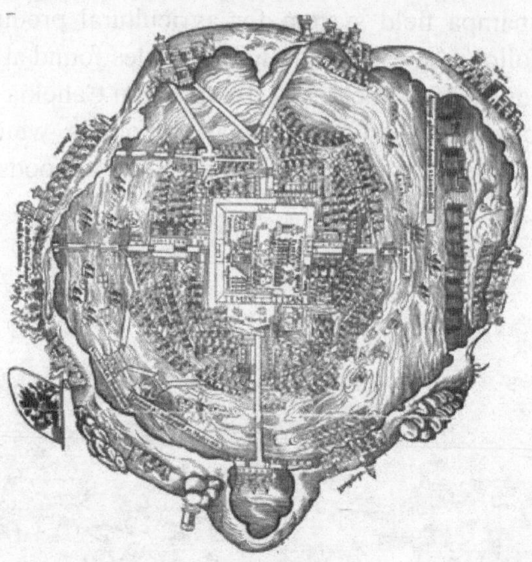

Fig. 3.16. Ancient Mexico – Tenochtitlan Correns Plan

Fig. 3.17. Machu Picchu in Peru, a UNESCO world heritage site is a symbol of Inca civilization

Byzantine and Islamic Culture

The Byzantine empire spanned a period of more than 1000 years (330-1453 A.D.) and a geographic area from modern day Spain and Britain to the Middle East and North Africa. Due to this temporal and geographic spread, there is no single dominant style that can be labeled "Byzantine style." However, the cities were full of pleasure gardens, parks and mosques. Constantinople, Madrid, Córdoba in southern Spain, the Morocco and Naranjos are the examples of Byzantium cities established during 8th century onwards.

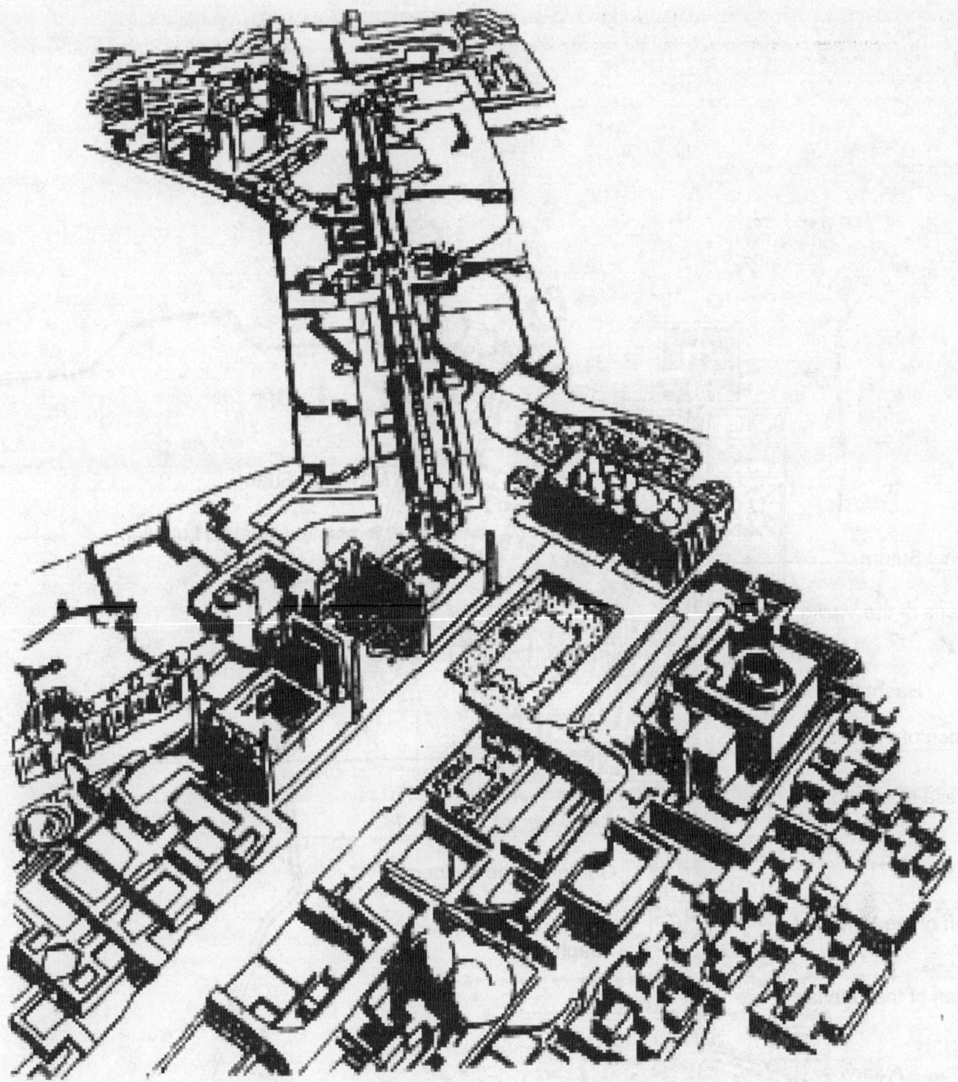

Fig. 3.18. Isfahan: One of the earliest classical city with a central vista and large open spaces around public buildings

Isfahan

The centre-piece of Isfahan, Shah Abbas city, was the central square known as the Maydan-i-Shah or imperial square. It was used for markets and ceremonies, including wild beast fights, court pageants and the playing of polo. Around this square are the major buildings and the great royal mosque Masjid-i-Shah. This is magnificent structure with a jewel like finish encrusted with mosaic. To the north, royal bazaar linked the old city. On the east is a magnificent mosque for the royal ladies, the Masjid-i-Shaykh Lutfullah, facing the Ali-Qapu or lofty gateway, a seven storey building which acted as a state gateway to Shah Abbas paradise garden beyond. On top of it was an audience chamber and grandstand overlooking the maidan. The Ali-Qapu linked the palace complex with the public maidan.

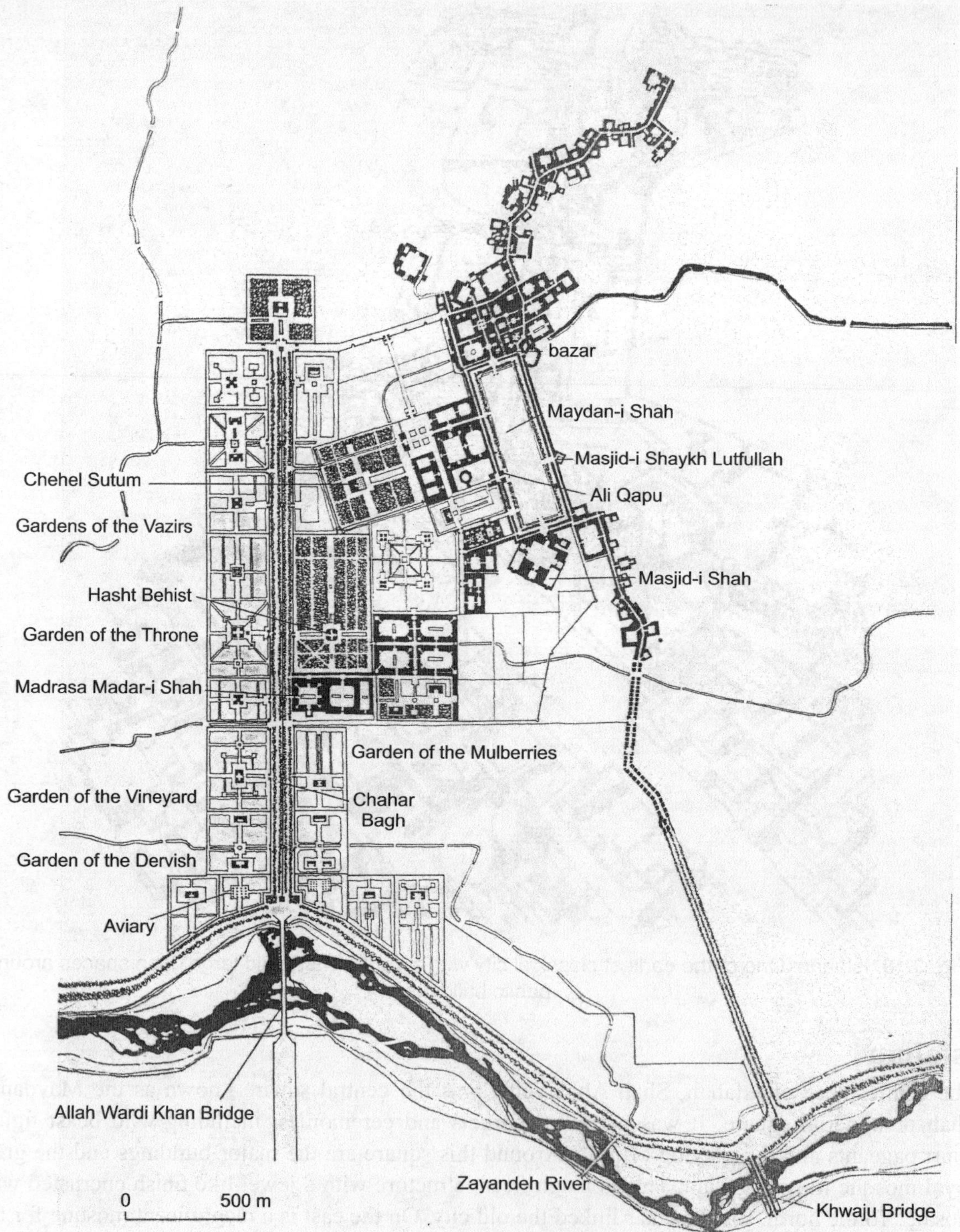

Fig. 3.19. Plan of Isfahan in 17th Century

Santa Sophia, Istanbul

Santa Sophia in Constantinople (Istanbul) achieved a new feat of architectural technology - that of placing a vast circular dome on top of a square formed of four arches.The link between the curves of two arches (diverging from a shared supporting pillar) and the curve round the base of the dome is made by a complex triangular shape known as a pendentive. Santa Sophia is not the first building in which a pendentive is used. But it is the most impressive. Following the example of Santa Sophia, it became a tradition for churches to have a dome over the central space of the interior. In what becomes the conventional design, the dome sits at the centre of a cross (one with four equal arms) formed by the nave and transept.

Fig. 3.20. Istanbul, 6th Century A.D.

The walls supporting the dome are buttressed at ground level by side chapels, each with a domed or partially domed roof. The result is the non-linear, gentle and organic-seeming exterior of a typical Byzantine church. The dome has a rich display of mosaics.

The Dome of the Rock, Jerusalem (691 A.D.)

The Dome of Rock is a wooden structure which is lavishly decorated in a combination of polished marble and glittering glass mosaic against a gold background. Jerusalem is Islam's third holiest shrine, after Mecca and Medina, where the Dome of the Rock is a familiar image. This became model for a mosques and tombs in many parts of the Islamic world, in Cairo, Kairoun, Teheran, Delhi and many other places. In Bukhara - the rulers of the Samanid dynasty built a mausoleum which consists of a simple square building surmounted by a dome.

The 14th century Mongol tomb at Soltaniyeh in northern Iran, Mameluke tombs in Cairo, Tughluq tomb in Delhi and the tomb of Timur in Samarkand are embellished by domes and geometric decorations or blue tiles. Brunelleschi is believed to have been inspired by Islamic dome who adopted these in his designs in Florence and elsewhere.

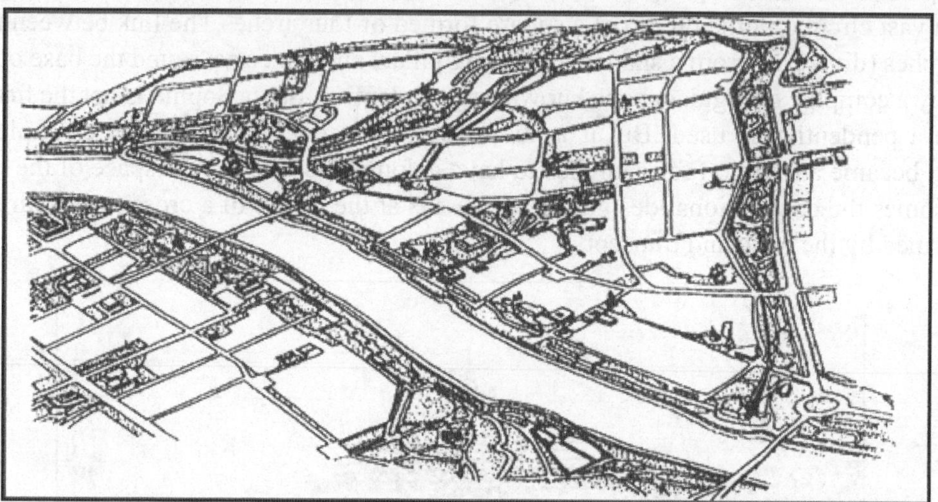

Fig. 3.21. Water being the life-line, the cities have developed along the rivers

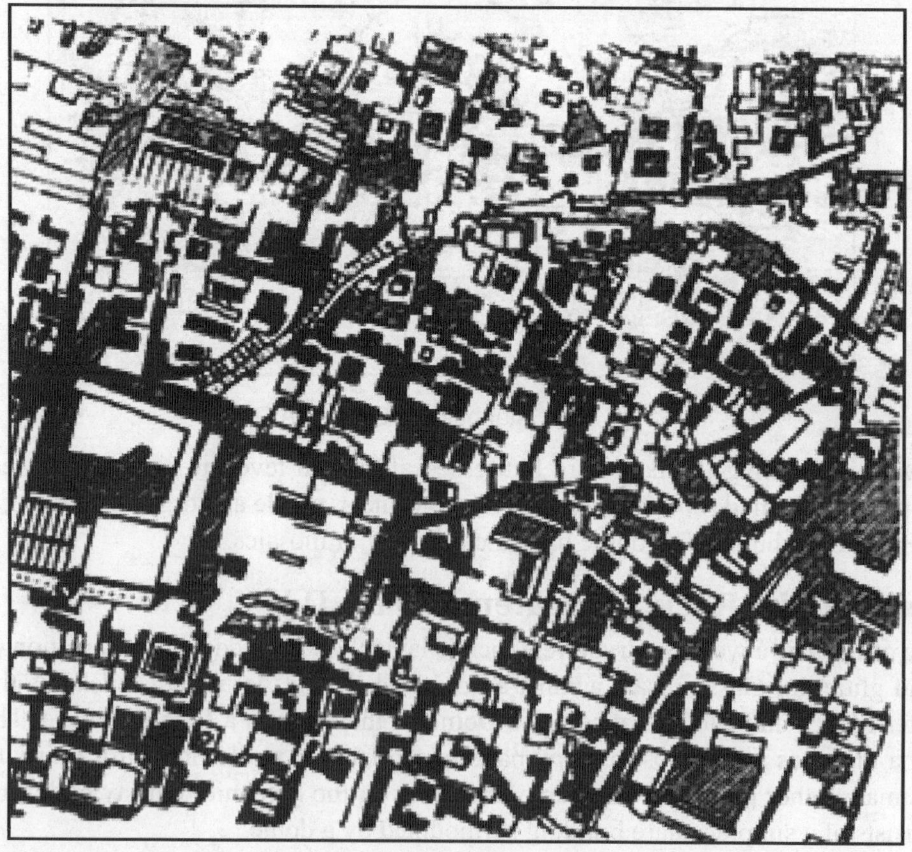

Fig. 3.22. Tunis, Tunisia

Hellenistic and Roman Architecture

In Greece and Rome Hippopotamus, Vitruvius, Pythagoras and other stalwarts developed the principles of town planning and architecture. The greatest achievement of architecture was the development of arch, vault and dome in the 1st century. Earlier the architecture of India, Egypt, Rome, England and Greece had been exclusively trabeate, using flat horizontal lintels to span the opening. This was related to cosmic movement of stars, sun and moon. The Stonehenge, in Salisbury England depicts such a composition by raw stones.

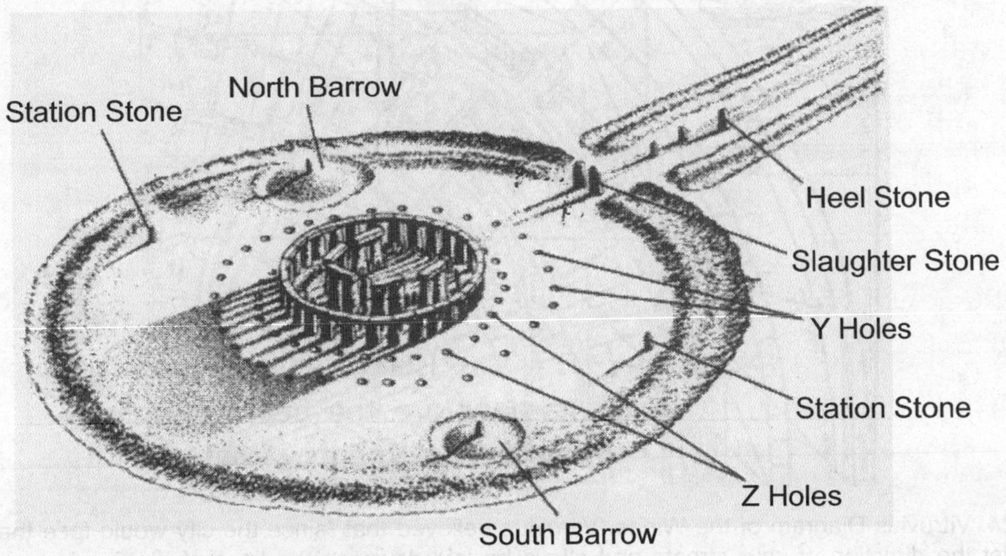

Fig. 3.23. Stonehenge, Salisbury, England

The arch has far greater capabilities than the lintel, as it is made of smaller units of stone or brick. In Greek architecture a single vast stone lintel can reach between columns at most 7 yards apart spanned much more and a Roman brick arch can. The vault is an exceptionally deep arch and the dome as a collection of arches were versatile tools for architecture, which allowed larger openings and spanning a large roof. An arch or dome bonded into solid form by a strong inner layer of concrete sits as one unit, exerting its weight downwards rather than outwards.

Vitruvius (1st century B.C.)

Vitruvius, a Roman architect, set out the principles of architecture in his seminel book De architectura ('On architecture'). He deals with all aspects, from general principles to materials and from the Orders of architecture to stucco work, painting, aquaducts and machinery. This treatise is the most influential text in the entire history of architecture. Its precepts subsequently guided the classical revival in the Renaissance. Since then the proportions and theories of Greek and Roman architecture as enshrined by Vitruvius have remained the basis of architecture.

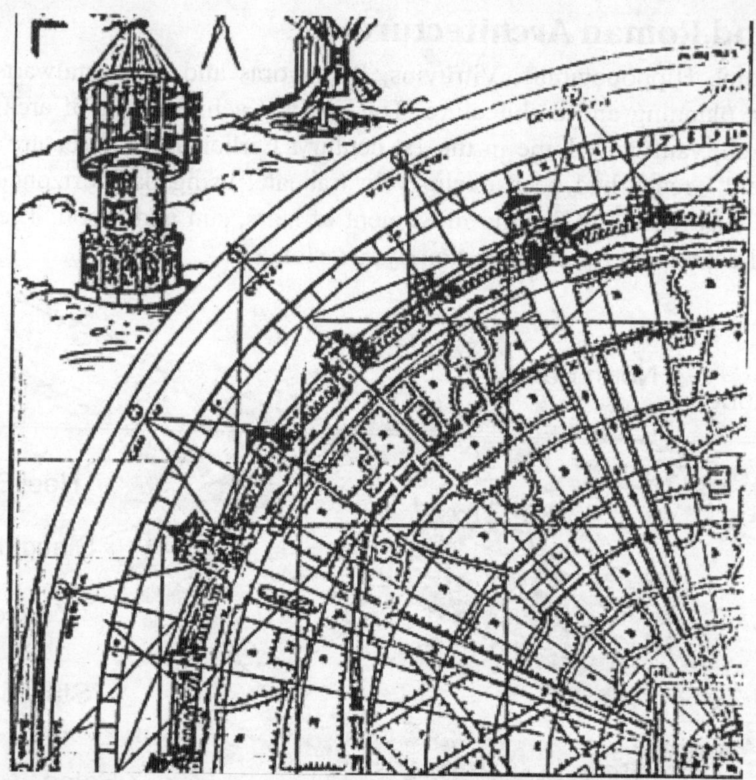

Fig. 3.24. Vitruvius Diagram of the Winds. Vitruvius believed that "since the city would face the eight winds, let the direction of your streets and alleys be laid down on the lines of division between the quarters of two winds so no wind would blow directly down them, and would be dispersed. Vitruvius prescribes locations of major temples, the forum, the basilicas, which should be in the warmest possible quarter. The city would be walled with defensive towers. Access roads should slope upwards towards the city gates which should be approached from the right so that enemies, carrying their shields. In their left hands, would expose their unprotected flanks to the defenders." Vitruvius suggested that towns should be laid out in circular form to give view of enemy from many points

Greek and Roman Cities

Priene, perched on a precipice above the meander valley, has a sequential placement of architectural elements. Temples, theatres, shops, streets, and ways conform to grid arrangement. East-west streets run parallel to contours which had public spaces, like the agora, temples and shops. Persian influences extended to post-Alexander's Greece. Around 350 B.C. there were several cities and gardens at Athens and other parts of Greece.

The later Crete cities were characterised by fortress towns due to increasing invasion from Greece and Asia Minor. The cities in Greece developed from 6th century B.C. till Alexander's period (4th Century B.C.), were characterised by dominance of nobles and emergence of democracy. This led to the development of House of People or Council Chamber, Assembly House, Open Air Theatre and Agora.

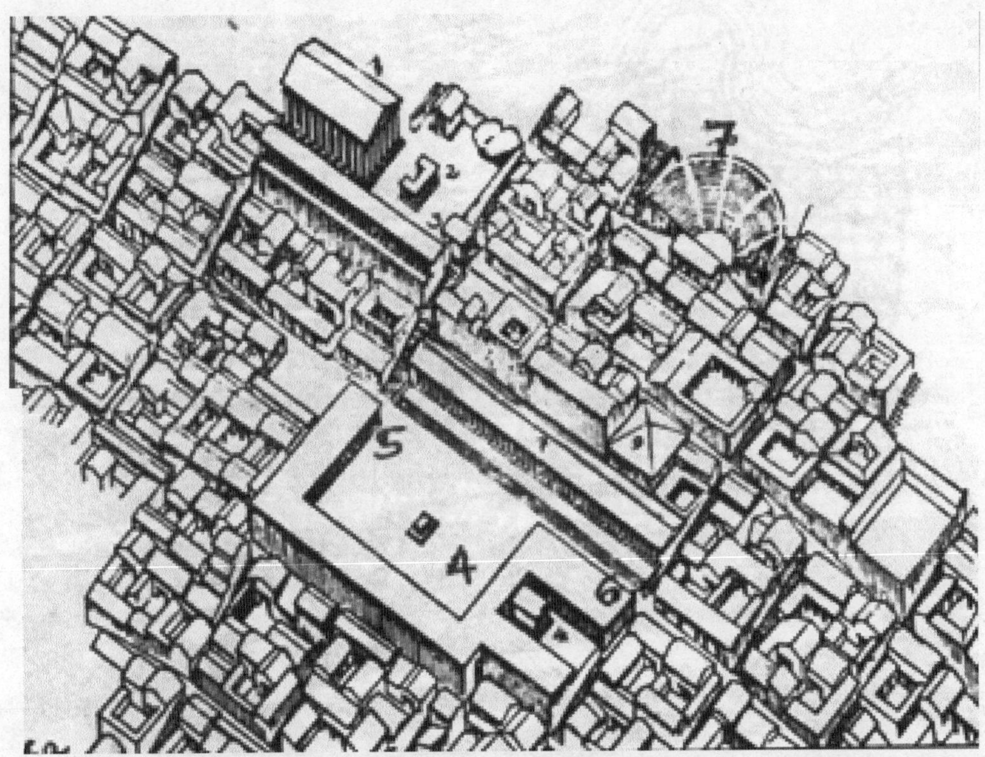

Fig. 3.25. Plan of Priene, (sixth-century B.C.), Greek city in Hippodamian mode

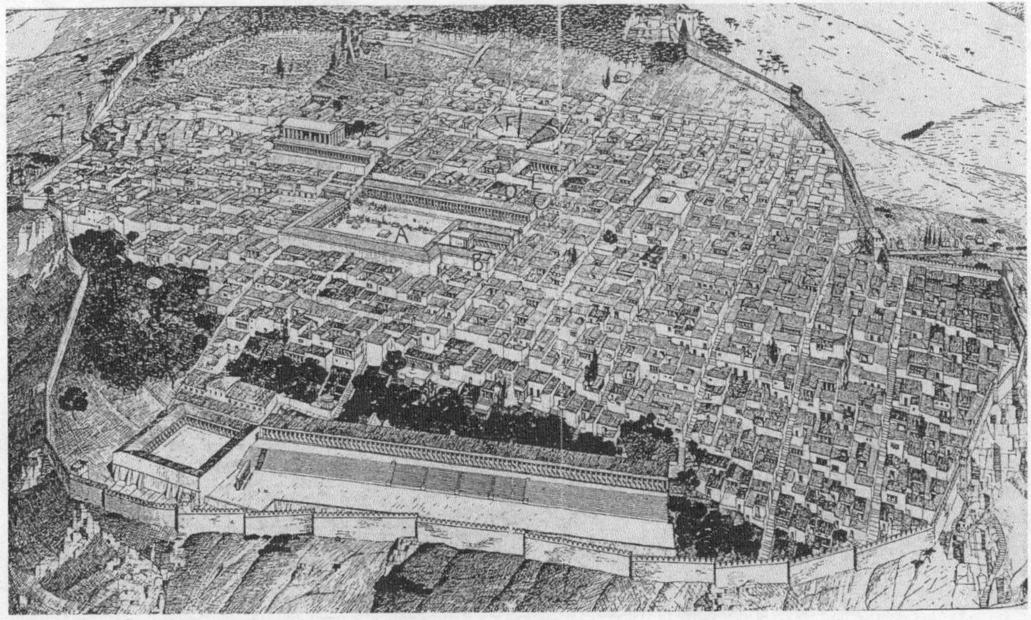

Fig. 3.26. Aerial Perspective of Priene

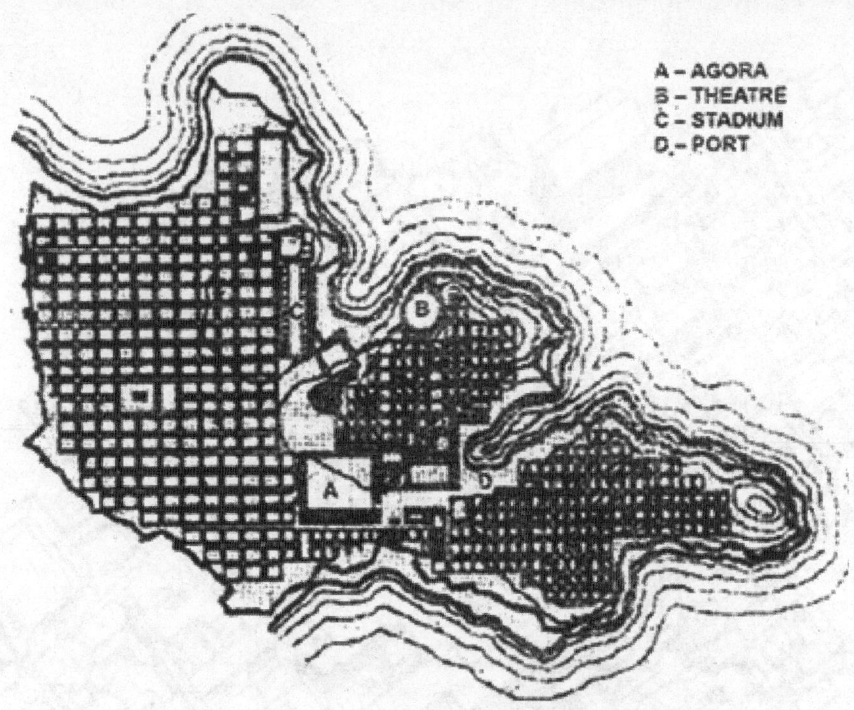

Fig. 3.27. Miletus (700-500 B.C.)

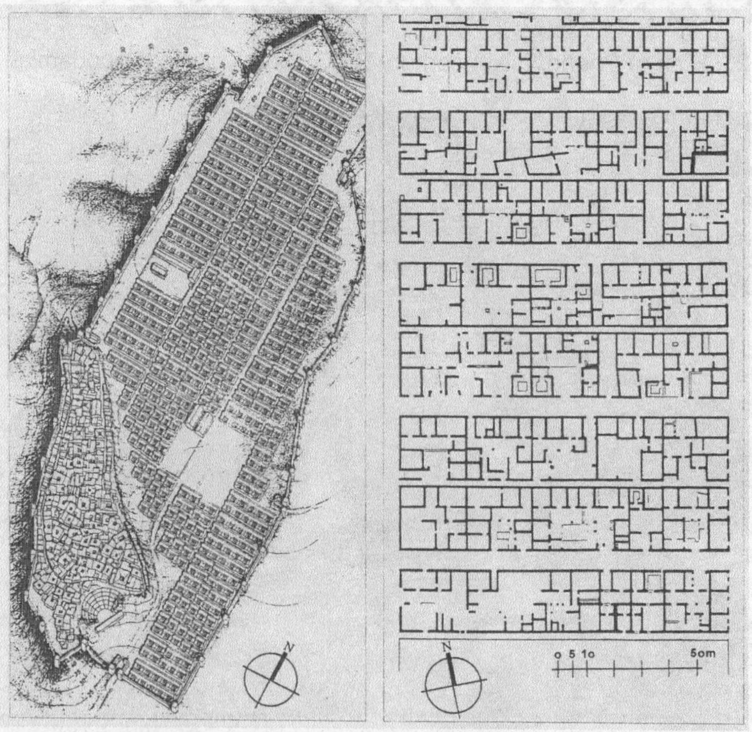

Fig. 3.28. Olynthus in Greece followed a geometric grid pattern with N-S orientation. It had courtyard houses (appx. 35 × 90 m), an Olympic Stadium, Agora, theatre, markets and temples

Fig. 3.29. Parthenon, Athens is one of the most endured piece of architecture, which initiated the design of orders, proportions and balance. It is considered building as a climax of trabeated building design

Fig. 3.30. The Greek architecture epitomised refinement of post and beam construction and order's that were further developed by the Romans

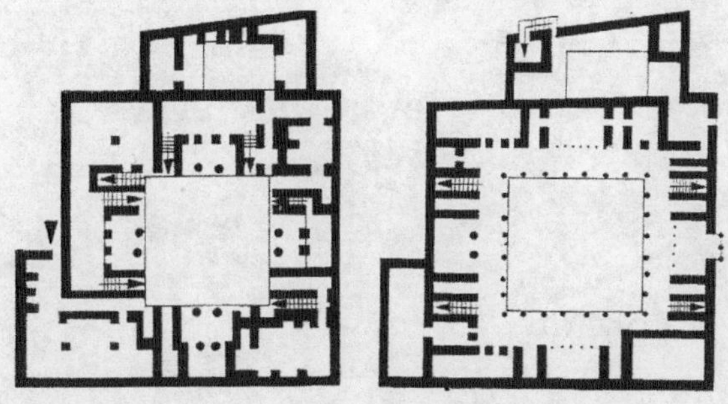

Fig. 3.31. The houses with courtyards provided climatic comfort, privacy and security (Baghdad)

The ancient cities like Rome were full of gardens and the classical architecture. Wall paintings in Pompeii attest to elaborate, extensive villa gardens with water features and topiary. Archaeological evidence survives at sites such as Hadrian's Villa.

The great aqueduct at Nîmes, known as the Pont du Gard was constructed in about A.D. 20. It is a channel bringing water from the river Eure to the new Roman town of Nîmes. The water flows gently downhill for a distance of almost 50 km. The Pont du Gard, with its three towering tiers of arches, carries it over the deep valley of the river Gard, in itself a source of water nearer to Nîmes, but too low-lying to reach the town by gravity.

Fig. 3.32. Roman Aqueduct in Segovia, Spain

Some of the most impressive Roman bridges are over ravines. A fine surviving example, built for Trajan in A.D. 105, spans the Tagus in Spain at Alcántara. Its two massive central arches, 110 feet wide and 210 feet above the normal level of the river, are made of uncemented granite. Each wedge-shaped block weighs 8 tons. During construction these blocks were winched into place by a system of pulleys, powered perhaps by slave labour on a treadmill. They were supported on a huge timber structure standing on the rocks below - which was removed when the arch was complete.

An equally remarkable feat of Roman construction is the building of bridges across the rivers where no rock or island emerges from the water to carry the piers. An example survives in Rome - the Sant'Angelo bridge, built for Hadrian in A.D. 134 as an approach to his great circular mausoleum, now the Castel Sant' Angelo.

Fig. 3.33. Dome: Interior of the Pantheon in Rome

The Pantheon in Rome is the most remarkable example of the Roman genius. The centre of the dome is open to the sky, which adds architectural and visual thrill. The Pantheon was built by Hadrian in around 120 A.D., demolishing an earlier *Pantheon* on the site.

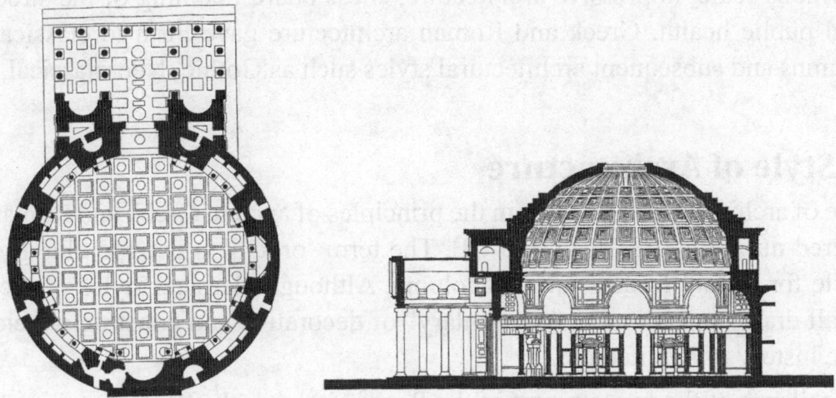

Fig. 3.34. The Pantheon in Rome has a dome spanning a diameter of 43.2 metres. The dome over a round plan has an occular opening in the centre

Fig. 3.35. Piazza del Campo, Siena, Italy. 700-year-old plaza was originally the site of the Roman Eorum. The square has acted as the cultural heart of the city since the construction of the town hall in the 12th century. The Piazza del Campo is a champion of the place making, and functions as a vibrant social space

During the Roman Empire, the Greeks and Etruscan groups, who occupied different regions of Italian peninsula during the eight century established cities and city states. By 500 B.C. the Roman monarchy was overthrown and replaced with republic. Julius Caesar annexed many States of Africa, Spain, France, England and other smaller countries. Roman cities became highly developed as the administrators of the Roman Empire (c. 100 B.C. - 500 A.D.) actively pursued their development. The Gardens of Lucullus (Horti Lucullani) on the Pincian Hill on the edge of Rome about 60 B.C. introduced the Persian garden to Europe.

Borrowing from the Greeks, the Romans improved the construction techniques and developed large span structures, such as stadia for games, circuses, amphitheatres for gladiatorial contests, theatres, basilicas and temples. Most of the Roman cities were characterised by their commanding position, enormous scale, impressive architecture, chess board planning of the streets, aqueducts, sanitation and public health. Greek and Roman architecture gave birth to classical architecture, orders of columns and subsequent architectural styles such as Gothic, Neo-classical, Palladian and Baroque.

Classical Style of Architecture

Classical style of architecture derived from the principles of ancient Greek and Roman architecture, which prospered during 600 BCE to 400 CE. The term 'orders' is used to classify columns, the word hexastyle for a front fecade with six column. Although classical styles of architecture vary greatly, they all draw on a common "vocabulary" of decorative and constructive elements, which dominated the history of architecture.

With the collapse of the western part of the Roman empire, the Roman architectural traditions ceased to be practised in large parts of western Europe. The first conscious efforts to bring back the disused language of form of classical architecture can be traced to the Carolingian Renaissance of the late 8th and 9th centuries. The gatehouse of Lorsch Abbey (c. 800) in present-day Germany displays a system of alternating attached columns and arches which could be an almost direct paraphrase that of the Colosseum in Rome. Byzantine architecture, just as Romanesque and even to some extent Gothic architecture, also incorporated classical elements and details but not to the same degree.

With the demise of Gothic style, major efforts were made by architects such as Leon Battista Alberti, Sebastiano Serlio and Giacomo Barozzi da Vignola to revive the language of architecture of first and foremost ancient Rome. This was done in part through the study of the ancient Roman architectural treatise De Architectura by Vitruvius, and to some extent by studying the actual remains of ancient Roman buildings in Italy. Nonetheless, the classical architecture of the Renaissance from the outset represents a highly specific interpretation of the classical ideas. In a building like the Ospedale Degli Innocenti in Florence by Filippo Brunelleschi, one of the very earliest Renaissance buildings (built 1419–45), the treatment of the columns for example has no direct antecedent in ancient Roman architecture. During this time period, the study of ancient architecture developed into the theory of classical architecture; somewhat over-simplified.

The elements of classical architecture have been applied in radically different architectural contexts. For example, Baroque or Rococo styles, which although classical at root, display a language very much in their own right.

As a reaction to late Baroque and Rococo forms, architectural theorists from circa 1750 through what became known as Neoclassicism and attempted to emulate antiquity, supported by recent developments. Claude Perrault, Marc-Antoine Laugier and Carlo Lodoli were among the first theorists of neoclassicism, while Étienne-Louis Boullée, Claude Nicolas Ledoux, Friedrich Gilly and John Soane were among the more radical and influential. Neoclassical architecture held a particularly strong position on the architectural scene around 1750–1850. The competing neo-Gothic style, however, rose to popularity was characterised by a variety of styles, some of them only slightly or not at all related to classicism.

An English style using the folk manner of construction developed in Britain in the 16th century, named as the Tudor.' New features are labelled after the rulers-Queen Anne and Georgian.

From the 18th century neo-Gothic style became popular.Also, European countries began to establish trading centres or colonies. From the 18th century, the Portuguese, the Dutch, the French and the British used their own architectural styles and fort building techniques in their colonies. Local materials were used as local craftsmen employed to build imposing secular buildings and homes in European designs-the 'Cape Dutch' style of Dutch settlers of the Cape of Good Hope and Imperial style for major British buildings in India. Numerous Neo-Palladian and Indo-Sarcenic buildings were built in Chennai and Kolkata and Neo-Gothic in Mumbai.

Indo-Saracenic Style

From the mid-19th century, the elements from Indian buildings, particularly Mughal and Buddhists, viz-chhatris, jaalis, chhajjas, doors, door frames-were incorporated into civic buildings. This style was called Indo-Saracenic or Hindu-Islamic, a term used by James Fergusson for pre-British architecture which had a mixture of Hindu and Islamic elements.

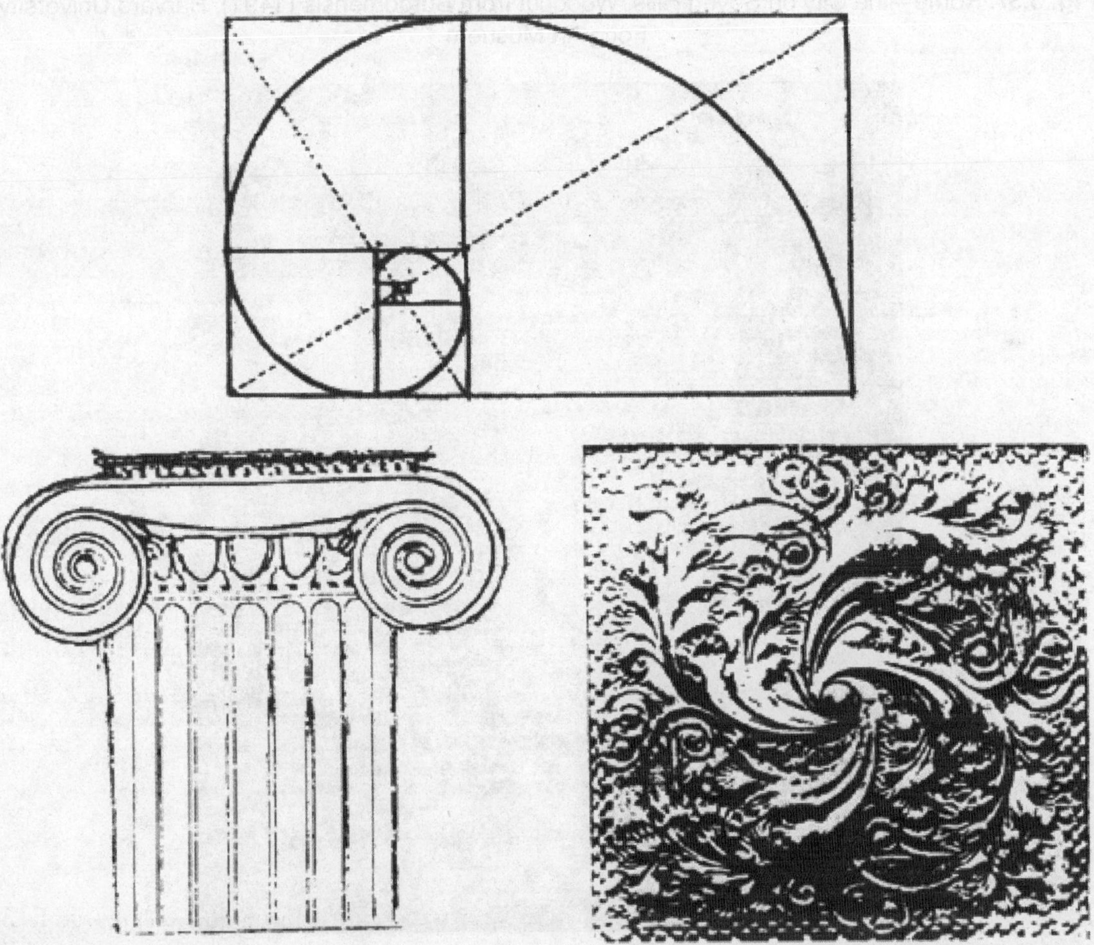

Fig. 3.36. The Golden Section and its application in architectural design

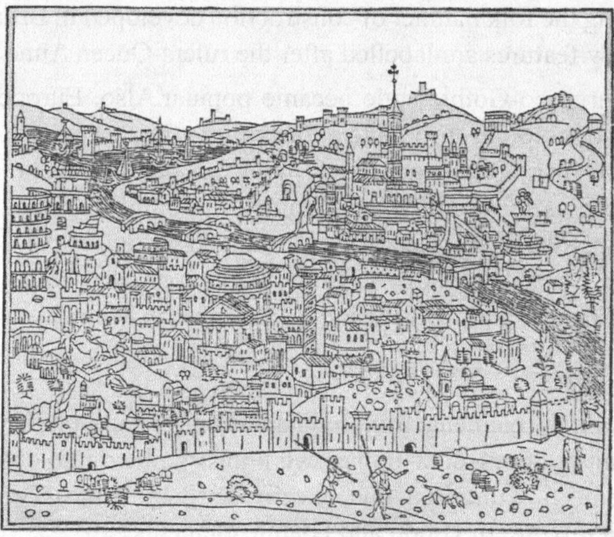

Fig. 3.37. Rome—the City on Seven Hills, Woodcut from Burgomensis (1491), Harvard University, Fogg Art Musuem

Fig. 3.38. Cathedral Dome, designed by Brunelleschi provided Florence with a visual reference to the Renaissance architecture (1420)

Fig. 3.39. Venice, Piazza de St Marco

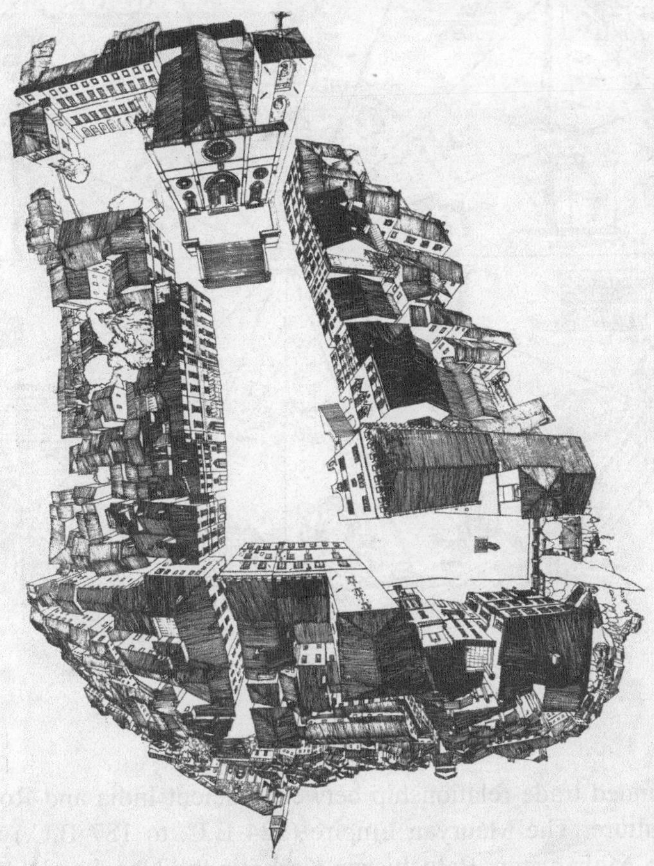

Fig. 3.40. Todi, Italy is a medieval city with interlocking squares. The simplicity of design is such that the citizen never looses his relationship with the city

Fig. 3.41. Rome (18th Century)

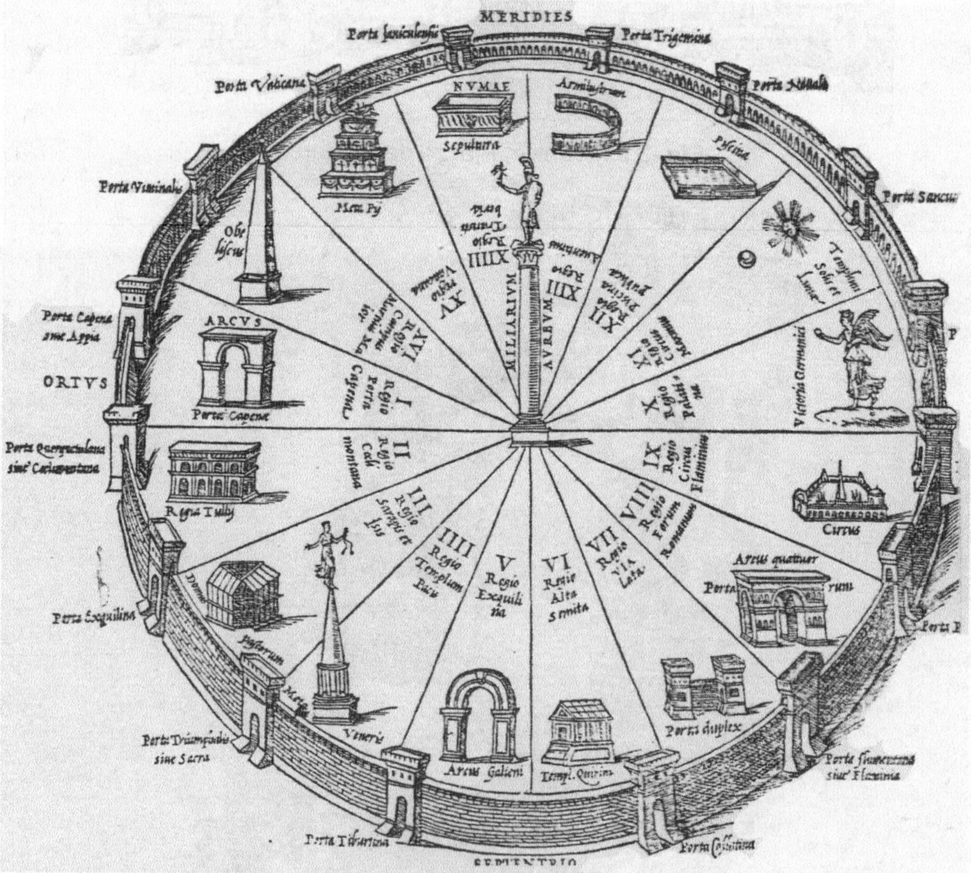

Fig. 3.42. Rome (1527 A.D.)

There was a continued trade relationship between ancient India and Rome, which gave rise to the Indo-Roman culture. The Mauryan Empire (324 B.C. to 187 B.C.) under Samrat Ashok extended his empire to Afghanistan, Baluchistan, Kashmir and Nepal and witnessed the exchange of Indian and Roman arts, architecture and culture.

The Italian Renaissance inspired a revolution in architecture. The period between 1400-1750 was the golden age of Italy, where public buildings, cathedrals, markets, roads, stadia, theatre, canal, waterways, gardens luxurious villas were built in and around Venice, Milan, Florence, Coevorden, Karlsruhe, Charleville, Amsterdam, Rome and other cities. Some of these include Tivoli and the Villa d'Esta (1549) at Frascati and the Villa Dobrandini (1518), Torlonia (1621), Mondragon (1567) at Bagraia and the elegant Villa Lente (1566). The Roman culture and design approach spread to Britain, Switzerland and many other European countries. The industrial revolution saw profound influence of science and technology. Changes in building technology, invention of the steam engine and railway, motor car, telegraph, radio, electricity during the industrial revolution changed the concepts of architecture and city planning.

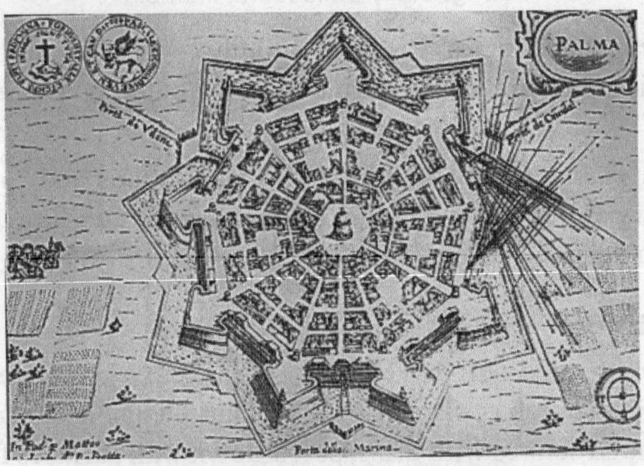

Fig. 3.43. Palma Nova (1713 A.D.)

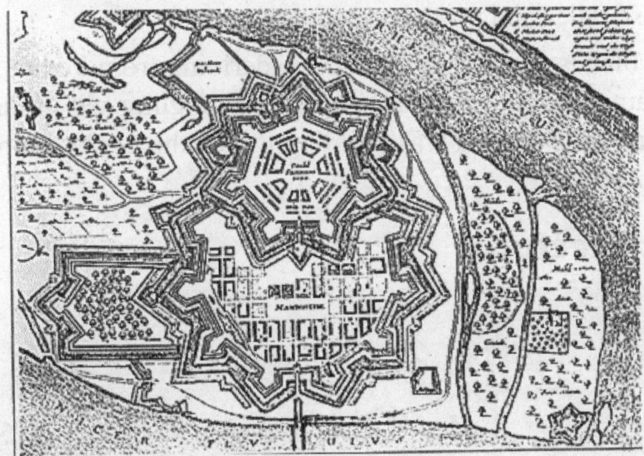

Fig. 3.44. Mannheim—A Military Cantonment in Germany

Romanesque Architecture

Romanesque (11th and 12th centuries) was the first pan-European style since Roman Imperial architecture and examples are found in every part of the continent. It is similar to Roman architecture in form and materials, but with use of round or slightly pointed arches, barrel vaults, and cruciform piers supporting vaults.

Fig. 3.45. Colloseum, Rome

The round arch is characteristic of a Roman building - whether in their great aqueducts and bridges, in emperors' triumphal arches, or astride classical columns (for example, in the churches of Ravenna)

Charlemagne's Chapel in Aachen, with its classical columns and round striped arches, also recalls the little baptistery at Fréjus. And both are echoed in the full flowering of the Romanesque style, as seen in the 12th-century Nave at Vézelay.

Gothic Architecture

The Gothic architecture emerged during 11th and 15th century, particularly in the France, such as the 12th century Abbey church of Saint-Denis in Saint-Denis, near Paris. Gothic architecture, features tall skeletal stone structures with glass, pared-down wall surfaces flying buttresses, pointed arches using the ogive shape, ribbed stone vaults, clustered columns, pinnacles and sharply pointed spires. Windows contain stained glass, showing stories from the Bible and saints. These design allowed cathedrals to rise taller and more spectacular.

This Gothic design blends with other influences, deriving from Venice, Byzantine and Muslim east. The result is a beauty, purely Venetian, which can be glimpsed in many of the older houses on the city's canals. But while Venice was building the Gothic style, Florence was busy with the architecture of the Renaissance.

Renaissance Architecture

Fig. 3.46. St. Peter's Basilica in Rome

Italian Renaissance began in the 14th century. This period of cultural rebirth witnessed the development of a new style of architecture. The invention of perspective brought a sense of infinity into the realm of architect's comprehension. Perspective represented a new understanding of space which expressed a sense of conceptual clarity and back into reality.

Brunelleschi is the pioneer in Renaissance architecture. His greatest claim to fame is building a dome over Florence's cathedral (the Duomo, built during the 14th century) which has only a temporary covering over the central space. The space spanned is 140 feet across. In 1418 he won a competition to erect the dome over the cathedral. Brunelleschi found a way of building the dome without any support from the ground. Using aerial scaffolding supported within the drum, he erected a double skin for the dome, with the outer and inner structures held together by bonds of masonry. The double structure not only adds strength, also enables the outer profile to be impressively high without the interior of the dome seeming too remote. Pioneered by Brunelleschi, the double skin dome later became common place, which was also used in St Peter's in Rome, and St Paul's in London.

Fig. 3.47. Roman Temple: Maison Carrée, Nimes, France

Fig. 3.48. Triumph Arch (Constantine) Rome

Fig. 3.49. Villa Rotunda, Italy, Architectural Classicism

The Renaissance spread to France in the late 15th century, when Charles VIII returned in 1496 with several Italian artists from his conquest of Naples. Renaissance Chateaux were built in the Loire Valley, and the style became dominant under Francis I (1515–47). The Château de Chambord is a combination of Gothic structure and Italianate ornament, a style which progressed under architects such as Sebastiano Serlio, who was engaged to work at the Château de Fontainebleau (1540).

Architects such as Philibert Delorme, Androuet du Cerceau, Giacomo Vignola, and Pierre Lescot, were inspired by the new ideas. The southwest interior facade of the Cour Carree of the Louvre in Paris was designed by Lescot and covered with exterior carvings by Jean Goujon. Architecture continued to thrive in the reigns of Henry II and Henry III.

In England the first great exponent of Renaissance architecture was Inigo Jones (1573–1652), who had studied architecture in Italy where the influence of Palladio was very strong. Jones returned to England and began to design such buildings as the Queen's House at Greenwich in 1616 and the Banqueting House at Whitehall. These works with their clean lines and symmetry, were revolutionary in a country still enamoured with mullion windows, crenellations and turrets.

In late 17th-century France, the ultimate architecture was created in Versailles. The size and glitter of Versailles reflects very precisely the power and prestige of the emperor Louis XIV. Rivals may attempt to match the architectural statement of French predominance but Versailles remains the supreme example of the palace as a gesture of power.

Baroque architecture

The Baroque style that followed the Renaissance was characterised by the embellished development under the decorative tastes of Rococo.

In the transformation of Rome into a Baroque city, no one played a part comparable to that of the sculptor and architect Giovanni Lorenzo Bernini. In 1629 he was appointed architect to St Peter's, the creation of which has given a new dignity to the ancient city.

Bernini achieved a perfect solution in the form of an open curving colonnade. The four concentric rows of columns provided covered walkways and a shape for the piazza, without closing it for there is no back wall. The balustrade above the columns is an ideal pedestal for the gesticulating stone saints who were an indispensable part of monumental baroque.

Sculpted golden rays stream up from St Peter's throne towards heaven. In an extra dimension to the illusion they are joined by real rays of golden light, shining from the afternoon sun through an amber window in which the holy dove spreads his wings. This glorious blend of sculpture and architecture was achieved between 1657 and 1666.

Palladian Architecture

In the late 17th and 18th centuries, the works of Andrea Palladio (16th century Venice) were again spread by the English translation of his dell Quattro Libri'Architettura and pattern books, such as Vitruvius Brittanicus by Colen Campbell. This Palladian architecture and classical imagery influenced Thomas Jefferson and other architects of the United States in their search for a new architecture.

Fig. 3.50. Facade of Gesu, Vignola: Baroque example

Palladian architecture tended to be more restrained in decoration but by usage of authentic classical forms. Palladio's skill in applying his classical principles brought him commissions for public buildings in Vicenza, churches in Venice and private villas, that won him lasting influence and fame. Most of these villas are built in Venice's hinterland, the Veneto. Palladio's designs for them become widely known after he published Quattro Libri dell'Architettura (The Four Books of Architecture) in 1570. It became as a pattern book. The single most imitated aspect of Palladio's style is his use of columns and pediment as a portico in front of a house. In broader terms the balance and the relative simplicity of classical design are its hallmark.

Palladio's most striking influence is seen in the great houses of 18th-century England. By then part of his appeal in reaction against a very different and far from the Baroque style.

The style of the great Venetian architect Palladio is known in England from his four books of designs (the Quattro Libri) and from the London masterpieces of Inigo Jones. These are the Banqueting House in Whitehall (1622) and the Queen's House in Greenwich (1629-40). Inigo Jones' pioneering work in the Palladian style was imitated for the rest of the 17th century, a period dominated by Baroque.

A collection of classical designs in the Palladian style was published in 1715, under the title Vitruvius Britannicus by a British architect, Colen Campbell. Vitruvius Britannicus launched a new fashion in 18th-century England. In 1717, the Earl of Burlington employed Campbell to remodel his London house in Piccadilly in the Palladian style. In 1722 Robert Walpole commissioned him to build Houghton Hall, a large Palladian country house in Norfolk.

Neo-Classicism

During the 18th century a quest for classical authenticity was undertaken with a new vigour. Archaeological sites such as Pompeii were being excavated and interest was shifting from the Roman classical heritage to the Greek. In 1755 Johann Joachim Winckelmann, a German archaeologist, published a work on Greek paintings and sculpture in which he argued that the art of Greece provides the best example of ideal beauty.

The avant-garde greeted this notion with enthusiasm. Over the next century Greek themes increasingly pervaded the decorative arts. Greek porticos and colonnades graced public buildings. Greek refinement became the ideal for neoclassical sculptors and painters.

By the turn of the century a more rigorously Greek style became the architectural fashion in many parts of Europe.A version of the Parthenon rises from 1806 in Paris on Napoleon's orders, to become eventually the church of La Madeleine. Another Parthenon begins to be built on Calton Hill in Edinburgh in 1822 as a memorial to the Scots who have died in the Napoleonic wars. The design chosen for the new British Museum, on which work begun in 1823, is a Parthenon with extensions.

Fig. 3.51. Castle of Milan from the Vitruvius Teutsch (1548 A.D.)

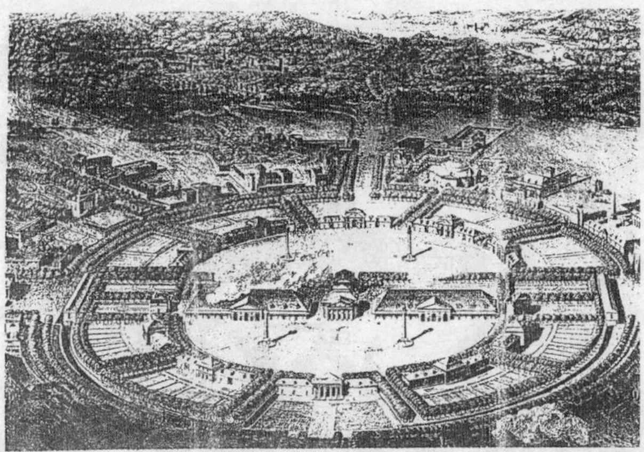

Fig. 3.52. Chaux Ideal Town (18th Century) From Ledoux (1804)

Fig. 3.53. Palmanova, Italy, founded 1593

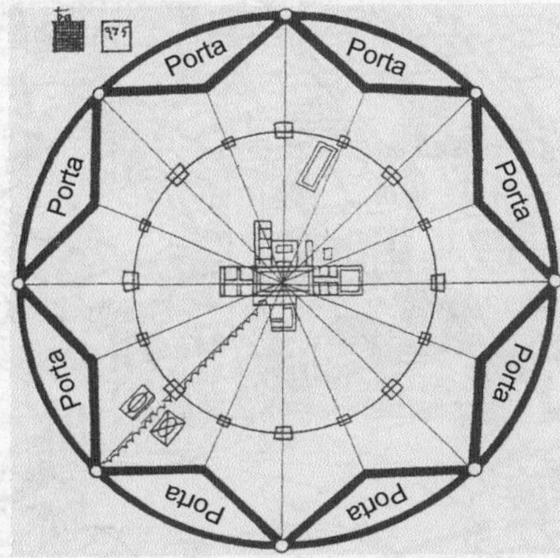

Fig. 3.54. Filarete's Sforzinda, the most famous ideal city plan of the Renaissance, (1465)

Fig. 3.55. Engraving of Rome published in 1612

Fig. 3.56. Piazza Long Champs, Marseilles 1862–69, H.J. Esperandieu

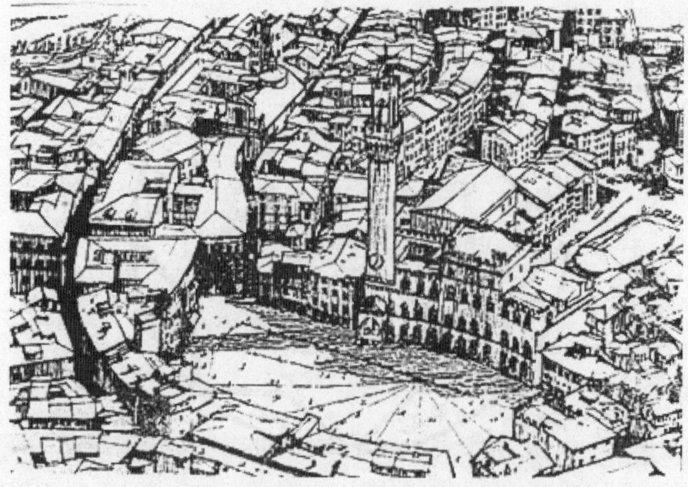

Fig. 3.57. Piazza del Campo Siena, Italy

Fig. 3.58. Palace de L'opera, Paris 1858-62, Rohault de Fleuys and Henri Blondel

Fig. 3.59. Canale Grande layout with Church of Antonio di Padova at end of Vista Trieste, 1826-49 (Peter von Nobile)

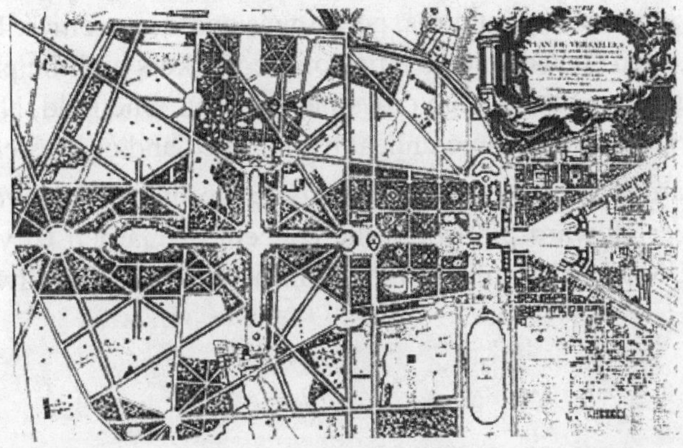

Fig. 3.60. Gardens of Versailles (1746) : The Vaux le Vicomte is one of the most admired French Baroque landscape and is the first great work of André Le Nôtre. The garden spans more than 1,000 acres and encapsulates the essence of a Baroque-era landscape in the French formal style asserted monarchical power and taste

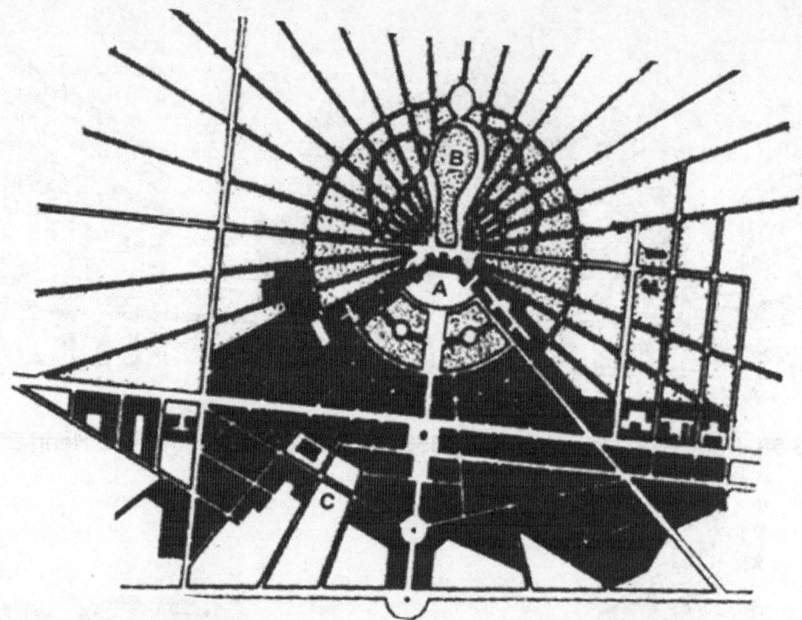

Fig. 3.61. Karlsruhe was designed to radiate from the Palace de la Concorde which was one of the most magnificent features of the city, designed by Jacques Ange Gabriel during reign of Louis XV

Industrial Revolution and New Urbanism

With the Industrial Revolution, (18th and 19th centuries) cities faced severe problems like sanitation, housing shortage and pollution. The advent of railways and motors changed the concept of urban mobility which needed a new type of infrastructure and wider corridors. The rapid urbanisation was not in pace with the city planning.

The industrial revolution saw the opening up of new industrial areas and cities. It led to decline of nobles and landlords and rise of industrial entrepreneurs and middle class. Changes in building technology, invention of steam engine and railway, motor car, telegraph, radio, electricity and other technologies led to development of suburbs, peri-towns and dense cities. It also gave rise to rapid urbanisation with congested shacks and shanties of the workers and the problem of pollution and public health. By 1870s many of the large cities like London, Sheffield, New York, Paris, etc. had high densities, poor services and became unhealthy, polluted and congested.

In response, the Garden City Movement attempted to offset negative industrial effects such as pollution. Sir Ebenzer Howard pioneered the concept of Garden City, which was applied in several new towns in UK and also in planning of Imperial Delhi by Edwin Lutyens in the early 20th century.

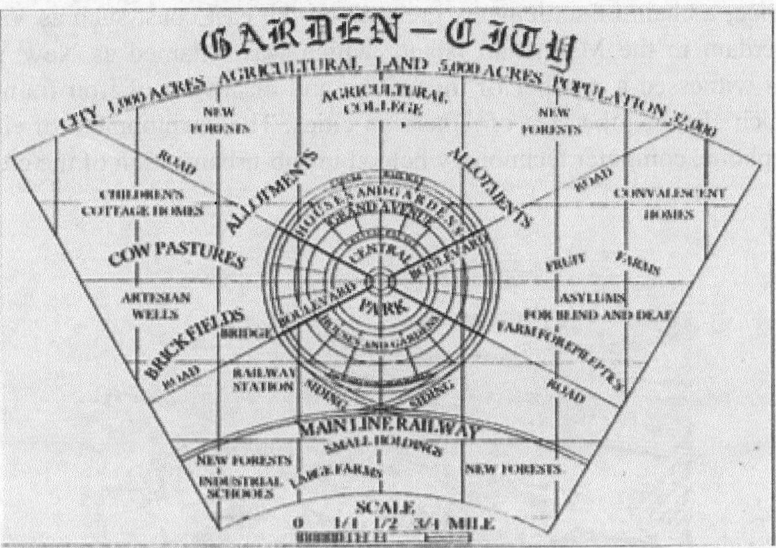

Fig. 3.62. Sir Ebenezer Howard's Garden City: The Garden City and Rural Belt was to cover about 1,000 acres at the centre of a 6000 acre tract. It was planned for a population of 32,000. Six magnificent boulevards-each 120 feet wide traverse the city from centre to circumference, dividing it into six equal parts or wards. In the centre the circular space of five and a half acres, laid out as beautiful and well-watered gardens. Each ward has ample grounds, and the larger public buildings-town hall and concert and lecture hall, theatre, library, museum, picture gallery and hospital

Source: *Ebenezer Howard, Garden Cities of Tomorrow, Cambridge, MIT Press, 1965*

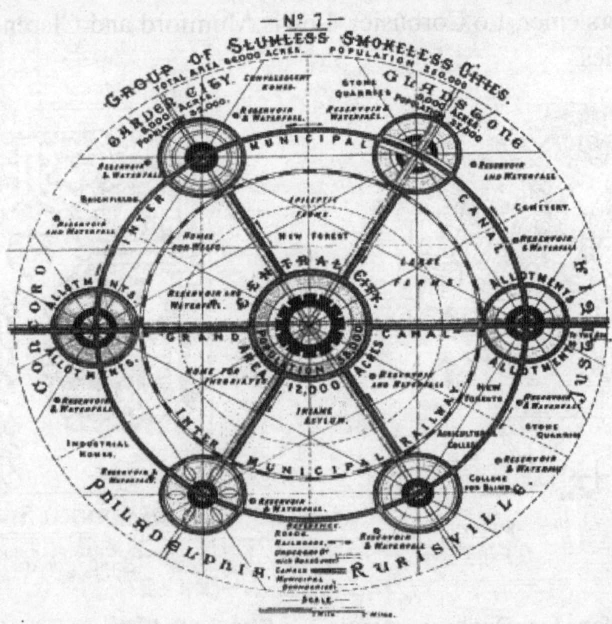

Fig. 3.63. Diagram of Sir Ebenezer Howard's Garden City in Garden City of Tomorrow, 1902. City planning principles proposed by Ebenezer Howard in 1898 reflected a desire for self-contained communities based on English country life in the face of rapid industrialisation and crowding of cities

Source: *Ebenzer Howard, Garden Cities of Tomorrow (Cambridge, MA: MIT Press, 1965)*

In the America, a chain of settlements grew along the east coast such as Virginia, New Port and New Amsterdam in the Manhattan Island, which was renamed as New York. The era of great metropolis witnessed a number of inventions and discovery of iron frame, steel structure and elevator which changed the face of American cities. The development of electric power and automobile, telephone, computer technology helped in sub-urbanisation of the cities.

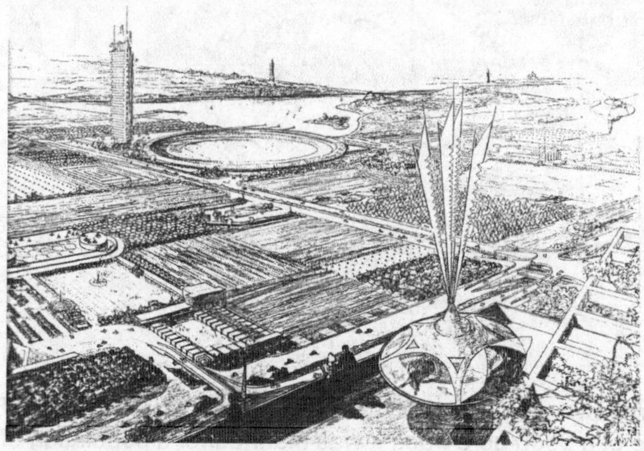

Fig. 3.64. Broadacre City by Frank Lloyd Wright

The chaotic growth of the cities led to the development of building and zoning regulations and application of restrictions for light, air and plot coverage. Various theories and city planning concepts were put forward by a number of visionaries like Patrick Geddes, Tony Garnier, Soria Y. Mata, Ludwig Hilbersiemer, Le Corbusier, Lewis Mumford and Clarence Stein to enhance the quality of life in the cities.

Fig. 3.65. In the plan for Radburn, New Jersey pedestrian and vehicular traffic was segregated, connected green spaces, separated housing clusters; and the cul-de-sac avoided through traffic in the residential area

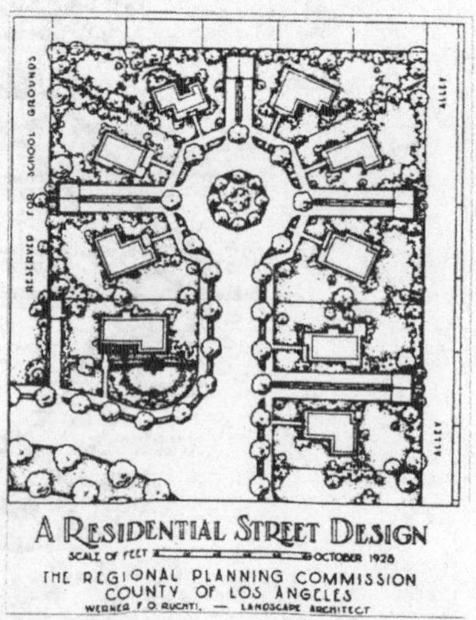

Fig. 3.66. In the residential community design for Los Angeles, California (1930), street pattern became curvilinear and housing communities were less dependent upon public transport

Fig. 3.67. Le Corbusier: International style architecture for Vila-de-Radieuse

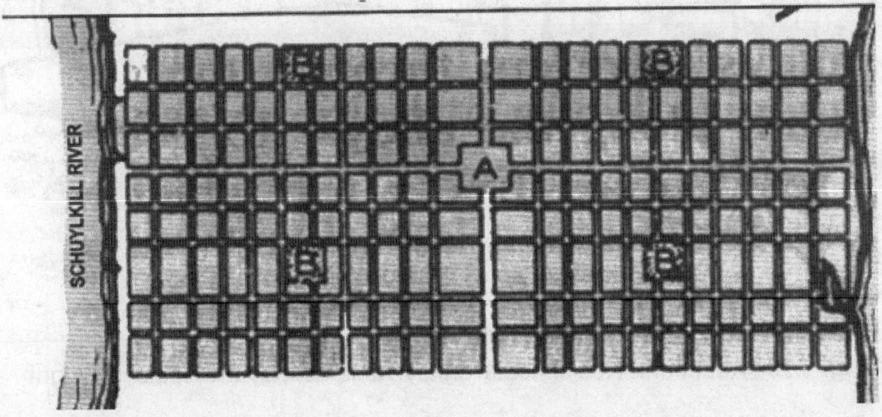

Fig. 3.68. Philadelphia was planned by William Penn Thomas Holman (1882) on a grid iron pattern with markets, parks (B) and a public square (A) in the centre of the city

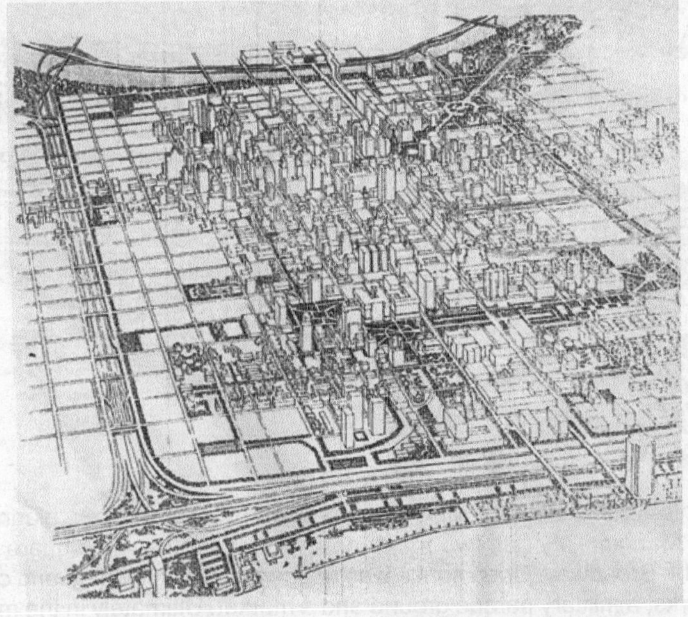

Fig. 3.69. City Centre, Philidelphia (USA)

Fig. 3.70. Kaufmann Residence, Pennsylvania built by Frank Lloyd Wright

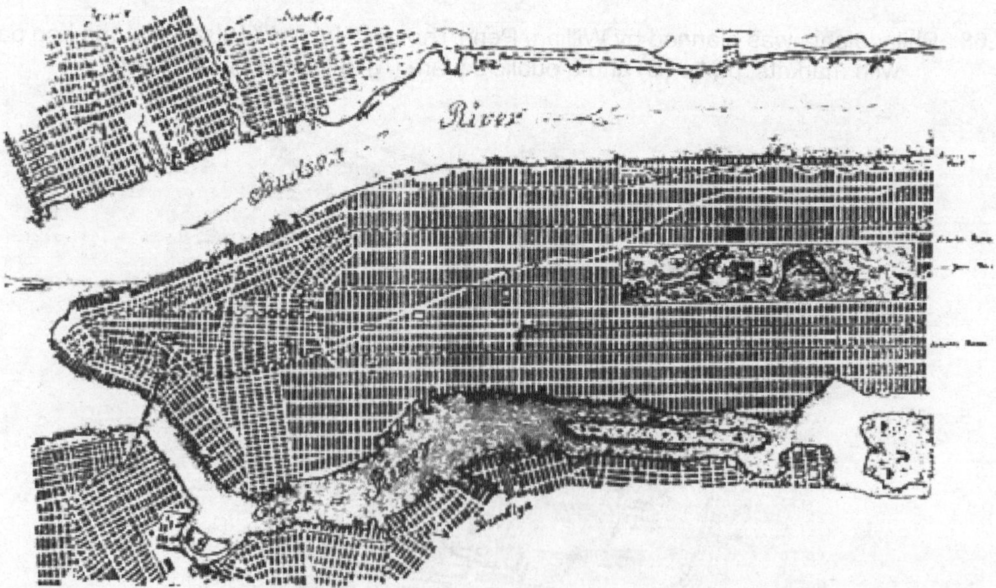

Fig. 3.71. The Commissioner's Plan for Manhattan Island (1811) New York, planned by City Surveyor and Architect Joseph Mangin. City had two major north-south streets with square and plazas and one major angular street-the Broadway. Open space was not generously allocated and city became cramped with only five small parks, a military parade ground and a market. Ultimately in the middle of 18th century Central Park was established

Fig. 3.72. New York City, Broadway near Cortlandt Street and Maiden Lane—The urban street was chaotic, foul smelling and congested, though it was the public meeting and market place. The automobiles made it dangerous and inaccessible. (Lithograph by J.J. Fogerty)

The colonial era of America (1600-1800) was marked with the formation of a chain of settlements along the east coast. Important cities of this period are Virginia, Boston, Newport and the New Amsterdam in the Manhattan. The era of growth and expansion (1800-1870) was characterised by trade and industrialisation, that led to unprecedented growth of cities. The era of great metropolis (1870-1940) witnessed a number of inventions, such as framed, steel structures and elevators, which changed the skyline of American cities and development of suburbs. The City Beautiful Movement in 1893 emphasised the need for a city that would be big, broad and beautiful. The plans were of colossal scale with monumental proportion failed to meet the needs of the common man. Boston-Washington was the first American megalopolis. Office towers multiplied very fast and many residential areas of the cities got totally transformed.

The fall out of industrial revolution was mass production, industrialised construction and development of new buildings, mainly built with reinforced concrete and steel. The advent of electricity, railways, motorised vehicles, lifts, etc. changed the whole approach towards cities and their urban form. The demand for green and pollution free neighbourhood and towns included river front landscape, conservation of forests, sports facilities, parks and recreational clubs. This was beginning of a new era of 'modern' style where important buildings were being designed with an eye toward innovation and streamlining their functional roles, removing unnecessary references and embellishment. The building design, followed the philosophy of "form follows function." In post-war United States people's residences and domestic lives became more outdoor oriented.

Beaux-Arts Architecture

Beaux-Arts architecture denotes the classical architectural style that was taught at the École des Beaux Arts in Paris. The style "Beaux-Arts" is the cumulative product of two and a half centuries of instruction at the Académie royale d'architecture and the Académie des Beaux-Arts. This provided a new template of codes and aesthetics of architecture, The Beaux-Arts architecture continued without a major renovation until mid-twentieth century.

Fig. 3.73. The Bauhaus building built in the earlier part of the twentieth century is an example of minimising eliminating all form of decoration. Architect Watter Groupies

Fig. 3.74. Cities like Manchester and Glasgow have been revived by place making, pedestrianism and conservation of heritage

Art Nouveau

Around 1900, a number of architects around the world began developing new architectural solutions to integrate traditional antecedents with new social demands and technological possibilities. The work of Victor Horta and Henry van de Velde in Brussels, Antoni Gaudí in Barcelona, Otto Wagner in Vienna and Charles Rennie Mackintosh in Glasgow, among many others, are the examples of Art Nouveau style of architecture. This was the beginning of the modern style of architecture.

Cast-iron architecture is linked with the name of Joseph Paxton. As superintendent of the duke of Devonshire's gardens at Chatsworth, he built in 1837-40 a great conservatory, shaped like a tent (277 feet long and 67 feet high), consisting entirely of cast iron and glass.

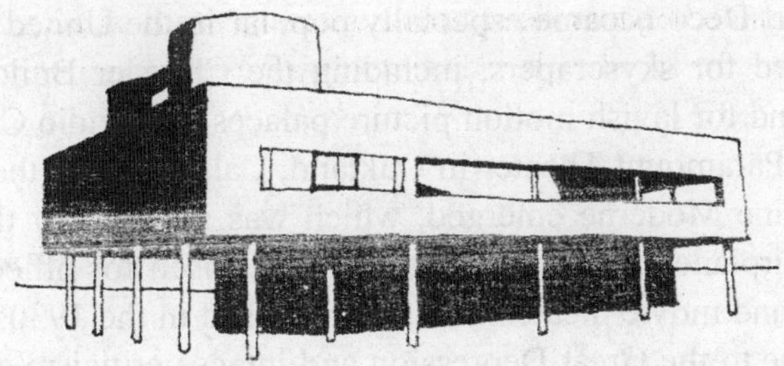

Fig. 3.75. Le Corbusier, Villa Savoye, Poissy, 1931

Queen Victoria noted in her diary in 1842 that it is 'the most stupendous and extraordinary creation imaginable.' Two years later a similar building is commissioned from Richard Turner and Decimus Burton for the royal gardens at Kew. Since 1841 these gardens have been open to the public, so that the beauty of the Palm House, completed in 1848, becomes more widely known than the Chatsworth Conservatory.

Paxton's building for the Great Exhibition of 1851, the Crystal Palace, revealed the potential of new architecture. The Crystal Palace is gigantic compared to its predecessors in cast iron and glass. The Crystal Palace had 3300 iron columns, 2150 iron girders, 250 miles of sash bar, and 293,635 panes of glass. These all conformed to a basic 24-foot module. The manufacture of the pieces was subcontracted to several foundries and glass factories, which were assembled on site in less than 200 days. It was dismantled in 1852 and moved to another site at Sydenham.

Expressionist Architecture

An important trigger towards a change in classical and conventional styles had been the maxim credited to Louis Sullivan: "form follows function." This is the principle that architects should design a building based on the purpose of that building. Expressionist architecture was an architectural movement that developed in Northern Europe during the first decades of the 20th century in parallel with the expressionist visual and performing arts.

The style was characterised by an early modernist adoption of novel materials, forms and very unusual massing, sometimes inspired by natural biomorphic forms, sometimes by the new technical possibilities offered by the mass production of brick, steel and glass. Many expressionist architects fought in World War I and their experiences combined with the political turmoil and social upheaval that followed the German Revolution of 1919, resulted in a utopian outlook and a romantic socialist agenda. Economic conditions severely limited the number of built commissions between 1914 and the mid-1920s, resulting in many of the most important expressionist works remaining as projects on paper. Ephemeral exhibition buildings were numerous and highly significant during this period.

Art Deco

The Art Deco style in architecture emerged in Paris before World War I with the Théâtre des Champs-Élysées by Auguste Perret (1911-1913) and the Majorelle Building by Henri Sauvage (1913). Its revolutionary use of reinforced concrete, geometric forms, straight lines and decorative sculpture applied to the outside of the building in plaques of marble, ceramics and stucco, and later in stainless steel, were a departure from Art Nouveau. The style reached its peak in the 1920s and 1930s, and took its name from the International Exhibition of Modern Industrial and Decorative

Arts in Paris in 1925. Art Deco became especially popular in the United States in the late 1920s, where the style was used for skyscrapers, including the Chrysler Building (1930) and Empire State Building (1931), and for lavish motion picture palaces viz. Radio City Music Hall (1932) in New York City and the Paramount Theater in Oakland, California. In the 1930s a stripped-down variation called Streamline Moderne emerged, which was inspired by the curving aerodynamic forms of ocean liners, airplanes and trains. Art Deco was used for office buildings, government buildings, train stations and movie theaters around the world in the 1930s, but declined rapidly at the end of the decade due to the Great Depression and intense criticism of the style by modernist architects such as Le Corbusier, who denounced its excessive ornament.

Fig. 3.76. Erich Mendelsohn, Einstein Tower, Rotterdam

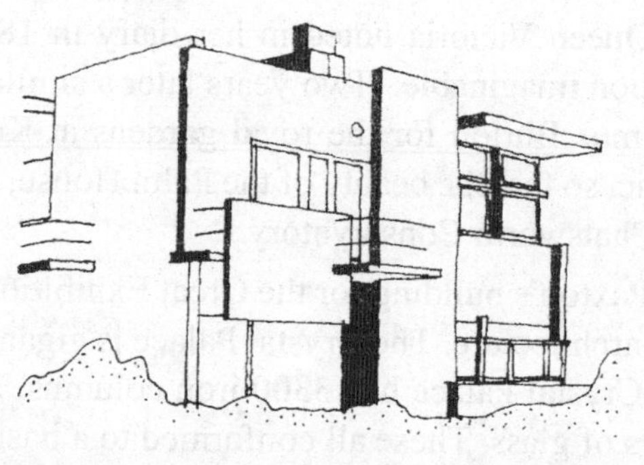

Fig. 3.77. Gerrit Rietveld, Schroder House, Utrecht, 1924

Fig. 3.78. During early 20th century, the British created art deco style fountains in Bombay, besides Calcutta, Madras and New Delhi

Fig. 3.79. Barcelona (Spain) has iconic structures designed by Architect Antonio Gaudi with his inimitable style of curvatures, glazed tiles, torrets and minarets. It was a new beginning of art–nouveu, a new aesthetics. Sagrada Familia (1893–1905) is his most famous landmark

International Style

The International style was a major architectural trend of the 1920s and 1930s. The term usually refers to the buildings and architects of the formative decades of modernism, before World War II. The term had its origin from the name of a book by Henry-Russell Hitchcock and Philip Johnson which identified, categorised and expanded upon characteristics common to modernism across the world. As a result, the focus was more on the stylistic aspects of modernism.

The ideas of Modernism were developed especially in what was taught at the German Bauhaus School in Weimar (from 1919), Dessau (between 1926–32) and finally Berlin between 1932–33, under the leadership of its founder Walter Gropius, then Hannes Meyer, and finally Ludwig Mies van der Rohe. Modernist theory in architecture resided in the attempt to bypass the question of what style a building should be built in, a concern that had overshadowed 19th-century architecture, and the wish to reduce form to its most minimal expression of structure and function. In the United States, Philip Johnson and Henry-Russell Hitchcock represented a new International Style. The core effort was to pursue an abstract, scientific programme but issues of style dominated its puritan goals.

Fig. 3.80. Seagram Building. New York by Mies van der Rohe Architect

Fig. 3.81. Saynatsalo City Hall, Finland designed by Alvar Aalto

Modern architecture

Modern architecture is generally characterized by simplification of form and creation of ornament from the structure and theme of the building. It is a term applied to an overarching movement, with its exact definition and scope varying widely. Modern architecture has continued into the 21st century as a contemporary style.

Fig. 3.82. Sydney Opera House designed by Jorn Utzon

In order to counter the placelessness and lack of meaning in Modern architecture, the concept of critical regionalism was developed by Alexander Tzonis, Liane Lefaivre and Kenneth Frampton.

Frampton put forth his views in "Towards a Critical Regionalism: Six points of an architecture of resistance." He evokes Paul Ricœur's question of "how to become modern and to return to sources; how to revive an old, dormant civilization and take part in universal civilization." According to Frampton, regionalism should adopt modern architecture critically for its universal progressive qualities but at the same time should value responses particular to the context. Emphasis should be on topography, climate, light, tectonic form and the sense rather than the visual.

Postmodern architecture

Postmodern architecture heralded the return of "wit, ornament and reference" to architecture in response to the formalism of the International Style. The functional and formalized shapes and spaces of the modernist movement are replaced by diverse aesthetics styles. Classic examples of modern architecture are the Lever House and the Seagram Building and the architecture of Frank Lloyd Wright or the Bauhaus movement. Transitional examples of postmodern architecture are the Portland Building in Portland and the Sony Building (originally AT&T Building) in New York, which borrows elements and references from the past and reintroduces colour and symbolism to architecture. A prime example of inspiration for postmodern architecture lies along the Las Vegas Strip, which was studied by Robert Venturi in his 1972 book Learning from Las Vegas celebrating the strip's ordinary and common architecture. Venturi opined that "Less is a bore", inverting Mies van der Rohe's dictum that "Less is more."

Fig. 3.83. The Portland Building, New York designed by Michael Graves

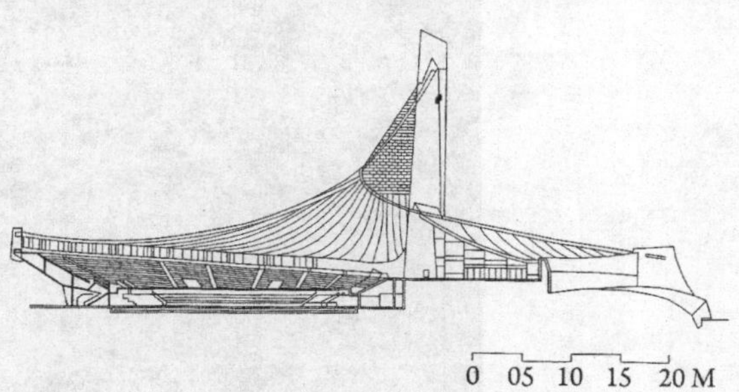

Fig. 3.84. National Gymansium, Small Olympic Arena, Tokyo, 1961–1964 by Kenzo Tange

Following the postmodern movement, the architectural ideals of New Urbanism and New Classical architecture emerged. It also produced Constructivism in architecture which characterized by the idea of fragmentation, non-linear processes of design, manipulating a structure's surface or skin, and non-Euclidean geometry, which distort and dislocate some of the elements of architecture, such as structure and envelope.

Fig. 3.85. Chrysler Building, New York (1930)

Source: *Campi Mario, Zurich (2000) Skyscrapers, Birkhauser, Basel.*

Important examples of deconstructivist movement include the 1982 Parc de la Villette architectural design competition (especially the entry from Jacques Derrida and Peter Eisenman and Bernard Tschumi's winning entry), the Museum of Modern Art's 1988 Deconstructivist Architecture exhibition in New York, organized by Philip Johnson and Mark Wigley and the Wexner Center for the Arts in Columbus, designed by Peter Eisenman. The style includes the works by Frank Gehry, Daniel Libeskind, Rem Koolhaas, Peter Eisenman, Zaha Hadid, Coop Himmelblau, and Bernard Tschumi. Sustainable architecture is an important topic in contemporary architecture, including the trends of New Urbanism, New Classical architecture and Eco-cities.

Fig. 3.86. Vitra Design Museum, Wellam Rhein, Germany designed by Frank Gehry

Fig. 3.87. CCTV Hq designed by Rem Koolhass

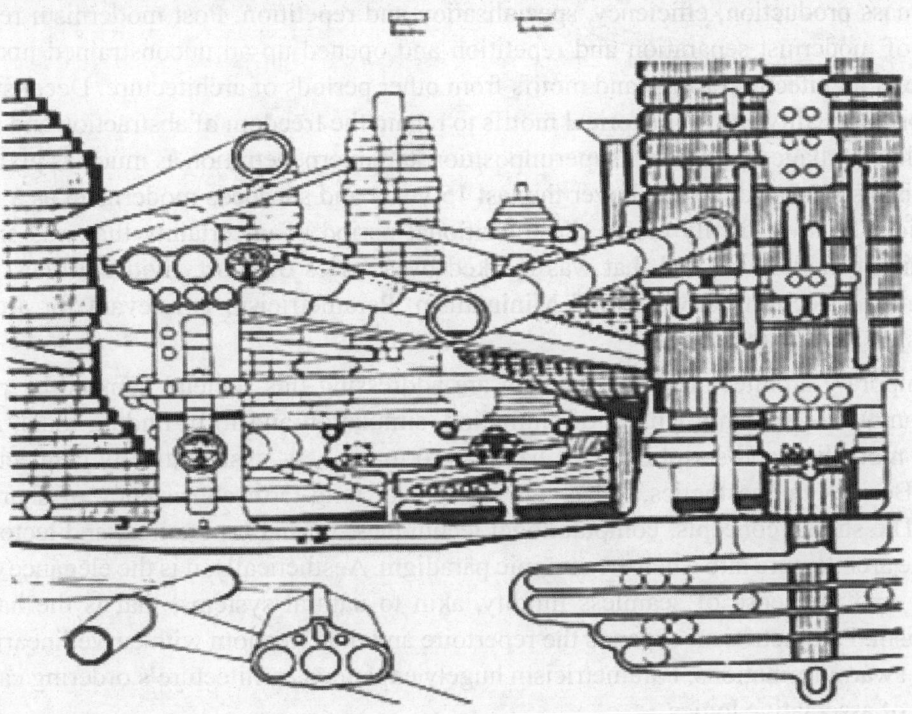

Fig. 3.88. Ron Herron and Warren Chalk, Interchange Project, 1965

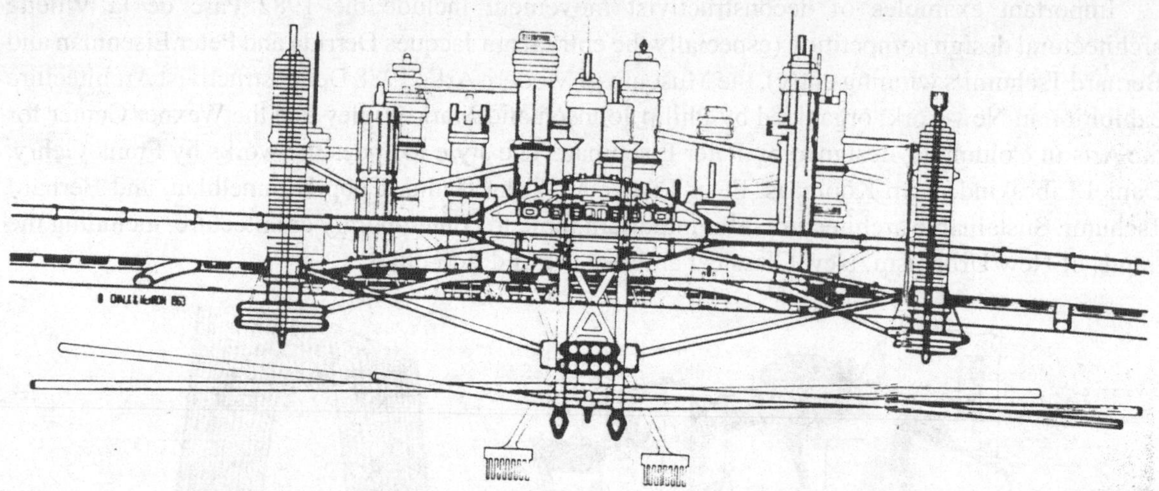

Fig. 3.89. Interchange City, Ron Herron and Warren Chalk, 1965

Parametricism

Since the classical style, which was primarily concerned with the expressive qualities of form and space, architecture has come a long way.The ordering principles of symmetry and proportion gave classical architecture the capacity to compose and order the city around the institutional ensemble of church and palace. Modernism did let go the constraints of symmetry and proportion and gained the freedom of abstraction. It maintained orthogonality and worked with the ordering principles of industrial mass production, efficiency, specialisation and repetition. Post modernism rejected the monotony of modernist separation and repetition and opened up an unconstrained juxtaposition and collage of architectural forms and motifs from other periods of architecture. Deconstructivism abandons orthogonality and all historical motifs to regain the freedom of abstraction and intensifies the principle of collage by allowing superimposition and interpenetration as much as juxtaposition. Parametricism style has developed over the last 15 years and succeeds modernism as a new wave of innovation. Its style finally closes the transitional period of uncertainty that was engendered by the crisis of modernism and that was marked by a series of short, livid episodes, including Postmodernism, Deconstructivism, and Minimalism. Parametricism is relevant for architecture, interior design and urban design.

Contemporary architecture and urbanism are addressing this societal demand by parametric design techniques—the employment of animation, simulation and form-finding tools, as well as parametric modelling and scripting. This has lead to many new, systematically connected design approach. Besides the aesthetics, it has a wide-spread, long-term consistency of shared design solutions. The shared concepts, computational techniques, formal repertoires, and tectonic logics characterize architecture into a new hegemonic paradigm. Aesthetically, it is the elegance of ordered complexity and the sense of seamless fluidity, akin to natural systems, that is the hallmark of parametricism. Parametricism expands the repertoire and thus freedom with curve linearity as well as gradient swarm formations. Parametricism hugely expanded architecture's ordering capacity via emergence of associative logics.

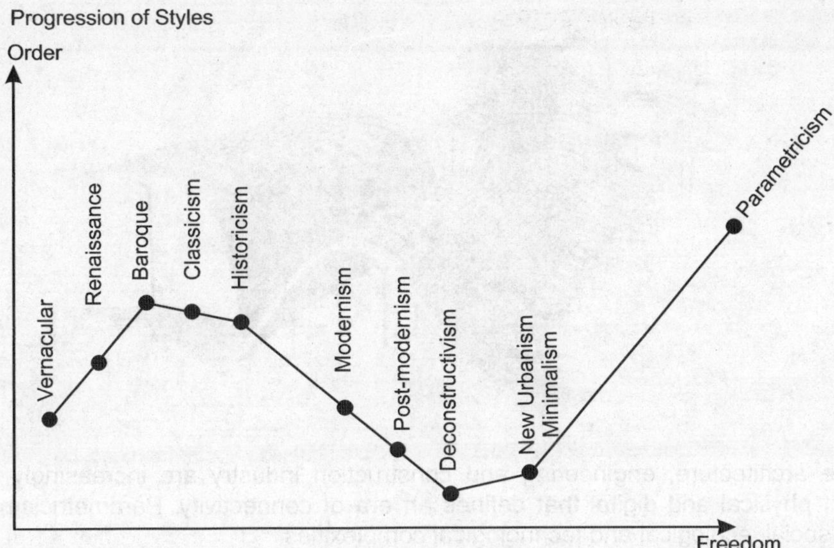

Fig. 3.90. Progression of Architectural Styles: Freedom vs Order, graph by Patrik Schumacher

Source: *Parametricism, Rethinking Architecture's Agenda for the 21st Century, March/April 2016, Volume 86, Issue 2, edited by Patrik Schumacher*

Parametricism can emerge as an epochal style. Parametricism has the capacity to combine complexity with a simultaneous increase in order, via the principles of differentiation and multi-system correlation. Parametricism can overcome the visual chaos of laissez faire urbanisation. It seeks to focus upon local identity and a bottom up process, which is based upon local contexts, topography, climate, etc. Parametricist order does not rely on the uniform repetition of patterns as Modernist urbanism, Parametricist compositions are inherently open ended.

Cities have become sources of extreme inequality and environmental degradation, which are even threatening their own subsistence, and are pointing at unsurmountable contradictions at the core of the current modes of economic integration. Urban planning has long been governed by the classification of human activities—work, residence, leisure and transport. However, this approach is ill-suited to address the pressing environmental concerns of our age. There is a need to adopt a broader urban design and technology to enhance the democracy of urbanism.

Citizens are increasingly aware that they inhabit ecosystem, which are crucially mediated by technology. For cities to address the challenges of the cosmic environment in which primeval elements—air, water, energy and earth, have become monetised, artificial and politicised, architects will have to develop a perspective which is no longer limited to the conceptualisation of the buildings, but mediated by technologies, condition of environment, recycling of refuse, producing food, shelter and clothes.

Fig. 3.91. The architecture, engineering and construction industry are increasingly operating with the merging of physical and digital that defines an era of connectivity. Parametricism can articulate contemporary social, ecological and technological complexities

Fig. 3.92. Design of Rubyovo-Arkangelskoye Neighbour hoot, Moscn by Zaha Hadid has been a pioneer in parametric architecture that synthesises social, ecological and technological complexity

Fig. 3.93. Zaha Hadid Architects' design of the new Rublyovo-Arkhangelskoye neighbourhood in Moscow aims to create an urban environment and ecological and technology that seamlessly integrates natural and human-made systems

Fig. 3.95. Zaha Hadid Architects' Rubyovo-Arkangelskoye in Moscow will include new homes for 66,500 residents in addition to new schools, medical clinics, transport infrastructure, shopping, civic and cultural institutions. The neighbourhood will accommodate 800,000 sqm of office space for Moscow's growing financial sector. In total, 4 million sqm of new buildings will be developed over 460 hectares to the west of Moscow. A third of the neighbourhood will be parklands and forest bordering the Moscow River with a 30 hectare lake at its centre

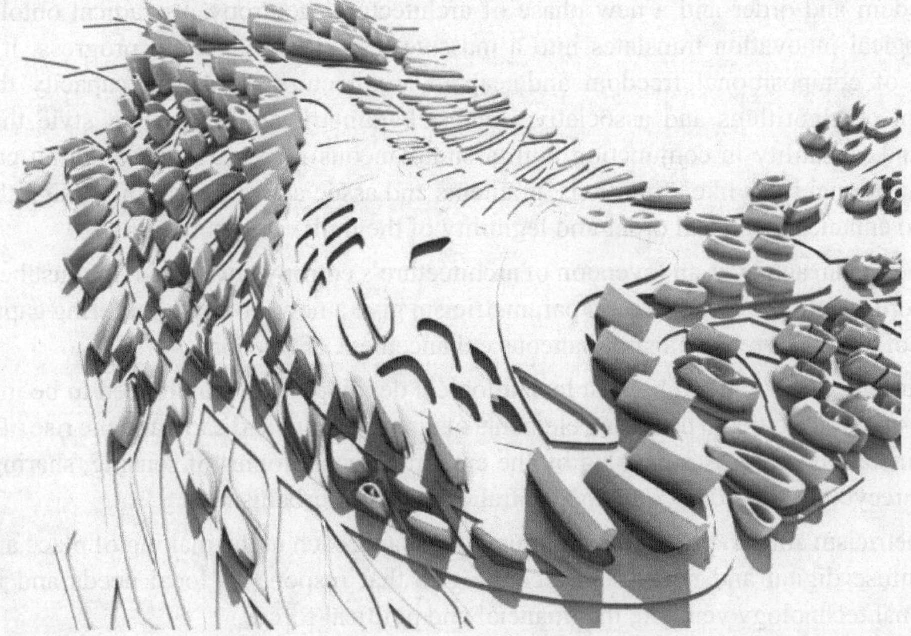

Fig. 3.96. Parametricism Pronounces Increase in Freedom and Order, Zaha Hadid Architects, Masterplan for Appur Istanbul

Fig. 3.96. South Asian Human Rights Documentation Centre, Anagram Architects, Brick work detail

The trend of a negative correlation of freedom and order has to be reversed. The parametricism. offers freedom and order and a new phase of architectural gentropy. Its radical ontological and methodological innovation translates into a massive leap in architectural progress. It entails an expansion of compositional freedom and leap in architecture's ordering capacity through the deployment of algorithms and associative logics. Parametricism is the first style that delivers freedom and versatility in conjunction with a simultaneous increase in its ordering capacity via new compositional rules like affiliations, gradients and associative logics. The design thus has the potential to enhance the visual order and legibility of the built environment.

Parametricism achieves an inversion of architecture's entropy law. Freedom must be bought by giving up order until the techniques of parametricism give a new, powerful ordering capacity to the discipline of architecture, and a simultaneous enhancement of freedom.

Our current age is marked by vast technological developments which need to be incorporated into the design of the cities. The arcane elements of air, water, fire and earth and the rise of artificially mediated metabolic processes enabled by the emerging technologies of sensing, sharing, moving, making or recycling should become the central concerns of urbanism.

Parametricism aims to provide a minimum viable approach to the making of place and imagine ways to infuse digital and networked technologies that respond to local needs and not that of multinational technology vendors, the financial and political forces.

According to Patrik Schumacher, by parametricism urban and architectural environments receive an inbuilt kinetic capacity that allows those environments to reconfigure and adapt themselves in response to prevalent occupation patterns. The real time registration of use-patterns drives the real time kinetic adaptation. The built environment thus acquires responsiveness, at different time scales. The systematic modulation of morphologies produces powerful urban effects and facilitates field orientation. Parametric urbanism might involve parametric accentuation, parametric figuration, and parametric responsiveness as registers to fulfill its ambition of deep relationality. Patrik Schumacher notes that parametric urbanism aims to construct new field logics that operate via the mutually accentuating correlation of multiple urban systems: fabric modulation, street systems, system of open spaces, etc. The agenda of deep connectivity implies that the fabric modulation also extends to the tectonic articulation. Both massing and fenestration might - each in its own way – be driven by sunlight, orientation, producing a mutual enhancement of the visual effect.

New Urbanism

New Urbanism, also called Smart Growth, New Community Design, Neo-traditional Design,Traditional Neighbourhood Development, Location Efficient Development and Transit Oriented Development, is a set of development practises to create more attractive, efficient and liveable communities. These can significantly improve accessibility and reduce per capita automobile travel. New urbanism focuses on the community and has a discernible Activity Centre. This is of ten a plaza, square or green, and sometimes a busy or memorable intersection. A transit stop should be located at this centre. Special attention is paid to protecting the public realm and creating quality public spaces, including sidewalks and paths, parks, streets capes and public buildings. This helps create community identity and cohesion, leading to stronger and healthier communities. Buildings are placed close to the sidewalk and to each other, creating an urban sense of spatial definition. Buildings towards the edges are placed further away and further apart from each other, creating a more rural environment. Most dwellings are within a five-minute walk (a quarter mile) from the centre. Streets are designed for walking and cycling with sidewalks on both sides, bike lanes, good crossings, traffic calming and other features to encourage non-motorized travel. There are a variety of dwelling types. These take the form of houses, row houses, and apartments, such that younger and older, single and families, the poorer and the wealthier can find places to live. There are places to work within and adjacent to the neighbourhood, including shops, office buildings, and live-work units.

New Urbanism reflects neighbourhood and local level planning, while access management, location-efficient development and clustering reflect similar principles at the site and block level. New Urbanism has gained increasing attention among professionals and the general public, particularly in regions experiencing growth-related conflicts. Many see the New Urbanism as a way to accommodate growth while enhancing community and environmental objectives.

DEBRIEFING QUESTIONS

1. Explain the architectural concepts of Egyptian pyramids.
2. Describe the salient features of:
   - (*i*) Ancient Babylon
   - (*ii*) Persian Architecture
   - (*iii*) Ancient Chinese Architecture
   - (*iv*) Ziggurats at Teotihuacan
   - (*v*) Machu Picchu
   - (*vi*) Byzantine Architecture
   - (*vii*) The Pantheon
   - (*viii*) The Parthenon
3. Explain how the invention of arch, vault and dome revolutionised the architecture?
4. Explain the principles of architecture by Vitruvius.
5. Explain the following styles of architecture:
   - (*a*) Gothic
   - (*b*) Neo-classical
   - (*c*) Palladian
   - (*d*) Baroque
   - (*e*) Renaissance
   - (*f*) Romanesque
   - (*g*) Beaux Arts
   - (*h*) Art Nouveau/ Art Deco
   - (*i*) International Style
6. What are the unique features of designs of :
   - (*a*) Florence
   - (*b*) Venice
   - (*c*) Amsterdam
   - (*d*) Versailles
   - (*e*) St. Peter's Rome (Bernini)
   - (*f*) Barcelona (Antonio Gaudi)
7. Explain the following :
   - (*a*) Ebenezer Howard's concept of Garden City
   - (*b*) L'Enfant's concept of Washington
   - (c) Parametricism
   - (*d*) New Urbanism

Chapter 4

VASTU IN MODERN CONTEXT

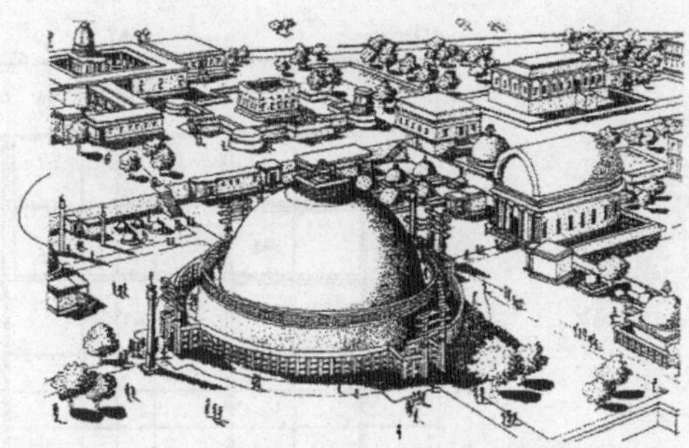

There is a renewed and growing interest in traditional knowledge systems, such as Vastu Shastra. This needs a detailed understanding of architecture, vastu principle and its application in site selection, orientation, site planning and building design.

Vastu is the energy manifest—Vastu is substantial—Vastu is the micro-space. Vastu is the macro space. Indwelling energy is Vastupurusa—the 'Vastu-Brahman.' The living place of devatas and human beings is known as 'Vastu.' According to Kautilya's Arthshastra, houses, fields, gardens, buildings of any kind, lakes and tanks are Vastu. Broadly, Vastu consists of Bhumi (earth), Prasada, Vahan and Shayan.

1. Bhumi is land where buildings are built
2. Prasada is buildings, palace, and other structures
3. Vahan means vehicles like Rath (chariot), Gaadi (cart), Vimana, Nauka (boat), etc.
4. Shayan is furniture like cot, table, cupboards, chairs, etc.

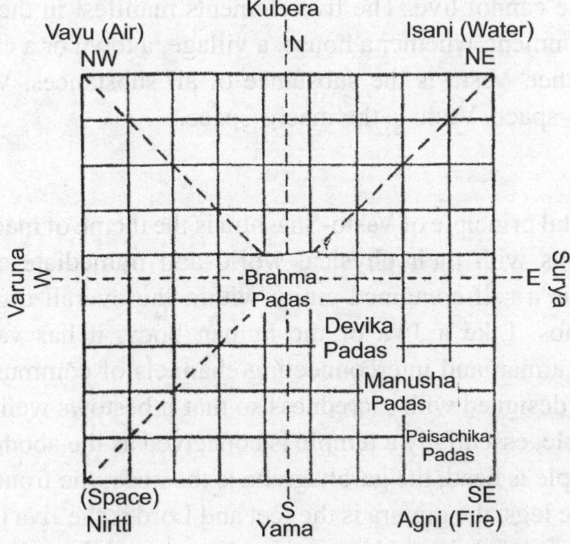

Fig. 4.1. Pad Vinyas and Deity Zones in Space

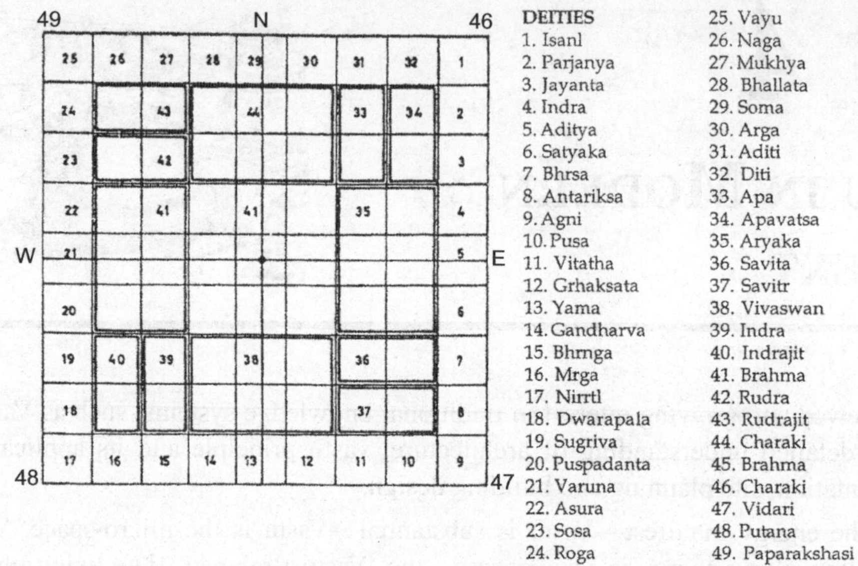

Fig. 4.2. Vastu Paramsayika Mandala based on spaces for deities (including demons)

All these four aspects of Bhumi are the resting place. Land (bhumi), the structures (prasada), together with vehicles (vahan) furniture (shayan) comprise 'Vastu', and the rules and guidelines are termed as 'Vastu Shastra.'

The term Vastu is derived from Vas or a place where living beings reside. Vastu Shastra deals with the process when Streee (nature) and Vastupurusha (jiva and kala) joins together Shristi (creation) takes place and 'Panchabhutas', that is five elements (earth, water, fire, air and space) are created without which one cannot live. The five elements manifest in the human being and these comprise the living environment, whether a house, a village, a town or a city. Both Vastu and Stree are dependent on each other. Vastu is the substance of all substances. Vastu is the Purush—the Brahaman. Vastu is micro-space. Vastu is the macro-space.

Basic Principles

The underlying fundamental principle of Vastu-Shashtra is the theme of macrocosm and microcosm, which binds human beings with their physical world and immediate environment. Whether a city, village or house, it is a self-contained entity within the overall organisation, structure and composition of the cosmos. Like a Jiva or the human body, it has various limbs to perform different functions, head, atman and interconnecting channels of communications (spinal chord). Accordingly, it should be designed with sacredness so that it bestows well being, happiness, peace and prosperity. For example, essentially a temple is conceived as the abode of God with Jiva in the centre. The top of the temple is head, the garbhagraha is the neck, the front mandap is the stomach, the parikaram walls are the legs, the gopura is the feet and Lord is the Jiva in the body. Every part of the temple is limb of the Lord and should be considered as sacred. Its spire transfers cosmic energy to garbhagriha. Pyramidical shape of the Shikhar (mountain) of the temple helps in optimising the concentration of the energy and conservation of the body, brain and atman. This principle is amazingly also seen in the pyramids of Egypt and main civilisations, indicating certain common link between ancient India and other civilisations in far-off lands.

Vastu Shashtra had been a holistic discipline, and as such as architect should have insight of religion, languages, literature, astronomy, mathematics, astrology, philosophy, sculpture and music and other arts, science and technology. In short, he or she should be an enlightened person and a complete (yogi) purush.

Process of Integration

"*With these shilpas Prajapati strengthened the heaven. With these he made the heaven shapely. With these he expanded the speech thoroughly." O Agni you make the king imbued with those splendours by which the Aditya shines with enhanced brilliance; by which the sun is seen with numerous rays; by which the speech is made complete and capable of denoting all meanings.*"

The essentials of Vastu and Shilpa are yoga (complete and integral vision), bala (capacity), and samarthya (efficiency) by which the entire world is invested with form, even as from it the cosmic elements derive their origin and strength. Prajapati is its source and also the one who manipulates and renders it active. Shilpa is conspicuous as tattva (active element) in primal creation, and it has among other things, the power or propensity to attract and control.

Vastu and shilpa compose 'prana' (breath) in the 'purush', which personifies sacrifice. It has the same efficacy in the purusa that breath has in a body; it enlivens it and activates it. As prana, it is same as atman (soul), for the two are perpetually inseparable. Thus vastu or shilpa manifest organic unity between purush and its counterpart. As such the concept of Vastu is similar to Sarira (human body). Like Sarira, Vastu has the following five dimensions:

1. At the functional level it is organic, i.e. it has a structure.
2. At the conceptual level it is the abode of atman (sarira with soul) i.e. it is not chetana (sentient) by itself.
3. In the time-dimension it is transient or ephemeral.
4. Speaking of its composition, it is made up of the five elements (bhutas) and is associated with impurity.
5. It is an instrument of atman.

Thus Vastu is organic or structural, it is dependent on a sentient or intelligent principle and is an instrument, is transient, and is composed of bhutas (elements). The association of sarira and Vastu is explicit in the concept of temples. The temple is the body or abode of God and the garbhagraha (womb-house) is like the hrdyaya-guha (heart-cave), the dwelling of the atman. The pratima (image) installed in the garbhagraha is again consecrated with a ritual of pranapratistha (installation of prana or life) implying that atman is 'entering' the body. A cyclic process by way of the 'structure' of the body being formed on the basis of bindu, the atman and the body thus created being again occupied by the atman is implied.

Vastu and Panchabhuta

Vastu Shastra is essentially the art of correct setting whereby one can optimise the benefits of the Panchbhutas and the influence of magnetic fields surrounding the earth. The scientific planning creates a perfectly balanced environment which enhances health, wealth and prosperity by concentration or dispersion of cosmic energies. Vastu Shastra lays down the importance of selection of a site, its shape, proportions, direction, location, etc.

Properly designed and pleasing house will be an abode of good health, wealth,intelligence, children, peace, happiness and will redeem one from debt of obligations. Negligence of canons of architecture will result in unnecessary travels, bad name, loss of fame, sorrows and disappointments. The character of the house built disregarding prescribed codes cannot be determined. All houses, villages, towns and cities shall be built according to Vastu Shastra. Therefore, Vastu Shilpa Shastra is brought into light in favour of and for the betterment and overall welfare of the Universe.

Vastu-Jnan

The enlightened gurus divided knowledge into metaphysical and physical sciences. Gyan was the outcome of the mind, Vigyana was the benevolent interface for the development of the mankind. The abstract thought was rendered into tangible scientific modes. Mutation of concepts was achieved by transition through Shastra Vidya and Kala; that comprised thinking process and realising. Ancient knowledge was preserved through Shruti, Smriti and Purana that is "what was heard, memorised and committed to texts."The Vastu texts available today, may not be 'divine scriptures', however, these are enough to inform the ability of the ancients to relate the effect of the astral bodies in the universe and solar radiation on human life.

The Vedas, Puranas as Samhitas contain a wealth of guidance for all the spheres of life. 'Vedas', the ancient scriptures of Indian thought, culture and sacred lore pave the path of final release or moksha through righteousness. The four Vedas are: Rig Veda, Yajur Veda, Sama Veda and Atharva Veda. Historical facts and stories in Puranas are called the fifth Veda. Vedas, Vedanta Sutras and Brahmanas, Aranyakas and Upanishads are all considered to be 'Shruti', the original revealed knowledge. Other parts of Vedic literature consisting of Mahabharata, Bhagavad Gita, Ramayana and other Puranas are called 'Smriti.' A person who follows the path as directed by Shruti and Smriti is called Arya.

Though there are four Vedas, traditionally they are spoken as 'Trayi', the Triple Vidya or the threefold knowledge, because they deal with Jnan, Bhakti and Karma and are in prose, verse and songs. The Rig Veda underlines the path of Jnan or knowledge, the Yajur Veda that of Karma or Action, and Sama Veda that of Bhakti or Devotion. Atharva Veda represents a synthesis of the three. The Vedas are referred to as the "Triple Eternal Vedas" (Trayam Brahma Sanatana), because the fourth one, the Atharva Veda is relatively of a late origin. These four together form the foundations of Indian social, political, philosophical and cultural systems and practice.

Vastu Shastra the ancient science of designing and constructing buildings finds its origin in Sthapatya Veda, which is a part of Atharva Veda. Some of the ancient texts on the subject are Kashyapa Shilpa Shastra, Brihat Samhita, Viswakarma Vastu Shastra, Samarangana, Sutradhara, Vishnudharmootara Purana, Aparajitha Praccha, Jaya Praccha, Pramana Manjari, Vastu Shastra, Maya Vastu, Bhrigu Samhita etc. Some of the great sages who enriched the ancient knowledge on Vastu Shilpa are Bhrigu, Brihaspathi, Shukra, Kashyapa, Vasistha, Atri, Maya,Viswakarma, Varahamihira, Bhoja and others.

'Vastu Shastra', the ancient Indian compendium deals with the art and science of building, covering soil testing, orientation, measurements and proportions, Astrology and ceremonies were linked with the construction work. The principles of Vastu Shastra are abundantly found in various Puranas and other ancient texts such as Mansara and Mayamata, which provide religious validation of construction of buildings.The Manasara, a major work on Vastu Shilpa mentions 32 Shastras while the Manusara mentions additional 18 shastra. By 11th century, about 25 books on Vastu Shastra were written. In the 11th century, Raja Bhoj from Dhar (Madhya Pradesh) compiled all these works and brought out a comprehensive book 'Samarangan Sutradhar' on Vastu Shastra. The science of design, construction and maintenance of a Vastu and planning of towns are the themes of this book, which outlines three aspects of a Vastu namely: Utility, Aesthetics and Durability.

1. Manasara 2. Mayamatam 3. Viswakarma Vastu Shastram 4. Vastu Vidya 5.Kasyapam 6. Shilpa Vignana Sangraham 7. Shilpa Ratnam 8. Tantra Samuchayam 9.Viswakarma Prakasaka 10. Viswakarma Vidya Prakasaka 11. Manushyala Chandrika 12. Samarangana Sutradhara 13. Aparajita Pruhcha 14. Kamikagama 15. Suprabhagam16. Vikha Gamadyagamas 17. Nandi Vastu 18. Jaimini Vastu (not printed) 19.Hiranyakesi 20. Kalamrutham 21. Vidyonodhoyuyam 22. Bruhat Samhita (Varahamihira) 23. Vashistamatam 24. Kasyapa Silpam 25. Divajan Vilasam.

The Hindu arts, science and culture reached a climax during Gupta period (6th century AD). It was the era of geniuses like, Aryabhatta, the famous mathematician; Varahamihira, the astronomer; Shusruta, the surgeon; Kalidasa, the poet and Vikramaditya who is credited with the authorship of Barihata Samhita, a notable work on astrology, which was one of the earliest texts on the science of architecture in this period. Matsya Puran and Kautilya's Arthshastra incorporate chapters on literature. By the medieval period independent architectural manuals were compiled. These texts deal with the whole gamut of building science covering all the aspects of construction of buildings. The Matsya Puran gives a list of eighteen legendary preceptors who are referred to as instructors in the science of architecture. The most important amongst them is Viswakarma, the architect of gods for building palaces for divine beings. Next to him is Maya, the architect of demons. From Dravidian India originated Mayamata and Manasara. By the end of Gupta age, architecture had absorbed many current scientific disciplines like mathematics, geometry, semantics of form, myths and narratives, the arts and crafts. The Sthapati, the architect had to undergo learning of all these subjects.

Matrix of Prakriti and Vastu

Prakriti, Purush, Pran and Kala are all interlinked and interlocked. The Vedas provide an insight into their inter-relationships. The five elements (panch mahabhutas) of the external world, five levels of personality (the panch kosas), five levels of mind (ahamkara), ego or personal identification, chitta-will, buddhi-intellect, manas-qualitative mind or sensibility, antahkarana-the 'inner faculty' or understanding), five vital functions (pranas), five senses (jnanendriyas), and five external functions of action (karmendriyas) envelop the spheres of cosmology. The sphere of 'earth' is enveloped by spheres of 'water', 'air', 'fire', and 'ether'; and finally enveloped by the infinite reality of God. This leads to the concept of interlinked macrocosm and microcosm.

If the three gunas are compared with the five elements, an evident correspondence emerges. Tamas (inertia and obscurity) evidently corresponds to 'earth', since both correspond to objects of action. Rajas (stimulation and energy) evidently corresponds to 'fire', since both correspond to motive energy. Sattva (harmony and clarity) corresponds to 'ether', since the harmony and continuity of nature imply one another.

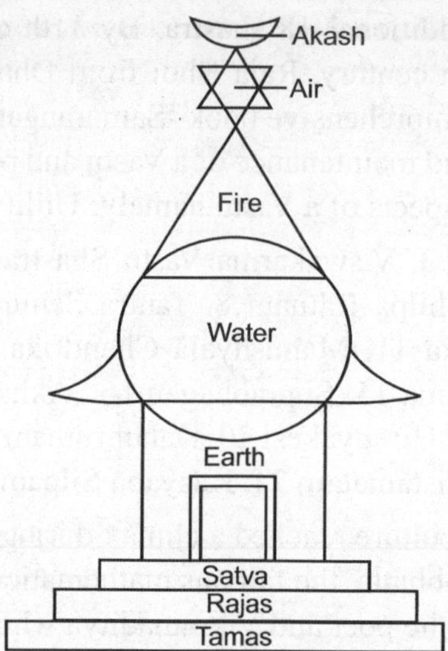

Fig. 4.3. The Five Elements of Prakriti (Nature)

Through a little further interpretation, 'water' and 'air' can also be seen as aspects of rajas. 'Water' can be interpreted as the element of fluid transformation, brought about by the motive energy of rajas. 'Air' can be interpreted as the element of relative conditioning, through which the energy of rajas is propagated. Hence the five elements can be interpreted as arising from the three gunas, by a further division of rajas (into 'water', 'fire' and 'air').

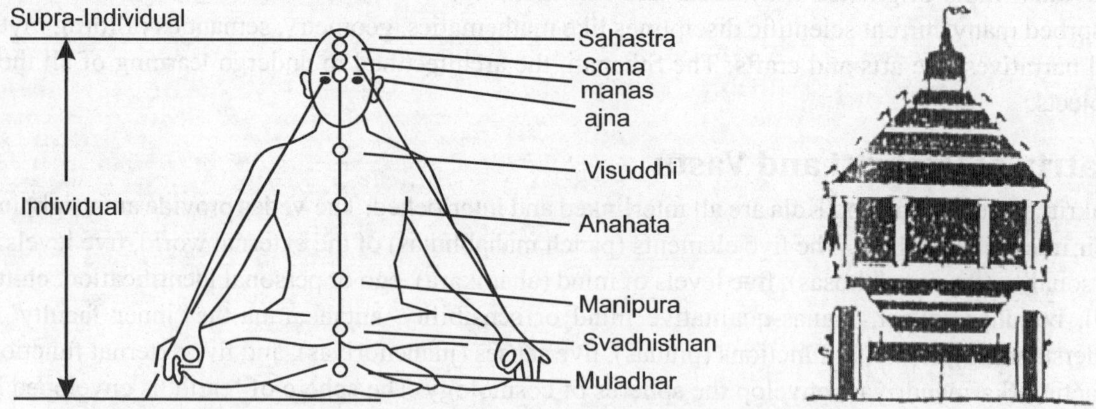

Fig. 4.4. The eight "wheels" (chakra) forming the chariot of fire of the psycho-physiological body. The ascent of the serpent power through the rising of the sun of knowledge, microcosmic counterpart of the heavenly realms and purification of the gunas the same principle is applied in Vastu, implying ascent of life (Prana) and sacred power

How the mahabhutas become instrumental in the formulation of this universe is described in the Vedas. There are three states of Mula Prakriti called tamas, aksara and avyakta all of which are very subtle. The other transformations following these states, namely mahat, ahankara and tanmatras are also subtle and when they attain the state of vikasa they get the name bhutas. As the seeds kept in a storage do not sprout, but when combined with water and mud gradually sprout, in the same manner the non-transformed state of the seeds represents Mula Prakriti, because, when it attains vikasa it represents the sprout. This is how the universe takes shape. All the created things dissolve into their origin.

In the Indian classical text, the five primal elements are linked with other elements or aspects of nature such as colour, form, sense organ, physical character, property, functions, etc. Elements have both personal (material) and universal (spiritual) attributes. Water and egg, which appeared in the beginning, have a fundamental feature of sacredness. The other elements earth, air, fire, and sky (with the sun, moon and stars) also have a similar in dwelling sacred attributes. However, not all elements are spiritually vibrant all the time and at all places; but they can be made so in a ritual way. The elements exist in two spheres—material and spiritual—simultaneously with different ranges of time and space.

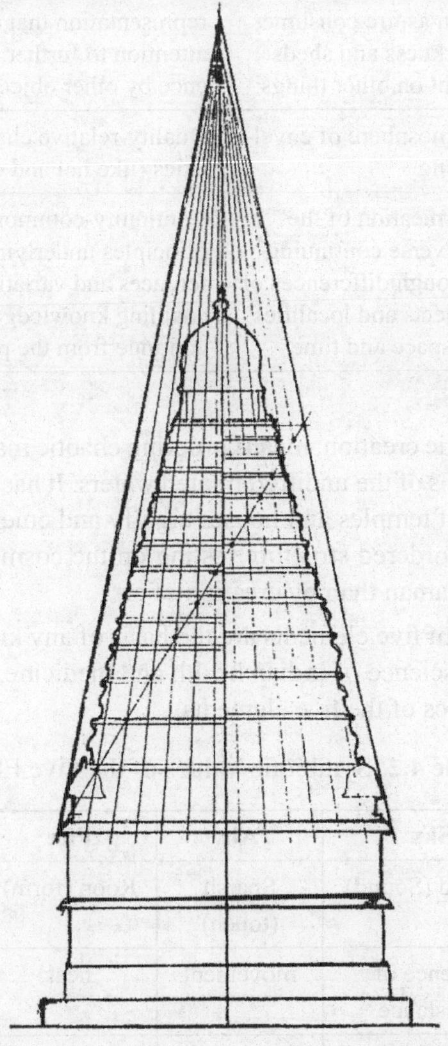

Fig. 4.5. Shikhar as an antenna of cosmic energy.

Source: *Pichard Pierre, Tanjavur, Brhadisvara*

Table 4.1. The Five Elements—Basic Characteristics

Element	Element of	Traditional Characterisation	Level of experience	Level of personality
'Earth'	Solidity	Differentiation into objects as clay made into different objects	Matter-differentiated into pieces of matter and thus formed into objects	Body and senses
'Water'	Fluidity	Change and transformation as water flows in changing shapes and forms	Form relating component pieces, though patterns recognised by similarity with other objects	Practical mind, will and observation
'Fire'	Inner illumination	Destruction and radiation as fire consumes darkness and sheds light on other things	Meaning of symbolic representation that directs attention to further experience by other objects	Intellect-formulation and interpretation
'Air'	Transparent	Atmosphere of enveloping	Quality-relative characteristics (like hot and cold)	Emotional judgement and intuition
'Ether'	Pervasion	Permeation of the universe continuing through differences of objects and localities in space and time	Continuity-common principles underlying differences and variations, enabling knowledge to continue from the past	Understanding, coordination and comprehension

Source: *IGNCA, Prakriti*

Artistic creation, like cosmic creation, means ordering chaotic material. The original chaos, has always been understood in terms of the undifferentiated waters. It has been recognised that the lotus petals surrounding the plinth of temples and houses signify and emergence of the temple from the primeval ocean, the solid and ordered structure resting on the cosmic chaos. Symbolically, Vastu interpretes the myth of samudraman than by creation of art.

The values and properties of five elements are the basis of any knowledge dealing with Purush and Prana. The Ayurveda, the science of Indian health and medicine, provides a detailed matrix of the properties and characteristics of the five elements.

Table 4.2. Symbiotic Values of the Five Elements

	Five elements	Sky	Air	Fire	Water	Earth
1.	Property	Shabad (Sound)	Sparsh (touch)	Roop (form)	Rasa (taste)	Guna (smell)
2.	Physical character	absence of resistance	movement	heat	liquidity	roughness
3.	Sensory organ	ears	skin	eyes	tongue	nose

4.	Functions	porousness, distinction	lightness activity	colour digestion, bereaveness, brightness, intolerance	heaviness, coldness oleaginous, semen	solidity, heaviness
5.	Psychological property (guna)	sattva	rajas	sattva	tamas	tamas
6.	Dosa	vata	vata	pitta	kapha	kapha
7.	Colour	crystal white	dark	red	white	yellow
8.	Form	circle	hexagon	triangle	half moon	square
9.	Mark	bindu sakti (point of power)	six points	svastika	lotus	vajra
10.	Bija-mantra	haun	hyaim	hrum	haum	haim
11.	Kala	Santya	sanll	vidya	pratistha	nivriti
12.	Presiding deity	isana	tatpursua	aghora	vanadeva	sadyojata
13.	Karnesvara	Widasiva	Isavara	Rudra	Visnu	Brahma

1 to 6 as pereceived in the Avurveda (Sharma, 1976), Nos. 7 to 13, as recognised in the Saivite system in South India (Janaki)

Source: *IGNCA, Prakriti*

These elements are also linked with psychological attributes called gunas. Each element is tied with a divinity and its related aspects such as mantra, etc. All the five elements are inter-related and act in conjunction with one another. The following matrix indicates their inter-relationship:

Table 4.3. Matrix of Panchbhuta (five elements) and Prana (life)

Element	**Ether**	**Air**	**Fire**	**Water**	**Earth**	**Function**
Either	Antahkaran	Vyana (moving throughout body)	Ear	Speech	Sound	Hearing & speaking
Air	Mind	Samana (helping digestion)	Skin	Hands	Touch	Touch, giving, taking
Fire	Intellect	Udana (taking food etc. upwards)	Eyes	Feet	Form	Seeing & walking
Water	Citta	Prana (air inhaled and exhaled)	Tongue	Penis	Flavour	Eating & enjoyment
Earth	Ego	Apana (air passing through lower parts)	Nose	Rectum	Smell	Smelling, excreting

Source: *IGNCA, Prakriti*

Fig. 4.6. Mahadeva Temple, Khajuraho (1017-1029), illustrates the perfection in design by following the vastu-jnan Samarangana Sutradhar and Mansara

Vastu and Energy

According to Hindu epics, the cosmos is omnipresent—from the scale of universe to an atom, from a city to a house, form a whole human body to hand. The hand is a microcosmos,where each finger is representing each of the five elements. The ring finger represents water while the thumb—sky, the index finger—air, the long finger—fire and the little finger—earth. The lines on the hand represent the glands inside our body. The sacred knot symbolizes 'kundalini', the divine force which flows through the spinal chord to the lotus of knowledge—the brain. As such, the concept of cosmos is not physical and spatial, but metaphysical and supernatural.

When all the elements are in balance in the body, one experiences good health and energy. Energy is basically of 2 types—one with which one is born and the constant flow which is maintained by eating, sleeping, meditation and yoga. According to Vastu, energy can be optimised by proper planning and design of a building for the benefit of its occupants.

According to the scriptures, the whole world, including the human body, comprises five essential elements, viz. earth, water, fire, air and sky. The principles of 'Vastu' are mainly dependent on the arrangement and balancing of these five elements in their proper order and proportions so that one can have better conditions in his physical environment.

The principles of 'Vastu' are based on the cosmic influence of the Sun, its light and heat, the direction of the wind, the magnetic field of the earth and the influence of the cosmos and various other heavenly bodies on the earth. The balancing of the five elements in their proper proportions is essential to keep the spirit and mind in perfect harmony for peace and happiness. It is a method to synthesise purity and environment with reverence to nature's elements, fire, water, air, earth and sky (space). Before laying the foundation of house, one has to pay respect to the earth through the ritual of Bhoomipuja with chantings from the Atharva Veda:

"Facing you, O House, who are facing me, I approach you peacefully: Sacred fire and water are within the main doors to Cosmic Order. I bring here these waters free from disease, destroyer of disease. In this House, together with Fire immortal, I take up thy abode!"

The mantras brings out the need to exist in synergy with nature's elements. The house, as fulcrum of the individual's existence, requires the energy of mantras more than anything else.

The plans of Indian temples were based on Vastu Purush Mandala or the yoga of nature, man and cosmic energy. Fundamental to the design are nine squares, each square representing one planet. Architecture starts with planets. The philosophy of the Vastu Purush Mandala is that everything must be in harmony and bring order into chaos.

The Silpa Shastra deals with the construction of houses, temples, palaces, etc. which is deeply connected with astronomy and mathematics, 'Vas', the place of residence, is not only place of comfort and convenience, but also health, longevity, safety, security and prosperity. It is believed that a town or a structure, if built rightly, according to ancient Vastu Shastra shall lead the occupier to happiness and prosperity, whereas ignorance of main principle shall cause hurdles in happiness and health.

The Sun

The ancient treatise on 'Vastu' are based on the basic principle of securing maximum benefit from the solar radiation. All buildings should be so oriented to give importance to East, the rising of sun. This is one of the main fundamental principle of architecture. The angular momentum of the Earth due to its rotation from West to East and its axis of rotation, attractions and repulsions are considered in planning and designing of dwellings.

The effect of Solar radiation on the body and on the mind must have been well understood by the ancient thinkers. The rays of the sun that propell the protons at a fantastic speed created energy fields on the Earth; Geo-magnetic and Electromagnetic, which cause an effect on the nervous system of the human body. The solar spots and flares produce temperature variations at the source.

Apart from sun, other heavenly bodies in the celestial space exert influence activity on the surface of the earth. Their influence on the well being, energy levels and radiation depends upon the location of site, birth time of the inhabitants and other factors.

Geo-magnetic Fields

The magnetic field between the North and the South poles of the earth affects the bio-organisms. The magnetic field also creates sensitive spots on the earth's surface which were used to advantage especially in communication whether marine or extra-terrestrial navigation. As such, orientation of buildings and occupants is an important aspect.

The above considerations are important factors in locational rules of Vastu Shastra. The awareness that 'urja' or energy related in the cosmos is responsible for making of the 'vishwa' or the universe and the man is the very basis of Vastu-Shastra. The Vastupurusha once laid on the ground is measured out in squares, from east to west, with the course of the Sun, from light to darkness. Space and time are its measures and form its body. All cultures took into consideration the subtle effect of the environment, both natural and built on the body. With this knowledge ancient architects created forms that were in harmony with the laws of nature and creation.

Instinct of Solar Architecture

Living creatures by instinct adjust their environment for physical and climatic comfort. Whereas man depends much on artificial means of comfort, the animals, birds and insects discern an amazing ability to choose and design their natural habitat for climatic comfort. The unique example is that of anthill, the colony of the termites.

Fig. 4.7. Termite's Nest by Henry Smeathman (1781) shows that a nest contains streets, bridges, canals, food stores, nurseries, guard rooms and a royal palace. In hot zones termites construct their highly developed structures along principle of natural ventilation, thermal storage and overheating in hot climate zones. Each nest is separated from the outer walls and stands on columns. Spaces are connected via bundles of vertical tubes. During the day the outer walls are hotter than the inner walls. Warm air is exchange through the porous walls and cooler air is sucked up from the basement. During the night, the inner walls are warmer than the outer walls, so the direction of air circulation changes

The compass termites of Western Australia build anthill which maintains its internal temperature within one degree of 31°C, throughout the summer and winter, while the external temperature may vary between 8°C to 42°C. Termites regulate the temperature by controlling the flow of air through the anthill. The shape and orientation of the anthill, which goes up to 3 meter height, influence its internal temperature. The towers are wedge shaped and always point towards the North. As the anthill tower heats up, the air inside rises, drawing fresh air currents through the living quarters. Wind blowing across the top of the tower is sucked through the nest by stack effect. The termites regulate the airflow by blocking and opening of the channels.

Sun and Health

The Sun emits two types of rays: ultra-violet and infra-red. These rays have various effects on the human body and the environment. This is one of the basic principle of the Vastu Shastra. The Sun emits ultra-violet rays in the morning hours, which have a good effect on the human body and the environment surrounding him. These rays have a tendency to kill bacteria. This is why the kitchen is preferred to be located on the eastern side. It is also good to have morning rays fall on our eyes, and which is why the kitchen platform should be oriented towards eastern side so that while cooking food ultra-violet rays will enter the eyes. The Sun emits infra-red rays during evening hours which are harmful. Water bodies at south-west corners are therefore not desirable. The reflected infra-red rays from the water body in this direction enter the house and have adverse effect on human body.

South-west side of the building is to be higher than others; walls facing south-west side to be thicker than other sides are meant to reduce the penetration of hot sun rays inside. Areas like the toilet, stores are to be located also on the west or south-west side. South being the direction of windows, living space are to be located here for better ventilation. A central court is useful for lighting and ventilation of the internal spaces.

A higher elevation of south-west side is necessary as it relates to location of a site, which should be towards the south-west of a river, stream, lake or water body. Thus a slope towards north-east will facilitate proper drainage of the site. It is necessary to understand vastu codes in a rational context and not to be dogmatic about them. Most of the scholars have found the old texts obscure and are not sure of late additions and alterations to original texts.

The movement of sun towards northern hemisphere is beginning of the Uttarayana (March 21), while its movement towards the southern hemisphere (September 23) is the beginning of Dakshinayan. Uttarayana and Dakshinayan are of great scientific importance. Day time will be more than the night time in Uttarayana, with availability of more sunlight. According to ancient traditions all the important functions like marriage and graha pravesha are held in Uttarayana and it is believed to be auspicious even for the death of a person. Bhishma waited lying on the bed of arrows for Uttarayan to commence to leave the world.

Fig. 4.8. The Surya Temple, Modhera, Gujarat stands on the longer side of the tank

Seeing the Invisible

We live surrounded by visible manifestations, but it is the invisible that actually adds meaning to our lives. The non-manifest lies embedded in us our cultural memory, rituals and history. To draw this infinite source and create a new with the help of today's technology for people and their aspirations is to invent the future. One must look back in order to look ahead. According to Charles Correa, "*we have inherited the cultural accretions of thousands of years. Nothing has been wiped out. New ideas do not replace old ones. They co-exist. Where does Rangoli pattern come from? The Bindi on a Hindu women's fore-hgead? A woman who wears that mark also wears a nylon sari; the woman who makes mysterious rangoli patterns at her doorstep also watches Hindi films on television. An architect working in such a cultural environment is in a uniquely fortunate position. To carry that traditon forward, all the links with the past, present and alive, in a culture of vast multiplicity, the task of architecture has always been to define the place of the individual in relation to an infinitely cosmos.*"

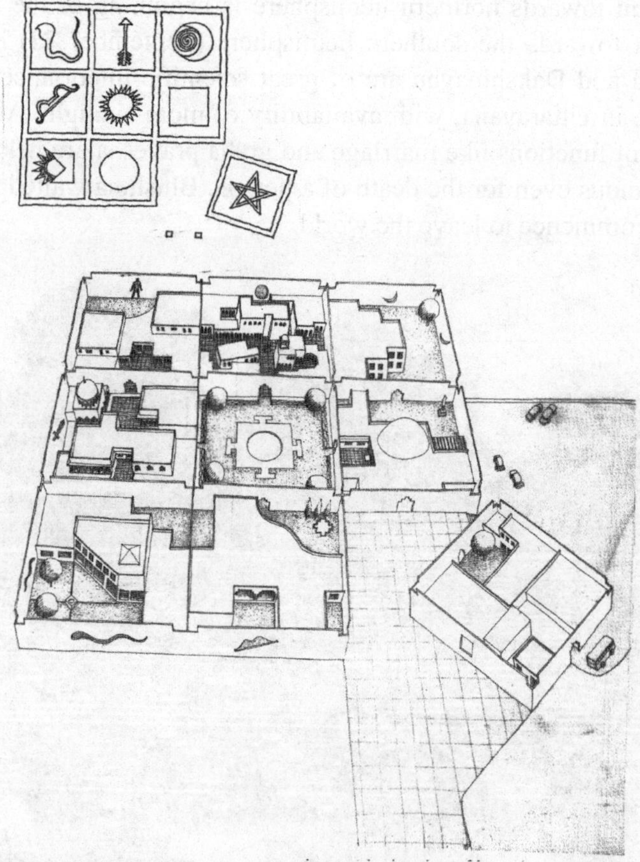

Fig. 4.9. At the Jawahar Kala Kendra, Correa uses the Navagraha, the 9-square mandala based on the mythological Vedic texts to define the enclosure of the museum. The squares correspond to real and imaginary planets, such that each becomes the symbolic representation of the setting. Externally the planets appear on the red sand stone facades as symbols inlayed in white marble and granite, while the plan configuration of nine squares corresponds to the mythical qualities associated with each planet. Isometric drawing of layout drawing: courtesy of charles corres foundation

The Mysterious Energy

Ancient cultures tried to look at the subtle effects of natural and built environment on the human system through divination skills known as Geomancy. The form of an object or a structure determines its energy absorbing capacity. The pyramids in Egypt are believed to have attracted a strong magnetic force and it is believed that these conserved biological energy. The ancient Roman road system was also based on magnetic forces as reaction to energy lines. There were negative and positive energy grids and roads were laid on the basis of this. Water, minerals and metals all have energy. The ancient architecture (Vastuvidya) in the form of building rules, codes and planning paradigms, was an attempt to capture this energy. Like the paradox of 'Shunya', which is nothing and everything, it tried to concentrate implosive and explosive forms of energy for the benefit of Purusha.

The 'Mandal' is the geometric form of space and manifestation of energy sphere around the Punish. It is an idea and a model of the cosmos, at the centre of which is the Vastupurush, the cosmic man.

The human aspect of 'Purusha' remains constant while the Vastu the buildings, 'keep on transforming with the location, space and time. This is illustrated by various classical examples of Indian architecture, which include the Sun Temple of Modhera in Gujarat, the City of Srirangam in Tamil Nadu, the Kailasa Temple of Ellora and the Stupa at Sanchi, the Castle of Datia near Gwalior, the Jain Temple at Ranakpur, the Padhanapbapuram a place in Trivandrum and the city of Jaipur.

The word 'Akash' connotes much more than just the sky. It is a symbol of enlightenment, which is experienced though several level of spaces. The monumental temple of South India are experienced not just as shrines and Gopurams but as a movement through the sacred open to sky spaces that lie betwen them. This movement in the dimensions of time (Kala) is a ritualistic pathway, a 'Pradakshina' a pilgrimage. To move along such a path towards a sacred centre must trigger off some primordial memory, embedded in the deep structure of the human mind since the beginning of time.

Movement in space is integrated with the aspect of time (Kala). This has been a basic component of Vastu or any creative work. The fascinating Jantar Mantar (Time Instrument) built by Sawai Jai Singh II of Rajasthan (1686-1743) for the gigantic observatory that was completed in 1734 in the city of Jaipur. Jantar-Mantar is not just a collection of astronomical instruments used to deduce time concepts from the movements of the heavenly bodies. They not only give visible expression to the passage of time, their form embodies the underlying celestial three-dimensional manifestation of these process. These forms function both as a spatial sculpture and a measurement of time which provide possibility of interchanging space and time. The form of these large scale sculptures points to the time dimensions as a hub, as a hinge between space and time.

The Vastu-Vidya, following various adaptations, to building concepts, describes a team of four mythological experts:

1. The Sthapati (Architect) is the master builder, well-versed in all traditional sciences.
2. The Sutragrahin (engineer) must be skilful in measurement and construction of building in proper proportions.
3. Taksaka, the carpenter is also the sculptor.
4. Vardhaki is the expert in painting and decoration.

All the four need to work in union. In vedic times, the buildings were models of the cosmos because man's central concern was to define himself and his actions in relation to the cosmos. With the arrival of western values, cultural and education the central mythical image underlying architecture changed as man's relationship with the cosmos was replaced by a relationship with an all powerful divinity. The Age of Reason became man's context.

Reinterpretation of Vastu

The context is changing again. The myths of technology and progress are being replaced by environment and ecology. At the same time, there is a widespread resurgence and interest in the ancient knowledge of Vastu. This stems largely from unsatisfactory response by modern architecture, tensions and lack of psychological fulfilment in spite of higher levels of physical comfort. Whereas many architects have started relating their work with the non-authentic and superfluous codes of Vastu and astrologers and quacks have jumped into the scramble, there are some very few examples, which juxtapose architecture deeply with the ancient Vastu Shastra. Charles Correa was one of them.

The recent works of Correa explore a number of vital issues for India today, from the position of the traditional artist and craftsman vis-a-vis contemporary architecture. The galleries of the National Crafts Museum in Delhi, displaying the incredibly rich and diverse crafts of India are arranged around a succession of courtyards, all interconnected by an open to the sky pathway which becomes a metaphor for the Indian street. It starts with ambience of the mud houses and then proceeds to the sacred precincts of the Temple Crafts and finally to the opulence of the Durbar Crafts. The ritualistic pathway acts as a powerful device by which each section retains its own ambience authenticity. There is an easy harmony between part and the whole and the natural environment. In the Crafts Museum, Correa with inherent colours and textures in mud has conceived unique atmosphere, which is appropriate to its functions and objectives. It weaves an image of a local vernacular in tradition village. Leela that is the visual wit, colour and unexpected juxtaposition plays an important concept in aesthetic aspect of complex.

Table 4.4. Symbiotic Relationship of Various Planets with Activity, Space and Colours

S. No.	Planet	Colour	Activities/Space
1.	Ketu	Brown/Black	Textile/Costume
2.	Budh	Golden Yellow	Public Space/Exhibition
3.	Chandra	Milky White	Cafeteria
4.	Shani	Earth Red	Craftsmen
5.	Surya	Red	Public function
6.	Mangal	Red	Administration
7.	Rahu	Iridescent	Weaponry
8.	Guru	Lemon Yellow	Library/teaching
9.	Shukra	White	Theatre/Entertainment

Note: This concept has been applied in Jawahar Kala Kendra, Jaipur by Architect Charles Correa

The Library and Headquarters of the British Council in Delhi is organized along a formal linear axis with a series of layers symbolising the various interfaces, represented by three mythic axes mundi. At the end is the oldest one: the interfaces with Hinduism, symbolized here by the ancient Vedic Bindu (the source of all energy). In the middle is the interfaces with the Islam, here represented by the Charbagh (the Koranic Garden of Paradise). The third axis Mundi, brought by the English who arrived with their own mythic beliefs in science and rationality, is a traditional European one.

The Jawahar Kala Kendra, a museum in memory of Nehru is based on Vastupurush Mandala wherein architecture has been conceived as a model of the Cosmos. The Mandala invoked here is the Navagraha, which consist of nine squares-each representing a planet (including two imaginary ones, Rahu and Ketu). The city of Jaipur, built by Maharaj Jai Singh was based on this spatial matrix with one of the squares moved because of the presence of a hill. The Jawahar Kala Kendra directly invokes this original mandala, with one of the squares displaced so as to create a main entrance, recoiling the gesture of the original plan of Jaipur.

In this complex, Correa has conceived architecture from parts to whole and vice-versa. The concept of whole is intrinsic. According to him we can never visualise a building in its entirety. The mental image is synthesised from a sequence of partial views. Jawahar Kala Kendra has been built like a fort in red sandstone with no windows the facade. This cultural complex is submerged in a local context. The relation of line and shape is simple. The flatness and the horizontal structure of the complex create a spatial envelope. The Vastu Purush Mandal concept gives the whole composition a form of squares and a series of courtyards. The interiors are decorated by Tantra paintings with emphasis on proportions, light and shade effects and architectural balance.

The Inter-University Centre for Astronomy and Astrophysics in Pune has also been conceived by Correa as model of the Cosmos based not on archaic notion but on 20th century concept of the expanding universe. Thus, one arrives between black (local black basalt), surmounted by even blacker Kuddapth stone, capped by glossy black polished granite, reflecting sky and clouds. Black on black the infinity of outer space. The whole complex is arranged around a central kund symbolizing the ancient archetype for the cosmos which is expanding into peripheral systems of spaces. In the projects of Charles Correa, colour and animation are combined with building techniques in a unique architectural vision. His projects have a richness that seems undeniably Indian, but there is also a deeper and broader cultural vitality.

Amazingly another striking reinterpretation of Vastu Shastra is by a foreigner. It is the Lotus temple, built during the eighties in Delhi, symbolises the renaissance of intrinsic values of architecture, superseding functionalism. Its architect Fariburz Sahba evolved a unique concept to infuse Bahai ideals into an Indian symbol. The form of the temple represents universal principles and a true symbolism, far from those invented by men but springing from the nature itself. The lotus represents the universe and enshrines the ideas of light and growth. In Indian philosophy, it is associated with the notion of purity and Sattva. From Sattva springs the Dharma and Gyana. The tranquil effect created by the Lotus Temple is achieved by arrangement of the petals, geometrical symmetry and the alluring form. The combination of large open spaces all round gives a spacious feeling and lightness to the environment. The nine pools around the building represent green leaves of the lotus floating on water.

DEBRIEFING QUESTIONS

1. Explain the concept of Vastu Purush Mandala.
2. Explain the interaction between Vastu and Panchbhuta.
3. Explain the concept of Prakriti Stupa and its applications in traditional temples.
4. How the principles of Vastu have been applied in:
   (*a*) Varanasi
   (*b*) Jaipur
5. Write short notes on:
   (*a*) Geometric fields
   (*b*) Mandala
   (*c*) Sun Temple at Modhera
   (*d*) Srirangam (Tamil Nadu)
   (*e*) Kailash Temple (Ellora)
   (*f*) Datia Castle, Datia
   (*g*) Padanabhapuram Palace, Trivandrum
6. How the concept of Vastu have been applied in the following modern buildings:
   (*a*) Jawahar Kala Kendra, Jaipur by Charles Correa
   (*b*) Indian Institute of Management, Bangalore, Sangath, Ahmedabad and other works of B.V. Doshi.

Chapter **5**

TRANSLATING ARCHITECTURAL THEORY INTO DESIGN

The architects have an enormous responsibility of creating a sustainable, equitable and aesthetic built environment. This demands understanding architecture beyond conventional building design and construction.

Architecture is a performing profession. This means the application of theory and ideology by way of creative and lateral thinking. The dreams, fantasy and innovations need to be translated into design in the context of human, financial, social and cultural dimensions. As such, the architectural profession needs to connect more closely with the realms of people, traditions, culture, ecology, technology, economics, management and humanities. This requires an architect to understand the living pattern of the people and design the building in close consultation with the people. Many government built housing remains unoccupied or is dratistically transformed as it is not responsive to the culture of the people. A study of traditional building and housing can enrich and contribute toward a liveable design.

A sense of interdependence can break down the rigid boundaries and make the profession more human centric, value based, relevant to cultural and environmental context and sustainable. The greatest enterprise of the mind has always been the manifestation of the linkages of these constituents. Architects must endeavour developing a creative mindscape which facilitates both, the individual and overall excellence, leading to an attractive and sustainable environment.

As such, the design process involves three dimensions–a horizontal dimension of technical knowledge, hard skills, a vertical dimension of soft skills–arts, aesthetics, ecology and humanities, and a third dimension of tools, processes, methods and values. A building has to be functional, aesthetic, comfortable, economical, safe and requiring less maintenance.

The most important aspect of its design is how best the given space is utilised. Spatial composition is a fundamental premises in the act of designing. Whether a house, a office, factory or shop there is always a shortage of space. Especially in the metropolitan cities, like Delhi, Mumbai, Kolkata, where demand of space is much higher than the supply, there is no option but to use every inch of space. The family keeps growing but space remains static. Expanding the space is a major challenge of house design. It is therefore logical to evolve human based anthropometric modular standards which provide a golden rule for spatial proportions.

Fig. 5.1. A house tucked in a corner of a street

In a tight space or small plot, it is always logical to start planning on a modular grid. The size of the grid is determined on the basis of minimum room sizes required for various functions, economy of structural frame (columns, walls, beams, slab, etc.), standard sizes of various components available in market (e.g. roof sheet, windows, doors, modular kitchen, bathroom fittings, tiles, etc.) and building bye-laws requirements. The modular grid offers flexibility to expand the house at a later date, as well as making changes in the plan which may be necessary in the future.

Site Reconnaissance, Surveys and Analysis

Before architect proceeds for planning and design, he/she carries a site reconnaissance, record the basic information of the site and its surroundings such as its area, dimensions, existing trees, structures, slopes, roads, service network, etc. The site analysis identifies issues, opportunities and constraints. A list of important points and free hand sketches are made to understand the site.

On-site considerations include the following:

- Orientation, north point, dimensions, area, shape, contours, etc.
- Trees and other significant vegetation
- Building landmarks or heritage characteristics
- Roads, access, boundaries and easement
- On-site drainage and other service like water supply, sewage, electricity and sanitation
- Geotechnical investigation–type of soil, bearing capacity, water table, etc.

Off-site considerations:

- The location, use and heritage value (if any) of surrounding buildings
- The surrounding road network, connectivity and traffic pattern
- The difference in levels of surrounding development
- The built form, scale and character of surrounding development
- Significant vegetation on surrounding properties
- Nallas, streams and water bodies

- Servies around the site
- Climatic conditions and climatic data like temperature, rainfall, humidity, prevailing wind direction and speed, sun path diagram, local microclimate, options/regrading orientation, fenestration, sunshades and other corrective measures
- Areas of visual interest.

Surveying

Larger and undulating sites require detailed surveying, which include measurement, setting out survey stations, open and closed traverse, chaining and offsetting, direct and indirect ranging, log-book, site boundaries, area, levels/contours, etc. The method of surveying include plane table, theodolite, tachometric, photometry, etc.

Survey of larger sites is usually undertaken by drones, aeroplanes, GIS and satellite. These techniques require digital image processing, techniques of urban information extraction and conversion of data into maps, which can overlay land/revenue maps, survey maps, etc. Often the GIS and remote sensing maps need to be corrected and updated by ground surveys.

Site Planning

After the site reconnaissance and survey, site analysis is undertaken to understand the topography, hydrology, soils, vegetation, climate, surface drainage, accessibility, size and shape, infrastructures available and natural/ecological, cultural and aesthetic factors around the site. Accordingly, a sound criteria for the siting of various types of building, parking, circulation of landscape areas and services are worked out.

The biosphere, ecosystems, natural resource and their implications with respect to soil, water, land, plants, animals, energy and waste are the critical determinants in the site planning. Large projects need environmental impact assessment and strategies of design and development with least environmental impact by cost benefit analysis, planning balance sheet and goal achievement matrix.

The decisions regarding planning, design, structure and construction must be logged into a database, site analysis and clients brief. A three-dimensional model helps in the visualisation of the project. Sustainability has emerged as a key issue in architectural design. Passive design approach, net zero energy, renewal energy and recycling of salvaged building materials are no more subsidiary issues but the core issue of design.

While exploring uncharted territory of the process of sustainable design, it is useful to heed Albert Einstein's advise that "*don't listen to his words, examine his achievements.*" The same applies to architecture.

Space Standards

A house is defined as the inhabited space, including all the installations necessary from technical and social point of view. As the problems of housing concern predominantly for low income sector of the population, minimum requirements in relation with local conditions, should be defined in terms of economy and liveability. However, there should be a balance line below which the standards must not be lowered. Firstly because beyond these limits, it is not able to satisfy the essential needs and secondly the production below these limits may be cheaper but not economical. The minimum requirements for adequate housing are not bound to be absolute values but should be determined at each stage as the economic level improve.

Buildings should be designed so that they fulfil the minimum requirements of way in which the prospective occupiers are likely to live and work in them, furnish them and store their possessions. Storage of possession should be given some extra stress here since some of the main utility and functions of houses for the low income group is the safe storage of their belongings and this needs extra attention.

There are various planning and building standards prevailing in India. The Master Plan Committee of Government of India recommended minimum two room dwelling unit.

Strict functional planning of space, does not mean designing without any consideration for aesthetics, style and psychological needs of openness and freedom. An important aspect of design is to create a feeling of freedom and spaciousness. The design should evolve from a simultaneous consideration of functional activities to which a room will be put, and the personal and aesthetic requirements. Any space, particularly a house, is not just a container of activities like sleeping, eating and sitting combined with entertainment, working and cooking, but is a place for building relationships, expressing feelings of love and concern and a channel of communications. A vital element in making the limited space work efficiently is its ability to function for multiple activities. For example, a dining area can also be used as a study or a designer's studio. The drawing room can become a guest bed by converting the sofa into a bed at night. Alternatively, a bed can be jacked into the wall niche to create a sitting room during the daytime. A children's room can have a double decker bed to save floor space.

A basic premise of multiplying the space is to save the floor space as much as possible. About one-fourth of the floor space is consumed by the walls. It should be explored if some non-load bearing walls can be avoided or removed to create more space. By erecting columns and providing lintels, load bearing walls can be avoided to provide valuable space. This needs careful planning, keeping in view structural safety.

Sometimes people compartmentalise a big room into smaller spaces and cubicals. This destroys the feeling of spaciousness and is counter-productive. Instead, it is preferred to avoid full height partitions and divide the space by built-in furniture. In this way the functions can be defined and privacy can be obtained without sacrificing the spaciousness, openness, light and ventilation. This also allows flexibility of space and its multiple use.

The rooms with high ceiling can have a mezzanine or a loft. This can be very useful for keeping unused goods. For the goods which are not in use so frequently, deep shelves can be created above the circulation area or under the staircase. It is a common practice to project out the masonry niche for almirahs, so that it does not occupy the floor space.

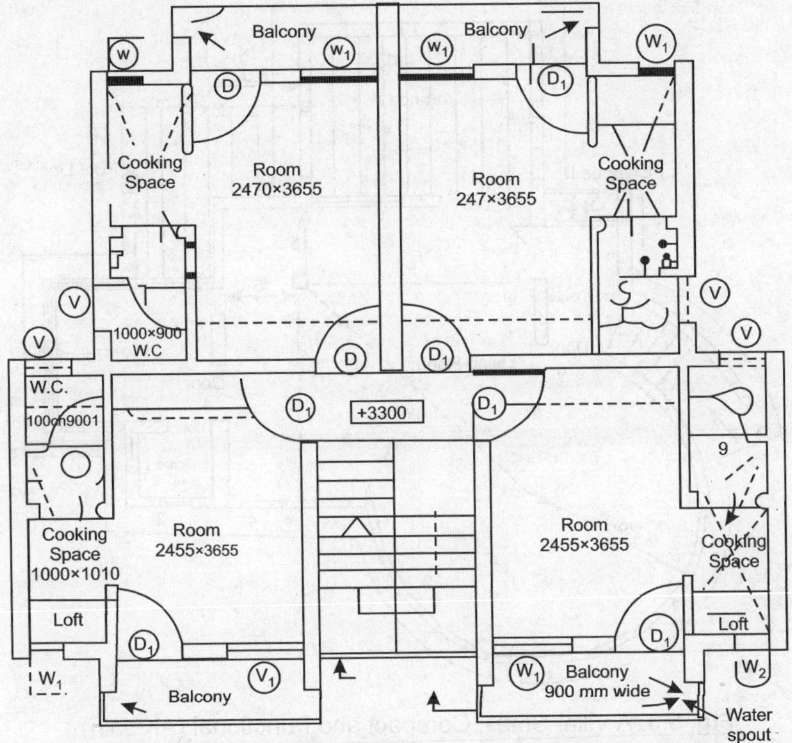

Fig. 5.2. Low Cost Housing—Typical Floor Plan of 18 sqm built up unit with common walls, service area and minimum circulation area

In a small house, some openings can be either without a door or with sliding shutter to gain more space. If a room is not well lighted, then a partially or fully glazed door can be used. Sliding and folding doors also save valuable floor space. Fold open type door consists of two vertical leaves, which fit within the door. As it opens, the leaves fold together for which only half the space is occupied. In a bay window seats can be built, either with or without storage.

It is essential to design a building to make it climatically comfortable and provide proper ventilation and day lighting. Passive design of building, orientation and simple methods such as courtyards, chajjas, brickwork, greenery in modular concrete unit and rainwater harvesting can improve the living comfort and micro-climate. The traditional buildings revolve around courtyards. They are essentially for climatically comfort, shaded space, ventilation, natural lighting, privacy and multiple functions. Large amount of space can become waste in absence of proper lighting or due to wrong position of the fans. Lights, fans, switches and electric points can have enormous impact on the use of space. These should be well planned and strategically placed so that the space is used to full potential, is comfortable and efficient to live and work.

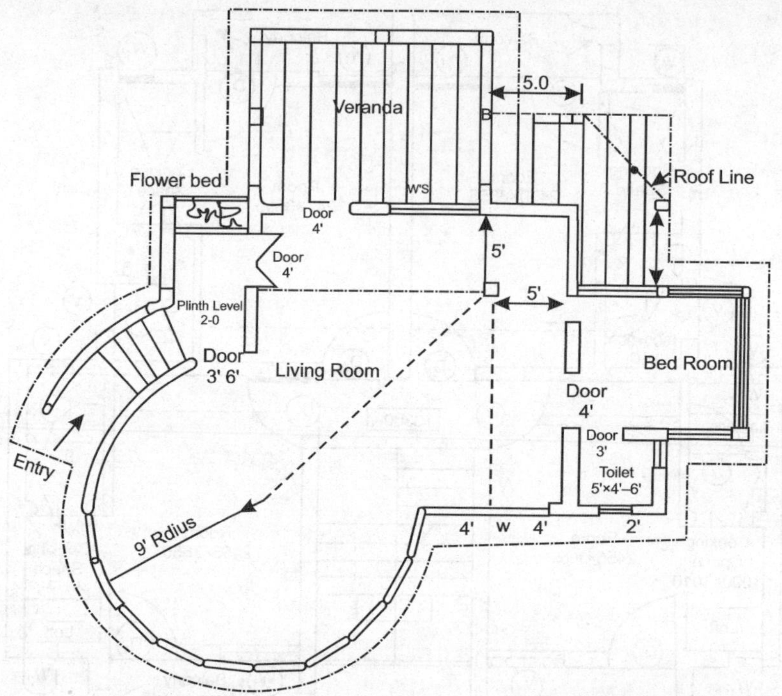

Fig. 5.3. A Villa–Small, Compact and Functional (AK Jain)

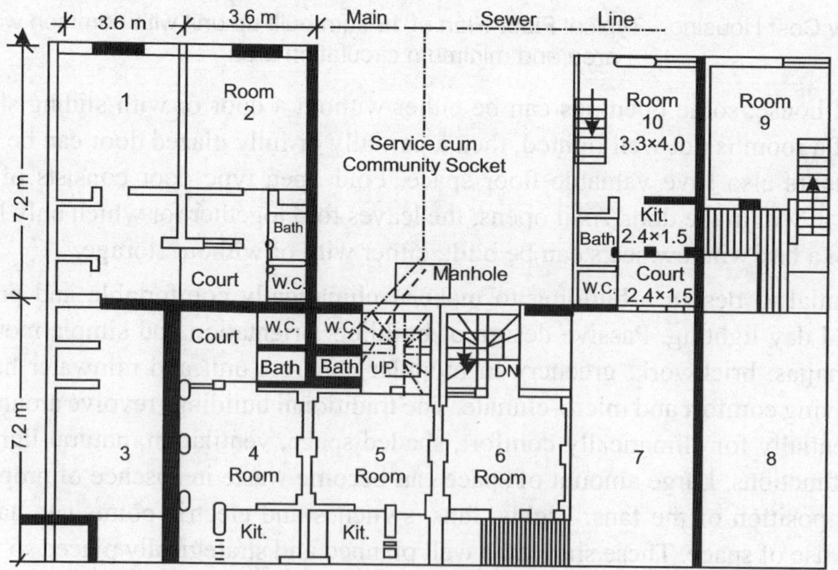

Fig. 5.4. Low Income Housing Cluster, Dwarka, New Delhi (Architect A.K. Jain)

Visual spaciousness is articulated by the effect of colours and patterns. Shade and tone of the colours immensely effect the impression of spaciousness. Light, plain, pale colours and small patterns reflect the light, hence the room looks larger. On the other hand, dark, bright colours and large, broad patterns advance and give a closer look. The stripes make a low ceiling appear higher. Breaking up of the surfaces, walls and floors in different colours, patterns or shades by way of materials, colours or texture makes a room to appear smaller. Highly reflective paints and mirrors can visually extend the space. Less can be more, if the space is designed meticulously.

Building Planning and Design

Building planning begins with site specific survey, development, control stipulations, permissible land use, zoning controls, Floor Area Ratio, Road Right of Way, orientation to the street, parking, circulation, height, setbacks, etc. The zoning entitlements vary according to land use and location. The ownership right of the site or legal arrangement with the owners is a basic pre-requisite. Other mandatory regulations, viz. planning controls, heritage, environmental, airport zoning, etc. should be considered when the plan for a building is prepared.

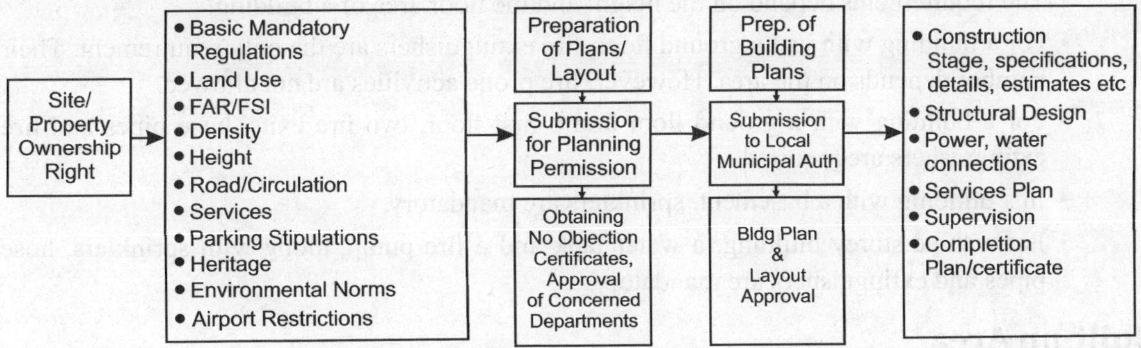

Fig. 5.5. Broad Sequence of Building and Site Planning

The Plans must conform to zoning, or the studies may be required to seek zoning entitlement changes to meet the site constraints and opportunities.

Land use is the principal use for which a plot of land or building thereon is used or intended to be used for the purpose as per the land use classification.

Plotted Development: A premise for one or more than one dwelling unit and may have on it a main building block and an accessory block for garage and servant quarter.

Road/Street: Any highway, street, lane, pathway, alley, passageway bridge over which the public have a right of passage and includes bends, channels, ditches, storm water drains, culverts, sidewalks, traffic islands, roadside trees and hedges, retaining walls, fences, barriers and railings within the right of way.

Set-back line: A line usually parallel to the plot boundaries or centre line of a road and laid down in each case by the Authority in Zoning/Development Control Regulations Building Bye laws beyond which nothing can be constructed.

Ground Coverage: The maximum ground area covered by a building, which varies according to the size of plot.

Floor Area Ratio: The quotient of the ratio of the combined gross floor area on all floors to total area of a plot multiplied by 100.

Parking (Equivalent Car Space): The space occupied by a car to be provided for mandatory parking for various land use/building types.

Front air plane: The plane contained between the ground in front of the building and the straight lines drawn downwards and outwards from the line of intersection of the outer surface of any front wall of the building with the roof perpendicular to that line, and at an angle of 63-1/2 degree to the horizontal. The 63-1/2 degree angle has a tangent of 2:1 so that if the ground is the level, the air plane reaches the ground at a distance from the exterior wall equal to half the height of the above level of that ground for the purpose of the definition of light plane, the outer surface of any veranda abutting on an interior or side open space shall be considered to be the exterior wall of the building.

Fire Clearance Thumb Rules

- The requirements depend on the height and the floor area of a building.
- For a building with just a ground floor, fire extinguishers are the only requirement. Their number depends on the area. However, fire prone activities are not allowed.
- For a building with a ground floor and a first floor, two fire exits, hose pipes and fire extinguishers are required.
- In a building with a basement, sprinklers are mandatory.
- For a three-storey building, a water tank and a fire pump, along with sprinklers, hose pipes and extinguishers are mandatory.

Built-up Area

Built-up area includes the carpet area and the space covered by the thickness of the inner and outer walls. Built-up area comprises the following:

- Carpet area refers to the area on which a carpet can be laid. Builders generally sell on the basis of the super area that includes the entire built-up area and common spaces such as corridors, lifts and stairs.
- Plinth area refers to the entire carpet area along with the thickness of the external walls of the apartment. It obviously includes the thickness of the internal walls and the columns, if any, lying within the four walls of an apartment.
- Super built-up area refers to the plinth area of an apartment as added by the balconies and other common areas like corridors, staircase, lift room, motor room, security room, meeting hall, gymnasium and indoor games.

The Building Bye-Laws prescribe the mandatory requirements for preparation of building plans of various types of buildings, which may vary from city to city. However, the provision of National Building Code and Model Building Bye-laws, 2016 (Ministry of Housing and Urban Affairs) should be followed in general.

DEBRIEFING QUESTIONS

1. Name two international and two Indian architects who have changed the approach to architecture. Highlight the major innovations in their works.

2. Write notes on:

(*a*) Organic architecture

(*b*) Spatial composition

(*c*) Form follows function

(*d*) Site selection and site planning

(*e*) FAR and Density

(*f*) Minimum space standards

(*g*) Vernacular architecture

3. Discuss the approach for climatic design of buildings.

4. How building safety is ensured?

5. Write notes on the following:

(*a*) Pattern language

(*b*) Cluster housing

(*c*) Reconnaissance Survey and Site Analysis

(*d*) Heritage Regulations

(*e*) Remote Sensing and GIS

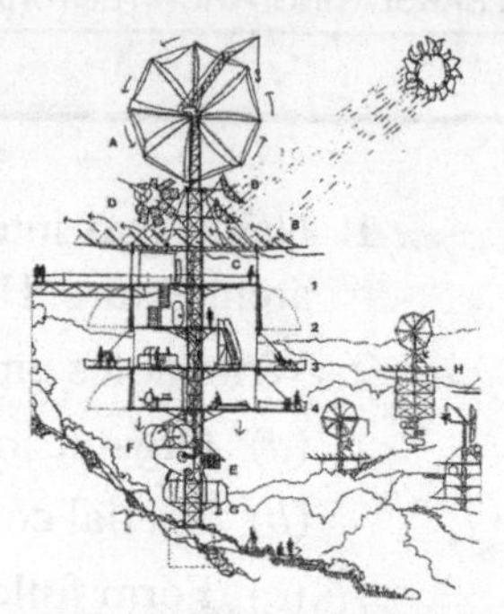

Chapter 6

Green Building

The term "green building" encompasses the entire built environment, buildings, landscapes, communities and physical and social infrastructure that connect the quality of life with the least ecological consequences. Green building manifests the principles of resource and energy efficiency, healthy buildings and materials, and ecologically sensitive land-use to achieve a sustainable and aesthetic environment. The USGBC (United States Green Building Council) defines, the term 'green building' as a synonymous with 'high-performance building', 'sustainable design and construction' as well as other terms refer to a holistic approach to design and construction. Green building design strives to balance environmental responsibility, resource efficiency, occupant comfort and well-being, and community sensitivity." According to the TERI green building is one that is designed, constructed and operated to minimize the total environmental impact while enhancing user comfort and productivity."

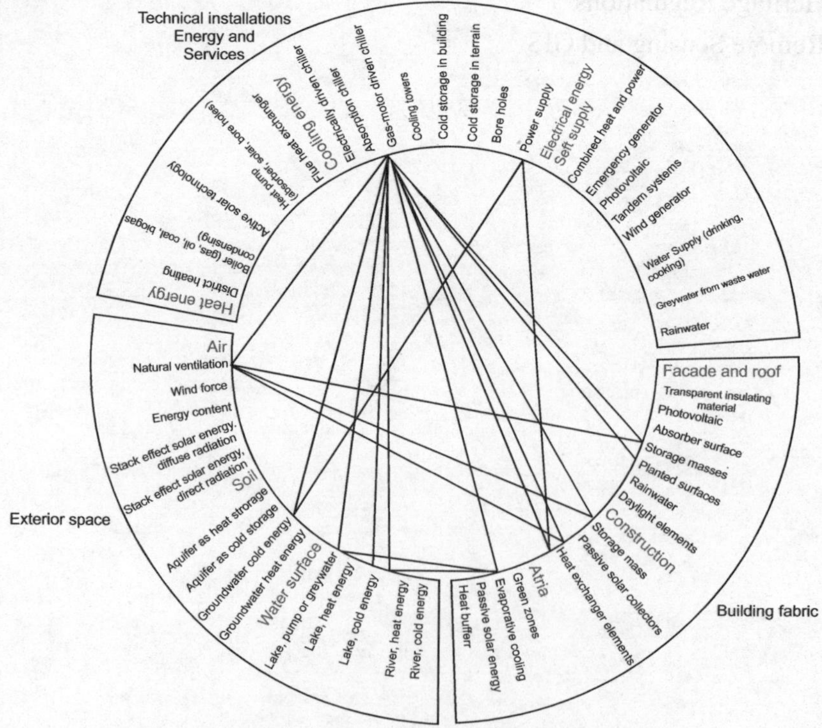

Fig. 6.1. Ecological Circle of Buildings

Source: *Daniel, Klaus, 1994, Technology of Ecological Buildings, Birkhauser, Verlag, Basel*

Every building exists in an ecological sphere comprising its external environment, internal ambience and building itself. Its external components comprise air, soil, water, urban matrix, energy, services, etc. The internal components include micro-climatic comfort, temperature, ventilation, lighting, furnishings, furniture, fittings, etc. The building components include building envelope, openings, façade, roof, construction materials, etc.

Site planning, conserving the natural vegetation/greenery, soil and drainage channels, organisation of land use, circulation pattern and decisions regarding density, Floor Area Ratio, building construction and land development impact the urban ecology and sustainability. The spatial model should be based upon the principle of "less travel, more energy saving." As such, a compact development can significantly help in saving fossil fuel consumption, climate change and environment. Critical instruments for this policy option include synergy with public transport, infrastructure development, mixed land use and e-governance, which reduce the need to travel.

Carbon Emissions in India

The following is the scale of carbon emission in India according to incitive groups.

- HIG with car and AC: 4.52 tons CO_2 equivalent per year
- LIG: 1.11 tons CO_2 equivalent per year
- Average India 1.2 ton/capita/year
- Benchmark: 2.5 ton/capita/year, expected to double up in next ten years.

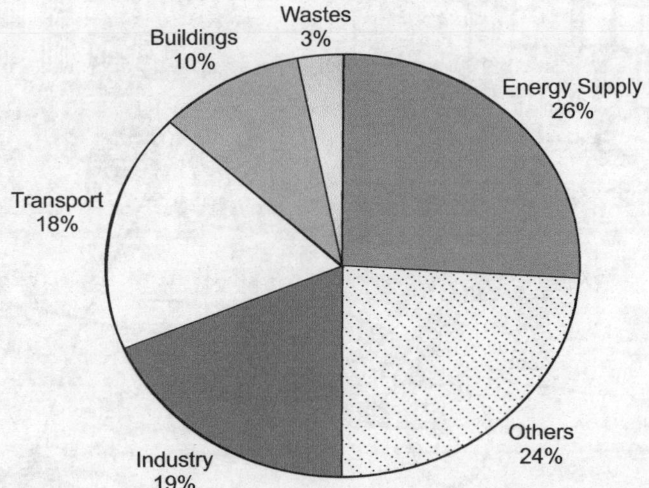

Fig. 6.2. Sources of GHG/Carbon Emission. Energy, transport and industry are responsible for about two-third of emissions

A low carbon urban form protects the blue and green networks by merging them together. It promotes walkablity and transport conservation by transit oriented development. Much can be learned from traditional cities which respond to local climate, culture and conservation of natural resources.

Fig. 6.3. A green building involves conservation of water, land materials and energy

Fig. 6.4. A Green Street with space for hawkers, pedestrians, cyclists, rickshaw and public toilets

Source: *DUAC/Divya Kush, 2014, New Ashok Nagar*

Building Design For Energy Efficiency

Building design for climatically comfortable environment depends upon its orientation, shade and ventilation, together with building design, materials use and its envelope. The exterior surface should be minimum while providing maximum internal volume. Natural ventilation, atriums and internal courtyards reduce glare and dissipate heat. Compact grouping and clustering of buildings minimise expose of wall surface and heat gain.

Table 6.1. Passive and active measures for Green Building Design

Passive measures		Active measures	
1.	Tim facade	11.	Absorber surface
2.	Passive solar utilization/evaporative cooling in winter garden (plants)	12.	Wind generators
3.	Natural ventilation	13.	Low temperature heating
4.	Natural lighting (daylight quotient)	14.	Cooling towers
5.	Cooling load reduction through storage messes (supported ventilation)	15.	Chilled ceiling
6.	'Air well'	16.	Chiller as heat pump (HP)
7.	Planted roof surface	17.	Absorption installation ('refrigeration energy)
8.	Rainwater utilization (greywater)	18.	Combined heat and power station (CHP)
9.	Photovoltaic units	19.	Filter installation for surface or groundwater heating (HP)
10.	Solar collectors		

The passive measures are integrated at the design stage, which are preventive, economical and long range. The active measures are usually add-ons and mechanical. A balanced mix of two approaches is necessary for a green building.

Concept of Sustainability

Thermal comfort is the condition of mind which expresses satisfaction with the thermal environment. It is not necessary to heat offices above 20°C nor cool them below 25°C for a sustainable thermal environment. Four environmental factors (air temperature, radiant temperature, humidity and air velocity) and two personal factors (clothing, insulation and heat produced by individual) form the six basic parameters determining thermal comfort. For a person to be in thermal comfort, the body must be in heat balance, the sweat rate and the mean skin temperature within comfort limits. Behavioural thermo-regulation allows people to adapt via measures such as opening a window, adjusting clothing, lighting fire, etc. The equivalent clothing index takes the adaptation into account.

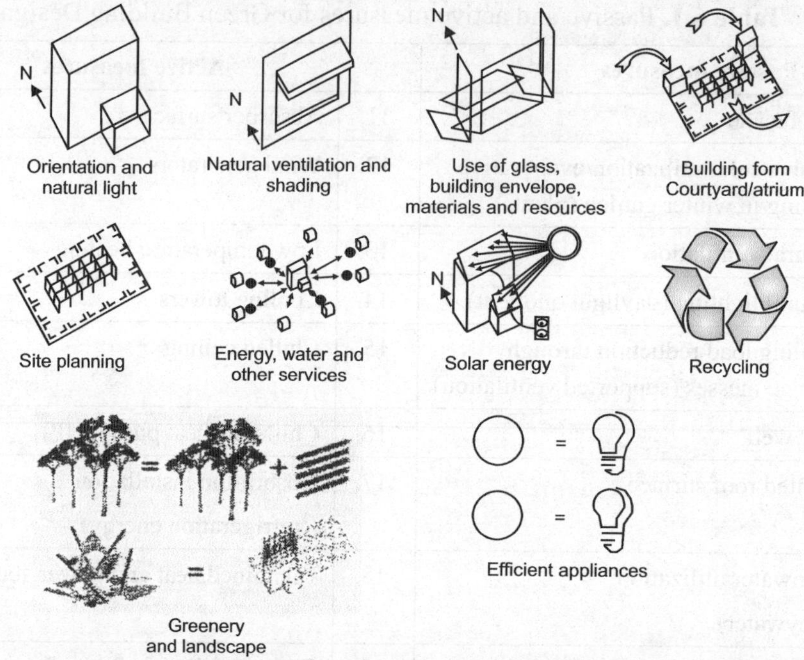

Fig. 6.5. Ten Basic Principles of Green and Energy Efficient Building Design

Comfort includes a comfortable temperature, adequate lighting, good quality air, low noise, and the ability to control the environment. One way to limit the use of fresh resources is to recycle and reuse. The push for energy efficient building is strongly linked to conserving fossil fuel usage. The heating, lighting, cooling, ventilating and general powering of buildings are responsible for bulk of the energy use. As buildings are the largest energy users, incorporating energy storage will increase the resilience of the energy distribution network and enable the more widespread use of renewable energy. Collecting rain water and growing food locally, the building can respond to the challenges of bio-diversity, social equity, waste minimization, embodied energy and energy in use.

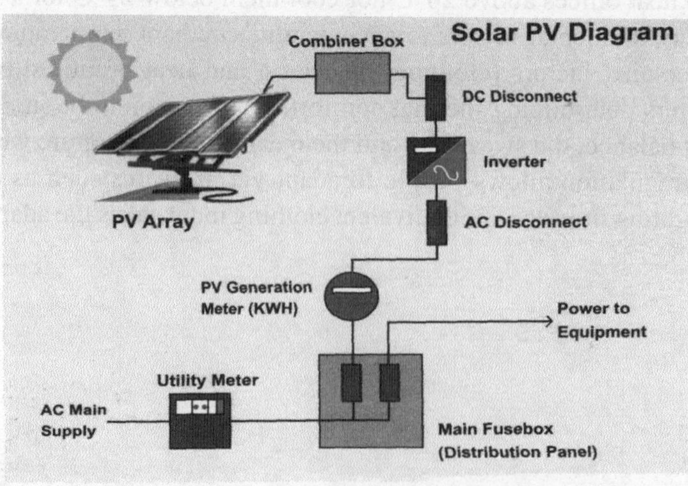

Fig. 6.6. Solar Photovoltaic Energy

Non-domestic buildings use much more energy than they should and are 'major energy-wasters.' The average office emits less operational carbon dioxide but more embodied one, and the variation in operational carbon dioxide is significantly more than that associated with dwelling houses. Among other things, the office dress code narrows the band of comfort condition, office equipment and glazed facades which lend themselves to enhanced internal heat gain. These, along with climate change, put some serious strain on the cooling requirement. Some what bizarre is the cooling of shopping malls below 15°C to lure passers-by who want to escape the heat and humidity outside. Another serious waster is the use of extravagant lighting. The energy efficient LED lighting is showing significant promise. The shift from heavy to light engineering and service industries has led to factories and warehouses having energy performance similar to that in new office buildings. The embodied energy in the building materials and maintenance is becoming a significant issue. With steel and concrete as the prevailing material choice, discussions continue regarding their embodied energy, reusability, and thermal mass effect. The Building Energy Management System, where sensors monitor the condition of a building, is recommended for large buildings. Recycling and reducing materials and energy use, quality of workmanship and increasing the amount of factory-made building components are emerging areas of green buildings.

To reduce building overheating and the use of air conditioning, along with mitigation of the heat island effect, the use of reflective materials and vegetation (such as reflcctive roofs, green roofs and green walls) are becoming more common. In the hot summer, plants on the building, through their shading and evaporation, can reduce the heat load. Courtyard, atrium, louvers, tiered sunshades and shaded envelope, combined with the vertical, hanging and spiral gardens have been used innovatively to achieve green building and energy efficient compatible buildings. The architect Ken Yeang has been a pioneer in this kind of designs. Urban vegetation has other benefits such as flood risk mitigation, promotion of bio-diversity, health and well-being.

The energy guzzling air-conditioning can be avoided by innovative methods like variable refrigerant volume (VRV) system, earth air tunnel (EAT) and thermal storage. By EAT system inside temperature of building can be maintained within 27 degree Celsius during summer and 19 to 24° celsius during winter. Lower ambient lighting with bionic controls and integration of natural light with high performance glazing combined with light sensors can save energy use in a building. Optimum day lighting and glazing design can help to reduce energy use. Synchronized lighting and HVAC systems can be designed to match building loads and schedules, which are segmented into multiple zones to allow more controllability. The use of a heat exchanger for recovering energy between the inlet and outlet flows can reduce the heating load by as much as 70%; when reasonable air-tightness with permeability of less than two is achieved. Controlled natural ventilation (e.g. via wind catchers), rather than purely mechanical ventilation can also save energy associated with driving the air through the ventilation ducts in a HVAC (Heating, Ventilation and Air Conditioning). Green roof, light coloured finishes and vertical gardens help economically to insulate the structure. The 'building design led' approach leads to off-site construction principles or 'modern methods of construction' (MMC). This involves using new, sustainable materials and technologies which improve building performance (comfort, operation, fire, sound, thermal, etc.), speed, durability and economy of construction. The 3L principles in building design are long life (> 50 years), low energy and loose fit. The building has to be able to absorb and deal with climate change and change of use without major remodelling. Annexure 6.1 gives details of energy efficiency and Annexure 6.2 gives definitions of energy terms.

Green Building Resources

Some of the key attributes of green building are as under:

- Consideration of sustainability aspects in all phases of building design and planning
- Consideration of sustainability aspects during construction and production of building material
- Use of healthy and environment friendly building material and product
- Use of energy and water efficient system
- Use of construction and system which are easy to maintain and service
- Safeguarding of high functionality, flexibility and adaptability
- Safeguarding health and comfort of the users
- High aesthetic and urban design quality; high public acceptance
- Appropriate location with good access to public transportation services and network in a nutshell, sustainable buildings use less energy and water, generate less greenhouse gases, use materials more efficiently, and produce less waste than the conventional buildings.

Energy Conservation Building Code formulated by the Bureau of Energy Efficiency (BEE), provides for the establishment of state energy conservation agencies to plan and execute programs. It is a voluntary code for buildings with connected load of 500 kW and covers minimum requirements for buildings envelope performance as well as for mechanical systems and equipment, including heating, ventilation and air-conditioning (HVAC) system, interior and exterior lighting system, service hot water, electrical power and motors in order to achieve energy efficiency in different climatic zones of India.

Some new green resources and technologies include the following:

- Swales, bio-drainage, porous paving, rainwater harvesting, waste water recycling, dual piping
- Aerators for water fixtures
- Waterless urinals and other water saving systems
- Micro irrigation systems, xeriscaping
- Building Integrated Solar Photovoltaic, wind energy, parabolic solar cookers
- Green roof, vertical garden, urban farms
- High CoP chillers
- Wind towers /tunnels/chimney/ High Albedo materials
- Geothermal systems
- LED, CO_2 Sensors, Intelligent, Bionic Sensors and Controls
- Building Information systems
- Rapid walls, precast, prefabricated component
- Low emitting adhesives and sealants
- Insulation products
- High SRI coatings
- High performance glass, intelligent, insulating windows
- Certified wood, engineered timber product
- Nano-technology, nano-adhesives
- Carbon–negative cement and concrete

Building Resources

The built environment at all stages consumes energy and resources, and contributes to a significant amount of emissions. The Life Cycle Assessment (LCA) can be used to indentify the different environmental impacts arising throughout a system's life cycle; that is, all inputs and outputs are included, for example, extraction of raw materials, heat and water consumption, emissions to air, water and land. Low-energy building resources are the cornerstones of the durable, comfortable, energy efficient, affordable and healthy buildings.

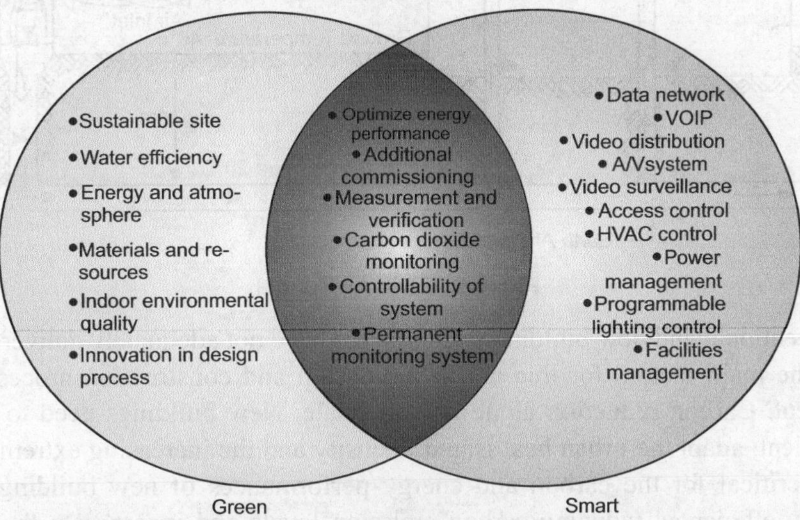

Fig. 6.7. Synthesis of Green and Smart Building Concepts

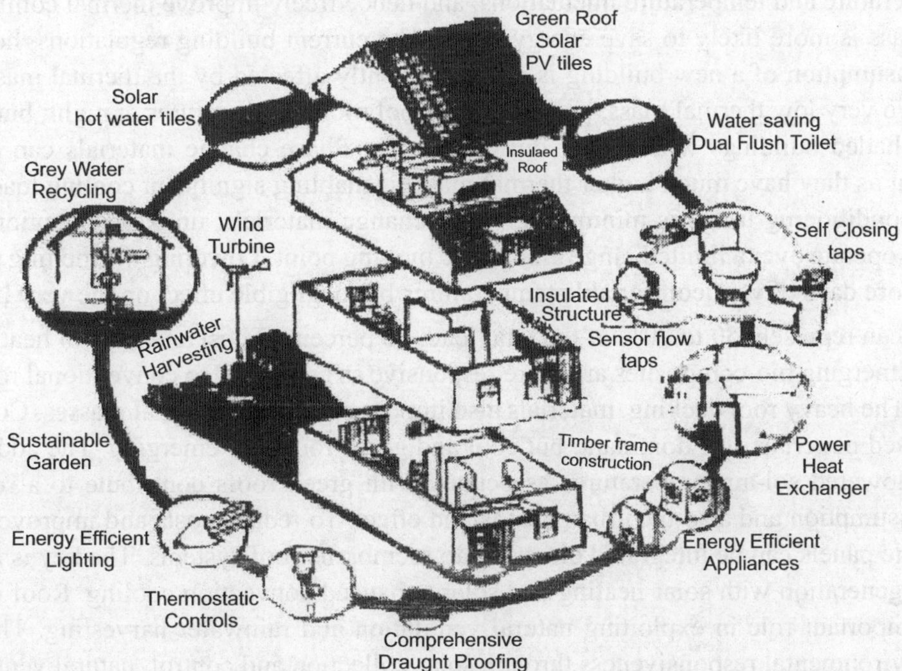

Fig. 6.8. Components of an Energy Efficient, Green Building

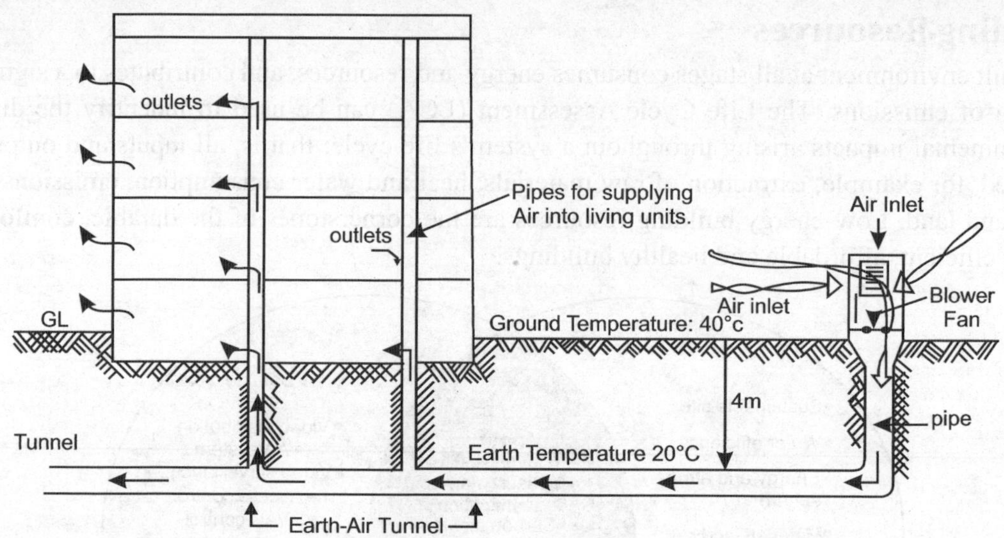

Fig. 6.9. Earth Air Tunnel

Some conventional and new building technologies have not adequately delivered performance as intended. The main factors for this are in the design and construction process, maintenance and management. Carbon reduction alone is inadequate. New buildings need to be designed to be energy efficient, adapt the urban heat island intensity and the increasing extreme temperatures. Legislation is critical for the carbon and energy performances of new buildings. Zero carbon involves energy efficiency, reducing carbon emission levels and incorporate the solutions such as renewable energy. Thermal mass can reduce space heating during the cool hours, and also the peak temperature and temperature fluctuations, and hence freely improve thermal comfort. Higher thermal mass is more likely to save energy. Under the current building regulations, however, the energy consumption of a new building is not significantly affected by the thermal mass. The stilt houses have very low thermal mass, providing for cool room temperatures at night; but high mass and well-shaded buildings work better during the day. Phase change materials can absorb and release heat as they have much higher thermal masses, enabling significant cooling load reduction if the air-conditioning usage is minimised. Phase change materials, unlike conventional thermal mass, only operate over a limited range around the melting point. Lowering the melting point could result in more days of very comfortable temperatures but negligible effect on the very hot days.

Roofs can represent 50 to 70% of the total load, 30 percent of cost and 50% of heat intake of a building. Emerging bio-composites are more responsive as compared to conventional roof decking materials. The heavy roof decking materials also impose significant thermal masses. Conventional asphalt-based materials still dominant, but cool and green roofs are emerging. The added thermal mass and lowered sol-air temperatures associated with green roofs contribute to a reduction in energy consumption and also the urban heat island effect. To reduce costs and improve durability, photovoltaic panels can be integrated directly into membrane roof systems. The key is to integrate electricity generation with solar heating and solar enhanced convection cooling. Roof design also plays an important role in exploiting natural ventilation and rainwater harvesting. The roof can express environmental responsiveness through solar collection and control, natural ventilation and rainwater harvesting.

Fig. 6.10. Common public spaces cause people to interact and come together

Source: *Design Principle—Safety and Surveillance, www.healthplaces.org.as.*

Some Tips for Reducing Carbon Footprint

- As every unit of electricity produced at the power station generates 0.82 kg of CO_2. By switching over to LED bulbs can reduce CO_2 emission by 5552 kg annually.
- Sensor lights in house, offices, bathroom and pathways can reduce annual CO_2 emission by 2542 kg.
- Reducing consumption of 1 ream of paper a month, reduces CO_2 emission by 75 kg.
- Composting food wastes can reduce CO_2 emission by 10604 kg annually.
- Water efficient faucets and dual flush toilets can conserve 10,000 liters of water per day/ 1000 sqm area, and can reduce annual CO_2 emission by 3718 kg.
- Every car goes off the road it reduces annual CO_2 emission by 1263 kg.
- Using the bus instead of personal car can reduce annual CO_2 emission by 24565 kg per 50 passengers.
- An LED lamp reduces annual CO_2 emission by 57 kg.
- To reduce the carbon footprint plant maximum number of trees as these absorb CO_2 and release O_2.

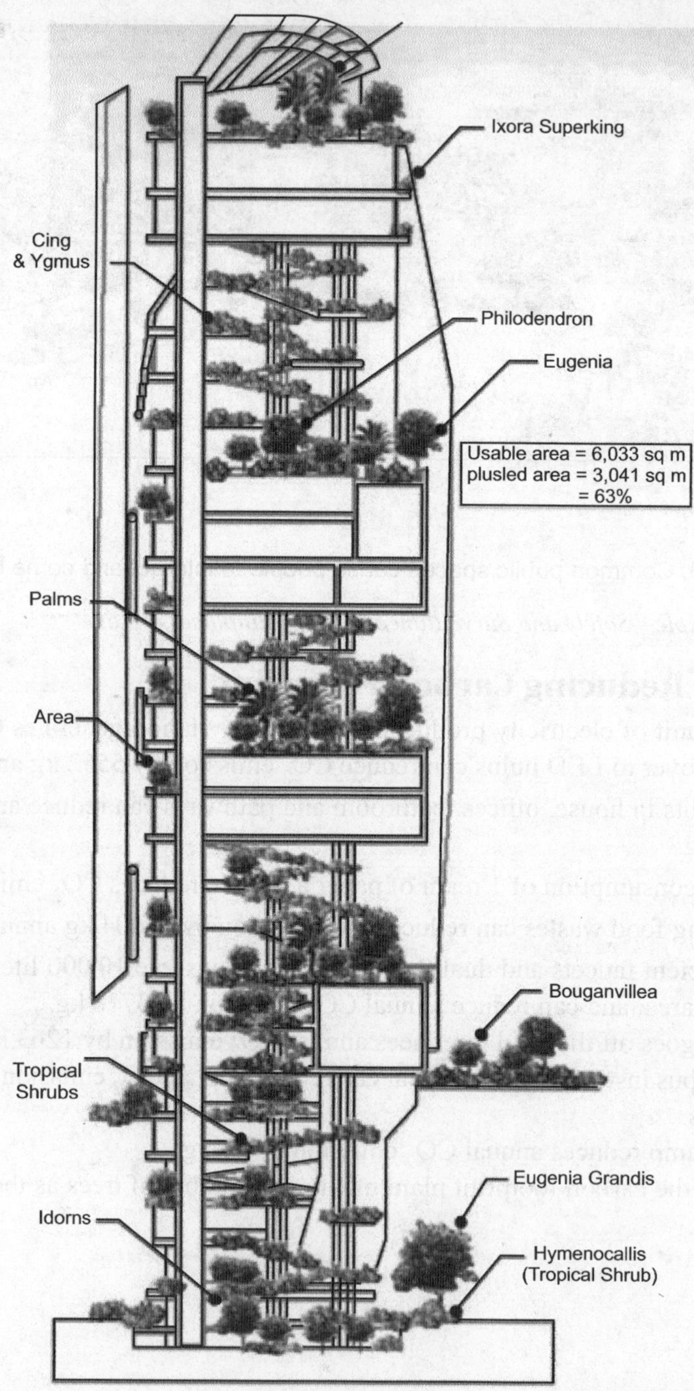

Fig. 6.11. Bio-climatic skyscraper: Vertical, spiral hanging gardens, terraces, courts, atriums, louvers, tiered sun shades and shaded envelope with bionic controls and mechanical systems. Architect Ken Yeang

Source: *Yeang Kenneth (1999) the Green Skyscraper, The Basis for Designing Sustainable Intensive Buildings, Prestel, New York*

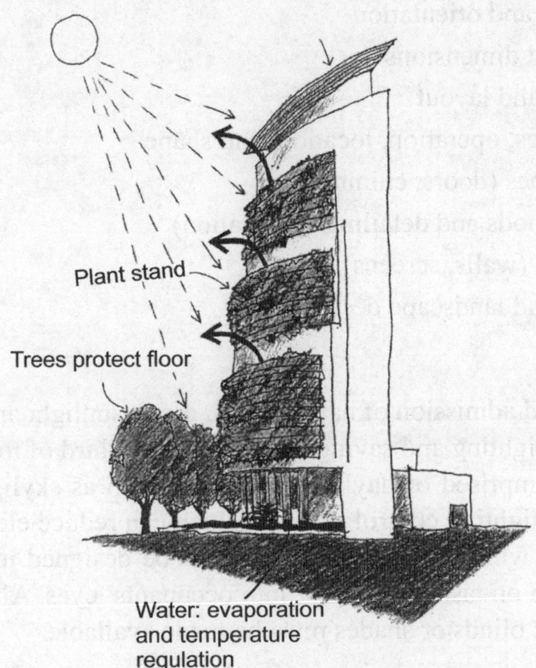

Fig. 6.12. Green wall: Street level trees shade the first three floors and vertical planting for upper floors (Credit Enrique Browne)

Source: *CTBUH (2014) Green Walls in High Building, Image Pub, Victoria.*

Natural Ventilation and Day Lighting

Natural ventilation is the process of supplying air and removing air from an indoor space without using mechanical systems. It refers to the flow of external air to an indoor space as a result of pressure differences arising from natural forces. There are two types of natural ventilation occurring in buildings: wind driven ventilation and buoyancy-driven ventilation. Wind driven ventilation arises from the different pressures created by wind around a building or structure, and openings on the perimeter. Buoyancy-driven ventilation occurs as a result of the directional buoyancy force that results from temperature differences between the interior and exterior. Since the internal heat gains which create temperature differences between the interior and exterior are created by natural processes including the heat from people, and wind effects are variable, naturally ventilated buildings are sometimes called "breathing buildings."

The impact of wind on a building affects the ventilation and infiltration rates through it and the associated heat losses or heat gains. Wind speed increases with height and is lower towards the ground due to frictional drag.

The impact of wind on the building form creates areas of positive pressure on the windward side of a building and negative pressure on the leeward and sides of the building. Thus building shape and local wind patterns are crucial in creating the wind pressures that will drive airflow through its apertures. Wind pressure will vary by its interaction with elements of the natural and built environment (trees, hills, buildings, structures), which effect thermal comfort conditions in the enclosed spaces. As such for comfort conditions the following design aspects need to be considered:

- Building location and orientation
- Building form and dimensions
- Indoor partitions and layout
- Window typologies, operation, location, and shape
- Other aperture types (doors, chimneys)
- Construction methods and detailing (infiltration)
- External elements (walls, screens)
- Urban planning and landscape design

Daylighting

Daylighting is the controlled admission of natural light, direct sunlight and diffused skylight into a building to reduce electric lighting and saving as much as one-third of total building energy costs. A daylighting system is comprised of daylight apertures, such as skylights and windows, along with a daylight-responsive lighting control system, which can reduce electric lighting power. The fenestration, or location of windows in a building, must be designed in such a way as to avoid the admittance of direct sun on task surfaces or into occupants' eyes. Alternatively, suitable glare remediation devices such as blinds or shades must be made available.

Daylighting requires an integrated design approach which involves decisions about the building form, siting, climate, building components (such as windows and skylights), lighting controls and lighting design criteria.

It involves carefully balancing heat gain and loss, glare control and variations in daylight availability. The following factors including window size and spacing, glass selection, the reflectance of interior finishes, the location of any interior partitions, etc. must be evaluated:

- Daylight-optimized building footprint
- Climate-responsive window-to-wall area ratio
- High-performance glazing
- Daylighting-optimized fenestration design
- Skylights (passive or active)
- Tubular daylight devices
- Daylight redirection devices
- Solar shading devices
- Daylight-responsive electric lighting controls
- Daylight-optimized interior design (such as furniture design, space planning, and room surface finishes).

A successful daylighting system will make use of the following devices and construction methods:

Exterior shading and control devices: In hot climates, exterior shading devices often work well to both reduce head gain and diffuse natural light before entering the work space. Examples of such devices include light shelves, overhangs, horizontal louvers, vertical louvers, and dynamic tracking of reflecting systems.

Glazing materials: The simplest method to maximize daylight within a space is to increase the glazing area. However, three glass characteristics need to be understood in order to optimize a fenestration system:

- U-value: represents the rate of heat transfer due to temperature difference through a particular glazing material.
- Shading coefficient: a ratio of solar heat gain of a given glazing assembly compared to double-strength, single glazing. A related term solar heat gain coefficient is beginning to replace the term shading coefficient.
- Visible transmittance: a measure of how much visible light is transmitted through a given glazing material.

Glazing can be easily and inexpensively altered to increase both thermal and optical performance. Glazing manufacturers have a wide variety of tints, metallic and low-emissivity coatings, and fritting available. Multi-paned lites of glass are also readily available with inert-gas fills, such as argon or krypton, which improve U-values. For daylighting in large buildings in most climates, consider the use of glass with a moderate-to-low shading coefficient and relatively high visible transmittance.

- Aperture location by simple side lighting strategies allow daylight to enter a space and can also serve to facilitate views and ventilation. Typically, the depth of daylight penetration is about two and one-half times the distance between the top of a window and the sill.
- Reflectance values from room surfaces will significantly impact daylight performance and should be kept as high as possible. It is desirable to keep ceiling reflectances over 80%, walls over 50%, and floors around 20%. Of the various room surfaces, floor reflectance has the least impact on daylighting penetration.

Integration with electric lighting controls: A successful daylighting design not only optimizes architectural features, but is also integrated with the electric lighting system. With advanced lighting controls, it is now possible to adjust the level of electric light when sufficient daylight is available. Three types of controls are commercially available:

- Switching controls: on-and-off controls that simply turn the electric lights off when there is ample daylight.
- Stepped controls: control individual lamps within a luminary to provide intermediate levels of electric lighting.
- Dimming controls: continuously adjust electric lighting by modulating the power input to lamps to complement the illumination level provided by daylight.

Other lighting control schemes: In addition to daylight controls, other electric lighting control strategies should be incorporated where they are cost effective, including the use of:

- Occupancy controls: using infrared, ultrasonic, or micro-wave technology, occupancy sensors respond to movement or object surface temperature and automatically turn off or dim down luminaries when rooms are left unoccupied. Typical savings have been reported to be in the 10% to 50% range depending on the application.
- Timers: are simply time clocks that are scheduled to turn lamps or lighting off on a set schedule. If spaces are known to be unoccupied during certain periods of time, timers are extremely cost-effective device.

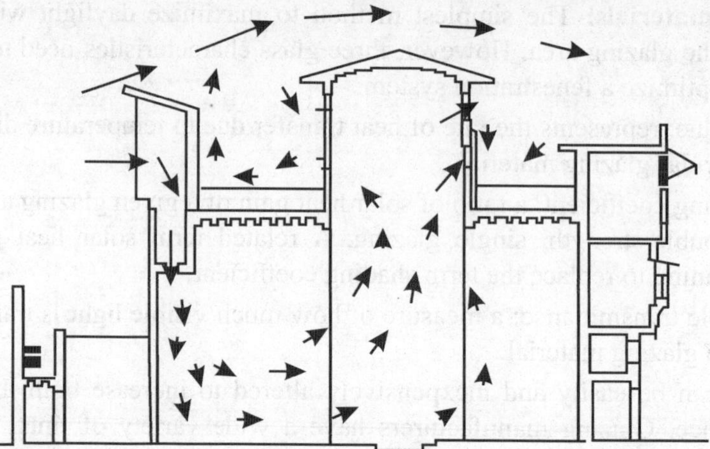

Fig. 6.13. Natural Cooling and Ventilation by Chimney Effect and Air Scoop

The use of a heat exchanger for recovering energy between the inlet and outlet flows can reduce the heating load by as much as 70%; when reasonable air-tightness with permeability of less than two is achieved. Controlled natural ventilation (e.g. via wind catchers), rather than purely mechanical ventilation can also save energy associated with driving the air through the ventilation ducts in a HVAC (Heating, Ventilation, and Air Conditioning). Internal air motion is important in indoor air quality as well as uniformity of thermal comfort. Adventitious leakage should not be reduced too far, for some domestic fuel-burning appliances rely on this to provide combustion air, and eliminating this can lead to lethal consequences. Although not yet a mature technology, phase-change material such as paraffin waxes, fatty acids, and hydrated salts are slowly being employed for night cooling. Using porous materials for providing dynamic insulation and for lowering heat gain seems promising.

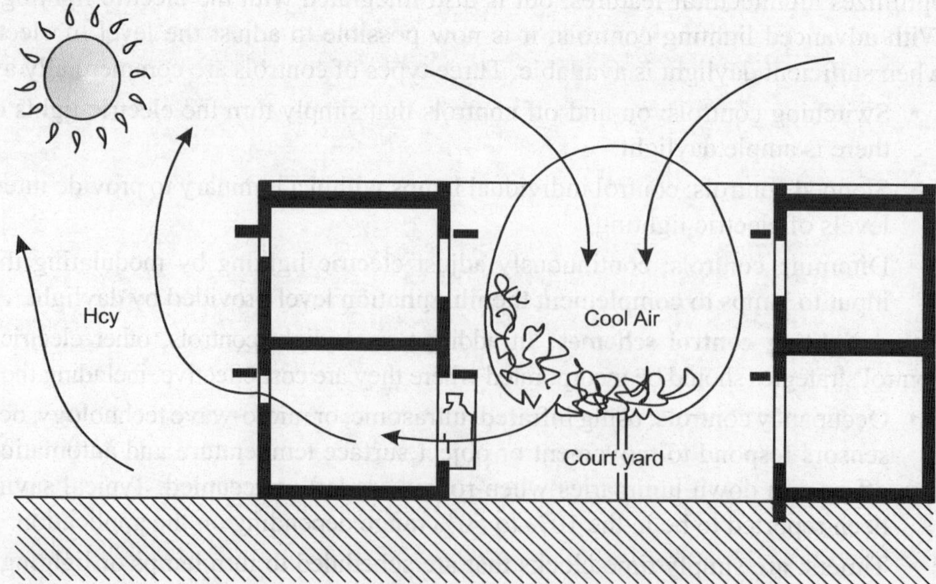

Fig. 6.14. Natural Cooling, Ventilation and Daylight by Central Courtyard

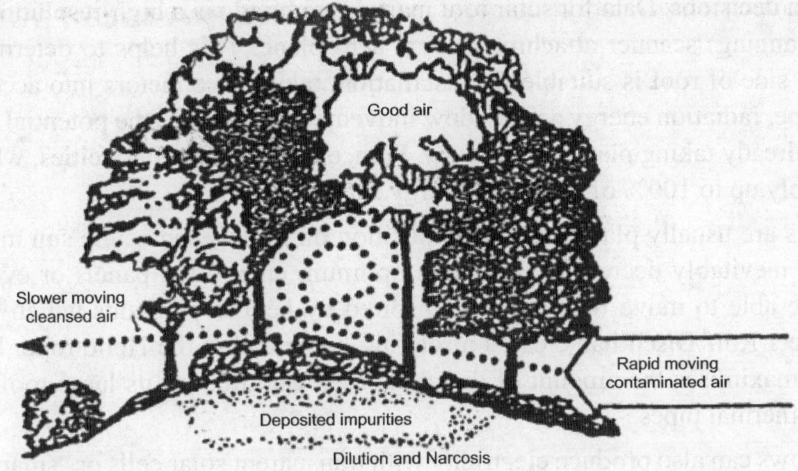

Fig. 6.15. Tree as a Green Air Filter

Some measures for lowering carbon retrofit include the insulation of roof, wall and floor, improving ventilation, insulating hot water tanks, switching to fluorescent or LED lighting, usage of high efficiency condensing boilers and renewable energy, installing double or triple glazing, and employing zoned energy with timers and sensors for energy savings.

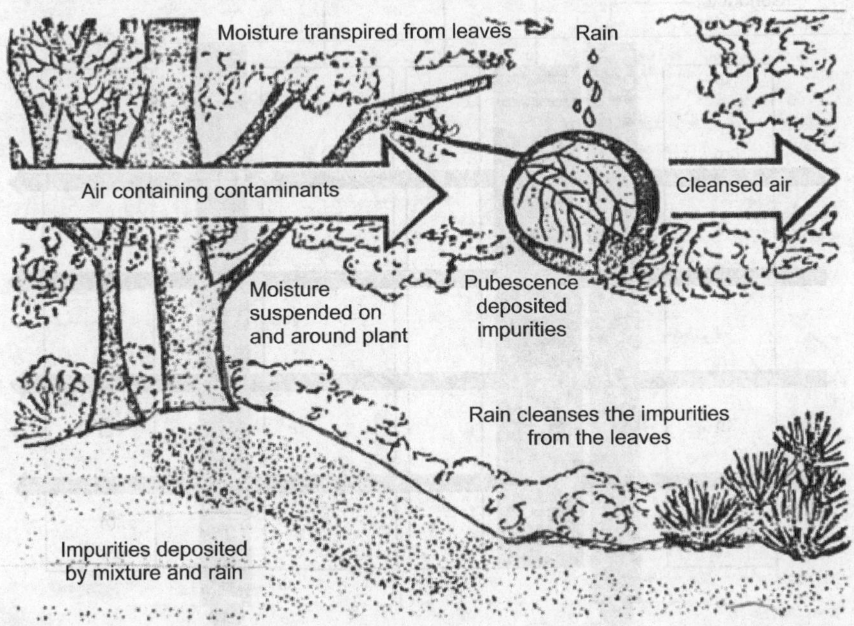

Fig. 6.16. Plants as Sinks of Air Pollution

Solar Renewable Energy

In spite of India receiving round the year sunshine and a dedicated ministry propagating the use of solar energy, it is difficult to gauge overall solar power capability on a regional or national scale. What is needed is that at local levels solar maps are made available for homeowners to help them in their installation decisions. Data for solar roof maps is captured via a high-resolution LIDAR (light detection and ranging) scanner attachment to an aero-plane. This helps to determine how much area and which side of roof is suitable for installation, taking five factors into account; roof area, orientation, slope, radiation energy and shadow movements. Mapping the potential for solar panels on rooftops is already taking place in Germany, France, Australia and US cities, where it has been possible to supply up to 100% of domestic energy needs.

Solar panels are usually placed at a fixed position on a roof, and as the sun moves across the sky, their yield inevitably decreases. To obtain optimum energy the panels or even the building itself, should be able to move with the sun. Inspired by heliotrope plants which follow the sun, German Architect Rolf Disch has created a rotating home called the Heliotrope. By tracking the sun, the house maximises the amount of direct sunlight captured by its large roof-mounted solar array and solar thermal pipes.

Solar windows can also produce electricity with transparent solar cells or "smart energy" glass, transparent photo voltaic cell that fits between two panes of a window. Although the costs are high, smart glass technology saves on air-conditioning and high energy cost. This is being used for Boeing 787 Dreamliner Jet planes and also in some high speed trains in Germany.

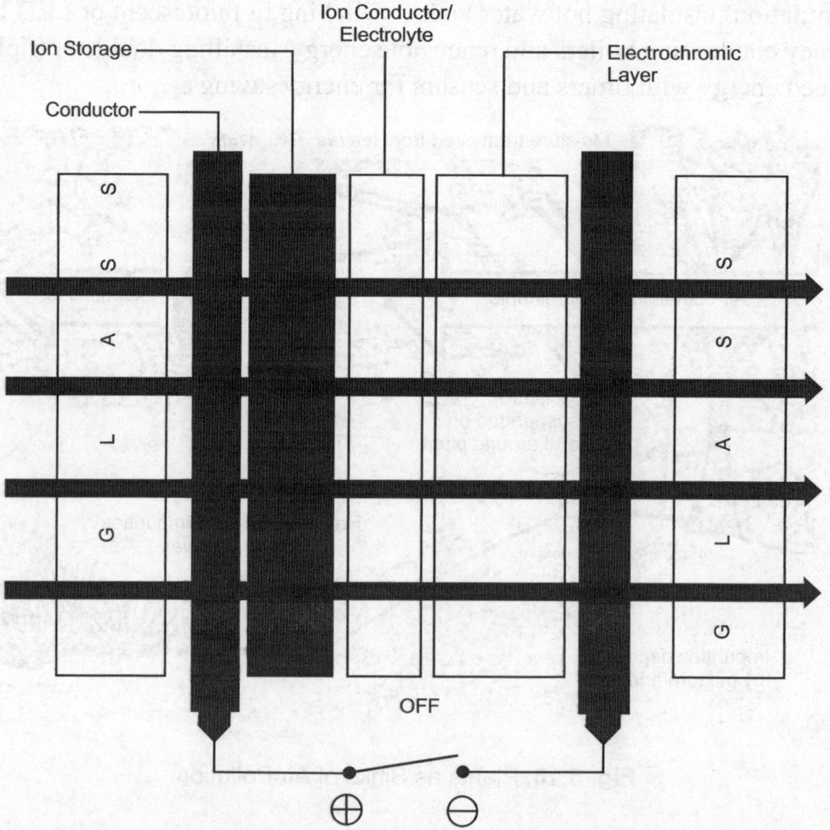

Fig. 6.17. The Electro-Chromic Smart Window, when switched off remains transparent and when switched on, a low volt of electricity makes the Electro-Chromic window translucent

Transparent insulation allows deep transmission of the incident solar flux. Advanced glazing can change demand using switchable thermo, photo- and electro-chromic coatings to reduce heat loss using low emissivity coatings and attached light shelves, and/or integrated mechanical devices such as shading devices and shutters. Double envelopes can provide solar ventilation, air preheating and/ or passive cooling, in addition to lowered thermal transmission and daylight control.

High-altitude wind power has advantage over solar energy, which is not always available. Research by California State University and Carnegie Institute at Stanford estimates that there is enough wind energy at altitudes between 7 and 12 km, where the jet stream blow to meet the global electricity demand a hundred times over. Due to their abundance and strength, jet stream winds to 15 km above the earth, provide tremendous potential to generate wind energy by installing turbines. In 2009, scientists had proposed an inflatable tower up to 20 km tall, which can carry people and payload into space cheaper than rockets and space shuttles. They proposed 100 wind turbines on a 15 km pneumatic tower made of Kevlar, a synthetic fibre with high tensile strength. India's total demand at present is 200 GW, that can be met by 10 floating turbines on the sea bed.

Carbon Negative Cements and RCC

Traditional cement production delivers green house gas, using fossil fuels to heat calcium carbonate to high temperatures, which then releases more CO_2 along with lime. Cement production currently accounts for around 2% of global man-made CO_2 emissions. In this light, several companies are developing carbon-negative cements that actually absorb CO_2 during their production and use. Super-heat steam is used to make cement from calcium magnesium carbonate particles that takes up large quantities of CO_2 as it hardens. By using magnesium oxide, carbonates and silicates, low-temperature process absorbs carbon dioxide during cement production.

In conventional RCC, steel is used which is produced by using huge kinetic energy and causes large amounts of greenhouse/carbon emissions. Innovative alternatives to steel reinforcement are being developed incorporating space-age technology for bridges and buildings that could reduce the carbon emission and steel consumption. Basalt fiber composite bars were recently used in reinforced concrete for a road bridge in Northern Ireland. Basalt fiber is incredibly strong–twice the tensile strength of regular steel–but just a quarter of its weight, and is also corrosion resistant.

Translucent concrete which allows daylight to pass through has recently been invented by Hungarian architect Aron Losonczi. Litracon contains thousands of optical fibres running parallel between the two main surfaces of the blocks. The manufacturers believe that a wall built from the light transmitting blocks could be several meters thick, as the fibres work up to 20 m without almost any loss of light. They can also be used for load bearing structures. Tiny glass fibres only constitute 4% of the blocks' overall volume and therefore do not affect their strength.

The University of Michigan in the US has developed self-healing concrete that fills up the cracks and cavities by itself. Small amounts of hydrated cement form a tiny calcium carbonate 'sear', sealing the cracks within a concrete structure. British scientists have developed a genetically modified bacterium which can knit together cracks in concrete structures by producing special glue. The microbe has been programmed to seal fine cracks in the concrete. Once in contact with surface, it produces a mixture of calcium carbonate and a bacterial glue which combines with the filamentous bacterial cells to "knit" the cracks together, ultimately hardening to the same strength as the surrounding concrete.

Nano-technology

The idea of nano-technology was born over 50 years ago, when Nobel Prize-winning physicist Richard Feynman noted that 'there's plenty of room at the bottom.' He envisaged tiny robots, who in turn would build even tinier robots, until you had a hoard of miniature solar-powered cyborgs that could manipulate individual atoms and molecules.

A nanometer is a billionth of a meter. This material is totally new and unique and there are already several of nano-scale products on the market, most used in sunscreens and electronic component. In construction, carbon nano-tubes and nano-coated metals may provide incredibly strong and corrosion-resistant building materials.

Some of the new building products are functionally gradient materials, polymers, carbon ceramic composites, diamond fibers, micro-infiltrated macro-laminated composites and nano-structured/ nano-composite materials. As a result of manipulating the microstructure and controlling the chemistry of cements, it is possible to develop more advanced cement matrix composites crossing the conventional boundaries of cementing materials. Among these could be strong macro-defect free cements; chemically bonded ceramics; and reactive powder concretes having very high ductility and compressive strength in the range of 200 to 800 MPA.

Recently scientists have developed a method which can turn cold water directly to steam using solar energy and light absorbing nano-particles. When submerged in water and exposed in sunlight, nano-particles in the solar steam device heat up very quickly due to their extremely small size. This makes the water vaporize instantly. The device has an efficiency of 24 percent, compared to 15 percent efficiency of solar panels. It can be used for water purification for heating and cooling and cooking (replacing electricity, CNG/LPG, etc.). The next generation of nanotech promises ultra-lightweight solar power films that could be painted onto exterior walls, energy-absorbing paint to replace bulky insulation, and printable, flexible electronic circuitry. Nano-tech adhesive is already in market, which is super-sticky in one direction but can be pulled off easily from another. Nanotech ultraviolet coatings for glass are invisible to humans but clearly visible to birds, so they won't fly into windows.

Researchers are working on self-healing nano-materials that can repair environmental or physical damage, and ways to 'mine' contaminated dirt to separate out the extract valuable and dangerous elements. Researchers in Japan have invented a new shock-resistant material that can withstand extreme temperatures. Made entirely of carbon, it can flow and stretch slowly like thick honey and spring back to its original form. It looks like a metal sponge that is porous. It is made from trillions of entangled carbon nano-tubes, when you stretch and release it, it can come back slowly to its original shape. Grown in a mixture of silicon, iron and water, the carbon nano-tubes are 5 nanometers in diameter, and can retain their form and function within a huge temperature range between minus 196°C and 100°C in an oxygen-free environment.

Dynamic nano-materials which can self-clean, heal and self-assemble along with environmental control, energy collection and storage are part of the future building resources.

Bio-mimicry and Bionics

Bio-mimicry is a field of science that investigates biological processes for effectively using them in the development of innovative building resources. It is a new field of emergence in material science in which lessons learnt from biology form the basis for application of novel technological and nano-electronics to civil/structural engineering. Bio-mimicry can help to create products and processes that are sustainable, perform well, save energy, reduce materials cost and redefine and eliminate waste. A fundamental biological principle is that of minimizing the use of materials in non-critical areas which can reduce weight and cost.

Bionics is the discipline that combines biology and technology. One example is the climbing robots that can walk up smooth glass facades like geckos, using a special micro-patterned tape on their feet. There are also beetles that can see infra-red light and form the model for sensors in fire alarms. Shark skin has inspired researchers to imitate its "rib-let" surface: the low level of drag of this surface reduces an aircraft's or ship's friction in the air or in water. An elephant's trunk was the model for the robot arm. The special feature is that the top of the trunk-like robot consists of sensitive gripper fingers with which it can hold even fragile items.

Biological processes have influenced material science on bio-deposition and bio-mineralization treatment (biology's ability to nucleate and grow inorganic materials), such as the microbial precipitation towards evolving a new technology for production of sustainable construction materials and processes for structural durability and strength.

An example is self-cleaning paint, Lotusan, which is based on lotus effect, the unique ability of lotus leaf surface to avoid wetting. The "lotus effect," is mainly due to the presence of micro-scale protuberances covered with waxy nano-crystals on their surface. Both the protuberances and the wax crystals make the surfaces of lotus super-hydrophobic in nature, which means water droplets easily roll over leaf surfaces taking contaminants and dust particles with them. This "self-cleaning property" has lead to find a new self-cleaning paint.

Honeycomb structures, biomes, lightweight stone veneer cladding products and pneumatic roofs have generated interesting architectural pieces. For example, branching tree-like roof supports at Stuttgart Airport, Tensairity beam structures, Jeddah Airport and Munich Olympics Stadium are based on a combination of cylindrical membranes filled with compressed air and supporting struts and cables. These systems combine rigid pneumatic beams integrated with opposing compressive and tensile forces. These have found applications in deployable structures, bridges, canopies and roof structures. Current areas of research in bio-mimicry include energy resource and efficiency, innovative building materials and structures, robotics, lightweight structures, etc.

Infrastructure Services and Systems

The performance of present urban services and systems needs to be reassessed with reference to environment, hygiene and public health. About 50 to 60 percent area in Indian cities do not have clean drinking water supply, drainage, effluent treatment, wastewater recycling, sanitation, sewerage and solid waste management facilities, leading to serious issues in public health. Widespread method of land filling for solid waste disposal is an environmental disaster. In order to safeguard public health the urban society has to adopt re-cycling (e.g. water, solid waste, land), regeneration (dilapidated, old areas), recovery (wastelands, encroached areas), restructuring (networks, land use, transport), recharging (traditional areas) and rejuvenation (river, water bodies, parks, etc.). Instead of conventional drainage, the concepts of micro-runoff, swales and bio-drainage need to be adopted. Ponds/reservoirs and sediments traps can be planned in the catchment zones on low-lying grounds. The concepts of watershed development, rainwater harvesting and conservation and recharging of groundwater need to be institutionalized and legalise. Various options can be explored for augmentation of physical infrastructure, such as technology upgradation, dual piping system, rain water harvesting, energy audit and exploring alternative sources of energy. Several technologies, such as decentralized and compact water treatment units, solar/aerobic/oxidation and root zone systems can be employed to purify potable water from the natural sources.

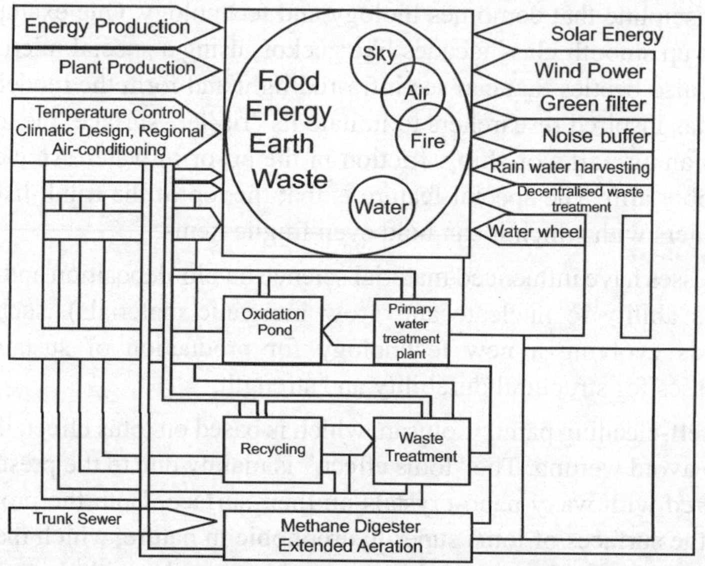

Fig. 6.18. Intelligent, Integrated and Inter-connected Infrastructure

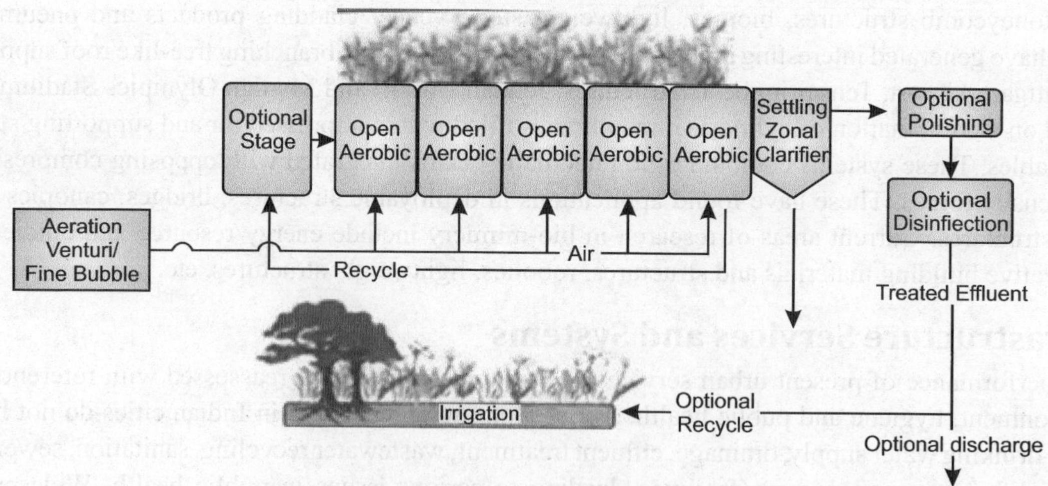

Fig. 6.19. Septic tank for first level treatment of black water

Source: *DUAC/M.N. Ashish Ganju, 2014, Aya Nagar Urban Development*

Planted Landscape

Landscape, earthen embankments, mounds, hedges, plantation, etc. act as the buffers to heat, wind and noise. Landscape planning of a site should be based upon the following principles:

- Preserve the existing vegetation
- Select each plant to serve its intended function
- Group trees to simulate natural stands; explore vertical gardening and roof scaping
- Use canopy trees to unify the site
- Install intermediate trees for under-story screening, windbreak and visual interest
- Install ground covers on the base plane to retain soil and soil moisture, define paths and use area and provide turf where required
- Utilise shrubs for supplementary baffles and screens
- Choose as a dominant theme tree a type that is indigenous, moderately fast growing, and able to thrive with little care
- Use secondary species to complement the primary planting installation and define the spaces of lesser magnitude
- Use trees to sheathe the traffic ways, but keep the sight line clear
- Use planting to reinforce the alignment of paths and roadways
- Install screen planting to hide unpleasant views, eliminate glare, and reduce noise level
- Provide evolving sequence of spaces to enclose and link the various uses
- Keep the planting simple
- Consider climate control in all landscape planting
- Complement the topographical forms
- Use plants as space definers and dividers

It should be carefully assessed how much area can be available for plantation after meeting the requirements of building, parking, and driveways. By skilful planning the landscape area and building can be merged together.

Medicinal, aromatic, flowering and fruit bearing trees adaptable to local climate, such as Neem, Citronella, Marigold, Floss flower, catnip, etc. should be chosen. Mosquitoes repellent plants and herbs like Lemon grass, Cedar, Basil, Marigold should be planted in open spaces of group housing projects near water bodies. For keeping environment free from mosquitoes certain fishes that feast upon mosquitoes, can be reared and maintained in small water bodies around the plants.

Fig. 6.20. Kitchen plants in trays and on a window

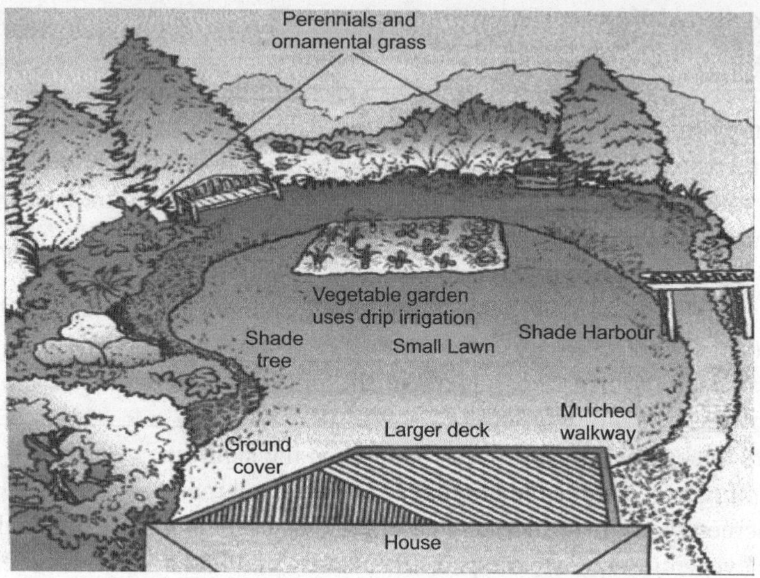

Fig. 6.21. Xeriscaping is landscaping in water stressed areas

Fig. 6.22. A geodesic dome as a glass house as a glass hours for urban agriculture

Fig. 6.23. Rendered view of the kiosk and bench

Fig. 6.24. View of seating with solar panel

Source: *DUAC/Sameer Mathur and RB Singh, 2014, Delhi Greenways*

Fig. 6.25. Landscape Court

Source: *DUAC/Sameer Mathur and R.B. Singh, 2014, Delhi Greenways*

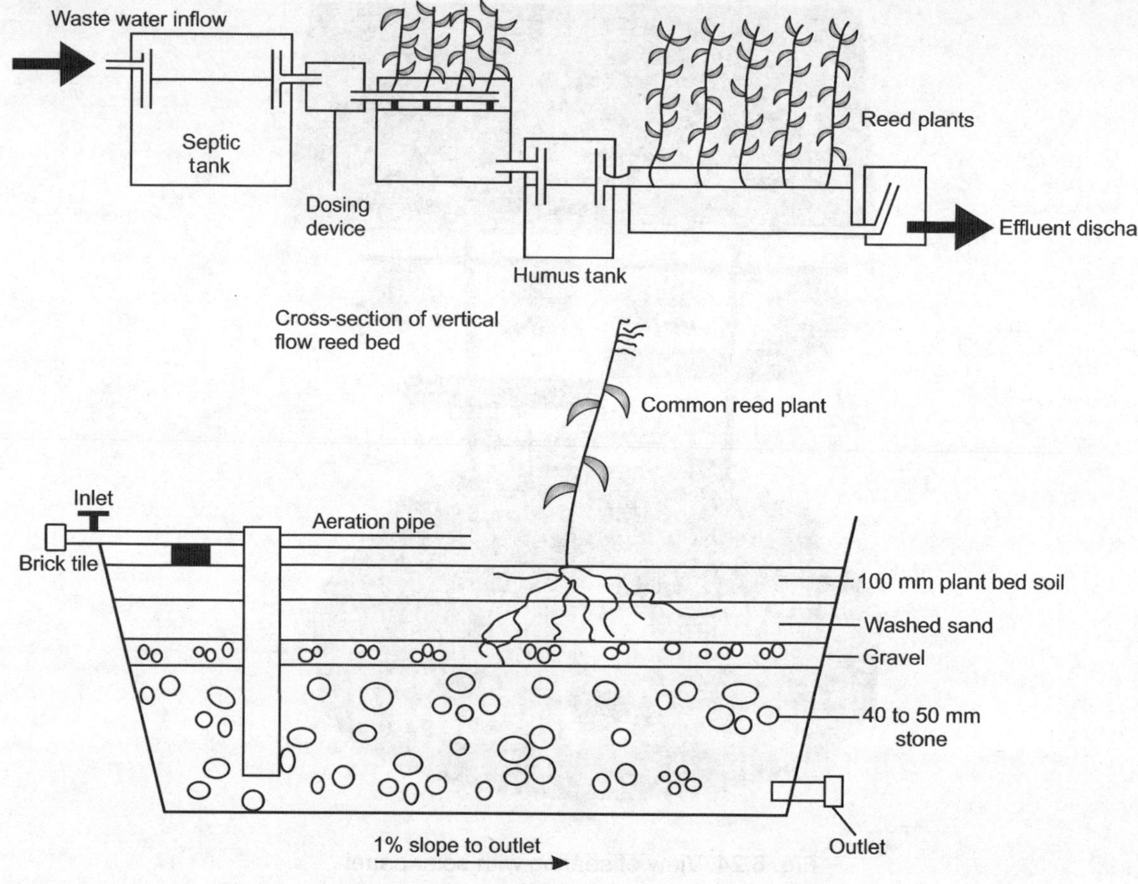

Fig. 6.26. Using reeds as constructed wetland

The idea of green building is a creative process that links the external and internal built environment with the human health and comfort, water, energy, bio-diversity and other natural resources. The endeavour is to create sustainable built environment which uses less energy and water, generates less green house gases, uses the resources and building materials more efficiently, and produces less wastes over the life cycle. The building design responds to the changing micro-climate and varying conditions of natural ventilation and light. The design obviates outdoor and indoor pollution, avoids use of materials with high energy demand and makes best use of space. It provides for water conservation, rainwater harvesting, recycling of wastes, explores sources of renewable energy, and the use innovative resources and of intelligent bionic systems. It is estimated that 60 per cent of buildings which will exist in the year 2030 are yet to be built. This provides a unique opportunity to redefine and reinvent the architecture and engineering for creating resource efficient, comfortable, healthy, intelligent, smart and sustainable buildings.

Suzlon One Earth

Pune is the headquarter of the Suzlon One Earth, which is named after the five elements of nature—air, aqua (water), tree (earth + wood), sky (ether space and sun). Some of the unique features of Suzlon One Earth building designed by architect Christopher Benninger are a storm and rainwater management system, efficient sunlight screening, low energy materials usage, etc. Sensors and modulating dampers are used in all densely occupied spaces for monitoring CO_2 levels. The sensors allow additional inflow of fresh air as soon as the CO_2 differential rises above the certified limit. Daylight sensors have been used in the work station area for optimized use of artificial lighting. Occupancy sensors control task lighting in unoccupied work stations, ensuring savings of about 20% of energy. The headquarter building is 100% powered by a combination of on-site and off-site renewable energy sources. Out of this, 7% of the total energy consumption comes from 18 on-site hybrid wind turbines, solar panels and photo voltaic cells and 93% of the remaining is from off-site wind turbines.

Instead of a regular tall, glass box structure it is spread out in the form of a campus. Three glass chimneys, facilitated by sky courts suck air out from the basement. The electricity converted from solar cells is used for producing hydrogen and oxygen in a compression electrolyser. Gas tanks store energy required for the season. The gases can be reconverted into the requisite energy. Hydrogen and oxygen are released by electrolysis. This offers new ways for a closed and pollution-free energy.

Fig. 6.27. Suzlon One Earth Building, Pune, Architect Christopher Benninger

Green Building Rating Systems

A green building is environmentally responsible and resource-efficient through its life-cycle: from design, construction, operation to maintenance, renovation and demolition. The following aspects are integrated in a green building : sustainable site planning, building envelope design, building system design, HVAC (heating, ventilation and air conditioning), lighting, electrical and water heating.

According to TERI, a green building aims to achieve reduced energy consumption without sacrificing comfort levels, reduced depletion of natural habitats and biodiversity, reduced air and water pollution with direct health benefits and reduced water consumption. A green building generates less wastes due to recycling and reuse, reduced pollution loads, increased user productivity and gives an enhanced image. Green building ratings are based upon these aspects.

The following are the main green building rating systems in India:

1. **Leadership in Energy & Environmental Design (LEED)** developed by US Green Building Council (USGBC) and adapted in India in collaboration with Indian Green Building Council (IGBC), is one of the most recognised rating system in India, LEED India rating system has been designed to suit the Indian construction industry, relevant to the local climate and regional practices.

2. **IGBC Green Homes Rating system:** IGBC Green Homes is a rating programme developed to address the residential sector across the country. Green concepts and techniques in the residential sector can help to address issues like handling of wastes, water efficiency, reduction in fossil fuel use in commuting, energy efficiency and conserving natural resources. Most importantly, these concepts can enhance occupants health, and well-being. A diverse group of stakeholders of the construction industry participate in the programme.

Salient measures to be adopted by the green buildings include the following:

- Preservation and reuse of top soil
- Reduced building footprints
- Internal Courtyards, Day Lighting and Ventilation
- Roof gardens to reduce heat-island impact
- Use of treated grey water for irrigation, air conditioning and cooling
- Root-zone treatment for wastewater
- Efficient Envelope
- Use of energy efficient air-conditioning systems
- On-site renewable energy
- Wind Towers
- Monitoring procedures, post occupancy
- Recycling of construction waste
- Use of materials with recycled content
- Use of Paints, Sealants, Adhesives with low VOC

3. **Green Rating Integrated Habitat Assessment (GRIHA)** developed by The Energy and Research Institute (TERI), is recognised by the Ministry of New and Renewable Energy (MNRE) as a national rating system, which takes into account ECBC and the National Building Code (NBC).

The GRIHA rating starts with the selection of the site that conforms to legal planning framework, the URDPFI (Urban and Regional Development Plans Formulation and Implementation) guidelines. The site must also be within half a kilometre distance from key amenities such as banks, place of worship, grocery shops, public transport terminals/ bus stops/metro halts, and the likes. The reason for this is that buildings may be energy-efficient in terms of design, but the people have to drive long distances to access the facilities. The GRIHA rating emphasises the site development considering the following:

- Trees are protected, preserved, or transplanted. Even if the trees are to be cut, trees of the same species are to be planted in a 1:3 ratio.
- Top soil is preserved so that it can be reused for landscape development.
- Construction activities (major civil works and structure) are organized in a manner that they are completed before the rains, so that activities like interior works and finishing can be carried out during the rains.

- All utilities are located in designated utility corridors that are easily accessible and are positioned right next to the vehicular/pedestrian pathways, so that no excavation or digging is required at a later date for repairs.

GRIHA attempts to quantify aspects such as:

- **Energy / power consumption** (in terms of electricity consumed in kWh per square meter per year)
- **Water consumption** (in terms of litres per person per day)
- **Waste generation** (in terms of kilograms per day, or litres per day)
- **Renewable energy** integration (in terms of kW of connected load)

The rating criteria of building is based on concept of following 5 'Rs':

- **Refuse** - to adopt trends, materials, technologies, products, etc. specially in areas where local substitutes/equivalents are available
- **Reduce** - the dependence on high energy products, systems, processes, etc.
- **Reuse** - materials, products, traditional technologies, so as to reduce the costs incurred in designing buildings as well as in operating them
- **Recycle** - all possible wastes generated from the building site during construction, operation and demolition
- **Reinvent** - engineering systems, designs, and practices that create green examples.

The design of a building should follow climate responsive strategies, such as:

- Solar path analysis to ensure that the building orientation is perfect.
- Minimal glazed areas on the side of extensive solar radiation.
- Optimal window to wall ratio (that is not having a 100% glazed facade).
- Ensuring the building openings are designed to allow the natural winds to flow through the building.
- Shading analysis to cut down on expenditure on high-performance glass. Lower performance glass, if used with shading strategies such as canopies and verandahs, can work just as well as very high performance glass without shading. However, very high performance glass also has a very high cost attached to it. Materials are selected carefully, such that they are available locally and not too much energy is wasted on their manufacturing as well as transportation. Constant coordination and interaction is maintained with all the consultants for proper design and execution.

The construction is carried out in a systematic manner and materials are stored carefully on the site. No material is wasted and all the waste products are safely discarded or recycled.

- The site should be barricaded so that air borne pollution does not affect the people around.
- The site should have a sedimentation basin or a pit to catch any water that may collect on site, especially during rains. This ensures that no water borne pollutants leak into the aquifer or the surrounding sites. Waste and water management strategies are formulated such that the building takes care of its own waste through either recycling or reuse methods.

- Labour is brought onto the site and provided with proper safety, health, and sanitation conditions.
- The energy systems, such as lighting and space conditioning, are designed after considering all the natural options available such as natural light and natural ventilation. The system is designed in an optimal way so as to minimize the system size and save capital cost, as well as to minimize the operational energy use and the operational costs. Electrical systems, such as cabling, transformers, and generator sets, are also downsized because the demand of the building is reduced. Wherever possible, solar thermal systems, solar photovoltaic systems, wind and biomass, supplement buildings' energy demand.

The GRIHA rating system of green building stresses on passive solar techniques for optimising indoor thermal comfort. The rating system sets benchmarks for air-conditioned and non-air-conditioned buildings in five climatic zones, namely hot-dry, warm-humid, composite, temperate, and cold.

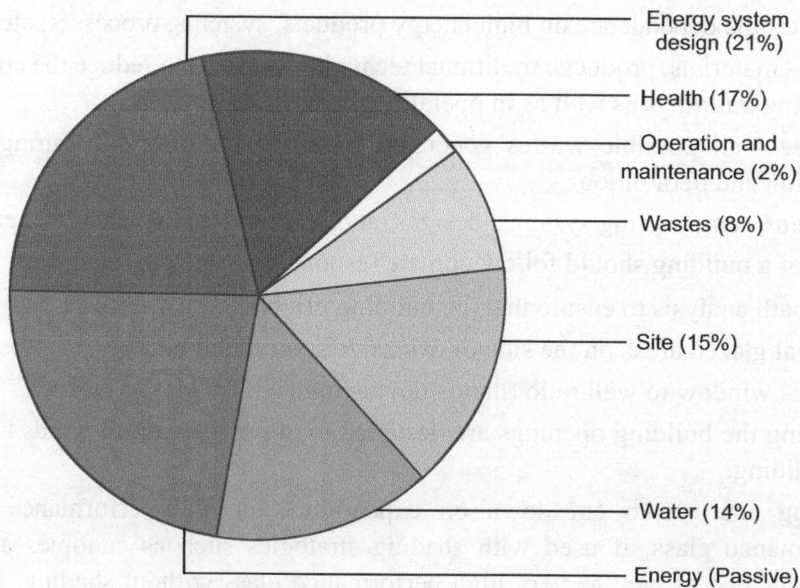

Fig. 6.28. Weightage allocated to various GRIHA criteria

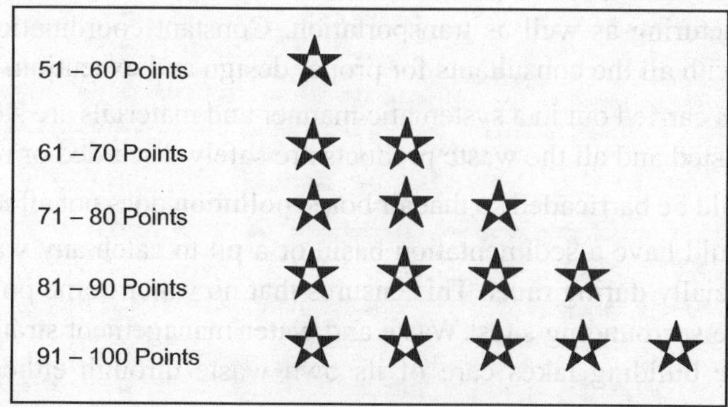

Fig. 6.29. GRIHA Star Rating

In order to address energy efficiency, GRIHA encourages optimization of building design to reduce conventional energy demand and further optimize energy performance of the building within the specified comfort limits. A building is assessed on its predicted performance over the entire life cycle from inception through operation.

GRIHA comprises a set of 34 criteria that address sustainable site planning, optimized energy performance, use of efficient materials and construction practices, integration of water and waste management strategies, indoor environmental quality, and health, comfort, and safety of human beings. It is a 100+4 point system where differential weightage is allocated on various criteria :

Table 6.2. Criteria for GRIHA Rating

	Criteria	Points
Criteria 1	Site Selection	1
Criteria 2	Preserve & protect landscape during construction	5
Criteria 3	Soil conservation (post cons)	4
Criteria 4	Design to include existing site features	2
Criteria 5	Reduce hard paving on site	2
Criteria 6	Enhance outdoor lighting system efficiency and use renewable energy system	3
Criteria 7	Plan utilities efficiently and optimise on site circulation efficiency	3
Criteria 8	Provide minimum level of sanitation/safety facilities	2
Criteria 9	Reduce air pollution during construction	2
Criteria 10	Reduce landscape water requirement	3
Criteria 11	Reduce building water use	2
Criteria 12	Efficient water use during construction	1
Criteria 13	Optimise building design to reduce energy demand	6
Criteria 14	Optimise energy peformance of building within specified comfort	12
Criteria 15	Utilisation of flyash in building structure	6
Criteria 16	Reduce volume, weight and time of construction by adopting efficient technology	4
Criteria 17	Use low-energy material in interiors	4
Criteria 18	Renewable energy utilization	5
Criteria 19	Renewable energy based hot water system	3
Criteria 20	Waste water treatment	2
Criteria 21	Water re-cycle & re-use (including rainwater)	5
Criteria 22	Reduction in waste during construction	2

Criteria 23	Efficient waste segregation	2
Criteria 24	Storage and disposal of waste	2
Criteria 25	Resource recovery from waste	2
Criteria 26	Use of low VOC paints/adhesives/sealants	4
Criteria 27	Minimize ozone depleting substances	3
Criteria 28	Ensure water quality	2
Criteria 29	Acceptable outdoor and indoor noise levels	2
Criteria 30	Tobacco and smoke control	1
Criteria 31	Universal accessibility	1
Criteria 32	Energy audit and validation	1
Criteria 33	Operations and maintenance protocol for electrical and mechanical equipment	2 Mandatory
	Total Score	100
Criteria 34	Innovation (4) Total	104

Source: *TERI (2010) Green Rating Integrated Habitat Assessment*

GRIHA Thresholds

In some projects (especially smaller ones), systems required are considerably small, such as Hot water requirement < 500 litres per day, Waste water recycling and reuse (< 10 KL per day), Solid waste recycling and reuse, particularly organic waste < 100 kg per day.

In such cases, investing in technology intensive solutions may unnecessarily lead to cost increments with poor returns. At a smaller scale it may be judicious to adopt conventional systems/ small-scale resource-efficient systems and technologies.

Site Planning

- Select appropriate site
- Ensure sedimentation/erosion control/save trees (if there)/plant more trees
- Design as per site conditions
- Air pollution control
- Ensure safety and health of construction workers
- Control hard paving / run off/ manage utilities efficiently
- Use energy efficient outdoor lighting fuse RE based lighting
- Use trees and native species for landscaping to reduce landscape water demand over GRIHA benchmark by 40%.

Energy/Water/Waste

- Save 25% water demand on GRIHA benchmarks (based on National Building Code)
- Save water in construction
- Follow mandatory provisions of ECBC (in case of air conditioned buildings)
- Meet prescriptive shading norms of ECBC, provide daylight, avoid over-design of artificial lighting
- Reduce energy performance index from GRIHA benchmark by 10%
- Provide 1% equivalent connected load of lighting and HVAC through RE power (meet10% lighting consumption through RE power)
- Use fly ash/other industrial waste based products in minimum two of the following three areas: (structure/walling/finishing)
- Recycle water and reuse 25% of treated waste water (if waste water quantity is higher than 10 kl/day)
- Segregate and store waste appropriately.

Small Versatile Affordable GRIHA (SVAGRIHA)

SVAGRIHA (Small Versatile Affordable GRIHA) was jointly developed by ADaRSH and TERI. ADaRSH (Association for Development and Research Sustainable Habitats) was founded jointly by TERI (The Energy and Resources Institute, New Delhi) and MNRE (Ministry of New and Renewable Energy, Government of India) along with the experts. GRIHA (Green Rating for Integrated Habitat Assessment) is promoted by ADaRSH as a design and evaluation tool for green buildings and habitats. Svagriha has been designed as an extension of GRIHA and has been specifically developed for projects with built-up area less than 2500 sqm. Svagriha can help in design and evaluation of individual residences, small offices and commercial buildings. The rating comprises of only 14 criteria (instead of 34 of GRIHA) and the interface comprises simplified calculators. These can be filled using information from construction drawings like areas and quantities of materials, by an architect handling the project. Once completed, the tool will tell the consultant the number of points that they are able to achieve in that particular criterion and provide recommendations in order to improve the environmental performance of the building.

Rating Process

- Registration of a project with the ADaRSH
- Submission of completed calculations, drawings and other documents as required (quantity estimates) to ADaRSH
- Assessent/review as per Svagriha
- Site visit and due diligence check post-construction (mandatory)
- Evaluation by GRIHA certified evaluator
- Award of rating

The site audit to check compliances is verified at the completion stage. In order to achieve a Svagriha rating each project must achieve a certain number of points in each category.

Table 6.3. SVAGRIHA Criteria to evaluate the performance of projects

Criterion number	Criterion	Points
1	Reduce UHIE and maintain native vegetation cover on site	6
2	Passive architectural design and system	4
3	Good fenestration design reducing direct heat gain and glare while maximising daylight penetration	6
4	Efficient artificial lighting system	2
5	Thermal efficiency of building envelope	2
6	Use of energy efficient appliances	3
7	Use of renewable energy on site	4
8	Reduction in building and landscape water demand	5
9	Rainwater harvesting	4
10	Generate resource from waste	2
11	Reduce embodied energy of building	4
12	Use of low-energy materials in interiors	4
13	Adoption of green lifestyle	4
14	Innovation	2
	Total	50

Based on the number of points the project achieves, the award is given as mentioned below:

Table 6.4. SVAGRIHA Award of rating as per points earned

Sub-group	Maximum points	Minimum points to be achieved
Landscape	6	3
Energy	21	11
Water and wastes	11	6
Materials	8	4
Others	4	1

Points achieved	Rating
25-30	★
31-35	★★
36-40	★★★
41-45	★★★★
46-50	★★★★★

Green Roads Rating System

Green Roads rating system was developed by researchers in Washington State in 2007. It is based on assigning point values to a road much like the United States Green Building Council's (USGBC) LEED rating system. Green Roads system was modelled closely after the LEED green building rating system TM 2.0. Table below shows the system points model for the Green Roads rating system and it has been found that the system can be implemented with promising outcomes. It indicates the critical aspects of design materials storm water management energy and construction to which impact the green road. Green Highway Association India (GHAI) has undertaken studies to formulate the general characteristics suitable to the Indian environment and to promote the use of green aspects of highways wherever possible. This association and its branches work at the project, Taluka (sub-district), district, state, and national levels to promote the concept of green highways after formulating the characteristics and rating methodology for green highways. A rating system must be designed for each region of India to evaluate regional needs and then assign a point scale accordingly.

Table 6.5. Green Roads Rating System

Category	Description	Credits available	Total credits
Sustainable Design (SD)	SD-1: Alignment Selection	1	10
	SD-2: Context Sensitive Design	1	
	SD-3: Traffic Flow Improvement	1	
	SD-4 Safety Improvement	2	
	SD-5 Long Life Pavement Design	3	
	SD-6 Public Input	2	
Materials & Resource (MR)	MR-1: Construction Waste	1	11
	MR-2: Reuse of Pavement	2	
	MR-3: Recycled Content	4	
	MR-4: Pavement Life Cycle	3	
	MR-5: Regionally Produced Material	1	
Storm Water Management (SM)	SM-1: Stormwater Management	2	8
	SM-2: Runoff Treatment	1	
	SM-3: Permeable Area	3	
	SM-4: Innovative Stormwater	2	

Energy & Environment (EE)	EE-1: Cool Pavement	1	12
	EE-2: Quitet Pavement	3	
	EE-3: Light Pollution	1	
	EE-4: Lighting Efficiency	1	
	EE-5: Eco-Connectivity	1	
	EE-6:Visual Quality	1	
	EE-7: Pedestrian Access	1	
	EE-8: Bicycle Access	1	
	EE-9: Environmental Management	2	
Construction Activity (CA)	CA-1: Reduce Diesel Emissions	1	9
	CA-2: Reduce Fossil Fuel	1	
	CA-3: Temporary Stormwater	1	
	CA-4: Noise Mitigation Planning	1	
	CA-5: Paving Emissions	1	
	CA-6: Construction Quality	2	
	CA-7: Quality Process	2	
Innovation (IN)	IN Innovation	4	4

Total Credits = 54; Certified = 19; Silver = 26; Gold = 32; Evergreen = 38+

Source : Bryce, J. M. (2008). Developing Sustainable Transportation Infrastructure: Exploring the Development and Implementation of a Green Highway Rating System. ASTM International. University of Missouri. http://www.wiseintern.org/journal/2008/James Bryce Final. pdf

Leadership in Energy and Environmental Design (LEED)

The Leadership in Energy and Environmental Design (LEED) Green Building Rating System is a voluntary standard for developing high-performance, sustainable buildings. Members of the U.S. Green Building Council (USGBC), representing all segments of the building industry, developed LEED and continue to contribute to its evolution. The USGBC works to promote buildings that are environmentally responsible, profitable, and healthy places to live and work. LEED standards are currently available for the following. New commercial construction and major renovation projects (LEED-NC). Existing building operations (LEED-EB)

- Commercial interiors projects (LEED-CI)

Standards are under development for:

- Core and shell projects (LEED-CS); Neighbourhood developments (LEED-ND); and Homes (LEED-H).

According to the USGBC, LEED was created to:

- Define "green building" by establishing a common standard of measurement;
- Promote integrated, whole-building design practices;
- Recognize environmental leadership in the building industry;
- Stimulate green competition;
- Raise consumer awareness of green building benefits; and
- Transform the building market.

LEED defines a quantifiable threshold for green building and provides a tool to promote and guide comprehensive and integrated building design. LEED is self-evaluating and self-documenting, but not self-certifying. Certification is done solely by USGBC. The LEED Green Building Rating System new commercial construction and major renovation projects (LEED-NC) has four levels of certification, based upon the number of points achieved by a project out of a total of 69 point :

LEED certified : 26 to 32 points, or 40% of base points

Silver : 33 to 38 points, or 50% of base points

Gold : 39 to 51 points or 60% of base points

Platinum : 52 plus 80% of base points

Table 6.6. Project Score Card Components

1. Sustainable site	**Possible points 14**
Prereq I Erosion and Sedimentation Control	0
Credit 1 Site Selection	1
Credit 2 Urban Redevelopment	1
Credit 3 Brownfield Redevelopment	1
Credit 4.1 Alternative Transportation, Public Transportation Access	1
Credit 4.2 Alternative Transportation, Bicycle Storage, and Changing Rooms	1
Credit 4.3 Alternative Transportation, Alternative Fuel Refuelling Stations	1
Credit 4.4 Alternative Transportation, Parking Capacity	1
Credit 5.1 Reduced Site Disturbance, Protect or Restore Open Space	1
Credit 5.2 Reduced Site Disturbance, Development Footprint	1
Credit 6.1 Stormwater Management, Rate, and Quantity	1
Credit 6.2 Stormwater Management,Treatment	1
Credit 7.1 Landscape and Exterior Design to Reduce Heat Island	1

Credit 7.2 Landscape and Exterior Design to Reduce Heat Islands and Roof Heating	1
Credit 8 Light Pollution Reduction	1

2. Water Efficiency	**5**
Credit 1.1 Water-Efficient Landscaping, Reduce by 50%	1
Credit 1.2 Water-Efficient Landscaping, no Potable Water Use for irrigation	1
Credit 2 Innovative Wastewater Technologies	1
Credit 3.1 Water-Use Reduction, 20% Reduction	1
Credit 3.2 Water-Use Reduction, 30% Reduction	1
3. Energy and Atmosphere	**17**
Prereq 1 Fundamental Building System Commissioning	0
Prereq 2 Minimum Energy Performance	0
Prereq 3 CFC Reduction in HVAC&R Equipment	0
Credit 1.1 Optimize Energy Performance, 20% New 10% Existing	1
Credit 1.2 Optimize Energy Performance, 30% New 20% Existing	1
Credit 1.3 Optimize Energy Performance, 40% New 30% Existing	1
Credit 1.4 Optimize Energy Performance, 50% New 40% Existing	1
Credit 1.5 Optimize Energy Performance, 60% New 50% Existing	1
Credit 2.1 Renewable Energy, 5%	1
Credit 2.2 Renewable Energy, 10%	1
Credit 2.3 Renewable Energy, 20%	1
Credit 3 Additional Commissioning	1
Credit 4 Ozone Depletion	1
Credit 5 Measurement and Verification	1
Credit 6 Green Power	1
4. Materials and Resources	**13**
Prereq 1 Storage and Collection of Recyclables	0
Credit 1.1 Building Reuse, Maintain 75% of Existing Shell	1
Credit 1.2 Building Reuse, Maintain 100% of Existing Shell	1
Credit 1.3 Building Reuse, Maintain 100% of Shell and 50% Non-shell	1
Credit 2.1 Construction Waste Management, Divert 50%	1
Credit 2.2 Construction Waste Management, Divert 75%	1
Credit 3.1 Resource Reuse, Specify 5%	1
Credit 3.2 Resource Reuse, Specify 10%	1
Credit 3.2 Resource Reuse, Specify 25%	1

Credit 4.1 Resource Reuse, Specify 25%	1
Credit 4.2 Resource Reuse, Specify 50%	1
Credit 5.1 Local/Regional Materials, 20% Manufactured Locally	1
Credit 5.2 Local/Regional Materials, 20% or above Harvested Locally	1
Credit 6 Rapidly Renewable Materials	1
Credit 7 Certified Wood	1
5. Indoor Air Quality (IAQ) and Environment	**15**
Prereq Minimum IAQ Performance	1
Prereq 2 Environmental Tobacco Smoke (ETS) Control	0
Credit 1 Carbon Dioxide (CO_2) Monitoring	1
Credit 2 Increase Ventilation Effectiveness	1
Credit 3.1 Construction IAQ Management Plan, During Construction	1
Credit 3.2 Construction IAQ Management Plan, Before Occupancy	1
Credit 4.1 Low-Emitting Materials, Adhesives and Sealants	1
Credit 4.2 Low-Emitting Materials, Paints Credit	1
Credit 4.3 Low-Emitting Materials, Carpet Credit	1
Credit 4.4 Low-Emitting Materials, Composite Wood	1
Credit 5 Indoor Chemical and Pollutant Source Control	1
Credit 6.1 Controllability of Systems, Perimeter	1
Credit 6.2 Controllability of Systems, Nonperimeter	1
Credit 7.1 Thermal Comfort, Comply with ASHRAE 55-1992	1
Credit 7.2 Thermal Comfort, Permanent Monitoring System	1
Credit 8.1 Daylight and Views, Daylight 75% of Space	1
Credit 8.2 Daylight and Views,Views for 90% of Space	1
6. Innovation and Design Process	**5**
Credit 1.1 Innovation in Design: Specific Title	1
Credit 1.2 Innovation in Design: Specific Title	1
Credit 1.3 Innovation in Design: Specific Title	1
Credit 1.4 Innovation in Design: Specific Title	1
Credit 2 LEED™Accredited Professional	1

Some other building rating systems

BREEAM: Developed in Britain, scores are given on health, energy consumption, water consumption, environmental treatment of site, etc. of buildings and rating given are: fail, pass, good, very good and excellent.

DCBA: Developed in Holland, the DCBA method categorises buildings into following categories:

1. Autonomous zero energy impact
2. Little environmental impact
3. Conventional construction with reduced environmental damage
4. Conventional construction

DCBA aims to reduce energy consumption of new buildings by 25%, water consumption by 10% and greenhouse gas emission significantly.

BEAT 2000: Developed in Scandinavia, it uses a software tool known as Building Environmental Assessment Tool. It combines a database on values of life-cycle, energy sources and greenhouse gas emissions.

Gronlund LCA tool software: Developed in Finland, it gives data on life cycle of buildings.

HQF system: Developed in France, HQF is a continuously evolving tool and not an assessment tool. It has four main themes:

- environmental construction,
- environmental management
- comfort
- health

Minergie: Developed in Switzerland, Minergie aims to reduce CO_2 emission by 10% Minergie aims to promote rational use of energy, use of renewable energy services, reduced pollution, etc. For new buildings, it sets standards of < 45 KWh/m^2/year of heating consumption and for pre1990 buildings it is < 90 KWh/m^2/year. For electricity, both for old and new buildings, Minergie proposes < 15 KWh/ m^2/year.

RT 2000: Developed in France, it is mandatory for all new buildings since 2001. It aims at reduced energy consumption of buildings by 20%. It is reported that most old buildings' consumption is around 250 KWh/m^2/year and retrofitting of these buildings is mandatory.

Low Energy House: Developed in Germany, the Low Energy House System recommends consumption of energy as under:

< 70 KWh/m^2/year for detached houses

< 60 KWh/m^2/year for terraced houses

< 55 KWh/m^2/year for apartments

BASIX: Developed in Australia, it is a web-based assessment tool to calculate water and energy efficiency of new housing.

Assessment Indicators

Based on the findings, using the outlined assessment categories, indicators, and parameters and their weightage coefficient, a spread sheet can be prepared. This system can be classified as a criteria-based tool that can be defined as a system of assigning point-values to a selected number of assessment items on a certain scale levels involving various levels of satisfaction like partially satisfied, satisfied, and not satisfied. The scope of this system includes the residential buildings and their immediate surroundings. This system can be implemented during the preliminary stages of design, considering building life cycle at different stages. This system defines environmental, economical, social and other aspects of sustainability. Thus, the assessment items are classified at three levels; category level, indicator level, and parameter level.

A computer program can be prepared to estimate the overall level of greenness of the structure. A simple program can also be used applying various options available in the popular MSExcel software. The excel spread sheet may consist of the main sheet, which includes information like building site, location, climatic regions and the main green categories. Further, seven other sheets may be prepared for seven categories; site, energy efficiency, water efficiency, materials, indoor environmental quality, waste and pollution, and cost and economics. Each sheet related to one of the categories includes its indicators and parameters with their weights derived from the AHP method by using a software or other methodology. The total score of each category comes by multiplying the score of each parameter where three ordinal scales are used to indicate the applicability of greenness for each parameter and thereafter the score result will be multiplied by the specific parameter weight. The total sum of each parameter will appear on the indicator level and finally the sum of indicator level will be shown on the category level with their relative weights. These values will be shown on the main result-sheet, indicating the contribution of each category and the summation of all weights. The final results can be presented graphically showing the overall level of greenness of the building. The result obtained in each assessment item level can be calculated by the following formula :

Parameter result (Rp) = Parameter weightage (Wp) × Parameter Score (Sp) ...(1)

Indicator result (Ri) = Indicator weightage (Wi) × Indicator score (Si) ...(2)

Category result (Rc) = Category weightage (Wc) × Category score ...(3)

Total assessment result = ΣRc ...(4)

Sp = (I) or (0.5) or (0) ...(5)

Si = ΣRp ...(6)

SC = ΣRi ...(7)

Table 6.7. Assessment Categories and Indicators (CEPAS, BREEAM and CASBEE)

	Assessment categories	Assessment indicators
1.	Site	Microclimate Site design Landform (s) Land use (s) on-site energy resource, available infrastructural efficiency, interaction between building and the surroundings, Landscape design, Low-environmental impact construction site techniques, Housing density (no. of units/area), Transportation facilities
2.	Energy efficiency	Building envelope performance, Use of renewable energy, Natural ventilation and lighting, Energy-efficient heating/ cooling system, Other mechanical system used, Greenhouse gases emission (Direct), Machine/appliances for domestic uses
3.	Water efficiency	Water conservation system/practices, Innovative water use reduction technologies, internal/external water uses, Water efficient landscape

4.	Materials	Use of local/regional materials, Renewable material(s), Resource recycle and reuse Environmental impact of various materials
5.	Indoor environment quality	Occupants health and safety, indoor air quality, Quality of life, Ventilation efficiency, thermal efficiency day light, acoustics and noise control, visual quality
6.	Waste and pollution	Waste and pollution reduction strategies
7.	Cost and economics	Site Energy efficiency, Material(s) and construction practice, Water efficiency, Waste(s) management

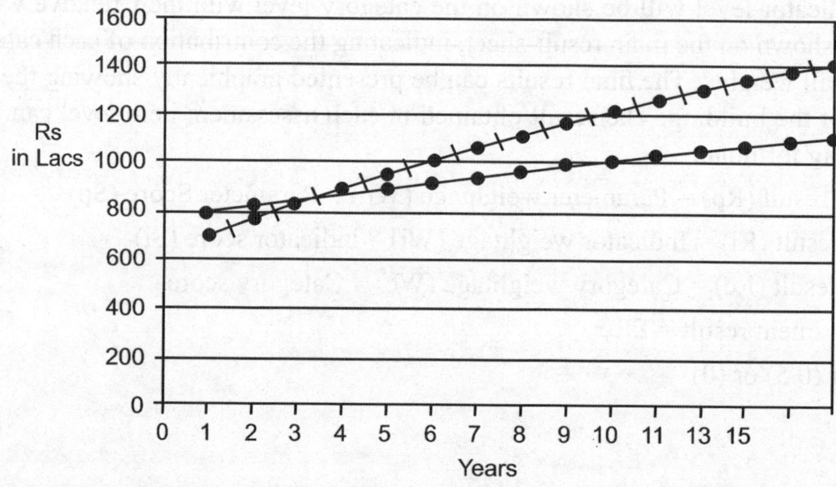

Fig. 6.30. Life Cycle Cost of a conventional and green building. The money spent on energy and resource consumption over the entire life of a green building is much lesser than that spent on a conventional building

Source: *GRIHA, TERI*

Green Rating for Business and Industry (CII)

This is a voluntary programme which aims to encourage and reward the greening of business and industry in India.

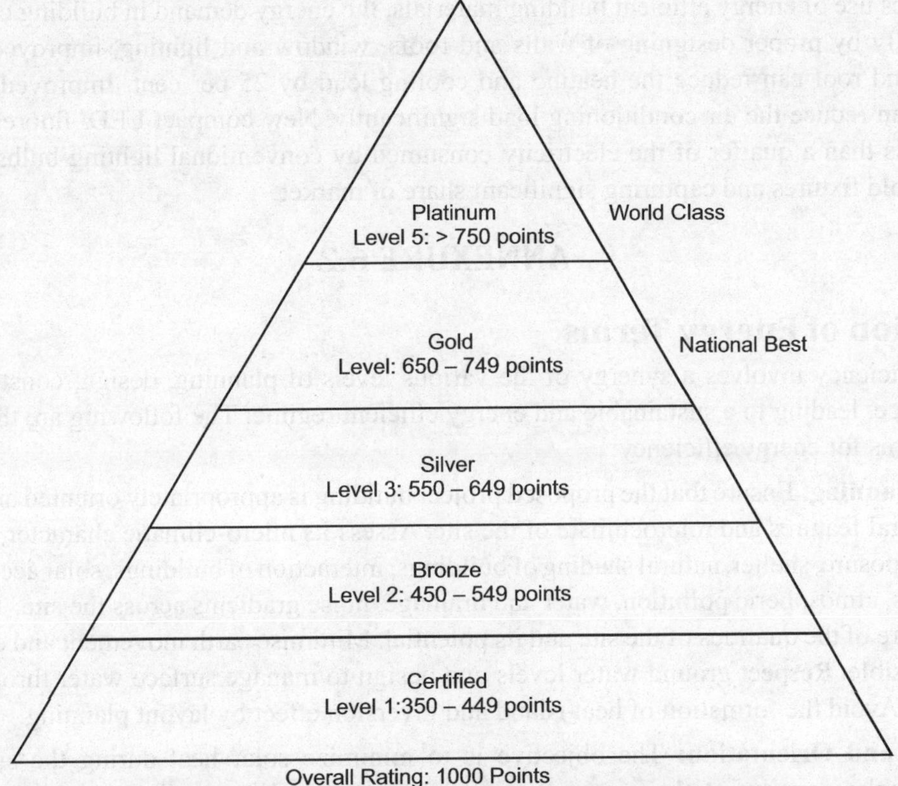

Fig. 6.31. Green Rating for Business and Industry (CII)

ANNEXURE 6.1

Energy Efficiency

Out of total electricity used in domestic sector generally, the utilisation ratio is as follows:

• Incandescent lamps	23%
• Fluorescent tubes/LED/Compact lamps	10%
• Space cooling, fans, etc	17%
• Desert coolers	4%
• Air conditioners	0.5%
• Refrigerator, toaster, iron, geyser etc.	30%
• Others, computer/ equipments	15.5%

The Asian Development Bank report (1997) indicates that the potential in saving due to better overall efficiency in domestic sector is about 20%. There exists a strong case for replacing low efficiency incandescent lamp with high efficiency LED/Compact/fluorescent and kitchen requirements which account for 30% of total electricity consumed, measures like increased thickness of foam insulation, use of high coefficient compressors, increased evaporator surface, use of tighter door seals and through other technical improvements can reduce consumption from 540 KWH/year to 300 KWH/year (for a 165 liter refrigerator).

Besides use of energy efficient building materials, the energy demand in building can be saved substantially by proper designing of walls and roofs, window and lighting, improved insulation of walls and roof can reduce the heating and cooling load by 25 per cent. Improved multi-pane window can reduce the air conditioning load significantly. New compact LED/ fluorescent lamps require less than a quarter of the electricity consumed by conventional lighting bulbs. These are replacing old fixtures and capturing significant share of market.

ANNEXURE 6.2

Definition of Energy Terms

Energy efficiency involves a synergy of the various levels of planning, design, construction and maintenance, leading to a sustainable and energy efficient regime: The following are the basis and critical terms for energy efficiency:

Site Planning: Ensure that the proposed project building is appropriately oriented and sensitive to the natural features and microclimate of the site. Assess its micro-climatic character, taking into account exposure, shelter, natural shading of buildings, interaction of buildings, solar access through the seasons, atmospheric pollution, water and drainage, noise gradients across the site. This gives a basic picture of the qualities of the site and its potential. Minimise earth movement and excavations where possible. Respect ground water levels and design to manage surface water through natural processes. Avoid the formation of heat island and inversion effect by layout planning.

Form and Orientation: The objective is to minimize solar heat during the summer and maximise solar gain during the winter so as to reduce the need for cooling, heating and lighting, thus reducing the demand for energy. Design to reduce surface area for heat transfer by avoiding elongated thin forms, spread out, and low-density development. Compact forms are preferred with grouping of the buildings for multiple use zoning.

Volume and Building Envelope: Generally avoid oversized interior height spaces in designing for specific functions. Thermal character of building envelope, roof, walls and fenestration should be compatible to U and R values.

Internal Layout: To reduce need for artificial light and for optimum heat efficiency cluster uses which need similar environmental conditions. Avoid open plan to allow for better control of services by the users.

Windows/Doors: Consider the percentage of fenestration on different facades and plan to minimise different temperature zones. Use southerly orientation for passive solar gain. Consider type of glazing and summer/winter ventilation. Use blinds, curtains, shutters draught lobbies and air curtains. Use energy efficient glass with spectrally selective coating to take the maximum advantage of day-light.

Ventilation/Air-Conditioning: Use natural ventilation where possible. Consider the use of atria to achieve some of these requirement and to provide amenity space for building users. Minimise the use of air conditioning. Consider the interaction between energy and ventilation strategies to balance potentially conflicting demand. Avoid the use or wet cooling where air conditioning is installed. Specify low-energy, high efficiency plant and fittings, sensor controls and appliances, as per BEE certification. Explore new methods of air-conditioning, such as Passive Energy Draft

Cooling (PEDC), High Efficiency Chilling Systems, earth embedded cooling, thermal storage system, etc.

Greenery: Landscape development of the site should improve the shaded areas, micro-climate and visual amenity by the greenery, green roofs, climbing plants on walls, window boxes and balcony gardens.

Passive Design: Major components of passive architecture are orientation of building, sun shades, double-glazed windows, smart glazing window overhangs, thermal storage wall/roof, roof painting, ventilation, evaporative cooling, day lighting, wind towers and earth air tunnel. The active and passive systems can be used simultaneously to make an integrated system.

Solar Energy: Sunshine is one of the desired aspects, especially in the residential buildings. As matter of planning and design, as well building bye-laws, the ratio of road width to building height becomes a very important factor.

Wall to Window Ratio, U Factor, SHGC and VLT Values: ECBC (2017) recommends a maximum U- factor of 3.3 w/m^2, SHGC of 0.25 for a wall to window (WWR) ratio of upto 40%, and SHGC of 0.2 for WWR of 40-60%. A glazing area in excess of 60% of gross external wall area is not recommended. The VLT value linked to WWR should be as ECBC. SHGC value is particularly critical for South, East and West facade. For glazing U factor and Solar Heat Gain Coefficient (SHGC) should be minimum, whereas VLT (Visible Light Transmittance) should be maximum.

Lifts: Consider buildings forms and heights to economise the reliance on lifts subject to meeting the needs of people with mobility problems.

Resource Recovery: Specify the reuse of material arising from demolition on site and recycled materials brought in from other sites locally. Shuttering, etc. should be reused wherever possible, rather than destroyed on completion. Allocate space for the future recycling of waste glass and other materials, and provide a composting facility, where appropriate.

Materials: Avoid over-designed structures, footing, etc. that may result in the wastage of materials. Consider alternative foundations and structures, where appropriate. Specify timbers from sustainable forests. Minimise the use of toxic chemicals and hazardous materials.

Environment Compatibility: The building design help in enhancement of indoor air quality for human safety, comfort and use of non-toxic paints, glues and building material to prevent additional environment impact and high waste treatment/disposal costs during demolition; maximum use of locally available renewables non-radioactive recyclables and durable material/resources, such as fly ash bricks, hollow bricks, stabilized mud blocks, etc. for building construction.

Landscape: Proper landscaping reduces direct sun from striking and heating up building surface. Landscaping creates different airflow patterns and can be used to direct or divert the wind advantageously by causing a pressure difference. The shade created by trees and the effect of grass and shrubs reduce air temperatures adjoining the buildings and provide evaporative cooling. Trees are the primary elements of energy-conserving landscape.

Plant location: To reduce distribution loses to a minimum locate plant close to areas of high energy consumption. Lag pipe runs to high specification, use low temperature storage, time controls and intelligent systems.

Waste heat recovery : Consider the use of a heat exchanger if the building is mechanically ventilated.

Building fabric: Specify insulation standard above the current regulation, where possible. Avoid the use of CFC blown insulation.

Controls: Employ controls that can respond to internal and external conditions. Time and temperature should be sensor controlled according to need of the occupants.

Decorative Finishes: Light coloured finished improve lighting conditions time and intensity controls.

Details/Standard of work: Joints, ceiling, insulation, ventilation and thermal installations should be checked to ensure that the work has been carried out to a high standard.

Operation: A user-friendly manual for occupants should be provided to explain the efficient operation of building and equipments.

Commissioning: Before occupancy, a building should be flushed to remove solvents, gases, vapours, smells, etc. that could affect future users. Check the performance of the components, machinery and the equipment against standards and to put right any defects found that could have major long term effects on the energy consumption of the building.

Incentives: Incentives like bonus floor area ratio, training and users participation in energy efficiency should be encouraged.

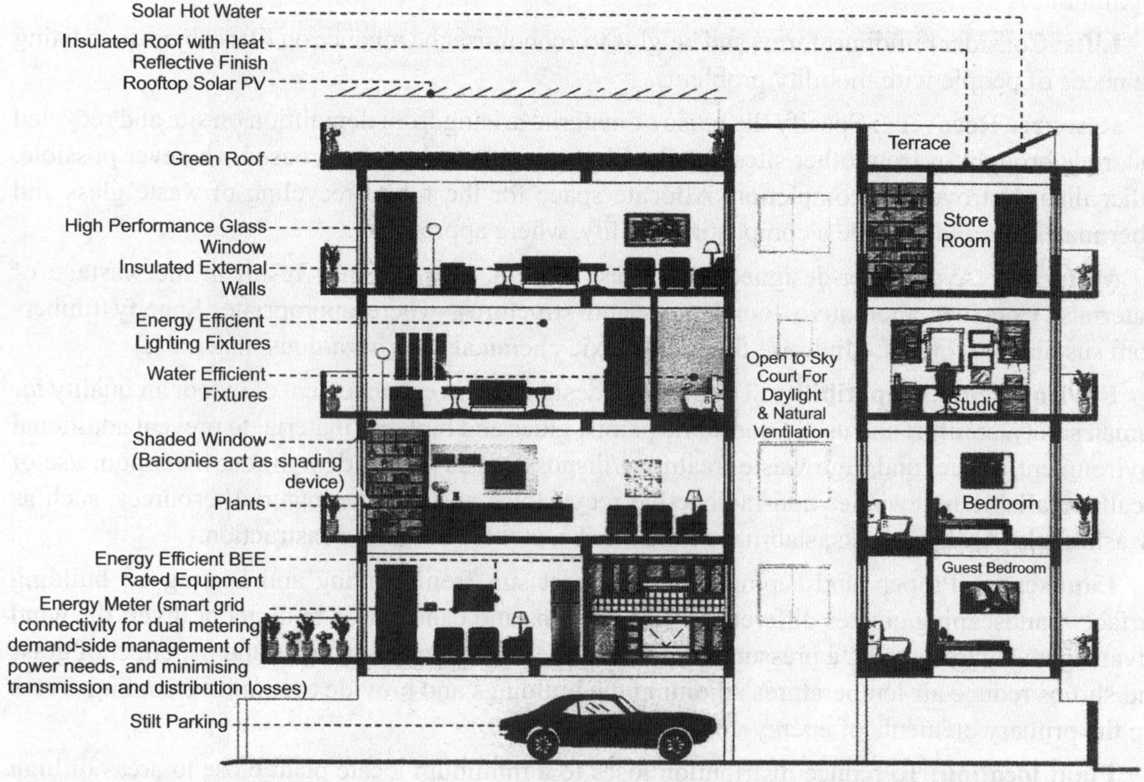

Fig. 6.32. Residential Building Compliant with Energy Conservation Building Code (2017)

Source: *DUAC/Amit Ghosal (2015) City Level Projects, Punjabi Bagh, DUAC, New Delhi.*

Absorptance

The percentage of energy incident on the glazing not directly transmitted or reflected % Absorptance = 100% - Direct Transmission - % Reflected.

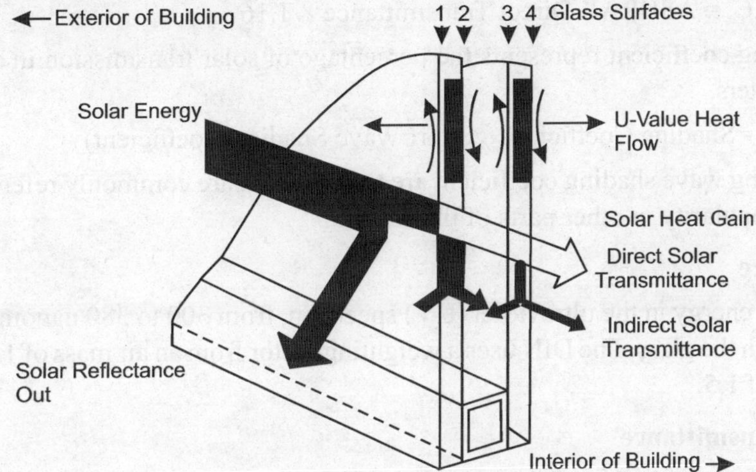

Fig. 6.33. The Solar Heat Gain equals the Direct Solar Transmittance plus the Indirect Solar Transmittance

K-Value

The European equivalent of the American (ASHRAE) U-Value. The Units are W/m^2K and are based on a wind speed of 4.4 m/sec at 0°C with an indoor temperature of 20°C.

Shading Co-efficient (SC)

A measure of the heat gain through glass from radiation specifically, the shading coefficient is the ratio between the solar heat gain for a particular type of glass and that of double-strength clear glass. The lower the shading co-efficient, the lower the solar heat gain.

R-Value

A measure of the resistance of the glazing to heat flow. It is determined by dividing the U-Value into 1, (R-Value = 1/U-Value). The Higher the R-Value, the better the insulating properties of the glazing.

U-Value (U-Factor)

A measure of the heat gain or loss through glass due to the difference between indoor outdoor temperatures. It is also referred to as the overall coefficient of heat transfer. The lower the U-value, better the insulating properties.

The unit is $Btu/(hr)/ft^2$. The Winter U-Value conditions are based on a wind speed of 15 mph at 0°F with an indoor temperature of 70°F. The Summer U-Value has wind speed of 7.5 mph at 89°F and indoor temperature of 75°F.

Short and long wave shading coefficients

Shading coefficient (S.C.) can be broken up into two components knows as long and short wave shading coefficients.

Short wave shading coefficient represents the percentage of solar transmission in the range of 300 to 4,000 nanometers.

Short Wave S.C. = DIN Direct Solar Transmittance × 1.15

Short Wave S.C. = ASHRAE Direct Transmittance × 1.16

Long wave shading coefficient represents the percentage of solar transmission in a range of 4,000 to 50,000 nanometers.

(Long Wave S.C. = Shading Coefficient – Short Wave Shading Coefficient)

Short wave and long wave shading coefficient are terms which are commonly referenced in Europe and are gaining popularity in other parts of the world.

UV Transmittance

The percentage of energy in the ultraviolet (UV) spectrum, from 300 to 380 nanometers, is directly transmitted through the glass. The DIN uses a weighting factor from an air mass of 1.0 and ASHRAE uses an air mass of 1.5.

Visible Light Transmittance

The percentage of energy in the solar spectrum, ultraviolet, visible, and near infrared energy, 300 to 4,000 nanometers, that is directly transmitted through the glass.

Air Mass = 1.0 for DIN and 1.5 for ASHRAE.

Relative Heat Gain (RHG)

The total heat gain through for a specific set of conditions. This value considers indoor/outdoor air temperature difference and the effect of solar radiation. The units are Btu/(hr)(ft^2), RHG = (Shading coefficient) {200 Btu/(hr)/ ft^2} + (U-Value, Summer) (14°F)

DEBRIEFING QUESTIONS

1. Explain the purpose and concept of 'Green Building.'
2. What do you understand by the ecological circle of building?
3. What are the Passive and Active measures for 'Green Buildings'?
4. Explain the basic principles of 'Green Building Design.'
5. Explain carbon negative building resources and techniques of 'Green Building.'
6. Write brief notes on:
   (*a*) Energy efficiency
   (*b*) Earth Air Tunnel
   (*c*) Natural Ventilation and Daylighting
7. Explain the standards and evaluation criteria for 'Green Rating for Integrated Habitat Assessment' (GRIHA) and 'LEED India Green Building Rating System.'

Chapter 7

BUILDING DESIGN FOR CLIMATIC AND THERMAL COMFORT

Climatic comfort has been a basic reason for building. Climate is a changing phenomenon of heat, temperature, radiation, sunlight, humidity, rain precipitation, wind, green house gases, biochemical cycles, etc. which are transferred over the land surface.

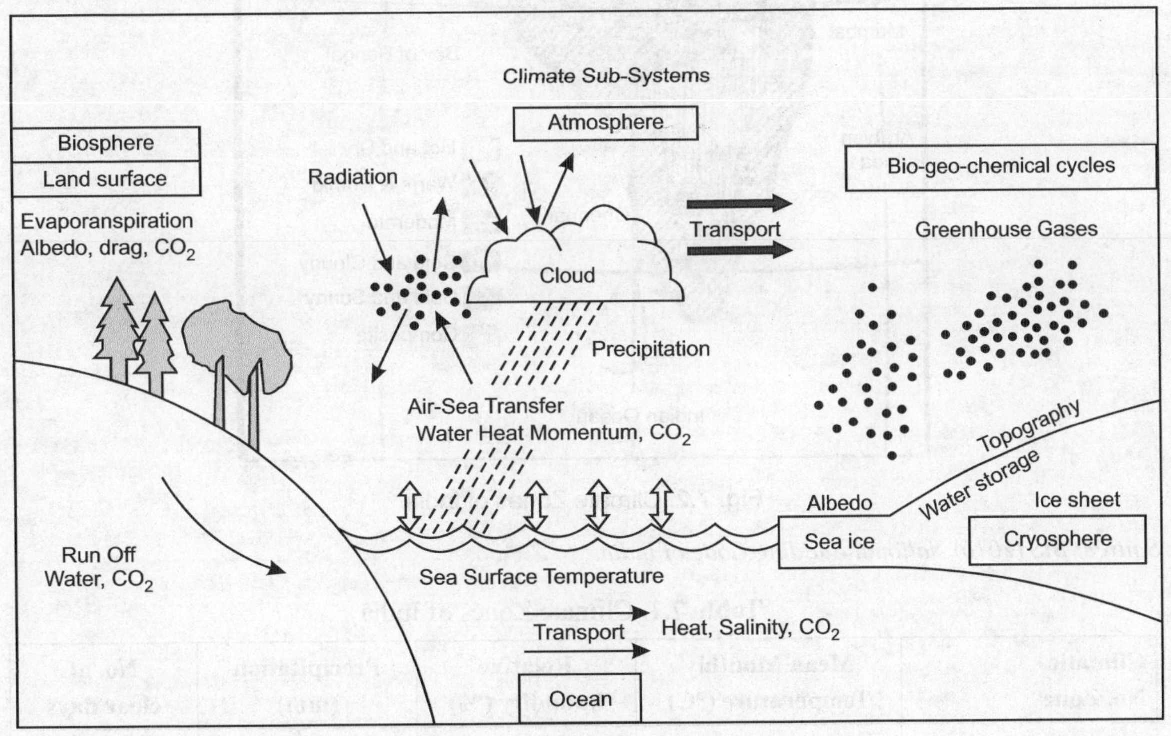

Fig. 7.1. Climate Sub-Systems

India with 3.2 million sq.km area has vast variations in climatic conditions. According to the National Building Code of India, for the purpose of design of building, the country has the following major climate zones:

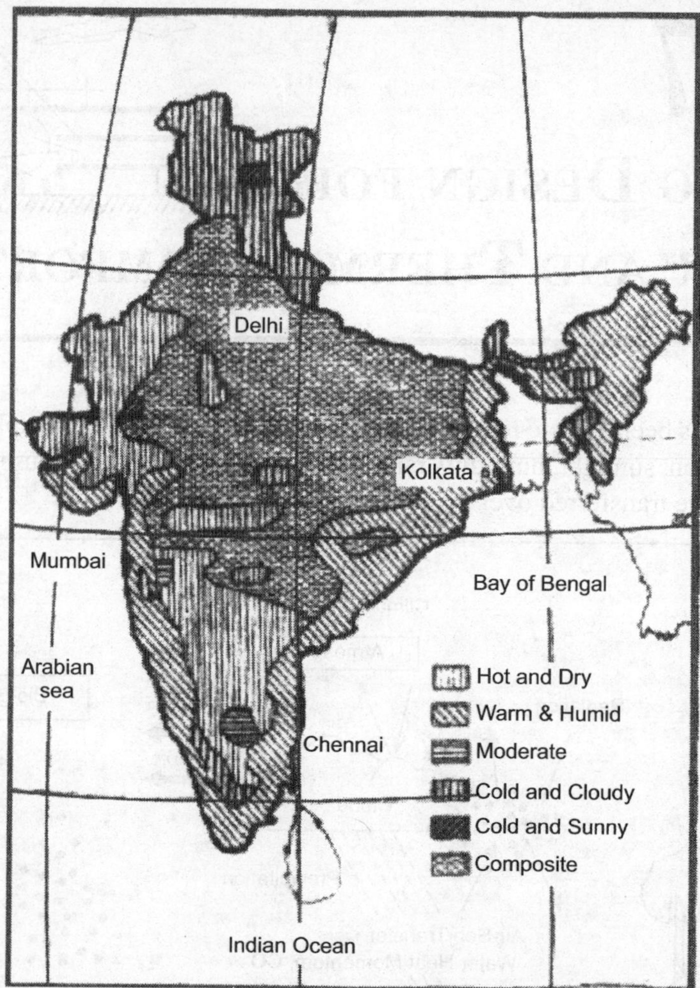

Fig. 7.2. Climate Zones of India

Source: *BIS (2016) National Building Code of India.*

Table 7.1. Climate Zones of India

Climatic No. Zone	Mean Monthly Temperature (°C)	Relative humidity (%)	Precipitation (mm)	No. of clear days
1. Hot-Dry	> 30	< 55	< 5	> 20
2. Warm-Humid	> 30	> 55	> 5	< 20
3. Moderate (M)	> 25	> 75	> 5	< 20
4. Temperate	25–30	> 55	> 5	< 20
5. Cold	< 25	< 55	< 5	> 20
6. Composite	A climatic zone that does not have any season for more than six months is called composite zone.			

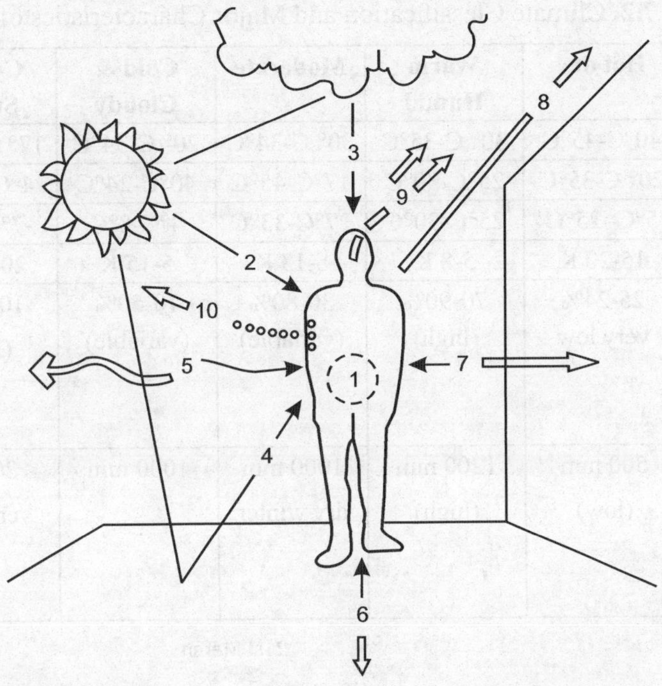

Heat gain	Heat loss
1. Body processes	5. Conduction to cooler air (assisted by airflow and convection)
2. Direct solar radiation	6. Conduction to cooler surfaces
3. Reflected radiation from the sky	7. Radiation to surface
4. Reflected radiation from surface	8. Radiation to space
5. Conduction from warmer air (assisted by airflow and convection)	9. Respiration
6. Conduction from warmer surface	10. Perspiration
7. Radiation from surfaces	

Fig. 7.3. Components of Thermal Balance. The human body, spatial envelope and micro-climate combine to give comfort conditions. The sun directly effects the temperature, humidity, micro-climate, wind flow and thus human comfort

The climatic characteristics of six climatic zones in India when related with human processes and comfort conditions provide the basis to micro-climatic design of building for comfort conditions.

Effects of Sun on Earth

The sun effects the amount of radiation coming on the earth surface. The intensity of the sun's radiation is measured in W/m^2. The intensity of the radiation reaching the upper surface of the atmosphere is taken as the solar constant (1,395 W/m^2) but may vary $\pm$ 2% due to the output of the sun, and $\pm$ 3.5% due to the changes in the earth sun distance.

Table 7.2. Climate Classification and Major Characteristics of Each Zone

Climate Features	Hot dry	Warm Humid	Moderate	Cold & Cloudy	Cold & Sunny	Composite
Summer midday	40°C-45°C	30° C-35°C	30° C-34°C	20° C-34°C	17° C-24°C	32° C-43° C
Summer Night	20° C-35°C	25°C-30°C	17°C-45°C	40°C-24°C	4°C-11°C	27°C-32°C
Winter midday	5°C- 25°C	25°C-30°C	27°C-33°C	4°C-8°C	-7°C-8°C	
Diurnal Variation	15-20 K	5-8 K	8-13 K	5-15 K	20-25 K	3-22 K
Relative Humidity	25-24% very low	70-90% (high)	30-80% (variable)	10-50% (variable)	10-50% (low)	20-55% dry season 55-95% wet season
Precipitation (annual)	500 mm (low)	1200 mm (high)	1000 mm dry winter	1000 mm	< 200 mm very low	500-1300 mm, 250 mm wet month

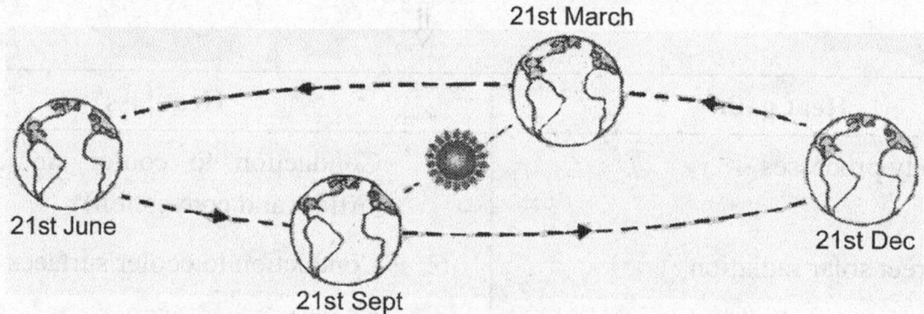

Fig. 7.4. Path of the Earth around the Sun

Due to the tilted position, the area receiving the maximum intensity moves north and south, between the Tropic of Cancer (23½°C) on 21st June (summer solstice) and Tropic of Capricorn (23½°S) on 22nd December (inter-solstice). This is the main cause of seasonal changes. On March 21st and September 21st the Sun is exactly over the equator (equinox).

The solar altitude angle (A1) is the vertical angle at the point of observation between the horizon plane and the line connection the sun with the observer.

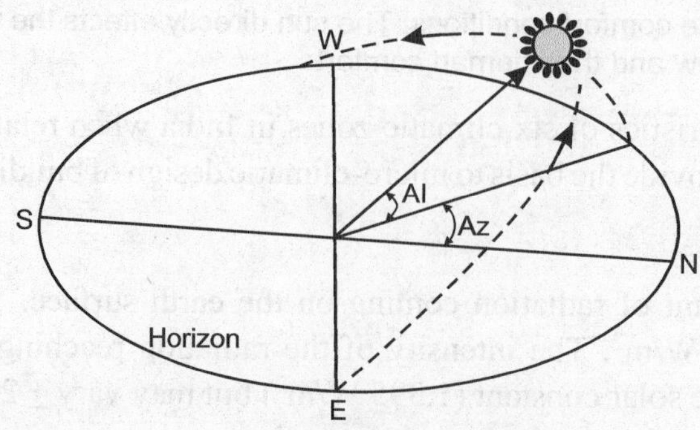

A : Southern Hemisphere

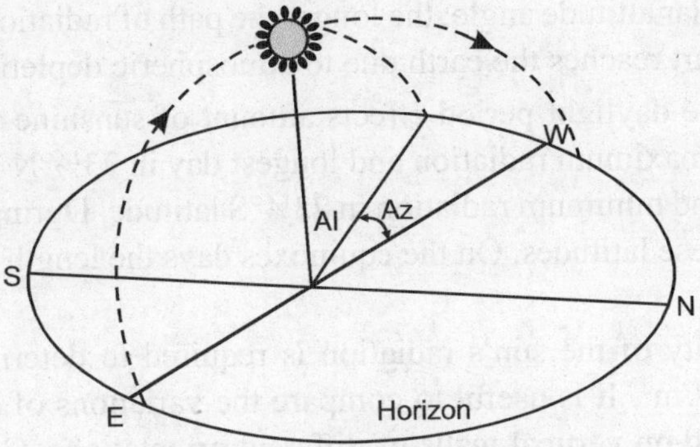

B : Northern Hemisphere

Fig. 7.5. A and B Solar Altitude and Azimuth

Sources: Solar Radiation Control Over Building, Harkness and Mehta; Wiley eastern, 1972; Meenakshi Dhote, Orientation of Buildings in Master Plan, Envis Journal, School of Planning and Architecture, New Delhi.

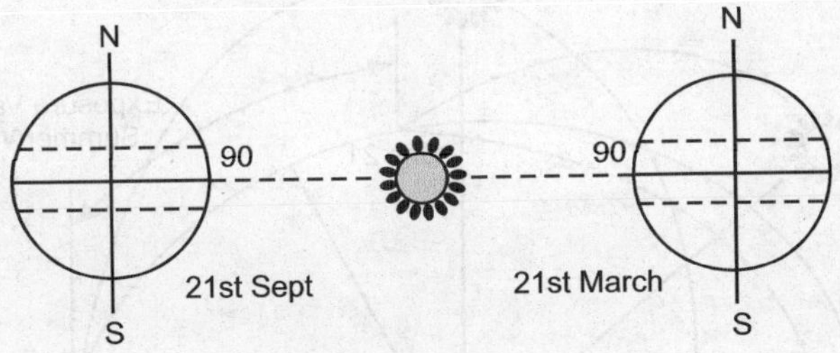

Fig. 7.6. Equinoxes

This change in the position of the sun effects the amount of radiation received at a particular point on the earth's surface in three ways:

– The intensity of radiation on a tilted surface equals the normal intensity times the cosine of the angle of incidence. The amount of radiation is distributed over a larger area, therefore intensity is reduced.

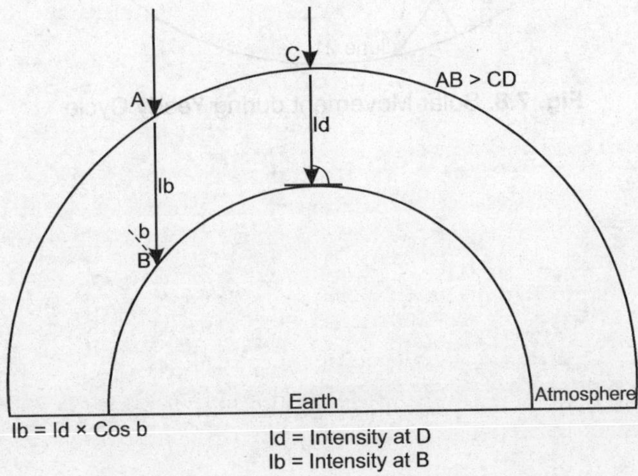

Fig. 7.7. Angles of Radiation Received on the Earth

– The lower the solar altitude angle; the longer the path of radiation through the atmosphere, thus a smaller part reaches the earth due to atmospheric depletion.
– The length of the daylight period effects amount of sunshine received. During summer solstice there is maximum radiation and longest day in 23½°N latitude. This corresponds to shortest day and minimum radiation in 23½°S latitude. During winter solstice the effect is reversed on these latitudes. On the equinoxes days the length of the nights and days are equal.

An idea of the intensity of the sun's radiation is required to determine the over-heated and under-heated periods in W/m^2. It is useful to compare the variations of solar radiation intensities on a horizontal surface and on vertical walls of different orientations. General observation is that the daily total of direct radiation on horizontal surface is considerably more (especially near the equator) than that on a vertical surface, especially in summer months.

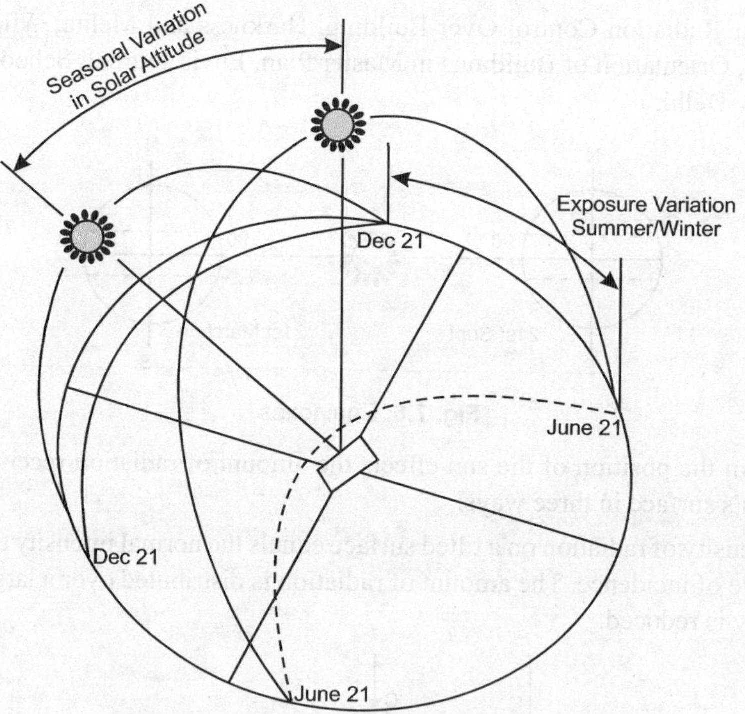

Fig. 7.8. Solar Movement during Yearly Cycle

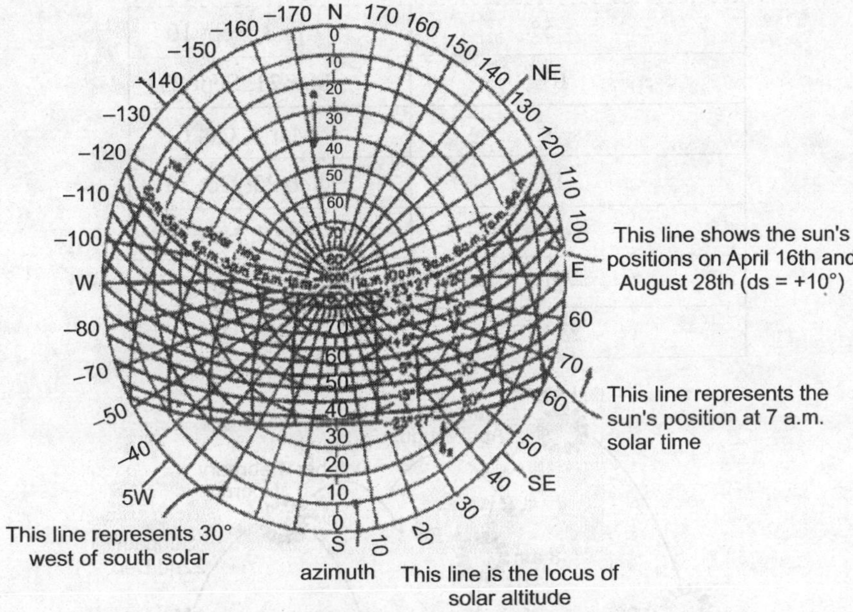

Fig. 7.9. Solar chart for 30°N latitude

The solar azimuth angle (Az) is the angle at the point of observation measured on a horizontal plane between the northerly direction and a point on the horizon circle where it is intersected by the arc of vertical, going through the zenith and the sun's position.

Climate and Buildings

The weather/climatic data is available for all major cities and towns, which is essentially collected for multipurpose applications by the meteorological department and related to general climate conditions over a large areas such as whole city. Within these large areas, the climate conditions do vary to a large extent, and this is why we find some zones or packets cooler and comfortable during different times of the year and at different hours. Therefore, one needs to take care in siting of building and its orientation to make best use of these elements that influence micro-climate in and around buildings.

Building orientation is a significant design consideration, mainly with regard to solar radiation and wind. With careful design, shading and deflecting devices can be incorporated to exclude the sun or redirect it into the building, just as wind as be diverted or directed to the extent desired. These factors need to be considered at the design stage, which help in obtaining a building environment as per the micro-climatic conditions.

Table 7.3. Declination Angles of Sun for 30°N Latitude

Angle	Approx. Dates
+ 23°27'	June 22
+ 20°	May 21, Jul 24
+ 15°	May 1, Aug 12
+ 10°	Apr 16, Aug 28

+ 5°	Apr 3, Sept 10
0°	Mar 21, Sept 23
–5°	Mar 8, Oct 6
–10°	Feb 23, Oct 20
–15°	Feb 9, Nov 3
– 20°	Jan 21, Nov 22
– 23° 27'	Dec 22

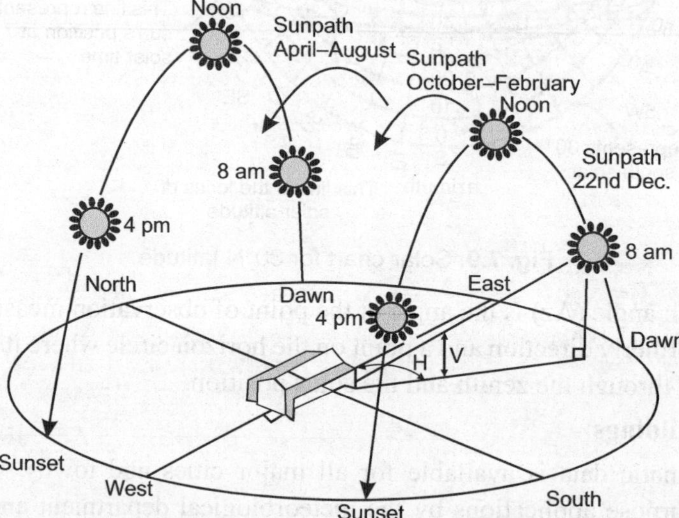

Fig. 7.10. The Sunpath: Direct sunshine should be kept out of building the summer. Sunshades should be large enough to exclude the Sun on 22 June

The determining factor for comfort is not only air temperature, but also the radiant heat. Radiant heat has 40% more effect on comfort than the air temperature. The rate at which the body releases heat in relation to the surroundings is an important consideration to ascertain heating or cooling loads. However, much of the air-conditioning load can be reduced by skillful design of the building, correct orientation, ventilation, hot air exhaust, roof insulation, light coloured painting of walls and roof, etc.

Climatically Compatible Building Design

Based on the above parameters, certain generic principles of energy efficiency a climatically comfortable building design can be worked out which comprise the following:

- Integration of energy efficiently concept from project outset to demand management
- Compact shape, minimize exposure to overheated period
- Daylight design
- Energy efficient lighting, ventilation and space conditions, site planning and landscape design
- Shading, green roof, building envelope

- Fenestration and window/opening design, glazing design
- Efficient use of passive solar energy, renewable energy
- Energy-efficient, easy-to-use technical systems
- Low water use sanitaryware
- Low-energy electrical appliances
- Use of low embodied energy, recyclable construction materials, increased insulation, elimination of thermal bridges, wherever possible
- Safety against fire and other hazards
- Landscape, earthen embankments, mounds, hedges, plantation, etc. to cool the air and to provide shade.

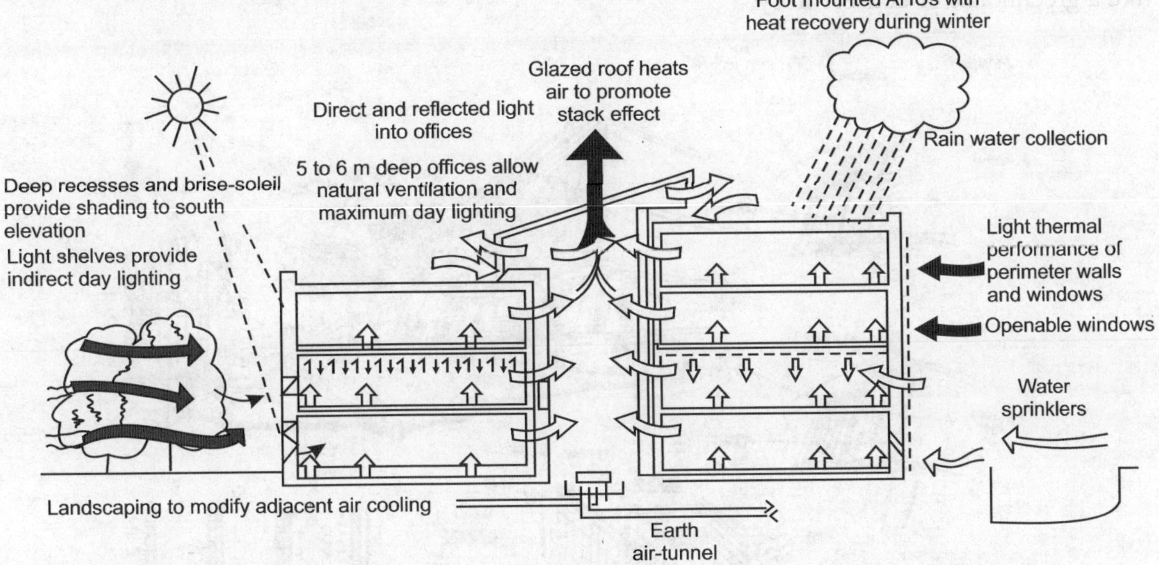

Fig. 7.11. A conceptual translation of principles of Low Energy Building Design

Building Envelope Design: In hot climate the object of building form and orientation is to minimize solar gain and to reduce the need of cooling thus reducing the demand for energy. As such, building should reduce surface areas and demand for energy by avoiding elongated thin forms, spread out single storeys or high rise. Compact forms are preferred. Group buildings for multiple uses and mixed use zoning are more appropriate.

Designing with the meteorological data of the location inevitably means certain physical and economic departures. For instance, sun shading increases the thickness of the external wall; external lift cores may be less efficient than a central-core layout. Designing with climate, would result in a reduction of the overall energy consumption of the building by the use of passive (non-mechanical) structural devices. Saving in operational costs derives from less use of electrical energy. The lowering of energy consumption would further reduce overall emission of waste heat, thereby cutting the overall heat-island effect on the locality.

The energy demand can be saved substantially by proper designing of walls and roofs, windows and lighting. Improved insulation of walls and roof can reduce the heating and cooling load significantly. New compact fluorescent lamps require less than a quarter of the electricity consumed by conventional lighting bulbs.

Buildings are exposed to the higher impact of external temperature and radiant heat. Accordingly, the overall building orientation has an important bearing on energy conservation. In general, arranging the building with its main and broader openings facing north and south gives the greatest advantages in reducing insulation and the resulting air-conditioning load. Generally, window opening should orientate north and south unless important views require other orientations. If required for aesthetic reasons, curtain walling may be used on non-solar facing facades. On other faces of the building some form of solar shading is required, while the quality of light entering spaces should also be considered. In temperate zones, transitional spaces can have adjustable glazing at the other face so that balconies or recesses can act as 'sun space', collecting solar heat, like a greenhouse or conservatory.

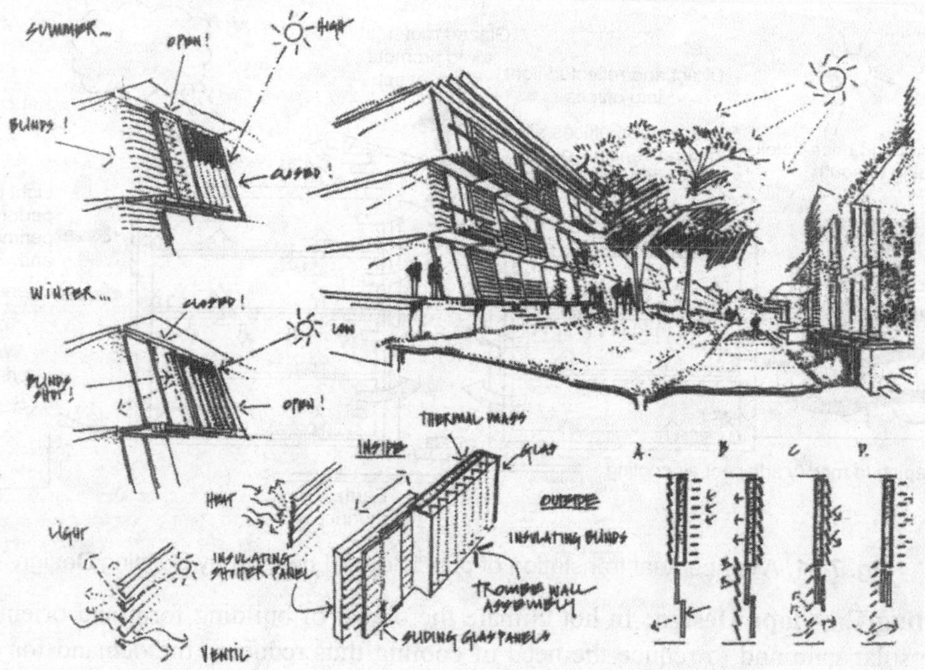

Fig. 7.12. Envelop study with Trombe Facade for Housing at Solar City, Linz Pichling (Austria), Architect Sir Norman Foster

Deep recesses may provide shade on the building's hot sides. A window can be totally recessed to form a balcony or small skycourt that can serve a number of function besides shading. Placing balconies on hot elevations permits glazing in these areas to be full-height clear panels. Large transitional spaces may be provided in the central and peripheral parts of the building as air spaces and atriums. These serve as 'in-between' zones located between the interior and the exterior. Atrium tops could be shielded by a louvered roof to encourage wind-flow through the inner areas of the building.

Green Roof: Cooler green roofs can be achieved by innovative design, which can be aesthetically pleasing and functional. A green roof is a combination of vegetation. hydrology, and architecture. Originally conceived in Iceland, where sod roofs and walls were used for centuries, modern green roof technology was developed more than 30 years ago in Germany, which now is a popular approach throughout the world. Such roofs consist of several layers of protective materials, including a waterproof membrane at the base, a roof barrier, an optional insulation layer, drainage layer, a filter fabric for fine soils, the growing medium, and the plant material.

Rooftop gardens are designed and engineered to conform to heavier load requirement. Green roofs should support deep soil base or shallow soil base for which additional structural strength may be required.

Reducing Solar Heat Gain: Generally avoid oversized building and spaces exposed to sun. External walls should be designed as permeable, environmentally interactive membranes with adjustable openings, rather than a sealed skin. In the tropics the external walls should have moveable parts that control and enable good cross-ventilation for internal comfort, provide solar protection, regulate wind-driven rain, and facilitate its rapid discharge.

Solar shading is essential for all glazed walls facing the sun (generally east and west in the tropics). A number of configuration of passive devices can be used depending on facade orientation. Shading blocks insulation in summer and prevents heat penetration of the buildings all year round in the tropics. Cross ventilation should be used (even in air-conditioned spaces) letting fresh air in and exhausting hot room air. Good air movement allows heat emission from the human body surface and gives a feeling of comfort. Skyfort, balconies and atriumns as open spaces and transitional spaces at the upper parts of the building encourage wind flow into internal spaces. Side vents operating as wind scoops located at the edges of the facade capture wind and make use of high wind found at upper levels.

Good thermal insulation of the building skin reduces heat transfer, both from solar gain and loss of coolness from the inside. A second skin (a rain wall) can be built over the inner wall with an air gap in between. Structural building mass may be used to store heat. The mass loses heat during the night and keeps internal spaces cool during the day.

Applications of Glass: The deterrent for use of day light is mainly glazing, heat transfer, prone to adverse climatic conditions and noise penetration. With the rapid development in glass technology, one can not only effectively control above factors but can also improve working conditions. Various types of glass are available as described below :

Photochromic devices change transmission in response to prevailing radiation levels. Small examples have been in everyday use in the form of sunglasses and spectacles. These react automatically to light levels. There are considerable technical problem to scaling up photochromic glass to normal window size.

Thermochromic glass has changing optical properties in response to temperature variations. It has a laminated structure incorporating a chemical which turns opaque at around 30°C, reducing insolation by about 70 per cent. For this reason an ideal application is as external solar shading.

Electrochromic glass, is an innovative option, the properties of which can be changed by the application of a small current. Their construction consists of complex multilayered transparent coating. The electrical signal reduces the transmission capacity of the electrochromic layer between two sheets of glass affecting not only daylight but also solar heat.

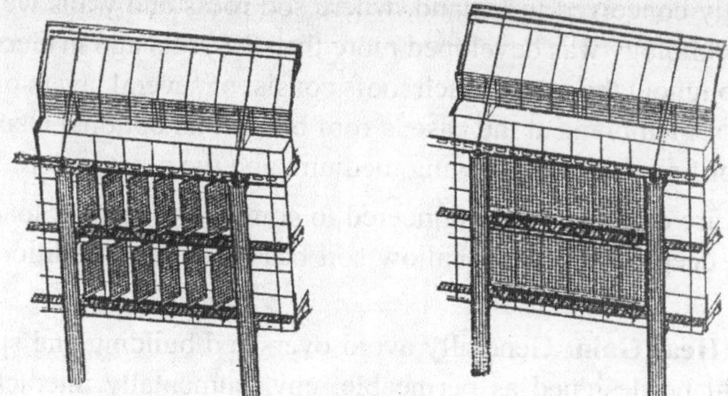

Fig. 7.13. The "Smart" facade filters sunlight according to internal temperatures, thus regulating solar gain and light effects. The automatically controlled system may be manually overridden

South facing verandahs, balconies, doors and windows are most livable area throughout the year. Another important feature, which is desirable in most parts of India, is that there should be easy flow of air and cross ventilation. Air exchange should be automatic to replace warm, stuffy used air and to eliminate smoke and odours. Vents should be proper size and so placed that every room or corner receives natural air. The vent should be insulated and properly sealed. Apart from size of opening of vents, doors and windows, their orientation should be according to wind direction so as to maximize the fenestration.

Wind Rose

In order to record the direction, intensity and duration of the wind, wind-roses are drawn for location, These may be drawn for annual wind pattern, seasonal wind pattern or monthly wind pattern. Thus we can construct single, four or twelve wind roses for a place depending on the requirements. The wind rose plots the direction of the wind around a circle indication whether the wind is blowing from N, NE, SE, S, SW, W or NW direction. These are represented by radial lines. The length of the radial is scaled to the duration of the wind whereas the thickness is scaled to the intensity to the wind. Landscaping such as location of trees, mounds, water bodies in relation to building cold also control the sun penetration, heat gain or loss. The choice of trees, their height, spread, foliage; size of mounds could be altered for better wind and sun control. Water bodies located in the direction of wind could add coolness to the breeze.

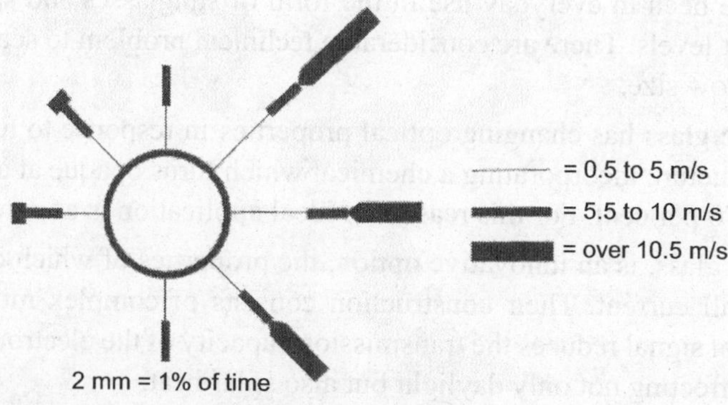

Fig. 7.14. Wind Rose

Solar Radiation

The radiation from the Sun travels in the space as electromagnetic wave. Above the earth's atmosphere, sunlight carries 1367 watts of power per square meter. This is known as the solar constant. We define solar constant as the amount of solar radiation received outside the earth's atmosphere on a unit area perpendicular to the rays of the sun, at the mean distance of the earth from the sun. The Earth receives 1.8×10^{17} W of incoming solar radiation continuously at top of its atmosphere.

But only half of its reaches the earth's surface. Factors like absorption, scattering and reflection of light during its passage through the atmosphere responsible for reduction of the amount of solar radiation available on the earth's surface. Solar energy is, by nature, a low-density energy source.

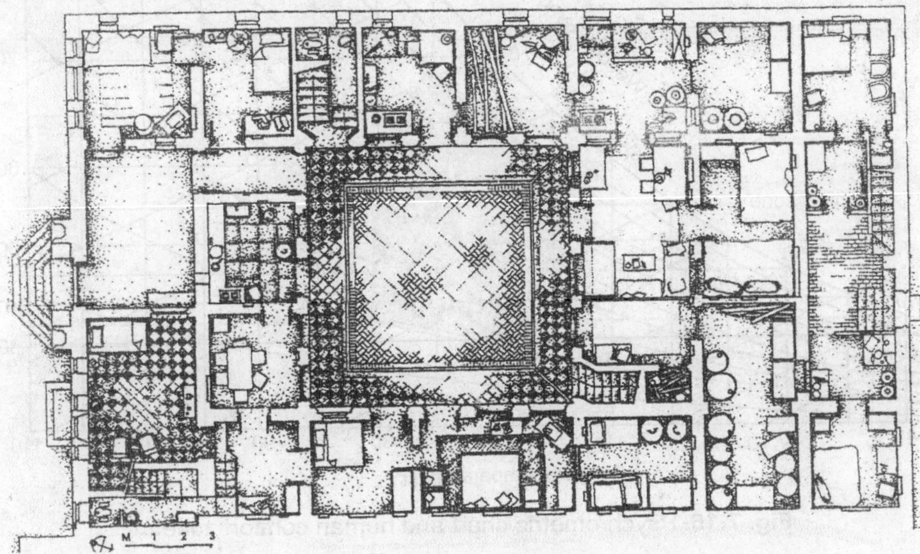

Fig. 7.15. Courtyard as the centre-piece of climatically comfortable traditional house. It acts like a sink of cool air and is shaded most of the day

Humidity

The humidity of air is measured as the amount of moisture present in it. The usual term used to express humidity is relative humidity (R.H.), which gives a direct indications of the evaporation potential. Relative humidity is defined by the expression:

$$\text{R.H.} = \frac{\text{Absolute vapour pressure at temperature T}}{\text{Saturated vapour pressure at temperature T}}$$

This is equal to :

$$= \frac{\text{Absolute humidity (A.H.)}}{\text{Saturated humidity (S.H.)}} \times 100 \text{ per cent}$$

Humidity is usually measured by noting the wet and dry bulb temperatures. The wet bulb temperature is measured in the same way as the dry bulb temperature, but the bulb (or sensor) in this case is covered with gauze or wick, which is kept wet. The evaporation of moisture cools the thermometer and hence the wet bulb temperature will always be lower that the dry bulb temperature, except at relative humidity of 100%, when the wet and dry bulb temperature will show identical readings. From the recorded observation of the Wet Bulb Temperature (WBT) and Dry Bulb Temperature (DBT) one can read the value of R.H. on the psychrometric chart. For example, if the DBT is 15°C (59°F) and the WBT is 10°C (40°F), the R.H. is about 53%, as shown in the Fig. 7.16.

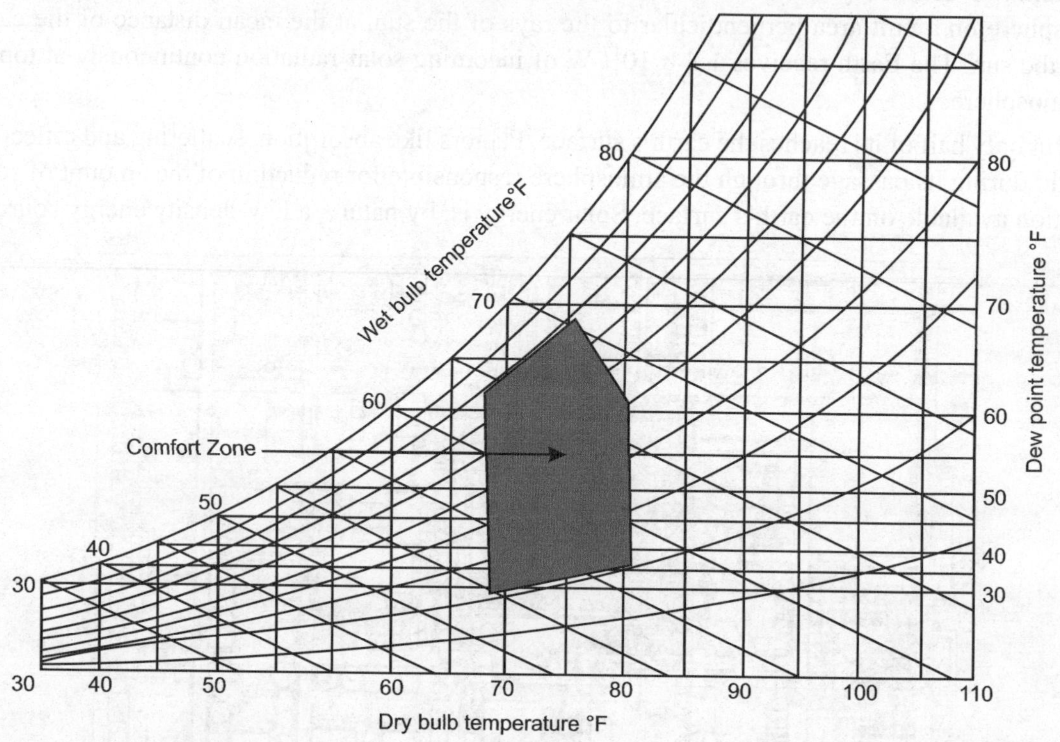

Fig. 7.16. Psychrometric chart and human comfort zone

Micro-Climatic Design of Buildings

Orientation, insulation and sun shading devices, ventilation, wind pattern and temperature variations are major factors for micro-climatic design of building. The building shape, form, and the choice of material for walls and roofs would also effect the thermal loss or gain. However these factors could be tackled at the building design level to ensure overall thermal comfort. For control of heat the main purpose of building orientation is to place the building in such a way that the facades with large openings face towards the direction which receives less sun. At locations near the equator it is not desirable to place large opening in east and west walls, except small ones.

For various climate zones, a differentiated passive design approach can help in making a building comfortable with little or even without use of mechanical and electrical devices. This necessitates placement and orientation of a building of a building according to sun, wind and rain. Design of walls, roof, fenestrations/openings, shading devices, glazing systems, overhangs and louvers, verandahs and courtyards, plantation, and building materials are the basic elements of micro-climatic comfort.

In latitudes remote from the equator openings on walls facing the equator are ideal because shading of the glass may be readily achieved during summer by the use of simple sunscreens and the winter sun can be let. In all cases, the roof should be properly insulated. Sizes of courtyards could be placed on the east and west side. The west side should preferably by blank due to the oppressive heat. In equatorial location, if solar heat gain is to be avoided the main windows should face north and south.

Setbacks (front, rear and sides) are worked out considering the sun parameters and climatic conditions. These would vary for different types of massing. The massing of building can be examined to study the changes in the setbacks to afford sun shading or sun ingress into the intervening spaces. At the layout planning stage, the street pattern should consider sun and wind movement. In locations north of equator roads moving north to south, with buildings on either sides; could afford maximum shade due to the longer shadows of the rising and setting sun. The width of the road and the height of the building would have to be correlated, so that unnecessary glare to the building facade is avoided. FAR, height and zoning would correspond to these factors.

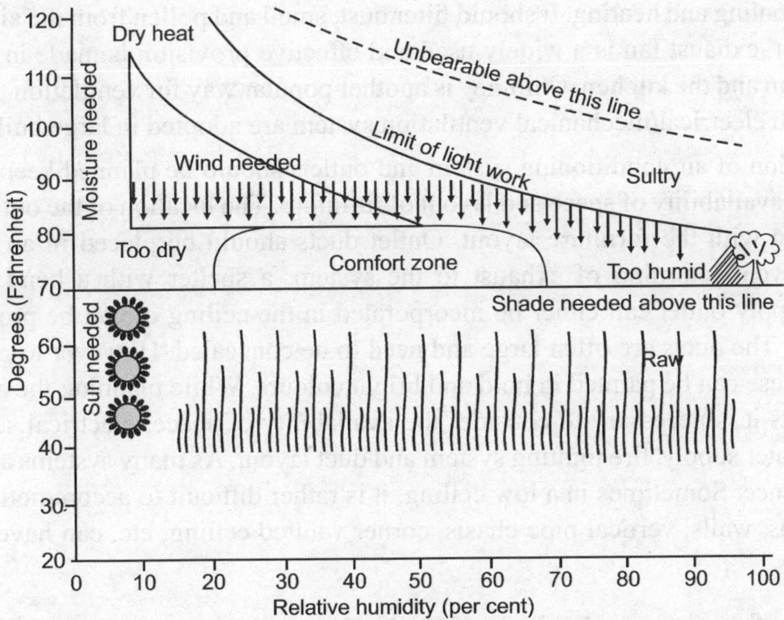

Fig. 7.17. Comfort zone in a building is a relative concept integrating several factors of which temperature and relative humidity are critical

The following design interventions can help in climatic comfort:

- Provide sun–shades, especially towards North and West and balconies, verandah towards the East and South to receive morning and winter sunshine
- Let natural light and air flow in the building, use daylight to minimize electrical lights
- Use underground space, which is cooler
- Provide air shaft for continuous exhaust of hot air
- Provide roof-insulation, paint in light colour
- Paint outer walls in light colours/white

- Use solar energy, minimise energy consumption and optimize energy efficiency
- Collect rainwater

Climatic comfort is an evolutionary state of mind and body. From the stage of cooling by shade, *i.e.* a simple roof over the head, cooling by electrical fans has become common. In hot dry arid zones desert coolers, *i.e.* fans combined and cooled by circulating water have been widespread. However, for cooling with controlled humidification and filtration of air, air conditioning is being increasingly adopted in the homes, offices and other building, and is becoming a necessity in the modern buildings. Bulk of air conditioning at present in the form of window unit, though split units and central system are being adopted for prestigious buildings, like the hotels. If the volumes of AC are heavy split unit are more appropriate. Height of the ceiling in an important factor as it effects the volume. It may restrict the laying of ducts if the ceiling slab or beams are too low.

In Indian cities, because of noise, dust and pollution, the windows are most of the time kept closed. Electrical heating and air conditioning systems provide filtered air. As the air is made stale by breathing, smoking and cooking, it is essential to incorporate proper ventilation system as an integral part of cooling and heating. It should filter dust, smell and pollen from the air. For removing smoke and odour, exhaust fan is a widely used and effective provision is made in the bathrooms, toilets, auditorium and the kitchen. Chimney is another popular way for ventilation. However, now-a-days ducts with electrical/mechanical ventilation system are adopted in large buildings.

The orientation of air conditioning system and outlets should be planned keeping in view the overheated side, availability of space and layout of furniture. The location of the outlet ducts should be planned along with the furniture layout. Outlet ducts should be placed in an unconspicuous location. To prevent returning of exhaust to the system, a shelter with a bend or undercut is provided, the supply outlet can either be incorporated in the ceiling or can be provided as an air handling fixture. The ducts are often large and need to be concealed. However to give a high-tech interior effect, these can be painted in bold and bright colours. While planning the air conditioning ducts and circuits it is necessary to consider the availability of space, electrical services, wiring, power supply, water supply, fire fighting system and duct layout. As many systems are incorporated without interference. Sometimes in a low ceiling, it is rather difficult to accommodate all these. In that case columns, walls, vertical pipe chasis, corner vaulted ceiling, etc. can have hidden spaces for these services.

Thermal Performance Index of Buildings

Thermal performance of a building is the result of the process whereby the design, layout, orientation and construction materials of the building modify the prevailing outdoor climate to create a comfortable indoor climate. In a building this is generally perceived by the occupants in terms of the extent to which the building seems cool in the heat of summer and warm in cold winter, taking into account the amount of heating or cooling required to create comfortable thermal conditions. Thermal performance can be expressed in numerical or quantitative terms in various ways. Building component properties may be interpreted as "low-level" performance indicators, whereas room performance descriptions may be interpreted as "high-level" behavioural properties. Thermo-physical properties (for example U-value, shading coefficient) may be defined as attributes of discrete components whereas energy performance (e.g. environmental temperature, heat gain or loss) may refer to room properties. The Bureau of Indian Standards have formulated the Building

Index, a high level thermal behavioural property for the building and Thermal Performance Index, a low level thermal behavioural property for the building envelope.

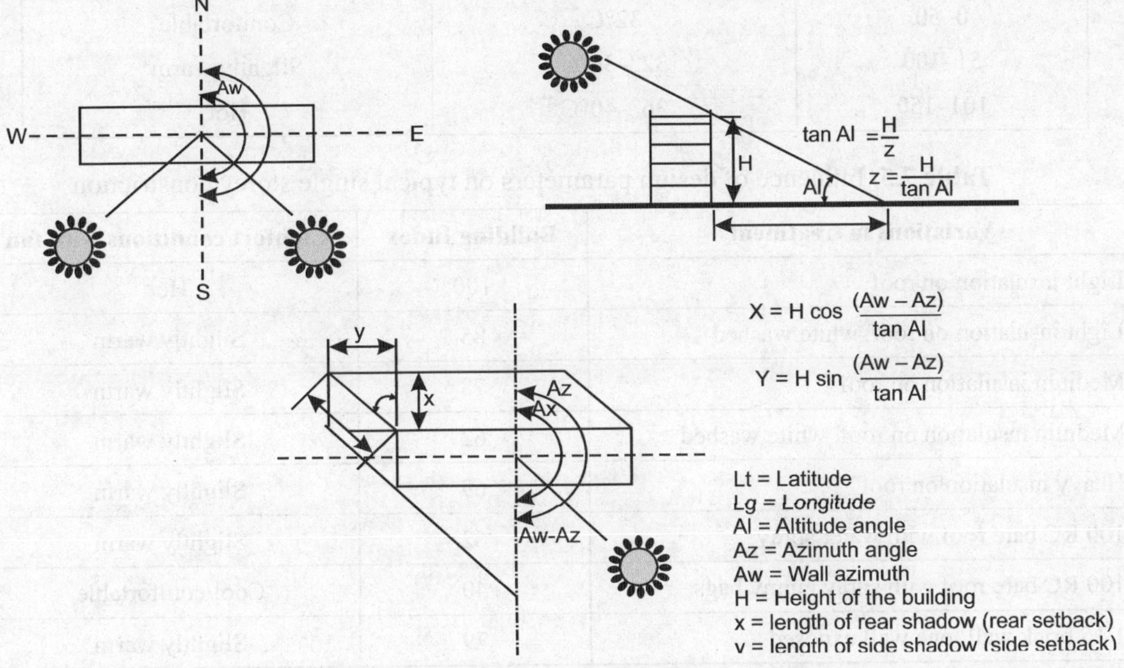

Fig. 7.18. Building Shadows and Setbacks

Building Index (BI): Thermal design of building is influenced by various parameters, such as:

- Building materials and building fabric specifications
- Orientation
- Glass area
- Insulation
- Shading
- Fenestration
- Ventilation
- Location of rooms

Building Index (BI) is defined as the percentage ratio of total maximum heat gain, averaged over the entire surface area of the building envelope to the acceptable limit of heat gain for achieving comfortable conditions indoors. It was developed at the Central Building Research Institute and later adopted by Bureau of Indian Standards. Acceptable limit of heat gain has been taken as 46.52 W/m^2 (40 $kcl/m^2/hr$) and corresponds to a building index value of 100. Unlike prevalent star rating, this scale uses a descending scale, *i.e.* lower score means better performance because it corresponds to low heat gain. Maximum limits of building index for different thermal comfort conditions and the corresponding indoor air temperature with fan are given in the Table 7.4. General features of typical single storey building and effects of different treatments are given in the Tables 7.5 to 7.7.

Table 7.4. Building Index corresponding to air temperature and comfort conditions

Building Index	Indoor air temperature	Comfort conditions with fan
0–50	32°C	Comfortable
51–100	32°–36°C	Slightly warm
101–150	36°–40°C	Hot

Table 7.5. Influence of design parameters on typical single storey constriction

Variations in treatment	Building Index	Comfort conditions with fan
Light insulation on roof	100	Hot
Light insulation on roof, white washed	85	Slightly warm
Medium insulation on roof	78	Slightly warm
Medium insulation on roof, white washed	62	Slightly warm
Heavy insulation on roof	69	Slightly warm
100 RC bare roof with water spray	62	Slightly warm
100 RC bare roof with spray gunny bags	40	Cool/comfortable
1 15 brick wall, one wall exposed	79	Slightly warm
230 brick wall, one wall exposed	73	Slightly warm
230 brick wall, two wall exposed	78	Slightly warm
230 brick wall, three wall exposed	87	Slightly warm
345 brick wall, one wall exposed	70	Slightly warm

General Features of a typical construction

Walls	230 mm brick with plaster on both sides	Glass area	15% of floor area, shaded
Roof	100 mm RC roof with 75 mm lime concrete	Orientation	Longer axis along east-west
Window	3 mm glass	Ventilation	3 air changes per hour
Door	25 mm teak wood	Aspect ratio	1:1.5
Exposure	Only one wall		

Source: *CBRI, 1985, Thermal design of buildings (no. 17)*

Performance limits are defined keeping in view the tropical climate of India. Although the conditions and type of construction are not specified, the concept of average heat flow could be useful in different climatic zones of the country.

Table 7.6. Relative Thermal Performance of Building

Sl. No	Type of Treatment	Building Index	Comfort Index Condition with fan
Multistorey Construction			
01.	Top floor, unshaded glass area 15% of floor area, North orientation	85	SW
02.	Top floor, unshaded glass area, 15% of floor area, South orientation	87	SW
03.	Top floor, unshaded glass area, 15% of floor area, East orientation	112	H
04.	Top Floor, unshaded glass area, 15% of floor area, West orientation	125	H
05.	Top foor, shaded glass area, 15% of floor area, South orientation	73	SW
06.	Top floor shaded glass area, 30% of floor area, South orientation	85	SW
07.	Ground floor, shaded glass area, 15% of floor area, South orientation	56	C–SW
Single storey construction			
08.	Light insulation on roof, glass are shaded	100	H
09.	Medium insulation on roof, glass area shaded	78	SW
10.	Heavy insulation on roof, glass area shaded	69	SW
11.	Light insulation on roof, glass area shaded	85	SW
12.	Medium insulation on roof with white wash, glass area shaded	62	SW

13.	Water spray on bare roof (RCC)	62	SW
14.	Water spray with gunny bags on bare roof (RCC)	40	C
15.	One wall exposed	73	SW
16.	Two walls exposed	78	SW
17.	Three walls exposed	87	SW
18.	12.5 cm brick wall, one wall exposed	79	SW
19.	37.5 cm brick wall, one wall exposed	70	SW

Note : *SW-slightly warm, H-Hot, C-Cool/Comfortable*
Source: *CBRI, Roorkee*

Table 7.7. Thermal Performance of different Roofs in Various Zones

Sl. No.	Basic Element	Treatment Interior	Treatment Exterior	Zone-1	TPI Zone-2	Kcal/ m² hr°C Zone-3	U-value (Kcal/m²hr°C) Zone–4
1.	10 cm R.C.C	1.5 cm cement Plaster	Tarfelt	225	215	222	3.143
2.	10 cm R.C.C.	1.5 cm cement Plaster	9.0 cm lime Conc. white wash	(91)	(86)	(90)	3.143
3.	10 cm R.C.C.	1.5 cm cement Plaster	5 cm brick tile+10 cm mud Phuska (100)	(100)	(16)	(98)	1.695
4.	13 cm Channel unit		Tarfelt	312	297	308	3.913
5.	13 cm Channel unit		12 cm lime conc + white wash	(96)	(93)	(95)	2.317
6.	13 cm Channel unit		5 cm brick tile + 10 cm mud phuska + white wash	(84)	(80)	(80)	1.909
7.	7.5 cm Cellular unit		Tarfelt	232	222	229	2.807

8.	7.5 cm Cellular unit		10 cm lime conc. + white wash	(93)	(90)	(94)	1.988
9.	7.5 cm Cellular unit		5 cm brick tile + 12mm mud phuska	(100)	(97)	(99)	1.500
10.	5 cm R.C. Plank		Tarfelt	324	309	320	3.876
11.	5 cm R.C. Plank		15 cm lime conc + white wash	(94)	(91)	(94)	2.092
12.	5 cm R.C. Plank		5 cm brick tile + 10 cm mud phuska + white wash	(91)	(86)	(90)	1.900

Notes: (*i*) The figures in brackets satisfy the thermal standards as per IS : 3792 (1978).

(*ii*) Water proofing treatment should be done as per B.S.I standards.

***Source:** CBRI (1985) and IS: 3792 (1978)*

Air Scoop

The builders in India, Pakistan, Iraq and other hot climate usually resort to heavyweight solutions to cool down the interior of their houses. Structures are massive with dense walls to absorb heat. Buildings may be dug into the ground to use the earth mass for cooling and to increase ventilation. In Hyderabad, Pakistan, the cool after-noon winds mostly come from the same direction. Therefore most buildings are equipped with enormous wind catchers which redirect the airflow down into the living quarters. Traditional homes in Baghdad may contain a badgir or an air scoop that face the north-westerly air stream. A *badgir* is a flue in the wall of house which rises to the highest point of the roof parapet. It is typically 50 by 20 cm in cross-section. *Badgirs* are most effective when built into walls transverse to the prevailing wind, with wide openings. Once the air is taken in, it sinks as it take on moisture and cools. This is an example of an air-conditioning system in its most sophisticated and energy-efficient form.

Fig. 7.19. Wind catcher (Barjeels in Arabic) or Air Scoops for cooling in hot dry climate

The air is taken in as before but rises through a central space which has opening at the top. Courtyards help to lower the temperature. They act as a vertical vent through the storeys of a buildings and create a comfortable microclimate. The temperature differential between ground floor and roof can be as much as 20 degree celsius.

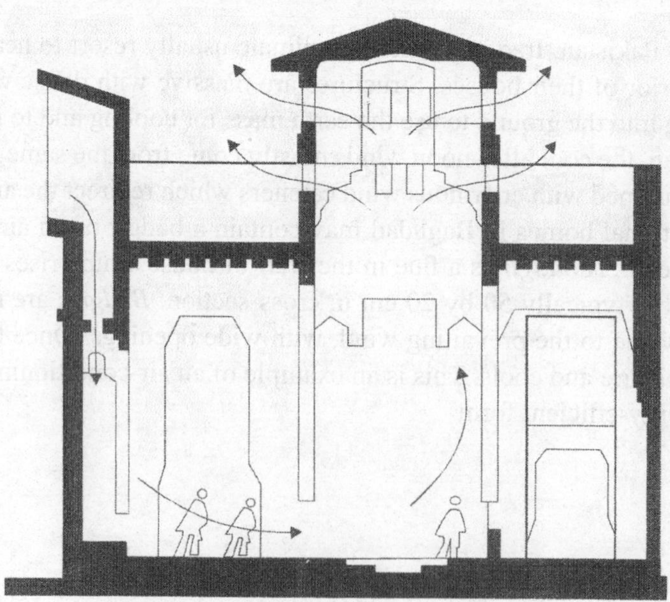

Fig. 7.20. Cooling by an Air Scoop

Earth Air Tunnel

Earth is an effective moderator of climate. Though surface thermal condition show patterns of yearly cycles warming the surface during summer and cooling it during winter, at depths below 4-5 meters yet this affect is negligible and the temperature remains more or less constant equal to yearly mean solar temperature. The moderating characteristic of earth, *i.e.* variation of temperature with depth is shown in Table 7.6.

Table 7.8. Summer earth temperature 4 meters below the surface in selected cities

Sl. No.	Name of City	Climate zone	Earth Temperature
1.	Bangalore	Composite	24°C
2.	Mumbai	Warm and Humid	28°C
3.	Delhi	Composite	25°C
4.	Jodhpur	Hot and Dry	29°C

Source: *Kachru, U (1994)*

Average earth temperature for some Indian cities in the following table shows that even in the hottest locations, earth temperature remains below 30°C. The capacity of the earth to condition the air by effectively damping the ambient air temperature can be used for cooling and filtering out the effects of solar radiation, used in combination by transmission in buried pipes or underground tunnels as were used in the traditional Persian architecture,

The main barrier to design of envelopes in building is the lack of cheap technology for the formation of small-gap continuous horizontal cavities, such as in the roof slab. Major heat gains in summer are through the roof. In Delhi, for example, 45-50 percent of the total summer solar radiation is transferred through the roof. The envelope system becomes ineffective unless techniques are developed to produce inexpensive horizontal cavities to enclose the roof area.

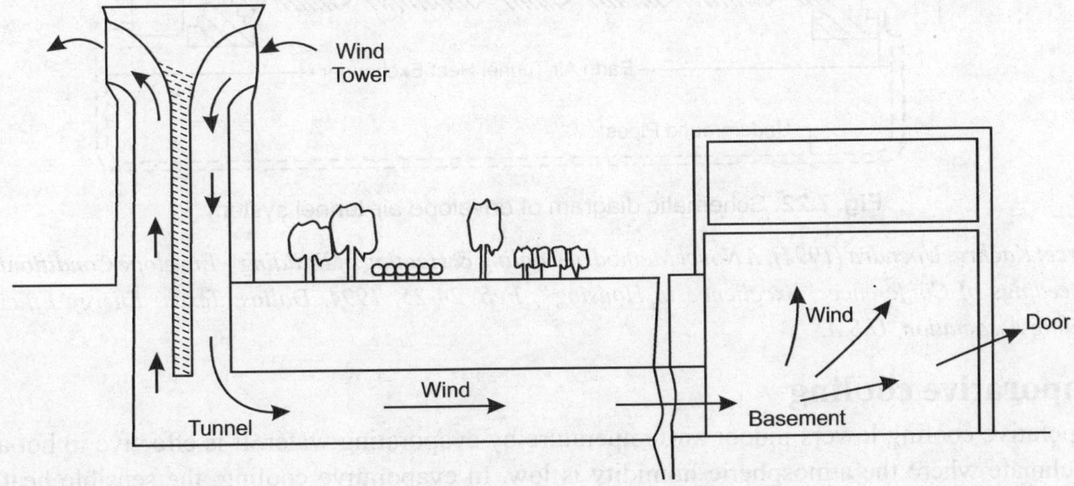

Fig. 7.21. Earth-Air Tunnel

A system of promoting wind flow through the building and reducing heat intake is earth berms with wind shafts opening within the rooms. The temperature of subterranean air is almost constant at any time of the year. The ambient air ventilated though this tunnel gets cooled in summer which is used for cooling in summer. The combined impact of improved temperature differential, increased surface area and turbulent forced air-flow improve the efficiency of transfer of thermal energy over conventional passive methods.

However, for large cooling loads, the cost of the tunnel may become prohibitive. Other limitations of the system can be the following:

- The ducts provide access to foul smells, fungi, micro-organisms, insects and rodents and thereby may create a health hazard;
- The conditioned air does provide cooling during period of high humidity, including monsoons; and
- Cold air delivered is not at low temperature, therefore large quantities of air are required.

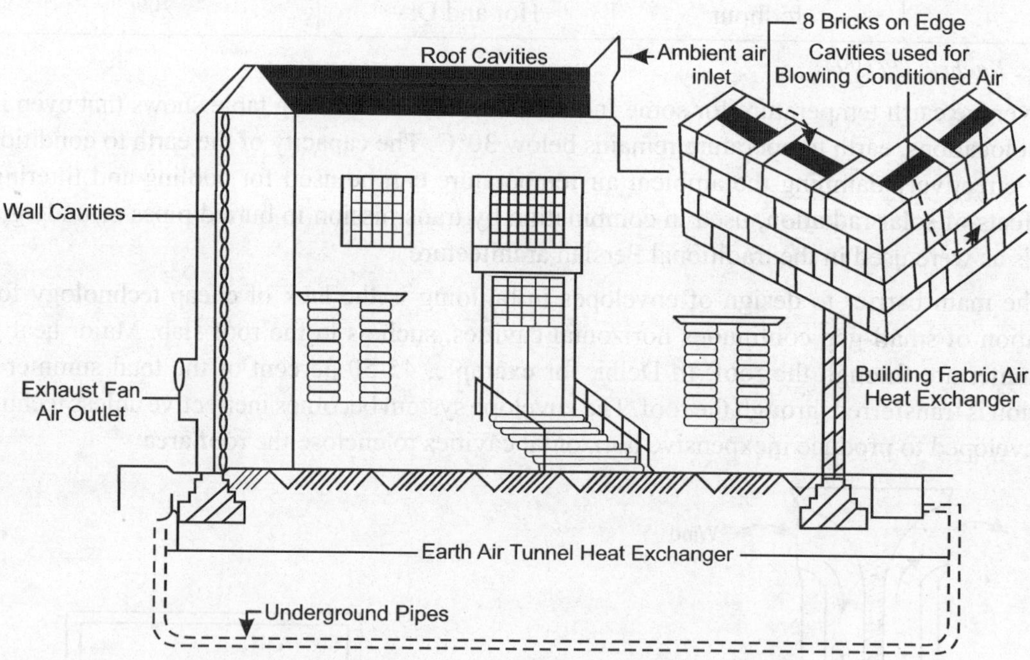

Fig. 7.22. Schematic diagram of envelope air-tunnel system

Source: *Kachru, Upendra (1994), A Novel Method of Cooling & Heating of Building – Envelope Conditioning, Proceedings of Conference "Excellence in Housing", Feb. 24-25, 1994, Dallas, Texas; Energy Efficient Building Association, U.S.A.*

Evaporative cooling

Evaporative cooling lowers indoor air temperature by evaporating water. It is effective in hot and dry climate where the atmospheric humidity is low. In evaporative cooling, the sensible heat of air is used to evaporate water, thereby cooling the air, which, in turn, cools the living space of the building. Desert coolers are the most economical and commonly used for evaporative cooling.

Wind catchers guide outside air over water-filled pots, inducing evaporation and causing a significant drop in temperature before the air enters the interior. Such wind catchers become primary elements of the architectural form also.

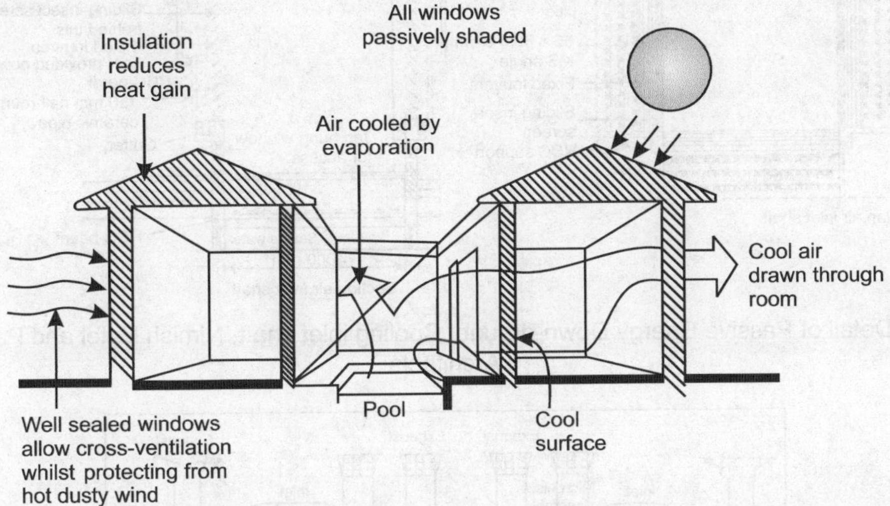

Fig. 7.23. Evaporative Cooling can be obtained by Desert Coolers, small pool/fountains, water filled pots and wind catchers

Passive Energy Down-draught Cooling (PEDC)

The PEDC combiners evaporative cooling, wind shafts with simulated configurations, cooling micronisers and dust control for low energy cooling. It is particularly suitable for hot-dry climates, white during the monsoon months the ventilation is induced.

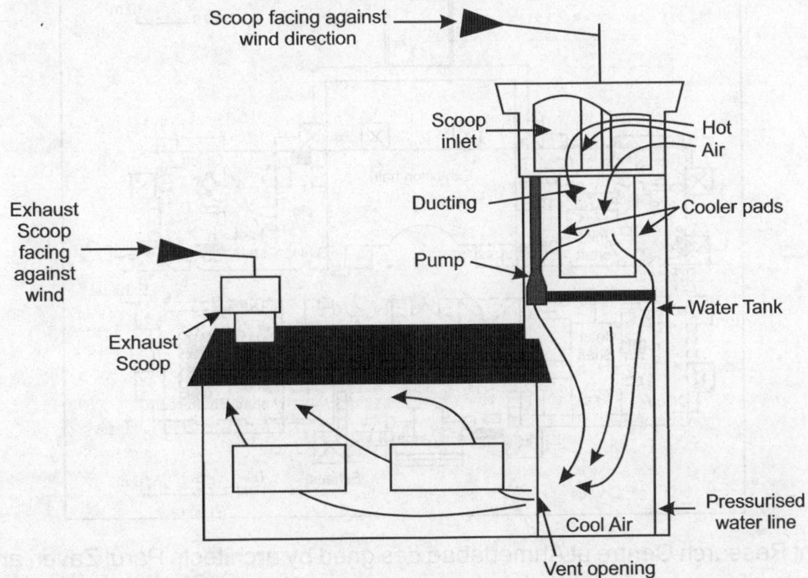

Fig. 7.24. Passive Energy Down-draught Cooling

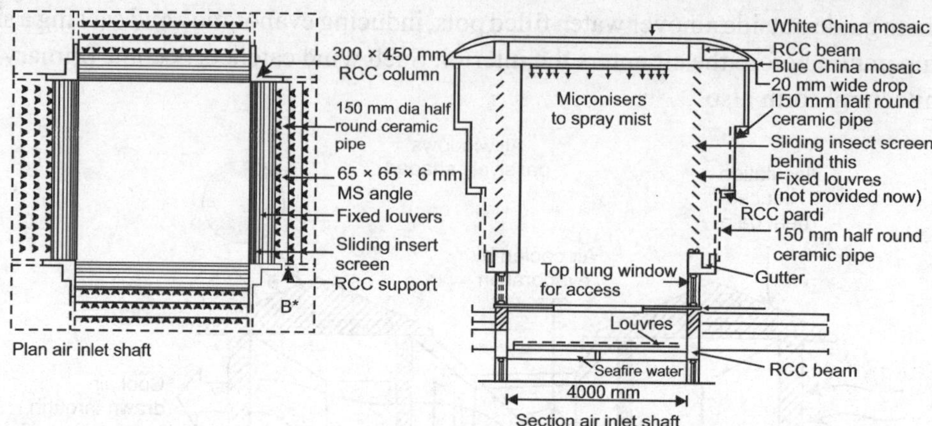

Fig. 7.25. Detail of Passive Energy Down-draught Cooling inlet shaft, Nimish Patel and Parul Zaveri, Architects

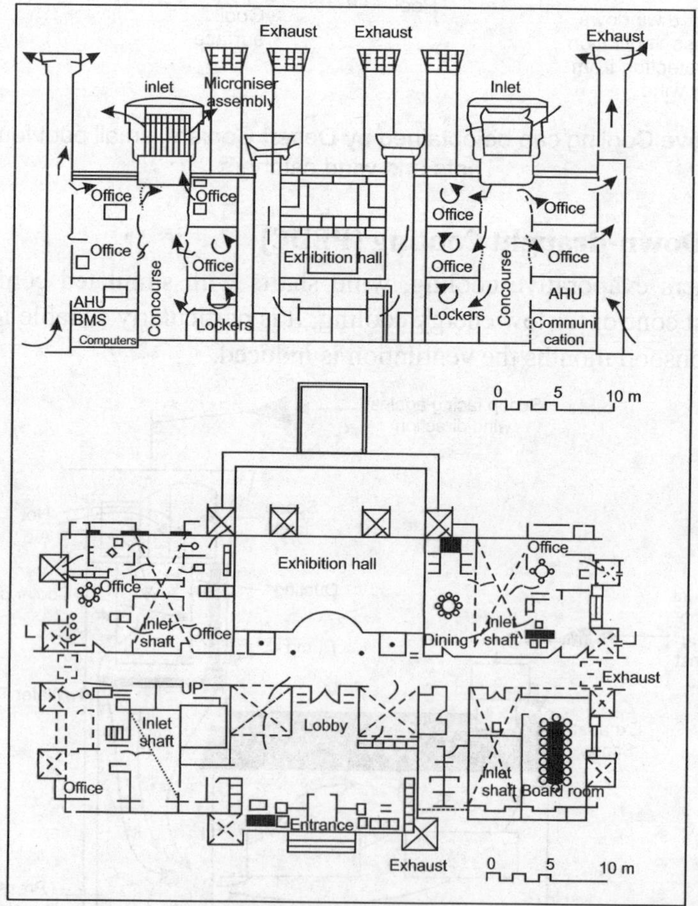

Fig. 7.26. Torrent Research Centre at Ahmedabad designed by architects Parul Zaveri and Nimish Patel, is a good example of energy efficient climatic architecture. The pharmaceutical laboratories minimize the use of air conditioning by Passive Down-draft Evaporative Cooling (PDEC) system. This is done by simulated design of inlet and outlet shafts for circulation of air through a fine spray of water that cools it. The buildings work on natural light and have dust control.

The shafts as a consequence of their design, location, size height, and their simulated configuration generate the required movement of air in different types of spaces without using any mechanical or electrical energy. The building has a climatically-sealed environment with air cooled at the point of entry using a fine spray of water. In the summer when the outside temperature is 43 to 44°C, the inside temperature remains at 29-30°, a 13-14°C drop. Six to nine air changes per hour are provided on each floor. Temperature fluctuations inside the building do not exceed beyond 4°C over 24 hours period, while the fluctuations outside are as much as 14-17°C. As such cooler inside temperatures provide comfort to its occupants.

The PEDC system is adaptable according to seasonal climatic variations. During the hot season strategy (March-June) passive evaporative cooling micronisers provide a down draft of cool air. Insulated building mass and roof and high air change rates (8 – 15) reduce the heat load. Air moves across the laboratory through short circulating and the micronisers control automatically the ambient humidity. During the monsoon season (July to September), the ventilation rate is increased with micronisers switched off. Ceiling and wall induce air movement. During the cool season (October - February), the inlets and exhausts are closed. Insulated walls and roof reduce heat loss. During the hot days the building is evaporatively cooled while the inlets and exhausts are closed at night.

Indoor Air Quality (IAQ) and Outdoor Air

IAQ refers to the air quality within the indoor space. It especially relates to the health and comfort of the building occupants. IAQ is affected by microbial contaminant (mould, bacteria), gases (carbon monooxide, radon, VOCs), particulates or any other ingredient that can induce adverse health conditions, Sick Building Syndrome (SBS) and Building Related Illnesses (BRI). Indoor air is, therefore, a health concern. It can be improved by using ventilation to dilute contaminants, filtration and pollutants source control. Various studies conducted worldwide clearly reflect the economic impact of IAQ on health and productivity.

Result shows that reducing SBS symptoms by 20% to 25% can reduce asthma by 8% to 25%, other respiratory illness by 23% to 76%, and the savings due to these reductions are phenomenal.

The outside air, however, while solving this problem, poses a great challenge for the HVAC system. The saviour of IAQ brings along with it the quandary of high latent load, the HVAC equipment and resulting in high RH inside in a tropical country like India. Lack of RH control leads to growth of mould and mildew, which in turn, lead to various health related issues. Mould releases tiny spores which waft through the indoor air and start developing in damp areas. This needs adoption of the Dedicated Outdoor Air System (DOAS) in air-conditioning. Various DOAS options are available which should be designed according to the climatic context, building need and costs involved.

Urban Heat Island (UHI)

UHI is mainly the urban area which is significantly warmer than its surrounding area. The phenomenon was first investigated by Luke Howard in the 1810s. The temperature difference usually is larger at night than during the day, and is most apparent when winds are weak. Seasonally, UHI is seen during both summer and winter. The main cause of the urban heat island is modification of the surface by urban development which uses materials which effectively retain heat; beside waste heat generated by energy usage. As population in urban centres grows they tend to have a corresponding increase in average temperature, which is consistenly hotter than the surrounding area. There are three types of heat island:

1. Canopy Layer Heat Island (CLHI)
2. Boundary Layer Island (BLI)
3. Surface Heat Island (SHI)

The first two terms refer to a warming of the urban atmosphere and the last one refers to the relative warmth of urban surfaces. The urban canopy layer (UCL) is the layer of air closest to the surface in cities, extending upward to approximately the mean building height. Above the urban canopy layer lies the urban boundary layer, which may be 1 kilometer or more in thickness by day, shrinking to hundred of metres or less at night. It is the BLI that forms a dome of warmer air that extends downwind of city. Wind often changes the dome to a plume shape. The typology of heat island varies from spatial form to temporal form, and also on some of the underlying physical process that contribute to their development.

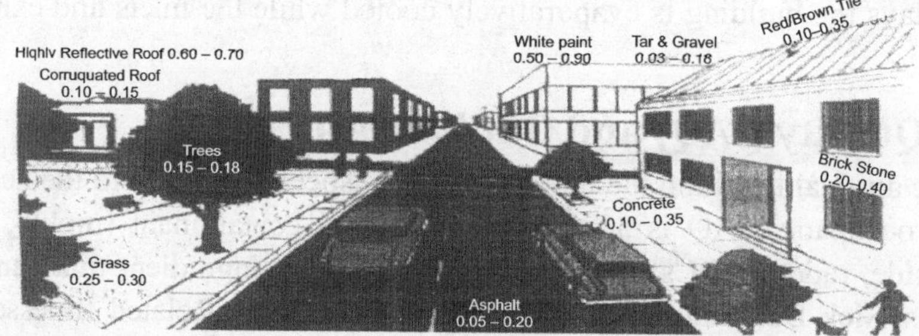

Fig. 7.27. Albedo and Heat Island Effect: As a city grows, new factors modify the local climate and have a complex character consisting of a mosaic of different surface materials. Each surface material has a different albedo, a measure of the amount of solar radiation reflected back into space. For a city as a whole, the albedo can be as low as 10–15%, which means that a lot of material used in the construction are characterized by a high heat capacity and high heat conductivity. Increased heat enhances photochemical reactions, which increases the particles in the air and thus smog. Urban heat island also can impact local weather, altering local wind patterns, spurring the development of clouds and fog, increasing the number of lightning strikes, and influencing the rate of precipitation.

***Sources:** http; yosemite. epa. gov.oar/globalwarming.nsf/content*

There are several causes of an urban heat island (UHI), as given below :

- The principal reason for the night time warming is building block surface heat radiating into the relatively cold night and sky.
- The rapid rate of urbanisation, increasing concrete surface area, less green dark colour roof tops are the primary driving forces behind UHI.
- The urban sprawl, road building programs, and high- and medium-rise buildings contribute to the UHI.
- Surface radiative properties (albedo and emissivity) in the highly concrete core urban areas vary; it becomes lower than the surrounding rural areas. This causes a change in the energy balance of the urban area, often leading to higher temperature than surrounding rural areas.

- The energy balance is also affected by the lack of vegetation of urban areas, which inhibits cooling by evapo-transpiration.
- The tall buildings within urban areas provide multiple surfaces for the reflection and absorption of sunlight, increasing the heat. This is called the "urban canyon effect."
- The blocking of wind by the buildings inhibits cooling. Waste heat from automobiles, air conditioning, industry, and other sources also contributes to the UHI. High levels of pollution in urban areas can also increase the UHI, as many forms of pollution change the radiative properties of the atmosphere.

Some cities exhibit a heat island effect largest at night. Seasonally, UHI shows up in both summer and winter. The typical temperature difference is several degrees between the centre of the city and surrounding fields. The difference in temperature between an inner city and its surrounding suburb is frequently mentioned in weather reports. The colour black absorbs significantly more electromagnetic radiation and causes the surface of roads and highways to heat up substantially. Aside from the effect on temperature, UHIs can produce secondary effects on local meteorology, including the altering of local wind patterns, the development of clouds and fog, the humidity, and the rates of precipitation. The extra heat provided by the UHI leads to greater upward motion, which can induce additional shower and thunder storm activity. Rainfall rates downwind of cities are increased between 48% and 116%. Partly as a result of this warming, monthly rainfall is about 28% greater between 20 miles (32 km) to 40 miles (64 km) downwind of cities, compared to upwind.

Research has been done in a few areas suggesting that metropolitan areas are less susceptible to weak tornadoes due to turbulent mixing caused by the warmth of the urban heat island. Using satellite images, research indicates to that city climates have a noticeable influence on plant grown up to 10 kilometers away from a city's edge. Satellite based thermal imagery data indicates that the causes for occurrence of urban heat island are mainly due to removal of vegetation cover, and paving of the land surface by non-evaporating and non-porous materials, such as asphalt and concrete.

While the "heat island" warming is an important local effect, there is no evidence that it indicates a trend in historical temperature record. The Third Assessment Report of the IPCC says:

"*However, over the Northern Hemisphere land areas where urban heat island are most apparent, both the trends of lower-troposphere temperature and surface air temperature show no significant differences. In fact, the lower-troposphere temperature warm at a slightly greater rate over North America (about 0.28°C/decade using satellite data) than do the surface temperatures (0.27°C/decade), although again the difference is not statistically significant.*"

With increasing vehicular emissions, fossil fuel usage and urban growth, coupled with growing air conditioning demand, it is projected that the urban heat island effect can add from 6 to 12°C the normal summer temperature of surrounding areas. The population's health and productivity will be affected in major cities by high ambient summer temperature due to climate changes. In such circumstances, action to reduce the urban heat effect must become a priority. Measures can include reducing heat from buildings and vehicles, green roofs, using paving materials with high albedo and improving air circulation between buildings.

Rural and urban areas obtain energy from radiative process, ultimately gaining energy from the sun and subsequently losing energy back to the upper atmosphere in space. Shortwave radiation from the sun is absorbed only during the daytime, but the long-wave radiation emitted by the earth system is lost all the time. Consequently, the earth warms up during the day and cools at night by these radiative processes. The incident solar radiation, QI, is 8.9 kWh/m^2/day for both locations because the same sun shines on both environments with equal intensity. With an albedo of 0.23 typical of a rural forest ecosystem, the reflected solar radiation, QR is 0.8 kWh/m^2/day in India. However, because of a high density of low reflecting building and roadway surfaces in most cities, urban ecosystems may have an average albedo as low as 0.04 resulting in an urban reflected sunlight of only 0.4 kWh/m^2/day. Thus the net energy obtained from the sun in the rural area is 6.5 kWh/m^2/day while in the urban area it is 8.9 kW/m^2/day, or 2.4 kWh/m^2/day more. An increase of 1.5 kWh/m^2/day in solar radiation could result in a temperature increase of almost 20°F. Surface albedo is indeed a very important factor in urban heating, that can be addressed by a change in the reflectivity of construction materials.

Every material substance gives off radiant energy, characteristic of the temperature of that substance. The long-wave upward radiation from both rural and urban environments will depend on the average effective temperature of the respective surfaces. The long-wave length downward-radiant energy back to the earth surface originates in the higher atmosphere when upward energy is absorbed. Warming the atmosphere and causing it to remit this energy. High level of pollutants in the urban atmosphere may be heat trapping and cause the urban upper atmosphere to be hotter. The existence of pollution would then cause the downward radiant energy, increasing urban heating.

The latent heat required for the vaporization of water. Lack of trees and shrubs in the city reduce the amount of water that can be evaporated by transpiration, especially in industrial, commercial, and densely populated high-rise residential areas. In a situation with a healthy ground cover of green, shrubs and trees, half of the evaporative water loss is through the plants. In a city, buildings, roads, and parking lots cover large portions of the surface.

Sensible heat refers to the back and forth transfer of heat between the atmosphere and various surfaces. It is heat transferred by conduction with various materials and by convection (vertical) or advection (horizontal) as air moves from one place to another. Storage heat is energy that is absorbed by the various materials of the surface environment, buildings, pavements, soil, etc. During the day the energy from the sun heats different areas of the city to different degrees. The main energy inputs in any micro-climate system are shortwave radiant energy from the sun and long-wave radiant energy exchange between the surface and the atmosphere. Human beings can affect the radiation energy by changing the albedo (by land use change) so that more of the sun's energy is reflected back into space. Wherever possible, dark (low aldedo) surface should be replaced by light (high albedo) surface so that less sun light is absorbed. Some practical and simple measures that can be adopted are the following:

- Replace high radiation absorbing surfaces such as dark roofs, asphalt streets and parking lots with highly reflecting materials.
- Adopt passive design to minimise energy use, utilize higher efficiency of air conditioning systems, industrial processes, and transportation system that produce less anthropogenic heat.

- Inclusion of green space, city forests, spaced buildings, and better public transportation, including non-motorised transport.
- Landscape development, green cover, plantation, trees and vegetation and also maintaining natural drainage slopes and channels of wind flow, ensuring the soil conditions, especially porosity to permit absorption of surface water.

These measures can bridge the gap between adaptation and mitigation to avoid urban heat island syndrome.

DEBRIEFING QUESTIONS

1. What are the main climatic zones of India?

2. What are the major components of climatic comfort in a building?

3. Write notes on the following:

(*a*) Building Orientation

(*b*) Overheated Area

(*c*) Green Roof

(*d*) Building Envelope

4. Explain the following:

(*a*) Earth Air Tunnel

(*b*) Air Scoop/Wind Catchers

(*c*) Urban Heat Island

(*d*) Albedo

(*e*) Thermal Performance of Building

(*f*) Building Index

5. What is the approach of Passive Design of a Building for climatic comfort?

Chapter 8

Sustainable and Resilient Habitat

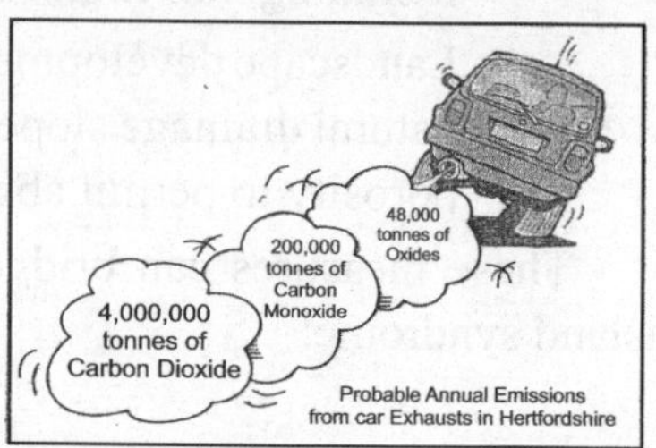

Probable Annual Emissions from car Exhausts in Hertfordshire

There is an umbilical relationship among natural environment, human settlements and societies. The ecology and environment have a major role in sustainable habitat. This calls for understanding the environment and its legal and institutional frameworks, together with study if the impact of land, air, water, flora and fauna, and health energy on the habitat.

174 countries of the world have signed the Sustainable Development Goals (SDGs), which aim to control pollution of air, water, soil, marine, noise, and arresting the climate change that impinge upon ecological systems. Sustainable development is closely related to architecture, energy, water conservation, waste management and landscape development. Sustainable strategies involve a trans-disciplinary collaboration in design, land use planning, transportation planning, renewable energy, water conservation and resilience to climate change and disasters.

India, with more than 1210 million people living in 7936 cities and towns and 6,41,000 villages, is second largest populous country of the world. India's cities and towns, having a population of 377 million, generate 60% of GDP and 70% of the jobs.

In India, millions of people every year migrate from villages to the cities in the hope of finding jobs and basic sustenance. However, many of them live in pathetic conditions in the slums and squatter settlements with pollution, shortage of the basic services and insensitivity towards the women, children, disabled, and elderly. Urban livelihoods are threatened by the risks of natural disasters, flooding, landslides, heat waves and droughts. The deterioration of urban environment by increasing carbon emission from fossil fuels, traffic, insanitation, poor drainage, open defecation and by inadequate solid and liquid waste disposal are major issues.

It is estimated that urban India generates 68.8 million tons of municipal solid waste per year, which is projected to grow to 160.5 million tons per year by the year 2041. Presently, only half of the municipal solid waste is collected and processed, resulting into insanitation and poor hygiene. Emissions and wastes from transport, industries, dairies, refineries, quarrying, power generation, etc. are major sources of air pollution, groundwater deterioration and soil contamination.

Fig. 8.1. Growth of private vehicles is a major threat to urban sustainability and resilience

Cities account for three-quarters of the total energy demand, including fossil fuels used for transport and produce almost 80% of CO_2 emissions making the urban air very unhealthy.

Almost every Indian city is situated along a river or water body, which is not only the source of water, but also has social, cultural and religious values. However, with indiscriminate urbanization these have become polluted and dirty. River Ganga was ranked among the top five most polluted rivers of the world (2007).

The form of urban planning and management prevalent in the country is generally bureaucratic and involves conservative controls. With the 74th Constitutional Amendment Act (1992), the urban local bodies have been assigned greater role in urban planning and governance. However, this has not happened, as most of the governments are reluctant to part with their powers. Poor capacity and finances are also acting as barriers in devolution of the municipal functions.

New Urban Agenda

The New Urban Agenda, an internationally negotiated document, calls for compact cities, polycentric growth, mixed use, prevention of sprawl and transit oriented development. The Habitat III New Urban Agenda (2017) aims at the following:

- Basic services for all including shelter, potable water, sanitation, food, health-care, education and access to communication.
- Equality of opportunity, with special attention to the needs of the women, children, people with disability, the elderly, indigenous people and organized groups.
- Cleaner air, by using renewable energy, greener public transport systems and sustainable practices with natural resources.

- More resilience and less risk of damages from disasters through better planning, resilient infrastructure and improved response capabilities.
- Safe and accessible greens public spaces, walkways, cycling lanes, squares and parks.

Sustainable Development Goals

Climate change has become an imminent reality with a rise in global temperature, changes in rainfall, floods, droughts and intense heat waves. A drastic increase in atmospheric concentration of water vapours, carbon-dioxide, methane and nitro-oxide, and other greenhouse gases help trap heat near the earth's surface.

With increasing vehicular and industrial emissions, fossil fuel usage and urban growth, coupled with growing air conditioning demand, it is projected that the urban heat can increase by 3 to 4.8°C. The population's health and productivity will be affected by high ambient summer temperatures. In such circumstances, action to reduce the climate change effect must become a priority. The Sustainable Development Goal (SDG) 11 aims to make cities and human settlements inclusive, safe, resilient and sustainable by the year 2030. Also the SDG 13 aims to combat climate change and its impact. Mitigation and adaptation to climate change imply new ways of habitat planning, energy, construction, infrastructure development and transport.

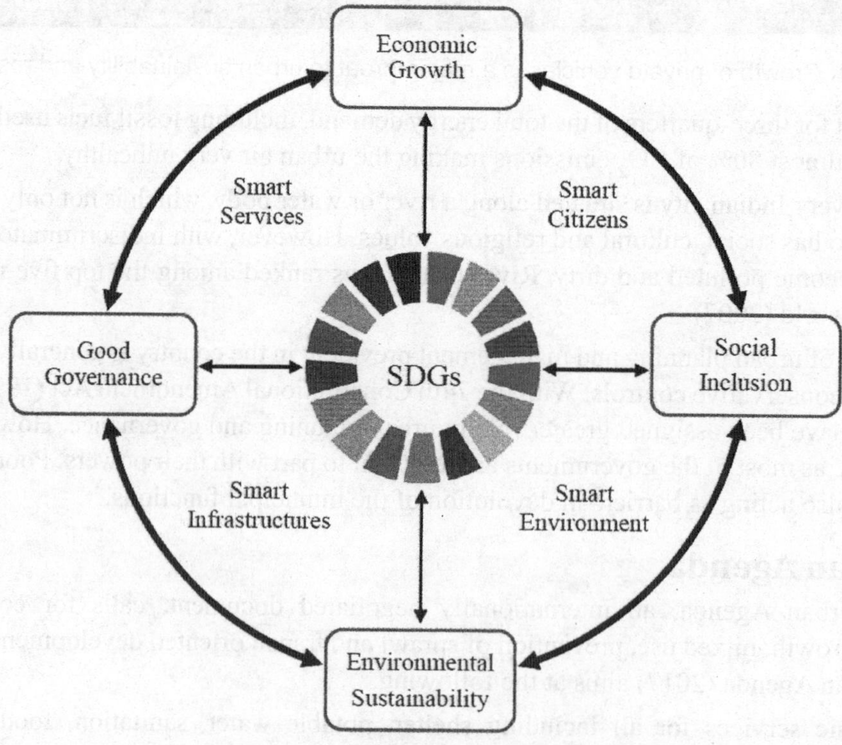

Fig. 8.2. The relation between urban components and the SDGs

Targets of SDG 11

SDG 11 aims to make the cities inclusive, safe, resilient and sustainable by the year 2030 with the following ten targets:

1. Access for All to Housing and Basis Services.
2. Sustainable Transports for All.
3. Sustainable Planning and Management.
4. Safeguarding the Cultural and Natural Heritage.
5. Disaster Resilient, Safety and Management.
6. Reducing the Environment Impact and Pollution.
7. Universal Access to Green and Public Spaces.
8. Strengthening Integrated Development Planning.
9. Mitigation and Adaptation to Climate Change.
10. Sustainable and Resilient Buildings and Resources.

In this pursuit, it is necessary to adopt an approach which engages with the identity of the city and meets the challenges of its population growth, housing, slums, jobs and employment, gender safety, and provision of adequate infrastructure services. The approach has to be visionary, keeping in view the following core principles of the SDG 2030 Agenda:

- Leave no one behind
- Localization
- Leave no place behind
- Access to development resources

National Agenda

In order to make the cities more livable, the Government of India have launched new urban missions, viz., smart Cities Mission, Atal Mission for Rejuvenation and Urban Transformation (AMRUT), Pradhan Mantri Awas Yojana, Historic City Development and Augmentation Yojana (HRIDAY) and Swachh Bharat Mission (SBM). These missions target the provision of core infrastructure services like water supply, sanitation and solid waste management, efficient urban transport, affordable housing for the poor, 24 × 7 power supply, IT connectivity and e-governance. These missions emphasise upon participatory planning and governance towards enhancing the diversity, livelihoods, connectivity and provide better education, heath-care, urban safety and services. This is an opportunity to indigenize urban planning and make it part of larger eco-system of sociology, which addresses our own demographics, culture, humanity and local geography.

These mission envisage to harness the public, private and community resources together with Central Government grants. Planning has to be based on comprehensive information system, digitized mapping and geo-portal, which relates with local culture and climate. It should be inclusive that provides jobs, livelihoods, local economic dynamism and venues to cultural expression. About 100 smart city project have been initiated, along with a network of cities on Delhi-Mumbai Industrial Corridor, Gift City, Gandhi Nagar and State capitals such as Amravati, the new capital of Andhra Pradesh.

The principles of Smart City underline the need to develop high quality streets and public spaces, mixed uses, connectivity, social structure, urban resilience and energy efficiency.

Liveability and Sustainability Index

To evaluate the liveability quotient of the Indian cities, a comprehensive assessment criteria comprising institutional, social, economic and physical factors has been developed. The data is being collated from 116 cities which will be weighted against 79 indicators covering approximately 134 million people.

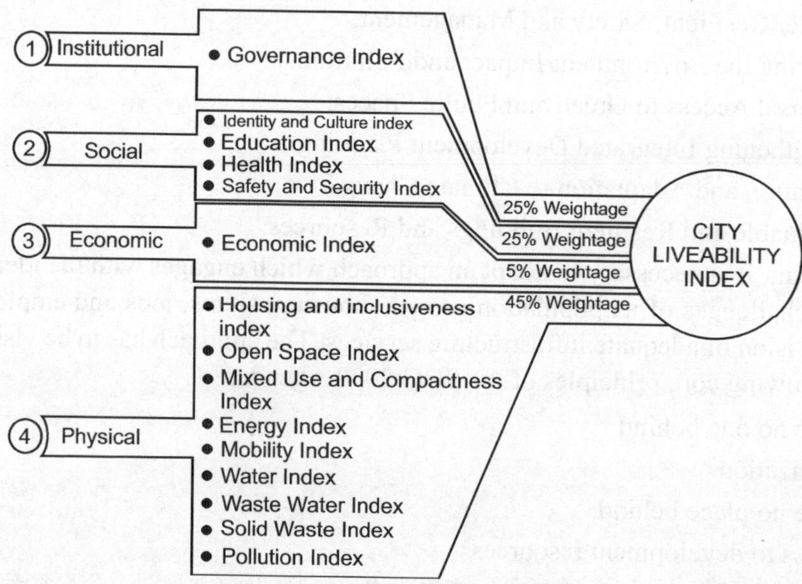

Fig. 8.3. City Liveability Index comprises four pillars of sustainable development (MOHUA 2018)

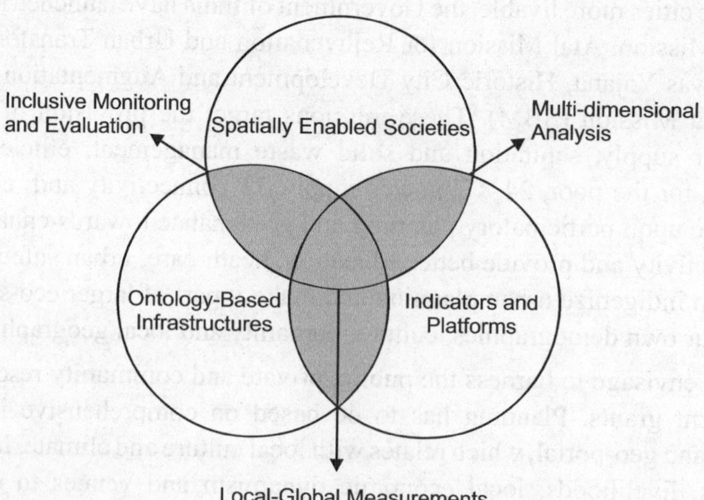

Fig. 8.4. Three major socio-spatial dimensions of sustainable development

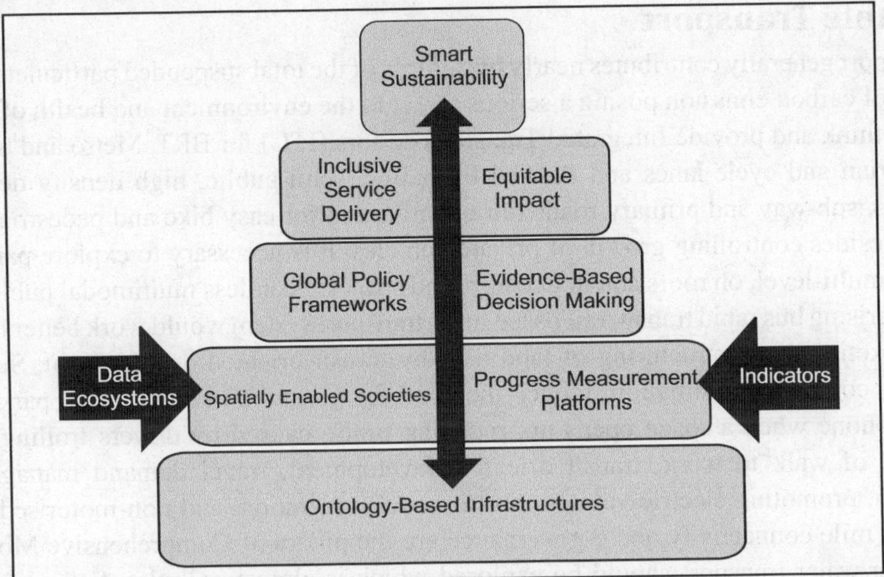

Fig. 8.5. Sustainable Cities Framework

STRATEGIES FOR SUSTAINABLE AND RESILIENT HABITAT

The following broad strategies need to be adopted to address the SDG-11, targets:

Access for All to Housing and Basic Services

There is a need to promote and incentivise housing for all with basic services, including in-situ slum rehabilitation, regularization and redevelopment, densification and upgradation of unplanned colonies/villages and old residential areas. This requires the reservation of minimum 15 percent of land/FAR or 35 percent of the total dwelling units for the society in every housing scheme. Compact high rise and high density housing pattern can enable optimum use of land and other resources. By using land as a resource, market sale component of housing upto 40% of FAR can subsidize social housing. This requires:

- Promoting a broader concept of upgrading with services, jobs and community participation,
- Variations rather than standard solutions,
- Promoting rental social housing,
- Local economic promotion and poverty reduction, and
- Security of tenure.

Inclusive housing involves the provision of mixed land use, jobs, social facilities and sustainable services, viz. drainage and flood control, sewerage, water supply, waste water recycling, rain water harvesting, solid waste management, public and individual toilets, roads, electricity, street lights, etc. The concept of bundling of land-infrastructure-housing can subsidize slum rehabilitation and social housing.

Sustainable Transport

Urban transport generally contributes nearly two-thirds of the total suspended particulate matter and 18 per cent of carbon emission posing a serious threat to the environment and health of the people. It is time to think and provide Integrated Transit Corridors (ITC) for BRT, Metro and trains linked with pedestrian and cycle lanes and flanked by public, semi-public, high density development. Metro, trains, sub-way and primary roads run underground for easy bike and pedestrian traffic on the grade. Besides controlling growth of private vehicles, it is necessary to explore parking space under stilts, multi-level, on roofs and in underground spaces. Seamless multimodal public transport system comprising bus rapid transit, rail based mass transport system would work better by adoption of single ticketing and restructuring of land uses by transit oriented development. Subterranean garages near commuter destinatioin reduce the need for ground parking. Digital parking meters tell mobile phone when a space opens up, reducing traffic caused by drivers trolling for space. The concept of walk to work, transit oriented development, travel demand management and smart growth, promoting electric vehicles multi-modal integration, and non-motorised transports (NMTs), last mile connectivity and e-governance are the pillars of Comprehensive Mobility Plan (CMP). River/water transport should be explored which is almost pollution free and most cost-effective. The concepts of cordon pricing, minimum occupancy vehicles, ceiling on registration of private vehicles and establishment of Unified Metropolitan Transport Authority can contribute in sustainable and coordinated urban transport.

Sustainable Planning & Management

The pursuit of sustainable development requires striking a balance between economic goals, human needs (social, cultural, liveability and health) and environmental integrity. It is "design with nature", which means development and human interventions in natural system to the extent of carrying capacity of an area that can be sustained for a given length of time without depletion of the resources or breakdown of the natural systems. Sustainability is all embracing—the ecology, landscape and cultural processes, the physical context, *i.e.* geography, geology, hydrology, vegetation and climate. The urban process, including consumption, food production, energy and waste management based on the principles of circular metabolism and recycling ensures the integrity of the natural resources.

Urban development of existing areas or new development should be based on preserving the green areas, conserve fertile land and protect ground water recharge areas. This implies maintaining an inter-dependence between natural and built environment.

The objective of sustainable development is to provide a healthy living environment to the citizens, which is based on the following considerations:

- Conservation of green areas, fertile land, forests, geology and hydrology
- Rejuvenation of rivers and water bodies, ground water augmentation
- Pollution prevention (water, air, noise, transport)
- Management of pollution sources (industries, transport, households)
- Provision of efficient sustainable infrastructure (energy, water supply, sewage, sanitation, liquid and solid waste management, etc.)
- Provision of compatible land uses and compact and smart growth.

A comprehensive digitised and geo-referenced survey and a parametric study of eco-determinants and their relationship of humans to the natural and man-made environment provide the basis for a sound land use planning. It translates into the following urban planning agenda:

- Higher level of mixed land use and compact urban form based on environmental performance criteria.
- A coherent urban form, place making, controlled streetscape, enveloping of inner city areas, landmarks, nodes, pedestrian precincts, chowks and squares.
- Wide variety and intermixing of socio-cultural activities, relationship of commercial and public activities with public transportation.
- Built from consistent with historical, socio-cultural context and particular potential of an area/region.
- Exclusion of environment endangering land uses.

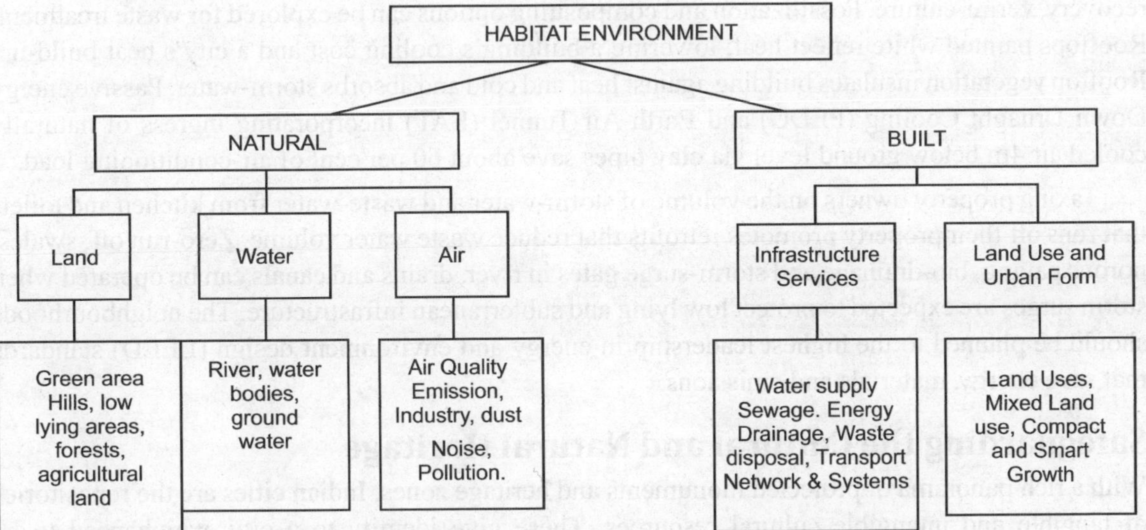

Fig. 8.6. Components of Sustainable Urban Environment

Fig. 8.7. Skolkovo Gardens, RU Moscow, Russia designed by Maxwan/Arteza

The cities, particularly slums, and unplanned settlements, are almost without hygienic sanitation, drinking water facility and a clean place to urinate and defecate. The public and individual toilet facility, particularly for women and children, is a critical area of concern. Intelligent, alternative and innovative ways to provide services, *i.e.* water, power, drainage and solid waste management and renewable energy have to be introduced with emphasis on servicing the informal, unplanned settlements. Common utility ducts or tunnels carrying electricity, water, pneumatic waste ducts, cable television and broadband internet minimize damage from traffic, road repairs, rains, etc. and make repairs easier. A series of low carbon zones across the city with co-located tri-generation energy systems (combining power, cooling and heating), dual piping for recycled water and automated, segregated waste collection and recycling would lead to bundling green infrastructure together. Solid waste extracted from sewage at treatment plants is burned to make electricity. Three bins recycling is adopted with separate bins for trash, recyclable and compost. Collection charges drop as trash drops. Bio-technology, enzyme based STP, bio-remedial treatment, sludge gas/energy recovery, vermi-culture. Fossilization and compositing options can be explored for waste treatment. Rooftops painted white reflect heat, lowering a building's cooling cost and a city's heat build-up. Rooftop vegetation insulates building against heat and cold and absorbs storm-water. Passive energy Down Druaght Cooling (PEDC) and Earth Air Tunnel (EAT) incorporating ingress of naturally cooled air 4m below ground level via clay pipes save about 60 per cent of air-conditioning load.

Taxing property owners on the volume of storm-water and waste-water from kitchen and toilets that runs off their property promotes retrofits that reduce waste water volume. Zero-run off, swales, porous paving, bio-drainage and storm-surge gates in river, drains and canals can be operated when storm surges are expected to protect low lying and subterranean infrastructure. The neighbourhoods should be planned to the highest leadership in energy and environment design (LEED) standards that save energy, materials and emissions.

Safeguarding the Cultural and Natural Heritage

With a rich panorama of protected monuments and heritage zones, Indian cities are the repositories of tangible and intangible cultural resources. These give identity to a city, which need to be conserved. A comprehensive approach integrating conservation of natural and cultural heritage involves the following:

- Listing and mapping of heritage/iconic buildings and zones, and working out conservation guidelines and plans thereof, including taking up the repairs, retrofitting and maintenance. This requires creation of dedicated units for conservation of cultural heritage in local bodies.
- The rivers, drains and water bodies in urban areas usually have a high level of pollution, which is mainly from the untreated sewer and waste from adjacent urban areas. This needs control of unauthorised development and land uses which are incongruous with the environment, e.g. sanitary landfills, industry, thermal power station, etc. The development of greenways along drainage corridors and harvesting of rain water in balancing lakes and ponds can be a new frontier in city development.

Disaster Resilience and Safety

Indian cities and towns are vulnerable to droughts, floods, cyclones and earthquakes. Landslides, avalanche and forest fires also occur frequently. Among the 36 States/Union Territories in the country, 22 are multi-disaster prone. On an average 18.6 million hectare of land is flooded annually. About 57% of area of the country is vulnerable to seismic activity. 18% of country's total area and about 68% of total sown area is drought prone, affecting approximately 50 million people. India has a long coastline of 8040 km, which is exposed to tropical cyclones and tsunami.

Devastating floods, typhoons and a series of hurricanes are being associated with climate change. According to the initial report of the United Nations Framework on the Convention on Climate Change, the predicted impacts of climate change in India include rise in a surface air temperature, up to 30% decline in agriculture yield in rain-fed areas and an increase in incidence of extreme events, such as droughts, floods, cyclones, urban heat islands, earthquakes and changes in microclimate due to shortwave radiant energy from the sun and long-wave radiant energy exchange between the surface and the atmosphere. The planning for climate and disaster resilience involves the convergence of various sectors into a strategy that establishes a link between climate change and GHG/CO_2 emissions. The spatial area can be delineated as natural conservation zone based on its vulnerability (coastal areas, cyclone, earthquake, landslide, droughts, etc.). Accordingly, a series of geographically linked and disaggregated regional-district-local-sectoral plans, all telescopically connected, can be developed. The local action plan is connected both ways—up and down in geographical scale and also on its sides with various sectoral plans.

Some practical and simple measures that can be adopted are the following:

- Replace high radiation absorbing surfaces such as dark roofs, asphalt streets and parking lots with highly reflecting materials.
- Adopt passive design and renewable energy for heating, cooling and cooking, utilize higher efficiency air-conditioning system, industrial processes, and transportation systems that produce less anthropogenic heat,
- Inclusion of green space, city forests, better spaced buildings, and better public transportation, including non-motorised transport.
- Landscape development includes plantation, trees, vegetation, maintaining drainage slopes and channels of water and wind flow, ensuring the soil conditions, especially porosity to permit absorption of water by avoiding unnecessary paving and roads. These measures can bridge the gap between adaptation and mitigation and avoid urban heat island syndrome.
- Comprehensive digitized and geo-referenced surveys and a systematic investigation of 'eco-determinants', which deal with relationship of humans and other forms of life to the natural and man-made environment and local climate provide the basis for a sound land use planning. Micro-zonation surveys may be referred for land use planning, layout plans and building design.
- Building bye-laws may incorporate the aspects of multi-hazard safety and retrofitting. Priority should be given to public buildings such as Hospitals, Educational. Institutional. Power Stations, Infrastructure, Heritage monuments and lifeline structures which attract large congregations.

The safety of women is a central issue. Various initiatives include the setting of the rescue and rehabilitation centres, re-integration of victims of trafficking; the setting up of 'One Stop Crisis Centre' provision of shelters, police desks, legal, medical and counselling service and 24x7 help lines. This also needs incremental actions, such as enhancement of street lighting, establishment of 'Multi-Utility Zones (MUZs)', pedestrian safety, safer roads, provision of public toilets for women, especially in the slums and streets and safer public transport with CCTV and alarm system.

The planning of a city can contribute in crime prevention by gender sensitive design of shared, lively and defensible spaces, mixed land use and adequate shelter/tenements for the poor, together with spaces for vending and informal trades that promote livelihood and community surveillance.

Reducing the Environmental Impact and Pollution

The air quality in terms of pollution levels is a matter of serious concern and is responsible for a number of respiratory diseases, heart ailments, eye irritation, asthma, etc. The three main sources of air pollution are vehicular emission (around 70 percent), industrial emissions (around 20 percent) with a major element of this coming from the thermal power plants, and from other sources such as diesel generator sets and domestic cooking, burning of biomass, etc.

With the phenomenal growth in the number of vehicles, the most significant aspect is the congestion and pollution. Deficiencies in sanitation, sewerage, drainage and solid waste management add to environmental disaster.

The need to save air, water and land from pollution is a major concern. Drinking water, sanitation, solid waste treatment and drainage are important aspects of the human environment. The performance of present sanitation systems needs to be reassessed with reference to environment, hygiene and their accessibility. The future city will be low-carbon, low energy, smart, sustainable, safer, more efficient, and resilient. It will optimize the use of IT, simulation, automation and robotics that will make it smart and intelligent. Renewable, efficient energy and solar mapping would be key concerns in its planning and design. In contrast to emphasis on complex EIA, end of pipe pollution control measures, cleaner energy and fuels, car emission norms, etc. What most urban centres need is an environmental planning approach that facilitates meeting deficits in provision of basic services, e.g. water, sanitation, drainage, electricity, healthcare, emergency services, schools, public transport, etc.

Various alternative technologies, based on decentralized services, like Extended Aeration Technique, Bio-gas production, Bubble Diffusion Process, Flotation, Anaerobic reactors, etc. which are already in vogue, can be explored for urban sanitation. In place of land filling for solid waste disposal, decentralized systems based on recycling, energy generation and organic decomposting should be explored. Bio-reactor composting and vessel system, vermi-composting, etc. are new generation technologies for waste treatment.

The concepts of energy efficiency, renewable energy and Zero-fossil Energy Development (ZED) can reduce the level of energy demand and slow down the rate at which resources are depleted. Energy efficiency involves a synergy of various levels of planning, design, construction and maintenance.

Smart and green buildings can give energy saving up to 30%, reduce carbon emissions, provide higher efficiency and comfort with lesser energy consumption. The city and buildings have not only to be comfortable, green and efficient but also intelligent and integrated. The following measures are necessary in this regard:

- Replace high radiation absorbing surfaces such as dark roofs, asphalt streets and parking lots with highly reflecting materials.
- Adopt passive design to minimize energy use, including space heating, cooling and cooking, utilize higher efficiency air conditioning systems.
- Inclusion of green space, city forests, better spaced buildings, and better public transportation, including non-motorized transport.
- Landscape development, plantation of trees, vegetation, ensure maintaining drainage channels, recharging of sub-soil water by porosity for absorption of water. By proper land use planning, mixed land use, location of public/semi-public and commercial activities along major transport arteries, a green buffer can be created for residential zone. The green buffer with thin leave trees, land formation, mounds, embankments, etc. provide effects barriers to transmission of noise.

Water, plantation, shade and channelling of cooling breeze are the prime elements for a comfortable micro-climate. Minimum exterior surface to maximum internal volume, correct orientation, atriums and internal courtyards reduce glare and heat. Drainage and flood control strategy may be linked with water supply and pollution control.

Universal Access to Greens and Public Spaces

The open spaces and public building in the cities are often encroached upon and are inaccessible, especially for the disabled, children, women, elderly and others. It is mandatory to make public spaces universally accessible with a safe passage for wheel-chair users. The Persons with Disabilities (Equal Opportunities, Protection of Right and Full Participation) Act, 1996 requires the mandatory provision of ramps in buildings, adequate space in corridors, lifts, kitchen, pathways and toilets for wheelchair users, along with Braille symbols and auditory Signals, signage and other facilities for sight and hearing impaired.

Strengthening Integrated Development Planning

In view of emerging issues of sustainability and climate and disaster resilience, it is necessary to review the present practice of master planning and institutional frameworks, which favour participatory, local planning. This involves the following key actions :

- Strengthen urban planning capacity and constitute empowered Local Area/Ward Planning Committees for Local Area Planning.
- Enact/review the Town Planning and Municipal legislations
- Take up the preparation of a Regional Plan
- Constitute a Land Management Committee and bring a legislation for on-line registration, transactions transfers and land pooling
- Take up Physical, Social, Environmental and Financial Audits
- Bridge the gap between planning and implementation by constitution of monitoring and coordination groups at policy, strategic and operational levels.

Mitigation and Adaptation to Climate Change

The mitigation and adaptation to climate change and resilience to disasters and risk management involves integrated policies and plans covering strategies for natural resource conservation, water and energy efficiency, enhancing green cover, reducing GHG emissions and pollution. For this, it is necessary to adopt the concepts of Transit Oriented Development, walk to work, decentralised solid and liquid waste management systems, passive design and alternative low energy space cooling systems. Resilience to disaster needs holistic planning in line with the NDMA guidelines and Hyogo framework. This involves the following:

- Development of Mitigation and Adaptation Plans and pollution control strategies for climate change and disasters.
- Development of networked emergency response and safety centres integrating police, fire, disasters, accidents, crimes, traffic and women's safety. Avoid left over, undefined spaces such as roadsides, backyards, waste dumps, etc.
- Development of a network of mohalla clinics, health infrastructure, dispensaries, trauma and accident centres.
- Improve urban infrastructure - CCTV, GIS, variable and Intelligent Traffic Signage, lighting, maps, pavements, public transport, parks, drinking water points, public toilets, lighting, police post, and street furniture.
- Signage in all public places giving details of helpline numbers and persons to be contacted in case of emergency.
- Provision of clean and well functioning toilets on all public roads, in schools, markets and public buildings.
- Discourage unoccupied, speculative property ownership, urban deterioration, dereliction and "broken window" syndrome.
- Safety of children in educational institutes, buses, playgrounds and on roads. Sustainable and safe transport needs a review of planning and engineering specifications, norms and practices, improvement of public transport, non-motorized vehicles, sidewalks, cycle tracks, underpasses and over-passes.
- Upgrading traffic control systems, public transport, alarm system for safety of women passengers, intelligent signal control, drivers' training and management.
- Review and simplify building codes for non-engineered buildings and mandatory structural and fire safety approvals.

Sustainable and Green Buildings

It is estimated that 60% of the buildings required in Indian cities by 2030 are yet to be built. This is a unique opportunity to shift towards sustainable, resilient and green buildings. For this the following principles and strategies can be adopted:

- Sustainable site planning
- Building envelope design
- Building system design, energy efficient, alternative HVAC (heating, ventilation and air conditioning), lighting, electrical, and water heating

- Integration of renewable energy sources to generate energy onsite.
- Selection of ecologically sustainable materials (with high recycled content, renewable resources with low emission potential)
- Passive design of buildings for climatic comfort
- Optimum use of energy and reducing its need by daylighting, courtyards, green roof, ventilation, etc.
- Water conservation and recycling
- Solid and liquid waste management
- Energy efficient transport
- Efficient building systems, construction and maintenance

It is always better to specify building materials which are locally sourced, require less energy for production and transportation to the site. These should have low embodied energy and should be preferably natural. Promote use of recycled materials in place of high embodied energy materials like steel and aluminium. Use of reclaimed materials such as construction and demolition waste should be promoted. Some new green materials and technologies include the following:

- Swales, bio-drainage, porous paving, rainwater harvesting, waste water recycling, dual piping.
- Aerators for water fixtures
- Waterless urinals and other water saving systems
- Micro-irrigation systems, xeriscaping
- Building Integrated Solar Photovoltaic, wind energy, parabolic concentrated solar cookers
- Green roof, vertical garden, urban farming
- High COP Chillers
- Wind towers/tunnels/chimney/high albedo materials
- Geothermal system
- LED, CO_2 Sensors, Intelligent, Bionic Sensors and Controls
- Building Information Modelling System
- Rapid wall, precast, prefabricated components
- Low emitting adhesives, sealants and insulation products.

Achieving the Outcomes

A sustainable and resilient habitat can't be accomplished without a roadmap which gives a clear orientation and a series of steps to be taken in a long journey. These steps include the following:

- Setting up the benchmarks, standards and norms
- Preparation of action plans for each target of the SDG-11.
- Institutional/organizational capacity building and competencies
- Legal framework and procedural reforms
- Financial planning, outcome budgeting and harnessing the resources of government, private and community sectors.

There is a need to develop a comprehensive insight into urban problems and policies and evolve a vision with the imperatives of decentralization, localization, partnership, equity, transparency and accountability. Civic engagement and participatory development should be the basis of sustainable and resilient habitat.

The planning of a sustainable and resilient city involves planning and actions at the local, regional and national levels. In order to uphold the 'leaving no one behind' promise, future infrastructure, technologies and policies must encompass inclusive and multilevel mobilisation and address social, economic, technical, spatial and other dimensions. The socio-spatial approach towards city that engages the citizens is necessary. Capability to overcome the urban challenges this enhancing the competencies, connectivity and coordinated implementation.

Principles of a Smart City

UN-Habitat has been promoting the principles of sustainable and smart urban development and adoption of new technologies to achieve competitiveness, and improve the quality of life of citizens. It recommends smart and new systems to address the urbanization challenges, such as population growth, urban sprawl, biodiversity, urban mobility and energy. It also emphasises planning at the national, regional and metropolitan scales to achieve integrated, connected, socially inclusive and resilient cities.

It has developed a Smart City Vision which aims to achieve sustainable development compact and efficient development, walkable neighbourhoods, promoting foster employment and providing a diversity of housing options.

The Smart City promotes a street network that not only works for vehicles and public transport, but also aims to attract pedestrians and cyclists. The principle entails:

- 50 percent of the land should be used for public space. Of this, 30 percent should be allocated to streets and 20 percent to squares, parks and open spaces.
- At least 18 km of street length per square kilometer.
- At least 80 crossings per square km are required in order to build a well connected grid in cities.

Mixed Urban Uses: This principle aims at developing a range of compatible activities and land uses close together and flexible enough to adapt over time to the changing market. This entails:

- Avoid zoning and avoid dividing neighbourhoods by highways or hard infrastructures
- At least 40 percent of floor space allocated to economic uses in any neighbourhood
- Single use blocks should cover less than 10 percent of any neighbourhood.

Connectivity: This principle proposes a grid and a hierarchy of streets with arterial and secondary roads that are well connected through intersections. This principle encourages walking, public transport and ICT accessibility.

Mixed social structure: This principle aims at promoting cohesion and interaction between different social classes in the same community and to ensure accessibility to equitable urban opportunities by providing different types of housing. This entails:

- Spatially combined rental and ownership property models
- A range of different rent levels to achieve integration and disseminate cosmopolitan values

- Dedicate 20-50 percent of residential space for low and affordable income residents who have a role in climate change and its mitigation.

Urban Resilience: Resilience recognizes the role of cities in climate change mitigation and adaptation, disaster preparedness and natural resources management. This entails:

- Reduction of GHG emission
- Assessment of high risk areas inside settlements
- Disaster preparedness strategies

Energy and Resource Efficiency: By using resources in a sustainable manner, cities will minimize impacts on the environment, creating more with less and delivering greater value with less input. This entails energy efficiency in sectorial policies, promotion of renewable energies, resource management and preservation, recycle, reuse, reduce and closed loop strategies.

Practical and enforceable norms and rules: It is critical to provide policies, plans, norms and rules that respond to the current needs of municipalities and at the same time are flexible enough to accommodate different growth scenarios of urban areas.

Smart City Extensions: One key methodology developed by UN-Habitat to accommodate rapid growth in cities is the Planned City Extension. The methodology addresses sustainable urban growth at a required scale including the provision of sufficient public space and buildable plots to unleash the housing process. The benefits of this approach include economic agglomeration advantages, including lower infrastructure; reduced mobility demand and increased social heterogeneity as a result of mixed land use.

Urban Environmental Accord

Signed on United Nations Environment Programme World Environment Day (June 5, 2005) in San Francisco, California

Energy : Renewable Energy | Energy Efficiency | Climate Change

Action 1 : Adopt and implement a policy to increase the use of renewable energy to meet ten percent of the city's peak electrical load within seven years.

Action 2 : Adopt and implement a policy to reduce the city's peak electric load by ten percent within seven years, through energy efficiency, shifting the timing of energy demands, and conservation measures.

Action 3 : Adopt a citywide greenhouse gas reduction plan that reduces the emissions by twenty five percent by 2030, include a system for accounting and auditing greenhouse gas emissions.

Waste Reduction: Zero Waste | Manufacturer Responsibility | Consumer Responsibility

Action 4 : Establish a policy to achieve zero waste to landfills and incinerators by 2040.

Action 5 : Adopt a citywide law that reduces the use of a disposable, toxic or non-renewable product category by at least ten percent in seven years.

Action 6 : Implement "user-friendly" recycling and composting programs, with the goal of reducing by twenty percent per capita solid waste disposal to landfill and incineration in seven years.

Urban Design: Green Building [Urban Planning | Slums

Action 7 : Adopt a policy that mandates a green building rating system standard that applies to all new municipal buildings.

Action 8 : Adopt urban planning principles that advance higher density, mixed-use, walkable, bikeable and disabled-accessible neighbourhoods which coordinate land use and transportation with open space systems for recreation and ecological restoration.

Action 9 : Adopt a policy or implement a program that creates environmentally beneficial jobs in slums and/or low-income neighbourhoods.

Urban Nature: Parks | Habitat Restoration | Wildlife

Action 10 : Ensure that there is an accessible park or recreational public open space within half a kilometer of every city resident.

Action 11 : Conduct an inventory of existing canopy coverage in the city; and then establish a goal based on ecological and community considerations to plant and maintain canopy coverage in not less than fifty percent of all available sidewalk planting sites.

Action 12 : Pass legislation that protects critical habitat corridors and other key habitat characteristics (e.g. water-features, food bearing plants, shelter for wild life use of native species, etc.) from unsustainable development.

Transportation: Public Transportation | Clean Vehicles | Reducing Congestion

Action 13 : Develope and implement a policy which expands affordable public transportation coverage within half-a-kilometer of all city residents in ten years.

Action 14 : Pass a law or implement a program that eliminates leaded gasoline (where it is still used); and that phases down sulfur levels in diesel and gasoline fuels, concurrent with using advanced emission controls on all buses, taxis, and public fleets to reduce particulate matter and smog-forming emissions from those fleets by fifty percent in seven years.

Action 15 : Implement a policy to reduce the commute trips by single occupancy vehicles by ten percent in seven years.

Environmental Health: Toxic Reduction | Healthy Food Systems | Clean Air

Action 16 : Every year, identify one product, chemicals, or compounds, that is used within the city that represents the greatest risk to human health and adopt a law to provide incentives to reduce or eliminate its use by the municipal government.

Action 17 : Promote the public health and environmental benefits of supporting organic foods. Ensure that twenty percent of all city facilities (including schools) serve locally grown and organic food within seven years.

Action 18 : Establish an Air Quality Index (AQI) to measure the level of air pollution and set the goal of reducing by ten percent in seven years the number of days categorized in the AQI range as "unhealthy" to "hazardous."

Water: Water Access & Efficiency, Water Conservation and Wastewater Reduction

Action 19 : Develop policies to increase adequate access to safe drinking water; aiming at access for all. For cities with potable water consumption greater than 100 litres per capita per day, adopt and implement policies to reduce consumption by ten percent in next 5 years.

Action 20 : Protect the ecological integrity of the primary drinking water sources (*i.e.* aquifers, rivers, lakes, wetlands and associated eco-systems).

Action 21 : Adopt municipal wastewater management guidelines and reduce the volume of untreated wastewater discharge by ten percent in seven years through the expanded use of recycled water and the implementation of a sustainable urban watershed planning process that includes participation of all affected.

DEBRIEFING QUESTIONS

1. What do you understand by Sustainable and Resilient Habitat ?

2. Explain the concept and components of Sustainable Development Goal 11.

3. Explain the Habitat III New Urban Agenda.

4. How and why environmental degradation takes place ?

5. Write note on :

(*a*) Environmental Impact Assessment

(*b*) Environmental (Pollution Control) Act, 1986

(*c*) Energy Efficiency

(*d*) Water Conservation

(*e*) Bio-diversity

(*f*) Recycling

(*g*) Solid and Liquid Waste Management

(*h*) Sustainable Public Transit

(*i*) Disaster Resilience

(*j*) Mitigation and Adaptation

(*k*) Climate Change.

Chapter 9

BUILDING RESOURCES AND TECHNOLOGY

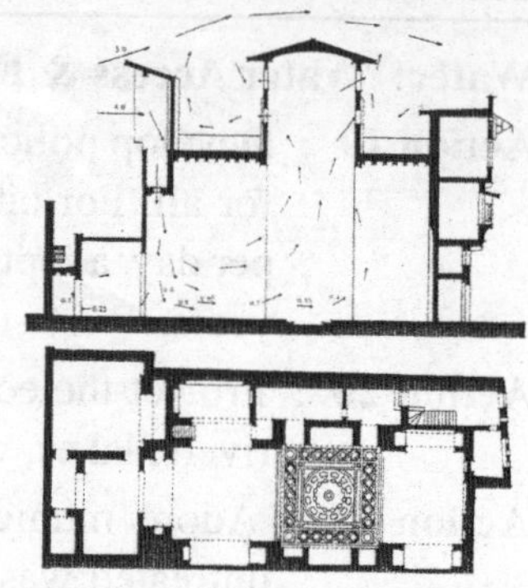

Turning the pages of history, it is evident that the building designs were limited by the technical achievement of that time, materials and labour available. Egyptians erected mountainous pyramids with immense labour and largely available stones with technical ability of quarrying and transporting. They adopted columnar form in their buildings. Further, Greek construction was entirely post and lintel. The maximum spacing of columns was determined by the amount of labour and the largest piece of stone available. They used the columns to support the roofing.

The Romans exploited the arches, which allowed large openings to be spanned and the construction was possible conveniently, because small elements were capable of being handy. It was a milestone in the history of architecture when the dome was introduced which developed from the arch. In the beginning the dome was formed by corbelling out the stone brick or tiles to form desired shape for the roofing over a circular plan. But afterwards the problem of dome on rectangular plan was brilliantly solved by introduction of pendentives.

The arch was used for spanning the openings in the form of barrel vault. There was a steady and increasing progress towards a pure structure form. As the social pattern changed and industrial revolution took place the building methods advanced with new materials and structural systems.

With the industrial revolution cast iron, steel, and reinforced concrete came as new building materials. These enabled erection of roofs of greater span and graceful appearance. These were first used in exhibitions and then in railway stations, factories, etc. These structures have their own characteristic, interior spaces and exterior shapes. Plasticity in design was possible by the use of new building materials and found its expression in works of many architects.

With the increasing urbanization, buildings and houses were erected. The structures for transport, bridges, viaducts, tunnels, etc. were erected. Here comes the engineer to provide an honest solution in a scientific term. This was fine engineering and to answer the problems architects coordinated with engineers in civil projects. This gave birth to a new aesthetics, which could be both structural and decorative. From the age of Vitruvius and Leonardo da Vinci a new generation of architects emerged which included Frank Lloyd Wright Le Corbusier, Gropius and Nervi. Steel, concrete, plastics, glass and non-ferrous metals like aluminium joined the list of building materials.

The concepts of construction materials and processes vary with the context of time and space. The celebrated American architect Frank Lloyd Wright, would ask his students–what materials are essential for construction? As usual the students would reply–stone, brick, glass, cement, steel, wood, etc. The master would then ask what about light and shade, air and water, sun and space? As such, the materials need to be seen in the light of composite design and potential of their transformation into an art, a sustainable structure. The celebrated architect Le Corbusier also looked at the building materials beyond their practical utility:

"You employ stone, wood and concrete, and with these materials you build houses and peaces. That is construction. Ingenuity is at work. But suddenly you touch my heart, you do me good, I am happy and I say: 'This is beautiful.' That is architecture. Art enters in. My house is practical. I thank you, as I might thank railway engineers, or the telephone service. You have not touched my heart."

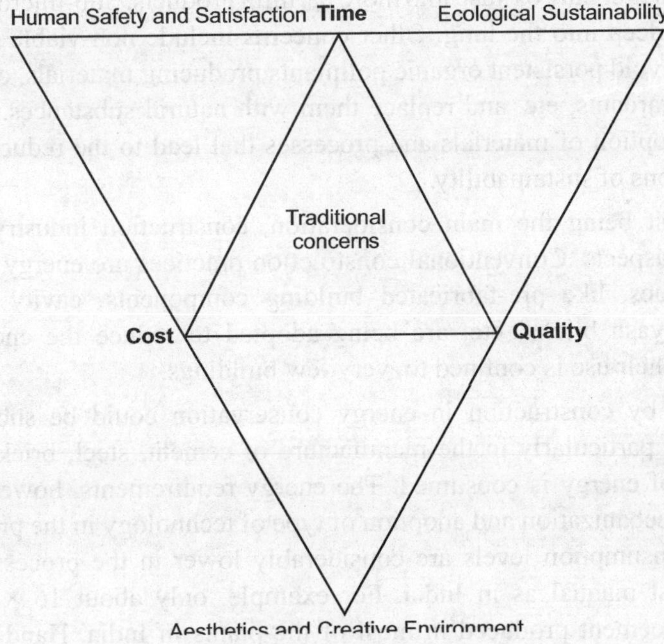

Fig. 9.1. New Paradigm

Time, quality and cost have always been the traditional factors in materials and construction. Today a new value system is emerging which is enveloping these traditional concerns. These are human safety and satisfaction, ecological sustainability and aesthetics.

We have come long way since H.G. Wells wrote the following in respect of building construction process and materials:

"I find it incredible that there will not be a sweeping revolution in the methods of building during the next century. The erection of a house wall, come to think of it, is an astonishingly tedius and complex business; the final result is exceedingly unsatisfactory. Everything in this was hand work, the laying of the bricks, the dabbling of the plaster, the smoothing of the paper, it is a house built of hands and some I saw were bleeding hands–just as in the days of the pyramids when the only engines were living men. I fail to see the necessity of (and, accordingly, resent bitterly) all these coral-reef methods. Better walls than this, and better and less life wasting ways of making them, are surely possible."

Buildings are the major consumers of energy, with existing stock responsible for more than 40% of the world's total energy consumption and 24% of world carbon dioxide emissions. The refurbishment of the existing building stock can assist in mitigating these problems. Energy conservation implies tightening up the buildings and tends to leave more room for indoor air quality problems, a host of adverse health outcomes associated with hazards in the environment, for example, asthma and allergy. The poor, women and the elderly are particularly vulnerable. Outdoor pollutants can infiltrate and react or stick with indoor materials. The magnitude of the deportation velocity can vary with indoor conditions such as humidity.

Volatile organic matter may oxidise into more harmful products. Sub-micron, particles produced via ozone can reach deep into the lung. Other concerns include non-viable particles, spores and bacteria. We should avoid persistent organic pollutants producing materials, chlorinated materials, brominates, flame retardants, etc. and replace them with natural substances. Modern approaches should favour the adoption of materials and processes that lead to the reduction of risks and are compatible with notions of sustainability.

Reduction of cost being the main consideration, construction industry generally neglects energy conservation aspects. Conventional construction practices are energy intensive. Improved construction techniques, like pre-fabricated building components, cavity walls, light weight concrete products, flyash bricks, etc. are being adopted to reduce the energy requirement of buildings. However, their use is confined to very few buildings.

The role played by construction in energy conservation could be substantial. Production of building materials particularly in the manufacture of cement, steel, brick, lime, plastics, etc. substantial quantity of energy is consumed. The energy requirements, however, vary depending upon the degree of mechanization and adoption of type of technology in the production of building materials. Energy consumption levels are considerably lower in the processes which are semi-mechanised or almost manual as in India. For example, only about 16 × 10' Kcal energy is consumed per kg of cement produced in most of the plants in India. Hand moulded bricks per 1000 nos. consume about 880×10^3 Kcal against 1020×10^3 in fully mechanised plant assuming the average calorific value of bituminous coal used as 5500 Kcal/kg. Similarly, conversion of wet process in cement manufacturing to the dry process results in 37 to 40 per cent reduction in fuel consumption. Considering reduced energy consumption a number of cement manufacturers in India have converted their wet process plants to the dry process. The basic approach toward reducing embodied energy and resource depletion include the following:

- Use locally sourced materials
- Use materials found on site or vicinity
- Minimise use of imported materials
- Use materials from sustainably managed sources
- Keep use of materials from non-renewable sources to a minimum
- Use low energy materials, keeping high embodied energy materials to a minimum
- Use second hand/recycled materials
- Re-use existing buildings and structures instead of new buildings.
- Use non-toxic or low-emission materials

- Avoid fibres from insulation materials getting into the atmosphere
- Try to minimise extraction of materials unless good environmental controls exist and avoid materials which produce damaging chemicals as by-products
- Do not dump waste materials off site but re-use on site

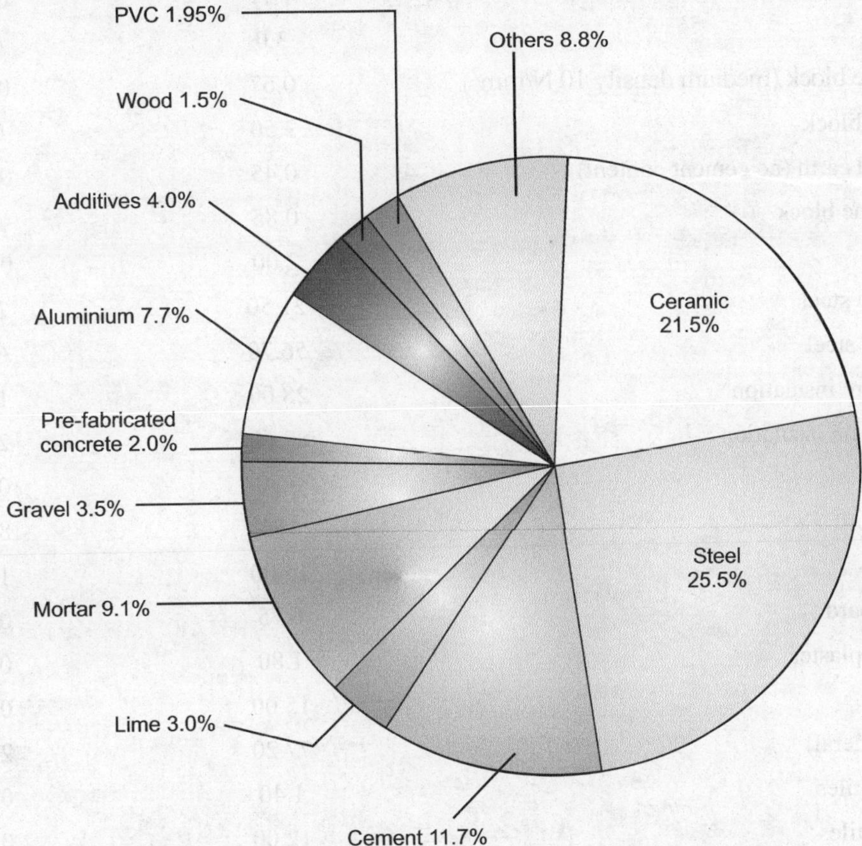

Fig. 9.2. Building Materials' contribution to embodied energy

Source: *Report of Centre of Research for Energy Resources and Consumption, (2010) Down to Earth, Jan. 16-31, 2013*

The embodied energy in buildings is related to the production of materials, during construction and transportation. On the basis of gross energy requirement for manufacturing unit weight of building materials, these can be classified in three categories:

- Low energy intensive materials like sand, aggregates, flyash, soil, adobe;
- Medium energy intensive materials like lime, bricks and tiles, concrete blocks, timber;
- High energy intensive materials like cement, steel, glass, aluminium, plastics, copper.

Low energy materials combine local materials and new technologies. The low embodied energy materials can be both conventional/traditional and evolved or modern, of which some examples are given in the following table.

Table 9.1. Embodied Energy and Embodied Carbon used in making products till they reach the factory gates

Material	Energy MJ/kg*	Carbon CO_2/kg
Concrete	1.11	0.159
Bricks	3.0	0.24
Concrete block (medium density 10 N/mm^2)	0.67	0.073
Aerated block	3.50	0.30
Rammed earth (no cement content)	0.45	0.023
Limestone block	0.85	—
Marble	2.00	0.116
Recycled steel	21.50	1.42
Stainless steel	56.70	6.15
Glass fibre insulation	28.00	1.35
Polystyrene insulation	88.60	2.55
Clay tile	6.50	0.45
Aluminium	155	8.24
Plywood	15.00	1.07
Plasterboard	6.75	0.38
Gypsum plaster	1.80	0.12
Glass	15.00	0.85
PVC (general)	77.20	28.1
Terrazzo tiles	1.40	0.12
Ceramic tiles	12.00	0.74
Iron (general)	25	1.91
Ceramic sanitaryware	29.00	1.51
Paint		
Water-borne paint	59.0	2.12
Solvent-borne paint	97.0	3.13
Photovoltaic cells		
Monocrystalline (average)	4750	242
Polycrystalline (average)	4070	208
Thin film (average)	1305	67

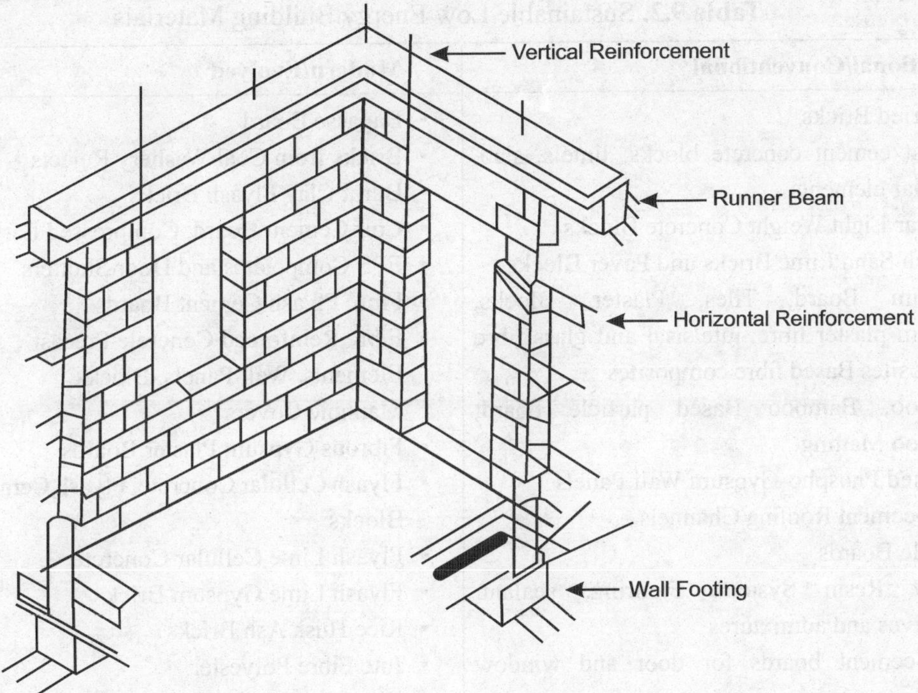

Fig. 9.3. Shear Wall in Concrete Block. 8" × 8" × 16" concrete blocks with two holes are laid one upon another by staggered joint. Vertical reinforcement is placed through these holes which are grouted

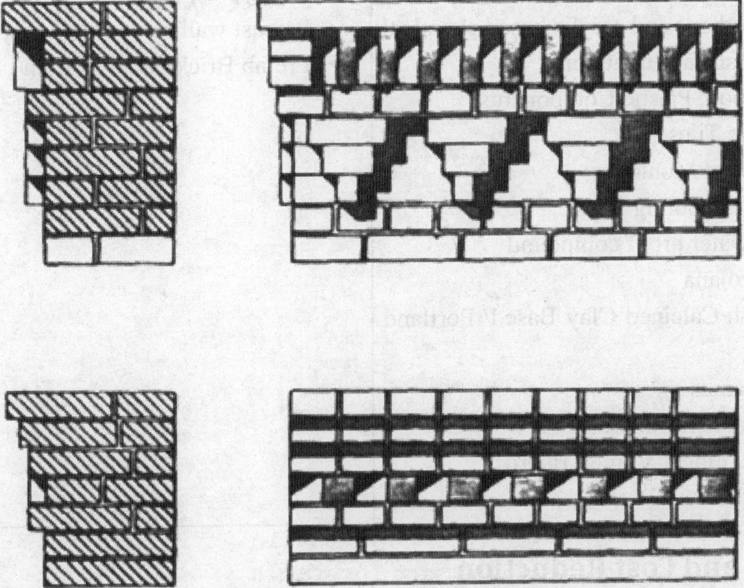

Fig. 9.4. The soffit in brickwork below roof and above openings for sun and rain protection, designed with attractive light and shade patterns

Table 9.2. Sustainable Low Energy Building Materials

Traditional/Conventional	Modern/Evolved
• Sun dried Bricks • Precast cement concrete blocks, lintels, slab, modular elements • Cellular Light Weight Concrete Blocks • Fly-ash Sand Lime Bricks and Paver Blocks • Gypsum Board, Tiles, Plaster, Blocks, gypsum plaster fibre, jute/sisal and glass fibre composites Based fibre composites • Bamboo, Bamboo Based particle board, Bamboo Matting. Calcined Phospho-Gypsum Wall Panels • Ferro-cement Roofing Channels • Particle Boards • Epoxy Resin System, Flooring, sealant, adhesives and admixtures • Ferro-cement boards for door and window shutters • Calcium silicate boards and tiles • Cement Paint • Clay roofing tiles • Water, polyurethane and acrylic based chemical admixture for surface treatment • Laminated Wood, Plastic Components • Marble Mosaic Tiles • MDF Boards and Mouldings • Micro-concrete Roofing Tiles • Polymerised water proof compound • Portland Pozzolana • Cement Flyash/Calcined Clay Based/ Portland Slag Cement • RCC Door Frames • Ready Mix Cement Concrete • Rubber Wood, Finger Jointed Board • Stone dust	• Bagasse Board • Bricks from Coal Washery Rejects • Burnt Clay Flyash Bricks • Coir Cement Board, Compressed Earth Blocks • EPS Composites and Door Shutters • Fibre Flyash Cement Boards • Fibre Reinforced Concrete Precast Elements, Wall Panels, Blocks, Manhole Covers • Fibrous Gypsum Plaster Boards • Flyash Cellular Concrete, Flyash Cement Brick, Blocks • Flyash Lime Cellular Concrete • Flyash Lime Gypsum Brick • Rice Husk Ash Bricks • Jute Fibre Polyester • Non Erodable Mud Plaster • Polystiles • Timber alternatives, such as poplar, rubber, eucalyptus, bamboo • Precast walling roofing components • Prefab Brick Panel System

Energy Saving and Cost Reduction

In the construction of a typical house in India, it has been observed that about 30% of cost is accounted for brickwork and the rest for other elements. Labour typically contributes 27% of total construction of a house, cement 18%, bricks 17% and timber, iron & steel, sand and other materials share the rest of the cost.

The materials account for 60-70% of the total cost of construction and therefore, the judicious use of materials can save the cost. Nowadays, there is plethora of alternative building materials such as blended cement, bricks from different waste materials, steel from recycled steel, replacement of partial sand component with stone dust, aggregates from different sources other than natural ones are being used extensively. These options not only optimise the cost, but also help in energy efficient building.

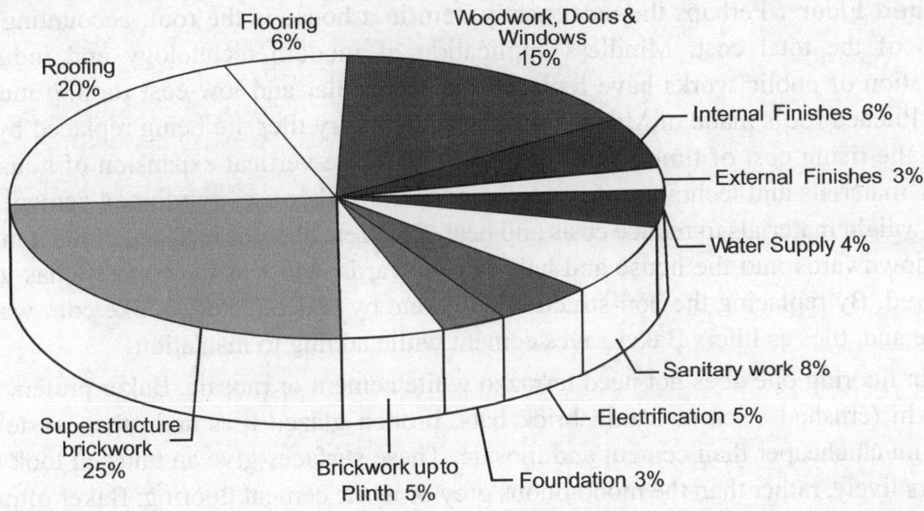

Fig. 9.5. Approximate Break-up of total Construction Cost for Different Elements of Building

Source: *BMTPC*

The cost effective technologies in place of conventional foundations, walls and roofing and use of recycled materials, wastes (industrial, agriculture, building construction, etc.) not only reduce the cost of building construction, but also provide the saving of energy and resources.

Low Cost, Local and Indigenous Construction of Laurie Baker

Laurie Baker's houses are harmonious with nature, honest with building materials, comfortable for the climate and meet the socio-economic realities.

In 1972, the Chief Minister of Kerela, sought Baker's ideas for streamlining the numerous housing programmes of the State. These were incorporated in a handy manual for laymen as a simple, illustrated guide. The manual was published in 1986 by the Centre of Science and Technology for Rural Development (COSTFORD) and was subsequently reproduced by the Housing and Urban Development Corporation and was used by several housing boards and educational/ training institute in India. The manual provides a guide on how to design, produce and assemble various components of building in a simple and economical manner.

Baker's houses manifest the basic principles of green buildings, that is 'less in more' and 'small is beautiful'. He organises space so that it provides maximum habitable space, with minimum use of building materials–stone, bricks, cement, wood, etc. He examines the usefulness of every component, walls, window, doors, etc. which can be built with local materials local skills and construction techniques. With multiple use of space, he saves on circulation area, length of walls and number of doors.

Shorter spans which are suitable for a cheaper kind of roofing, like brick vaults, one-ways slab, Reinforced Brick Concrete (RBC) roof, stone slab purlins and country tiles, etc. are the salient features of Laurie Baker houses. The location and agglomeration of wet areas and building services in relation to the municipal services and hygiene requirements make the houses more functional and economical. Baker's designs allow flexibility in growth, improvement and alterations, commensurate with the economy and changing needs of a family.

Roof and Floor : Perhaps the most costly item in a house is the roof, accounting for about one-fourth of the total cost. Mindless application of modern technology and indiscriminate standardisation of public works have replaced the vernacular and low-cost roofing methods and materials. Pitched roofs made of Mangalore tiles and country tiles are being replaced by the RCC slab. With the rising cost of timber and tiles, and due to the vertical expansion of housing in the cities, new materials and techniques have to be adopted. Baker uses reinforced cement filler slab with light-weight materials to reduce costs and heat. Concrete absorbs heat and emits it in the night: half of it downwards into the house and half of it upwards. Most of the concrete has to be filled and shuttered. By replacing the non-structural concrete by waste materials like coir, waste wood, thermocole and, tiles as fillers Baker saves cement while adding to insulation.

Even in flooring one does not need terrazzo white cement or mosaic. Baker prefers to use red chips, surkhi (crushed brick or sand), brick bats, broken glazed tiles and other waste materials which are much cheaper than cement and mosaic. These surfaces give an unusual look and make the interiors lively, rather than the monotonous grey or white cement flooring. Baker often used the waffle or filler slab for roofing. The basic idea of such a slab is to replace these portions of concrete which do not contribute to the strength of the slab with rejected Mangalore tiles, thus considerably reducing costs and the dead weight of concrete. In a brick vaulted roof its parabolic 'corrugations' allow it to bear its own weight. A cavity wall insulates the rooms from heat and dampness.

Local Building Materials : The use of local materials, which are generally more appropriate to the local climate, is the indispensable element of Baker house. Brick, tile, lime, surkhi, palm thatch, stones and country timber usually replace cement, steel and glass. Generally these are more suited to the humid climate than a heat guzzling concrete structure. They do not make the local masons and craftsmen redundant, who are less expensive than the specialists in modern materials and techniques. At the same time, the use of local materials also minimizes the use of the country's scarce and non-renewable resources and encourages small-scale industry.

Unplastered Walls : Baker rarely provided plaster on his brick walls, whether inside or outside. This affects enormous saving. Baker designs adequate overhangs or chajjas for protection of the wall surface. If necessary, he would isolate a wall which needs protection from excessive moisture and dampness, and cover it with a good lime-surkhi (crushed stone or sand) plaster. Such plaster is as good as cheaper than the usual cement plaster. The use of traditional materials (lime, lime-surkhi plaster or mud mortar in preference to cement) is low cost and helps in sustaining the dying crafts, skills and small industry, like the lime kilns. According to Baker, the old system of using lime involves a long and tedious process as compared to cement, which demands innovation and research. Unless old crafts and techniques are married to current technology, the appeal of exposed walls or lime mortar and plaster will remain restricted. Baker does not choose tradition for antiquarian reasons or because he wishes to avoid living in the present. Baker is conscious of the need for quality assurance while reducing the construction cost.

Bricks : Baker displays great faith in bricks, which are low cost, locally available, recyclable and user friendly. The bricks are made of universally available raw materials, that is soil. They prove to be climatically more comfortable and appropriate as compared to concrete, steel, stones, etc. Yet, these offer unlimited variety of design, use and alternative patterns. Sadly, because of the look of uneven hand-made bricks or due to the presence of under-fired bricks which disintegrate at the first monsoon, cement plastering has been commonly adopted. Under-firing is corrigible: taste and preferences can be modified. Bricks are not inherently unsuitable, but in fact adaptable, normal and congruent with the needs of society. Baker developed strong walls and attractive brickwork by introducing new bonding techniques which can accommodate dimensional variations. Baker creates interesting textures and patterns by skilful use of ordinary bricks which do not need any plastering. Thus there are cost savings, and as well good looking.

Jalis (Perforated Stone/Wood/Bricks) : Recreating the nostalgia of traditional Mughal architecture. Baker's uses perforated screens, usually in bricks, locally called the jali. These screens produce delightfully interesting patterns of light and shade and refreshing interiors. The brick honeycomb jali brings in both light and air and diffuses glare, while allowing privacy and security. A jali opening high up on walls will allow hot air to escape and insulate the room from the heat of the roof.

Doors and Windows : According to Baker, doors and windows are among the costliest items in the construction of a building. This is because expensive materials and skilled labour are involved in their manufacture and there is the additional expenditure on items such as hinges, locks, bolts, sills, lintels, etc. In most public low cost housing the effort is to economise on quantity and quality. Baker feels that usually the openings are excessive to the needs of living and for climatic comfort. Lintels and steel, glass, timber, etc. used in shutters may be ten times more costly than a simple wall. In many cases it is found that doors and windows are kept permanently closed or paper is pasted over the glazing. As such in order to save cost, it is necessary to rationalize the size and number of openings. Baker's answer lies in his questions What does it do? What is its function? What are its components? Are they necessary? He suggests a number of design simplifications. *"Many doors need not be there at all. If a door is not necessary, do not put it in. Considerable and immediate cost reduction is achieved. A doorway usually consists of a frame and a shutter or leaf."*

Lintels and Arches : By reverting to corbelling and arches, the expenditure on lintels, steel cement and form work can be avoided in the construction of houses. Baker uses a corbelled arch or simple stepped brick work wherever small openings are needed in a house. Reinforced brickwork or a flat arch can be adopted to allow a plain offset in a rectangular opening.

Attention to detail : Baker's care with detail led him to evolve alternative, low cost and innovative solutions. For example, as an alternative to plastering damp-prone walls he evolved the concept of a cavity wall. He stressed that it is necessary to use these measures only for those walls which need them and not to repeat them blindly all over the structure. Baker's approach to any problem in low cost construction is always to go back to first principles: What does something do? Is it locally available? Can it be used by local craftsmen and masons? What is its function? Is it affordable and cheap? Is it low-tech and recyclable? Is it beautiful? This kind of standard makes houses designed by Laurie Baker interesting, logical and beautiful. For instance, simple nailed wood and old-fashioned tiles can create interesting patterns in the ceiling.

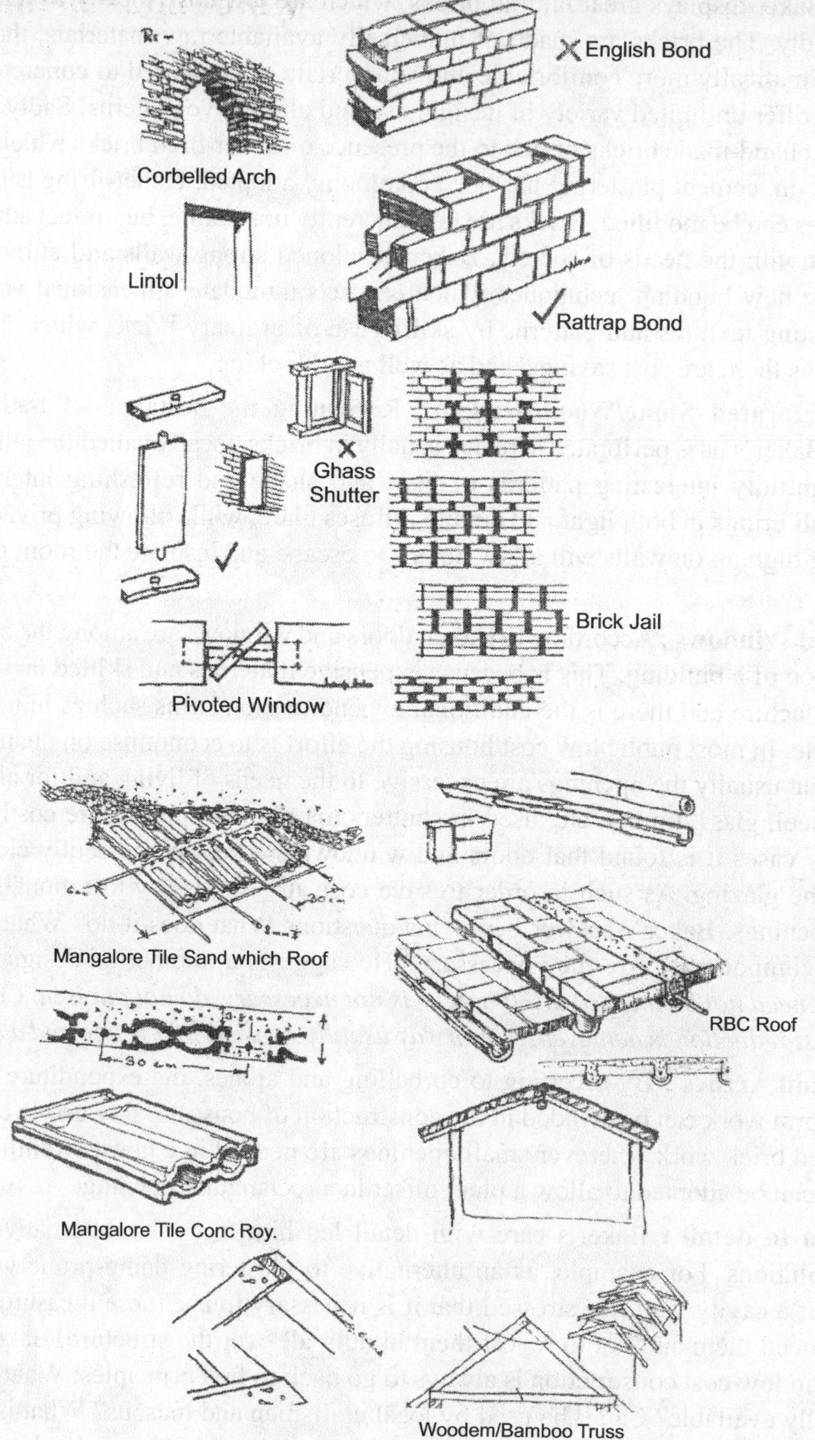

Fig. 9.6. Laurie Baker's simple ideas for economical, participatory and efficient building construction

Source: *Gautam Bhatia, 1987, Laurie Baker's Life, Works and Writings, Viking /HUDCO New Delhi*

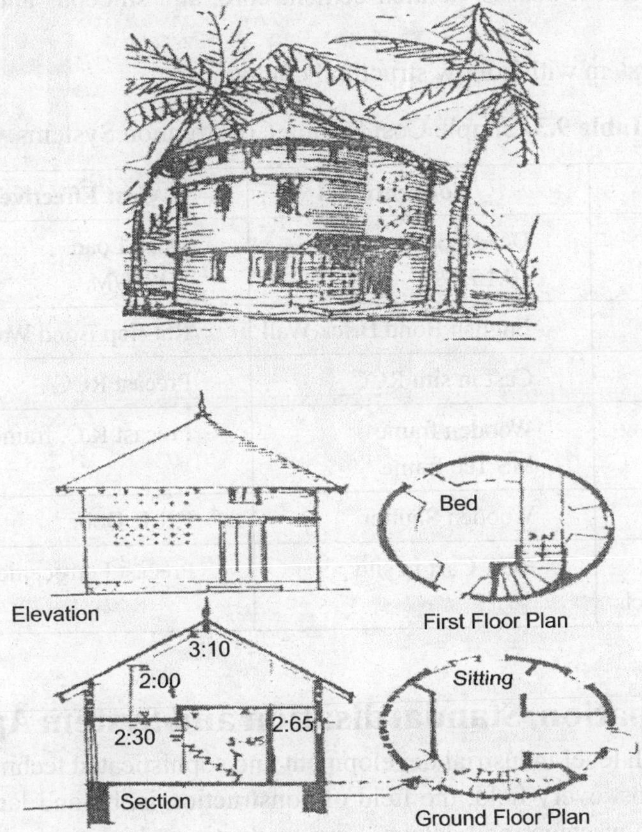

Fig. 9.7. Nambodripad house in Kerala by Laurie Baker

Source: *Gautam Bhatia, 1991, 'Laurie Baker's-Life, Works and Writings, Viking/HUDCO, New Delhi.*

Emerging Technologies

With ever-increasing need to build efficient, more sustainable and economic buildings, various technologies are emerging in the construction sector, such as:

- Rapid wall systems
- Monolithic concrete construction technologies
- Mortar-less masonry (interlocking)
- Confined masonry
- Light-weight construction methodology
- Technologies based on agro-industrial waste
- Bamboo-based technologies
- Pre-engineered systems
- Fibre cement board with expanded polystyrene (EPS), blocks and concrete light steel studs and concrete.
- Light-weight interlocking sandwich panels with 4 mm facing fiber sheet

- Reinforced cement boards, aerated cement core, and siliceous and micaceous material aggregate
- 3-S Prefab system with hollow structural components.

Table 9.3. Simple Cost Saving Construction Systems

Item	Conventional	Cost Effective	Saving
Foundation	Dead Load 10.15 T/M	Dead Load 8.13 T/M	20% 20%
Walls	English Bond Brick Wall	Rat-trap Bond Wall	20%
Roofing	Cast in situ RCC	Precast RCC	21%
Door and Window Frames	Wooden frame MS Tee frame	Precast R.C. frame	35%
Door Shutters	Wooden Shutter	F.R.P. Door	20%
Staircase Sun shades, Lintels	RCC Cast in situ	Precast Ferrocement	25%

Source: *BMTPC & NBO*

Modular Coordination, Standardisation and System Approach

In spite the fact that high level industrial development and sophisticated technological innovations have permeated in almost every field, the field of construction is, by and large, functioning in a primitive way involving wastages and delays. Low productivity, high costs, long building cycles, high energy contents, non-standardization and poor quality are the main challenges of building and housing. At present, a large proportion of building activity in the country is carried out by the individuals in a sporadic, semi-industrial manner, outside the monetary sector, employing mostly the local resources. Socio-economic changes make it necessary to change these traditional methods by others more in accordance with the present technological era. This is underlined by the key position of building within the national economy. It is the second largest sector after agriculture. Building and supporting economic activities account for/on the average about one half of the total value of investments and represent about 10% of the gross national product. To tackle the problem, it is necessary to evolve integrated systems approach in planning, design and development of building.

Close coordination and consistency between planning, design, production and management of buildings are pre-requisites of systems approach. This is difficult to obtain since quite often the objectives and interests of architect, builders, investors and users are not identical. To overcome this problem, an interdisciplinary approach together with modular coordination and standardization is necessary. A systems building comprises pre-fabricated, standardized components and systems that meet the functional, structural and design requirements in an efficient, quick and economical way. Art, science and technology in their inter-relation are the basis of architecture. This implies that a pre-engineered building need not be dull, box like structure, but can be designed beautifully. The basic principles of 'less is more', efficiency and economy are the pillars of 'systems building.'

Industrialised Building

Architects and engineers have always endeavoured to construct the buildings the way the car are produced. They evolved variety of pre-fabricated, standardized component systems that meet the functional, structural and design requirements in an efficient, quick and economical way. Science, technology and architecture have been working together to build the structures, which are beautiful, sustainable, green, economical and efficient.

The earliest attempt of systems building goes to pioneering genius of Leonardo da Vinci. As early as in 1516, Leonardo da Vinci planned a utopian city on the Loire consisting of knock-down serial houses. Only the foundations were to be built in situ. In 1854, four knock down timber houses at the Paris International Exhibition were shipped to Australia and reassembled in Sydney. It was the use of cast wrought iron in the 1840s that inspired the beginning of modern architecture. It started with Henri Labrouste's Bibliotheque Ste. Genevieve (1843-1850), Bibliotheque Nationale (1850-1851), Joseph Paxton's Crystal Palace in London, followed by the Eiffel Tower in Paris and Palais des Machines, Paris (1886-1889). The use of steel and reinforced concrete facilitated pre-engineered design and construction at the end of 19th century. In 1894, Christoph and Unmack patented a military tent/camp which was a simple structure that could be transported in a jeep and assembled by nuts and bolts. Edison in 1907 began the production of houses with a process analogue to the assembly line production of his friend Henry Ford. In collaboration with the architect Mann and NcNaillie, he developed a model for a house in reinforced concrete which could be mass produced.

During the first World War (1914), numerous bridges, railway stations, auditoria, factories and other structure were built. In Frankfurt, Earnest May founded a concrete panel factory to supply new suburban housing colonies. Emigrants then carried the idea to the like Bailey Bridge and steel frames for railway stations and large halls/sheds were imported in India, mainly by the military engineers.

The Bailey bridge is a portable, pre-fabricated, truss bridge which was developed by the British during World War II (1941-42). It had the advantage of requiring no special tools or heavy equipment to constructs bridge elements could be carried in a truck and lifted by hand, without the use of a crane. The bridges are strong enough to carry trucks and tanks. Bailey bridges continue to be extensively used in India especially by the military for border roads, spanning the rivers, drains and mountains. Its most recent use was during the Commonwealth Games 2010, when the footbridge being built at Jawaharlal Nehru Stadium at New Delhi collapsed just few days before the opening of the Games. The Army Engineers erected a Bailey Bridge of 30 m span within 6 days. This was extensively used as a footbridge by thousands of spectators and visitors. Both the cost and time taken for its construction were miniscule (about one-thirtieth) as compared to the original bridge. This raises an important question that why in spite of proven pre-engineered construction technology our civil engineering institutions continue ignoring them and maintain the status-quo.

Fig. 9.8. Charles Eames Catalogue House (Los Angeles, 1949) is a landmark pre-engineered building. The design was based on readymade components-roof truss, doors, windows, roofing, ceiling, furniture and fittings available from the catalogues. All these were skillfully chosen to make a unique composite design. It was widely published for its original style, economy and speed

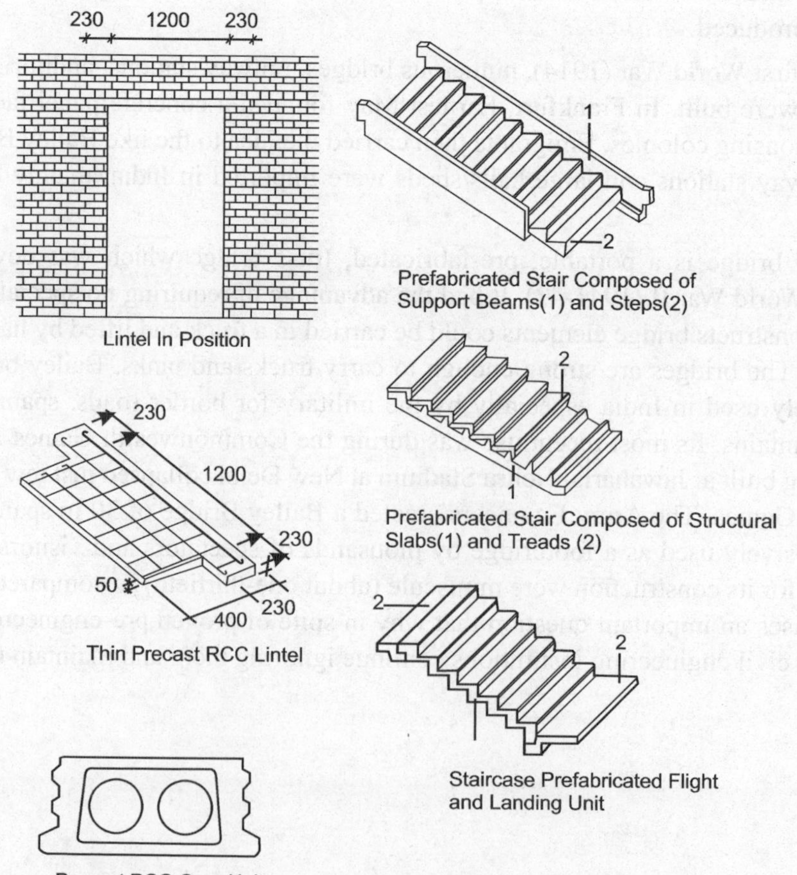

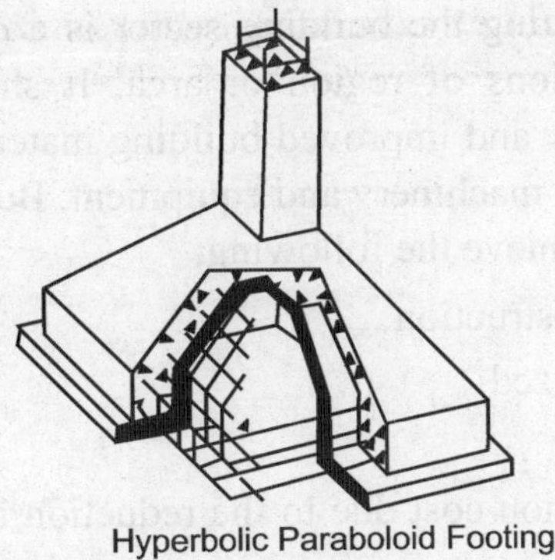

Fig. 9.9. Some Modular Building Components

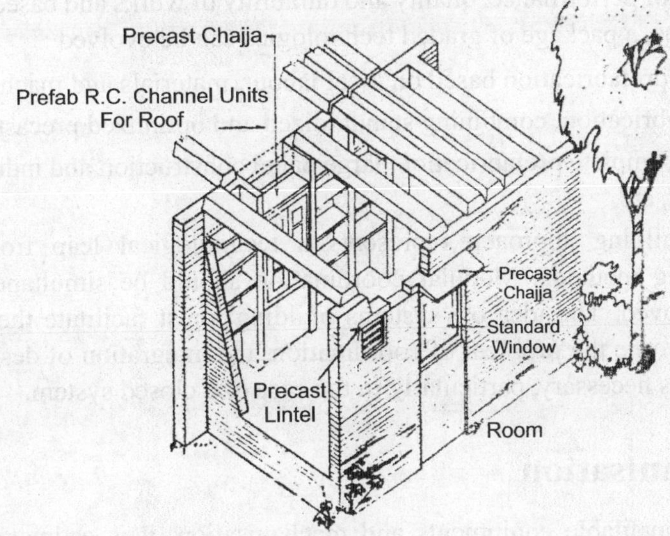

Fig. 9.10. Use of Prefab and standardise Components for Construction

***Soruce:** CBRI, Roorkee*

Systems Building

In any structure, equilibrium, resistance and stability are the basic pre-requisites. In the past the gravity was added to defeat gravity, resulting in massive masonry, compression structures, such as the pyramids. The new materials like steel and carbon fiber brought higher values of tension capability of structure, reducing the consumption and weight of building materials. System building is based on the dictum of enclosing the given space with more flexibility and stability by using lesser materials. This implies the adoption of Newton's law in design of a structure, that is, counteract the pull and push forces by ranging them off against each other, a game of action and reaction. While the minimalist philosophy has permeated everywhere computers, telephone and vehicles, buildings are still to witness this phenomenon. This is essential not only for economy, speed and quality of construction, but also for the reasons of ecological sustainability and inclusive growth.

The key concept in mechanizing the building sector is a differentiated and gradual process responding to the actual conditions of region or area. It should begin with standardization, rationalization, production of new and improved building materials, sections and units as well as the introduction of effective tools, machinery and equipment. Building processes and materials are considered progressive, if they achieve the following:

- Reduction in cost of construction
- Reduction in labour utilized
- Reduction in time
- Reduction in transportation cost due to the reduction in weight of materials and shorter distances
- Lower rates of pollution, dust, noise, accidents, GHG emissions, etc. in construction.

Higher standards of performance, quality and durability of works and based on local conditions and regional variations, a package of graded technologies can be evolved :

- Small scale prefabrication based on local labour, materials and machinery.
- Partial prefabrication, combining standardized and optimized precast components
- Full fledge/complete prefabrication, large panel construction and industrialized structural components, etc.

The Systems Building approach represents a technological leap from conventional to industrialized building methods. Modular coordination should be simultaneously adopted and standardization improved. The idea of 'systems building' must facilitate the pooling of mutual cooperation. To overcome the problem of coordination, the integration of design, production and assembly operations is necessary, particularly in the case of a closed system.

Building Mechanisation

By adopting readily available equipments and mechanisation, it is estimated that at least one third of time, energy and costs of construction be saved. Mechanisation is a process in which a construction activity is optimised in terms of cost, labour, time, productivity and accuracy, either by using a tool or an equipment or even a technology. Some of the activities which can be covered by mechanisation are given below :

Table 9.4. Scope and Fields of Building Mechanisation

S.No.	Field Activity	Options/Possibilities
1.	Surveying	Modern instruments like total station automatic levelling, laser based tools can be adopted.
2.	Earthwork	Earthwork related activities are more or less mechanised. Plethora of choices available in the market.
	Excavation Ground improvement Earth transportation Compaction	Dozers, Loaders, Excavators Modern techniques Tractors, trailers, tippers and trucks Compactors, rollers

3.	Formwork	Modern framework systems which are strong, durable, light and repetitive.
4.	Concrete production	Batching plants, mini-mobile batching plants, mixers with and without hoppers, weight batches.
5.	Concrete transportation	Immersion, surface, screed type vibrators.
6.	Concrete transportation	Transit mixer, dumpers, buggies, conveyors, concrete pumps, cranes, mechnical distributors, placer booms.
7.	Ground water control	Pumping, DPC barriers, osmosis methods.
8.	Reinforcement	Bar bending and cutting machines, typing tool, factory fabricated.
9.	Material Handling	Tower crane and lifting hoists, winches and accessories, self-climbing platform.
10.	Plastering	Ready plaster mix, plaster machines, levellers, plaster board, drywalls, auto rendering plaster machines.
11.	Curing	Curing pumps, curing compound, steam curing, accelerating curing.
12.	Infill walls/masonry	Wall panels, dry wall system, light weight blocks, mortarless joints.
13.	Structural elements	RCC components like lintels, sill beams, stairs, decorative elements, precast blocks.
14.	Water proofing	Modern water proofing systems.
15.	Flooring-Concrete flooring Tile flooring	Vacuum pumps, power trowels, polishing machines, groove cutters, screed vibrators compactors. Polishing machine, tile cutters, laser grid locators, cutting and grinding tools.
16.	Site monitoring	Cameras, GPS and other communication devices.
17.	Miscellaneous	Drilling and cutting tools, grouting guns nailing guns laser based diagnostic and measuring instruments, pipe cutter/vices, threading and bending machine, gas detectors, infrared thermometers, welding machines, protective equipment, power distributors, fire extinguishers, etc.

Pre-Engineered Building: The main objective of pre-engineered building has been to achieve quality, productivity and flexibility, together with reducing time and costs. Automation and robotics give precision to pre-fabricated building components and enable accuracy and customization. Computer Aided Manufacturing (CAM) and Computer Integrated Manufacturing (CIM) for prefabricated components, viz. ceilings, walls, roofs, etc. are integral to the process of pre-engineered construction. The simulation of construction process enables better control of time, machine, expenditure and the manpower, which could be reduced at least by half to one-third in comparison to the conventional construction. Innovative pre-engineering technology, bridges and buildings could reduce the carbon emission and steel consumption.

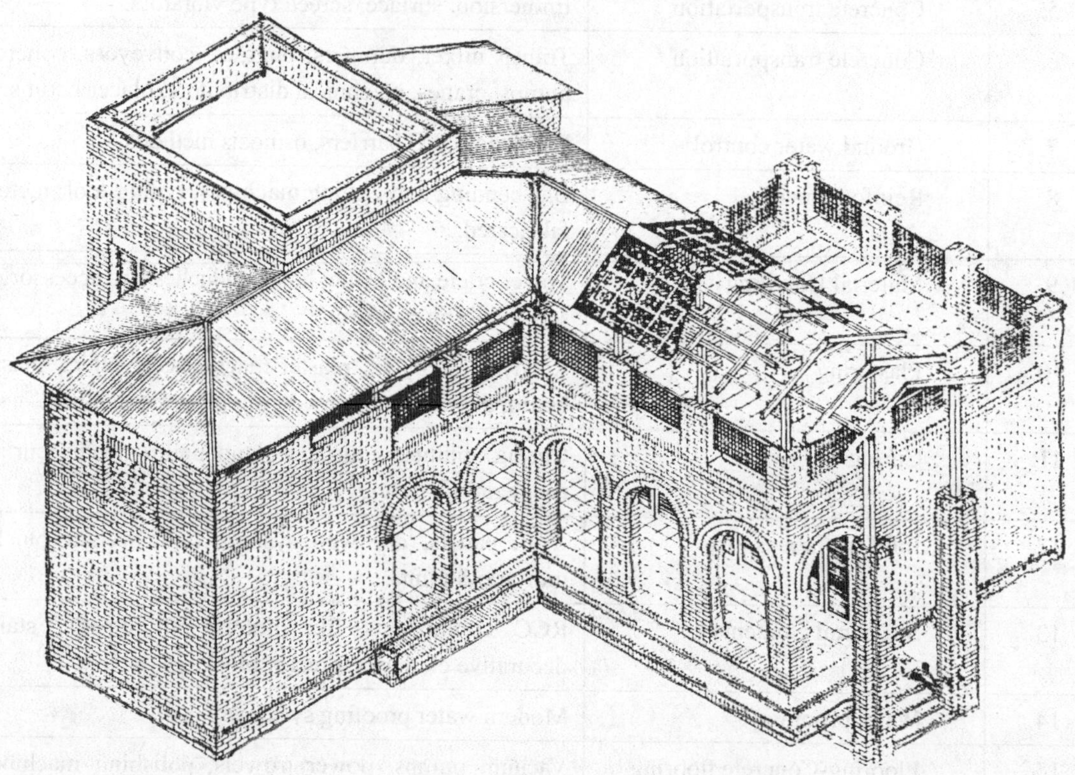

Fig. 9.11. Exposed Brick House, Bhatsaia, Brahmanbaria, Bangladesh, Architect Bashirual Haq

Fig. 9.12. School System developed by Foster Associates in conjunction with manufacturers

In India millions of tons of Sulphur-Gypsum waste is produced as by-product of coal fired power stations and chemical fertilizer industries, disposal of which is a huge environmental problem. The Rapid Wall helps to overcome these problems by turning waste into rapid wall panels that can be manually erected and are energy efficient, aesthetically pleasing and save time and costs.

Space Structure

Konrad Wachsmann (1901-1980) was the master of prefabrication and space structures. In 1959 he was asked by the US Air Force to design a demountable system for large aircraft hangars which suited his interest in industrialized production methods. Wachsmann used a constant tetrahedral module made out of 10 feet long tubes connected with three dimensional swivel nodes allowing the attachment of up to 20 members. This principle allowed every possible combination of construction and geometry. All the building elements could be prefabricated by mass production method. The principle of space frame has been further developed and is being extensively adapted for skyscrapers, such as Hong Kong and Shanghai Bank at Hong Kong.

Cable Net Roof

Montred Expo (1967) witnessed innovative German Pavilion with a large span. The 140120 m roof in a pre-stressed steel cable net roof with the skin made of translucent PVC coated polyester fabric. Designed by Rolf Gutbrod and Frei Otto, the roof was inspired by the spider's web and the strength of the fisherman's nets. The shape of cable roof structure is defined by a net, where the spatial coordinates of a finite set of the intersections fix its shape.

Fig. 9.13. Rolf Gutbrod, Frei Otto, Cable Net Roof, German Pavilion, Expo 1967, Montreal

Geodesic Dome

In 1959, Buckminster Fuller invented the Geodesic Dome applying the tensegrity principle using light aluminium alloy tubing and aircraft control wires. This enabled him to design enclosures of over 3 kilometers in diameter. He illustrated this by proposing to cover fifty blocks of Manhattan Island with tensegrity dome. Geodesic domes are made of rigid struts, connected into triangles, pentagons or hexagons. Each strut is arranged to constrain each joint at a fixed position, thus stabilizing the structures. All structural members are pre-stressed. Within the structure, the rigid struts stretch or tense the flexible tension cables, while the tension members compress the struts. The counteracting forces equilibrate throughout the structure and stabilize it, in contrast with normal building structures that derive their stability from continuous compression. Buckminster Fuller designed several geodesic domes. His United States Pavilion at Expo 67 in Montreal was 76 meter high using 90 millimeter diameter steel tubes to form a three-dimensional frame of hexagonal and pentagonal components. The frame was covered with a crylic panels. The concept demonstrated a minimalist approach in the design of structure where strength is derived from its composite form rather than the individual structural elements.

Fig. 9.14. Geodesic Dome by Standard Components (Buckminster Fuller), Expo 1967, Montreal

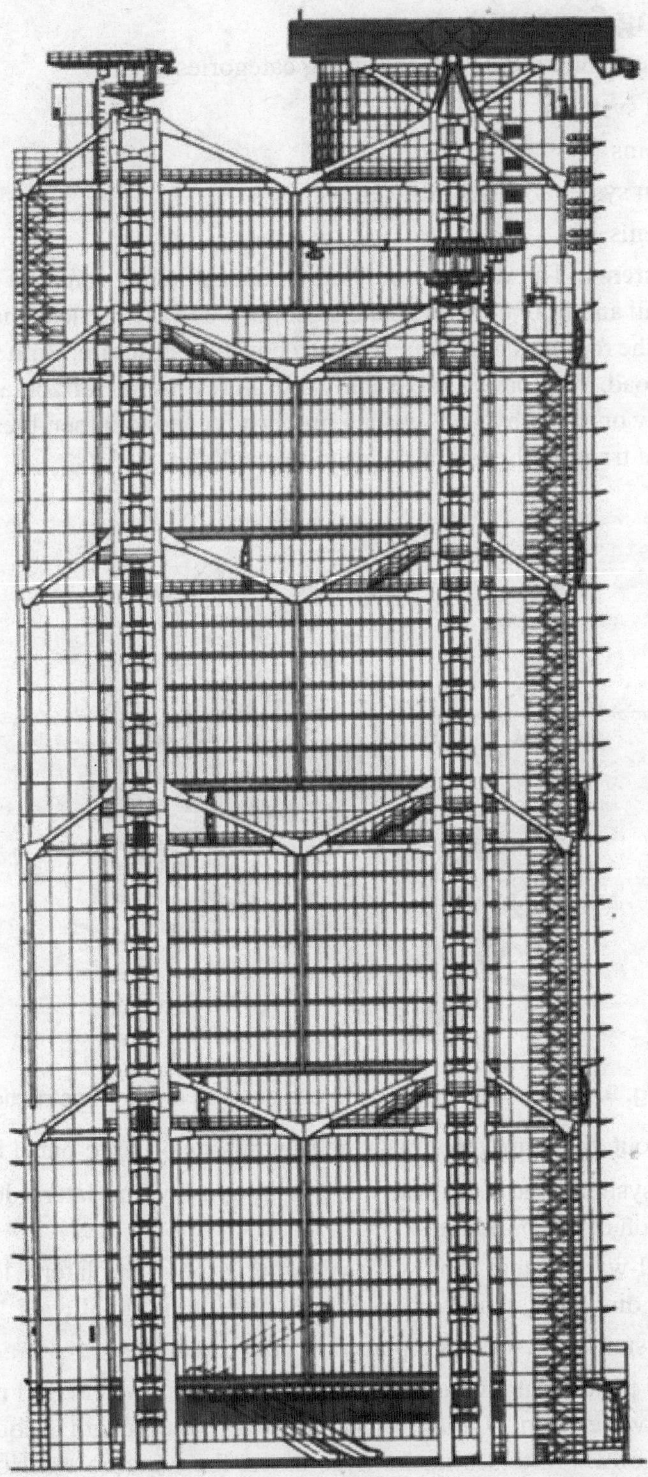

Fig. 9.15. Hong Kong and Shanghai Bank, Hong Kong, Architects Foster Associates, Engineers: Ove Arup and Partners

Precast Building Systems

The precast systems are divided into the following categories:

- Large-panel systems
- Frame systems
- Slab-column systems with infill walls
- Mixed systems

Large-Panel Systems: The designation "large-panel system" refers to multistorey structures composed of large wall and floor concrete panels connected in the vertical and horizontal directions to enclose spaces for the rooms. These panels form a box-like structure. Both vertical and horizontal panels resist gravity load. Wall panels are usually one storey high. Horizontal floor and roof panels span either as one-way or two-way slabs. When properly joined together, these horizontal elements act as diaphragms that transfer the lateral loads to the walls.

Fig. 9.16. A Large-Panel concrete building under construction

Depending on the layout, there are three basic configurations of large-panel buildings:

- Cross-wall system. The main walls that resist gravity and lateral loads are placed in the short direction of the building.
- Longitudinal-wall system. The walls resisting gravity and lateral loads are placed in the longitudinal direction; usually there is only one longitudinal wall.
- Two-way system. The walls are placed in both directions.

Thickness of wall panels ranges from 120 mm for interior walls to 300 mm for exterior walls. Floor panel thickness varies from 60 mm to 150 mm. Wall panel length is equal to the room length, typically in the order of 2.7 m to 3.6 m. In some cases, there are no exterior wall panels and the facade walls are made of lightweight concrete.

Panel connections represent the key structural components in these systems. Based on their location within a building, these connections can be classified into vertical and horizontal joints. Vertical joints connect the vertical faces of adjoining wall panels and primarily resist vertical seismic shear forces. Horizontal joints connect the horizontal faces of the adjoining wall and floor panels and resist both gravity and seismic loads.

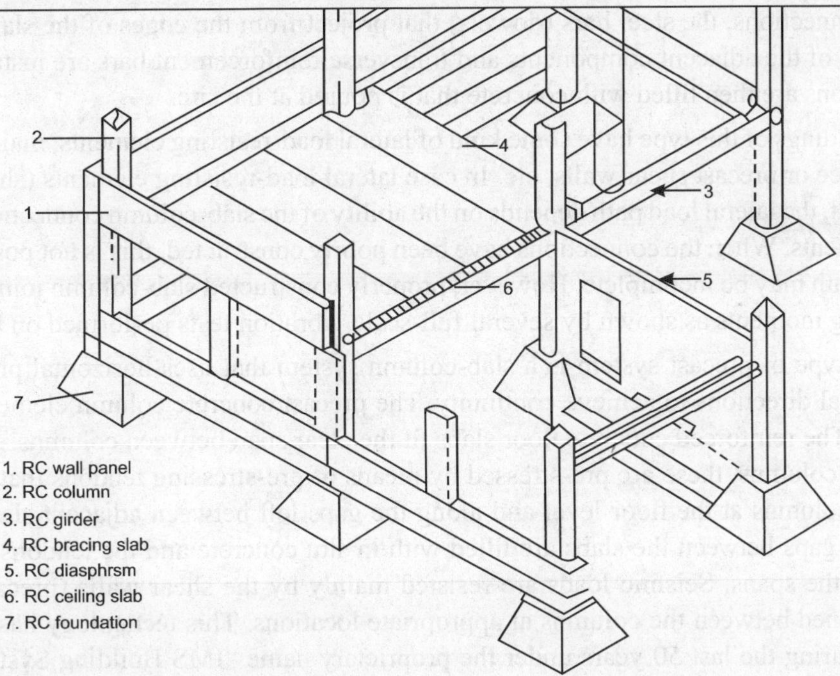

Fig. 9.17. Components of a precast reinforced concrete frame system

Depending on the construction method, these joints can be classified as wet and dry. Wet joints are constructed with cast-in-place concrete poured between the precast panels. To ensure structural continuity, protruding reinforcing bars from the panels (dowels) are welded, looped, or otherwise connected in the joint region before the concrete is placed. Dry joints are constructed by bolting or welding together steel plates or other steel inserts cast into the ends of the precast panels for this purpose. Wet joints more closely approximate cast-in-place construction, whereas the force transfer in structures with dry joints is accomplished at discrete points.

Frame System: Precast frames can be constructed using either linear elements or spatial beam-column sub-assemblages. Precast beam-column sub-assemblages have the advantage that the connecting faces between the sub-assemblages can be placed away from the critical frame regions. However, linear elements are generally preferred because of the difficulties associated with forming, handling, and erecting spatial elements. The use of linear elements generally means placing the connecting faces at the beam-column junctions. The beams can be seated on corbels at the columns, for ease of construction and to aid the shear transfer from the beam to the column. The beam-column joints accomplished in this way are hinged. However, rigid beam-column connections are used in some cases, when the continuity of longitudinal reinforcement through the beam-column joint needs to be ensured.

Slab-Column System with Shear Walls: These systems rely on shear walls to sustain lateral load effects, whereas the slab-column structure resists mainly gravity loads. There are two main systems in this category:

- Lift-slab system with walls
- Pre-stressed slab-column system

In the connections, the steel bars (dowels) that project from the edges of the slabs are welded to the dowels of the adjacent components and transverse reinforcement bars are installed in place. The connections are then filled with concrete that is poured at the site.

Most buildings of this type have some kind of lateral load-resisting elements, mainly consisting of cast-in-place or precast shear walls, etc. In case lateral load-resisting elements (shear wall, etc.) are not present, the lateral load path depends on the ability of the slab-column connections to transfer bending moments. When the connections have been poorly constructed, this is not possible, and the lateral load path may be incomplete. However, properly constructed slab-column joints are capable of transferring moments as shown by several full-scale vibration tests performed on buildings.

Another type of precast system is a slab-column system that uses horizontal pre-stressing in two orthogonal directions to achieve continuity. The precast concrete column elements are 1 to 3 stories high. The reinforced concrete floor slabs fit the clear span between columns. After erecting the slabs and columns, these are pre-stressed by means of pre-stressing tendons that pass through ducts in the columns at the floor level and along the gaps left between adjacent slabs. After pre-stressing, the gaps between the slabs are filled with in situ concrete and the tendons then become bonded with the spans. Seismic loads are resisted mainly by the shear walls (precast or cast-in-place) positioned between the columns at appropriate locations. This technology has been used in Yugoslavia during the last 50 years under the proprietary name "IMS Building System," and can also be found in other countries.

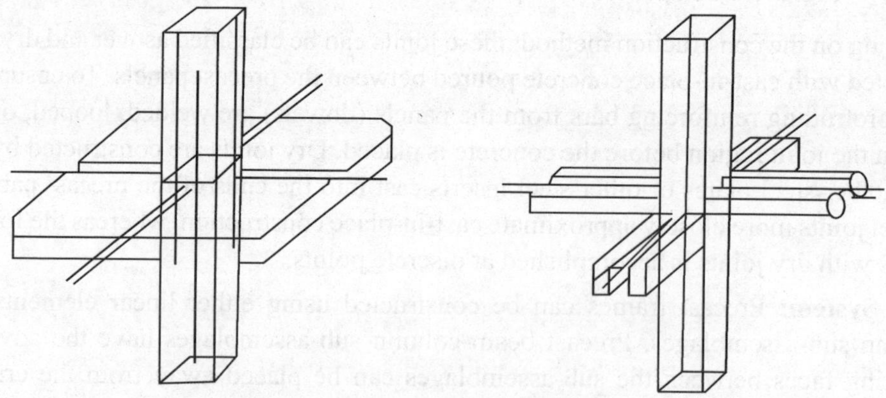

Fig. 9.18. Post-tensioned slab-column connection

Modular Plug-in Units

Portable modular home units have been around for quite some time, but have not been able to make an impact largely due to problems of costs, services, transportation, land and sprawl. If properly defined, they could have a modest carbon footprint compared with traditional, permanent housing. Brazilian architect Felipe Campolina has proposed high-density trailer parks in the sky. Steel framed skyscrapers provide a plug-in skeleton into which modular homes can be slotted as required. The homes would be built from standard 1.2 m × 2.4 m panels and could telescope in and out for transportation or installation. Each unit would have thermo-acoustic insulation, water recycling, a combined heat and power unit, and tempered glass windows. When the time comes to move house, residents could use a lift to lower their unit to ground level and ship it to a new location.

Innovations in Building Materials and Processes

Conventionally, the construction materials are divided into the following broad categories: Natural or Organic, Engineered (recycled, manufactured, precast or prefabricated), Hybrid, and New Generation. An emerging category of construction materials is that of recycled materials, agro-wastes, fly-ash, plastics, etc. Nanotechnology is opening up a new door of construction technologies and materials. The sustainability of materials and building processes is becoming an essential pre-requisite.

Construction automation has 4 fundamental components:

- An-on site, all weather enclosed factory
- Automated jacking system
- Automated material conveying system
- Centralized information system.

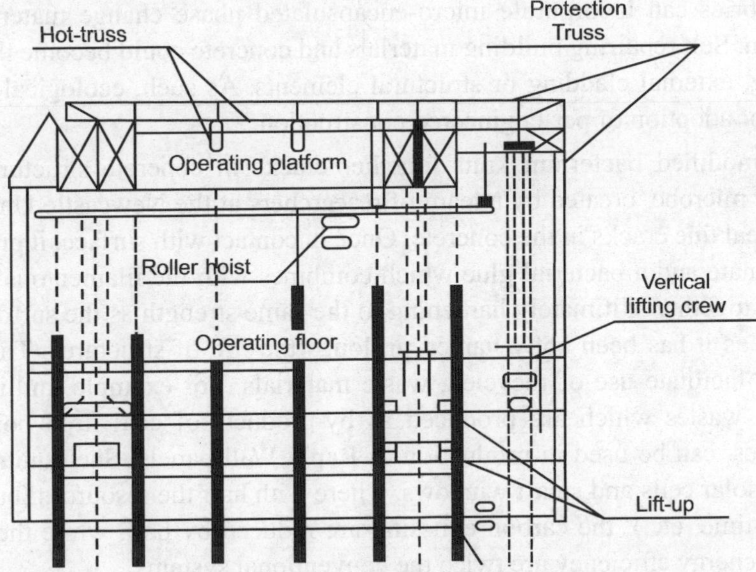

Fig. 9.19. Integrated Automotive Building Construction unit with Robotic Trolley and Hoists for Logistics and Positioning

These systems use JIT principle for delivery of materials and bar coding for tacking and materials management at site. The simulation of construction process by automation, gives information about time, expenditure and the number of workmen, skilled tradesmen and other staff needed; this way the time of on-site construction could be reduced at least by half to one-third in comparison to the conventional construction. However, it demands increasing efforts in project planning, process planning and logistics. Accordingly, the on-site staff have to be more specialized as most of the no-nergonomic work on site is reduced.

A new surge has led to Computer-Aided Manufacturing (CAM) and Computer Integrated Manufacturing (CIM) for prefabricated components, ceilings, walls, roofs, etc. Construction robots range from simple tools to fully automated robot. In Japan and other countries single task and automated construction system are becoming common. To address the shortage of shilled labour and workforce in construction sector, single task robots are developed to supplement skilled labour to achieve construction speed, precision and quality. Various single task robots are used for jobs like concrete and steel structural erection, external and internal finish work, maintenance and demolition work, etc.

During recent times the purpose of automation has been shifting from increasing productivity and reducing costs to broader issues, such as increasing sustainability, energy efficiency, quality and flexibility of the building. Automation and robotics are being in construction for prefabrication of building components and also for speed, accuracy and customization. The flexible production system using robotic cells could execute various tasks such as setting moulds, placing reinforcement bars or mats distributing concrete for various products such as floor, roof, wall, beam and column.

The future of system and pre-engineered building and design lies in its response to in environmental sustainability. Metal alloys such as nickel-titanium can change form as directed. Super fibres, such as carbon and glass fibers, provide greater stiffness, strength, flexibility and economy, coping with higher tensile and compressive stresses achieved with the least amount of mass. Techno fabrics can incorporate micro-encapsulated phase change material for improved thermal insulation. Self repairing building materials and concrete could become the ideal materials for roof covering, external cladding or structural elements. As such, ecological advantage is the greatest reason for adoption of per-engineered construction.

Genetically modified bacterium knits together cracks in concrete structures by producing special glue. The microbe, created by a team of researchers at the Newcastle University has been programmed to seal fine cracks in the concrete. Once in contact with surface, it produces a mixture of calcium carbonate and a bacterial glue which combines with the filamentous bacterial cells to "knit" the cracks together. Ultimately hardening to the same strength as the surrounding concrete, the "bacila filla" as it has been aptly named prolongs the life of structures. The pre-engineered components also facilitate use of recycled, waste materials. For example, millions of tonnes of Sulphur-Gypsum wastes which are produced as by-products of coal fired power stations and fertilizer industries, can be used in production of Rapid Wall panels. Such units can incorporate solar/PV panels, solar cells and smart windows, where with half the resources (building materials, labour, finances, time, etc.), the carbon emission are reduced by half, while the space, speed of construction and energy efficiency are twice the conventional systems.

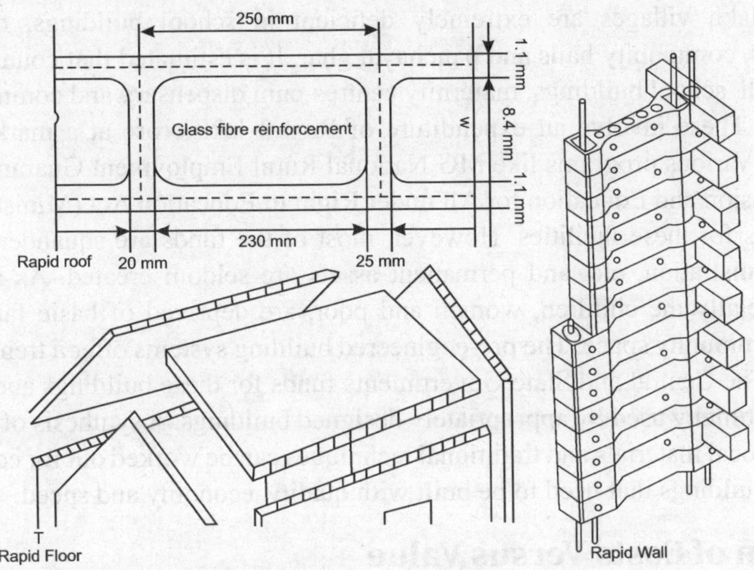

Fig. 9.20. Rapid Wall, Roof and Floor Panels

System Building for Rural Development

In India various pre-engineered building systems have been experimented. These have been used generally for large buildings–railway stations, warehouses, hangers, sports complexes, stadia, etc. For small building construction, these are yet to be accepted and recognized in the normative government system. It is time that pre-engineered building systems are institutionalised, encouraged and adopted on a large scale.

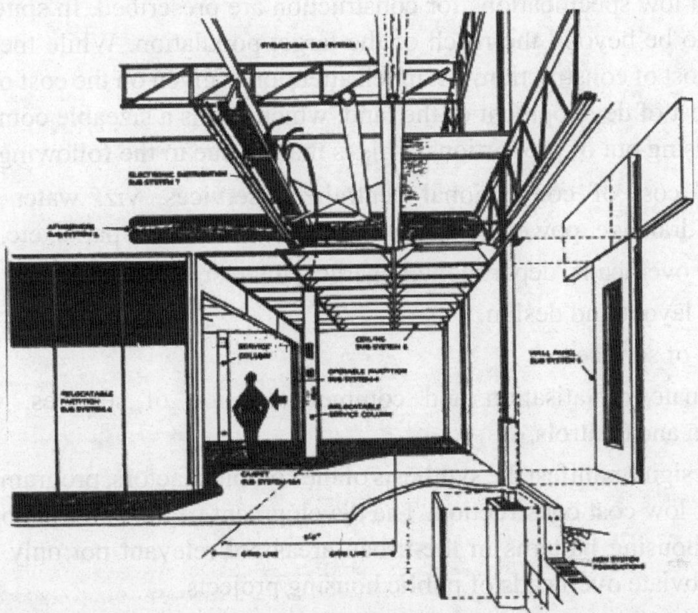

Fig. 9.21. SFS system derives from compatibility of a large number of sub-systems and inter-systems for a school building

India's six lakh villages are extremely deficient in school buildings, dispensary/health/maternity centres, community halls and panchayat ghar. It is estimated that country needs to build about 74,000 each–school buildings, maternity centres-cum dispensary and community halls-cum-Panchayat Ghar. These involve an expenditure of Rs 1.3 lakh crore at a market rate of Rs 60 lakh per facility. Various programs like MG National Rural Employment Guarantee Act, National Rural Health Mission and Education for All under Right to Education Act (Ministry of HRD) have budget provisions for these facilities. However, most of the funds are squandered in manpower, equipment, administration, etc. and permanent assets are seldom created. As a result the rural population, especially the children, women and poor, are deprived of basic facilities of health, education and community space. The pre-engineered building systems offer a tremendous scope to bridge this gap. The Central and State Governments funds for these buildings and facilities can be efficiently and optimally used by appropriately designed buildings. A synthesis of modern building technology with local materials and traditional techniques can be worked out for educational, health and community buildings that need to be built with quality, economy and speed.

Optimisation of Costs Versus Value

Land development and building costs are defined as the monetary value of the inputs and resources used up in the production of the output. The costs could be divided into fixed and variable costs. There are the costs which can be directly and fully attributed to a cost unit, and indirect costs are those which are incurred on behalf of more than one cost unit and, are usually shared by apportionment formulae. Further, there are hidden costs, which are mainly attributed to unexpected overhead, inefficiencies, kickbacks, delays, strikes, etc. which are part of the working culture and cannot be written off.

While dealing with the reduction of the cost of housing, the plinth area of dwelling is reduced to the minimum and low specifications for construction are prescribed. In spite of subsidies, such housing continues to be beyond the reach of the target population. While the efforts are to save every penny in the cost of construction, not much attention is given on the cost of land development and services. The cost of development of the land, which forms a sizeable component of dwelling cost has been increasing out of proportions. This is mainly due to the following factors:

(*a*) Increasing cost of conventional centralized services, viz. water supply, sanitation, sewerage, drainage, power, solid waste disposal, roads and parks, etc.

(*b*) Increasing overheads, departmental charges, interest and delays.

(*c*) Inefficient layout and design.

(*d*) Monopoly of services.

(*e*) Indiscriminate privatisation and commercialisation of services, without regulatory mechanism and controls.

The plans and designs manifest the synthesis of the complex factors, programme of requirements and various ideas of low cost construction. The development of the concepts of evolutionary, low rise - high density housing patterns in the urban areas are relevant not only in maximizing the output, but also to obviate overheads of public housing projects.

The costs are intrinsically connected with setting up of benchmarks- specifications, standards, norms, and parameters with respect to planning, design, engineering, safety, environment, finances, wages and labour welfare, etc. The concept of cost management and benchmarks has to be understood in a wider context of social, economic and national goals.

The magnitude of each of these cost components depend on the nature, size and location of the project as well as the management organization, among many considerations. The owner is interested in achieving the lowest possible overall project cost that is consistent with its investment objectives.

It is equally important to estimate the corresponding operation and maintenance cost of each alternative for a project in order to analyse the life cycle costs. The large expenditure needed for maintenance, especially for publicly owned infrastructure have the implications in operation and maintenance, allowance for contingencies or unexpected costs.

Elemental Project Cost Systems Approach

A building project is divided into various components called elements that usually perform a major function regardless of material used, specifications and construction method. The framework of elemental classification is fundamental to the elemental cost approach and is necessary to provide a common reference for the purpose of description, economic analysis and management during all the phase of a project. The basis for the identification and classification of elements are:

- Form substantial portion of total cost
- Provide hierarchical framework at various levels
- Allow summation of lower elements into higher elements
- Allow cost analysis during design and cost monitoring during execution
- Higher frequency of occurrence
- Elements are distinctive and easier for communication

The elements are usually divided into four levels;

- Major group elements
- Group elements
- Elements/sub-elements
- Components

Total Quality Management

With the increasing economic level, India is undergoing a rapid transformation. The consumers are more demanding and quality conscious. With the opening up of the economy, the building industry is facing a global competition. The privatization of construction activity is creating a competitive environment where it is the survival of the fittest. As such the concept of "total quality management" (TQM) has become an indispensable aspect of building industry, both for private and public sectors.

Through a combination of quality systems, modern statistical techniques, the belief and commitment that customers have to be involved at various stages of the product/service delivery system and through continuous improvement programmes. TQM seeks to influence business competitiveness in the areas of cost reduction and adding value to consumer products and services. It is generally agreed that quality has to be management led, to cover all aspects of organizational systems. It is everybody's responsibility; the emphasis has to be made on prevention rather than correction. The standard has to be right first time and every time; the effort has to be based on continuous improvement and control via quality costing. At the heart of any TQM effort is the establishment of the customer-supplier chain, with the following attributes:

- Customer satisfaction
- Common goals and objectives
- Integrated production process
- Equity without any distinction

Computerised Design, Co-ordination and Monitoring

Computer Aided Design (CAD) is three-dimensional coordinate system that allows people to "walk through" a facility before it is built. It significantly benefits design of construction by its display in three dimensions, not just the two dimensions of traditional drawings. The system automatically raises a flag when two components in the drawings occupy the same physical space, and allows corrections to be made before the problem reaches the field. Future improvements in design capabilities will allow closer linkage of design to operations and maintenance, better life-cycle costing linked to design alternatives, and improved methodologies for cost estimating and procurement linked to electronic design program software. Bar-code technology helps in tracking and locating materials and equipment, with identification codes linked directly to CAD systems.

Monitoring of Health of the Structures: Health surveillance of civil infrastructure and structures uses, sensor and wireless communication technologies, thereby recording in real-time condition of the structure.

Failure analysis is the technique of evaluating data to establish the origin of a failure and recommend the precautions necessary to avoid recurrence. It is a significant subject in the field of construction. It is dependent on the examination of the failed component to establish the cause of failure, using an extensive range of methods. The non-destructive testing approach is useful since the failed components are not affected by the examination. A software program is used to conduct the failure analysis based on the applied element method. It examines the causes for the collapse of structures due to extreme loads.

Mitigation of Reinforcement Corrosion: Predictive modelling of aging and performance levels of risk are necessary for safety, disruptions to services, economic loss, and environmental sustainability. It yields a broad array of options to maintain, remediate, strengthen, and choose the materials and processes that can mitigate aging-more sustainable and safer infrastructure can be achieved by technology choice, specifications and life cycle performance of materials, construction and corrosion mitigation.

Building Information Modeling (BIM) provides computerized layers of information, planned details of the structure containing everything from 3D drawing and planning documents, service plans and controls to the specifications of building materials, components, light fitting and fixtures. BIM is an integrated, collaborative process that enables engineers, architects, contractors and clients to work from a single, digital project model and share reliable, coordinated information at every stage of a project life-cycle.

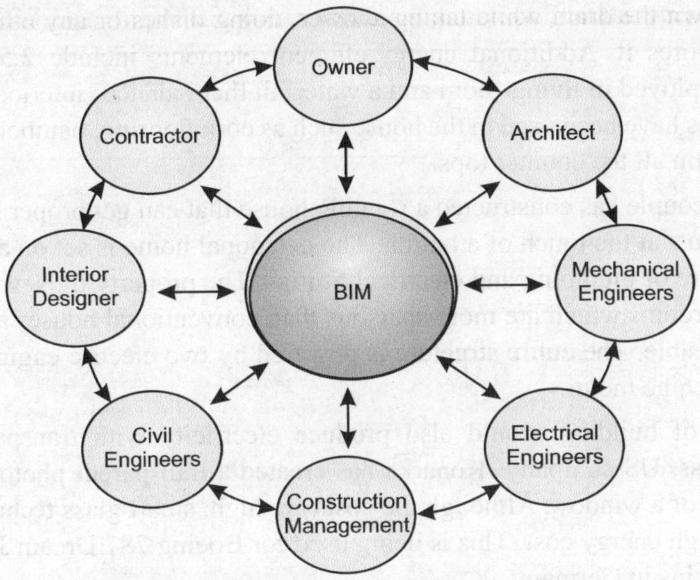

Fig. 9.22. Building Information Modelling

BIM tool can simulate the entire construction sequence beforehand addressing sustainability issues and reducing waste by choosing the best option. Global positioning systems are increasingly being used on construction sites, aiding the operators to build, lay underground services to cut exactly by satellite-guided tools. GPS devices, for example, can be attached to equipment grading the road. A GPS-linked computer indicates whether the grading is being done in the right place, or it is too deep. By BIM 'on-site' virtual system, pipe work installed in a building can be inspected by a worker. Before installation, a contractor digitally tags every pipe and electrical cables are computer tagged, which provides an augmented version of reality through 3D glasses that recognize the tags and displays exactly where a misplaced cable or pipe could be, relaying data back to a central control unit.

The 3 D cameras recognise the objects and material, and whether they are being used at the right place and with accuracy. The way of measuring distances could become more accurate with 'smart fingers.' Currently in the concept stage, two computerized plastic devices fit over the thumb and finger, and measure the distance relayed between the two points when they are moved apart. The data can be shown on a monitor and can be transferred via USB to a computer.

Solar Mapping and Renewable Energy

A demonstration house built in Kamloops, Canada, generates its own power and features a host of energy-efficient elements. A rooftop array of solar photovoltaic panels been installed in the house that generates power. A dual-purpose electricity meter has also been installed that tracks the amount of energy consumed as well as surplus power dispatched onto the grid when the home does not need it. The house features a lumber stud exterior wall that provides an insulation rating of R44 as compared to R12 for conventional fiberglass insulation and triple glazed windows with low-e coatings. A geothermal energy system in the house uses pipes extending about 66 m deep into the ground as an efficient means of heating and cooling. A hot water recovery system takes the hot water that goes down the drain while taking shower, doing dishes or any other activity, recovers that energy and stores it. Additional energy-efficient elements include 2.5 cm thick recycled rubber shingles employed in living-room and a waterfall that balances interior humidity. A host of renewable resources have been used in the house such as cork flooring, bamboo cabinetry, recycled glass and concrete on all the counter tops.

An Australian couple has constructed a rotating house that can get proper light all day long by following the sun just at the touch of a button. The octagonal home is set on a turntable and spins around a central core of plumbing and electrical fittings. The property in New South Wales has of irregularly-shaped rooms which are more spacious than conventional houses and capture as much natural light as possible. The entire structure is powered by two electric engines not much bigger than a washing machine motor.

The windows of buildings could also produce electricity with transparent solar cells or "smart energy" glass. US company Konarka has created a transparent photovoltaic cell that fits between two panes of a window. Although the costs are high, smart glass technology saves on air-conditioning and high energy cost. This is being used for Boeing 787 Dream Jet plane and also in some high speed trains in Germany.

Wind Energy

High altitude wind power has advantage over solar energy, which is not always available. Solar towers have reflecting mirrors that require frequent cleaning and maintenance. After sunset, batteries are required to store solar energy, adding to the cost. But space rowers can generate power in the giga-watt range, and do not require a storage medium. Research by California State University and Carnegie Institute at Stanford estimates that there is enough wind energy at altitudes between 7 and 12km, where the jet stream blow, to meet the global electricity demand a hundred times over. Due to their abundance and strength, jet stream winds to 15 km above the earth, provide tremendous potential to generate wind energy by installing turbines.

In 2009, scientists had proposed an inflatable tower up to 20 km tall, which can carry people and payload into space cheaper than rockets and space shuttles. They proposed 100 wind turbines on a 15- km pneumatic tower made of Kevlar, a synthetic fibre with high tensile strength. The main advantage of these insulating towers of strong polymer fabric is that electricity collected by the tower skin will not flow into the ground plane. The tower can be inflated with helium or ordinary air and would be able to sustain loads up to 270,000 tonnes. The estimated cost of a single tower with turbines, which can generate 20 GW of power is said to be a prohibitive $ 10 billion. India's total demand at present is 200 GW and that can be a met by 10 such towers.

A group of companies in Britain have come up with a radical proposal of floating windmills that will open up thousands of kilometers of coastline to zero-carbon power. Project Deepwater was launched to research ways of overcoming the engineering problems that limit offshore turbines to water depths of 40 meters or less. The floating turbines have the potential to open up vast amounts of power. The answer involves a windmill with a buoyant base held in place by cables attached to a steel and concrete disc on the seafloor. The deep-water turbine (300 m deep) would cost about the same as a normal single 3MW turbine ($ 20 m).

Stereo-lithography

Stereo-lithography is the practice of constructing complex structures from a bath of liquid polymer. A computer-controlled laser traces a precise path in the polymer, solidifying it into a tough resin. Once each layer is complete, the model is lowered slightly, more liquid flows over the top and the laser adds another microscopically thin layer. At present stereo-lithography devices (also known as 3D printers) are capable of building dwellings not larger than dolls' houses, and are used primarily for creating one-off components and small product prototypes. Belgian company materialise is pioneering mammoth stereo lithography, using larger machine boasting build areas of over 2m. The firm has already made full size body panels for concepts cars and large-scale architectural models. In the future, stereo-lithography is going to get lighter and cheaper, raising the possibility that builders may be able simply to print custom-made parts on site.

This will allow designs in free forms, even for skyscrapers. New kinds of lifts and escalators will glide on a vertical track positioned within a strong electro-magnetic field and will be built using a space age lightweight material. A revolutionary future escalator, the Levitator, named after its inventor Jack Levy is the world's first escalator is capable of following free-form curves.

Researchers in Japan have invented a new shock-resistant material that can withstand extreme temperatures. Made entirely of carbon, it can flow and stretch slowly like thick honey and spring back to its original form. It looks like a metal sponge that is porous. It is made from trillions of entangled carbon nano-tubes, when you stretch and release it, it can come back slowly to its original shape. Grown in a mixture of silicon, iron and water, the carbon nano-tubes are 5 nanometers in diameter, and can retain their form and function within a huge temperature range of between minus 196°C and 100°C in an oxygen-free environment.

Self-healing Concrete

Victor Li, a professor of materials science at the University of Michigan in the US, has developed Self healing concrete that fills up the cracks and cavities by itself. Small amounts of hydrated cement form a tiny calcium carbonate 'sear', sealing the cracks within a concrete structure.

British scientists have developed a genetically modified bacterium which can knit together cracks in concrete structures by producing a special glue. The microbe, created by a team of researchers at the Newcastle University, has been programmed to seal fine cracks in the concrete. Once in contact with surface, it produces a mixture of calcium carbonate and a bacterial glue which combines with the filamentous bacterial cells to "knit" the cracks together. Ultimately hardening to the same strength as the surrounding concrete, the "bacila filla" as it has been aptly named prolongs the life of structures.

Safety of Structures From Disasters

Safety in buildings and construction can be seen in different ways, viz. safety during construction, safety of structure and safety during occupation and use of the buildings. There are several elements which concern the aspects of safety.

Safety During Construction Process

- Securing construction sites from accidents, threats, hazards, thefts and entry of unauthorised visitors, etc.

- Safety of people, property, traffic and environment in the vicinity of site.
- Safety regulations, specifications, code and enforcements.
- Safe work practices and performance evaluation.
- Process hazard assessment.
- Safety of transportation, material movement and construction machinery, electric equipment and tools, including their maintenance.
- Communications, lighting and public address/warning system.
- Operational procedure, manuals and instructions.
- Insurance and medical cover.
- Accident Investigation System.
- Safety gear for workers/supervisors.
- First-aid, medical help, accident and trauma treatment.
- Materials management (including security, storage and transport).
- Safety audit.
- Training and awareness.

Structural Safety

- Structural design, specifications, standards and codes.
- Safety system, performance evaluation and managements.
- Fire safety, lifts, escalators, power system, cables, building services, etc.
- Access for disabled.
- Emergency preparedness, response, rescue and operational control.
- Operational procedure, manuals and instructions.
- Communications, lighting and warning systems,
- Insurance and medical cover.
- Maintenance, safety audit and inspections.
- Safety Management Information System (MIS).
- Safety drill, training and awareness.
- Continuance of relevant safety practices initiated during the construction process.

Occupational Safety

- Hazard assessment.
- Operational procedures, manuals and instructions.
- Fire safety, lifts, power system, cables, escalators, etc.
- Safe storage of hazardous goods, chemicals, gases, etc.
- Emergency planning, rescue and response.
- Access for disabled.
- Risk management and insurance.
- Occupational health safety.
- On the job and off the job safety.

- Building maintenance, services management and inspections.
- Checks, supervision, commitment and accountability.
- Safety Information and Warning System.
- Safety audit.
- Training and awareness.
- Continuance of safety practices taken up during planning, design and construction including periodic check of the structure, equipment, services, communications, safety MIS, certification, etc.

Potentially Hazardous Buildings

A hazardous building presents a potential for life loss or serious injury when an accident occurs. Types of buildings considered potentially hazardous include:

- Concrete frame buildings without special reinforcing;
- Pre-cast concrete buildings, including old structures;
- Soft-storey buildings (those with the lower storey lacking adequate strength)
- Buildings with pre-stressed concrete elements and/or post-tensioned concrete slabs;
- Steel frame or concrete frame buildings with unreinforced masonry walls;
- Reinforced concrete building with no special detailing or reinforcement;
- Unreinforced masonry wall buildings with wood or precast concrete floors;
- Theatres and auditoria having long span roof structures;
- Large unengineered buildings;
- Buildings with inadequately anchored exterior cladding and glazing;
- Building with poorly anchored parapets and appendages.

Often the common failures of a structure are the following:

- Roof sheets or tiles fly off
- Joints and connections are broken
- Anchorage of roof gets broken and whole roof collapses
- Frames collapse due to joint failures
- Corners splaying
- Bulging of walls
- Diagonal cracks in the walls
- Diagonal cracks from corners of openings
- Cracks wherever materials change
- Delamination of plasters
- Walls and columns giving because of roof load

It is generally not the natural hazard *perse* that kill people; rather unsafe buildings and construction that lead to loss of life and property. For ensuring safe construction, the following are the imperatives:

- Site selection, planning and architectural design

- Engineering and technologies that are cost effective, environment friendly, ecologically appropriate, energy saving and locally relevant
- Codes, specifications, regulations and enforcement

Disaster Rehabilitation Involves a systematic sequence of diagnosis, surrey, site selection, services planning and building/ Structural design

Site Selections Criteria

- Land ownership and possible of acquisition of land
- Proximity and condition of road infrastructure
- Proximity of facilities, fire station, hospital, dispensaries, service infrastructure
- Proximity to bus stands, transport, railways, metro station, etc.
- Constraints and vulnerability

Site conditions

- Topography and site gradients should be sufficient for drainage while being habitable for the expected density of occupation. The appropriate maximum site gradient depends on soil conditions, vegetation and possible drainage and erosion control measures, which need to be taken into consideration in order to prevent flooding and mudslides. The ideal gradient is between 2% to 4%.
- Ecology, agriculture, sub soil water, plantation, soil type, etc.
- Natural hazards, including earthquakes, volcanic activity, landslides or flooding.
- Permeability of the ground.
- Micro-climatic conditions.

Services

- Availability of sufficient drinking water within a suitable distance throughout the year.
- Height of the water table, whether it risks pollution by sanitation, flooding, etc.
- Wastewater disposal and treatment.
- Sanitation, sewerage, energy and power supply.

Space

- Whether there is sufficient space for the desired density of the population?
- Whether there is space for extension?
- Land use and development parameters and norms.
- Land ownership and possibility of acquisition of land.

Land use and town planning are the important aspects of disaster mitigation, prevention and management. Natural and man-made disasters neither can be prevented nor predicted. However, with the technological advancement to some extent mechanism can be developed to mitigate the after-effects of the disaster. Areas of vulnerability can be identified and necessary measures can be proposed by the concerned local bodies, who should keep updating the building byelaws to safeguard against disasters and ensure effective and impartial enforcement. Following strategies for disaster management are proposed:

Pre-Disaster Preparedness

Micro-zonation surveys should be referred for land use planning while preparing the Zonal Plans and Layout Plans.

- Seismic micro-zonation for selected areas having high growth rates should be taken up on priority.
- On the basis of vulnerability studies and hazard identification, which include soil conditions, probable intensity of earthquake, physiographic conditions of the area, fault traces, etc., local level land use zoning and planning should be undertaken.
- Building bye-laws should incorporate the aspects of Multi-Hazard Safety and Retrofitting.
- Priority should be given to public buildings (such as hospitals, educational, institutional, power stations, infrastructure, heritage monuments, lifeline structures and those which are likely to attract large congregation) for their ability to withstand earthquake of the defined intensity.

NDMA, State DMA or Fire Services should identify vulnerable areas. Disaster Management Centres should be established in every zone to deal with the disasters, including biochemical and nuclear disasters. It is also important to make people aware through media campaigns and advertisements about emergency procedures and location of emergency shelters, etc.

Post-Disaster Management

It has been observed that disaster is generally followed by breakdown of communication lines and disruption of essential services. Therefore, the key communication lines and disruption of essential services. Therefore, the key communication centres should be protected from natural disasters *i.e.* flood, fire and earthquake, etc. Services restoration should be taken up on top priority. Necessary set up should be created in the concerned department for such eventualities.

Engineering For Disaster Management

The major areas of damage are the walls and roof. According to the Building Materials and Technology Promotion Council (BMTPC), the matrix as mentioned in Table 9.5 provides a guideline of probability of damage for various type of roofs and walls. It is necessary to understand that the loss-susceptibility is an aspect of building and construction types and it largely varies with the ground/geological/subsoil conditions. A building infrastructure schedule for a district should be prepared to meet the damage risk to buildings. For this the format developed by the BMTPC provides comprehensive guidelines. Apart from the information on vulnerable buildings, the following aspects need due consideration for hazardous buildings survey:

(*i*) Visual description of failures of structures
(*ii*) Type and quality of soil strata including level of water-table
(*iii*) Type and quality of materials used in construction
(*iv*) Local level of workmanship/construction techniques available
(*v*) Terrain and topographic details
(*vi*) Size and shape of the structure

(*vii*) Age of the structure

(*viii*) Distance to the road and nearest highway

(*ix*) Engineering details of the structure, construction drawings

(*x*) Observed/inferred mechanisms of failure

Most of the housing in our country is built by people themselves with the help of semi-skilled artisans *i.e.*, non-engineered construction, which need special attention being hazard and accident prone. The categorization of various buildings helps to identify the extent of damage and strategy for redevelopment as given in Table 9.5.

Table 9.5. Vulnerability of Buildings to Hazards

Wall/Roof Type	**EO Intensity MSK**				**Wind Velocity (m/s)**				**Flood**		**out**
	≥IX	VIII	VII	<VI	55	47	33	Prons	Protected		side
A2. a. Unburned Brick Wall (Sloping roofs)	VH	H	M	L	VH	H	M	L	VH	M	L
A2. b. Unburned Brick Wall (Flat roots)	VH	H	M	L	VH	H	M	L	VH	M	L
A3.A. Stone Wall (sloping roofs)	VH	H	M	L	VH	H	M	L	VH	M	L
A3.B. Stone Wall (Flat roofs)	VH	H	M	L	H	M	L	L	VH	M	L
B.a. Burned Brick Wall (Flat roofs)	H	M	L	VL	M	L	L	VL	H	L	VL
Cl.a. Concrete Wall (Sloping roofs)	H	L	VL	NIL	L	VL	VL	VL	L	VL	VL
Cl.b. Concrete Wall (Flat roofs)	M	L	VL	NIL	L	VL	VL	VL	L	VL	VL
C2. Wood Wall (All roofs)	M	L	VL	NIL	VH	H	M	L	H	M	VL
C3. Ekra wall (All roofs)	M	L	VL	NIL	VH	H	M	L	H	M	VL
X1 Gl and other metal sheets (All roofs)	M	VL	NIL	NIL	VH	H	M	L	H	M	VL
X2 Bamboo, Thatch, Grass, Leaves, etc. (All roofs)	M	VL	NIL	NIL	VH	VH	H	L	VH	M	L

Legend: VH–Very High, H–High, M–Medium, L–Low, VL–Very Low

Source: *BMTPC*

Building Category

The building with respects to structural safety are categorised as below.

Category A: Buildings in field stone, rural structures, unburnt brick houses, clay houses

Category B: Ordinary brick buildings, building of large block and prefabricated type, half-timbered structures, building in natural hewn stone

Category C: Reinforced building, well-built wooden structures

Category X: Other types not covered in A.B.C. These are generally light.

Table 9.6. Earthquake loss-susceptibility data for different construction types Average damage (%) at Intensity (MM) (MM = modified Mercalli scale) (from Degg, 1992)

S.No.	Construction type	Average Damage (%) at Intensity (MM)				
		VI	VII	VIII	IX	X
1.	Adobe	8	22	50	100	100
2.	Unreinforced masonry, non-seismic design	3.5	14	40	80	100
3.	Reinforced concrete frame, non-seismic design	2.5	11	33	70	100
4.	Steel frames, non-seismic design	1.8	6	18	40	60
5.	Reinforced masonry, medium non-seismic design	1.5	5.5	16	38	66
6.	Reinforced concrete frame, seismic design	0.9	4	13	33	58
7.	Sheer wall structure, seismic design	0.6	2.3	7	17	30
8.	Wooden structure, seismic design	0.5	2.8	8	15	23
9.	Steel frame, seismic design	0.4	2	7	20	40
10.	Reinforced masonry, seismic design	0.3	1.5	5	13	25

***Source:** BMTPC*

Table 9.7. Seismic intensity increments

Ground conditions	Reid (1908)	Medvedev (1965)
Granite	0	0
Limestone, Sandstone	0-1.2	1-1.5
Gravel	1.2-2.1	1-1.6
Sand	1.2-2.1	1.2-1.8
Clay	1.5-2.0	1.2-2.1
Fill	2.1-3.4	2.3-3.0
Wet Gravel Sand Clay	2.3	1.7-2.8
Wet fill	3.5	3.3-3.9

***Source:** BMTPC*

Table 9.8. Average changes in intensity associated with different types of surface geology (from Degg. 1992)

Subsoil	Average change in intensity
Rock (e.g. granite, gneiss, basalt)	–1
Firm sediments	0
Loose sediments (e.g. sand, alluvial deposits)	+1
Wet sediments, artificially filled ground	+1.5

Table 9.9. Types of Damage and Remedial Measures

	Category of Damage	Extent of Damage	Remedial Measure
A.	Slight Non-structural Damage	Fine cracks in plaster, fail of small piece of plaster	Only architectural repairs needed
B.	Moderate Structural Damage	Small crack in walls fairly large pieces of plaster states slip off, cracks in parapet, walls	Architectural repair to achieve durability
C.	Heavy Structural Damage	Large and deep crack in walls, chimneys fall, load carrying capacity of the building is partially reduced	Building to be vacated and reoccupied only after structural restoration and seismic strengthening
D.	Severe Structural Damage	Gaps in walls, part of buildings may collapse separate parts of building lose cohesion and shown relative movement, inner walls collapse, Approx. 50 per cent of the main structural elements fail	Building has to be vacated. Either the building has to be demolished or extensive structure restoration and seismic strengthening work has to be undertaken
E.	Collapse	Total collapse of building	Clearing site and reconstruction

Source: *BMTPC, BSI and LBRI*

Key Elements of Safe Construction

A-Anchorage

B-Bracing

C-Connections

D-Detailing

E-External Environment

Safety and retrofitting of buildings and structures should be undertaken in the following priority:

(*a*) Public Buildings

(*i*) Educational: Schools, Colleges, Libraries, etc.

(*ii*) Health: Hospitals, wards, clinics, etc.

(*iii*) Essential Services: Telephone exchange, fire stations, water supply, pump houses, power houses, etc.

(*iv*) Congregation: Cinemas, theatres, auditoria, religious buildings, etc.

(*v*) Administrative: Offices and staff residences

(*vi*) Monuments

(*vii*) Critical hazardous industries (to prevent collateral chemical hazard)

(*b*) Other Critical Structures

These include those essential for water supply, transportation and communication.

(*c*) Suggested Actions

(*i*) Government initiative for securing and retrofitting the buildings in the government sector.

(*ii*) Incentives for public and private sectors, such as adjustment of insurance premia.

(*iii*) Models and prototypes illustrating retrofitting techniques for different building types.

(*iv*) Incentives and disincentives to motivate retrofitting of homes, along with loan or loan-cum-subsidy schemes.

(*v*) Technology transfer.

Lifeline and Temporary Shelters

In the event of a disaster, it is essential that rescue shelters are available for taking temporary refuge and for treating the injured. It has to be ensured that the community asset buildings and social infrastructure such as schools and hospitals are designed with provisions to serve the dual purpose of serving as rescue shelters. It is also advisable to adopt more stringent norms in the design and construction of these public buildings so that they would be able to withstand even disaster of intensity a level higher than the estimated vulnerability. The key lifeline structures such as major roads, bridges, railways, helipads, airports, jetties and communication systems in the vulnerable areas need to be designed, strengthened and retrofitted in advance to ensure uninterrupted access in the event of a disaster. For construction, reconstruction and repair of buildings, the following are the critical considerations:

Foundation

- Desist from foundations in loose sand, soft silt and expansive clays. It is necessary to provide a rigid raft foundation or piles resting on a firm stratum.
- Soil improvement measures for lighter buildings could be taken up through sand filling and soil stabilization.
- Individual footings or pile caps need to be connected with RCC ties of prescribed reinforcement, below plinth level in at least two directions at right angles to each other.

Super Structure

- Buildings in earthquake prone zones classified into categories from A (best case) to E (worst conditions) based on location and seismic co-efficient.

- Simple structural systems and diagonal bracing in the vertical panels of steel or concrete frame to withstand the seismic forces.
- Light weight construction, wherever possible.
- Avoid mud and rubble masonry in highly seismic areas.
- Well-braced timber framed structures and light-weight materials to prevent loss of life and property due to falling debris.
- Precaution against chain effects, such as landslides, floods, fires and disruption to communications.
- Separation sections in buildings asymmetric in plan, elevation or mass.
- To ensure a structural equilibrium of flexibility and rigidity by transferring stresses to adjacent structures and design of structures for 3D performance.

Walls

- For brick or laterite stone masonry in mud mortar, provide damp-proof course at plinth level to stop upward seepage of water.
- Eaves projection of minimum 50 cm to protect walls from driving rain.
- Water-proof plaster using bitumen cut-back and kerosene oil on outer face of walls.
- Free standing boundary wall to be checked against overturning.
- For brick work in mud mortar, the minimum wall thickness should be 9 inches in single storeyed construction; could be 1.5 brick thickness in construction upto 3 floors.
- Walls to be reinforced with reinforced concrete bands.
- Wooden beams with cross elements as alternative to RC bands.
- Load bearing walls not recommended above four storeys and beyond a height exceeding 15 m.
- Wall corners to be strengthened; proper bonding by stepped or toothed joints. Care be taken to reinforce the corners of walls and buttresses using alternating bands of thin bricks and stones in vulnerable corners. Thin bricks and stone act like a tying element with respect to the volume of masonry, and reinforce the wall. Stone can be used mainly in infill walls.
- Instead of bricks, in a few places, pressed large pieces of stone can be used at corner of building.
- Good masonry with proper interlocking and bonding.
- Use of thin fired bricks for a better structural performance of the wall. Use of earthquake resistant features such as diagonal stone masonry.

Non-Engineered Buildings

- Hand-formed walls tapering upwards keeping the minimum thickness 300 mm at top.
- Footing and masonry wall above foundation up to plinth level to be built of stone or fired brick in cement mortar.
- Height of plinth above High Flood Level (min. 30 cm above ground level)

- Water proofing layer of waterproof mud using bitumen cutback or heavy/thick polythene sheet at plinth level.
- For strengthening of existing damaged wall and floor diaphragms, steel mesh could be provided on the outside of the surface and nailed or bolted to the walls. It then may be covered with plaster or micro-concrete.

Wooden Members and Joints

Since wood is an easily workable material, it is easy to restore the strength of wooden members, beams, columns, struts and ties by splitting additional material. The weathered or rotten wood should first be removed. Nails, wooden screws or steel bolts will be most convenient as connectors. It is advisable to use steel stars to cover all such splices and joints to keep them tight and stiff.

- All poles and posts to be properly anchored into the ground or reinforced cement footing.
- Alternatively, the posts with cross members connected at the lower end be embedded in ground to a minimum depth of 75 cm.
- For earthen buildings, lintel band and roof band to be provided, wherever height of wall exceeds 2.5 m. Unfinished rough-cut or sawn lumber with diagonal bracing could be used for the bands.
- Collar beam to cover the buttresses where pilasters or buttresses are used at corners or T-junctions.
- Diagonal struts at corners for further stiffening of the collar beam.

Staircase

- Interconnection of the stairs with adjacent floors should be appropriately treated by providing sliding joints to prevent bracing effect on the floors.
- Alternatively, rigid walls enclosing the sides of the stair or stairs separated by a gap from the floor slab with provision of a tread plate.

Openings

- Opening at any level to be small with continuous lintel band. Width of opening should not exceed one third of total length of a wall.
- Length of openings not to exceed 3/5th to half of wall-length between adjacent cross walls.
- Offset from inside corner of the external wall to the outer edge of the opening 22 to 45 cm.
- Minimum vertical distance between openings one above the other 60 cm.
- Openings not compliant with requirements to be strengthened by provision of RCC band or reinforced brickwork.
- Arches to span openings not ideal in seismic areas unless steel ties are provided.
- Both lintel and sill stones of windows have a bearing at least 6" on each side. This prevents diagonal cracks originating at the corners.
- Minimum pier width should be 600 mm and the openings shall have a continuous lintel band.

- In earthen buildings, the width of a door or window not greater than 1.2 m with not more than one opening in a wall.
- The minimum offset between an inside corner and the opening should be not less than 90 cm.

Retrofitting of Old Buildings

Usually existing, old buildings are more prone to damage due to the fires, structural failure, overloading, cyclones and floods. The first and foremost need is to save them from falling down. For this bracing, scaffoldings and buttressing are required to provide support. Following guidelines, developed by Indian Trust for Arts and Cultural Heritage (INTACH) are handy:

- In cracked external corners place wooden planks across the crack and then support the planks with wooden members.
- Do not prop the damaged wall at the parapet level, it may cause more damage.
- Propping in a single storied structure support at ceiling level. Use supports at different levels, if necessary.
- In two storeyed structures use jute bags filled with rubble or sand till the lintel level of the ground floor and then use the planks and the wooden supports. Use folded jute bags at the end of the support. At the corner of the wall use support at various levels.
- Long length of damaged walls can be supported using rubble masonry of regular stones at regular intervals along the length of the wall. Mud mortar could be used.
- Jute or plastic bags filled with rubble or sand collected on site can also be stacked at intervals to support the walls.
- Do not support the arches at the centre or along the curve.
- Support them at the spring point of the arch. Use wooden supports. In case of metal support use folded gunny bags at the end of the support.
- In a column-beam situation, support the beam in the middle with either a masonry pillar or stacking sand filled jute or plastic bags.
- If a flat ceiling is being supported with wooden or metallic supports, do not forget to use folded jute bags at the end of the support.
- For tall structures erect a wooden scaffolding all around and care fully remove all the loosely hanging elements. In case you are dismantling arches, do not remove the keystone.
- On roofs tie the loose damaged parapet with Gl wire (Galvanized Iron). Collect the rubble either at the corners or on the periphery. Do not stack in the middle of the slab or on the cracks. Too many people should not get on the top of a damaged roof at the same time.

Codes of Structural Design and Safety

The structural design of foundation, masonry, timber, plain concrete, reinforced concrete, pre-stressed concrete and structural steel be carried out in accordance with Part-VI structural design, section-1 loads; section-2 foundation; section-3 wood; section-4 masonry; section-5 concrete; section-6 steel; of National Building Code of India, taking into consideration the Indian Standards for safety from structural failure, fires, earthquake, cyclone/windstorm and floods. The following codes, specifications and guidelines that can be referred to for planning retrofit measures and for designing new constructions in hazard prone areas:

1. **Vulnerability Atlas and Guidelines** prepared by the Expert Group on Natural Disaster Prevention, Preparedness and Mitigation (Ministry of Urban Affairs and Employment) published by Building Materials and Technology Promotion Council (BMTPC), New Delhi

   1.1. Vulnerability Atlas of India, 1997, BMTPC, New Delhi

   1.2. Techno-legal Aspects of Earthquake, Windstorm and Flood Hazards and Land use Zoning, 1998, BMTPC, New Delhi

   1.3. "Land Use Zoning in Hazard Prone Areas related to Earthquakes, Windstorms and Flood Hazard - Guidelines", 1998, BMTPC, New Delhi

   1.4. "Improving Flooding Resistance of Housing - Guidelines", 1998, BMTPC, New Delhi

   1.5. "Improving Wind/Cyclone Resistance of Housing - Guidelines", 1998, BMTPC, New Delhi

   1.6. "Improving Earthquake Resistance of Housing - Guidelines", 1998, BMTPC, New Delhi.

2. **Coder or General Structural Safety** published by Bureau of Indian Standards (BIS)

   2.1. IS: 1905-1987 "Code of Practice of Structural Safety of Buildings : Foundations", 1995

   2.2. 13:1904-1978 "Code of Practice of Structural Safety of Building: Foundation", 1995

   2.3. IS: 465-1978 "Code of Practice for Plain and Reinforced Concrete", 2000.

   2.4. 15:800-1984 "Code of Practice for General Construction in Steel", 1985

   2.5. 15:883-1966 "Code of practice for Design of Structural Timber in Building", 1967.

3. **Codes for Earthquake Protection**

   3.1. IS:1983-1984 "Criteria for Earthquake Resistant Design of Structures (Fourth Revision)", 1986.

   3.2. IS:13920-1993 "Ductile Detailing of Reinforced Concrete Structures subject to seismic forces - Code of Practice", 1993.

   3.3. IS:4326-1993 "Earthquake Resistant Design and Construction of Buildings - Code of Practice (Second Revision)", 1993.

   3.4. IS: 13828-1993 "Improving Earthquake Resistance of Earthen Building" - Guidelines, 1993.

   3.5. IS: 13935-1993 "Repair and Seismic Strengthening of Buildings."– Guidelines, Nov. 1993.

4. **Codes or Cyclone/Wind Storm Protection**

   IS: 875(3)-1987 "Code of Practice for Design Loads (Other than Earthquake) for Buildings and Structures, Part 3, Wind Loads", Bureau of Indian Standards, 1989.

Table 9.10. Building Performance Check List

	Category of Damage	Check List
1.	Stability requirements	Mechanical resistance to static and dynamic actions, both individually and in combination. Resistance to impacts, international and unintentional abuse, accidental actions. Cyclic (fatigue) effects.
2.	Fire safety requirements	Risks of outbreak of fire and of spread of fire. Physiological effects of smoke and heat. Alarm time (detection and alarm system). Evacuation time (escape routes). Survival time (fire escape).
3.	Safety in use requirements	Safety in respect of aggressive agents (protection against explosions, burning, sharp point and edges, moving mechanisms, electrocution, radioactivity, inhalation or contact with poisonous substances, infection) safety during movements and circulation (limitation of floor slipness, unobstructed passage, guard rails, etc.), security against human or animal intrusion.
4.	Tightness requirements	Water tightness (rain, ground water, drinking water, waste water, etc). Air and gas tightness, Snow and dust tightness.
5.	Hygrothermal requirements	Control of air temperature, thermal radiation, air velocity and relative humidity (limitation of variation in time and space, controls), Control of condensation.
6.	Air purity requirements	Ventilation, control of odours.
7.	Acoustical requirement	Control of external and internal noise (continuous and intermittent), Intelligibility of sound, Reverberation time.
8.	Visual requirement	Natural and artificial lighting (required illuminance, freedom from glare, luminance contrast and stability). Sunlight (insolation), Possibility of darkness, Aspect of space and surface (colour, texture, regular, flatness, verticality, horizontality, perpendicularity, etc). Visual contact, internally and with the external world (links and barriers for privacy, freedom from optical distortion).
9.	Tactile requirements	Surface properties, roughness, dryness, warmth, suppleness, freedom from discharge of static electricity.
10.	Dynamic requirements	Limitation of whole body accelerations and vibrations (transient and continuous). Pedestrian comfort in windy areas. Ease of movement (slope of ramps, pitch of staircase). Manoeuvrability (operation of doors, window, equipments, etc.)

Source: *BMPTC*

Table 9.11. Sub-Systems and Components of Building/Structure

Category of Damage		Examples of assemblies or components
1. Stability requirements	1.1 Foundation	Shallow (ground beam, raft, etc.)
	1.2 Walls	Deep (deep footing, pile, diaphragm wall, etc)
	1.3 Structure	Column, beam, panel, slab, shell, lattice structure, etc.
2. External envelope	2.1 Envelope below ground	Base, side and top envelope (solid floor, basement wall, underground roof, etc.) Openings (pipe entry, shaft, etc.)
	2.2 Envelope above ground	Base, side and top envelope (exposed floor over external space, wall, roof) Openings (door, window, roof-light, etc)
3. Spatial dividers (outside the envelope)	3.1 External vertical divider	Portions (wall, balustrade, etc) Openings (door, grille, etc.)
	3.2 External Horizontal divider	Floors (terrace, balcony, porch, roof, etc.) Opening (trap-door, etc.)
	3.3 External vertical divider	Stairs, ramps, etc.
4. Spatial dividers (within the envelope)	4.1 Internal vertical divider	Portions (wall, balustrade, cupboard, etc.) Openings (door, etc.)
	4.2 Internal horizontal divider	Floor opening
	4.3 Internal staircase	Stairs, ramp, lift, etc.
5 Building Services	5.1 Water distribution/ disposal	Water distribution (pipe, tap, tank, pump, softener, etc.) Sanitary appliances (basin, sink, bath, shower, bidet, WC, etc.) Waste water disposal (pipes, traps, chutes, etc.) Rain water disposal (pipes, tank, etc.)
	5.2 Heating and ventilation	Sewerage (pipes, Inspection Chamber, septic tank, cesspol, etc.) Gas fuel distribution (pipes, taps, tank, etc.) Liquid fuel distribution (pipes, tape, tank, etc.) Primary heat source (boiler, chemney, etc.) Water circuit (pipes, taps, circulator, expansion vessel)

	5.3 Gas distribution	Air circuit (ducts, air vent, ventilators, etc.). Compressed air distribution (pipes, plant, etc.).
	5.4 External	Gas distribution (pipes, plant room, etc.) High voltage grid lines, transformer, low voltage grid (wiring, switch, socket, lighting, etc.)
	5.5 Tele communication	Telephone system (wiring telephone) Internet, wi-fi etc. Intercom system (wiring, bells, door opener, intercom) Radio and television distribution (wiring, aerial, dish antenna etc.
	5.6 Mechanical and electromechanical	Lift (plant room, car, cables, etc.) Escalator and moving walkway Hoist (pulleys, etc.)
	5.7 Pneumatic and gravity transport	Refuse diposal (ducts, etc.), vacuum cleaning
	5.8 Safety	Pneumatic transporter (ducts, plant, etc.) Lighting protection (conductor, cable, earth connection, etc,) Fire Protection (pipes, tank, fire, alarm, smoke, detectors) CCTV, Gates/Doors, Grills, Escape Staircase, etc.

***Source:** BMTPC and Author (AK Jain)*

Maintenance Management

Our cities and buildings suffer from:

- Inadequate service coverage, lack of proper standards, norms and specifications and their enforcement
- Poor quality of service, and costly O & M
- Absence of qualified and competent personnel /supervision
- Lack of citizen/consumers' orientation, resistance to changes/reforms
- Wastage of time, human resource and finances
- Poor linkage between costs and pricing
- Degenerating equipment
- Lack of proper Management Information System
- Incompleteness and inaccuracies

Management of maintenance is an action oriented philosophy with the following attributes:

- User/Customer Satisfaction
- Common goals & objectives
- Integrated maintenance process
- Flexibility
- Speed of response
- Performance effectiveness

Major Forms of Maintenance Outsourcing

- Integrated contracts
- Programme management consultancy
- Management contracts
- BOT for bulk facilities
- Competitive tendering
- Participatory approach, including the involvement of Residents/Owners/Tenants Association.

Local Maintenance Company/Agency

- Electrical system, street lighting, power generators, transformers, CETP, etc.
- Water supply system, including filtration and recycling plants, booster pumps
- Sewerage system
- Storm water, Drainage system
- Roads and Parking
- Pavements, corridors, common circulation areas, including staircases, lifts, ramps, escalators, access for the handicapped, etc.
- Open space, landscape, plantation, street furniture, drinking water, benches, etc.
- Fire fighting equipment/installation
- Informal sector booths/khokas/booths, etc.
- A.C./Cooling/weather control systems
- Public toilets and urinals
- Taxi-stands
- Controlling construction and encroachments in common/public areas
- Collection/disposal and management of solid waste
- Security

Maintenance Cycle

- Twice a day
- Cleaning of public toilets and urinals
- Checking water supply in public hydrants

Once a day

- Scavenging of roads, paths and community areas
- Cleaning of roadside/minor drains
- Cleaning of dustbins and refuse dumps

Once a week

- Cleaning and disinfection of main drains and public toilets
- Cleaning of sanitary and sewer pipes and open drains
- Checking of daily and weekly jobs, registers and complaints
- Survey and checking of roadside vendors, encroachments and unauthorised constructions
- Checking of daily and weekly jobs, registers and complaints
- Survey and checking of roadside vendors, encroachments and unauthorised construction
- Checking roadside plantations, watering of parks and other horticultural jobs.

Once a month

- Repair/provision of signboards, including cleaning and removal of posters
- Maintenance of street lights, replacement of fused lights
- Removal/demolition of encroachments, checking of property registers, repair and fencing of public lands
- Checking the water supply system, testing of water, recommissioning of public hydrants and hand-pumps
- Cleaning open areas, parks, dressing of road berms, central verge, filling of depressions, including removal of malba and dismantled materials
- Repair, fencing of parks and tree guards
- Repair and replacement of broken drains and manhole covers
- Review of progress

Once Every Three Months

- Servicing and repair of water supply installations and pipelines
- Checking and repair of electrical installations, pumps and motors
- Desilting of drains, correcting their slopes, manhole covers, repair of sewers, culverts and dustbins
- Repair of paths and roads, parking, patching of potholes and damaged portions.

Once Every Six Months

- Painting road markings
- Repairing compound walls, railings and landing
- Repainting signboards/Signage
- Clearance of drains and outfall choke, including desilting
- Repairing public hydrants, pair of toilet blocks and culverts
- Repair and cleaning of overhead and underground water tanks
- Servicing and maintenance of road signals, traffic rotaries island, traffic stands and street furniture.

Annual

- Monitoring and review of progress
- Repair and whitewashing of buildings
- Re-carpeting of roads
- Review long term measures like construction of new roads, facilities and parking areas, shifting of godowns, goods, transport, etc.
- Construction of new dustbins, urinals and toilets, wherever required
- Stock-taking, annual monitoring and programming for the coming year.

The maintenance of built environment can no longer be treated as a footnote of planning, design and construction but has to be at the focus of the building management.

ANNEXURE 9.1

Quantities of Materials for Different Items

Concrete is a mixture of cement, sand (fine aggregate), crushed stone and water. It is made in different mixes for different applications. A general idea of the materials required for different mixes is given here. Approximate quantities are for one cubic metre of concrete.

Quantities of Materials for Different Concrete Mixes

Mix	Water in litres per 50 kg bag of cement	Cement by number of dogs	Sand in m^3	Crush stone in m^3
1:1:2	15.0	12.2	0.382	0.764
1:1:5:3	21.0	8.0	0.411	0.822
1:2:3	25.0	7.1	0.493	0.740
1:2:4	27.5	6.4	0.424	0.848
1:3:4	32.5	5.3	0.552	0.736
1:3:5	34.5	4.8	0.500	0.833
1:3:6	37.5	4.4	0.448	0.896
1:4:8	47.5	3.4	0.458	0.196

Note: Voids in sand and stone are assumed to be 40 and 45 percent respectively. No allowance has been made for bulking and wastage.

For Various Types of Construction

Concrete Mix	Consistency	Type of Usage
1:1:2	Medium	Heavy column a long span arches.
1:2:2	Medium	Heavily stressed members and small precast works like fencing, telegraph poles decoratives items, water tight construction, etc.
1:1.5:3 or 1:2:3	Medium	Column and beams subjected to medium loads, concrete under water.
1:2:4	Stiff to Medium	All general building works subject to moderate stresses, beams, slabs, basement, walls, pavement, etc.
1:3:6	Stiff to Medium	Mass concrete work in culverts, retaining walls, ordinary machine bases and foundation course for buildings.
1:4:8	Medium	Mass concrete for heavy walls, foundation under column footings.

Data for Brickwork

Material	Quantity
Bricks (normal size 20 × 10 × 10 cm)	50,000 nos. per 100 m^3
Dry mortar for brickwork (30%)	30 m^3 per 100 m^3
Brick ballast for lime concrete	37,000 nos. per 100 m^3
Brick-bats for lime concrete	105 m^3 per 100 m^3
Brick for rubble masonry work	42,000 nos. per 100 m^3
Bricks (20 × 10 × cm) as brick on edge for wall or floor	5,600 nos. per 100 m^2
Brick (20 × 10 × 10 cm) for honeycomb wall	3,500 nos. per 100 m^2

Permissible Stress for Masonry

Masonry		Stress in Kg/cm^2
Brickwork in cement Mortar Brickwork in Lime Mortar Brickwork in Mud Mortar	1:3	9.8
	1:4	8.7
	1:6	5.5
		4.4
		1.6

Stone Masonry ashlar		
in cement mortar	1:3	17.4
in Lime mortor	1:6	8.7
Coarse rubble masonry in cement mortar in	1:4	11
lime mortar	1:6	5.5
	1:6	5
Random rubble masonry in cement mortar	1:6	4.4
in lime mortar	1:6	3.3

Cement Required for Brick Masonry

Type		Cement in Bags (50 kg)
Full brick work in cement mortar	1:2	3.25/m^3
	1:3	2.60/m^3
	1:4	1.9/m^3
	1:5	1.6/m^3
	1:6	1.25/m^3
Half brick work in cement mortar	1:2	0.35/m^2
	1:3	0.28/m^2
	1:4	0.21/m^2
	1:5	0.17/m^2
	1:6	0.14/m^2
Ruled pointing in cement mortar	1:2	3.90/100 m^2
	1:3	3.06/100 m^2
	1:4	1.95/100 m^2
	1:5	1/8/100 m^2
	1:6	1.5/100 m^2
Cement plaster 20 mm (3/4 in.) thick	1:2	30.5/100 m^2
	1:3	22.80/100 m^2
	1:4	17/100 m^2
	1:5	1.8/100 m^2
	1:6	11/100 m^2
Cement plaster 12 mm (1/2 in.) thick	1:2	19.5/100 m^2
	1:3	14.7/100 m^2
	1:4	11/100 m^2
	1:5	8.9/100m^2
	1:6	7.2/100m^2

Compacted Mortar – Quantities

Mortar Mix (cement & sand)	Water in litres/Bag of cement	Cement in Bags (50 kg / cum)	Sand in m^3/ (cum)
1:1	12.5	20.4	0.7
1:1:5	14.0	16.2	0.84
1:2	15.0	13.6	0.94
1:2.5	17.5	11.6	1.0
1:3	20.0	10.1	1.05
1:4	26.5	7.6	1.07
1:6	35.0	5.0	1.17
1:8	45.0	4.4	1.22

DEBRIEFING QUESTIONS

1. What do you understand by:
   (*a*) Building Resources
   (*b*) Appropriate Technologies for Construction?
2. What are the methods of reduction of cost of a building? Give examples.
3. What is the relationship between building materials and embodied energy?
4. List out sustainable, low energy building materials.
5. What is the meaning and concept of Systems Building?
6. How standardisation and modular coordination can help in better buildings?
7. Write notes on the following:
   (*a*) Precast Building Systems
   (*b*) Pre-engineered Building Systems
   (*c*) Frame Systems
   (*d*) Construction Automation
   (*e*) BIM
   (*f*) NBC 2016
8. Explain the ways to achieve safety of civil structures, what are the ABCD principles of safe construction?
9. What is meant by the non-engineered buildings and how these can be made safer?

Chapter **10**

Building and Planning Codes

A building is a structure constructed for human habitation or other purposes. It comprises foundation, structural elements, plinth, walls, floors, roofs, plumbing and building services, platforms. verandas, balconies, cornices, projections, etc. along with appurtenant land, garden/lawn/courtyard, parking, swimming pool, etc.

Planning Codes and Building Regulations provide the mandatory norms with respect to land use, open spaces, setbacks and margins, norms for buildable ground coverage and Floor Area Ratio (FAR), building height, access, requirements of parking spaces, norms for fire protection, norms for building services, lighting, ventilation, etc. The codes and regulations also specify the administrative provisions for obtaining building permits, architectural control and approval of plans of building services, structure, etc.

Building Types

The buildings are generally categorised according to their functions and form. According to Building Codes the following are the major building types:

(*a*) **Assembly building** – A building where groups of people congregate or gather for amusement, recreation, social, religious, civil, travel and similar purposes. These include cinemas, theatres, drive-in theatres, assembly hall/city hall/town hall/auditoria, exhibition hall, museum, "mangal karyalaya" (marriage function venues), skating rink, gymnasia, restaurant, eating or boarding house, places of worship, dance hall, gymkhana, roads, railways, air, sea or other public transportation stations.

(*b*) **Business building** – are mainly for transaction of business and/or keeping of accounts and include offices, banks, professional establishments, court houses, etc.

(*c*) **Education buildings** – include schools, college, university, research institution, and quarters for essential staff, hostel and other amenities and facilities.

(*d*) **Group Housing** – A premises of size not less than 3000 sq.mt. (in NCT Delhi) comprising residential flats with basic amenities like parking, park, convenience shops, public utilities, etc.

(*e*) **Industrial Building** – includes a building wherein products or material are fabricated, assembled or processed, such as assembly plants, laboratories, power plants, refineries, gas plants, mills, dairies and factories, etc.

(*f*) **Institutional Building** – includes a building used for medical treatment, auditorium, cultural and allied activities, hospitals, care of orphans, abandoned women, children and infants, convalescents, destitute or aged persons, correctional detention of the inmates, dharmshala, sanatoria, custodial and other government and non-government institutions.

(*g*) **Mercantile Building** – includes shops, stores or markets for display and sale of goods or merchandise, office, storage and service facilities incidental thereto.

(*h*) **Multi-storeyed Building or high rise building** – A building exceeding 15 meter or more in height above the average level of front road.

(*i*) **Multi Level Car Parking building** – A multi- floor building having basements and upper floors for parking of vehicles.

(*j*) **Office Building** – includes offices, banking, public and private sector offices, stock exchange IT centres, etc.

(*k*) **Special Building** – includes special, industrial building, wholesale establishment, hotel, etc,

(*l*) **Storage Building** – A building used for storage of goods and merchandise, including a warehouse, cold storage, freight depot, transit shed, store house, hanger, truck terminal, grain elevator, barn and stable.

(*m*) **Wholesale Establishment** – An establishment for wholesale trade including related storage facilities, warehouses, transport, booking agencies and logistics.

(*n*) **Residential Building** – includes dwellings, apartment houses, flats, and condominiums. These may be detached, semi-detached, multi-storied, tenements, hostels, night shelter, etc.

(*o*) **Mixed Landuse Building** – A building partly used for commercial activities and partly for residential or other purpose.

(*p*) **Unsafe Building** – is a building which is structurally unsafe, or unsanitary, or not provided with adequate means of ingress or egress, constitutes a fire hazard or is dangerous to human and safety, health, and public welfare due to poor maintenance, dilapidation or abandonment.

A hazardous building includes a building used for storage, handling, manufacture or processing of radioactive substances, or highly combustible or explosive materials or of products which are liable to burn with extreme rapidity and/or producing poisonous fumes, or explosive emanations, or involves highly corrosive, toxic or noxious alkalis, acids, or other liquids, gases or chemicals producing flame, fumes and explosive mixtures etc. which may result in pollution and ignition.

All unsafe buildings/structures are required to be restored by repairs, demolition or dealt with as per the laws.

A Building is a Part of Urban Fabric

Like a human being every buildings has its own personality. This means every type of building, whether residential, commercial, governmental, industrial or institutional should be so planned and designed which reflects its typology, fits into the overall urban fabric, and is aesthetically pleasing while exploiting the optimum development potential of the site, (FAR, density, etc.).

Connaught Place is the Central Business District, at the heart of Delhi. In the Master Plan of Delhi (1962) its area was proposed to be enlarged from 200 acres to 350 acres by adding the bungalow plots along the radial roads, viz. Kasturba Gandhi Marg, Barakhamba Road, Janpath, Baba Kharak Singh Marg, etc. In place of bungalows on these roads, multi-storey buildings with 400 FAR (maximum ground coverage of 25%, 16 to 20 storied high) started coming around the iconic, double storied Connaught Place. This transformation created several problems with respect infrastructure services, traffic and parking and changed the skyline of New Delhi, which was conceived as a garden city with trees dominating the Skyline. The then Prime Minister, Smt. Indira Gandhi was not happy with such developments and asked the Ministry of Urban Affairs and Housing, how the high-rise buildings were allowed around the composite, classical and double storeyed Connaught Place and why the new developments were not in sync with the character of existing areas. As a result, by an Act of Parliament, Delhi Urban Art Commission was set-up in 1973. The Prime Minister also stated that New Delhi is the pride of country and not the real estate. As such, the plans and designs have to be worked out in a broader context, respecting the heritage and green character of an area. New buildings should not compete with each other, but form a composite urban design. This needs not to adopt a building regulations approach, but an urban design framework.

Site Planning Principles

Recognising the fact that human life, the built form and environment are inextricably inter-linked, a site plan should be based on the following principles:

1. **Community Module :** The site plan should provide walkability, efficient circulation and transport and provide space for the public greens and social infrastructure. The purpose is to creating a walkable, smart and compact development, control urban sprawl and promote mixed land use. Usually arterial roads (60 m right of way and above) should be spaced at 500 m, collector and sub-arterial roads (30 m to 60 m R/W) at 300 m and local streets (upto 40 m R/W) at 150 m. Accordingly, a module/sector can be designed, for example 800 m × 1200 m in Chandigarh. The industry, warehousing and transport terminals should be located outside in the urban periphery.

   Primary pedestrian access to buildings should be within a 5 to 8 minute walk (say 400 m) from nearest metro stations bus-stop. The main building facade should face the street with active use and transparent edge that contribute to street safety. Commercial frontages should have facades with minimum 50% transparency to facilitate visual surveillance of streets. Vending spaces should be marked along high pedestrian volume areas which activate the street and make it safer. Spaces should be planned for utilities, including drinking water kiosks and toilets. The following guidelines may be adopted for site planning:

   - All streets and public spaces shall be universally accessible.
   - Cycle tracks should be provided along with pedestrian walkways. Provide the shortest direct route to pedestrians and non-motorized modes of transit.
   - As far as possible, locate public transport stations, homes, jobs and civic facilities within easy access of each other, to encourage walking and cycling for short distances.

- Disincentivize private motor vehicle use. Limit supply and appropriately price private parking spaces. Explore common areas, underground and stilted parking.
- Create a safe, vibrant, comfortable urban place by providing round-the-clock active streets and incidental spaces to relax. Introduce mixed land use and informal street activities like vendors, etc.
- Encourage non-opaque fences that provide surveillance of public spaces.
- Maximize densities within Transit Oriented Development (TOD) zone in order to facilitate extensive use of public transit.

  In such areas, as per Delhi master Plan an FAR of 400 and a maximum density of 2000 persons per hectare (PPH) is permissible, besides mandatory components of social housing for which an extra FAR of 15% is provided. Further, 10% of FAR for commercial use and 10% of FAR for community facilities are permitted to facilitate mix of uses.
- Roads for vehicular routes network should be spaced at approximately 250 m c/c and pedestrian network at approximately 100 m centre to centre.
- 20% of the area of the plot shall be designated as green public open space. Social infrastructure may be provided in built-up area in the form of Accommodation Reservation.

2. **Street Design:** National Urban Transport Policy, 2006 recommends ensuring safe, affordable, quick, comfortable, reliable and sustainable access for the growing number of city residents to jobs, education, recreation and other such needs. This is sought to be achieved by incorporating urban transportation at the planning stage rather than being a consequential requirement. It seeks to bring about a more equitable allocation of road space with people, rather than vehicles, as its main focus. It encourages greater use of public transport, non-motorized need modes and multi-modal public transport system. The policy upon the need to establish institutional mechanisms for enhanced coordination in the planning and management of transport systems, along with intelligent transport system and reducing pollution levels through changes in travelling practices.

EPCA (Supreme Court) directive on increased use of Public Transport in Delhi:

"Over the years, it has become clear that each city is fighting a losing battle against air pollution and growing congestion – because of the growing number of vehicles. Economic progress of our cities will depend on their environmental health. A turnaround is only possible when cities recognize the need for transition to public transport and adopt it."

Table 10.1. Hierarchy of Roads

Type of Road	Function and Design Features	Spacing	R.O.W	Width Pavement	Maxi Grade	Max. Speed	Other Features
Freeway	Provide regional and metropolitan unity, Limited access, no grade crossing, no traffic stops.	Variable; related to regional pattern	200'-300'	Varies; 12' per lane; 8-12 shoulders both sides of each roadway; 8' to 60' median strip.	3%	60 mph	Depressed, at grade, or elevated. Preferably depressed though urban areas. Requires intensive landscaping, service roads, or adequate rear setback lines (75') where service roads are not provided.
Expressway	Provide metropolitan and city continuity. Limited access; some channelized grade crossings and signals at major intersections. Parking prohibited.	Variable; generally radial or circumferential	200'-250'	Varies: 12' per lane; 8-10' shoulders; 8-30' median strip.	4%	50 mph	Generally at grade, Requires landscaping, service roads adequate building setback.
Major Roads (Arterials)	Provide unity throughout contiguous urban area, form boundaries for neighborhoods. Minor access control; channelized intersection; parking prohibited.	$1\frac{1}{2}$ to 2 miles	120'-150'	84' maximum for 4 lanes, parking and median strip.	4%	35-45 mph	Require's 5' wide detached sidewalk planting strips (5'-10' wide or more) and adequate setback lines

Secondary Roads (Minor Arterials)	Main feeder streets, Signals where needed, stop signs on side streets. Occasionally form boundary neighbourhood.	$\frac{3}{4}$ to 1 mile	80'	60'	5%	35-40 mph	Requires 5' wide detached sidewalk, planting strips between sidewalks curb 5' to 10' or more, and adequate building setback.
Collector Street	Main interior streets. Stop signs on side streets.	$\frac{1}{4}$ to $\frac{1}{2}$ mile	64'	44' (2 traffic lanes)	5%	30 mph	Require at least 4' wide detached sidewalk; vertical curbs: plating strips are desirable; building setback lines 30' from right of way.
Local Street	Local service streets. Non-con-ducive to thorough traffic.	At blocks	50'	36' where street parking is permitted	6%	25 mph	Sidewalks at least 4' in width for densities greater than 1 dw.unit/acre.
Cull-de-sac	Street open at only one end, with provision for turnaround.	Only wherever practical	50' (90' dia. turnaround)	30'-36'	5%	15 mph	Should not have a length greater than 500 feet.

***Source:** Time Saver Standards for Architectural Design, Mc-Graw Hill.*

Table 10.2. Recommended Width of Residential Roads

Road type	Recommended carriageway width (m)
One way four lane, divided carriage way	14.6
Two lanes each way with central refuge	14.6
Two-way, four lanes with no refuge	13.5
One-way, three lanes	11.0
Two-way, three lanes (Recommended only for tidal flow)	9.0
One-way, two lanes	7.3

***Source:** Indian Roads Congress*

3. **Urban Form:** The site should manifest:
   (*i*) A coherent urban form, streetscape, pedestrian precincts, chowks and squares
   (*ii*) Wide variety, inter-mixing of socio-cultural activities and public activities
   (*iii*) Built form in harmony with the historical, socio-cultural context
   (*iv*) Exclusion of environment endangering land uses and activities.
4. **Climate:** Water, shade, channelling of cooling breeze are the prime elements of a comfortable micro-climate, besides minimum exterior surface to maximum internal volume, correct orientation, atrium and internal courtyard to reduce glare and dissipate heat, compact grouping and clustering of buildings to maximise exposure of wall surface, use of open spaces, platform, chowks, porch and squares for social and traditional attributes of urban design.

   Orientation and the placement of a building should be such that it may obtain the best advantages in relation to the following:
   - Sunlight
   - Prevailing breeze/wind
   - Views

   In general in most parts of India, South orientation is preferred. Sunlight will occur from late morning to early afternoon. During the summer months, the sun will appear high in the sky and during the winter months sun will appear low in the sky. The hot summer sun can be controlled by properly designed overhangs. The low angle of the sun during winter months will enable the rays to penetrate deep into the room. West orientation should be avoided because during the summer west sun will be very intense.
5. **Decentralised Services and Recycling:** In the context of emerging environmental awareness, the need to save air, water and land from pollution is a major concern. Drinking water, sanitation and waste treatment and drainage are important aspects of the human environment. The performance of present sanitation system needs to be reassessed with reference to environment, hygiene and their accessibility. Various alternative technologies based on decentralised services, like Extended Aeration Technique, Bio-gas production, Bubble Diffusion Process, Floatation, Anaerobic Reactors, etc., which are already in vogue, should be explored for urban sanitation.

   Widespread method of landfill for solid waste disposal is an environmental disaster. Decentralised system based on recycling, energy generation and organic decomposing were explored for solid waste treatment. Bio-reactor composting and vessel system, vermin composting, etc. are new generation technologies which can be employed for treatment of urban solid waste.
6. **Conservation of Surface Water Sources:** The drains and water bodies in urban areas usually have a high level of pollution, which is mainly from the untreated sewer and waste from adjacent areas. The site plan is based on the following strategies:
   (*a*) Linking of natural/water body/river with the population by access and landscape development.

(*b*) Control of pollution of water from industry, drainage, sewerage, flyash, garbage and waste dumping.

(*c*) A drainage and flood control strategy linked with water supply.

(*d*) Control of squatting/unauthorised growth and land uses which are incongruous with environment, such as polluting industry.

The revival of age-old concept of watershed development, harvesting and conservation of rainwater and recharging of underground water can substantively resolve the urban water crisis. Several technologies, such as decentralised and compact water treatment units, solar/aerobic/oxidation and root zone systems can be employed to purify and recycle waste water.

7. **Green Spaces:** About 10 to 15 per cent of the area should be planned for neighbourhood parks and playgrounds within the residential areas. In a city about 9 sq.m of recreational area per capita should be reserved as open space, 3 sq.m at city level, 3 sq.m at zonal level and 3 sq.m at local level. A system of landscaped linkages connecting various parts of the city, neighbourhoods and important monuments should be planned. The garden, both at community and building level, should provide a sense of oasis and shelter from oppressive climate. Green belts should act as wind breakers, filters of dust storms and as transition zone.

   The land uses identified as natural water bodies, forest and vegetation, green open spaces, coastal zone, wetlands, etc. should be protected and adequate buffer shall be provided from the planned establishments. For planning around these areas, the building norms and regulations as stipulated by the respective statutory bodies, such as Town Planning Departments, MoEF and State Environment and Forest Departments shall be applicable.

8. **Drainage:** The development of greenways along natural drainage corridors and harvesting of rainwater in balancing lakes and ponds has been a new frontier in water management. Instead of resorting of conventional drainage, the concept of zero run-off may be adopted by using retention ponds. Such ponds, reservoirs and sediment traps can be located in the catchment zones on low-lying ground, which is earmarked for greenery.

9. **Noise Control:** Noise is emerging as a major pollutant and irritant in the Indian cities. Its high intensity is constant source of pain and disturbance and a health hazard. Against a permissible level of 50 to 60 db (a), the sound level invariably exceeds 80 db (a). Faulty and leaking silencers, over-use of motor horns, screeching tyres, rattling bodies of vehicles plying on the roads accentuate noise level from the traffic. Besides this, the noise from commercial and industrial activities in residential zones, unabated use of sound amplifiers, generator sets and fire crackers often disturb the peace in urban areas.

   It is not desirable to locate residential areas along major arteries and non-residential activities inside the residential areas that would invite outside traffic. By proper land use planning, mixed land use, location of public/semi-public activities along major transport arteries, a buffer can be created for residential zone. Green buffers with thin leave trees, land formations, mounds, embankments, etc. Provide effective barriers to transmission of noise.

10. **Energy Efficiency:** The concept of energy efficiency, renewable energy and Zero-fossil Energy Development (ZED) can reduce the level of energy demand and slow down the rate at which resources are depleted. Energy efficiency involves a synergy of the various levels of planning, design, construction and maintenance, leading to a sustainable and energy efficient regime. The renewable energy not only helps in energy generation, but also in a pollution-free environment.
11. **Climate and Disaster Resilience:** The planning for climate change involves the convergence of various sectors into a strategy and establishes a link between climate change and GHG/CO_2 emissions. The site area can be delineated as natural conservation zone based on its vulnerability. The strategy of climate and disaster resilience depends on the unique natural features of the site, population size and rate of growth, the level of income and economic development, diverse spatial dimension of environmental problems and the roles of local actors.
12. **Gender Equity and Safety:** The safety of women, children and other vulnerable sections of the community is a central issue. Various initiatives include the setting of the rescue and rehabilitation centres, re-integration of victims of trafficking; the setting up of 'One Stop Crisis Centres' provision of shelters, police desks, legal, medical and counselling services, and 24 × 7 help lines. This also needs incremental actions, such as enhancement of street lighting, establishment of 'Multi-Utility Zones' (MUZs), pedestrian safety, safer roads, provision of public toilets for women, especially in the slums and streets and safer public transport with CCTV and alarm system.

    The planning can contribute in crime prevention by gender sensitive design of shared, lively and defensible spaces, mixed land use and adequate shelter/tenements for the poor, together with spaces for vending and informal trades that promote livelihood and community surveillance.

Planning and Building Codes

Planning of a building is based on planning and building codes, which include permissible land use, zoning controls, development control norms, *i.e.* Floor Area Ratio, Road Right of Way, ground coverage, parking stipulations, maximum height, setback, etc. These vary according to land use and location. Other mandatory regulations viz., planning controls, heritage, environmental, airport zoning, etc. should be considered when site and building plans are prepared.

Floor Area Ratio and Height

The limitation of area and height of buildings is specified in terms of Floor Area Ratio (FAR), taking into account the following aspects:

- Population Density
- Occupancy Class/activity
- Type of construction
- Width of street fronting the building
- Locality, and density stipulations
- Parking facilities

- Fire fighting facilities
- Water supply and drainage
- Earthquake prone zone
- Land use zone
- Carrying Capacity

Minimum Setbacks

The setbacks in a building layout are provided to meet the requirements of building height, ventilation and fire safety. Setbacks can be provided in two ways:

1. Based on plot size
2. Based on abutting road width.

These two methods as described below may be adopted for providing setbacks. However, the provisions shall also conform to the local building bye-laws.

Table 10.3. Minimum Setbacks

Sr. No.	Plot Size (in sqm)	Front (m)	Rear (m)		Side (m)	Side (m)
			Plains	Hill Towns	Plains	Hill Towns
1.	Upto 60	0	0	2	0	1.5
2.	Above 60 and upto 150	3	0	2	0	1.5
3.	Above 150 & upto 300	3	3	3	0	1.5
4.	Above 300 & upto 500	3	3	3	3	3
5.	Above 500 & upto 1000	6	3	3	3	3
6.	Above 1000 & upto 2000	9	3	3	3	3
7.	Above 2000 & upto 4000	9	6	6	6	6
8.	Above 4000 & upto 10000	9	6	6	6	6
9.	Above 10000	15	9	9	9	9

Notes:

(*i*) In case the permitted coverage is not achieved with setbacks, the setbacks of the preceding category may be followed.

(*ii*) In case a layout is sanctioned with more than the minimum prescribed setbacks, the same shall be followed in the sanction of the building plans.

(*iii*) The building plan sanctioning authority may relax setbacks in special circumstances.

(*iv*) In case of compact city planning, the margins to be altered upto at least 50%.

***Source:** 1996. MPD-2021*

The above table may be referred for deciding the minimum setbacks for different size plots in various use zones. The size of plots should be decided after taking into account the provisions of National Housing Policy and Urban Land (Ceiling and Regulation) Act. The setbacks, if necessary, may be changed depending upon the local situations and specified in the Development Plan and Building Byelaws.

Table 10.4. Front Setback with respect to Abutting Road

Sr. No.	Front Setback (m)	Width of street fronting the plot (m)	Remark
1.	1.5	Upto 7.5	For buildings upto a maximum height of 7m
2.	3.0	7.5 to 18	
3.	4.5	18 to 30	
4.	6.0	Above 30	

Note: For streets less than 7.5 m in width, the distance of the building (building line) shall be at least 5 m from the centre line of the street.

Source: *NBC, 2016*

Rear and Side setbacks for building height up to 10 m

Rear setback: The rear setback shall be minimum 1.8 m

Side setbacks: The side setback shall be as follows:

- For detached building: Minimum 3 m on both sides,
- For semi-detached building: Minimum 3 m on one side,
- For row type building: No side setback is required.

Table 10.5. Rear and Side Setbacks for Building Height Above 10 m

Sr. No.	Height of Building (m)	Side and rear setbacks (m)	Other Controls
1.	10	3	• For buildings above 24 mm in height, the minimum front setback shall be 6 m. • Where rooms do not derive light and ventilation from the exterior open space, the width of such space shall be reduced by 1 m subject to a minimum of 3 m. • Alternative setbacks for tower like structure: – Upto 24 m height minimum 6 m – Between 24 m and 37.5 m height minimum 9 m – bove 37.5 m height, two setbacks minimum 12 m
2.	15	5	
3.	18	6	
4.	21	7	
5.	24	8	
6.	27	9	
7.	30	10	
8.	35	11	
9.	40	12	
10.	45	13	
11.	50	14	
12.	Above 55	16	

Note: The building plan sanctioning authority may relax setbacks in case of a compact and TOD development.

Source: *NBC, 2005.*

Distance from Electric Lines

Following clearances shall be maintained between the building and overhead electric supply line in accordance with the Indian Electricity Rules as amended from time to time:

Table 10.6. Clearances Between Building and Electricity Mains

Sr. No.	Description	Vertical	Horizontal Distance(m)
1.	Low and medium voltage lines and services	2.5	1.2
2.	High voltage lines upto and including 11 kV	3.7	1.2
3.	High voltage lines above 11 kV and upto and including	3.7	2.0
4.	Extra high voltage line beyond 33 kV	3.7 (plus 0.3 m for every) additional 33 kV or part there of)	2.0 (plus 0.3 m for every additional 33 kV or part theory)

Source: *NBC, 2016*

Minimum Dwelling Size: The minimum dwelling units size could vary from State to State and region to region, owing to various factors, including the terrain and soil types, etc. However, a thumb rule is given in the following table.

Types 10.7. Indicative Minimum Dwelling Unit Sizes

Number of rooms	Dwelling unit size (sqm)
1 BHK	60-80
2 BHK	80-120
3 BHK	120-160
4 BHK	160-200
5 BHK	200-260

Source: *Naya Raipur Master Plan*

The residential areas are developed either as (*a*) plotted development or (*b*) group housing/ flatted development. The density pattern *i.e.* (high density, high medium density, low medium density or low density) are followed for working out the pattern of development with respect to the size of plot to number of dwelling units on each plot, setbacks, FAR and the number of storeys/ height of the building.

Table 10.8. Norms of Farm House

Size of Farm	Maximum FAR	Maximum Height	Horizontal Distance (m)
Min. 4000 sm	20 (including mezzanine floor) maximum 30 subject to payment of additional floor area charge	12 m max.	• Setback in front should be 15 m from any road in front
			• Where the property abuts an urban road the dwelling house should be 30 m from the centre line of that road. In case a village road, the building setback from the centre line of road should be 15 m. • No dwelling unit should be built within 400 m of the right of way of the National Highway.

Source: *DDA, MPD-2021*

Table 10.9. Norms for Primary Activities

Type	FAR	Ground Coverage	Max. Building Ht.
Agrobased uses	5	5%	15 m
Poultry Farm	25	25%	10 m
Religious, Educational, Hospital, Slaughter house, cold storage, transport truck terminal, Government godowns and warehouses	45 or as per development code/BBL	15%	15 m

Source: *Ahmedabad Development Plan*

Access Provisions for Differently-Abled: The minimum access provisions shall be provided as given in the following table, and as per 'Guidelines and Space Standards for Barrier Free Built Environment for Disabled and Elderly Persons', 1998.

Table 10.10. Minimum Access provisions for Barrier Free Built Environment

Sr. No.	Type of Building	Minimum Provisions
1.	Single detached dwelling units	A minimum of 2% of the total number of units to be constructed with barrier free features (adaptable units)
2.	Staff housing, multiple dwelling and high rise residential units	Minimum of 1 unit for every 25 units to be designed for barrier free built environment plus 1 additional unit for every 100 units thereafter
3.	Tenement house, row houses, apartments and town houses	A minimum of 1 unit for up to 150 units plus minimum of 1 additional unit for every 100 units thereafter entrances and exits to be designed for barrier free accessibility

4.	Post-office, bank and financial service institutions	(*a*) A minimum of 1 lowered service counter on the premises. (*b*) A minimum of 1 lowered ATM/ cash dispersal points on the premises.
5.	Shop houses and single storey shops	Barrier free access to/within shopping area.
6.	Places of worship	Entrances and exits and main area of the worship to be accessible
7.	Food centres, restaurants	(*a*) A minimum of 1 table without stools or seats attached to the floor for every 10 tables (*b*) A minimum of 2 tables without stools or seats attached to the floor for the whole premises (*c*) Accessible entrance
8.	Community centres, community halls, auditoria, assembly halls, theatres and other places of public assembly	(*a*) Accessible entrances, exits, aisles and main community or public gathering areas (*b*) Accessible toilet facilities (*c*) Seating for person with disabilities (*d*) Various seating/viewing choice to be provided for persons in wheelchairs (*e*) A minimum of 2 wheelchair spaces for seating capacity up to 100 seats (*f*) A minimum of 4 wheelchair space per 100 to 400 seats.

Source: *Guidelines and Space Standards for Barrier free Built Environment for Disabled and Elderly Persons, Central Public Works Department, 1998.*

External Ramp: Min. width 1200 mm. Max. gradient 1:12. When gradient exceeds 1:20, an unobstructed platform minimum 1200 mm × 1200 mm should be provided at top of ramp. When gradient exceeds 1:15 a handrail should be provided both sides. When ramp exceeds 2000 mm, a central rail may be provided.

External stepped approach should be not less than 280 mm and risers should be not higher than 150 mm. The vertical rise of any flight should not exceed 1200 mm. Handrail should be provided on each side.

Entrance doors: Minimum clear opening of 800 mm.

Lifts: Minimum depth 1400 mm and width 1100 mm. Door clear opening of 800 mm. Clear space in front of doors 1500 mm × 1500 mm.

Passageways: Minimum 1200 mm wide.

Internal stairs goings should be not less than 250 mm and risers not more than 170 mm. Vertical rise of a flight should not exceed 1800 mm.

Switches and controls: Light switches should align with door handles. No higher than 1400 mm above floors.

Signage should have large characters or numerals contrasting with the background.

Sanction of the Building Plan

A site plan is developed showing the streets, utilities, plot dimensions, building footprint and landscape plan to meet the requirements of the site approval process. Once a basic plan is in place, a project must seek the approval by various agencies which may include:

- Land use and land ownership
- Utility Service Plan
- Environmental clearance
- Traffic and Transportation/Parking Plan
- Urban Design/Heritage approval
- Fire/Security/Airport Clearance
- Zoning and Planning Approval
- Layout plan approval and building permit. This is usually granted when all other clearances/approvals are obtained.

A building plan shall be accompanied by necessary permit fee and various documents such as land ownership documents, Certificate of Architect/Engineer/Planner, Parking and Services plan, Affidavit, undertaking and indemnity bond necessary under the Building Bye-Laws.

The construction of building can be taken up after approval of the building plan by the local/ urban body. After the completion of the building, the owner shall submit a notice of completion along with the required documents and plans for approval of local authority. After inspection of completed building, the objections and compounding fee, if any, are intimated to the owner/ Architect.

Reviewing the Building Regulations

The building regulations encompass a range of various controls, such as given below:

1. **Planning Controls/DCR**
   - Development Controls
   - Land use zoning
   - Sub-division Regulations, infrastructure services, traffic/mobility and parking plan, landscape plan, etc.
2. **Building Controls**
   - Height
   - Ground coverage
   - Setbacks
   - Floor Area Ratio
   - Density
   - Parking/road in front
3. **Architectural Controls**
4. **Fire safety, earthquake and structural safety**
5. **Airports Regulations**

6. Environment Regulations

7. Urban Design Regulations

8. Heritage Regulations and Archaeological Stipulations

9. Others–NMAI, Revenue Department, Property tax, Labour Dept, Miner Deptt, CGWB, etc.

A builder may require as many as 34 kinds of permits before starting construction, which may take anywhere between six months to three years. The developer has to run to over two dozen Central Government ministries and agencies, including environment and forest clearance, Archaeological Survey of India, National Highways Authority, fire department, electricity department, Airport Authority of India, Ministry of Labour, Ministry of Mines, Central Ground Water Board, etc. to get No Objection Certificates.

Table 10.11. Number of Approvals Required and Time Taken

Country	No. of Approvals Required	Time Taken
India	34	6 months to 3 years
Hong Kong	6	Over two months
Singapore	11	26 days

The development control regulations and building bye-laws are made primarily for green-field development and not for redevelopment which is a major thrust of Housing for All, AMRUT and other programmes of urban development. Regulations have to respond to the needs of redevelopment and provide a facilitating framework. The constraints of redevelopment are the requisition of proof of land ownership, mechanism for approval of plans, joint ownership and development of small plots being amalgamated together. The regulations do not provide any system of assembly of small plots, so that the old dilapidated areas can be developed with proper layouts, adequate roads, services, amenities, parking and open space.

The planning and building codes act as exclusionary devices, which often exclude slums, hutments, poor households, small vendors and manufacturers. These often ignore the vital aspect of public importance, like public toilets, dustbins, drinking fountains, footpath design, street furniture, street vendors, utility booths, signage, public spaces, conservation of cultural heritage, etc.

The bottlenecks and overlapping jurisdictions can be reduced by a careful mapping of the regulatory jurisdictions, regulatory authority and regulatory laws.

The Government of India has initiated certain reforms for fast track clearance of building plans which include the following:

(*a*) The Union Ministry of Environment, Forests and Climate Change has come out with revised and simplified environmental laws. These have been notified in the Gazette of India 9th December 2016. This has been done with a view to streamline the permissions for buildings and construction sector with the following changes:

- The environmental clearance (EC) will be issued to all building constructions covering a built-up area between 20,000 to 1,50,000 sq. mtr. in an integrated manner, along with the building permission under building bye-laws.

- No consent will be required from the State Pollution Control Boards to establish and cperate under the Water (Prevention and Control of Pollution) Act, 1974 and the Air (Prevention and Control of Pollution) Act, 1981 for residential buildings with built-up area up to 1,50,000 square meters.
- The environmental clearance for building and construction projects with built-up areas from 1,50,000 to 3,00,000 sq. mtr. will be issued by the State Level Environment Impact Assessment Authority.
- The Township and Area Development projects with built-up area above 3,00,000 sq. mtr. or covering an area of more than 150 hectares will be approved and cleared by the Union Government.
- Projects with built-up area between 5000 sq. mtr. to 20,000 sq. mtr. will have to file a 'Self Declaration Form' to comply with the environmental conditions along with Form 1A and certification by the Qualified Building Environment Auditor. This online submission must be made by the project proponent along with the application for building permission. The buildings with built-up area between 5000 sq. mtr. to 20,000 sq. mtr. will have to follow environmental norms for construction and maintenance phase as enlisted in the notification.
- The Qualified Building Environment Auditors, who are in charge of assessing and certifying the building projects would be accredited by the Ministry of Environment, Forest and Climate Change (MoEF & CC). An Environmental Cell may be constituted in the local authority to this cell would be monitor the implementation of the amended Notification and oversight the Third-Party Auditing process.
- The project proponent of buildings with built-up area of more than 20,000 sq. mtr. must submit Performance Data and Certificate of Continued Compliance of the project for the environmental conditions parameters applicable after completion of construction from Qualified Building Environment Auditors every five years with special focus on:
  (*i*) Energy Use
  (*ii*) Energy generated on site from renewable sources
  (*iii*) Water use and water generated, treated and reused on site
  (*iv*) Waste segregated and treated on site
  (*v*) Tree plantation and maintenance
- After completion of the project, the Environmental Cell shall randomly check the projects compliance status including the five years' audit report. The notification provides for the State Governments to enact suitable laws to impose penalties for non-compliance of environmental conditions and parameters.
- The cases of false declaration or certification shall be reported to the accreditation body and to the local body for blacklisting of Qualified Building Environment Auditors and financial penalty on the owners/project proponents and Qualified Building Environment Auditors.

The Amended Notification has been brought under scrutiny before the National Green Tribunal (NGT) by the Society for Protection of Environment and Biodiversity, stating that this Notification may be quashed as it is in contravention to the provisions of EIA notification, 2006 and The Environment Protection Act, 1986. The NGT has asked the Ministries to refrain from acting under the new notification.

(*b*) The Ministry of Civil Aviation has asked the Airport Authority of India to standardize the norms for building height around airports. The Authority has issued Color-Coded Zonal Maps (CCZMs) for 12 airports which account for 58 per cent of such applications and make them available to the respective urban bodies. The ministry also commissioned an improved version of online NOCAS (No Objection Certificate Application System), eliminating human interface and expediting issues of NOC through automatic calculation of permissible height in airport zone and also enabling the applicants to track the status of their applications.

(*c*) Online filing and NOC for buildings falling outside restricted areas of national monuments can be obtained using 'app' developed by ISRO. Clearance under the Heritage bye-laws no. 281 (major monuments) have been fast tracked by the Ministry of Culture.

(*d*) Local military authorities and units have been directed to provide details and maps of restricted and unrestricted areas.

(*e*) Formulation of Model Building Bye-laws by the Ministry of Housing and Urban Affairs for on-line approvals on single window.

The Expert Committee appointed by Government of India for Streamlining Approval Procedure for Real Estate Projects (SAPREP) has come up with six reforms:

- Bring transparency, predictability and accountability to protect consumer interest
- Review existing systems and procedures by removing duplicity and conflict between regulations, bringing automation process and delegation of approvals
- Single window or 'one-stop shop' enabled by IT
- Reforms to promote affordable green housing
- Sharing of best practices
- Creating capacities in public (ULBs and UDAs and TP Departments), private sector and professionals (architects, engineers, urban planners, structural and other specialists) to carry out development responsibility and be empowered.

In view of the complexity of getting building permit, loss of time and corruption involved, there is a need to consider on-line processing, simplification and deregulation of planning and building controls, including the following reforms:

- Reduce the number of approvals required
- Time limit for grant of the approvals
- Devolve and delegate powers
- One window system, a computerised portal/platform for Building Plan approvals
- Replace building bye-laws by Planning and Development Permission
- Resort to a more flexible and local Development Zoning and White Zoning
- Invoke concepts of Transferable Development Right (TDR) and Accommodation Reservation (AR)

A graded and differential approach may be a possibility, comprising the following stages:

- No sanction/waiver
- Instant Prototype Sanction (on-line)
- Sanction of architectural plan and structural design by Registered Architects and Structural Engineers under intimation to the ULB, and within BBL, NBC and DCR of Master Plan
- Planning and development permissions by the ULB.

This involves the devolution of powers and responsibility to registered Architects/ Engineers and deletion of micro-details from the Building Regulations, which can be attended by the architects and engineers.

The Structural Design, Civil Engineering and Services Plans may be approved by a registered engineering, professional agency under the delegated powers. The reforms in Building Regulations should make it redundant for an inspector to enter a private buildings, and the regulations concerning the internal feature, like room size, ceiling height, ventilation; sanitary fitting, etc. may be the mandatory responsibility of the Architect.

Larger plots (say 4 Ha and above) may involve the approval of Services Plans, Transport and Parking Plans, urban design, heritage, environmental and other clearances. The Planning & Development Regulations and codes should also cover the approval of land pooling schemes, sub-division plans and building proposals, including mandatory social housing component.

For planning and Development Permission, an interdisciplinary platform representing Architects, Planners, Engineers, Service Agencies, representatives of Fire Department, Civil Aviation, NMA/ ASI, Pollution Control Committee and other concerned authorities can be created. The power for approval and clearance under various acts may be delegated to such an interdisciplinary platform.

For the unplanned areas (unauthorized colonies, urban villages, etc.) Planning and Development Permission can help to bring them within the fold and framework of planned development. This will need evolving comprehensive guidelines for amalgamation of plots, infill development, and conversion of isolated plots into development of group housing, with proper facilities, parks and parking.

The local authorities should ensure that on-street parking, congestion and traffic bottlenecks are avoided and provision of green, mixed land use, utilities and amenities are adequately provided in all built up areas.

A major emphasis of the policies of urban development and housing is on brown-field development and transit oriented development with the additional FAR. This needs the preparation and approval of redevelopment schemes, taking into consideration the surrounding area, mobility, parking, greenery and services. To ensure availability of the common areas, the tools of Transferable Development Right and Accommodation Reservation are essential. Also, it should ensure that through the redevelopment schemes and Transit Oriented Development, the poor are not out and at least half of the dwelling units are provided to EWS/LIG categories, for which 15 to 20 per cent incentive FAR may be provided.

The city should not have any unsafe building irrespective of status of a colony, land ownership or land use. As such, it is necessary to delink building safety from the process of the planning and development permission or approval of building plan. Every building should have a Structural

Safety Certificate which need not be linked with land use, approved layout and ownership. The Local Bodies can proactively help the building owners in making available the services of a panel of structural engineers/ institutions for guiding the owners to ensure the structural safety of non-engineered buildings. A simplified Structural and Fire Safety Code for non-engineered buildings can be introduced along with other regulations.

Ambiguity in various definitions such as Layout Plan, Site Plan, illegal, unauthorized, violation, deviation, non-compoundable, addition and alteration gives scope of harassment and corruption, which need to be clearly defined.

Online Building Plan Scrutiny System

The computerised scrutiny system AutoDCR and Building Information Modelling (BIM) are being brought in use by various local bodies in India. These systems have been adopted by Pune Municipal Corporation, Thane Municipal Corporation, Meera Bhayandar Municipal Corporation, Kolhapur Municipal Corporation in Maharashtra, Municipal Corporation of Delhi, NDMC, and Delhi Development Authority. Products are designed to get faster and accurate approval of building proposals. It brings uniformity and standardization of drawings and process to eliminate lengthy manual process and human errors. It reduces the time and effort of the architect and the Authority.

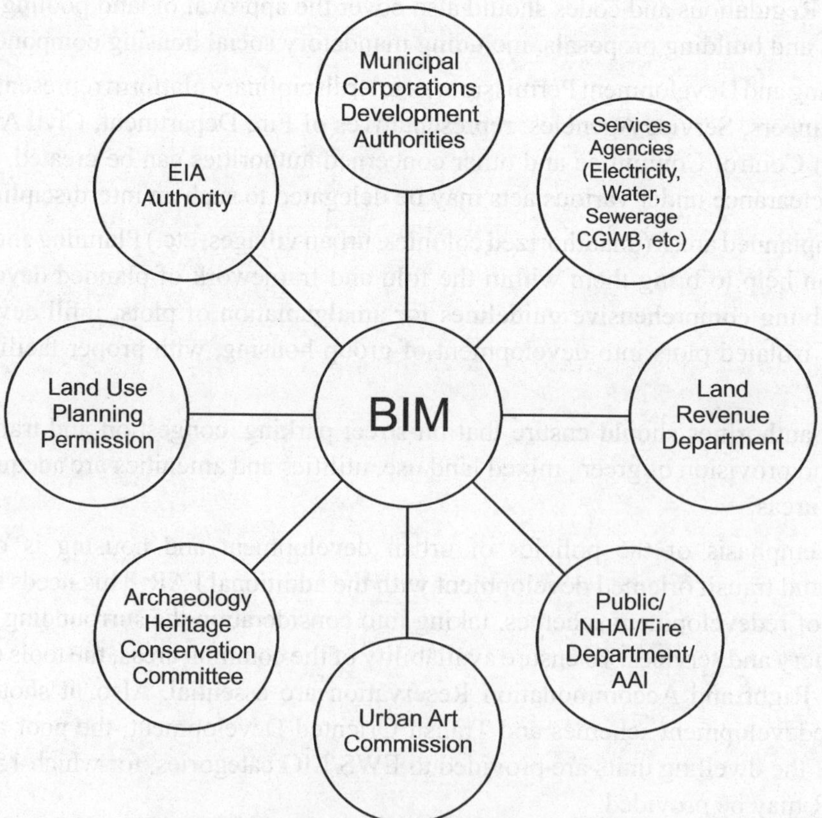

Fig. 10.1. Building Information Modelling (BIM) as a unified platform for Building Plan Scrutiny

BPAMS and Auto DCR integrate documental data with drawing. Auto DCR reads data from CAD drawing, establishes relationship between various entities, imposes specific proposal conditions, geometrically maps each and every entity by corresponding with complex and interlinked rules. By using AutoCAD objectivity, users can maintain the objectivity and speed. Analysis is done as per Development Control Regulations by AutoDCR. Tables and reports are saved with the drawing. It takes about 3-5 minutes to save a file. Reports are sent to BPAMS for making status available online.

Building Information Modelling (BIM) can be reversed department viewed with grant of NOC/ approval various platform, thus eliminating spermatic approval from various agencies. This is already in practice in Singapore, Europe and the USA, which needs to urgently adapted in India.

DEBRIEFING QUESTIONS

1. What are the major types of buildings?
2. Explain the approaches for planning of:
   (*a*) Group Housing
   (*b*) Residential Plot
   (*c*) Government Office Building
   (*d*) Shopping Mall
   (*e*) School
3. What are the general Development Control considerations while planning a building?
4. What are the Building Bye-laws and their purpose?
5. Write short notes on:
   (*a*) Floor Area Ratio
   (*b*) Building Permit
   (*c*) Architectural Controls
   (*d*) Fire Safety, Earthquake and Structural Safety
   (*e*) Environmental Regulations
   (*f*) Urban Design
   (*g*) On-line Building Plan Scrutiny System.

Chapter **11**

ANTHROPOMETRY AND ERGONOMICS

Anthropometry has been defined as the science of dealing with the measurement of the human body to determine differences in individuals, groups, etc. Ergonomics is the study of human body in a dynamic environment, the science that seeks to adapt working conditions, furniture, equipment, tools and spaces to suit human performance. As such, static and dynamic anthropometry encompasses the body types and various postures, measurements, structure and functions, body supportive devices, such as furniture, chair, work surface, table, work counter, etc. Ergonomic design provides performance support, occupational safety and convenience by reducing the potential fatigue errors, discomfort and unsafe acts.

Architecture is the organization of space around the human beings. The buildings and human settlements reflect the interplay between ideas, culture, society and anthropology. Like music, the beauty of spatial composition depends upon harmonious orchestration of heterogeneous factors–light and colour, surfaces, human comfort, solids and voids, functional and environmental parameters. Designing is like creating a stage set. It should speak and present a personality, character and image. Unlike mass produced match box office towers or rubber stamped apartment blocks the buildings often lack a personal touch and an identity. The recent trends indicate a search for emotional and human relationship with the space and built environment. The human relationship is not just physical, but also in terms of psychological and emotional feelings. The celebrated architect and progenitor of the modern movement, Le Corbusier in early 20th century employed the human form as a model and module of space. The human form gives harmony and proportions to space.

The Golden Section was the name given to the principle of proportions evolved by Euclid in 300 B.C. According to Euclid, a line is cut in such a ratio only when the 'whole line is to the greater segment, so is the greater to the less.' Luca Paccoli, a close friend of Leonardo da Vinci and a famous mathematician of 16th century wrote a book called 'Divina Proportione' (divine proportion) and contended that an aesthetic principle is found in architectural forms and in the human body, even in the letters of the Latin alphabet. Leonardo da Vinci in 16th century described the length of a man as equal to this width with arms extended. He created his famous drawing of the human figure based on the Vitruvian form. More than 2000 years after Vitruvius, Le Corbusier revived the human form in his modular figure.

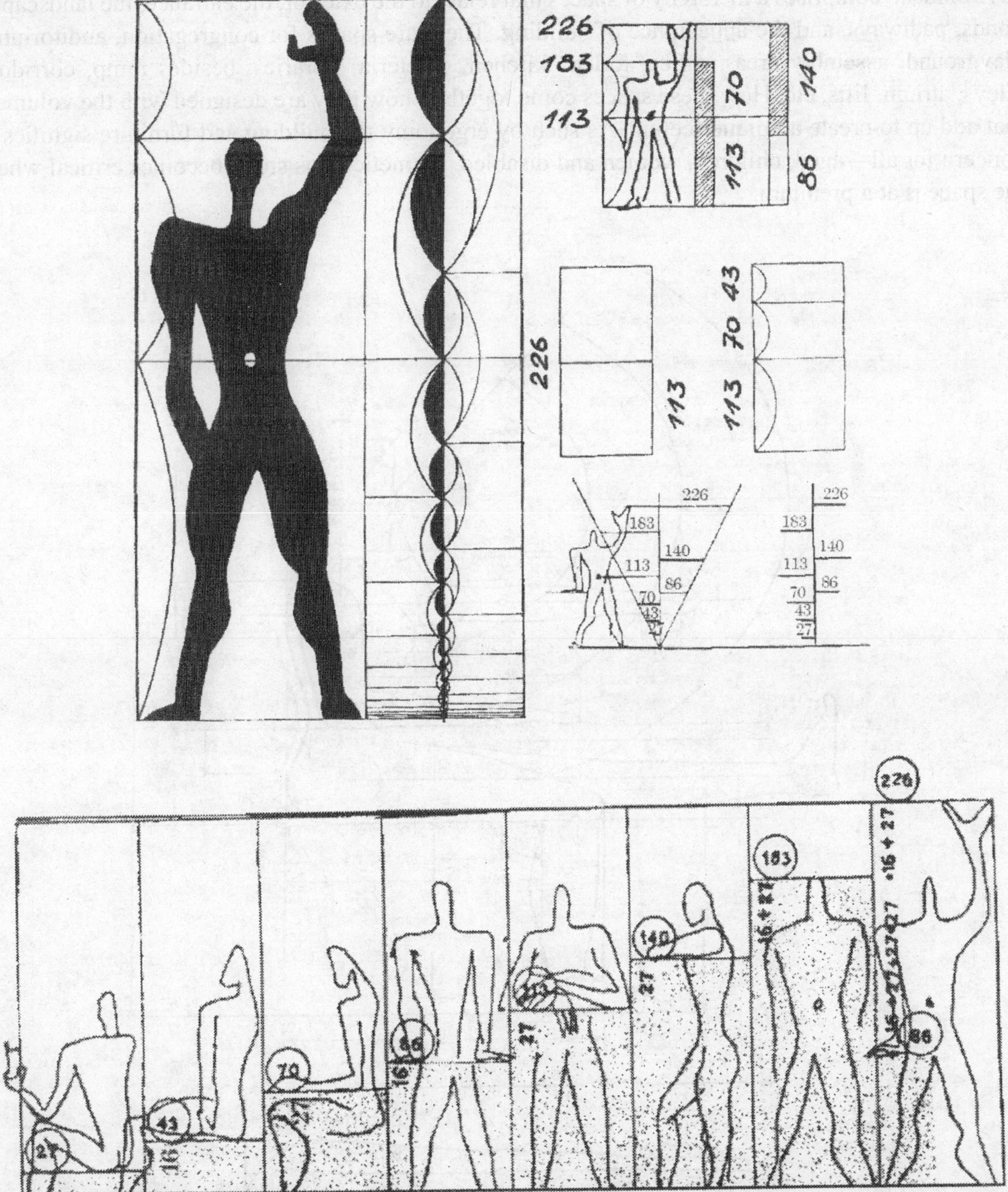

Fig. 11.1. Le Corbusier's Modular provides a relationship between human figure and the architectonic world. On one hand it employs anthropometric design of furniture, openings and building; on the other, it provides a golden rule for aesthetic proportions

A building, whether a minimum house or a university campus, designed on the basis of anthropometry and ergonomics can be economical, functional and comfortable. The architect gives a form to the building that embody the values while taking care of the functional needs. The built environment comprises a hierarchy of spaces that relate to the exterior, the entrance, the landscape, ponds, pathways, and the appearance of building. There are spaces for congregation, auditorium, playground, assembly areas, office, toilets, kitchen, cafeteria, libraries, besides ramp, corridor, alleys, atrium, lifts, etc. How these spaces come together, how they are designed with the volumes that add up to create a unique feeling. As such by ergonomy the building and furniture signifies a concern for all—aged, children, women and disabled. Its meticulous study becomes critical when the space is at a premium.

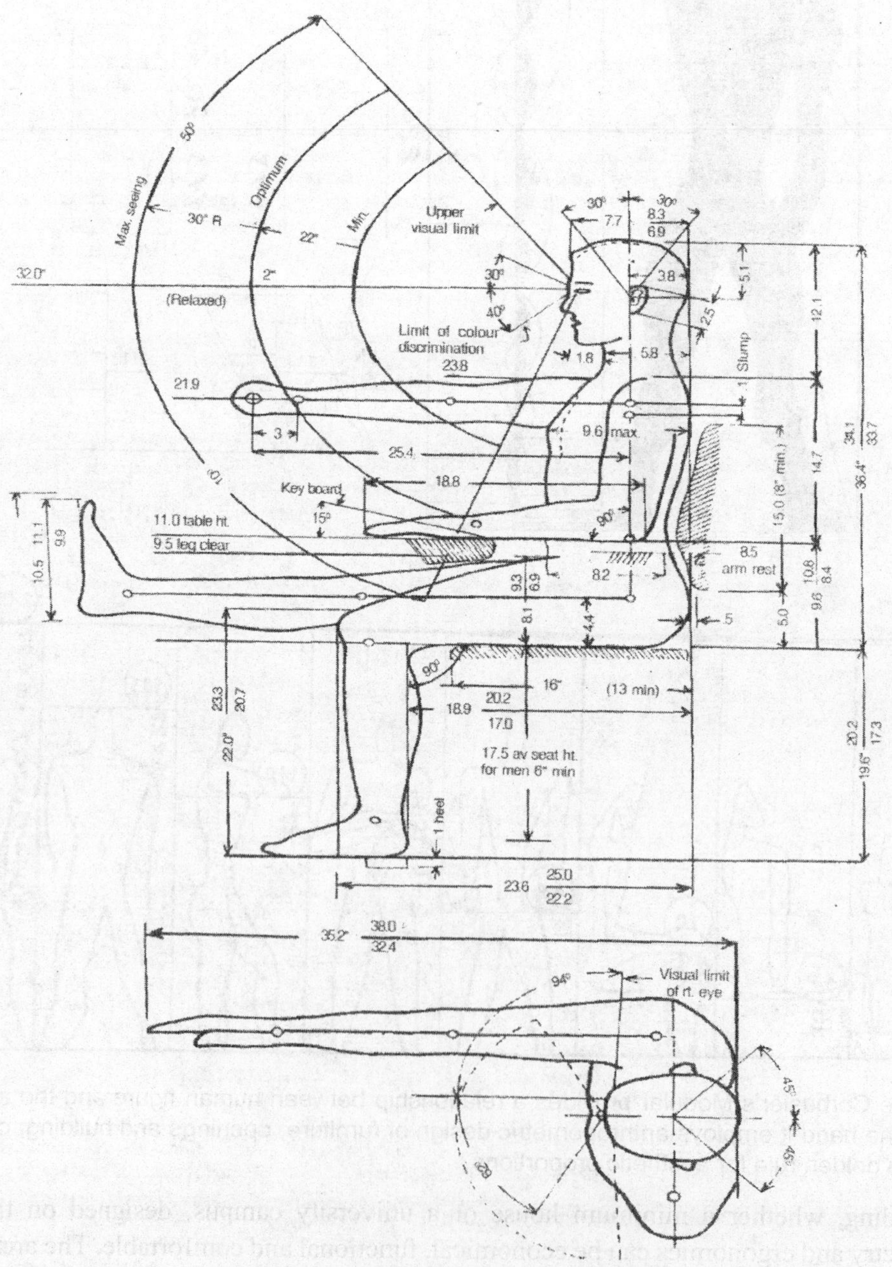

Fig. 11.2. The human form is the basis of the process of design

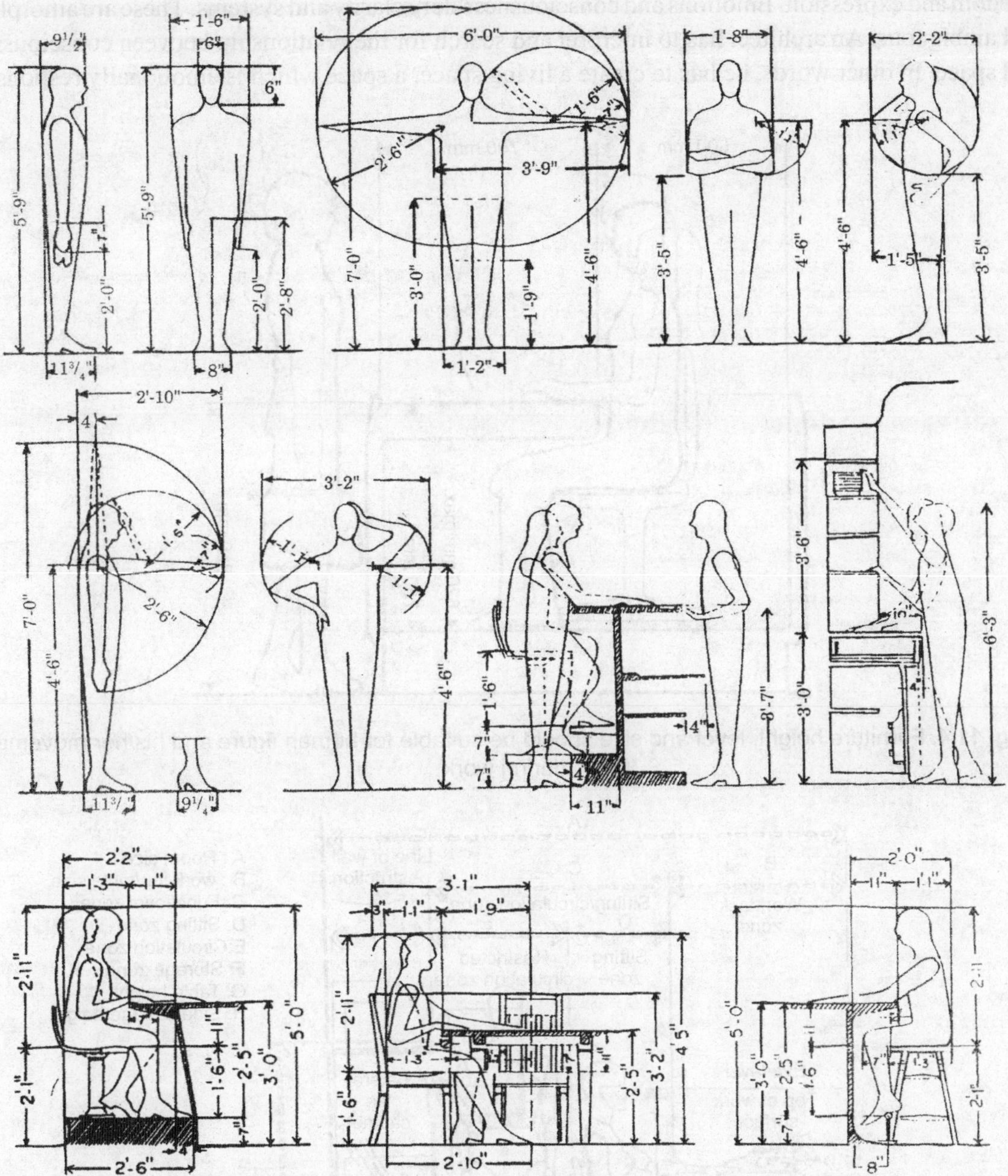

Fig. 11.3. Human dimensions based on the average or normal adult. As clearances are minimum, they should be increased when conditions allow

Space: The Container of Life

A home is the identity tag of family. For a designer, it involves striking a balance between the functional needs and aesthetic desire. A house should have a environment conducive to comfort, as well as facilitate congeniality and integration. Today it is better realised that the human consciousness and emotions dominate his physical world and the designers have to respect individual diversity, freedom and expression. Emotions and consciousness defy clarity and systems. These are amorphous and ambiguous. An architect has to interpret and search for the relationship between consciousness and space. In other words, he has to create a living space, a space which is emotionally responsive.

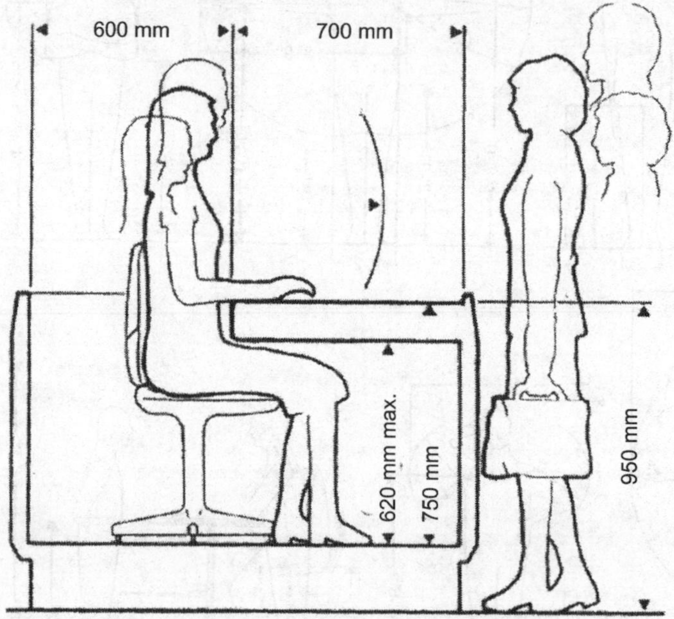

Fig. 11.4. Furniture height, level and size should be suitable for human figure and his/her movement during work

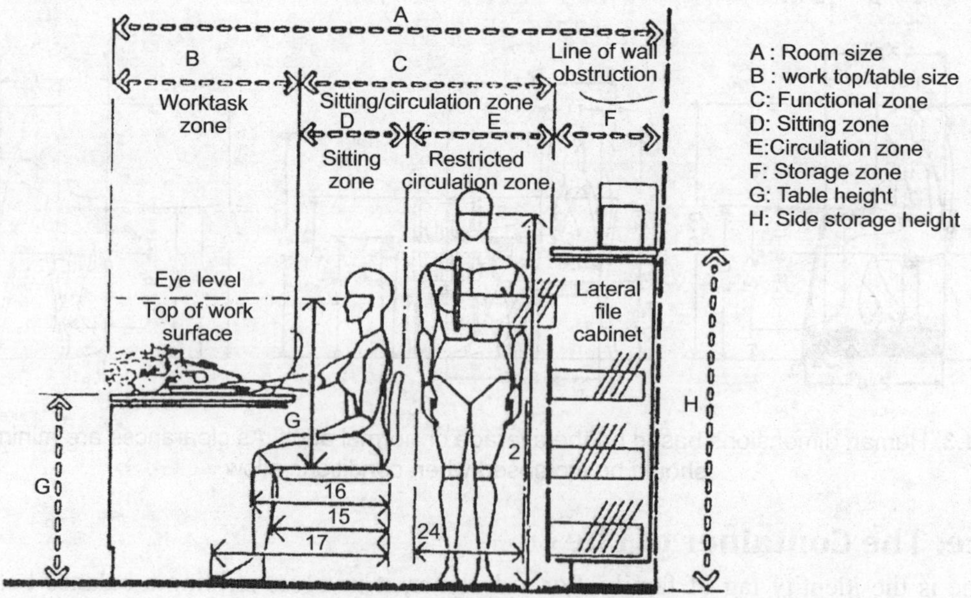

Fig. 11.5. Design of a desk for comfortable working depends on ergonomics and functions

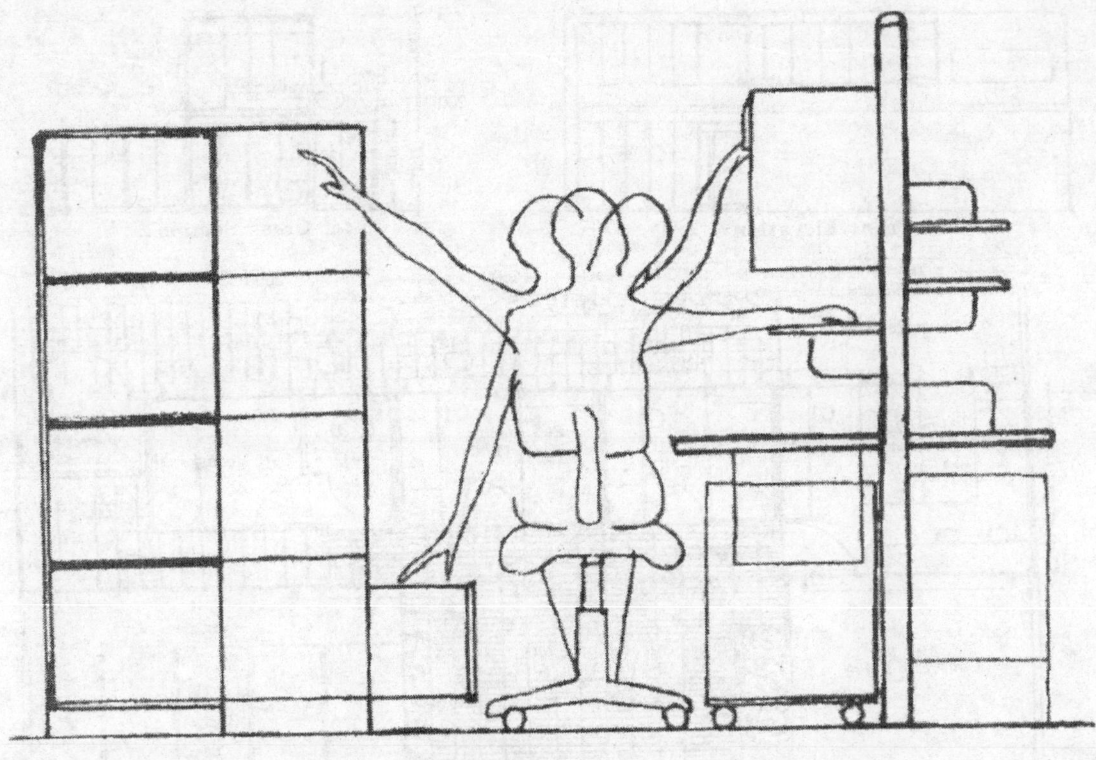

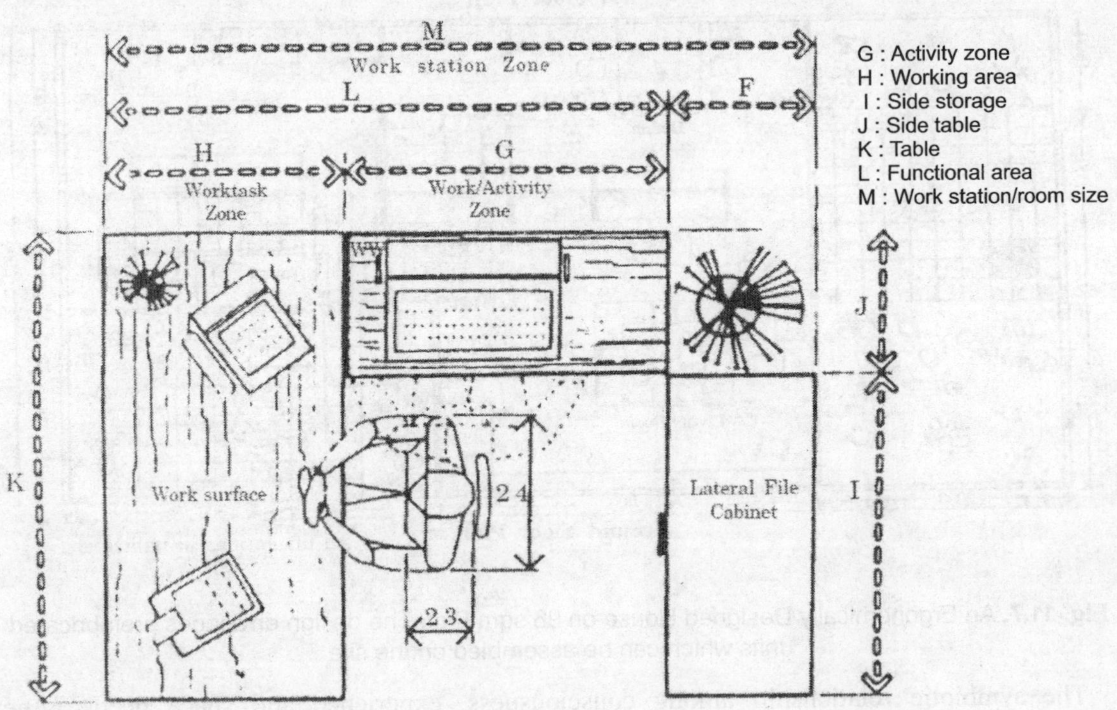

Fig. 11.6. Human dimensions articulate work space and furniture design

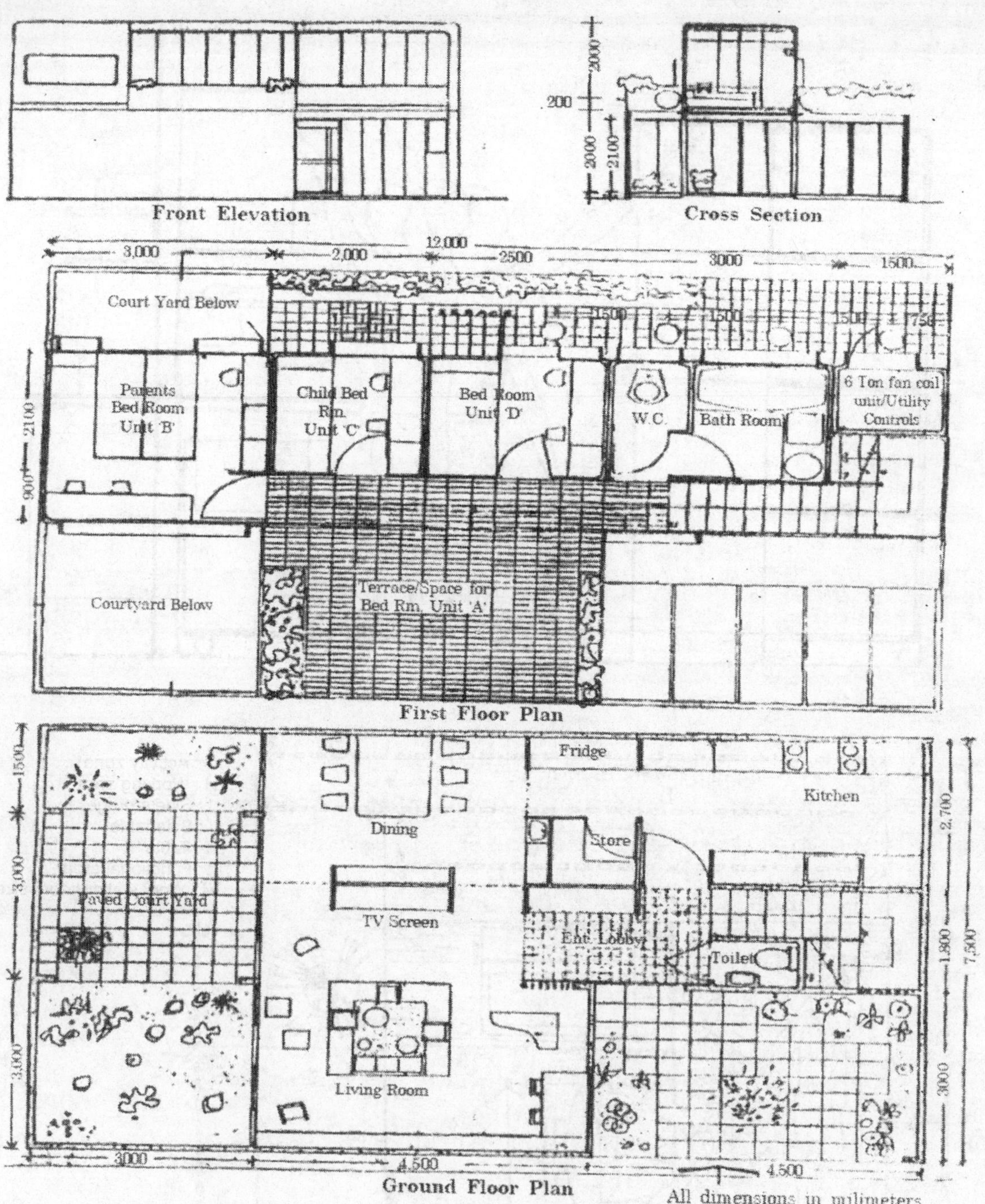

Fig. 11.7. An Ergonomically Designed House on 96 sqm Plot. The design envisages prefabricated units which can be assembled on the site

The symbiotic relationship among consciousness, experience and space needs a new understanding, approach and expression in terms of design. Like vast diversity of human minds and their individual nature, it is necessary to evolve a "heterogeneous option of diversification" while attempting to establish a condition of order through the process of design. This may require looking back at the ethnic and traditional design, which sometimes defy logic, but express an emotional relationship with space. This is evident in the recent advent of the 'post-modern' style in the West and revival of 'ethnic style' in India. However, in this age of fast fashion and commercial exploration, the treatment of the issue tends to be cosmetic and superficial. It is more of fashion, than a search of experience, emotions and consciousness related to space design. Emotions are not skin deep and interior design is not decoration. The architect of today must search for new values and diverse definitions of space.

Why is it that the lofty temples usually have a small which is lower than the human height? Why the figure of the God is placed in the centre of the circumambulating orbit? Is it by conscious design that a place is always strategically positioned at a focal point and at a commanding height? Is it to humble a visitor and glorify the king that he usually sits at the end of long hall? Why his seat is always higher than all the others?

The entrance, location, position, level, distance and dimensions of space and enclosures are important aspects of the status and the power structure. The red carpeted first floors of North and South blocks and various Bhavans in New Delhi are exclusively reserved for the ministers and their paraphernalia. Edward T. Hall, the famous anthropologist had said that man's experience of space is not only visual alone but multisensory and is related to action. That is why within a space, people move and interact with each other. They sense the atmosphere, smell the space, visualise it and hear it. Mostly the locus of power in corporate office is centred in the board rooms flanked by the heads in the corners, where the lines of power cross. Location status is vertical as well as horizontal. The importance of one's status is also recognised by the height, level or the floor.

Besides the knowledge of human dimensions, body movement and furniture, one has to take into account the bubble of privacy and psychological factors, while designing an enclosure. The body breadth of an individual is about 56 cms (23 inches). While planning corridors or passageways, the minimum width should be maintained in relation with the density of users including wheel chairs. It would vary, if the passage is meant for some particular persons and is also related with the scale of the building and its proportions.

While designing a building, the architect should be well-versed with the ergonomics. The ergonomics is an interdisciplinary science that studies the relationship between the human being and his environment. By ergonomy a working relationship can be established between the environment and the users. The space should be designed according to its use and keeping in view the efficiency, productivity, working environment, human development and users' satisfaction. The job satisfaction is closely linked with the facilities. It requires a close scrutiny of the functions and corresponding facilities required for their performance. The basic facilities, like furniture, storage, equipment, machinery, etc. provide functional efficiency. The symbolic facilities give the users a feeling of identity, importance and dignity. The different aspects of environment are climatic comfort, location, dimension of space, entrance, enclosures, distance, colour, lighting, privacy, etc. The amount of privacy needed depends upon the nature of the building. According to Franklin Becker there are two sides of privacy, viz. :

(*a*) Hearing and being heard, and

(*b*) Seeing and being seen.

He feels that any work place should have three kinds of privacy, viz:

1. Communicable privacy - where the flow of information is quick and informal. This is particularly necessary to perform the functions of public dealing.
2. Concentration privacy - freedom from visual and acoustical disturbances. It is required for creative worker, like the artists, writers, etc.
3. Contemplative privacy - to reflect on events, plan strategies or to take decisions.

Another kind of privacy which affects living and productivity is acoustical privacy. The users need protection from the noise of typewriter, telephones, machines, etc. However, the most distracting noise is the people's conversation. To provide acoustical privacy the background sound level should be higher than the speech level. Controlling noise involves curative and preventive measures. Locating or segregating noise emitting areas away from the quiet areas is a preventive measure which is necessary to provide acoustical privacy. Among curative measures noise absorbing surfaces, blocking and covering hard surfaces by soft surfaces, are common methods to control noise. Partial height partitions should be treated with sound absorbent materials. Sound waves travel like light waves. If we can see a person we can also hear him.

According to Edward T. Hall, there are four zones of "territorial distance", viz., intimate, private, social and public. The distance determines the proximity required for a comfortable working environment in a given situation. Intimate distance is 45 cms. from the human body, where one can touch the other person. The personal distance is assessed to be 45 cm to 75 cm for a close range and 75 to 120 cm (2.5 to 4 feet) for a far range. This proximity signifies a special relationship or suitability for personal conversation.

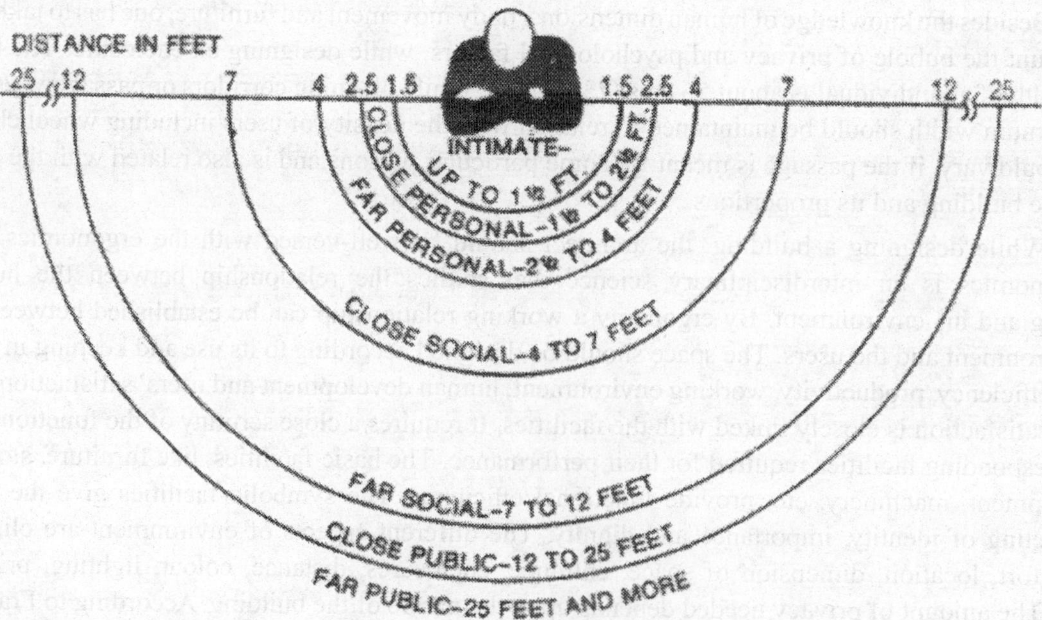

Fig. 11.8. The four zones of territorial distance: Intimate, Personal, Social and Public

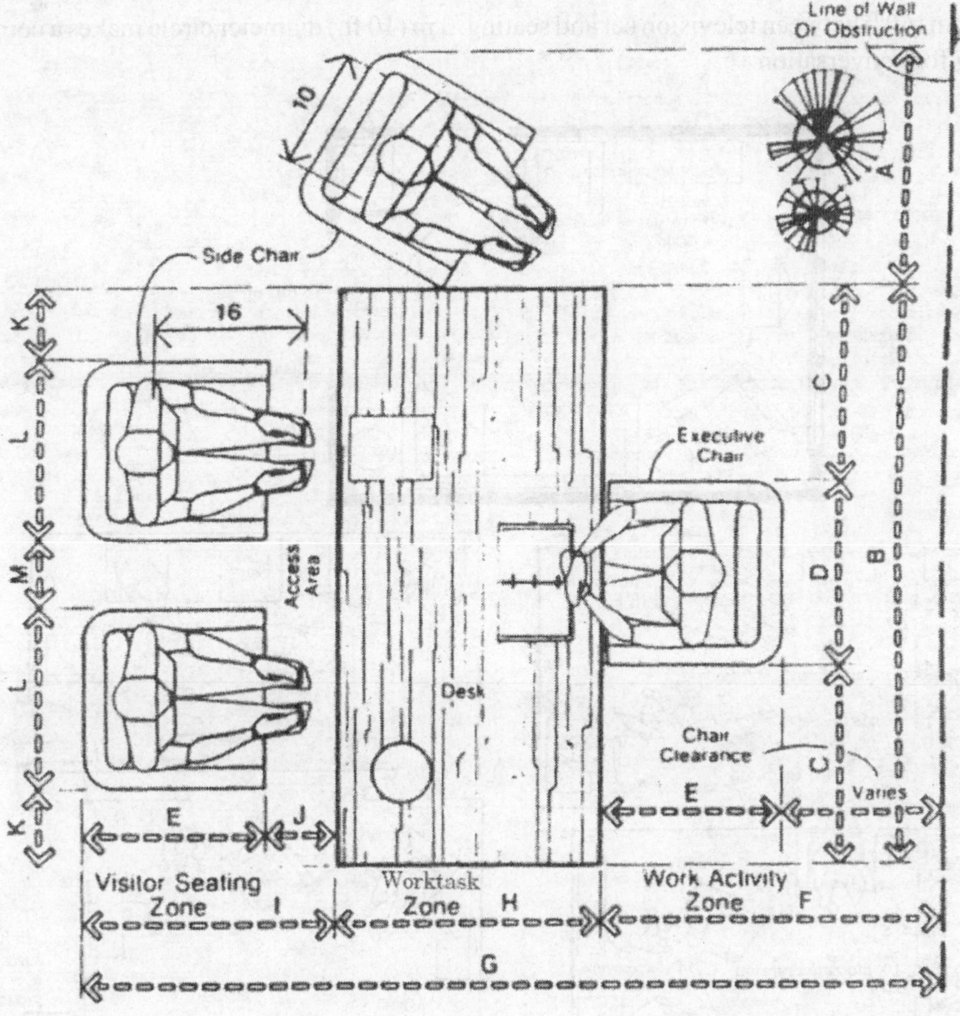

Fig. 11.9. The minimum size of an office worked out on the basis of ergonomics. A to M indicate the minimum space required for furniture, human movement, access, storage and clearances

Space and Furniture

The following are the critical considerations in space design from ergonomic and anthropometric point of view:

- Maximum liveable area.
- Through traffic should be separated from activity area.
- Opening should be located so as to give enough wall for furniture arrangement.
- Convenient access should be provided to doors, windows, electric outlets, etc.

For convenient use of furniture, the following clearances should be observed:

160 cm (60") between seatings

60 cm (24") for use of desk

90 cm (36") for main traffic

160 cm (60") between television set and seating. 3 m (10 ft.) diameter circle makes a comfortable grouping for conversation.

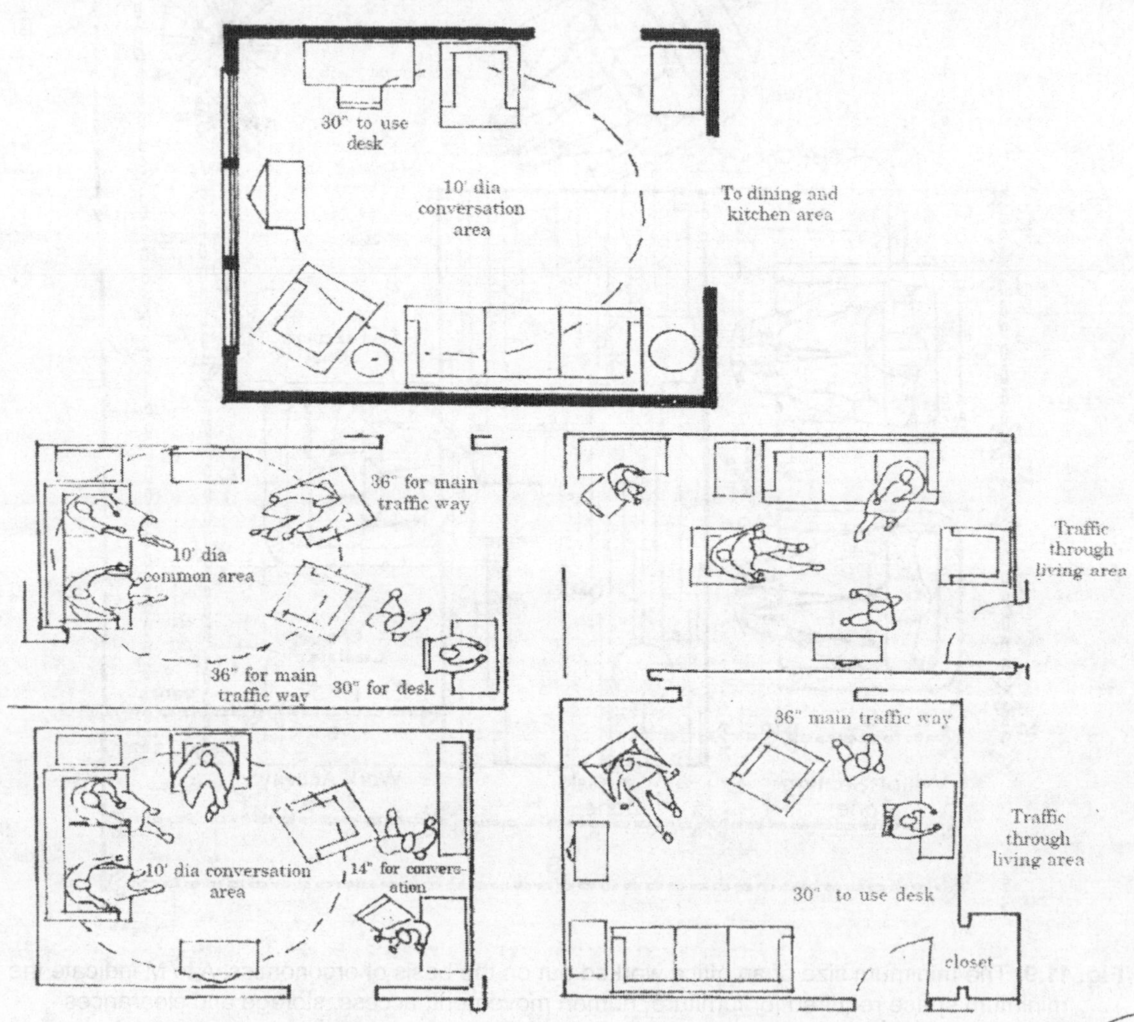

Fig. 11.10. Minimum dimensions of space are determined by human figure, movement and the activities

Social distance is between 1.2 to 3.6 m (4 to 12 feet) where one could work with his colleagues. It signifies a formal relationship. The public distance of 3.6 m to 7.5 m (12 to 25 feet) or more is suitable for public meeting or gatherings, where a speaker maintains distance from his audience. In terms of design these distance help to plan the space more functional. The position of furniture, size of rooms and shape of furniture can be accordingly planned and designed.

Ergonomic Design of a Kitchen

The kitchen is as much a workplace as a small factory. It requires services and environmental conditions which facilitate proper output, safety and convenience. It should be free from odour, smoke and excessive heat. It should be well lighted and ventilated. The exhaust fan not only helps in the circulation of air, but also dispels bad odour, smoke and heat. It can be installed just above the window. For fresh air and natural light, in place of conventional side-hung window, a combination of adjustable glass louvered and side hung panels may be more suitable for proper ventilation. The layout should ensure proper light, ventilation and movement. Apart from adequate natural light, kitchen needs proper artificial lighting. The worktop would be well lit and every part of the kitchen should receive direct light. The lighting should be so placed not to cast shadows on the counter nor its colour should temper the natural colours of food material. The level of lighting should allow doing minute jobs, like cleaning of pulses without any stress. Normally a level of 300 to 400 lux should be maintained. Incandescent lamps are more suitable as they allow the eye to see the natural colours. However, for additional lighting a concealed tube can be installed above the counter and below the shelves. A combination of pendent and luminescent lamps help to avoid the casting of shadows.

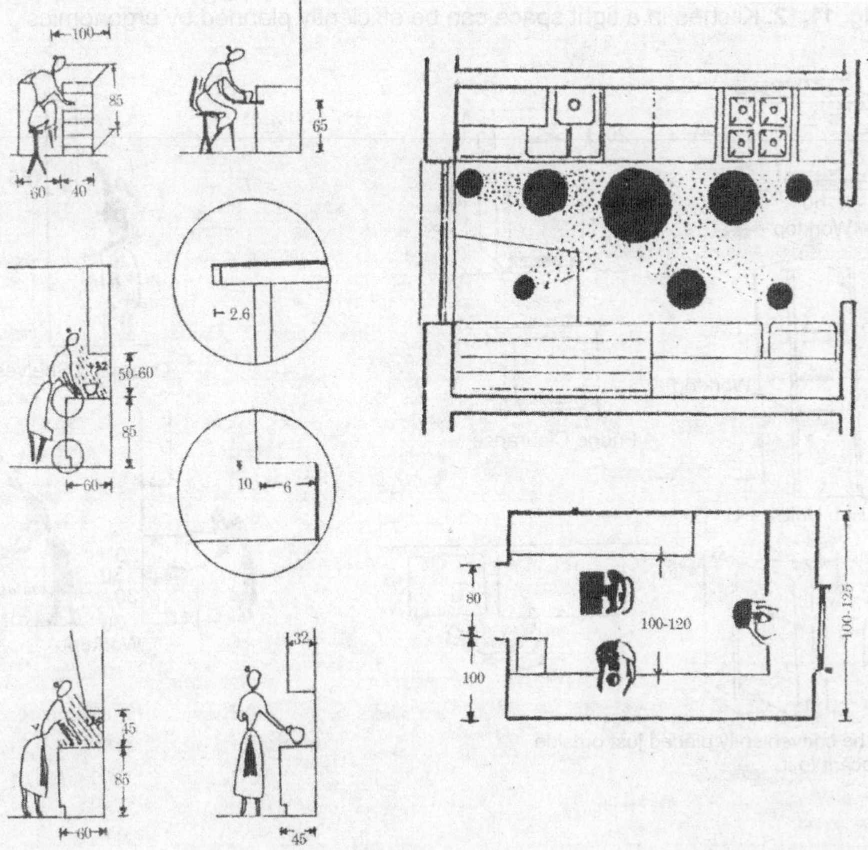

Fig. 11.11. Ergonomic design of a kitchen

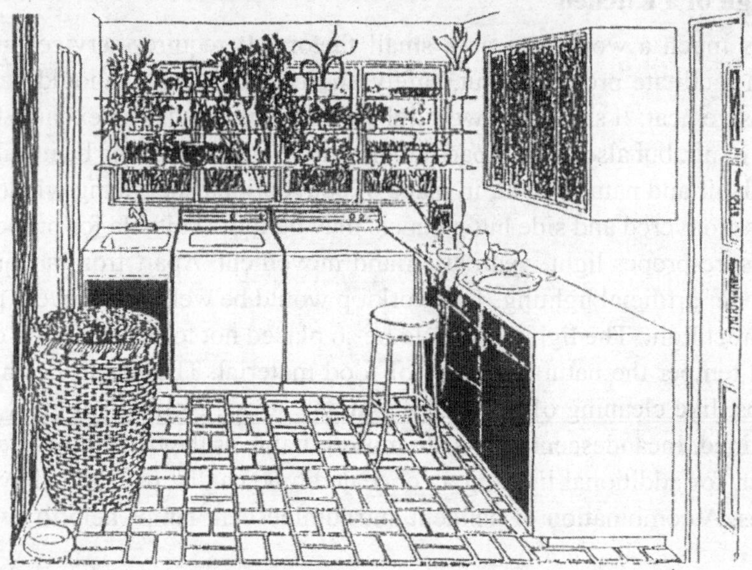

Fig. 11.12. Kitchen in a tight space can be efficiently planned by ergonomics

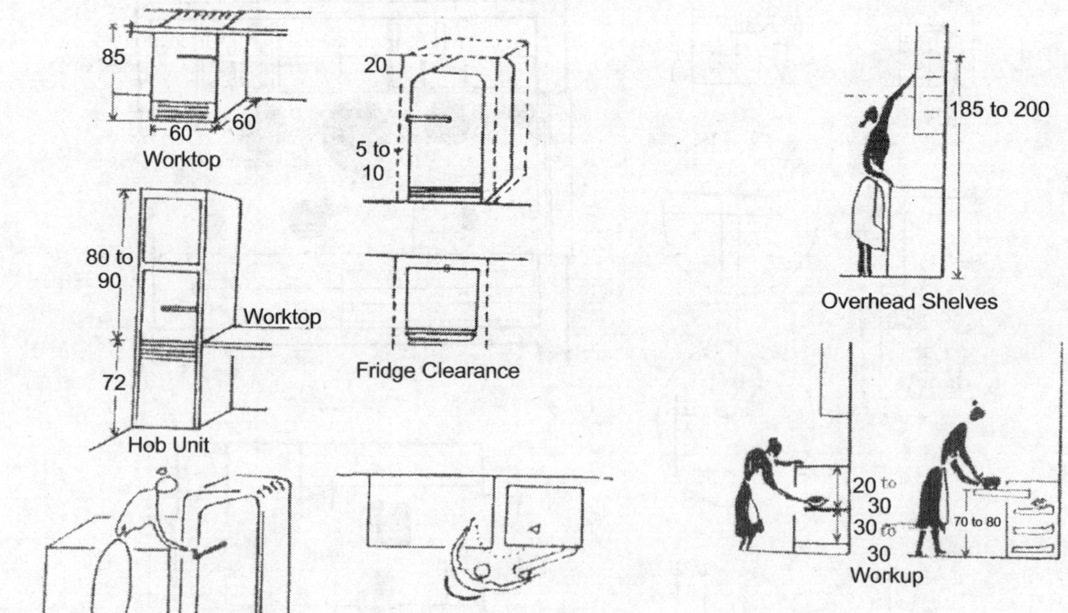

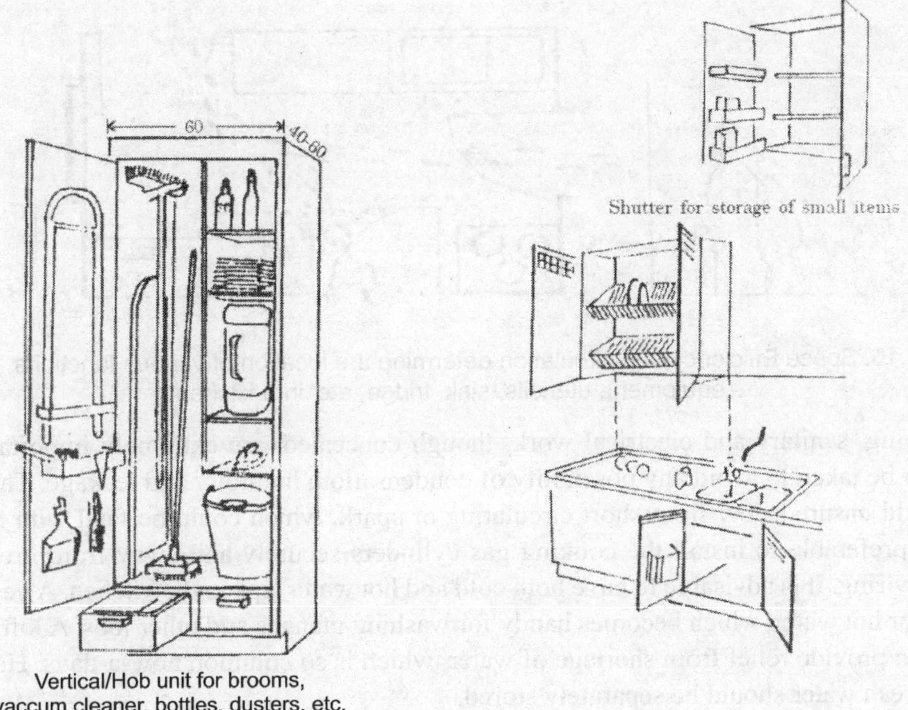

Fig. 11.13. The kitchen is like a small factory which should be designed ergonomically

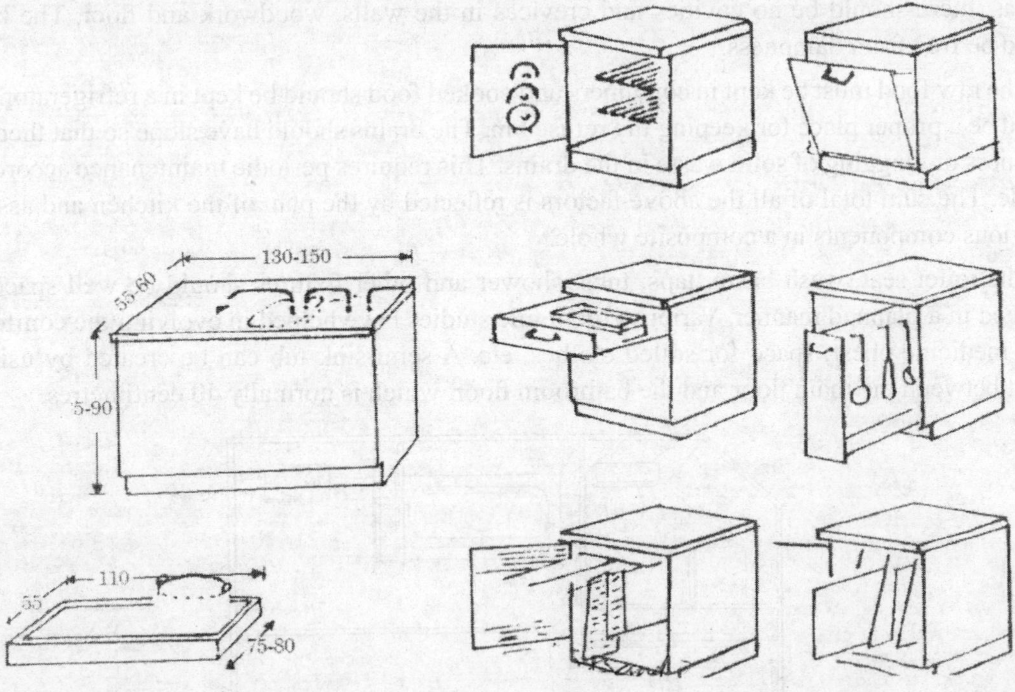

Fig. 11.14. Kitchen equipment, storage, and services include micro-oven, cooking stove, etc.

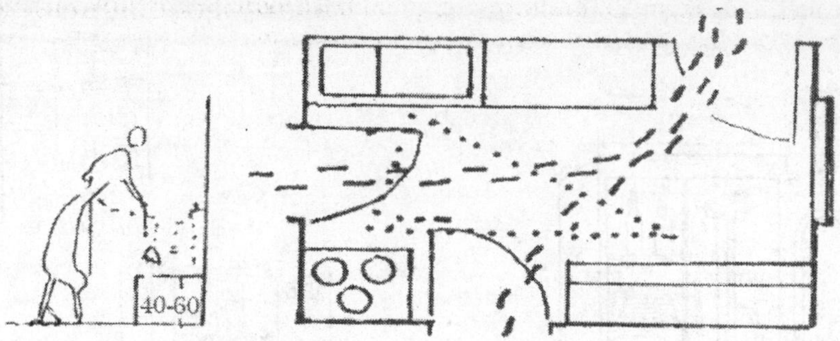

Fig. 11.15. Space Efficiency and circulation determine the location of various functions, cooking equipment, utensils, sink, fridge, etc. in a kitchen

Plumbing, sanitary and electrical work, though concealed, are extremely important. Special care has to be taken to avoid any possibility of condensation, humidity and leakage. The electrical work should ensure safety from short circulating or spark, which could be fatal with the LPG. It is always preferable to install the cooking gas cylinders securely and away from fire, oven and electrical wiring. It is advisable to have *both cold and hot water taps in the kitchen.* A geyser can be installed for hot water, which becomes handy for washing utensils and other jobs. A loft tank in the kitchen can provide relief from shortage of water, which is so common now-a-days. However, for drinking fresh water should be separately stored.

The kitchen should be protected from insects, flies, mosquitoes and cockroaches. For this, general cleanliness, ventilation and lighting are essential. It also depends on many other factors, such as, there should be no cavities and crevices in the walls, woodwork and floor. The kitchen should be free from dampness.

The raw food must be kept in containers and cooked food should be kept in a refrigerator. There should be a proper place for keeping the refuse bin. The drains should have slope so that there is no dampness or clogging of solid waste in the drains. This requires periodic maintenance according to a cycle. The sum total of all the above factors is reflected by the plan of the kitchen and assembly of various components in a composite whole.

The toilet seat, wash basin, taps, tubs, shower and other fixtures should be well spaced and arranged in a planned manner. Various ergonomic studies have helped in evolving the comfortable soap, medicine chest, space for soiled clothes, etc. A semi-sink tub can be created by using the height between the main floor and the bathroom floor, which is normally 40 centimetres.

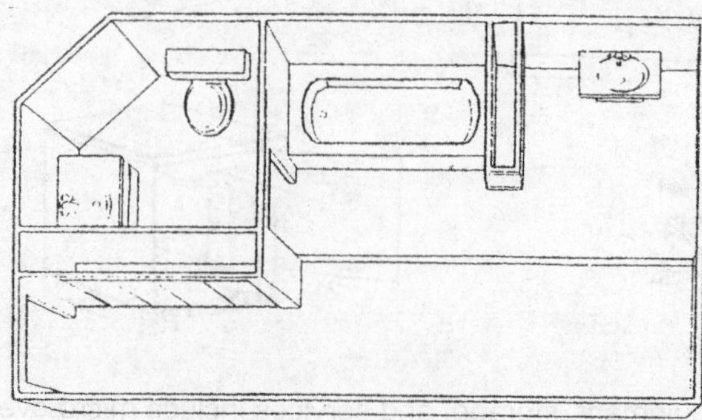

Fig. 11.16. Toilet layout should be according to living habits, ergonomic and hygienic requirements

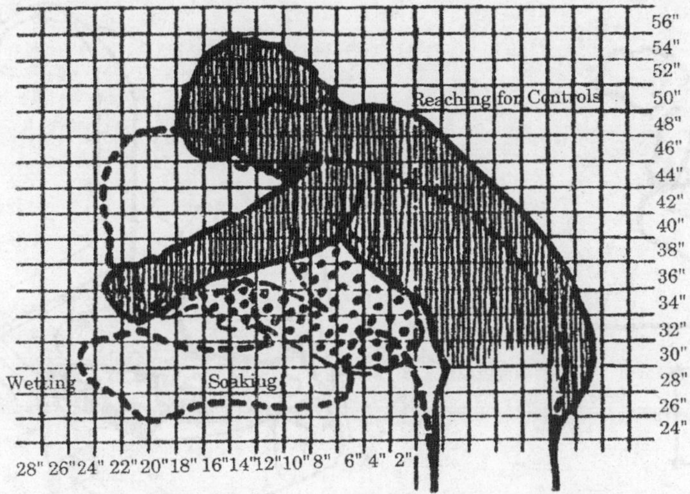

Fig. 11.17. Ergonomy of body and arm movement while washing face. Diagram is based on the photographs of models moving in front of calibrated background

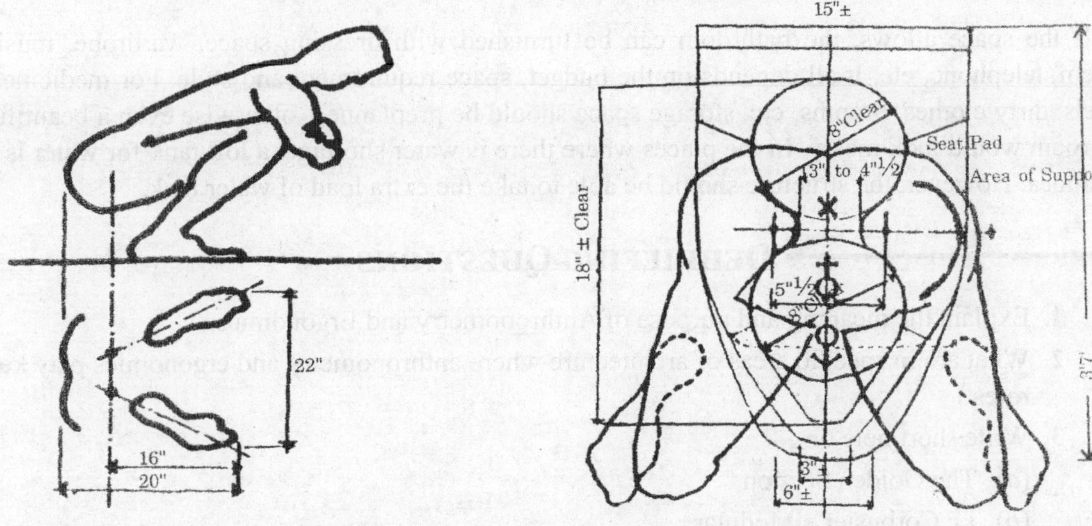

Fig. 11.18. Natural posture for male defecation

Fig. 11.19. Prototype unit designed by Alexandra Kira

It combines functions associated with water closet and the bidet. In addition to flushing action to carry away feces, new unit has two water jets for cleaning of genital and anal regions of both sexes. Height and configuration of seat are derived from analysis of physical and physiological aspects of act.

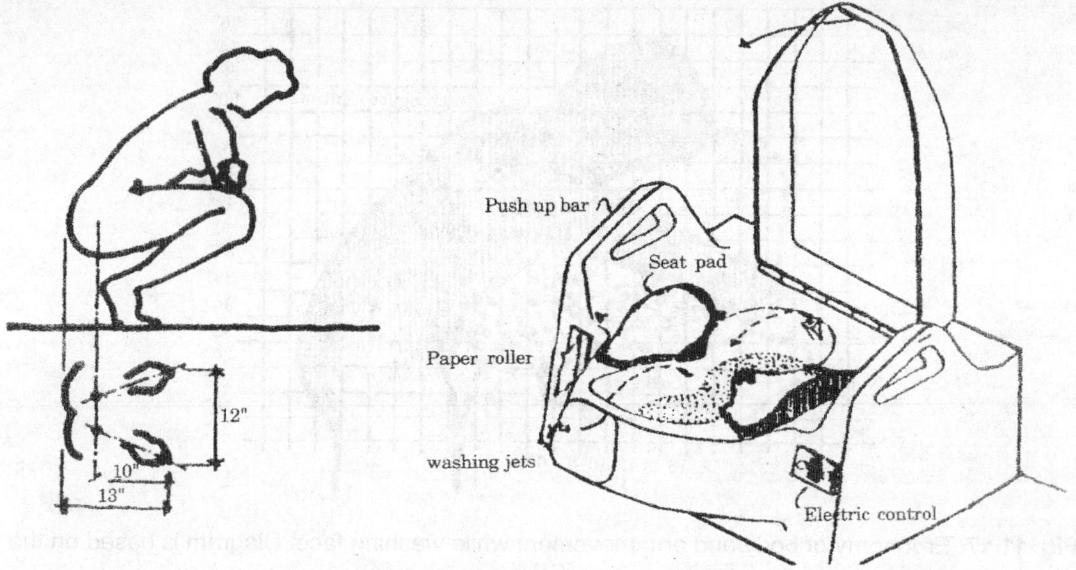

Fig. 11.20. Natural posture for female defection

Fig. 11.21. A portable W.C. Unit

If the space allows, the bathroom can be furnished with dressing space, wardrobe, music system, telephone, etc. It all depends on the budget, space requirement and style. For medicines, towels, dirty clothes, brooms, etc. storage space should be preplanned, otherwise even a beautiful bathroom would look messy. In the places where there is water shortage, a loft tank for water is a good idea. However, the structure should be able to take the extra load of water tank.

DEBRIEFING QUESTIONS

1. Explain the meaning and purpose of Anthropometry and Ergonomics.
2. What are in specific areas of architecture where anthropometry and ergonomics play key roles?
3. Write short note on :
   (*a*) The Golden Section
   (*b*) Le Corbusier's Modular
   (*c*) Territorial zones
4. How ergonomics based design of a kitchen and toilet are worked out?
5. Explain 'Ergonomics' based furniture design.
6. Explain the process of design of a minimum house based on ergonomics.

Chapter 12

BARRIER FREE ARCHITECTURE

The Barrier Free Architecture enables people with disabilities to move about safely and freely and to access the facilities within the built environment. This entails adoption of design and space standards for barrier free builts environment that include public and semi-public and educational, residential and, commerical buildings, industrial buildings, healthcare, institutions, community establishments, religious centres, hotels, restaurants and transport facilities. It also indicates the need to ensure the access for all, including disabled, wheel chair users to corridors, entrances and exits, paths, stairways, lift, toilet, and other facilities, such as water fountain, telephone, mailbox, vending machine etc. These have to be in compliance with the Persons with Disabilities (Equal Opportunities, Protection of Rights and Full Participation) Act, 1996, which requires mandatory provisions for pathways and ramps in buildings, adequate space in corridors, lifts kitchen, door width, toilets for wheel chair users, Braille symbols and auditory signals in elevators, etc.

Various disabilities, considered while planning the barrier free built environment are classified under four categories:

1. **Non-Ambulatory :** Impairment that regardless of causes or manifestation for all practical purposes, confine individuals to wheel chairs.
2. **Semi-Ambulatory :** Impairments that cause individuals to walk with difficulty or insecurity, individuals using braces or crutches, amputees, authorities, spastics and those with pulmonary and cardiac ills may be semi-ambulatory.
3. **Sight :** Total blindness or imperilments affecting sight to the extent that the individual functioning in public areas is insecure or exposed to danger.
4. **Hearing :** Deafness or hearing handicaps that might make and individual insecure in public areas because he is unable to communicate or hear.

Space For Persons Using Wheelchair

Adequate space should be allocated for persons using mobility devices, *e.g.* wheelchairs, crutches and walkers, as well as those walking with the assistance of other persons. The range of reach (forward and sides, with or without obstruction) of person in a wheelchair should be taken into consideration. Attention should be given to dimension of wheelchairs used. Standard size of wheel chair is 1050 mm × 750 mm.

The design guidelines for the special needs of the persons with disabilities are as follows:

Non-Ambulatory Disabilities

Persons restricted on wheel chair should be used the facilities within the built environment without a helper's assistance. The wheelchair design may assume that the user should be able to operate the wheelchair without help. The width and length of the wheel chair, its control and the diameter of the casters decide the following:

- Width of entrances and exits (clear 900 mm)
- Width of the passage/corridor (min. 900 mm)
- Slope of the ramp, slope levels and grooves
- Transferring from wheel chair (adequate space is required to transfer from wheel chair to chair, toilet and bed).
- Lift size.

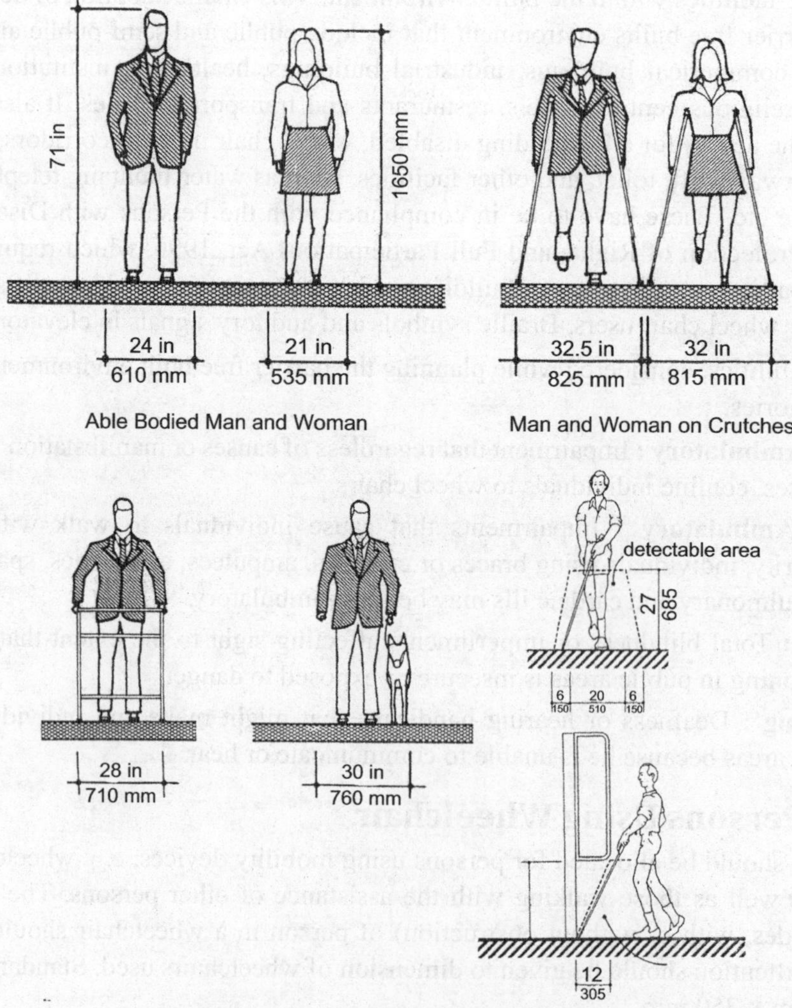

Fig. 12.1. Basic Human Dimensions (Handicapped)

Source: *Time Saver Standards for Architectural Design*

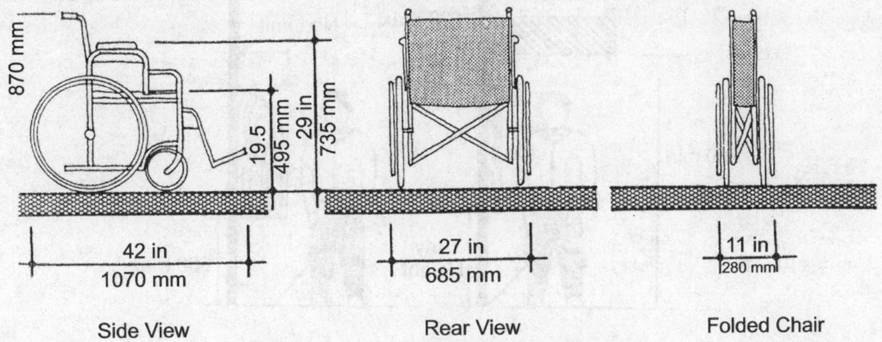

Fig. 12.2. Wheel Chair Dimensions

Height :	Arms from floor	29 in	(735 mm)
Height :	Seat from floor	19.5 in	(495 mm)
Foot :	Min. extension	14.5 in	(365 mm)
Foot rest :	Max. extension	20.75 in	(525 mm)
Wheel diameter front		8 or 5 in	(205 or 127 mm)
Wheel diameter rear		24 in	(610 mm)

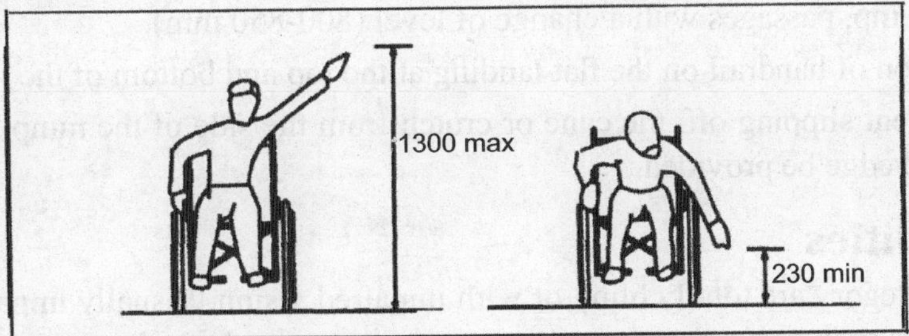

Fig. 12.3. Side reach without obstruction (dimensions in mm)

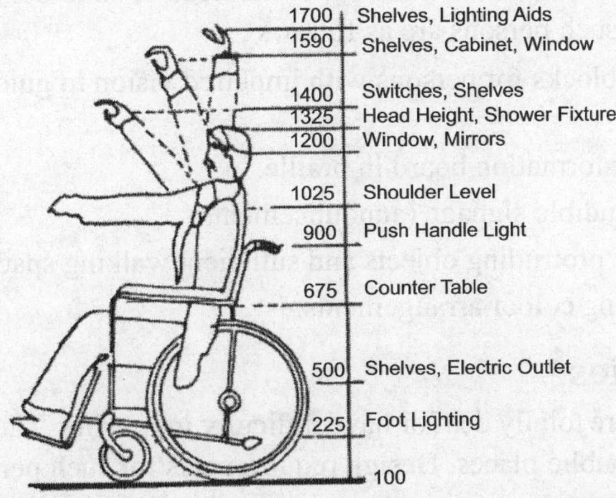

Fig. 12.4. Control Range and Furniture for wheelchair users (dimensions in mm)

Source: *Time Saver Standards for Architectural Design.*

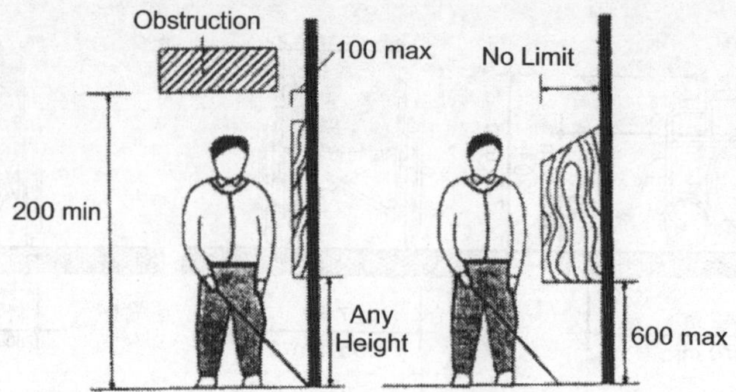

Fig. 12.5. Space Dimensions without Obstructions

Semi-Ambulatory Disabilities

Persons in this category are those who use walking aids such as crutches or canes, who are amputees, who have chest ailments or heart disease. Design requirements for such persons are as follows :

- Width of passage for crutch users (min. 900 mm)
- Finishes of floor surface with non-slip floor materials.
- Installation of handrail to support the body weight at the critical places *e.g.* staircase, toilet, ramp, passages with a change of level (800-850 mm).
- Extension of handrail on the flat landing at the top and bottom of the stairs (300 mm).
- To prevent slipping off, the cane or crutch from the side of the ramp 20 mm high lip on exposed edge be provided.

Sight Disabilities

Persons in this category are totally blind or with impaired vision. Visually impaired persons make use of other senses such as hearing or touch to compensate for the lack of vision. It is necessary to give instructions to access through the sense to touch (hand, fingers or legs). While walking with a white cane their feet near the tip of the cane his or her head or shoulder against protruding objects. Design requirements for such persons are as follows :

- Use of guiding blocks for persons with impaired vision to guide them within and outside the building.
- Installation of information board in braille.
- Installation of audible signage (announcements)
- Removal of any protruding objects and sufficient walking space for safe walking.
- Use of contrasting colour arrangements.

Hearing Disabilities

Persons in this category are totally deaf or have difficulty in hearing. They generally use their sight to gather information in public places. Design requirements for such persons are as follows:

- Provision of information board in an easily understandable manner.
- Provision of illuminated signage, layout diagrams to help the persons easily reach the desired place.

Elderly Persons

Elderly persons may suffer from impaired mobility, sight disability (partially or fully), hearing disabilities or any physical difficulties, for which the design guidelines within and outside the buildings and facilities shall be similar to physically disabled persons.

Accessible Buildings

The basic provisions to be incorporated in and around building should make it convenient for the disabled people, including those dependent for mobility on wheelchairs and those affected by hearing and sight impairments. These recommendations can also be used for adaptation of existing buildings.

Table 12.1. Minimum Access Provisions for Various Types of Buildings

Type of Building	Minimum Provisions
Single detached dwelling units	A minimum of 2 per cent of the total number of units to be constructed with barrier-free features.
Staff housing, multiple dwellings, high rise apartment units and tenements	A minimum of 1 unit for every 25 plus 1 additional unit for every 100 units thereafter. Entrances and exits to be accessible.
Tenement houses, row houses, apartments and town houses	A minimum of 1 unit for up to 150 units and a minimum of 1 additional unit for every 100 units thereafter to be accessible.
Post-offices, bank and financial service institutions	A minimum of 1 lowered service counter on the premises. A minimum of 1 lowered automatic teller machine (ATM)/ cash disbursement point on the premises
Shop houses and single-storey shops	Accessible shopping area
Places of worship	Entrances and exits and main area of worship to be accessible
Food Centre / Restaurant	A minimum of 1 table without stool or seats attached to the floor for every 10 tables A minimum of 2 tables without stool or seats attached to the floor for the whole premises
Community centres, halls, auditoria, concert halls, assembly halls, cinema, theatres, and other places of public assembly.	Accessible entrances, exits, aisles and toilet facilities. Seating for persons with disabilities to be accessible from main entrance and lobbies Various seating/viewing choice to be provided for persons in wheel chairs in the main seating area A minimum of 2 wheelchair spaces for seating capacity up to 100 seats A minimum of 4 wheelchair spaces for seating capacity over 100 to 400 seats

Source: *Time Saver Standards for Architectural Design.*

In spite of the mandatory stipulations, the built environment grossly lacks in catering to the persons with disabilities. This needs implementable, simple guidelines which can be adopted by the architects, planners and engineers for accessible and barrier free built environment.

Ramped Approach

Ramp shall be finished with non-slip material to enter the building. Minimum width or ramp shall be 1800 mm. with maximum gradient 1:12, length of ramp shall not exceed 9.0 mt. having double handrail at a height of 800 and 900 mm on both sides extending 300 mm beyond top and bottom of the ramp. Minimum gap from the adjacent wall to the handrail shall be 50 mm.

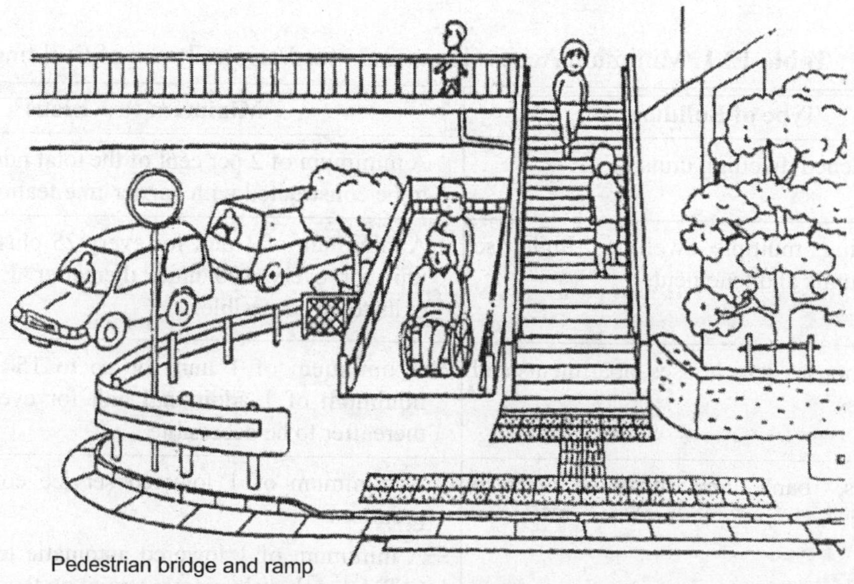

Fig. 12.6. Pedestrian Bridge and Ramp for wheelchair users

If possible, ramp gradient should not exceed 1:20, in which case a maximum distance of 10,000 mm between resting places is acceptable, With the steepest gradient of 1:12 the maximum distance is reduced to 6000 mm.

- Resting places should be provided at the top and bottom of the ramps and should take the form of an unobstructed platform with dimensions not less than 1200 mm long × 1500 mm wide, clear of any door swing. Where there are intermediate resting places, these should not be less than 1500 mm × 1500 mm.
- Strengthened handrails should be provided on each side of the ramp.
- A100 mm kerb upstand should be provided on each open side of the ramp with a rail at low level as a guide.
- The minimum width of the ramp should be 1500 mm, but 1800 mm is better to allow wheelchairs to pass each other.

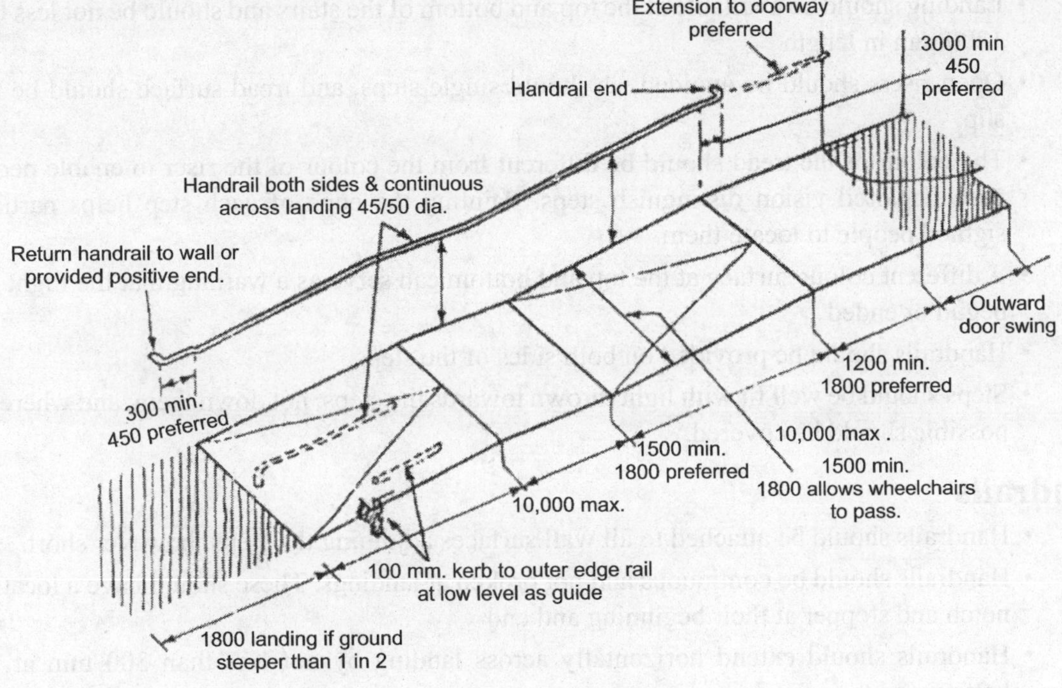

Fig. 12.7. Detail of a Ramp

External Steps

Steps are often easier to use than ramps by those who walk with difficulty. Access ramp must, therefore, be complemented by external steps. Dimensions of steps should be uniform and as follows:

– Tread not less than 280 mm (320 mm preferred)
– Riser not higher than 150 mm (130 mm preferred)
– Vertical rise of any flight, not more than 1200 mm.

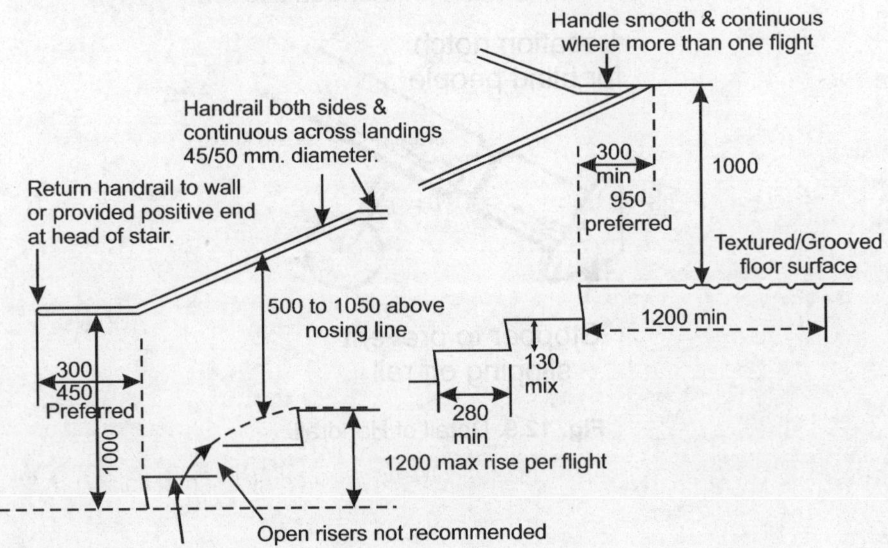

Fig. 12.8. Details of Staircase

- Landing should be available at the top and bottom of the stairs and should be not less than 1200 mm in length.
- Open risers should be avoided, as should single steps, and tread surface should be non slip.
- The colour of the tread should be different from the colour of the riser to enable people with impaired vision distinguish steps. Painting the edge of each step helps partially sighted people to locate them.
- A different colour surface at the top and bottom can serve as a warning that the flight has begun or ended.
- Handrails should be provided on both sides of the steps.
- Steps should be well lit with light thrown towards the steps, not down them, and wherever possible should be covered.

Handrails

- Handrails should be attached to all wall surfaces adjoining the steps, however short.
- Handrails should be continuous and not broken at landings. These should have a location notch and stopper at their beginning and end.
- Handrails should extend horizontally across landing by not less than 300 mm at the bottom and top of stairs.
- Handrails should either be returned to wall or a positive end at the top and bottom of the rail should be provided.
- The optimum height for a handrail is 850 mm on steps and 1000 mm on level ground.
- The distance between stair rails should be not less than 1200 mm, preferably not more than 1800 mm.
- Handrails should be easy to grip and non-slip even when wet. The preferable width or diameter for a handrail is 45-50 mm.
- There should be a clearance of 45 mm between wall and rail.

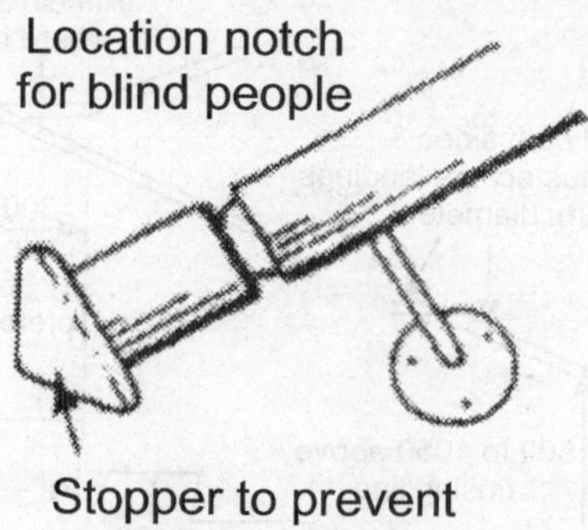

Fig. 12.9. Detail of Handrail.

Parking

Many disabled people are dependent on their vehicles and careful consideration must be given to the parking needs of disabled drivers and passengers. The following standards are applied:

- 3% of spaces provided in any car park should be reserved for disabled users, with a minimum of 1 space per 20-49 parking spaces. For less than 20 parking spaces, there is no specific requirement to allocate a space for disabled users, and the provision should be made, wherever possible.
- Reserved parking spaces should be provided close to an accessible entrance on level ground.
- If possible, covered spaces should be provided as transfer between car and wheel chair can take time.
- Where access to a public building is via a pedestrian area, reserved parking should be provided within 50 metres.

Spaces reserved for disabled people should be clearly marked and should display "Disabled" symbol both at eye level and on the ground. The location of the reserved parking bays should be signposted at the car park entrance. The route from the parking bays to the building entrance should be clearly signed, levelled and well-lit.

Parking spaces for disabled users should be a minimum 3200 mm wide to enable the car door to be fully opened within the bay.

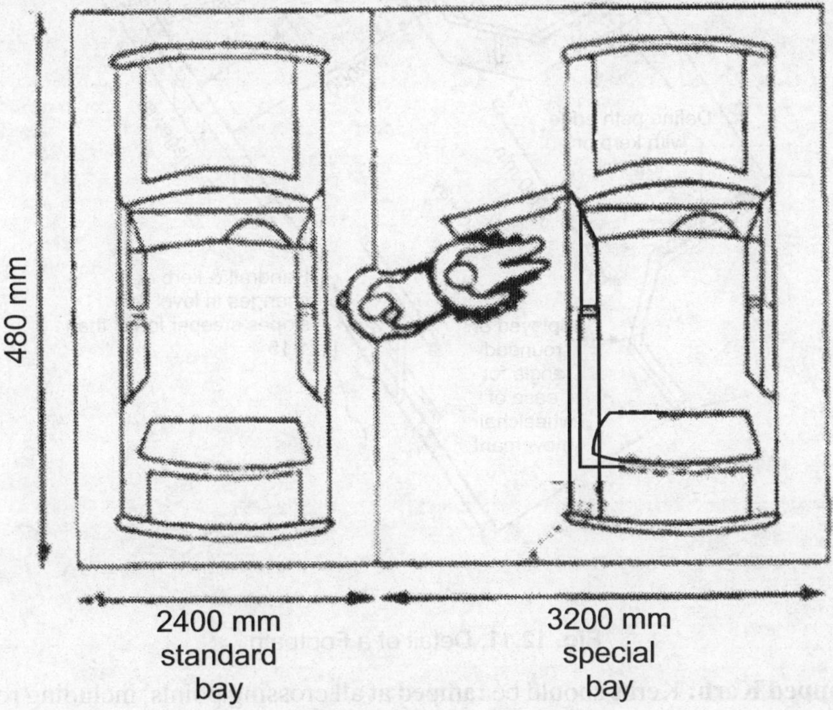

Fig. 12.10. Parking Space

Alternatively, standard spaces with transfer zones can be provided with a 1200 mm zone for transfer from car to wheelchair. Transfer zone should either serve two bays or be positioned in the corner of a parking area to avoid being used by other drivers. Kerbside space for disabled users should be provided with a dropped kerb access to the footway.

Footpaths

Footways adjacent to the carriageway, as well as footpaths where there is no contiguous carriageway, should be as level as possible without camber, and constructed of stable, firm, non-slip materials. External surface should be well laid and maintained. Cracked, uneven surfaces can be tracherous for disabled people. Ground surface should not deaden sounds and echoes which blind people depend on to gain direction guidance. Edges of footways and footpath should be well-defined. Footways and footpath should have a minimum width of 2000 mm to allow wheel chairs, prams and chairs to pass each other. Change of colours be designed for detection by blind people using canes. Handrails should extend beyond changes of levels. The minimum width between obstacles should be 900 mm.

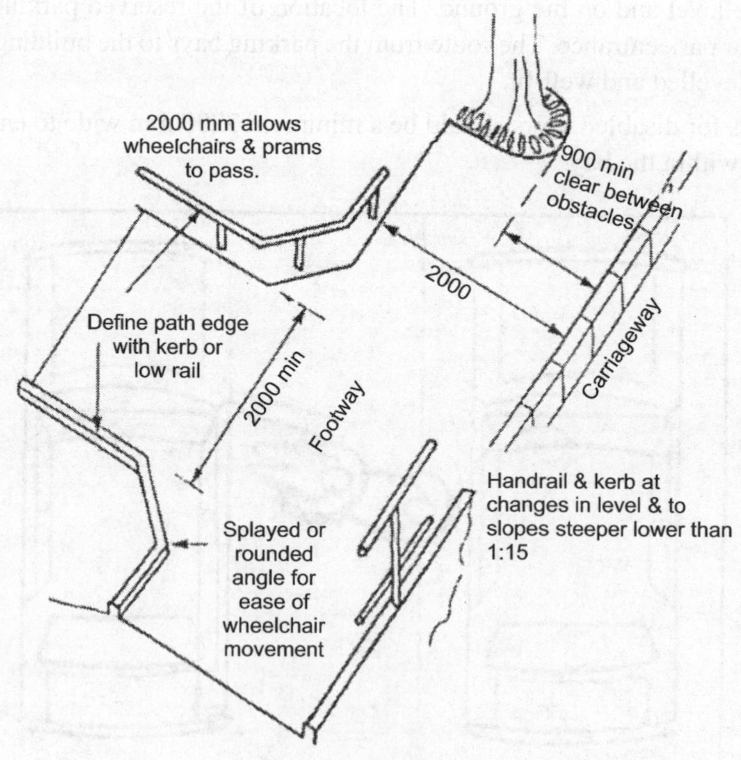

Fig. 12.11. Detail of a Footpath

Kerb and Dropped Kerb: Kerbs should be ramped at all crossing points, including road junctions. The gradient should be as gentle as possible with the maximum desirable gradient being 1:12. Special consideration should be given to crossing facilities in locations where they are most likely to be used for people with disabilities and for crossing to shops, clinics, public facilities and old people's homes.

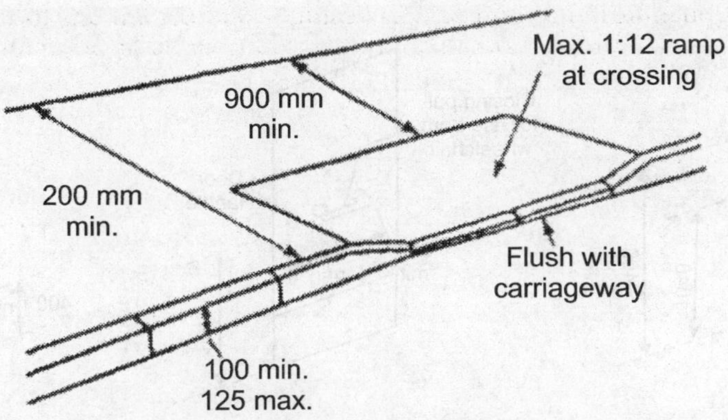

Fig. 12.12. Detail of a Kerb

The following guidelines should be followed:

- Kerb should be at least 100 mm high and not more than 125 mm high.
- Dropped kerb should be marked with a distinctive colour.
- A textured strip should be provided on the approach to the dropped kerb to alert blind people and their dogs.
- A mimimum width of 900 mm should be provided behind the ramp to allow safe passage along the pavement.
- Dropped kerb should be flush with the road surface, with no upstand.
- Dropped kerb and ramps on either side of vehicular route should be directly opposite one another. This is particularly important for guide dogs which are trained to cross at right angles.
- Dropped kerb should not be sited on the apex of a corner because this tends to lead the user out into the middle of the junction.
- A minimum distance of 2000 mm between the bollards should be provided to facilitate movement of wheelchairs.

Opening Doors

Doors should be sited so they can be approached easily and without obstruction to accessibility by wheelchair users. Standard 1000 mm door sets should be used having a minimum clear opening width of 870/875 mm or 855 mm in fire resisting construction. A minimum clear opening width of 900 mm would be preferred.

The following guidelines may be followed:

- On the leading face of any door to public, a clear wall space (panel equivalent) to the side should be not less than 300 mm.
- Door handles should be approximately 1040 mm above floor level.

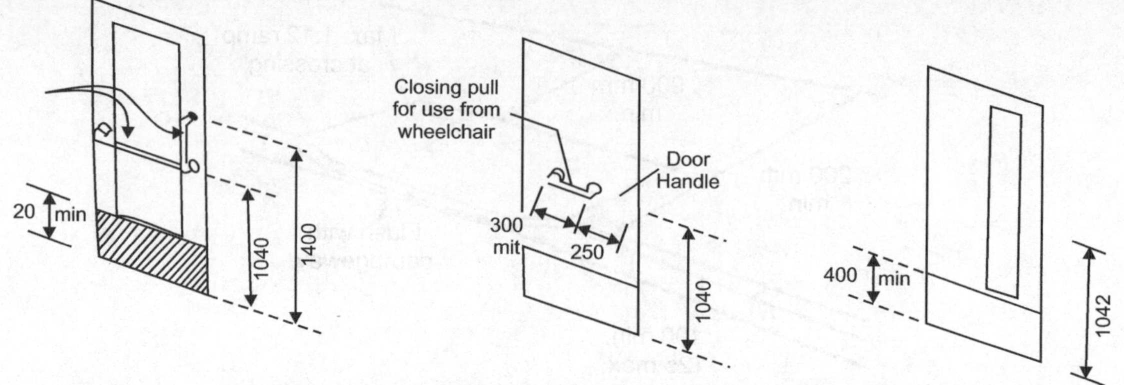

Fig. 12.13. Location and Size of Door Handles

- Handles should be large and robust and lever handles should be used, where doors are latched.
- An additional handle may be required to pull the door, if it is self closing.
- Clear, large printed signage can be used to indicate opening function *i.e.* PUSH/PULL.
- Bright coloured marking help identify plate glass doors. These should be set at approximately 1400 mm above floor level.
- Kicking plates are useful against general wear and tear and provide additional protection against wheelchairs. Plates should not be less than 400 mm in height.
- Where swing doors are installed, glazing is required to prevent accident. For wheelchair users, the lowest level of the glazing should be a maximum of 1040 mm above floor level.

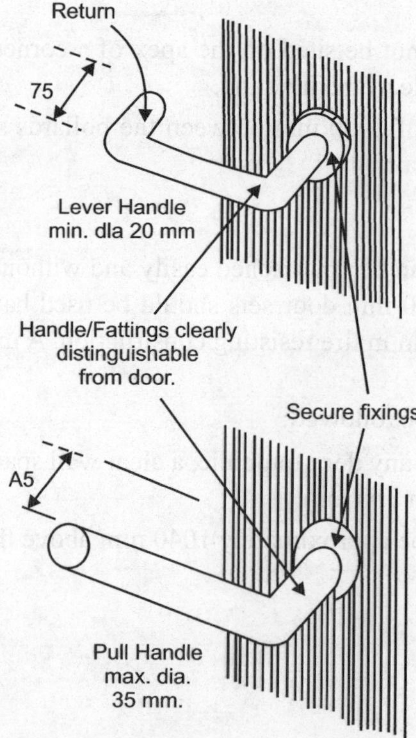

Fig. 12.14. Detail of a Door Handle

- Where doors are completely glazed, they should be marked by a contrasting colour band at a height of 1400-1600 mm.
- Glazing should be laminated safety glass, preferably plain and not dark tinted.
- Where privacy is not essential, corridor door should have a glass pane to allow people to see through. Deaf people cannot hear footsteps on the other side of a door, but they can see someone approaching through a glass pane.

Internal Lobbies

These should be free from steps and have a minimum width of 1200 mm to allow for wheelchair movement. Tight spaces and changes in direction create difficulties for disabled and for prams and push chairs. The dimension of door for wheelchair users to an accessible shall be minimum 1000 mm.

Internal Stairs

The dimensions of internal staircases should be uniform as follows:

- Tread not less than 250 mm
- Riser not more than 170 mm
- Vertical rise of any flight not more than 1200 mm
- Landing should not be less than 1200 mm long
- Nosing should not project, but may be splayed or rounded on a 7 mm radius.

Lifts

A seat with a minimum height of 600 mm should be provided at each floor for use whilst waiting for the lift. Lifts should be automatically self-leveling and the car should stop precisely at floor level. The minimum clear opening width of lift doors is not to be less than 900 mm.

Internal dimensions should be not less than 1100 mm × 1400 mm to allow movement in and out. 1500 mm × 1500 mm allows wheelchairs to turn through 180°. An internal handrail running around the sides of the lift car at 1000 mm above floor level is recommended. A pull down seat is also desirable. An unobstructed space of 1500 mm × 1500 mm in front of the lift should be provided, with a textured floor covering. Timing devices on lift doors should be set to allow sufficient time for people with disabilities and users with children to enter and leave comfortably. Lift controls inside and outside the cars should not be higher than 1400 mm floor level, and not lower than 1000 mm. Touch light controls, including floor/level numerals, should have embossed digits and there should be both illuminated and audible system, inside the car and at landing. Lift car with opposing doors should be provided with an audible indication of the opening set.

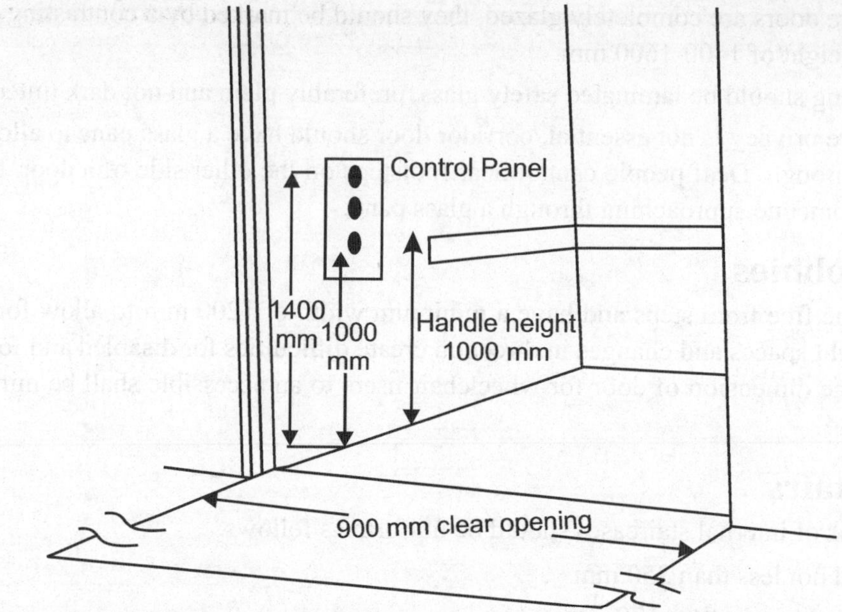

Fig. 12.15. Lift Detail

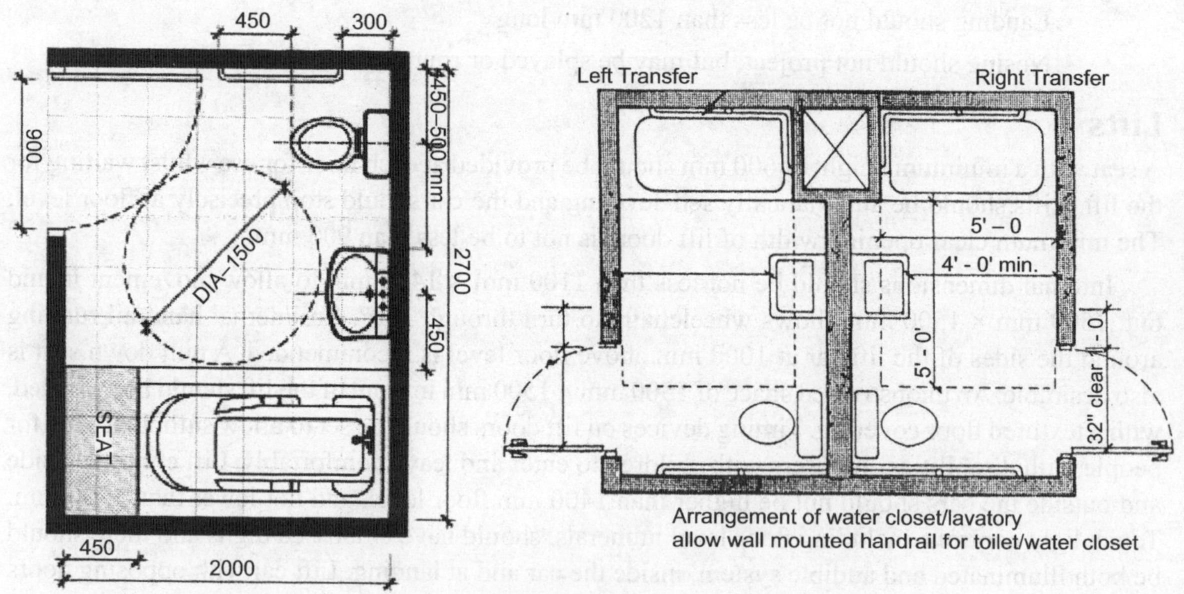

Fig. 12.16. Toilets for Handicapped

Source: *Time Saver Standards for Architectural Design*

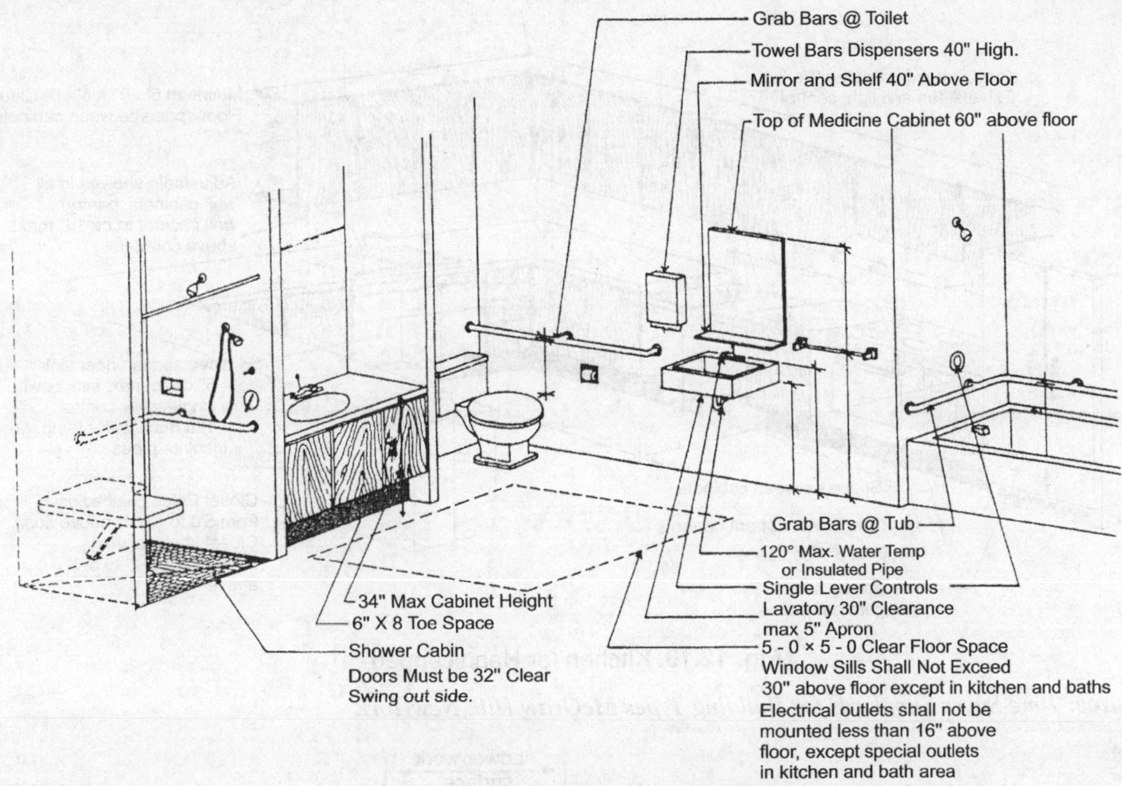

Fig. 12.17. Unisex Toilet for Disabled

Source: *Time Saver Standard for Building Types, McGraw Hill, New York*

Toilets

Toilets should be designed to allow access by wheelchairs and helpers. Separate unisex facilities enable helpers to assist disabled people of the opposite sex. A unisex facility should not be entered from single sex facility. In premises such as theatres or sports stadia where large number of people arrive and depart at the same time, it is desirable to have wheelchair accessible units in the male and female lavatories in addition to a separate unisex unit. Lavatories provided for people with disabilities should measure not less than 2000 mm long × 1500 mm wide. The door to any compartment must have a minimum clear opening width of 900 mm but 1000 mm is preferred. The floor surface of lavatories should be non-slip in both wet and dry conditions. An outward-opening, side-hung door is better than a sliding door. It should always be possible to open door from the outside in an emergency.

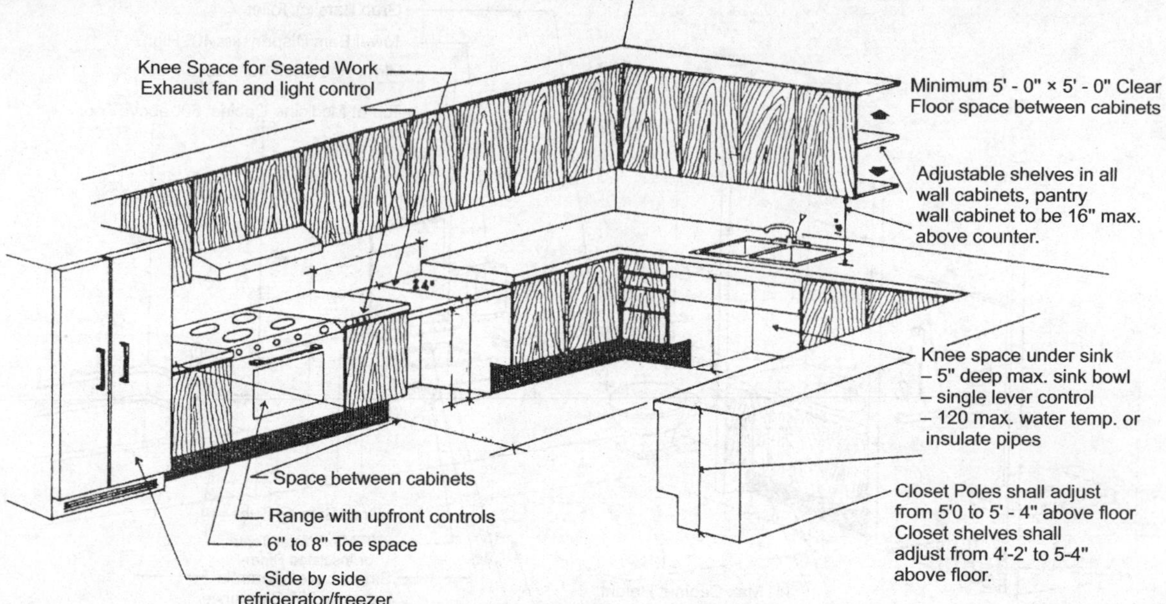

Fig. 12.18. Kitchen for Handicapped

Source: *Time Saver Standards for Building Types McGraw Hill, New York*

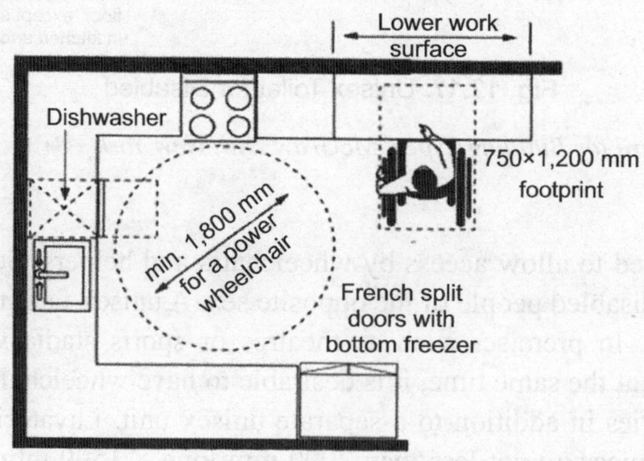

Fig. 12.19. Plan of a Disabled-Friendly Kitchen

Signage

It is important to let disabled people know about the facilities provided. As such the signage should indicate :

- Accessible entrance to the building
- Manageable route through the building
- Lifts that disabled people can use and operate
- Accessible W.C.s
- Specially reserved car parking spaces
- Any special service available in the building

Circulation

All basic facilities such as cloakroom, lift and accessible W.C. etc. should be available to people with disabilities and adults with young children. These facilities should be on the same level as the entrance door. Floor surface should be non-slip and well lit. The use of deep pile carpet and surfaces which make the passage of a wheelchair difficult should be avoided. Circulation space should be wide enough to allow prams, push chairs and wheelchairs to turn. A general turning space of not less than 1500 mm diameter is required. Passageway should be wide enough to allow double buggies and / or wheelchairs to pass each other. A minimum width of 1800 mm is needed for major circulation areas. Appliances such as fire extinguishers and radiators should be recessed so that circulation space is unobstructed. There should be no wall projections or surfaces hazardous to blind people. Splayed or rounded corners are desirable. Unexpected changes or level, particularly at doorways, are undesirable. All changes in level should be ramped, not steeper than 1:2. Where stairs are necessary, they should have handrails. They should also be clearly marked, ideally with a warning surface, such as a change of texture at the top and bottom.

Definitions/Short Notes

Architecture and Planning: The art and science of organisation of space and design of building bridging between technology and the humanity. It is the connective tissue between individual structures and the community as a whole.

Balcony: A horizontal projection with a hand-rail, balustrate or a parapet, to serve as a passage or sitting out place.

Fig. 12.20

Broadacre City: Frank Lloyd Wright's concept of urban living in rural ambience with more than half of all dwellings in higher-density clusters, with the rest on one acre or more. His concept was characterized by abundant open space and community features.

Building Code: Municipal Regulations that set forth the standards and requirements for the construction, maintenance and occupancy of buildings. The codes are designed to provide for the safety, health and welfare of the public.

Carpet Area: The carpet area of a property is defined as the net usable area from the inner sides of one wall to another. The following are included in the carpet area:

(*a*) Door and other openings in the wall;

(*b*) Intermediate pillars, supports or any other such obstruction within the plinth area irrespective of their location;

(*c*) Pilaster along wall exceeding 300 sq. cm in area;
(*d*) Flues which are within the wall;
(*e*) Built in cupboard, almirah and shelf appearing within a height of 2.2 m from floor;
(*f*) Fire place projecting beyond the face of the wall in living or bed room.

The carpet area may exclude the following:

(*a*) Veranda;
(*b*) Corridor and passage;
(*c*) Entrance hall and porch;
(*d*) Staircase and stair-cover (mumty),
(*e*) Shaft and machine room for lift;
(*f*) Bathroom and lavatory;
(*g*) Kitchen and pantry;
(*h*) Store;
(*i*) Canteen;
(*j*) Air-conditioning duct and plant room; and
(*k*) Shaft for sanitary piping.

Civic Sites identified at a prominent location should attract residents where they can meet neighbours or have scheduled community events. They also lead to a "sense of place", which increases pride in one's community.

Climate: It is the collective state of the atmosphere at a given place over a long period of time comprising of average as well as extreme weather events. Generally, 30 years of average values are considered in order to know the climate pattern of a given place. Climate is therefore a sum of the weather experienced at place is course of years and also over many years.

Micro-climate refers to the climate closer to Earth's surface in geographically defined sites in villages, cities and towns. The micro-climate of a place is affected by local factors such as variations in topography, the presence and density of vegetation, the presence of large water bodies and nature of built development.

Temperature and climate regimes determine the prevalence of particular vegetation types on a global scale. These regimes vary according to altitudes as well as latitudes. There will be similarities in temperature values between place at higher altitude located in latitudes closer to equator and other places at lower altitudes, but located further from equator at latitudes closer to North or South Pole.

Cluster Development: Higher-density structures arranged in proximity to create resultant open space. It is not simply higher density. In fact, clustering may or may not represent a change in the overall density.

Common Areas: Those portions of a building, land, or improvements and amenities owned by a planned unit housing, shopping, condominium, homeowners' association (or a cooperative) that are used by all of the unit owners, who share the common expenses of their operation and maintenance. Common areas include swimming pool, tennis court, recreational facilities, common corridors, parking areas, means of ingress and egress, etc.

Community Survey: Community survey, when properly conducted, can elicit important information about land-use patterns and physical features that could not be accessed in any other way. Surveys also need to account for land-use preferences. How people would prefer to use the natural resources around them? An understanding of people's preferences is an important step that will allow planners and architects to engage the community in a discussion around the long-term impacts of different kinds of use patterns. Surveys can either be collected by meeting the households or through community meetings where features are discussed in group settings. Household surveys may elicit more honest information from participants, leading to revelations that would not have otherwise been raised.

Connective Tissue: The understanding and coordinated design of open space, streets, trees, walls, fences, signage, lighting and other devices to create an overall community fabric.

Connectivity: Plentiful connections between different communities and land uses within a development reduce traffic on "connector" routes, by allowing diversion of traffic on a greater number of streets.

Conservation: Conservation means the process of looking after a place so as to retain its historical, architectural, aesthetic and cultural significance and includes maintenance, preservation, restoration, reconstruction and adaptation or a combination of these.

Development: The act of altering and modifying resources in order to obtain potential benefits.

Diverse Housing Types: Single family, townhouses and multi-family apartments and condos can be integrated into one development, as long as the scale and design of adjacent uses is compatible with each other. A mix of housing types ensures that people of various socio-economic classes may live in proximity to one another and share a common pride in one's community.

Environment: The combined features and natural resources that provide the basis for development, environmental management and conservation. Includes the processes and components of atmospheric, hydrological, geophysical, biotic, human and landscape.

Environmental Degradation : Adverse effects on bio-physical, social and economic resources, or reduction of the natural resources available to future generations.

Environmental Impact: Change in environmental quality due to external disturbance to a system includes positive and negative, primary and secondary, cumulative, synergistic, short, medium and long-term, reversible and irreversible. Described in terms of magnitude (of effect), direction (of change) and probability (of occurrence), with or without mitigation in terms of discussing "development" (the act of altering and modifying the resources of the natural environment in order to obtain potential economic and social benefits), it is important to note that it involves the application of human, financial and biophysical resources to satisfy social and economic needs, inevitably leading to some modification of the biosphere. The extent of development-induced modifications depend on the location, scale, intensity and duration of activities as well as adequacy of mitigation and compensatory measures, which define the scope for, and degree of balance in, environmental costs and benefits. Ideally, for a development to be "sustainable", it should be economically feasible and socially acceptable, without causing environmental impact or land, air and water degradation.

Environmental Maps: For planning purpose, environmental maps developed with a satellite imagery, aerial photographs, and data from soil, air and water samples. It includes the location and types of existing infrastructure and human settlements, as well as the geographical features of the chosen locality. Where data is available, layers can be added that will exhibit the current reach of water supply, sanitation, health, fire and other city services. Cadastral maps can be entered to show property ownership. Information compiled can be combined with demographic surveys and fed into a GIS mapping tool that acts as a "one-stop-shop", allowing city planners to view the environmental quality and services.

Environmental Quality: The status or value of the natural resource capital at a particular location at a specified time, relative to development, environmental management and condensation. Any reduction in environmental quality of a system, or depletion of the environmental resource capital. Adverse effect is defined in terms of and measured by environmental impacts.

Environmental Risk and Land Use Impact Analysis: Once the physical features of a locality have been mapped, analysis needs to be given to the compatibility of existing and prospective land uses. High density settlements, for example, are often highly vulnerable if located upon unstable land masses, steep slopes and wetland areas. Here it is important to collect specialists from a variety of fields. What is readily apparent to a health officer, may not be apparent to an environmental engineer. Here also, the input of community groups and NGOs is invaluable as they can analyse the impacts of land use from first-hand experience. It is extremely important, at this point, to consider the data collected in community surveys regarding preferred and actual land use patterns.

Environmental Sensitivity: The preservation of natural areas such as wetlands and woodlands, used as community amenity and buffers. These open spaces should be mandatorily designated as green areas and natural conservation zone.

Green Design: The name given to methods, systems and materials that seek to conserve land, energy and water, including all methods for the re-use of materials that would otherwise be discarded or used in a wasteful manner.

Heritage Building means and includes any building of one or more premises or any part thereof and/or structure and/or artefact which requires conservation and/or preservation for historical, architectural, or aesthetic, cultural, environmental, and ecological values.

Heritage Precinct means and includes any space that requires conservation and/ or preservation for historical, architectural, aesthetic, cultural, environmental and/or ecological purpose.

Hydrogeology: The study of the occurrence, distribution and movement of groundwater.

Hydrology is the branch of earth sciences that studies the occurrence, circulation and distribution of water in the Earth and its atmosphere primarily on or near the land surface. Ocean waters are the domains of oceanography and the marine sciences. On land, the science is concerned with the water in streams and lakes, rainfall and snowfall, snow and ice. Below the Earth's surface, it is concerned with water occurring in the pores of the soil and rocks.

The hydrological cycle describes the continuous movement of atmosphere onto the Earth's surface in solid or liquid state and atmosphere in vapor state. On the Earth surface, water stored in depressions, percolates below the land surface, evaporates through rivers and streams.

Increased Density: More units on smaller lots allow for preservation of open space, reduce infrastructure and maintenance costs, and allow for a more diverse mix of housing stock. Increased density is being perceived as a panacea to "urban sprawl."

Integrity: Anything true to itself, including the honest use of materials, architectural design and landscapes that complement their setting.

Listed Heritage Buildings/Precincts are those buildings, artefacts, structures, streets and areas of historic, architectural, aesthetic, cultural or environmental value as identified by the competent authority.

Live-Work Concept: One of the recent trends is the "Live-Work" concept, that started in the 1970s and 1980s, when many factories and warehouses were converted into residential flats, and business premises. This has gained momentum and now mixed use structures are popular.

Loft: An intermediate storage area in between two main floors.

Mezzanine Floor: An intermediate floor in between two main floors having minimum height of 1.8 m and a maximum height of 2.2 m and having proper access to it.

Mixed-Use: A complexity of functions allowing for community provisions, including work, home, shopping, school, restaurant, entertainment, and civic buildings within close proximity.

New Urbanism or Traditional Neighbourhood Development (TND) refers to the pedestrian friendly, more integrated land-use patterns characterized by streets arranged on an open, mainly rectangular grid, with alleys and traditionally styled houses on smaller lots.

Plinth Area means the built up covered area measured at the floor level of the basement or of any storey. For the purpose of plinth area, following shall be included:

(*a*) Area of the wall at the floor level, excluding plinth offsets, if any; when the building consists of columns projecting beyond cladding, the plinth area shall be taken up to the external face of cladding.

(*b*) Internal shaft for sanitary installations and garbage chute, provided these do not exceed 2 m^2 in area, vertical duct for air-conditioning, lift well, including landing.

(*c*) Staircase cover (mumty).

(*d*) Machine room and Porch.

The following shall not be included in the plinth area.

(*a*) Additional floor for seating in assembly building/theatre and auditorium, etc.

(*b*) Cantilevered porch

(*c*) Balcony

(*d*) Area of loft

(*e*) Internal sanitary shaft and garbage chute provided these are more than 2 m^2 in area

(*f*) Area of architectural band, cornice, etc.

(*g*) Area of vertical sun breaker or box louver projecting out and other architectural features, for example slabs projection for flower pot, etc.

(*h*) Open platform

(*i*) Terrace at floor one

(*j*) Spiral staircase

(*k*) Towers, turrets, domes projecting above the terrace level.

Porch is a cover surface supported on pillars or otherwise for the purpose of pedestrian or vehicular approach to a building.

Preservation means and includes maintaining the fabric of a place in its existing state and retarding deterioration.

Public Transportation: A compact high density pattern with mixed land use makes existing and potential public transportation service more accessible and feasible than conventional subdivisions.

Restoration means it includes returning the existing fabric of a place to a known earlier state by removing accretions or by reassembling existing components without introducing new materials.

Reconstruction means and includes returning a place as nearly as possible to a known earlier state by removing accretions or by reassembling existing components without introducing new materials. This shall not include conjectural construction.

Rentable Area means the usable carpet area at any floor level. The rentable area shall be the carpet area, but includes the following:

(*a*) The carpet area of kitchen, pantry, store, lavatory, bath room; and

(*b*) Fifty percent of carpet area of unglazed and 100 percent of glazed verandah.

It shall, however, exclude the carpet area of the following:

(*a*) Covered portion of the building within portion such as storage space on top, landings of staircase, under first landing and waist slab on floor one.

(*b*) Fifty percent of the carpet area of balcony.

While accounting the rentable area, one-fourth carpet area shall be accounted for when stilts have height more than 2.4 m.

Site Planning: The process of establishing a coherent and definitive scheme to organize buildings, open spaces and infrastructure on a site keeping in mind local planning regulations and character, its relationship with surrounding areas and activities required by the proposed design.

Smart Growth and Mixed Land Use (MLU): Smart Growth supports the integration of mixed land uses(MLU) as a critical component of achieving better places to live. By putting uses in close proximity to one another, alternatives to driving, such as walking or biking, once again become viable. MLU also provides a more diverse and sizable population and commercial base for supporting viable public transportation. It can enhance the vitality and perceived security of an area by increasing the number and attitude of the people on the street. It helps streets, public spaces and revitalizes community life.

Soil is a natural porous body that comprises solids, liquid and gases. It occurs as the upper most part of the earth's crust. Exposed to the atmosphere, it has horizon layers that are distinguishable from the initial material and has the ability to support rooted plants in a natural environment. Soil has depth and is therefore three-dimensional, whereas land is two dimensional, measured by length and breadth.

Top Soil/Surface Soil is the uppermost layer (0-300 mm) of soil, rich in organic matter. The roots of the plants largely depend on this layer for meeting water and nutrient needs. It has organic matter that increases the ability of the soil to retain moisture and make it available to plants. Organic matter also prevents and reduces erosion by binding the soil particles.

Subsoil layer under top soil it is usually poor in organic matter as compared to surface soil. It plays an important role in landscape construction. Subsoil drainage systems are provided to drain away excessive subsurface water in order to prevent waterlogging of soils and make them suitable for planting and construction purpose by reducing moisture content.

Table 12.2. Composition of Different Types of Soil

(*i*) Loamy Soil (50% sand, 50% clay or silt or both)
(*ii*) Sandy Soil (85% sand, 15% clay or silt or both)
(*iii*) Silt soil (90% sand, 10% clay or silt or both)

Table 12.3. Diameters of Various Kinds of Soil

Soil Particle	Diameter Range (mm)
Clay	Less than 0.0002 mm
Silt	0.0002-0.002
Coarse sand	0.020-2.0
Stone and gravel	Above 2.0

Staircase Cover (Mumty) is a space having a roof over a staircase and its landing, built for the purpose of providing protection from weather and not used for human habitation.

Street Scene: What one sees and feels along the building facades, edges and pathways of the city. It is shaped by adjacent buildings and articulated by landscaping and lighting, as well as by the colour and texture of paving and signage. The street as a community space is to be designed with great care.

Sustainable Community: Sustainability is not a matter of single-issue idea, but views the interaction of whole systems, which include the variables of land use, circulation, infrastructure, energy, transport, greenery, building systems and patterns of human behaviour.

Three-Dimensional Planning: Configuring urban studies with models of the topography, the character, perception and aesthetics of the built environment, which are more than the two-dimensional maps.

Transit Oriented Development (TOD). With the advent of cars in the early 20th century the city form came to celebrate the automobile, which manifested in the urban sprawl. The society transformed rapidly into a car dependent one; thereby increasing pressure on the infrastructure and more importantly on the environment. As now the understanding of the relationship between the urban form and climate change has been established, steps are being taken to remediate the damage from vehicular dependency to walkability, cycling, non-motorised means of transportation and public transit systems. A TOD is typically a master planned development that focuses upon a rapid transit station which provides employment, housing, shopping, and entertainment centres. Ideally, a rapid transit station should be not farther than a 10 minute walk, or one-quarter mile from housing units. This close proximity necessitates higher residential density and mixed use.

Vision is ability to see the invisible and big picture of the future that will stand the test of time. The most effective visions are long-term.

Walkability: Street design with sidewalks, linear parks and parkways, encourages residents to walk. This is particularly important for children and elderly reduces the burden on "chauffeur moms", as well as reduces fuel consumption and carbon/GHG emissions.

Wasteland: Barren or uncultivated land not producing anything or producing far below its optimal level. However, some ecologists believe that there is nothing like the wasteland.

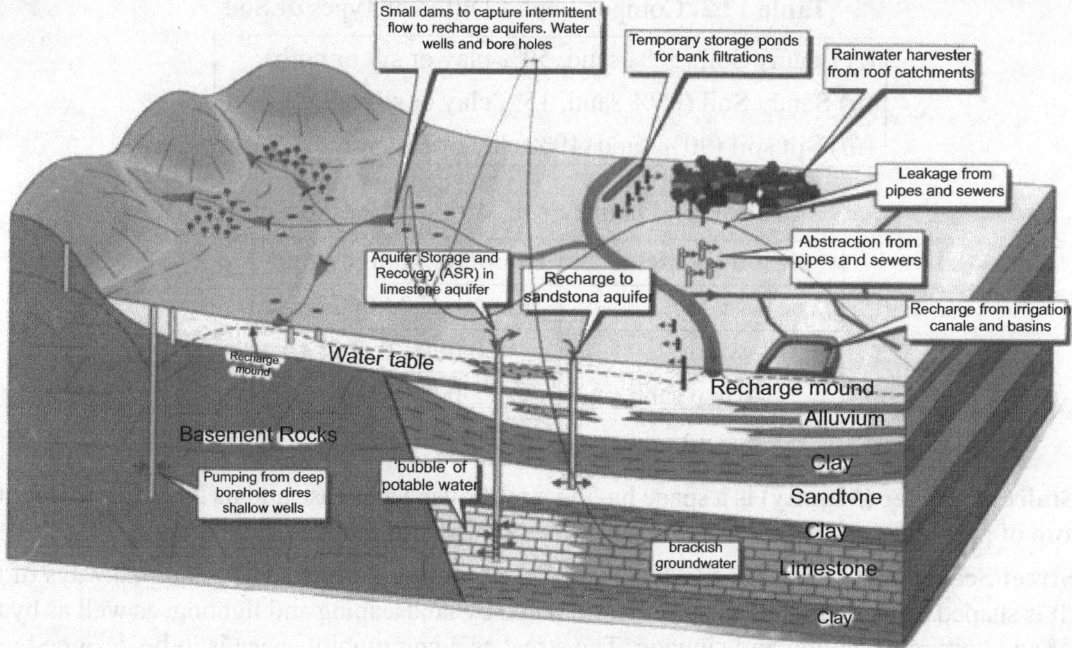

Fig. 12.21. Watershed approach envisages protection of natural drainage, land form and sources of water, conservation of valleys, drains, rivers and water-bodies

Watershed approach: An approach of treating an area by dividing it into watersheds based on drainage lines and to comprehensively treat the watershed as a unit of planning, aiming to conserve natural drains, streams, river, valleys and water bodies, besides the groundwater and natural landscape.

Watershed recharge: Amount of precipitation that percolates into the soils of a watershed and then appears as subsurface water in springs and wells.

DEBRIEFING QUESTIONS

1. Explain the concept of barrier free design in compliance with Persons with Disabilities (Equal Opportunity, Protection of Right and Full Protection) Act, 1996.
2. What are main kinds of disabilities?
3. What are the minimum wheelchair access provisions for a building ?
4. Write short notes on the following:
   (*a*) Ramp Approach
   (*b*) Parking for disabled
   (*c*) Footpaths
   (*d*) Dropped Curb
   (*e*) Internal Door
   (*f*) Bathroom/Toilet/WC
   (*g*) Kitchen

BIBLIOGRAPHY

Acharya Prasanna Kumar (1980) Architecture of Mansara, Munshiram Manoharlal Publishers, New Delhi.

Acioly, Claudio & Forbes Davidson (1996) Density in Urban Development, Building Issues, Vol. 8, 1996, Lund Centre for Habitat Studies, Sweden.

Adrian Smith and Gordon Gill (2011) Toward Zero Carbon, Images Publishing Victoria., Australia.

Aga Khan Trust for Culture (2011) Historic City Program, Prestel, New York.

Agarwal, Anil & Sunita Narain (1997) Dying Wisdom (India's Traditional Water Harvesting Systems) Centre for Science & Environment, New Delhi.

Agarwal K.N. & Prakash, C. (1987) Thermal Performance of Building's in Different Thermal Climatic Zones of the Country, CBRI, Roorkee.

Aijaz, Rumi (2015) India's Urbanisation Experiences, Observer Research Foundation, New Delhi.

Alexander, Christopher. A Pattern Language, OUP, London.

Ali S., Sharma, M.R. and Maitreya, V.K., Climate Classification for Building Design in India, Architectural Science Review, 36 (1): 31-36.

AMDA (2009) Land Policy for NCTD-2021, New Delhi: Association of Municipalities and Development Authorities.

American Planning Association (2006) Planning and Urban Design Standards, John Wiley, New Jersey.

Anurag, R. (2007) Green is not just a colour: architecture towards a sustainable development. Architecture + Design 24(10) 92-100.

Archaeological Survey of India (2007) Legislations http://asi.nic.in/asi_legislations.

Archer, R.W. (1993) Urban redevelopment with landowner participation using the land pooling/readjustment technique. Bangkok: Asian Institute of Technology.

Aslet, Clive (2015) The age of Empire, Britain's Imperial Architecture from 1880-1930, Auram Press, London.

Arvind, K., Baker, N., Yannas, S. & Szokolay, S.V. (Ed., 2001) Climatic Responsive Architecture, Tata McGraw Hill, New Delhi.

Bacon, Edmund N., (1974) The Design of Cities, Viking Press, New York.

Baker, Lee and David Sims. (1991) "India Public/ Private Partnerships in Land Development."1991.

Baker, N.V. (1987) Passive and Low Energy Building Design for Tropical Island Climates.

Bandhopadhya, Dr. Bibek (1998) Solar Water Heating, IREDA News, Jan.-March, 1998.

Bangalore Development Authority (2007) Report on Comprehensive Development Plan (Revised) Bangalore.

Banham, R. (1996) The Architecture of the Well Tempered Environment, Architectural Press, London.

Broadent, G. (1973) Design in Architecture; John Wiley and Sons, New Delhi.

Bansal, N.K. & Minke, G. (eds) (1995) Climatic Zones and Rural Housing in India.

Banshree, Mitra (1987) Land Supply for Low Income Housing in Delhi, Seminar IHS Rotterdam.

Barbara Harris-White, (ed) (2016) Middle India and Urban-Rural Development, Four Decades of Change, Springer, New Delhi/London.

Bachelard, Gaston (1969) The Poetic of Space, Beacon Press, Boston.

Barton, H., Davis, G. and Guise, R. (1995) Sustainable Settlements: A Guide for Planners.

BEE, (2017) Energy Conservation Building Code, Bureau of Energy Efficiency, Ministry of New and Renewable Energy, New Delhi.

Bell, Keith Cliford (2011) Land Governance in Coordinates, December, World Bank.

Benninger, Christopher (2011) Letter to a Young Architect, CCBA Pvt. Ltd., Pune.

Bharne, Vinayak (ed). The Emerging Asian City: Concomitant Urbanities & Urbanism.

Oxford: Routledge.

Benninger, Christopher, Rosa Favlo and Ram Prasad (2016) Architecture for Modern India, CCBA, Pune and Rizzoli. New York.

Bertaud, Alain (2014) "Converting land into affordable housing floor space," Policy Research Working Paper Series 6870, The World Bank.

Billand, Charles J. (1990) Delhi Case Study: Formal Serviced Land Delivery, Washington D.C. Prepared for A.I.D. PADCO.

BIS (2016) National Building Code of India, Bureau of Indian Standards, New Delhi.

Boesiger, W. (ed.) (1999) Le Corbusier-Complete Works, Birkhauser Publishers, Basel.

Brown, A. (2015) Planning for Sustainable and Inclusive Cities in the Global South, GIZ/DFID.

Browe, M (1992) From Idea to Building, Architectural Press, London.

Bunyard Peter (1978) Sewage Treatment in a Swedish Sculpture Garden, Ecologist, No.1, Jan-Feb.

Callender, John. (1974) Time-Saver Standards for Architectural Design, 5th ed. New York: McGraw Hill.

Calvita, Nico and Alan Mallach (2010) Inclusionary Housing in International Perspective: Affordable Housing, Social Inclusion and Land Value Recapture, Cambridge, MA, Lincoln Institute of Land Policy.

Census of India (2011) Census Report, Government of India, New Delhi.

Centre for Policy Research (2012) Governing Indian Mega-Cities, New Delhi.

Central Public Works Department (1998) Guidelines and Space Standards for barrier free built environment for disabled and elderly persons, Government of India, New Delhi.

Centre for Science and Environment, (2012) Excreta Matters, 71 Cities Survey, CSE, New Delhi,

Chen, M. Skinner, C. (2014) The Urban Informal Economy: Enhanced Knowledge, Appropriate Policies and Effective Organisation, Routledge, New York.

Chennai Metropolitan Development Authority, Master Plan for Chenai, CMDA, Chennai.

Chhaya, H.D. (1988) Vedic Spirit in Architecture, Architecture + Design, Sep-Oct.

Christ, Emanual and Christoph Ganenbein, (2015) Typology, Review No. III, ETH, Zurich (1914).

Chiara, Joseph (1994) Time Saver Standards for Housing and Residential Development, McGraw Hill, New York.

Chopra, Tarun (2016) Temples of India, Prakash Books, New Delhi.

Cities on Water, (1991) Impact of Sea Level Rise on Cities and Regions, Proceedings of the Commonwealth Science Council, London.

Courtney, J. (1978) Urban Land-Uses Regulation, in Urban Land Policy: Issues and Opportunities, edited by H. Dunkerly and C.M Whitehead, World Bank, Washington.

Crowe, Timothy D. (2000). Crime Prevention Through Environmental Design, Stoneham, MA Butterworth, Heinemann.

CRY (2012) Annual Survey report 2012-13, New Delhi.

CSE, (2010) Report of Centre of Research for Energy Resources and Consumption, Down to Earth, Jan. 16-31, 2013.

Curtis, W. (1982) Modern Architecture Since 1900, Phaidon.

Daniel Klaus (1994) Technology of Ecological Buildings, Birkhauser Verlag, Basel.

Davis, John Emmeus (ed) (2010) The Community Land Trust Reader, Lincoln Institute of Land Policy.

DDA (1981) Disposal and Development of Nazul Land Rules, New Delhi.

DDA, (2007) Master Plan for Delhi : 2021, New Delhi: Delhi Development Authority.

De Chiara, J., Callender, J. Time-Saver Standards for Building Types, Mass; The MIT Press.

Dora P. Crouch June, G. Johnson, (2001) Tradition in Architecture of Africa, America, Asia and Oceania, Oxford University Press, New York.

Doshi, Bal Krishna (2019) Paths Uncharted, Mapin, Ahmedabad.

Doxiadis, C. (1965) 'Islamabad, the Creation of a New Capital', Town Planning Review, 36(1).

DPU & HIC, (2015) Habitat III National Reporting Processes: Locating Right to the City and the Role of Civil Society, University College, London.

Drakatis Smith (2001) Handbook of Urban Studies, Sage Publication, London.

Dreyfuss, Henry (1966) The Measure of Man: Human Factor in Design. New York: Whitney Library of Design.

Dreze, Jean, and Amartya Sen (1996) India, Economic Development and Social Opportunity, New Delhi: Oxford University Press.

DUAC/Divya Kush (2014) City Level Project, New Ashok Nagar, New Delhi.

DUAC/M.N. Ashish Ganju (2014) City Level Project, Aya Nagar, DUAC, New Delhi.

DUAC/Sameer Mathur (2014) City Level Project, Delhi Greenways, DUAC, New Delhi.

DUAC/ Mohammad Shaheer (2014) City Level Project, Nicholson Cemetary, DUAC, New Delhi.

DUEIIP (2001) Status Report of Delhi 21, Delhi Urban Environment and Infrastructure Improvement Project, Government of India, Ministry of Environment and Forests and Government of NCT of Delhi Planning Department, New Delhi.

Dupont, V. (2008) Slum Demolition in Delhi Since the 1990s: An Appraisal, Economic and Political Weekly, Vol. 43, 28, (2008), Mumbai.

Correa, Charles. (2010) A Place in the Shade. The New Landscape and other Essays. Gurgaon: Penguin Book, India.

Ebenezer Howard (1965) Garden Cities of Tomorrow, Cambridge, MA: MIT Press.

Erpenstein, Annette, (2012) Back to the Future: The Rebirth of Public Place in Seoul, Trialog.

Evans, M., Shui, B. & Somasundaram, S. (2009). Country Report on Building Energy Codes in India, Pacific Northwest National Laboratory, prepared for the U.S. Dept of Energy.

Faetanini, M et al, (2011) Urban Policies and the Right to the City in India, CSH and UNESCO, New Delhi.

Fawcett A. Peter (1998) Architecture: Design Notebook. Architectural Press, London.

Fletcher David (ed) (2015) Rooftop Garden Design, Images Pub, Victoria.

Fonesca, Rory (1976) The Walled City of Old Delhi in Shelter and Society.

Frampton, Kenneth (1996) Charles Correa, Perennial Press, Mumbai.

Frampton, Kenneth (1980) Modern Architecture, Critical History, Oxford University Press.

Gehl Jan (2010) Cities for People, Island Press, Washington/London.

Ghertner, D Asher, (2015) Rule by Aesthetics- World Class City in Making in Delhi, Oxford University Press.

Gina Tsrouhas (ed) (2014) Green Walk–Green Roofs Images Pub. Victoria.

Giedion, Sigfired (1962) Space, Time and Architecture, Harvard University Press, Cambridge, Mass.

Giurgola, Romaldo/ Mehta, Jaimini (1975) Louis I. Kahn, Architect, Westview Press, Boulder, Colorado.

Girardet, Herbert, (1997) Sustainable Cities – A Contradiction in Terms, Architectural Design, London.

Goodall, Christ, (2007) How to Live a Low Carbon Life, Earthscan, London.

GOI (1956) Slum Areas (Improvement and Clearance) Act, Government of India.

Gill Tsarouhas (ed) (2014) Green Walls–Green Roofs, Images Pub. Victoria.

Government of Delhi (2013) Delhi Human Development Report, New Delhi.

Government of India (2007) National Urban Housing and Habitat Policy, Ministry of Urban Affairs and Employment, New Delhi.

Government of India (2008) PM's council on climate change, National Action Plan for Climate Change, New Delhi.

Government of India (2009) National Mission on Sustainable Habitat, MOUD, New Delhi.

Government of India (2012) Task Force Report on Urban Housing, Ministry of Urban Affairs and Employment, New Delhi.

Government of India (2006) National Urban Transport Policy, Ministry of Urban Affairs and Employment, New Delhi.

Government of India/Charles Correa (1986) Vistara, The Architecture of India, ICCR, New Delhi.

Grandjean, Etienne, (1973) Ergonomics of the Home. New York: Halstead Press, Division of John Wiley & Sons.

GTZ, (2006) Capacity Building for Ecological Sanitation, Paris: UNESCO.

H Kohn, E. & Katz, P. (2002) Building Type Basics for Office Buildings. John Wiley, New York.

Hardy, I. E., Mitlin, D., Satterthwaite, D. (1992) Environmental Problems in Third World Cities. Earthscan Publications Ltd., London.

Hardy Adam (1995) Temple Architecture, IGNCA, New Delhi.

Harris, Charles, Nicholas T Dines (ed) (1997) Times Saver Standards for Landscape Architecture, McGraw Hill, New York.

Howard, Ebenzer (1965) Garden Cities of Tomorrow, Reprinted, MIT Press, Cambridge.

Huang, J. & Deringer, J. (2007) Status of Energy Efficient Building Codes in Asia (China, Hong Kong, Taiwan, Japan, Korea, Malaysia, Philippines, Singapore, Thailand, India). The Asia Business Council, Hong Kong SAR. http://www.climateworks.org/download/status-ofenergy-efficient-building-codes-in-asia-june-2009.

IEA (2007) Energy balances of Non-OECD countries, International Energy Agency.

Intergovernmental Panel on Climate Change (2007) Climate Change 2007: Synthesis Report. Contributors of Working Groups I, II, and III to Fourth Assessment Report of the IPCC, Geneva.

IGBC (2007) LEED - India, Green Building Rating System, abridged reference guide for new construction & major renovations (LEED-India NC), version 1.0 Indian Green Building Council, Hyderabad. http://www.igbc.in/site/mmbase/attachments/48344/LEED.Abrid_Ver.pdf.

INTACH (1999) Delhi: The Built Heritage (2 vols), New Delhi–1999.

INTACH (1994) Special Issue on Heritage, Architecture + Design, May-June.

INTACH (2010) Delhi–A Living Heritage, New Delhi.

International Institute for Environment and Development (1992) Environment and Urbanisation, Volume 4, Number 2, London. ISO-9000 and ISO-14001 Compendiums.

Jacobs, Jane (1961) The Death and Life of American Cities, Random House, USA.

Jacobus, Ricks (2015) Inclusionary Housing Creating and Maintaining Equitable Communities, Cambridge MA, Lincoln Institute of Land Policy.

Jaggi, I.R. (1991) Readymade Housing, Indian Architect and Builder, October 1991.

Jain, A.K. (2009) Urban Land Policy and Public Private Partnership for Real Estate and Infrastructure Projects, Readworthy Publications, New Delhi.

Jain, A.K (2013) Dillinama, Synergy Books, New Delhi.

Jain, A.K (2013) Sustainable Urban Transport and Systems, Khanna Publishers, New Delhi.

Jain, A.K (2014) Revisiting Land Acquisition and Urban Process, Readworthy Publications, New Delhi.

Jain, A.K (2014) Right to Toilet, Readworthy Publication, New Delhi.

Jain, A.K (2017) Urban Transformation, Discovery Publishing House, New Delhi.

Jain, A.K. (2010) Urban Planning and Governance, Bookwell Publishers, New Delhi.

Jain, A.K. (2009) Planning for Inclusive Community and Social Infrastructure, Readworthy Publication, New Delhi.

Jain, A.K. (2018) City Planning for a Changing India, Synergy Books, New Delhi.

Jain, A.K. (2015) Transforming Delhi, Bookwell, New Delhi.

Jain, A.K. (2016) Building Twenty Million Homes, Discovery Publishing House, New Delhi.

Jain, A.K (2017) Landscape Architecture-Planning, Engineering and Horticulture, Discovery Publishing House, New Delhi.

Jain, A K. (2010) Urban Housing and Slums, Readworthy Publications, New Delhi.

Jain, A. K. (2011) Making Infrastructure Work, Discovery Publishing, New Delhi.

Jain, A. K. (2015) Conservation of Cultural Heritage, Discovery Publishing, New Delhi.

Jain, A. K. (2015) Regeneration of Rivers and Water Resources, Discovery Publishing, New Delhi.

Jain, A. K. (2015) Smart Cities: Vision and Action, Discovery Publishing, New Delhi.

Jain, A. K. (2015) Towards Cleaner and Hygienic Cities and Villages, Discovery Publishing, New Delhi.

Jain, A. K. (2011) The Informal City, Readworthy Publishers, New Delhi.

Jain, A.K. (2007) Water – A Manual for Architects, Engineers and Managers, Daya Publishing, New Delhi.

Jain, A.K. (2001) Ecology and Natural Resource Management, Management Publishing Co. Dehradun.

Jain, AK (2018) Affordable Housing and Infrastructure Services, Lambert Publishing, Litavia.

Jain, A.K. (2007) A Practical Guide to Disaster Management, Pragun, Delhi.

Jain, A.K. (2009) Low Carbon Cities–Policies, Planning and Practice, Discovery Publishing, New Delhi.

Jain, A.K. (2015) The Idea of Green Building, Khanna Publishers, New Delhi.

Jain, Kulbhushan and Meenakshi Jain (2000) Architecture of the Indian Desert, AADI Centre, Ahmedabad and the University of Virginia, US.

Jain, Kulbhushan (2012) Architecture Concept to Manifest, AADI Centre, Ahmedabad.

Jain, Minakshi, Kulbhushan Jain, Meghal Arya, (2009) Architecture of Royal Camp (Fort of Nagaur), AADI Centre, Ahmedabad.

Jain, Shikha, DRONAH (2008) Presentation on "Heritage Legislation in India—An Overview," IHCN, Second Biennial Conference, Hyderabad, AP, 18-20 Dec. 2008.

Jain, Shikha, (2004) Havelis: A Living Tradition of Rajasthan, Shubi Pub, Gurgaon, 2004.

Jain Shikha and Vanicka Arora (2017) Living Heritage of Mewar, Mapin Publishing, Ahmedabad.

Jodidio, Phillip (2015) Heritage of the Mughal World, Aga Khan Historic City Programme, Prestel, Munich.

Kabre, C. (2010) A new thermal performance index for dwelling roofs in the warm humid tropics, Building and Environment, 45: 727-738.

Kachru, Upendra (1994) A Novel Method of Cooling and Heating of Building Envelope Air Conditioning, Proceedings on Conference-Excellence in Housing, Feb-24th and 25th, Dallas, Texas, Energy Efficient Building Association, USA.

Kamiya, Takeo, (2003) Architecture of the Indian Sub-continent, Architecture Autonomous, Goa, India.

Khan Hassan Uddin (1987) Charles Correa, Singapore Concept Media Pvt. Ltd.

Klaus, Daniels, (1994) the Technology of Ecological Building, Birkhauser, Verlag, Basel.

Koenigsberger, Ingersoll, Mayhew, Szokilay; (1975) Manual of Tropical Housing and Building; Orient Longman, London.

Kollar L. Peter (2001) Symbolism in Hindu Architecture, Aryan Books, N. Delhi.

Kumar, S., Kapoor, R., Rawal, R., Seth, S. & Walia, A. (2010) Mission-Developing an Energy Conservation Building Code Implementation Strategy in India.

Laul, Anil (2011) Green is Red, ASHRAY, Anangpur, Haryana.

Le Corbusier (1950-1955) Le Modulor, Boulogne-Seine, Modulor 2, Boulogne-sur-Seine, London.

Le Corbusier (1964) When the Cathedral were White, McGraw-Hill, New York

Le Corbusier (1960) My Work, The Architectural Press, London.

Levitt Bernstein Associates, (1978) Supervisor's Guide to Rehabilitation and Conversion, Architectural Press, London.

Ling (1967) Runcorn New Town Master Plan, Runcorn Development Corporation.

Mansukhhani, Raju, Dipti Khera (2002) The City Within a City - Volume, Jagmandir on Lake Pichola, Maharana Mewar Charitable Trust.

Marcus Clare Cooper and Carolyn Francis, Design Guidelines for Urban Open Space, 2nd edition, Van Nostrand Reinhold, New York.

McHarg, Ian (1969) Design with Nature, New York, Natural History Press.

McKinsey Global Institute (2014) A Blueprint for addressing the global affordable housing challenge, New York.

McKinsey Global Institute (2010) India's Urban Awakening: Building Inclusive Cities, Sustaining.

Mehrotra, Nirmita (2013) Disaster Resilience, Architecture–Time Space and People, Council of Architecture, New Delhi.

Mehrotra, Rahul et al (2000) Building of the Kala Ghoda Art District, Mumbai: Max Muller Bhavan. Marg Publications and Urban Design Research Institute.

Mehta, Dinesh and Mira Mehta (1991) Land for Shelter Delivery of Serviced Land in Metropolitan India. Ahmedabad, India: Prepared for USAID Centre for Environmental Planning, Ahmedabad.

Meininger, Irmgard (2000) Palaces of Udaipur, Printworld (P) Ltd., New Delhi.

Michell George (1994) Royal Palaces of India, Thames and Hudson Ltd., London.

Ministry of Rural Development (1999) Total Sanitation Guidelines, Government of India.

Ministry of Urban Development Government of India, New Delhi, (2001) The Constitutional (Seventy-Fourth) Amendment Act (1992) The Nagarpalika Act.

Ministry of Urban Development (2011) Report of the High-Power Committee on Urban Infrastructure, New Delhi.

Ministry of Urban Development (2014) Swachh Bharat (Clean India) Campaign, Government of India, New Delhi.

Ministry of Urban Development (2015) AMRUT, (Atal Mission for Rejuvenation and Urban Transformation) Government of India, New Delhi.

Ministry of Urban Development (2015) HRIDAY (Historic City Redevelopment and Augmentation), Government of India, New Delhi.

MOHUPA, (NBO) (2012) Urban Housing Shortage, 2012-17, New Delhi.

Ministry of Urban Development, (2015) Smart City Mission Guidelines, Government of India, New Delhi.

MNRE (2010) Green Rating for Integrated Habitat Assessment, Ministry of New and Renewable Energy, Government of India, New Delhi, http://www.grihaindia.org/index.php.

MNRE (2014) Report on New and Renewable Energy, Ministry of New and Renewable Energy, Government of India, New Delhi, http://www.grihaindia.org/index.php.

Modi, Narendra, (2010) Convenient Action, Mcmillan, New Delhi.

MoEF (2016) Environmental Clearances, Ministry of Environment, Forests and Climate Change, Government of India, New Delhi, http://moef.nic.in/modules/project-clearances/ehvironment-clearances.

MOHUPA (Ministry of Housing and Urban Poverty Alleviation) (2015) Model Tenancy Act, Government of India, New Delhi.

MOHUPA (Ministry of Housing and Urban Poverty Alleviation) (2015) Pradhan Mantri Awas Yojana–Housing for All, (Urban), Scheme Guidelines, Government of India, New Delhi.

MOHUPA (Ministry of Housing and Urban Poverty Alleviation), (2015) National Urban Rental Housing Policy (Draft), Government of India, New Delhi.

MOHUPA, (NBO) (2013) State of Housing in India: A Statistical Compendium, New Delhi.

MOHUPA, (NBO) (2013) State of Slums in India, A Statistical Compendium, New Delhi.

Mostafavi, Mohsen, (2016) Archirecture and Plurality. Lars Muller Publishers, Geneva.

Murty, C.V.R. & Indian Institute of Technology, How to Reduce Earthquake Effects on Buildings, Kanpur, IITK-BMTPC, Kanpur.

National Council of Applied Economic Research (1995) India Infrastructure Report, New Delhi.

National Council of Applied Economic Research (2012) Land Pooling Policy for Delhi, New Delhi (unpublished).

National Council of Applied Economic Research (2015) Affordable Housing Sector in India, New Delhi (unpublished).

National Sample Survey Office (2010) Migration in India, NSS 64th Round Ministry of Statistics and Programme Implementation, New Delhi.

Norberg-Schulz, Christian (1965) Intentions in Architecture, The MIT Press, Cambridge, Mass.

OECD (2010) Organising Local Economic Development, the Role of Development Agencies and Companies, OECD.

Pandya, Y. (2007) Elements of Space Making, Mapin Publishing, Ahmedabad.

Pandya, Y. (2012) Concepts of Space in Indian Architeture, Mapin Publishing, Ahmedabad.

Pandya, Y. (2007) Towards symbiosis of nature and architecture, Architecture + Design.

Pabnero, Julius and Martin Tzelnik (1979) Human Dimensions and Interior Space, Whiteny Library of Design, New York.

Parry, M.N. Arnell, P. Berry, D. Dodman, S. Fankhauser, C. Hope, S. Kovats, R. Nicholls, D. Satterthwaite, R. Tiffin and T. Wheeler (2009) Assessing the costs of adaptation to climate change: a review of the UNFCCC and other recent estimates, International Institute for Environment and Development / Grantham Institute for Climate Change, London.

Pevsner, Nicholaus (1976) History of Building Types, Bollingen Series, Princeton University Press, Princeton, USA.

Plummer Jenelle (2012) Focusing Partnerships, Earthscan, London.

Punjab Government, (1988) A Gazetteer of Delhi 1883-84, Vipin Jain, Gurgaon.

Rai, G.D. (1989) Solar Energy Utilization. Khanna Publishers, New Delhi.

Rai, Markandey (2012) Creating Safe and Secure Metropolitan City: UN Perspective, UN Habitat, Nairobi.

Rao, P.K. (1991) Safeguards for Sound Concrete, Indian Architect and Builder, October 1991.

Raynolds, Johns (2002) Courtyards, John Wiley Sons, New York.

Rees, William E. (1997) Ecological Footprints and Urban Transportation, Velocity, Barcelona.

Replogle, M. (1993) Bicycle and cycle rickshaws in Asian cities, 6th conference on urban transport in developing countries, CODATU-VI, Tunis.

Ribeiro, E.F.N. (1985) Improved Sanitation and Environmental Health Condition with Evaluation of Sulabh International Low Cost Sanitation in Bihar, Patna: Sulabh International.

RICS (2010) “Making Affordable Housing Work in India”, RICS, CBRE and LEVVEL.

RTPI (2014) Fostering Growth–Understanding and Strengthening the Economic Benefit of Planning, RTPI, London.

Rudofsky, Bernard (1964) Architecture without Architects, University of New Mexico Press, Albuquerque.

Russel B, EL Maddox and Faroq Ameen (2015) Fifty under Fifty, Images Publishing, Victoria.

Sampat, Preeti (2013) Limits to Absolute Power: Eminent Domain and the Right to Land in India, EP Weekly, May 11.

Sanjay, P. (1992) Energy conscious architecture: an endless quest. Architecture + Design.

Saxena, K.B. (2011) Rehabilitation and resettlement of displaced persons. Chapter three in Development-Induced Displacement, Rehabilitation and Resettlement in India. Routledge Contemporary South Asia.

Scoenauer, Norbert (1984) 6000 years of Architecture, W.W. Norton & Co., New York.

Scriver Peter and Amit Srivastava (2015) India- Modern Architecture in History, Reaktion Books, London.

SEI, Your Guide to Building an Energy Efficient Home, Sustainable Energy Ireland, Dublin, Ireland. www.seai.ie/Publications/Your_Home.../RE_guide Jn_the_home.pdf. http://

Safdie, Moshe (1974/2015) For Everyone a Garden, MIT Press Publisher House Victoria.

Seonwook Kin and Pyo, Miyoung (ed.) Construction and Design Manual–Mobile Architecture.

www.nbmcw.com/articles/green-construction/25585-the-cost-of-going-green.html

Sekaran, Veera (ed.) (2015) Exterior Green Wall Design, Images Pub., Victoria.

Sheshadri, T. N. Sharma, M. R. & AS, Ali (1969) Climatological and Solar Data for India to Design Buildings for Thermal Comfort, Sarita Prakashan, Meerut.

UN Habitat (2016) Implementing Agenda 21, Nairobi.

Sharp Dennis (1972) Twentieth Century Architecture, A visual History, Image Publishing, Victoria.

Shivaramakrishnan K.C. (2015) Planning for Metropolitan Region, Oxford University Press, New Delhi.

Smart, James (2012), The Role of Post Disaster Institutions in Recovery and Resilience – a Comparative Study of Three Disasters–Victorian Bushfire (2009), Queensland Floods (2010-11) and Cantebury Earthquake (2010-12) Institute of Governance and Policy Studies, Victoria University, Wellington.

Smith, Adrian (2015) The Architecture of Adrian Smith–Toward a Sustainable Future, Image Publishing, Victoria, Australia.

Sorensen, Andre (2000) Conflict, Consensus or Consent: Implications of Japanese Land Readjustment Practice for Developing Countries, Habitat International Vol. 24.

Spreiregen, Paul D (1991) Architecture of Towns and Cities, McGraw Hill, New York.

Sterling, Henry (1988) Hindu India from Khajuraho to the Temple City of Madurai, Beredikt Taschen Verlag.

Steinberg, Florian (1996) Conservation and Rehabilitation of Urban Heritage in Developing Countries, Habitat International, June.

Steinberg, Florian: Concept of Evolutionary Housing Design for India, Hudco, New Delhi.

Subrahmanyum G.V., (2009) Revised Environment Clearance Process, Prescriptions of the Ministry of Environment and Forests, New Delhi.

Synder, Michael (2015) The Wealth of Nations, The Caravan, New Delhi (December).

Tadgell, Christopher (1994) History of Architecture in India, Viking, Penguin Books (India), Phaidan Press London.

TCPO (2011) Status of Town and Country Planning Departments and Acts in different States and UTs in India. Spatio-Economic Development Record, Vol. 18, No. 5, New Delhi.

Thatte, Ram Anant (2016) Ajanta, B.R. Publishing Corp. New Delhi.

The State of the World's Cities 2010/2011: Bridging the Urban Divide (2010), London/Washington D.C., Earthscan, UN-Habitat.

Thurow, C. (1983) Improving Street Climate Through Urban Design, Planning. Advisory/Service Report No. 376, American Planning Association, Chicago.

Tipple, A.G. (2005) 'The place of home-based enterprises in the informal sector: Evidence from Cochabamba, New Delhi, Surabaya and Pretoria' Urban Studies, April: 42(4): 1-15.

Uchida, Hirotsugu and Andrew Nelson (2008) 'Agglomeration Index – Towards a New Measure of Urban Concentration', Background Paper Prepared for World Development Report.

United Nations Centre for Human Settlements (UN-Habitat) (1994) Sustainable Human Settlements Development: Implementing Agenda 21, Nairobi.

UN Global Compact and Oxfam, (2015) Poverty Footprint: Overview, New York/London.

UN Habitat (2003) The Challenge of Slums - Global Report on Human Settlements, London.

UN Habitat (2007) Enhancing Urban Safety and Security, Nairobi.

UN Habitat (2014) A Practical Guide to Designing, Planning and Executing City-wide Slum Upgrading Programmes, Nairobi.

UN Habitat (2015) Habitat III Issues Paper, Nairobi.

UN (2013) A New Global Partnership: Eradicate Poverty and Transform Economies through Sustainable Development, United Nations, New York.

UNESCO (2010) Historic Districts for All, New Delhi, UNESCO.

UN-Habitat (2011) Cities and Climate Change, Global Report on Human Settlements, Earthscan, UK/USA/Nairobi.

UN-Habitat (2013) Planning and Design for Sustainable Urban Mobility, Global Report on Human Settlements, Earthscan, UK/USA/Nairobi.

UN-Habitat (2010) The State of the World's Cities: Bridging the Urban Divide, London/Washington D.C. Earthscan.

UN-Habitat/International Institute for Environment & Development (2010) Developing Local Climate Change Plans, UK/USA/Nairobi.

UNDP and UN Solution Exchange (2012) Social Inclusion of Manual Scavengers, A Report of National Round Table Discussion Organised by United Nations Development Programme.

UNEP (2015) District Energy in Cities: Unlocking the Potential of Energy Efficiency and Renewable Energy, New York.

UNISDR (2015) United Nations Global Assessment Report on Disaster Risks, UN Office for Disaster Risk Reduction, Geneva.

USAID (1991) Constraints Affecting the Efficiency of Urban Land Markets in India, New Delhi.

Vastu Shilpa Foundation (1995) Living Environment and Housing Designs by Balkrishna Doshi, Ahmedabad.

Vatsayan, Kapila (ed.) (1995) Prakriti-The Integral Vision, IGNCA, New Delhi.

Venturi, Robert (1996) Complexity and Contradictions in Architecture, Museum of Modern Art, New York.

Virasat (2006) Discovering Jaipur, Jaipur Virasat Foundation, Jaipur.

Volwahsen, Andreas (2002) Imperial Delhi, Prestel Verlag, Munich.

Volwahsen, Andreas (2001) Cosmic Architecture in India, Prestel, New York and Mapin Publishing, Ahmedabad.

Watson Donald, Crosbie Michael J. (2005) Time Saver Standards for Architectural Design, 8th Edition. McGraw Hill, New York.

Watson Donald (2009) Time Saver Standards for Building Materials and Systems, Tata McGraw Hill, New York, New Delhi.

Watson, V. (2009) The Planned City Sweeps Away the Poor: Urban Planning and 21st Century Urbanisation, Elsevier.

Yeang Kenneth (1999) The Green Skyscraper, the Basis for Designing Sustainable Intensive Buildings, Prestel, New York.

Zamos Alexender (1987) Forms and Structures in Architecture, New York, Van Nostrand Reinhold New York.